ROBERT CHRISTGAU

ROCK
ALBUMS
OF THE '70s

A CRITICAL GUIDE

ROBERT CHRISTGAU

ROCK ALBUMS

OF THE '70s

A CRITICAL GUIDE

A DA CAPO PAPERBACK

Library of Congress Cataloging in Publication Data

Christgau, Robert.
  [Christgau's record guide]
  Rock albums of the '70s: a critical guide / Robert Christgau.
    p.   cm.
  Originally published under title: Christgau's record guide. New
Haven: Ticknor & Fields, 1981.
  ISBN 0-306-80409-3
  1. Sound recordings — Reviews. 2. Rock music — 1971-1980 —
Discography. I. Title. II. Title: Rock albums of the seventies.
ML156.9.C53   1990   90-39074
781.66'09'0470266 — dc20   CIP
                                                 MN

This Da Capo Press paperback edition of *Rock Albums of the '70s: A Critical Guide*
is an unabridged republication of the edition, originally entitled *Christgau's Record
Guide: Rock Albums of the '70s,* published in New York in 1981, here supplemented
with author corrections. It is reprinted by arrangement with Robert Christgau.

Published by Da Capo Press, Inc.
A Subsidiary of Plenum Publishing Corporation
233 Spring Street, New York, New York 10013

Manufactured in the United States of America

TO CAROLA —

NEVER AGAIN

CONTENTS

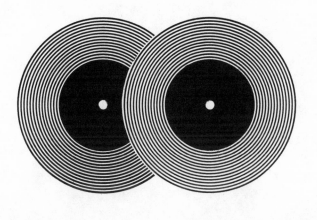

INTRODUCTION

The Guide

When I became *Esquire*'s "secular music" columnist in early 1967, I didn't know I'd found a vocation — I was just staking my journalistic claim to a subject I'd been passionately analytic about since Alan Freed hit New York in 1954. I could imagine myself in 1977 (at thirty-five, God) doing a record review column for *Cosmopolitan* or somewhere: rock and roll would be a professional base, something to fall back on, not a career, or an obsession. Hadn't I rejected criticism as a way of life when I decided to skip graduate school? Apparently not. When the column dried up two years later, I quickly hustled down to *The Village Voice*, where I was allotted one 2500-word piece per month, a deal that quartered my rock-related income as it tripled my workload. And still I craved more.

By then there were lots of rock critics — we gossiped at concerts, mooched meals at press parties, palled around. I even lived with one. We'd all fallen for a hype or two. We'd all learned to separate achievement from intention, real thing from phony, art from product, and maybe even to tell when those distinctions were meaningless. In short, we were all more or less skeptical. Yet for some reason I was less skeptical than most, as my unusual work habits proved — I tried to listen to everything the record companies sent me, a task so time- and soul-consuming that my rockcrit cohab, Ellen Willis, would banish me and my dreck to a backup apartment whenever the drone began to get to her.

It was strange that I felt compelled to do this. According to my theory of pop, in which rock and roll's broad appeal was intrinsic to its aesthetic value, record-bizzers and radio programmers comprised an unwittingly beneficent distribution system: given the inevitable exceptions and time lags, the way to find good music in 1969 was the same as in 1954 and 1964 — by turning on the radio and watching the charts. Admittedly, there was a polemical contrariness in this idea, a reaction against the elitist left sentimentalism in which The People are thwarted in their progress toward Good Music by a conspiracy of Establishment Reactionaries. But in 1969 I still believed it sincerely, and in 1969 it was still true. Not all of the most popular rock was good, but most of the good rock seemed to be popular. Of course, the meaning of popular was changing — it wasn't just top forty any more. While I continued to love AM and paid special attention to albums by the soul and teenybopper singles artists the counterculture ignored, I was aware that FM's free-form progressivism (har har) had proven essential to the pop process. But the new radio was only another example of the quirkish vitality of a new mass culture (call it youth, call it pop) that seemed destined to defy the status quo. Or so I argued.

Yet at the same time I felt it was somehow my duty to listen to the small mountain of LPs I was mailed each week. This was partly incipient workaholism, partly recompense for all those freebies. But it was also a way to join the distribution system. I didn't realize this at first because I knew that radio and personal appearances, not print, sold records; even the press coverage that did have discernible commercial clout (the MC5's *Kick Out the Jams* went to number thirty in the wake of a publicity blitz, for instance) began with corporate hype. Nevertheless, there I was with one piece a month and dozens of records bouncing around in my head — *The Original Delaney & Bonnie, Fairport Convention,* the Grateful Dead's *Aoxomoxoa,* and (I admit it) Procol Harum's *A Salty Dog,* all of which I loved, and *Sea Train, Cat Mother & the All-Night Newboys,* Country Joe's *Here We Are Again,* and (I admit it) Skip Spence's *Oar,* all of which I thought grossly overrated. I had heard whole albums that most rock fans knew only by cuts on the radio or even covers in the record store, and others — Mavis Staples's *Mavis,* say, or *Cleanliness & Godliness Skiffle Band's Greatest Hits* — to which they probably had no access at all. I felt obliged to share my findings even if only a few dozen or a few hundred buyers would do something as a result.

And so the Consumer Guide was born. The first one, which appeared July 10th, 1969, reviewed and rated sixteen records (including the ten named above) I knew well enough to comment on in a brief, first-draft sentence. Only occasionally did I go beyond such acute analysis as "unexceptional white blues, much below their excellent first album" (Linn County's *Fever Shot,* a D). Nevertheless, the feature was a hit — countless cards and letters begged for more. Soon my listening became more systematic, my grades more rational, my comments more thoughtful and detailed. Five months later I was still protesting: "This is business, folks, not criticism. You have a limited amount of money to spend on records and a limited quantity of data on which to base your allotments. The Consumer Guide is more data." But in fact I conceived the CG as complementing my monthly essay. It was criticism with an immediate, undeniable practical function — criticism in a pop form, compact and digestible.

The most essential component of this form was also the most controversial — the grades. It was 1969, remember; I was soon to spend two years teaching in college programs that didn't even permit the grading of coursework. And in fact I never suggested that grades were anything more than an imperfect shorthand. Granted, I was getting my polemical jollies — it was a pleasure to remind the minions of rock-is-art that if art could be quantified in a pricing system, it could damn well be quantified in a grading system as well. It was distressing to learn, however, how bare of nuance grades could be. In theory, mine stretched from A to E, and early on I would seek out horrible examples that merited inclusion at D or below. But since the main point was to find good music for people, and since ascertaining exact degrees of worthlessness was a depressing occupation, most of my ratings clustered up in the listenable range, B minus and above. I soon figured out that unless a record got a B plus or better, it was unlikely that I'd ever play it voluntarily again, and when the B plusses came in six and seven at a time, I even took to listing them top to bottom in an introduction.

Of course, what people hate about grades, even more than their arbitrariness, is their appearance of objectivity, of absolute authority. In a music of parricides I thought it prudent as well as accurate to emphasize that authority was not my goal — the grades summed up a private aesthetic response. Always big on relativism, I assumed that many kinds of rock fan utilized the service I provided, and that we were all equal. "I admit my prejudices — I dislike most rock improvisation, and am suspicious of even the most innocent pretensions, while I am perhaps unnaturally disposed in favor of soul music and anything that reveals a trace of wit," I explained, and went on: "There are records as low as C minus that may be worth owning if your tastes are very different from mine. But if you like many Ds and Es you might as well stop reading me altogether — we have nothing in common, intelligence included."

Well, there had to be a punchline, and basically, my humility was genuine. One prejudice I didn't even bother to mention was that I thought popular music should be popular — the Stooges' *Fun House* and Captain Beefheart's *Trout Mask Replica* ("JUST TOO WEIRD") were rated B plus on grounds of inaccessibility, as it's called. I realize now that my populist bias dulled my take on those two records (as well as others), although no more than a rock-is-art bias led "progressives" to kid themselves about experiments that didn't come off. My populism worked in the other direction as well — although aware of its unevenness, I named *Tommy* best album of 1969 in tribute to its pop impact. But I recognized that something else was going on — the distribution system appeared to be faltering, FM and all. After all, the Flying Burrito Brothers' *Gilded Palace of Sin,* which climbed all the way to 164 in *Billboard,* and *The Velvet Underground,* which never cracked 200, were also in my top ten. By the following summer, enamored of two more records that never made the charts — Randy Newman's *12 Songs* and *A Rainbow in Curved Air,* by the avant-garde minimalist Farfisa mystic Terry Riley — as well as many near misses, I was inspired to coin a new term for all this wonderful but commercially unsuccessful stuff. "Just as semiclassical music is a systematic dilution of highbrow preferences," I wrote, "semipopular music is a cross-bred concentration of fashionable modes." Semipopular music, that was the key, and as the decade wore on I became less snotty about it.

I'd always warned that critics, predisposed toward novelty by overexposure, perceived music differently from ordinary fans. But it gradually became clear that our readers weren't ordinary fans — they did read, after all. Like us, or at least not unlike us, they wanted provocation and formal acuteness from rock and roll. What's more, so did many of the most gifted musicians, although because the magic of the music was tied into a youthful lyricism (and anger) that couldn't be willed, wanting it wasn't enough. In any case, semipopular music — not the genteel if gratifying artiness of the late '60s, but arcane stuff with limited mass potential — had the power to pull people together. Not to inspire a mass movement, a disappointment for a comsymp like me, but to gather a sort of electronic bohemia, a conceptual community in which rock journalism played a crucial role. And over the years the Consumer Guide evolved into my report on and to that community.

Early in 1972, Long Island's *Newsday* hired me as music critic. The CG, conceived since its second installment as twenty alphabetically arranged reviews, wasn't suited to the daily's format; instead, I tied two "record capsules" thematically to my Sunday column and contributed 500-word batches of caps to the review section. This material was compiled by Dave Marsh at the Detroit-based rockmag *Creem* into a monthly feature. The *Creem* slot was one reason I lugged my portable phonograph on a long cross-country vacation in 1973 and wrote caps for the remainder of a six-month leave. And when I became music editor of *The Voice* in 1974, *Creem* decided to reprint the CG.

Writing for *Newsday* used up a lot of energy, but as an editor I had more to say than time to say it, and the Consumer Guide became my outlet. As a result, it took a quantum leap. Induced by my writers to make contact with music that didn't come naturally, I learned to like a lot of it, a lucky thing in a time when the mainstream had already turned to slush and Patti Smith didn't belong to ASCAP yet. I got into the habit of condensing one or two fairly complex ideas into most entries, which expanded to an average of eighty words. My one-liners became sharper, less willful. And while my evaluations still sprang from personal pleasure, I was no longer content merely to react and pass judgment — the first-person singular became an option rather than a matter of principle. None of which meant the Consumer Guide was turning respectable — not if I could help it. I'd always believed that rock criticism should piss people off, and every improvement made my gibes harder to sneeze at.

And who (besides publicists and other bizzers) would be doing the sneezing? It was all very well to posit a community, and I believed I had at least one reader in every segment of it, from upwardly mobiles on the streets of Harlem to Oregon radicalesbians. But I tried not to idealize my audience, even positing a rather unromantic typical consumer. Most likely he didn't exist, not down to the last detail. But he served as a useful paradigm. Just like me when I subscribed to *The Voice* at Dartmouth fifteen years before, he was a bright, white, college-age male. He listened to New York's free-form WNEW-FM with more reservations about its heavy metal than its singer-songwriters — not because he wasn't a rock and roll fan, but because his first commitment was to his own brain. He knew very little about top forty. Even though he liked a good beat he paid small attention to black rock, and he never listened to real country music even though he liked good songs. His basic sympathies were with the popular end of semipopular music, whatever form it might take. It was my mission to open him up.

To do this, I continued to monitor ninety percent of the albums that came my way — at least 1500 a year. My swag included all U.S.-release major-label pop (except for some country) and a good portion of the minor-label output, with the gaps falling among regional country and r&b/soul/disco specialists and the really tiny folk companies as well as in jazz, where my coverage has been enthusiastic but inexpert and quite haphazard. I definitely did monitor rather than listen — once half the stuff reached my changer I knew it would never get there twice. But lots of records I had to hear two or three times before I could put them aside. Everything B plus and above made the column, and so did most of the Bs; for color, vitriol, and news value, I added major-artist disappointments, records enjoying inflated word-of-mouth or sales, and the occasional horrifying curiosity. Sometimes I couldn't think of anything interesting to say about an eligible LP, sometimes I couldn't make up my mind, and too often I just missed things. But I paid my way — deciding a record is a B minus by playing it a dozen times feels a whole lot like work.

Initially, I figured that transforming this work into a book would be a piece of cake — a month or two of revisions and additions and I'd be ready for history. I ended up putting in fourteen hours a day seven days a week between February and July of 1980, and that was only the big push. I'd known that the early CGs were in need of expansion, that I'd have to grade compilations and go back to records that had passed me by, and that some artists merited complete reevaluations. But I hadn't realized how much of the pre-'76 material was inadequate by my later standards. I hadn't realized how many good albums I'd skipped; I hadn't realized how many best-ofs there *were*. And I hadn't realized how many major musicians I'd misunderstood, shortchanged, or avoided. In short, I hadn't realized I'd have to write two-thirds of the book from scratch.

The sheer effort this new project required presented a formal problem. Ordinarily, I listen to a new LP over weeks or months, so that it becomes a companion rather than a critical object, and yet my responses retain the freshness of recent acquaintance. Forced labor seemed inimical to this ideal relationship. I did my best, however, to simulate real-life conditions. I began listening early to artists who'd always given me trouble, going through careers chronologically to minimize hindsight. If possible, I based my capsules on Consumer Guides and essays written when the records came out, and included the original grades of those I'd changed my mind about (unless the information disturbed the tone or flow of my comment — this is a reference book, not a confessional). I always wrote in the present tense, though I sometimes gave into the "at first I thought" construction toward which so many problematic albums gravitate, and located each record in time by means of a U.S. release date (since it's hard enough to get years accurate, I didn't bother with months). I hope the result comes across both considered and immediate, like good rock and roll.

The other big problem was where it would all end. Since my material only dated back to mid-'69, a basic shape suggested itself — this would be a book about the albums of the '70s. I'd follow my own rules faithfully by including every B plus rock LP I could get my ears on and passing over very few Bs. Down below would be record-by-record rundowns (ignoring especially useless live albums) on all major artists (but what is art?) plus other matters of historical interest — which since this is rock and roll would mean giving the trivial, the venal, the ephemeral, and the absolutely forgettable their due. I didn't worry about what was in catalogue, partly because cut-out bins, used record shops, collectors' exchanges, imports, reissues, and simple time lag all work to make that distinction meaningless, partly because I wanted to honor art (but what is art?) over commerce. As there was no practical way to be comprehensive about imports, even English imports, I decided regretfully to omit the few I dote on (Big Youth's *Screaming Target,* Culture's *Two Sevens Clash,* The Plastic People's *Egon Bondy's Happy Hearts Club Banned,* X-Ray Spex' *Germ Free Adolescents,* the Heartbreakers' *L.A.M.F.,* Johnny Thunders's *So Alone,* the Beggars Banquet punk compilation *Streets,* and the original version of *The Clash*) and leave the discovery of others to a less harried time.

To some this schema may seem a little arbitrary, but that's the way it is with schemas. Within my guideline — worthwhile albums released in the U.S. in 197X — I've been as complete as possible. On the other hand, no record that missed the cutoff will be found here — not *London Calling* nor *Crawfish Fiesta* nor *Live/Dead* nor *Oh! Pleasant Hope,* all of which came within weeks and all of which I've written perfectly reprintable tidbits about. I should emphasize that my completeness warranty applies only to "rock," which in my usage (and it's an outrage that I should even have to explain this) encompasses all black pop since r&b. And I should point out that since the grades do reflect my tastes, devotees of such woebegone '70s genres as country-rock, heavy metal, fusion, and boogie will find many of their favorites missing. Although I've covered hundreds of LPs in the roots genres of country and blues, including every good one I could find, completeness in those fields was beyond my means. I've also reviewed many singer-songwriters who would have been called folkies before the advent of James Taylor, a few avant-gardey electronic experiments, some African music, and other oddities. But while I've rated dozens of comedy albums over the years, not even the Firesign Theatre made the book. I've omitted jazz, which is a whole different world, although I did cover a few records that speak to what I think of as my rock sensibility (specifically including all of Miles Davis, father of fusion and numerous black-sheep sons). And I've omitted gospel and salsa.

I hope a useful — nay, essential — buyers' guide has emerged from all this. Also a valuable reference work. And a great bathroom book. But I must admit that while I don't really expect anyone to sit down and read it from cover to cover, I nevertheless like to fantasize that I've also provided a kind of piecemeal critical history — the story of a much misunderstood musical decade, arranged alphabetically.

The Decade

The decade is of course an arbitrary schema itself — time doesn't just execute a neat turn toward the future every ten years. But like a lot of artificial concepts — money, say — the category does take on a reality of its own once people figure out how to put it to work. "The '60s are over," a slogan one only began to hear in 1972 or so, mobilized all those eager to believe that idealism had become passe, and once they were mobilized, it had. In popular music, embracing the '70s meant both an elitist withdrawal from the messy concert and counterculture scene and a profiteering pursuit of the lowest common denominator in FM radio and album rock. But soon after this process began, the spectre of the previous decade was invoked to rather different ends. Nascent punks reviled the '60s because they had spawned the '70s, blaming the excess and dishonesty of hippiedom for everything softheaded, long-haired, and piggy in a rock industry grown flatulent beyond its greediest fantasies. If the '60s were over in 1972, the '70s were in trouble by 1977. Don't get me wrong — the Eagles and Foreigner and Earth, Wind & Fire are, er, survivors. Good or bad they're careerists, they jog two miles a day, and they're all destined to outlast the Ramones. But you don't get the sense that these quintessential '70s bands conceive themselves as '70s bands. After all, what kind of a distinction is that?

Rock may have turned into a multibillion-dollar industry in the '70s, it may have doubled its market in ten years, but at the same time it suffered a loss of cultural prestige that not even a trade magazine could twist with statistics. Maybe the Bee Gees became more popular than the Beatles, but they were never more popular than Jesus. Insofar as the music retained any mythic power, the myth was self-referential — there were lots of songs about the rock and roll life but very few about how rock could change the world, except as a new brand of painkiller. Jerry Brown and Jimmy Carter — Jimmy Carter! — exploited the music to youthen up their images, not to affect opinion; even the antinukers acted more like bait than inspiration. And by most people's standards, a rough matchup of '60s and '70s artists — Smokey

Robinson vs. Gamble & Huff, Bob Dylan vs. Neil Young, the Beatles vs. Rod Stewart or Stevie Wonder or Elton John or Linda Ronstadt or Fleetwood Mac (or some combination of the five), the Stones vs. Led Zeppelin, Aretha Franklin or Sam Cooke or Otis Redding vs. Al Green, James Brown vs. James Brown, Jimi Hendrix vs. God, Sly Stone vs. George Clinton, Lou Reed vs. Johnny Rotten — pits genius against talent again and again.

Yet, somehow, unlike a lot of my generational and even critical colleagues, I've never been tempted to let my turntable go to seed or to keep it in trim wearing out copies of *Dictionary of Soul* and *The Who Sell Out*. Ever the incomplete skeptic, I remained unconvinced that such contests were as one-sided as rock mythmongers assumed. Not only did almost all my '70s superstars do decidedly less super work in the '60s (score one for artistic maturity) but at least six of my '60s heroes — Dylan, the Stones, Aretha, Hendrix, Sly, and Uncle Lou, plus John Lennon, if he counts — did some of their greatest work after their supposed time was over. For the most part, this was in the early '70s, but maybe a bad decade deserves credit for having the modesty to begin its spiritual life two or three years late. And even the staunchest neoreactionary will perhaps grant that the utopian/millenarian spirit of the '60s, outgoing and visionary though it was, was deepened in certain instances by the weary savvy that followed, self-pitying and cynical though it was. *Imagine*, *There's a Riot Goin' On*, *Exile on Main St.*, and *Blood on the Tracks* are all '70s albums in the best possible way — their distance from the action permits them a reflective complexity beyond the reach of rock and rollers in the '60s, though quite a few went for it.

Granted, it took more than an inspired synthesis of artistic sagacity and spiritual fatigue to create those records — they exploit an acumen about how to make albums that barely existed before the mid-'60s but has jes grew ever since. This in turn would seem to speak well for studio sophistication, the most widely touted "artistic" benefit of the decade's rampaging pop professionalism. But I don't hear it that way. For in fact *Riot* and *Exile* defy standards of punch and aural clarity that Sly and the Stones were instrumental in laying down, while *Imagine* was produced by mono maniac Phil Spector, not exactly a '70s fella. And *Blood on the Tracks*, like almost all of Dylan's albums, was recorded fast, to get a spontaneous feel; when some tracks didn't come out so good he rerecorded them with session men from Minneapolis, in retrospect a hilarious slap at the N.Y.-L.A. studio establishment. In short, the acumen these records exploited was the kind of conceptual audacity that began with, you know, *Sgt. Pepper* (*Rubber Soul*, actually, if not *Bringing It All Back Home*) and was later subverted by mealy-mouthed pros who talked art while rolling out product. Not that all four records — especially *Exile*, that apotheosis of murk — didn't capitalize on engineering expertise. But where such good-to-great albums as *Heart Like a Wheel*, *Aja*, and *Rumours* celebrate technology, these challenge its hegemony. Which may be one reason their particular mastery hits home.

Hits home here, I must emphasize once again. Tastes do vary, and mine are still with semipopular music. Although most of the records I consider the finest of the decade have made money, only a few have gone platinum, now the standard of public acceptance among rock professionals, and those by my very favorite bands, the New York Dolls and the Clash, haven't even made money (not in America, anyway). This fondness of mine for the nasty, brutish, and short intensifies a common semipopular tendency in which lyrical and conceptual sophistication are applauded while musical sophistication — jazz chops or classical design or avant-garde innovation — is left to the specialists. This isn't merely because we're suckers for snappy melodies with a strong beat, but because we find upon reflection that we value crudeness actively, as a means to some sort of vitality. And when rock pros define musical sophistication as an overlay of polish and/or flair on the same old snappy melodies and strong beat, they only encourage our atavism — such standards not only have nothing to do with artistic advance but spell an end to any sense of spontaneity, innocence, or discovery. We believe that what really tones up our beloved basics is the kind of conviction that can make change happen from the inside — even jazz chops or classical design or avant-garde innovation, if one (or all) should fit.

The semipopular is the crux of a decade. It's a truism now; for some it's been a truism longer than it's been true. But there's no way to proceed without reprising. If in the '60s rock and roll had cultural life, then in the '70s it had subcultural life. Even when it achieves multiplatinum, there's rarely any reason to feel that its millions respond to more than a fraction of what makes it as good as it is. Its consensus is no longer enough — it has to justify itself formally, *as art*. Not surprisingly, though, its gratifications still have a lot to do with its popular status — or rather, its semipopular status: the connection is as much to a mode of communication as to an audience. After all, in a world where all kinds of self-described avant-gardists believe the web of mass media is a key to the zeitgeist, it's only fair that a few formal advantages should accrue to artists who actually command the usages of a mass medium.

Sometimes these are simply thematic. The New York Dolls can say more about the Alienation of Modern Youth than *A Clockwork Orange* not just because they enact it from the inside, or because David Johansen is smarter (and more of a humanist) than Anthony Burgess, but because rock and roll was conceived as an outlet for adolescent yearnings, giving Johansen access to expressive material Burgess couldn't imagine. To make rock and roll is also an ideal way to explore intersections of sex, love, violence, and fun, to broadcast the delights and limitations of the regional, and to deal with the depradations and benefits of mass culture itself.

But beyond raw content there are resonances, in the '70s confined mostly to the head (whereas those of the '60s touched the spirit). Given their pop context, Steely Dan's bebop usages and Brian Eno's avant-gardey moves and the Ramones' pseudo-know-nothing minimalism and George Clinton's mocking mystagogic sci-fi lingo are attractive not only for themselves but for the criss-crossing recontextualizations they achieve. It's more than that, too. Ordinary rock and rollers are prisoners of their form, though since the form is part-ordinary by heritage they often make their jailhouse sound like home. But the great ones give off an aura of democratic grace; they make you feel they've *chosen* a colloquial voice, out of irresistible good-heartedness (or in the case of the nastier ones, an instinctive contempt for snobbery). And at their very best they can take you to that primordial, preverbal place where all human beings really are equal — without ever giving in to its dark power.

All of which suggests why those rough matchups I set up aren't as one-sided as they seem. Sure something's been lost — the democratic aura is healthiest when it's in contact with a vital audience. But the loss of the audience can't be blamed primarily on the artists. Most rock and roll stars succumbed knavishly to the pressures and temptations of the middle '70s, but even those few remarkable ones who had the guts to go against the grain — George Clinton, David Bowie, Bob Marley, Bryan Ferry, Bruce Springsteen, Patti Smith among the newcomers, Neil Young and Al Green among the already successful — failed to go all the way saleswise. And this was because the punks were right — among other things, the '60s were full of shit, generating good feelings (and good records) that were rooted in self-deception, especially about the malleability of power. In the '70s the powerful took over, as rock industrialists capitalized on the national mood to reduce potent music to an often reactionary species of entertainment — and to transmute rock's popular base from audience to market.

In effect, what the best artists did in response, whether they played guts ball against the new hegemony, or — like Steely Dan, Randy Newman, Brian Eno, Joni Mitchell, Allen Toussaint, and many others — merely circumvented it, was to act semipopular even when they were in fact much bigger. Think of Neil Young and Joni Mitchell and David Bowie refusing to repeat obvious successes, or of Steely Dan's apparently premature withdrawal from live performance, or of George Clinton's whitey-baiting, or of Al Green's religious fantasies, or of Eno and Toussaint using rock projects to bankroll more esoteric ventures. And if this seems like elitism, consider that only the most popular of all these, Steely Dan, seems elitist in the pejorative sense. The others were merely autonomous or trying to be, reacting defensively to a change we can only pin down in retrospect; at various times during the first half of the decade they all came to feel that they could no longer say what they had to say to an audience that was really listening. And so, with expansion through outreach cut off, they put their energies and their agape into expansion through form.

More charitable choices were still possible, but in 1974 or 1975 the mainstream was in bad shape. Among superduperstars, only Stevie Wonder, Fleetwood Mac, Bob Dylan (not for long), Pink Floyd (maybe), and Elton John (so prolific his misses don't count) did consistently good work in the heart of the '70s, while mortals like Lynyrd Skynyrd, Millie Jackson, and Bonnie Raitt (if they had any likes) were all but buried amid the garbage. And what made most of these mainstream artists special wasn't how eloquently they spoke for their fans, which was the way it was supposed to work in the '60s, but how honestly — or at least intensely or extravagantly, at least something that challenged expectations — they spoke *to* them. No matter how eager to zonk or mellow out the audience seemed to be, the music demanded alertness, conscious perception, sometimes even growth. Except that demanded is too strong a term — requested, or maybe permitted, is more like it.

Perhaps most important of all, the semipopular permeated two crucial, interrelated areas: failures and movements. Beautiful losers are a rock tradition that goes all the way back, as countless unjustly forgotten blues, rockabilly, doowop, and garage-band forty-fives attest. But heroic failed album artists — artists with half an hour in them rather than three minutes — are a legacy of the days of expanded consciousness that flourished in the era of corporate rock, with its habitual faith in venture capital. The worthwhile LP that neither portends the ripening of a long and honorable career nor sells diddleysquat is more a feature of the '70s than the '60s. Much of the best disco continued the fine old tradition of the one-shot, and without unprofitable but seminal albums by the Stooges and the Dolls, punk might never have happened. Most plentiful, however, have been spinoffs of the '70s' dominant movement. Admittedly, it's a conceit to refer to it as a movement, since it never announced or probably even saw itself as one, but that only serves a rabidly anticollectivist decade right. Torpedo a phrase of Harold Rosenberg's and call it the herd of independent voices — all the solo vocalist-composers fending for themselves on the fringes of the industry. These included substantial artists like John Prine and Leonard Cohen and Loudon Wainwright, fatuous pros like Paul Williams and John David Souther and Don McLean, and all manner of sports and oddballs: Thomas Jefferson Kaye, Andy Fairweather Low, James Talley, Terry Garthwaite, John Cale, Paul Pena, Randall Bramblett, Garland Jeffreys, Mary McCaslin, Kevin Coyne, and on and on. The whole mainstream aesthetic, with its cult of the studio and its revanchist individualism, could have been designed for such folks, and they came up with an enormous store of obscure but significant albums.

I used to think movements and their less ideological cousins, genres, were bad for rock and roll; they went with declining cultural prestige, living proof that the expansion of the audience entailed disastrous fragmentation. Fragmentation too is a '70s phenomenon. It goes back to whenever arty types began to find "the best" rock worthy of attention in the '60s, but in the '60s tolerance was the rule; it was easier to name rough substyles — say British invasion, folk-rock, psychedelic, and soul — than to analyze their separate audiences (even racial distinctions were fuzzy). Not until 1968 or 1969, when it became a hippie commonplace to dismiss soul as "commercial" and when bubblegum and "white blues" developed into clear categories, did the breakdown really begin. And only in the '70s did genres start asserting themselves: singer-songwriter and interpreter, art-rock and heavy metal and country-rock and boogie, fusion and funk and disco and black MOR, punk and new wave, and somehow straddling them all (except for punk, God bless) the monolith of pop-rock. Barren, a lot of these styles might seem. But every one of them produced good music.

A complication here is that semipopular music was invented by black people long before rock or for that matter bebop; every time Louis Armstrong sent up a pop tune he achieved recontextualizations the likes of which have rarely been heard since. So in the '70s, as in the '60s and '50s, there was a whole body of semipopular music that had just about nothing to do with rock and roll. I don't count fusion out yet, not with Ornette Coleman and Blood Ulmer working variations and a whole generation of real jazz players rediscovering the joys of blues and the 4/4, but that's not even what I mean — when I think about the decade's music, I think about all the new jazz I enjoyed and all I didn't have time or ears for. I also think of the music's greatest professionals, singers who rock the blues rather than swinging them, who interpret a song rather than transform it; crafty geniuses like Ray Charles, B. B. King, and Esther Phillips may not have released one great album in the '70s, but they did record twice as many good cuts as, for instance, Paul Simon. And I think about the persistence of Chicago blues, which was probably better documented in the '70s than in the '60s, thanks especially to the folkie Leonard Chess, Bruce Iglauer of Alligator Records.

In sum, I probably enjoyed the '70s' music as much as or more than the '60s', with movements and genres the key to my pleasure. Which means that it is now time once again to refer to my theoretical '60s–'70s matchups. First of all, I cheated. Bob Dylan vs. Neil Young wasn't a fair statement of the alternatives, because formally it was a decade of Dylans. I mentioned only Young because I regard the solo artists who've achieved major popularity — James Taylor, Jackson Browne, John Denver, and so forth — as lightweights, though I might have tipped my hand by bringing in Joni Mitchell. But once you accept the notion that the decade's best music has been semipopular, you can proceed immediately to Van Morrison, whom many sensible people (not me) prefer to Dylan. Then go to the brilliant Randy Newman, then to Prine, Wainwright, and Cohen, and then stick Richard Thompson and Arlo Guthrie in somewhere. Are the '70s looking better? Note that I cheated in other ways, too. There's no '60s equivalent to Steely Dan or Brian Eno or Miles Davis or Bonnie Raitt (keep your Joan Baez to yourself), so I left them out. The ska of the '60s had nothing on the reggae of the '70s, but since (like most Americans) I know Jamaican rock very sketchily, I left that out, too.

But beyond this innocent chicanery, my matchups were deceitful in a more fundamental way, because the whole idea, the very terms of the comparison, favored the '60s. Genius vs. talent indeed. For all its putative egalitarianism, what the previous decade seems to have bestowed on rock and roll is a shitload of Greatness. Now, I think that's great — *Let It Bleed* and Smokey's *Greatest Hits Vol. 2* still speak to me with startling fullness and authority. But by the late '70s I didn't actually listen to them all that much, because I was too busy catching up with the latest — and maybe the greatest, too, but that wasn't what mattered — new wave. Starting with punk and running through its various pop, reggae, funk, and avant-garde offshoots, this was an idea — that is, a movement — that occasioned a startling quantity of good rock and roll. About audiences, I remain something of a '60s holdout. But if music makers themselves are compared collectively instead of individually, something all '60s holdouts should be more than willing to do, the '70s come out earning all the attention I've given them, and more. And if records, especially long-playing records, are how we remember the musical past — which they are — then the '70s are going to end up sounding very fine indeed. Rock and roll's first quarter century produced well under a thousand excellent albums. Close to two-thirds of them appeared during its last and least romantic decade.

The Criteria

When I became a critic, I believed in the magic that could free my soul —
through the modern miracles of mass production and marginal differentiation,
rock and roll seemed capable of giving me pleasure for the rest of my life.
And it probably will. But if late-'70s power pop proved anything, it's that
the best melodies and snappiest beats don't in themselves guarantee spontaneity, innocence, discovery, conviction, youthful lyricism, youthful anger, or
democratic aura. The best artists have nurtured rock and roll's connection to
all these things by opening up their music and their audience — myself included.

It's not enough for me simply to identify my musical preoccupations as
beat, electricity, and song — rock and rollers keep revealing new possibilities
in apparently transparent forms. But it's a good start. In 1967 I was addicted
to the r&b backbeat, sometimes whitened and/or mechanized, sometimes softened with a Caribbean fillip. Now I listen for, and am turned on by, rhythm
(especially polyrhythm, in funk and the great world outside), repetition (rock
as electronic trance music and vice versa), and tempo (faster, faster). That's
what I mean by beat. Electricity comprises perfectionism (studiomania in the
manner of Steely Dan or the great L.A. producers at their young best), power
(as orchestrated by the few worthwhile heavy metal bands as well as many
raving punks), and galvanic noise (investigated most fruitfully by guitarists,
although explorers from other fields like Gram Parsons, Philip Glass, and
Miles Davis have taught us a lot). Song is most of what's left. Alec Wilder,
that renowned connoisseur of "American popular song," claims that it pretty
much died around 1950, so I guess I'm attracted to something else. Maybe
it's streetsong, or electric folksong, or (forgive me) songpoetry, or just American semipopular song, a neat term that unfortunately sounds too arty. For if
the '70s taught me to respect the idea of songpoetry, they also taught me to
treasure the common wisdom of the pop lyric.

Even in the '50s I appreciated a well-turned lyric, and in retrospect the
heightened vernacular of Leiber & Stoller and my man Chuck Berry seems a

clear precedent for both the colloquial specificity and the associative flights of writers as diverse as Randy Newman, John Prine, and August Darnell. But I was a big fan of nonsense syllables, too, and I liked the sincerely dumb stuff. In the late '60s I retained those affections, but not without condescension — for a while it got harder to hear Smokey Robinson for the wordmaster he was and is. I was never taken in by the image-laden versifying so many young composers served up as poetry — despite such literary lights as Leonard Cohen, Joni Mitchell, Van Morrison, and Tom Verlaine, I've always believed the basic evocative task of the words was to enrich the music's passionately conversational, often rough-hewn vocal stance. But only in the '70s did I realize that I'd never developed the habit of expecting philosophical or political apercus from a song. This isn't to say I never got them — thanks Clash, thanks Sly. But they were always lyrical rather than analytic — these were songs, after all. And usually, the song that made me say aha merely reminded me of something that had slipped my mind. One way I've gotten into country music is as the domain of the truest singer-songwriters (and interpreters) — there are a hundred cheatin' songs with more truth in them than any but five or so of Jackson Browne's. Banal, maybe, but remember that cliche about cliches — they only get that way by saying something real.

Music comes first; the songs I love include instrumental compositions/ performances from Hendrix to Eno to Hound Dog Taylor. And music is more than beat and electricity — in addition to the wonderful melodies (rock and rollers have uncovered a lot of sweet, simple ones, and some sour, sophisticated ones as well) there is the little matter of how those melodies are sung. Improvisation is also a major factor, though to these jazz-fledged ears rock's improvisatory integrity inheres more in choruses, riffs, licks, and sheer spirit than in the long solos that so few of its players have the chops or imagination to sustain. But lyrics do something for music —they bestow (or clarify) (or complicate) meaning. And thus they can make a context for music that by pop standards is quiet or spare or dry or lifeless or forbidding, so that in the end the most hyperactive ass-shake ideologue can learn to enjoy semipopular rock-by-historical-association — acoustic guitar meditations or synthesizer fantasias or rhythmic leaps or idealized raveups, sometimes even without drums. I know, because it's happened to me — with Taj Mahal, Pere Ubu, the Meters, John McLaughlin.

Just as a semipopular orientation has heightened my pleasure, it's also defined my displeasure — my aversion for all attempts to elevate the music into something "better" or reduce it to the lowest common denominator so beloved of marketing sharpies and mass culture theorists. Devotees of American culture have been battling the forces of the genteel since Melville, and though I can enjoy such art-lovers as Judy Collins and Jon Anderson once in a very great while, the bulk of their music has been fatuous and the entirety of their influence pernicious. Less annoying but even more dangerous are the exploiters who, instead of illuminating the unique vantage of kids (and others) untrammeled by education and big ideas, cater to everything lazy, cowardly, and brutal in the rock audience. For all its grandiose symphonic tendencies, heavy metal is a real rock and roll style, but with very few exceptions its content is egoistic at best and nihilistic at worst. And the cheap compassion and covert self-love of legions of nostalgia-mongers and pop-rock hitmakers have turned AM radio into the refuge from intelligence that fools have always believed it to be.

Despite that last caveat, though, I must admit that most of the records I like work some variation on good-melodies-with-a-snappy-beat. This formula is one of the best substitutes for intelligence known to humankind, and I'll forgive a lot of banality and even some stupidity in anyone who can bring it off with an iota of spirit or originality — if a record can get me humming or bouncing around, it has earned at least a portion of my approval. But one luxury of being a critic — by which I mean getting your records free — is that you have to hum pretty loud and bounce pretty hard before fully suspending your disbelief. In the preceding paragraphs I've tried to suggest what makes me hum loud and bounce hard and what doesn't. Though some gentle souls may find my judgments unnecessarily severe, I'm really quite lenient. In fact, one point of the Consumer Guide is that it's possible to enjoy rock and roll without compromise. I've found well over 500 A records in the '70s alone, and though I listen to music all the time I don't hear enough of them.

Judgments were simpler in pop's early days partly because rock and roll was designed to be consumed in three-minute take-it-or-leave-it segments. The rise of the LP as a form — as an artistic entity, as they used to say — has complicated how we perceive and remember what was once the most evanescent of the arts. The album may prove a '70s totem — briefer configurations were making a comeback by decade's end. But for the '70s it will remain the basic musical unit, and that's OK with me. I've found over the years that the long-playing record, with its twenty-minute sides and four-to-six compositions/performances per side, suits my habits of concentration perfectly. Unlike many of my colleagues and even some consumers, I rarely sit at my turntable playing the same track over and over. In fact, my turntable is that bane of discophiles, a changer — to aid my work I even shuffle records before I stack them so I can be caught up short by some work of genius that I had mistaken for dogshit. When the Consumer Guide started, I often listened casually, letting a few key songs determine the overall impression conveyed by the grade. Now it's my practice to scrutinize each cut (or take note when I find it impossible to do so) after letting an album sink in for five or ten plays. Almost any LP will include failed music, but you really can stick to records on which even the ordinary material affords some modicum of pleasure when you tune in. Most of those I recommend with a B plus or better fall into that category.

Overall impression still counts, though — there really is such a thing as a concept album. Concept intensifies the impact (and improves the grade) of the Who's *Quadrophenia* and Mary McCaslin's *Way Out West* and Millie Jackson's *Caught Up* in more or less the way Sgt. Pepper intended. But the sheer historical audacity of Joni Mitchell's *For the Roses* or *Never Mind the Bollocks, Here's the Sex Pistols* has a comparable effect. It's also a species of concept that pushes a rhythmically unrelenting album like *The Wild Magnolias*, or a vocally irresistible one like Shirley Brown's *Woman to Woman*, to a deeper level of significance. And while compilation albums by album artists (as opposed to stylistically unified singles specialists) are often useless, sometimes they present themselves as events: *The Kinks Kronikles* or *Changesonebowie* or *A 25th Anniversary in Show Business Salute to Ray Charles*. Similarly, most live doubles are profit-taking recaps marred by sound and format inappropriate to phonographic reproduction (you can't put sights, smells, or fellowship on audio tape). But for Joe Cocker and Bette Midler and Bob-Dylan-in-the-arena, the form makes a compelling kind of sense.

I've tried to grade every '70s rock album worth owning and most of those worth considering. If it's rock and not included, my implicit advice is to forget it. A few artists I respect have been relegated to ''Subjects for Further Research''; many I don't respect have been banished to ''Distinctions Not Cost-Effective'' and ''Meltdown.'' I haven't always rated later releases by performers who've fallen victim to the familiar rock and roll pattern, the fate of lyric artists since the dawn of romanticism — early peak, long and depressing deterioration. I've occasionally skipped albums in the middle of a mediocre career. And I've rarely searched conscientiously for the best LPs by artists I have no use for — if Harry Chapin has come up with a C plus, I don't want to know about it. A lot of serendipity and personal eccentricity obviously informed my more marginal choices. The decade eligibility of previously unavailable music was determined more by date of release than of recording; best-ofs had to cover material from the '70s (or at least 1969) to qualify. I've specified catalogue numbers only in the few cases where two albums of very similar artist and title appear on the same label. When an album runs less than fifteen minutes per side, I've added up the cut lengths (according to the label, which admittedly isn't always accurate) and indicated total time.

Ultimately, each grade represents a synthesis of aesthetic judgment, which is relatively objective, and function analysis, which isn't. When a grade originally appears, part of its intent is predictive — it asserts that I will (or won't) find rewards in a given record six months or six years hence. And a good many times I've simply been wrong — for the most part, the changed grades reflect the actual use I've gotten out of an LP. This is obviously a very personal approach, and you'd probably be well-advised to adjust my grades according to our differences of taste. That's why I've tried to outline what my taste is.

But on the other hand, it's impossible to make a life out of rationalizing/ explaining your own opinions without believing in some part of you that those opinions jibe with the zeitgeist. So if you find yourself valuing many of my C plusses and rejecting a lot of my As, maybe we'd better not have lunch.

The Grades

An **A+** record is an organically conceived masterpiece that repays prolonged listening with new excitement and insight. It is unlikely to be marred by more than one merely ordinary cut.

An **A** is a great record both of whose sides offer enduring pleasure and surprise. You should own it.

An **A−** is a very good record. If one of its sides doesn't provide intense and consistent satisfaction, then both include several cuts that do.

A **B+** is a good record, at least one of whose sides can be played with lasting interest and the other of which includes at least one enjoyable cut.

A **B** is an admirable effort that aficionados of the style or artist will probably find quite listenable.

A **B−** is a competent or mildly interesting record that will usually feature at least three worthwhile cuts.

A **C+** is a not disreputable performance, most likely a failed experiment or a pleasant piece of hackwork.

A **C** is a record of clear professionalism or barely discernible inspiration, but not both.

A **C−** is a regrettably successful exploitation or a basically honest but quite incompetent stab at something more.

A **D+** is an appalling piece of pimpwork or a thoroughly botched token of sincerity.

It is impossible to understand why anyone would buy a **D** record.

It is impossible to understand why anyone would release a **D−** record.

It is impossible to understand why anyone would cut an **E+** record.

E records are frequently cited as proof that there is no God.

An **E−** record is an organically conceived masterpiece that repays repeated listening with a sense of horror in the face of the void. It is unlikely to be marred by one listenable cut.

CONSUMER GUIDE

Albums of the Seventies

Abba: *Greatest Hits* (Atlantic '76). Although four of these songs have gone top twenty here, the title commemorates the band's conquest of such places as West Germany and Costa Rica, where Abba's Europop is the biggest thing since the Beazosmonds. Americans with an attraction to vacuums, late capitalism, and satellite TV adduce Phil Spector and the Brill Building Book of Hooks in Abba's defense, but the band's real tradition is the advertising jingle, and I'm sure their disinclination to sing like Negroes reassures the Europopuli. Pervasive airplay might transform what is now a nagging annoyance into an aural totem. It might also transform it into an ashtray. God bless America, we're not likely to find out which. **C+**

Abba: *Arrival* (Atlantic '77). Since this is already the best-selling group in the universe, I finally have an answer when people ask me to name the Next Big Thing. What I wonder is how we can head them off at the airport. Plan A: Offer Bjorn and Benny the leads in *Beatlemania* (how could they resist the honor?) and replace them with John Phillips and Denny Doherty. Plan B: Appoint Bjorn head of the U.N. and Benny his pilot (or vice versa) and replace them with John Lennon and Paul McCartney. Plan C: Overexpose them in singing commercials. Plan D: Institute democratic socialism in their native land, so that their money lust will meet with the scorn of their fellow citizens. **C**

Abba: *Greatest Hits Vol. 2* (Atlantic '79). Fourteen cuts, close to an hour of polyvinyl chloride, and only two of 'em made U.S. top ten. We have met the enemy and they are them. **C**

Ace: *Five-a-Side* (ABC '75). The single, "How Long," is welcomed by some desperate souls as a breakthrough for England's pub-rock movement. Bet if John David Souther lived in England he'd play pubs too. Super catchy, but even more banal than that term used as a superlative ordinarily implies, sung and played with a mildness infuriating in musicians of such skill but totally appropriate to lyricists of such underweening triviality. **C+**

David Ackles: *American Gothic* (Elektra '72). "I won't get maudlin," Ackles promises midway into the second side, locking himself in the barn as the dappled stallion gallops to join his brothers and sisters on the open range with his mane flying free in the breeze. **C−**

Aerosmith: *Get Your Wings* (Columbia '74). These prognathous New Englanders are musicianly (all things are relative) inheritors of the Grand Funk principle: if a band is going to be dumb, it might as well be American dumb. Here they're loud and cunning enough to provide a real treat for the hearing-impaired, at least on side one. Have a sense of humor about themselves, too, assuming "Lord of the Thighs" is intended as a joke. With dumb bands it's always hard to tell. Original grade: B. **B−**

Aerosmith: *Toys in the Attic* (Columbia '75). These boys are learning a trade in record time — even the sludgy numbers get crazy. Too bad the two real whompers are attached to rockstar lyrics, albeit clever ones, because Steve Tyler has a gift for the dirty line as well as the dirty look — anybody who can hook a song called "Adam's Apple" around the phrase "love at first bite" deserves to rehabilitate a blue blues like "Big Ten Inch Record." **B+**

Aerosmith: *Rocks* (Columbia '76). Dave Hickey compares the teen crossover of the year to a Buick Roadmaster, and he's right — they've retooled Led Zeppelin till the English warhorse is all glitz and flow, beating the shit out of Boston and Ted Nugent and Blue Oyster Cult in the process. Wish there were a lyric sheet — I'd like to know what that bit about J. Paul Getty's ear is about — but (as Hickey says) the secret is the music, complex song structures that don't sacrifice the basic 4/4 and I-IV-V. A warning, though: Zep's fourth represented a songmaking peak, before the band began to outgrow itself, and the same may prove true for this lesser group, so get it while you can. Original grade: B plus. **A−**

Aerosmith: *Draw the Line* (Columbia '77). The problem with the multiple-riff hi-test jobs that made *Rocks* rock was that when time came to follow up, the band was out of gas. The best of the three good ones here is a mold-breaking Joe-Perry-alone boogie that probably reflects the usual "internal tensions." Perry goes nowhere near the mold-breaking "Kings and Queens," synthesized medieval pomp-rock (cf. Styx, Rush) that proves beyond doubt that they won't bite "The Hand That Feeds." We knew it all along, guys. **B−**

Aerosmith: *Night in the Ruts* (Columbia '79). This opens with a promising song about their career called "No Surprize." Then they edge ever closer to the flash guitar, dull tempos, and stupid cover versions of heavy-metal orthodoxy. No surprise. **C+**

Africa Dances (Authentic '73). What *The Harder They Come* does for reggae this sampler attempts to do for the American-influenced urban music of Africa. Its scope is necessarily broad, but only once does an alien-sounding rhythm (Arabic tarabu) interfere with its remarkable listenability. The mood might be described as folk music with brass, for although the horn techniques are familiar from big-band jazz, r&b, and especially salsa, the overall effect is much less biting than that would imply. There's something penetratingly decent, humorous, and even civil about this music, as if the equanimity of tribal cultures at peace at least with themselves has not yet been overwhelmed by media-nourished cross-cultural complexities. If this is my misapprehension, perhaps it is reinforced by the fact that the lyrics aren't in English, although I don't get anything similar from salsa. Anyway, a find. Original grade: A minus. **A**

Charlie Ainley: *Bang Your Door* (Nemporer '78). The title cut is the raunchiest fuck-me song in years, and the funniest: when Charlie bellows, "I don't want you to fix my bed," the Misdemeanors chirp back, "I'm not." It just doesn't quit, and nothing else here comes up to it. But the overall level of rancor, humor, and genre experiment is gratifyingly high for what is basically an English r&b album. Bang on. **B+**

Air: *Air Lore* (Arista Novus '79). Demonstrating not only that ragtime (Scott Joplin) and New Orleans (Jelly Roll Morton) are Great Art consonant with Contemporary Jazz, but also that they're Corny. And that both Great Art and Corn can be fun. Which is why the somewhat stiff, if not corny, readings of the themes, especially "King Porter Stomp," don't get in the way. Although just what could get in the way of Henry Threadgill improvising over an explicit pulse for a whole album I can't imagine. **A**

Willie Alexander and the Boom Boom Band: *Willie Alexander and the Boom Boom Band* (MCA '77). I have hated these Beantowners steadfastly through independent singles, a guest shot at Max's, and *Live at the Rat*. White r&b with poor epiglottal hygiene, who needed it? Yet I've grown fond of this album. What seemed silly if not self-indulgent eccentricity in a failed thirty-five-year-old rock and roller is brave and funny on an honest-to-God major-label elpee. And "Lookin' Like a Bimbo" is an anthem for failed thirty-five-year-old rock and rollers. Original grade: B plus. **B**

Terry Allen: *Juarez* (Landfall '75). Cut to accompany a museum show by painter-sculptor Allen, who sings like a self-conscious Charlie Daniels, this explores Western-violence mythos with mucho grotesquery and nary a smile. Very, er, conceptual, as dissatisfied sculptor-painters like to put it. **C+**

Terry Allen: *Lubbock (on Everything)* (Fate '79). Maybe Allen meant *Juarez*'s overstatement to be funny, but it wasn't, because he wasn't. This time he sings like Kinky Friedman with a sense of humor, doing a lot better by his own words than Butch Hancock, the only lyricist in Texas (maybe anywhere) who merits a comparison. From football heroes gone wrong to noble floozies to farmers fiddling while Washington burns, he's a tale-spinning poet of the Panhandle, with local color provided by Joe Ely's homeboys. Like so many double-LPs — though a lot less than most — this could stand some editing. But since that would probably have meant omitting the songs about art, the one subject he knows better than Texas, I'll settle. **A–**

The Allman Brothers Band: *Idlewild South* (Atco '70). Anybody who can comp for Aretha Franklin and ghost as the fifth Domino is obviously on his way to titanhood. One guitarist never made an album, though, and this is a lot more than brother Duane's showcase. Backup guitarist Dickey Betts puts in two songs of inspiration — "Revival" shoulda been a hit — and Berry Oakley's bright "Hoochie Coochie Man" is a relief from the one-dimensional moan of the real leader of this band: little brother Gregg, whose "Midnight Rider" puts me in a forgiving mood anyway. [Reissued with *The Allman Brothers Band* as *Beginnings*.] **B+**

The Allman Brothers Band: *Live at the Fillmore East* (Capricorn '71). Four sides comprising seven titles — only two of them repeated (ad infinitum) from the band's studio albums — and they sure do boogie. But even if Duane Allman plus Dickey Betts does equal Jerry Garcia, the Dead know roads are for getting somewhere. That is, Garcia (not to bring in John Coltrane) always takes you someplace unexpected on a long solo. I guess the appeal here is the inevitability of it all. Original grade: C plus. **B–**

The Allman Brothers Band: *Eat a Peach* (Capricorn '72). Side three is a magnificent testament. It opens with Gregg doing Sonny Boy Williamson justice, wrenches through some of the most formally intense accompaniment Duane ever played, skips into a high-spirited Dickey Betts tune, and provides a coda for a whole sensibility in one two-minute acoustic duet. Side one sandwiches two subordinary Greggeries around an instrumental excursion that sounds like Dickey OD-ing on *Live/Dead*. And sides two and four comprise thirty-four minutes with an all-too-relaxing theme by Donovan Leitch. I know the pace of living is slow down there, but this verges on the comatose. And all the tape in the world isn't going to bring Duane back.　**B**

The Allman Brothers Band: *Brothers and Sisters* (Capricorn '73). Simplicity can be a virtue — the nice thing about the Allmans is that when they put two five-year-olds on the cover we know it's not some "decadent" joke. Gregg Allman is a predictable singer who never has an unpredictable lyric to work with anyway, and the jams do roll on, but at their best — "Ramblin' Man," a miraculous revitalization of rock's weariest conceit — they just may be the best, and on this album Dickey Betts's melodious spirituality provides unity and renewal.　**A−**

The Allman Brothers Band: *Win, Lose or Draw* (Capricorn '75). I've been telling cynics that the Brothers haven't broken up. Now I feel like maybe I was taken.　**C**

The Allman Brothers Band: *The Road Goes On Forever* (Capricorn '75). Not all of it is as great as those who crave it all believe. But given how poorly the Brothers' live extrapolations fare without their spectacular visuals, this seventeen-cut, two-record compilation is the one to own if one is all you need.　**A−**

The Allman Brothers Band: *Wipe the Windows, Check the Oil, Dollar Gas* (Capricorn '76). I suppose Duane (as well as Berry) is missed on this second ABB live double — Dickey's guitar ripples begin to sound like mirages over the long haul. But as boogie Muzak it's only marginally less useful than *Live at the Fillmore*. "Whipping Post"!　**B−**

The Allman Brothers Band: *Enlightened Rogues* (Capricorn '79). The heartening sense of overall conviction here doesn't extend to many specifics, with the surprising exception of Gregg's rough yet detailed vocals. But Ronnie Van Zant himself couldn't breathe life into these songs, most of which Dickey Betts was saving up for the third Great Southern album — now never to be heard, which is one good thing.　**C+**

Duane Allman: *An Anthology* (Capricorn '72). If Duane qualified as auteur, whatever that means, then he was the auteur-as-sideman. Over four sides (nineteen cuts, fifteen available elsewhere) he takes one vocal, contributes one original composition, and reserves his most definitive playing for other people's sessions — listen again to Boz Scaggs's "Somebody Loan Me a Dime," not to mention the overlays Clapton got out of him on "Layla." Since Duane's only concept was the open-ended jam that so many session players mistake for artistic fulfillment, this is just as well; any format that limits the Brothers to four-minute tracks has much to recommend it. It doesn't result in very coherent albums, though. For scholars and acolytes.　**B+**

Gregg Allman: *Laid Back* (Capricorn '73). Gregg still doesn't know the difference between drawling slowly and singing soulfully, and it isn't tragedy that makes him sound so doleful, it's a limited formal imagination. That said, it must be admitted that he puts a lot into "These Days" and "Midnight Rider," and that the reason you can listen to such originals as "Please Call Home" and "Multicolored Lady" isn't the writing. Original grade: C plus.　**B**

The Gregg Allman Band: *Playin' Up a Storm* (Capricorn '77). One expected the new band to cook, but the spiced-up song formulas are a surprise — and the timing, grit, and passion of Gregg's singing simply astonishing. My wife thinks Cher must be the first woman ever to make him feel something, while I suspect a sibling rivalry is brewing with Dickey. First round to (Cher) (big brother).　**B+**

The Alpha Band: *The Alpha Band* (Arista '76). Finally a decent record comes out of Rolling Thunder, from what sounds like a country-rock band shocked by city living into a credible, slightly surrealistic nastiness, rather than the usual sleazy lies. T-Bone Burnett is that rare combination, a tall, inspired crazy; David Mansfield is a precocious, multi-instrumental sound-effects man, and Steve Soles is a speed-rapping narcissist who can be thrown to the Poco fans. Plus a rhythm section that plays actual rock and roll. And Bobby Neuwirth in the background, where he belongs.   **B+**

The Alpha Band: *Spark in the Dark* (Arista '77). This unholy trio's second album is "humbly offered in the light of the triune God," but T-Bone Burnett still sounds like a helluva monad to me. He doesn't know as much as he thinks he does, but when he steps aside from the songwriting the group usually falls flat — and when he pitches in, these guys could almost pass for a country-rock Steely Dan without money.   **B+**

The Alpha Band: *The Statue Makers of Hollywood* (Arista '78). Now I learn that my man J. H. Burnett really is a born-again Christian, which must be why he feels so strongly about money changers and temples. Nonbelievers consider him shrill, but I find something sweet and reflective right beneath his cool, caustic self-righteousness. This is the weakest of three strong, oddball LPs, but David Mansfield's instrumental finesse makes the questionable cuts go, and Steven Soles keeps his mouth shut most of the time.   **B+**

Amazing Rhythm Aces: *Stacked Deck* (ABC '75). If you wanted to be stuffy about it, you could complain that Russell Smith's line about "two lovely lesbian ladies slow-dancin' on a parquet floor" is condescending, but I'll settle. There's enough natural hip here to last most Southern boogie bands a career, with the added attraction that this isn't a Southern boogie band, not hardly, despite the Memphis locus and blues inflections. Some of them worked with Jesse Winchester, but his magnolia rue didn't rub off either. Just

something else new under the sun.   **A−**

Amazing Rhythm Aces: *Too Stuffed to Jump* (ABC '76). The jazzy, boogie-based eclecticism and colloquial cleverness almost never transcend the cute and commercial, a major letdown after a debut album that may have fulfilled more promise than the group has.   **B−**

Amazing Rhythm Aces: *Burning the Ballroom Down* (ABC '77). Just figured out why I've always been attracted to Russell Smith's sly, sincere songs and lethargic though hardly shiftless phrasing — he's a kind of laid-back Ronnie Van Zant. Which must be why I don't like him as much as I liked Ronnie Van Zant.   **B−**

America: *History/America's Greatest Hits* (Warner Bros. '75). Randy Newman once described "A Horse with No Name" as "this song about a kid who thinks he's taken acid," and at least back then they were domesticating CSNY instead of CSN. More tuneful than Seals & Crofts but with less to say, which they've managed to conceal by establishing meaningless high-school verse as a pop staple, they might be remembered as the '70s' answer to the Association if they could come up with one song half as lively as "Windy" or "Along Comes Mary."   **C−**

Eric Andersen: *Blue River* (Columbia '72). I was ready to discard this but because it was so pretty I suffered second thoughts, which is too bad for both of us. In 1967, Andersen sounded like early electric Dylan, so now he sounds like . . . James Taylor. He's honest enough to back himself with a girlie chorus, but that's as far as his honesty goes. If I'm liable to run into noodleheads like Andersen walking down some country road, I'll feel safer in Central Park.   **C**

The Animals: **See the Original Animals**

Paul Anka: *Anka* (United Artists '74). Sure "You're Having My Baby" is a cute little single. But the rest of the album is the usual abortion. **C −**

Argent: *Argent* (Epic '70). "Dance in the Smoke" is to "Time of the Season" as "Time of the Season" was to "She's Not There," extending ex-Zombie keyboardist-vocalist-composer Rod Argent's pop breathiness another quantum away from cuteness and toward incantation. Add ex-Unit 4 + 2 guitarist-composer Russ Ballard's ceremonial "Liar," and the whole first side works as a catchy mystical ritual, with the worries of the world going up in flame at the climax. On side two, however, they reappear. **B**

Argent: *The Argent Anthology: A Collection of Greatest Hits* (Epic '76). Only on "Hold Your Head Up" did they ever get back to the gentle intensity that made their debut half a delight. With Rod Argent seeing Keith Emerson in the mirror and Russ Ballard contributing such FM fodder as "God Gave Rock and Roll to You," this is a more graphic document of what happened to the '60s than you want to hear. **C+**

Joan Armatrading: *Joan Armatrading* (A&M '76). It took me a long time to hear that this forthright (not to say stentorian) black Englishwoman was anything more than ' a postfeminist Odetta, but it's clear in retrospect that Armatrading was reaching for something more colorful and less pompous even on her apparently folky 1973 debut, *Whatever's for Us,* produced by Eltonian concertmaster Gus Dudgeon. Two years later, on *Back to the Night,* she had shucked both the portentous prettiness of Dudgeon and the vague portentousness of lyricist Pam Nestor, but only here, with production from Glyn Johns, does she find a context forceful enough to give her own maturing lyrics an edge. Helps that she's more comfortable singing, too. **B**

Joan Armatrading: *Show Some Emotion* (A&M '77). OK, I'm convinced. Sometimes funny, always real, and never ever pretentious, she proves that a big, husky voice needn't turn you

into a self-important fool. So why don't I have anything more specific to say about this record? Because most of the meaning of the ordinary-plus lyrics is conveyed by stance and nuance. **B+**

Joan Armatrading: *To the Limit* (A&M '78). The secret of Armatrading's songs is their plainness, but it's also their drawback. When she hits an image — "I read your letter yesterday/It fell between the covers/And my bare skin" — she lights up a real life. More often, though, she just says what she has to say with whatever unprepossessing idiom is at hand, and her melodies are even less inclined to witticism than her words. This style of candor, engaging in theory, escapes tedium in practice by way of Armatrading's bluntly dramatic singing. Rarely have less tuneful songs so impressed themselves on my mind. **B+**

Art Bears: *Hopes and Fears* (Random Radar '78). Despite rock instrumentation from Fred Frith, Chris Cutler, and friends and the rousing Who quote that kicks the best original song into high, this music is either consciously antipopular or "serious" with pretensions to accessibility. In either case it's Art — political Art, I know. The problem is, I don't get as much out of it as I do out of, say, the Cuban novelist Alejo Carpentier, or at least Bertolt Brecht and Hans Eisler, whose "On Suicide" announces the band's intent. Despite Dagmar's self-indulgent austerity, the stark, atonal music is often compelling, but while the lyrics are never stupid, they do depend on intellectual commonplaces — labyrinth imagery, reference to Greek myth, and other roundabout ways of saying not much. "In Two Minds," about a teenager's schizophrenia, is a commonplace too, but an illuminated one. And the envoi to Piers Plowman is a touch I like. **B**

Art Bears: *Winter Songs* (Ralph '79). With its tape loops, orchestral percussion, and artsong timbres, this is as far from rock as guitar-based music can be; it's also closer to Eno's hypnotic repetitions than Henry Co. has ever come. This time the lyrics aren't so much attempted myths as haiku-like apothegms set in some abstract historical space. They're not great poetry, but they're not bad poetry either, which combined with the music makes for pretty good poetry.   **B+**

Artful Dodger: *Artful Dodger* (Columbia '76). Having barely conquered my addiction to "Think Think," the supra-Beatles raver that opens side two, and having learned that "Think Think" stiffed as a single, I find myself clearheaded enough to report that if "Think Think" didn't make it this band will have to wait till next year, and to point out that next years sometimes come for bands this tight, melodic, and intense. Original grade: B plus.   **B**

Artful Dodger: *Honor Among Thieves* (Columbia '76). These kids deserve to turn into teen heroes everybody can be proud of. They respect the rock and roll verities, but in a dynamic rather than an arty or nostalgic way; their instrumental wallop is powerful enough to keep them in there with the heavies, but so deft that the lyricism of their songs is left untouched. A lot of bands around CBGB will spend their lives wishing they could have gotten it together like this.   **B+**

Artful Dodger: *Babes on Broadway* (Columbia '77). OK, two nice if slightly deliberate albums of power pop go virtually unnoticed, so you up the power, especially since you're running out of the cute tunes 'n' tricks that provide the pop. But then it isn't power pop any more — sounds almost like Angel, or Queen. Sounds pretty desperate, too.   **C+**

The A's: *The A's* (Arista '79). People say they take after the Dolls, but I hear the Boomtown Rats. At its best, their burlesque on a "teenage jerk off" (a title) who still gets "grounded" (another) is funny and a little nasty. At its worst it's boring and a little too nasty. In between it's got verve and you've heard it before.   **B**

Ashford & Simpson: *Gimme Something Real* (Warner Bros. '73). Can this marriage be saved? The problem: Good-but-not-great songwriters whose lush sentimentality would have been unforgivable had they worked for a white company instead of Motown leave Motown for white company. The doctor replies: if they develop the intestinal fortitude to go along with their own vocal limitations, they may not end up the Peaches & Herb of middle-class soul. What did they say? "Time is the space between you and me"? Well, sounds like a breakdown of communication as well.   **C**

Ashford & Simpson: *Send It* (Warner Bros. '77). They need more to get by, but they can call a filler instrumental "Bourgié Bourgié" if they want — they've earned it. The important thing is that after writing for Marvin & Tammi (& Diana) for all those years they've finally figured out how to sound like them. Upwardly mobile. **B**

Ashford & Simpson: *So So Satisfied* (Warner Bros. '77). As performers, these bigtime writer-producers have always struck me as a mite classy — by which I mean rich, among other things. Their genuinely eccentric romanticism only made their ad for the end of the rainbow more insidious, and so my tastes in nouveaux ran more to the showbiz vulgarity of Elton John and James Brown, or the lost-in-a-goldmine inconsistency of Stevie Wonder and John Lennon. Three strained, uneven albums didn't bend me, but *Send It* put a crimp in my bias, and this one rips it to shreds. It's not the songs per se, although just about every one finds a message in the new black elegance — that material success is good for the soul. It's the vocal detail — very eccentric, very romantic, and convincing both ways.   **A−**

Ashford & Simpson: *Is It Still Good to Ya* (Warner Bros. '78). Here, my friends, is what comfort and idiosyncrasy are for: adulthood. This couple hit a groove right off and explore it with an internalized virtuosity that seems completely natural, celebrating love over thirty with a compassion and sensuality that makes the smartest disco and cabaret sound shallow. And where *So So Satisfied* worked more by mood than by composition, the songs here — my favorites are the painfully sexy title showpiece and the disco-identified "Get Up and Do Something" — brim with confidence and stay with you.   **A−**

Ashford & Simpson: *Stay Free* (Warner Bros. '79). Not only is this token of tribute to the great god Disco notably less intense than the nonpareil *Is It Still Good to Ya,* it's notably less memorable than *Send It,* which offers three songs that beat anything here. Yet it's also the better record. How come? The great god Disco has bestowed upon them a groove.   **B+**

Robert Ashley: *Private Parts* (Lovely '78). I cannot tell a lie. On each side of this record, the composer reads an abstract prose fiction over "settings for piano and orchestra by 'Blue' Gene Tyranny," and that's it. The vocal style is a kind of hypnotic singsong; the quiet settings are dominated by piano, tabla, and what sounds like a string synthesizer. I like it more than *Discreet Music,* less than *Another Green World,* and about as much as *A Rainbow in Curved Air.* I suppose I prefer side one, "The Park," because I like the verbal content more, although in fact I perceive the reading as music, just like I'm supposed to, and have never managed to follow the words all the way through. A friend who's done yoga to this record — not an arty type, incidentally — is reminded of going to sleep as a child with adults talking in the next room. Then again, a rather more avant-garde friend who made me turn it off is reminded of the spoilsport who used to read the rosary for five minutes just before his favorite radio program.   **A−**

Ashton, Gardner, Dyke & Co.: *What a Bloody Long Day It's Been* (Capitol '71). Not your average record, since some of it is bloody awful. But at its best — the title tune, with its gently shuddering guitar line, and "Ballad of the Remo Four," a lament for the group's long-lost pre-Beatle Liverpool days that sounds like the best of Doug Sahm and Boz Scaggs in one cut —it's bloody terrific. Original grade: B.   **B−**

Asleep at the Wheel: *Comin' Right at Ya* (United Artists '73). Their coterie complains about flat recording and performance, but flatness is of the essence in Western swing, and the sly singing and positively underhanded songwriting here exploit it brilliantly. Beneath their unflappable veneer these country revisionists are seething subversives; it may even be that the protagonist of "Daddy's Advice" only plans his little murder to right a case of incest. Side one ends with a song of praise to a spaceship. Side two ends with a song of praise to the Son of God.   **A−**

Asleep at the Wheel: *Asleep at the Wheel* (Epic '74). This band has stopped trying to straddle their original home, West Virginia, and their spiritual one, Berkeley. Now comes the straight country push, and just in case the straight country isn't buying fetching Western swing with a '70's accent, once or twice those fiddles even sound like strings. The losses, in sprightliness and fantasy and danger, aren't fatal. But why not just listen to Bob Wills?   **B**

Asleep at the Wheel: *Texas Gold* (Capitol '75). If honest country music is what we need, then the mildly satiric mood of this is a blow for truth, especially considering the compromises of their second LP. But when I consider the matter-of-fact suffering and brutality of the first one, I conclude once again that honesty ought to go further than a commitment to good sound and good sounds.   **B+**

Asleep at the Wheel: *Wheelin' and Dealin'* (Capitol '76). Now that its musicianship and production values are established, the album quality of this excellent but marginal band will depend mostly on the song quality. Except for "Miles and Miles of Texas," this LP singles out no really striking nonoriginals, and Leroy Preston, touring hard of late, contributes only two new ones. **B**

Asleep at the Wheel: *The Wheel* (Capitol '77). I began by wondering what unsuspecting big band had provided the horn riff on "Am I High?" and ended by wondering whether they'd made it up themselves, as with so much that is good on this group's most satisfying post-debut. By now the songwriting has become almost straight; you might conceivably find "Somebody Stole His Body" on a white gospel album or "My Baby Thinks She's a Train" on a Sun outtake. The distance that remains comes across as healthy, good-humored respect, especially for banality, which with this band often turns into dumb eloquence, as on the love song "I Can't Handle It Now." Inspirational Verse: "In French Baton Rouge might mean red stick/But to me it means broken heart." **A−**

Asleep at the Wheel: *Collision Course* (Capitol '78). A lot of conceptual work went into the choice of material here. But what's made the Wheel's records come across have been new Ray Benson and Leroy Preston songs that played off and framed the borrowings and rediscoveries. This offers wonderful countrifications of Count Basie and Randy Newman; the other covers are nice, rarely more. Original grade: B. **B−**

Asleep at the Wheel: *Served Live* (Capitol '79). Side one is playable, although "God Bless the Child" was born under a bad sign, and the hot live performances don't suit the living room as well as the more delicate studio versions available on three out of five songs. Side two, however, sounds terribly forced. Not only does John Nicholas's overstated, bloozey original make clear that Leroy Preston's songwriting is going to be missed, but his duet with Chris O'Connell is too close to Peggy Scott and Jo-Jo Benson to remain so far away. And "Will the Circle Be Unbroken" might just as well be "Saints," or "Send in the Clowns." **C+**

Assalam Aleikoum Africa Volume One (Progressive and Popular Music of West Africa) (Antilles '77). Unlike John Storm Roberts's *Africa Dances* anthology, this LP and its companion come from one location — Abidjan, Ivory Coast. Thus, they're a little limited. On this one, the same musicians tend to reappear in different permutations, and their interests are more specifically "progressive" than "popular" (which can mean almost anything in a place where folk culture still thrives). That is, they like horns — great sax break on the catchy "Dogbo Zo N'Wene" — and are fascinated by electric guitars. Something called "Ode to Hendrix" is pretty remarkable, as is the title cut and much of Charles Atagana's bass playing, but the same cannot be said of "Live in Peace," which clocks in at a progressive 11:39 and supports neither its length nor its English lyric. **B**

Assalam Aleikoum Africa Volume Two (Traditional and Modern Folk Music of West Africa) (Antilles '77). Once again there's a key word in parentheses — "modern." A lot of this would seem to be popularized folk music in the manner of the Weavers if not the Kingston Trio, which might bother an ethnomusicologist or a tribal loyalist but needn't concern ignorant people like you and me. Basically, this is a selection of time-tested melodies translated into our (musical) language — and translated roughly enough to convey authenticity, since what passes for slick in Abidjan wouldn't last a hairdresser on Lenox Avenue till coffee break. **B+**

The Atlanta Rhythm Section: *Back Up Against the Wall* (Decca '73). A rather ordinary-sounding white Southern boogie band, except that this one has its roots in pop — they began as the Candymen, the greatest cover band in history. Only they actually began as Roy Orbison's backup band. As you might imagine, they're tighter and slicker than your ordinary boogie band, which all things considered is a small boon. I hope somebody on Capricorn covers "Wrong." And I hope they find something as good as, oh, "Good Vibrations" to cover themselves. **C+**

Atlanta Rhythm Section: *A Rock and Roll Alternative* (Polydor '77). If these guys actually sounded as if their studio were located (as it is) in a Georgia industrial park — fluorescent light through the pines and so forth — the general improvement in clarity and inventiveness might be interesting. But it's industrial only in the most predictable sense — more product. Even Charlie Daniels obviously has something to sing *about;* the vocalist here — why should I bother to look up his name? — might just as well be cuttin' another dog-food spot. **C+**

Atlanta Rhythm Section: *Champagne Jam* (Polydor '78). You can tell these guys are from Atlanta — it says so right in the name. So why do they sound like lazy Eagles? Why have they concocted a title that is the rock and roll equivalent of "cocktail jazz"? And when are they going to change their name officially to ARS, as in AWB? **C**

Audience: *The House on the Hill* (Elektra '71). You remember how in the old days when they wanted to convey how really *far out* "rock" was getting they'd say that a musician had "studied at Juilliard"? Always turned out to mean he or she was too dippy to play real rock and roll, but we were young. Well, now we're older, so when it says Howard Werth plays "electric classical guitar" we know what it means. No matter how desperate things get. Right? **C**

Average White Band: *Show Your Hand* (MCA '73). A cross between te Spinners and the Main Ingredient who grew up in Scotland and play their own instruments? If you wonder who needs

it, maybe you do. Not only do they write pretty and sing sweet, but unlike so many British r&b bands they've cultivated a sense of rhythm. And they've somehow gotten to compose with Joe Sample, Bonnie Bramlett, and Leon Ware. **B+**

Average White Band: *Average White Band* (Atlantic '74). These lyrics aren't banal, just plain-spoken (my favorite: "Keepin' It to Myself"), and in any case the passionate expertness of the vocal mix (like the Rascals, only the Rascals were never this tight), combined with a motion more Brownian than most black groups can manage, more than makes up. Original grade: B plus. **A−**

Average White Band: *Cut the Cake* (Atlantic '75). Have they lost their impassioned identification with their mastery of a nonwhite form? Has success (death?) (maybe just familiarity?) robbed them of their magic? Or have they just run out of songs? Next step: strings. **C+**

Average White Band & Ben E. King: *Benny and Us* (Atlantic '77). This cuts *Cut the Cake* and finds what *Soul Searching* was looking for, a tribute not to chemistry but to simple addition. Alan Gorrie and Hamish Stuart are OK vocalists themselves, and King isn't artist enough to turn AWB into a backing band. But "A Fool for You Anyway" and "A Star in the Ghetto" are King's meat, far superior to whatever ricky-tick originals AWB might have put in their place. And in the absence of ricky-tick, such AWB shtick as "Keepin' It to Myself" and Ned Doheny's "Get It Up for Love" sound quite rocky-tock. **B**

Average White Band: *Feel No Fret* (Atlantic '79). Once their name was a candid joke about their limits, their values, and their aspirations. Now it's a flat statement of fact. Swinging California pop in the manner of the Doobie Brothers and Pablo Cruise, cool in its passions and its rhythms and uninspired in its composition, and who cares who got there first. **C**

Babe Ruth: *First Base* (Harvest '72). This team socks pretty hard for the art-rock league, but since they're English I'd better tell them what I mean by calling them a fungo outfit. That means they'll find it a lot harder to get a hit in a real game. Original grade: B minus. **C+**

Bachman-Turner Overdrive: *Bachman-Turner Overdrive* (Mercury '73). For about three days I kept playing the first cut, "Gimme Your Money Please" — which is about a mugging, rather than their artistic ambitions. Soon I began to notice all the usual metal moves, but I found myself enjoying the rest of the side anyway — it may have been simpleminded but it was also fast. Wonder if they take checks. Original grade: B. **B+**

Bachman-Turner Overdrive: *Bachman-Turner Overdrive II* (Mercury '73). Here's what those of us who once kind of liked the Guess Who always hoped they'd become, and if that sounds dumb to the rest of you, you're missing something. This may be crude as a ploughboy, but Randy Bachman has always had a way with the catchy riff, and Turner, I suppose, provides the overdrive. **B+**

Bachman-Turner Overdrive: *Not Fragile* (Mercury '74). These vulgar Americans, have they no culture of their own? The Who, plodding slightly, is here rotated to reveal . . . guess who? Black Sabbath, that's who, without the horseshit necromancy. And I love every stolen riff, if not every original one. **B**

Bachman-Turner Overdrive: *Four Wheel Drive* (Mercury '75). Not only is number four their worst — only natural when you've already milked a formula for three pretty good albums — but people seem to know it: the surefire single didn't make top ten. Watch out for flying gear teeth. **C+**

Bachman-Turner Overdrive: *Head On* (Mercury '75). The bad-mouthing finally reached even a bemused admirer like myself, so that I was all ready with an alternate title — *Flat Tired*; pretty funny, eh? — until I listened one last time. Which is when I noticed that "Average Man" is a well-above-average cut, a typical paradox for this obstreperously ordinary group and album. Clomp on. **B−**

Bachman-Turner Overdrive: *Best of B.T.O. (So Far)* (Mercury '76). So far my foot — from "Roll On Down the Highway" to "Takin' Care of Business," two titles that encompass their vision quite aptly, this is as close as they'll ever come to a premium-quality album. In the end, though, I prefer their first, when the inspiration was fresh. And I do mean inspiration — in 1972, a rock and roll that spoke up loud and straight for the self-reliant but spiritually unambitious ordinary guy could only have been conceived by a clod like Bachman himself. **B+**

Bad Company: *Bad Co.* (Swan Song '74). Since a strong singer (Paul Rodgers, who's letting the hair on his chest grow out) usually dominates a strong guitarist (Mick Ralphs, who's devoting himself to Paul Kossoff impressions anyway), this is less Mott the Hoople without pretensions (which are missed) than Free poppified (but not enough, hit single or no hit single). Original grade: C plus. **B−**

Bad Company: *Straight Shooter* (Swan Song '75). This rocks even more consistently than *Bad Co.*, but to argue that it epitomizes hard rock as a style is not only to overlook its deliberate speed but to believe in one's (usually male) heart that Paul Rodgers is the ideal rock singer. You hear that a lot; what it seems to mean is that he doesn't shriek when he gets to the loud parts. Rodgers's power is no more interesting than Tom Jones's, and Jones is twice as subtle. If hard rock doesn't have more to offer, it's not worth arguing about. **B−**

Bad Company: *Run with the Pack* (Swan Song '76). Almost imperceptibly, album by album, they soften their Free-derived formalism — not only does this one include ten (why, that's almost eleven!) different tunes, but the dynamics shift and the tempos accelerate slightly and Paul Rodgers actually sounds a little soulful. Which needless to say is a mixed blessing. It's not just that the lyrics are dumb, although there are smarter ways of being dumb than this, but that Rodgers emotes these egregious hip-and-funky clichés as if he's never run across such sentiments before in his life. Ordinarily, that's what a (soulful) singer should do. This time, though, it adds a false note that endangers the entire illusion. Original grade: B. **B−**

Bad Company: *Desolation Angels* (Swan Song '79). This is supposedly a return to form after *Burning Sky,* and it may be. I'll just say that if I'd never mistake them for Free anymore, I'd never mistake them for Foreigner either. I don't think. P.S. Are those *syndrums* on "Evil Wind"? Naughty naughty. **C**

Badfinger: *No Dice* (Apple '70). I don't think these guys imitate the Beatles just so Paul will give them more hits — they've got hits of their own. But from the guitar parts (play "Better Days" right after "I Feel Fine") and harmonies (the Paul of "I've Just Seen a Face" atop the Paul of "Long Tall Sally") to concept and lineup, an imitation is what this is, modernized slightly via some relaxed countrification. They write almost well enough to get away with it, too. But somehow the song that stands out is "Blodwyn," a simulated (I think) English folk ditty about a swain and a spoon that has nothing to do with the Fab Four at all. **B**

Badfinger: *Straight Up* (Apple '71). Once again I'm forced to wonder whether I wouldn't like this record if it were by the Beatles. But without mentioning what the question says about the group, which is called Badfinger, the answer is that the Beatles couldn't have made this record. Except for "Day After Day" and "Perfection," not one of these unabashedly tuneful tunes has any magic to it, which isn't simply a matter of cautious tempos and harmonies — it's a matter of magic. Nor will any of them add any phrases verbal or musical to our common language, although they might keep a few in circulation. Also, the Beatles put nicer pictures on the cover — pictures of themselves. **B−**

Joan Baez: *Come from the Shadows* (A&M '72). How anyone whose concept of beauty is so well-bred can pretend to visionary politics has always baffled me, but for a start she could write songs in which the object always follows the predicate. I don't know about The People, but just plain people say "scattered upon the four winds," not "upon the four winds scattered." Actually, they don't say "scattered upon the four winds'' either, but we'll get to that next time. **C+**

Ginger Baker's Air Force: *Ginger Baker's Air Force* (Atco '70). Contrary to rumor, Baker is not the best drummer in the world. Elvin Jones is. (Not to mention Keith Moon. Or Tony Williams. Or whoever's at the Village Vanguard this week.) And I wouldn't want to hear Elvin Jones's ten-piece horn band, either — good horn players lead their own bands, and bands led by drummers tend to leave a lot of space for drum solos. Plus this is a live double album and the sound is terrible. Plus I'm starting a rumor that Stevie Winwood is no longer the best Stevie Winwood in the world. **D+**

Balcones Fault: *It's All Balcones Fault* (Cream '77). Three excellent songs on one side from this Austin-based unit — a New Orleans shuffle with country-rock vocal, a Jamaican polka, and a remake of the theme from Busby Berkeley's *42nd Street*. But somehow nothing coheres. This is eclecticism pushed over the brink of shtick, as if Dr. Hook bought out Asleep at the Wheel and got turned into Manhattan Transfer as punishment. **B−**

Long John Baldry: *It Ain't Easy* (Warner Bros. '71). You know how it is with English blues giants — he ain't so big, he's just tall, that's all. **C**

The Band: *Stage Fright* (Capitol '70). I've gone both ways with this group — if *Music from Big Pink* didn't tempt me away from my urban fastness, *The Band* did manage to make me jump around in my apartment. What gets in the way of this follow-up, however, is neither natural alienation nor critical overanticipation — it's the music itself, which simply overmatches the words. The tunes are so bright and doughty, and the musicians pitch in with so much will, that the domestic banalities of side one seem out of place

in a way those of Delaney & Bonnie, say, never do. And if the settings are too complex for what Robbie Robertson knows, they're too unfocused for what he doesn't know, as the confused politico-philosophical grapplings on side two make agonizingly clear. Memorable as most of these songs are, they never hook in — never give up the musical-verbal phrase that might encapsulate their every-which-way power. Which perhaps means that they don't have much to say. **B+**

The Band: *Cahoots* (Capitol '71). Whew, these fellows can really play. They cook on "Smoke Signal," and you should hear the guitar solo on "Last of the Blacksmiths." Seem overly worried about the passing of the world as they know it, though — not just blacksmiths, but eagles, rivers, trains, the works. **B−**

The Band: *Rock of Ages* (Capitol '72). This live double introduces a couple of covers, a "new" song they've been playing for years, and the seven-minute organ precede with which Garth Hudson protracts "Chest Fever" in advance, while finding room for only one song from their most recent (and worst) studio album. Yet admirers claim it as a masterwork rather than a commercial stopgap. Nonsense. Given the Band's ordinary woodenness in performance, the playing and singing are spirited, and Allen Toussaint's horn arrangements add genuine punch instead of the usual fuss, although they never reshape—as opposed to redecorate — the material. But this is clearly the testament of artists who are looking backwards because the future presents itself as a vacuum — a problem that has afflicted even their best work. **B**

The Band: *Moondog Matinee* (Capitol '73). Since I never expected this talented rock group to guide me through the travails of life — mostly because there was too much goddam travail in their music — I regard this album not as an aesthetic reverse but as an uncommonly well-selected and -performed buncha oldies. Not as many good tunes as on *Stage Fright*, I'll grant you, but the lyrics are better. **B+**

The Band: *Northern Lights — Southern Cross* (Capitol '75). I've always been put off by the sprung quality of the Band's music — the sense that if someone were to undo the catch its works would be propelled forth in all directions. Instead of energizing the impulse to piece together the lyrics — in the manner of the Stones, not to mention Bob Dylan — the sound of albums like *Music From Big Pink* and *Stage Fright* (though not *The Band* or *The Basement Tapes*) tends to reinforce their own metaphorical impenetrability. So the pure comeliness of every melody on this album led to an immediate infatuation. As I listened to the words, however, infatuation turned to mild affection, for the best of these songs is sentimental, and the worst (the two that are set in the city) are grossly sentimental. Only Garth Hudson, who has turned into a synthesizer natural, saves things in the end, and just barely. Original grade: A minus. **B+**

The Band: *Islands* (Capitol '77). Even true believers admit that this sounds like a listless farewell to old habits — recording as a group on Capitol, for instance. The best song is about the baby Jesus and almost made me gag first time I heard it; the second best is about a traveling evangelist and strikes a familiar note; and the third best is a remake that sounds like one. **C+**

The Band: *The Last Waltz* (Warner Bros. '78). The movie improves when you can't see it — Robbie Robertson and friends don't play anywhere near as smug as they look (or talk). And for an olio featuring eleven guest vocalists and a studio "suite," the soundtrack is remarkably coherent. The four new Band tunes are nothing special, but everybody lays into the oldies. The blues sequence — beefed up by Toussaint's horns, Butterfield's harp, Muddy's pipes, and a blistering if messy Robertson–Clapton duet — is a small landmark, Morrison and Young are worth going back to, and Dylan's "Baby Let Me Follow You Down" is spunky enough to make up for "Forever Young." Not only that, Joni Mitchell and Neil Diamond are on the same side. Bet this ages a lot better than *Woodstock* — in a way, it already has. **B+**

The Band: *Anthology* (Capitol '78). Well, it salvages *Stage Fright* and *Cahoots*. But not on the same side. **B−**

Moe Bandy: *I Just Started Hatin' Cheatin' Songs Today* (GRC '74). Whereupon the singing sheet-metal worker bequeaths to posterity a whole album of 'em — simple tales of pain, guilt, and hard-earned redemption, unadorned by violins or other self-indulgences. On side two especially he finds songwriters who take sin as seriously as he does — believe me, anybody who can top "This Time I Won't Cheat on Her Again" with "I Wouldn't Cheat on Her if She Was Mine" is covering all the angles. Time: 24:25. **A−**

Moe Bandy: *It Was Always So Easy (to Find an Unhappy Woman)* (GRC '74). Next line: "Till I started lookin' for mine." Time: approximately 24:30. **B+**

Moe Bandy: *Bandy the Rodeo Clown* (GRC '75). Look closely at the bull on the back cover and you'll note piss coming out of his pizzle, but even combined with Bandy's vinegar it's not enough. However much you admire his stylistic single-mindedness, hard honky-tonk doesn't pack quite enough wallop in itself — it requires a less austere singer, or inspired material, or the kind of thematic single-mindedness that can make a whole audience love cheatin' songs again. Time: 24:11. **B**

Moe Bandy: *The Best of Moe Bandy* (Columbia '77). Despite the definitive "Hank Williams, You Wrote My Life," Bandy's music on Columbia has followed the pattern of such GRC anomalies as "Bandy the Rodeo Clown" and "Cowboys and Playboys" — if not tinged with pop outright, then at least softer rhythmically or melodically. I like these songs when they're good. But they misrepresent him — the cheated-upon protagonist of "The Biggest Airport in the World" is *naive,* which misses Bandy's point completely. This compiles eight GRC hits (including the above-named anomalies) and the two CBS songs I've mentioned. It's an unusually solid country LP, and the GRC albums are all out of print anyway. But I miss "Smoke Filled Room" and "I'm Gonna Listen to Me" and "I Stop and Get Up (to Go Out of My Mind)." **A—**

Moe Bandy & Joe Stampley: *Just Good Ol' Boys Featuring "Holding the Bag"* (Columbia '79). Bandy and Stampley, honchos of the hard-assed nouveau honky-tonk style that is Nashville's answer to Texas outlawism, tend to sound pretty dolorous as solo artists. Bandy is still obsessed with cheating as both doer and done; Stampley's more cheerful, but as an ass man of the sincere-if-bearded school he spends a lot of time singing persuasive ballads. Like most country albums, theirs are spotty; recent song titles include "To Cheat or Not to Cheat" and "I Don't Lie," and those are *highlights.* As a duo, though, they whoop and holler and get hairy, lie to each other's wives and trade wedding rings for outboard motors. The material is still spotty, but since it's always Friday night they can shout right through the spots. All of which goes to show that male bonding is more likely to pick up the tempo than love and marriage. **B**

Bobby Bare: *Lullabys, Legends and Lies* (RCA Victor '73). I admit to a weakness for Shel Silverstein, who wrote all fourteen songs on this record — or rather, these two records, as this is Nashville's first country oratorio or something (subject: America or something). But even for a fan, Silverstein's jokes and tugs on the heartstrings wear thin after half an hour (if not ten minutes). Nor does the audience of cronies yukking it up and

singing along do much for Bare's interpretations, which verge on the obvious under the best of circumstances. Time: 58:39. **C+**

Bobby Bare: *Cowboys and Daddys* (RCA Victor '75). Bare's cowboys wonder how come they're in Calgary, eat stew just like in the movies, scoff at poets, fuck cows, and lie about their age. His daddys lie about cowboys. With two good-to-great songs apiece from Shel Silverstein ("The Stranger" comes complete with bleep), Dave Hickey ("Calgary Snow" is as intricate as good Jackson Browne and a lot wiser), and Terry Allen ("Amarillo Highway" melds Jimmie Rodgers and Bob Wills for a self-conscious age) plus Marty Cooper's theme statement, this does as much for the outlaw ethos as Waylon and Willie put together. **A—**

Bobby Bare: *Sleeper Wherever I Fall* (Columbia '79). In case you were wondering what Bill Graham's been up to, here he is directing the career of a Nashville veteran with a great ear who's never fulfilled his great expectations. His CBS debut, *Bare,* was a Shel Silverstein collaboration that offered its fair share of pleasures, but it didn't sell, so this one goes rock-schlock, befouling good songs with strings that aren't up to Parton and Byrdsy cadences that aren't up to McGuinn, Clark & Hillman. Fortunately, the new one hasn't sold either. **C+**

Elizabeth Barraclough: *Elizabeth Barraclough* (Bearsville '78). Her vocal intensity seems passionate when you're in the mood and affected when you're not. Her love songs are as desperate, committed, and possessed as her political ones. She tends to be a little long-winded. I hope the guitar riff on "Who Do You Think's the Fool" and "Shepherd's Bush" (almost the same riff) is hers. And I hope she keeps getting better. **B—**

Syd Barrett: *The Madcap Laughs/Barrett* (Harvest '74). This set comprises the two albums Barrett made after leaving Pink Floyd in early 1968. The second was released in England just before *Atom Heart Mother* in 1970, which must have made a striking contrast; in the wake of Floyd's triumph with *The Dark Side of the Moon* the contrast is even sharper. Barrett coughs when he's not wheezing, he can hardly strum his guitar, and his lyrics are off-the-wall in a modest, workaday way. David Gilmour and Roger Waters back him up (good for them), but sloppily (good for them again); there's no hint of their engineering-student expertise. Admittedly, a lot of what results is worthy of the wimp-turned-acid-casualty Barrett is. But a lot of it is funny, charming, catchy — whimsy at its best. I love most of side one, especially "Terrapin" and "Here I Go." And while my superego insists I grade it a notch lower, I know damn well it gives me more pleasure than *The Dark Side of the Moon*.   **B**

Ronnie Barron: *Reverend Ether* (Decca '71). Why do white guys from New Orleans sing so weird? Barron sounds like he took falsetto lessons from Geraldine. I can live with it — even like it when the songs are as good as "Chattanooga," about a redcap. But I don't think he could find an audience if he was writing nothing but "I'm in Love Again" and "Mother-in-Law."   **B−**

Bay City Rollers: *Bay City Rollers* (Arista '75). I was hoping I wouldn't have to mention this, but the single has made the push to the top. So . . . what you figured, too bland to be offensive yet, more Partridge Family than Osmonds. Noormal geeze just like yew.   **C**

Bay City Rollers: *Greatest Hits* (Arista '78). Rollermania in this country was pretty depressing — 1977's "You Made Me Believe in Magic," the last of their three top-tenners, could have been by Bread or Barry Manilow, and better the Partridge Family than that.

Still, they got to put their name on three great singles, more than most people who make albums (or singles) manage: the number-one breakthrough "Saturday Night," the semistiff "Rock and Roll Love Letter," and the completely stiff "Yesterday's Heroes," a 1976 song about how they had to take command or fade away that was written for them — at their command, I'm sure — by Vanda & Young.   **C+**

The Beach Boys: *Sunflower* (Brother/ Reprise '70). If you can feature the great candy-stripes grown up, then this is far more satisfying, I suspect, than *Smile* ever would have been. The medium-honest sensibility is a little more personal now, soulful in its Waspy way. Maybe they weren't really surfers or hot rodders, but they were really Southern Californians, and that's what their music was about. It still is, too, only now they sing about water, broken marriages, and the love of life. Still a lot of fun, too. Original grade: A.   **A−**

The Beach Boys: *Surf's Up* (Brother/ Reprise '71). Their worst since *Friends,* which just goes to show that making like a great group is as bad for your music as making like a buncha mystics. Except for the sophomoric "Student Demonstration Time," the songs on the first side are all right — "Take a Load Off Your Feet" is worthy of *Wild Honey* and "Disney Girls (1957)" is worthy of *Jack Jones's Greatest Hits* — but the pop impressionism of side two drags hither and yon. The dying words of a tree are delivered in an apt, gentle croak, but the legendary title opus is an utter failure even on its own woozy terms and there are several disasters from the guest lyricists — Van Dyke Parks's wacked-out meandering is no better than Jack Rieley's. I'll trade you my copy for *Surfin' Safari* even up, and you'll be sorry. Original grade: C plus.   **B−**

The Beach Boys: *Holland* (Brother/ Reprise '72). I admit that this *sounds* real good — it's engineered clear and bright as a redwood mountain stream — but to overlook what's doing the sounding is formalism as deliberate stupidity. That is, the actual music and words are murky and dim. I suppose that in time their tongue-tied travelogue of Big Sur may seem no more escapist than "Fun Fun Fun," but who'll ever believe it's equally simple, direct, or innocent? Original grade: C minus. **C**

The Beach Boys: *Carl and the Passions — So Tough/Pet Sounds* (Brother/Reprise '72). They can't have much faith in the new one if they're loss-leading with an old one (the one that turned them into a cult band, now finally — how did we stand the wait? — available in its pristine mono form). And indeed, there's no reason they should. Despite the title, it's not some sort of primitive surf doo-wop — sounds a lot like *Friends* and *Holland* to me. Fairly pleasant, but even the highlights aren't all that hot: a nice Brian Wilson oeuvre called "Marcella" (sounds like *Smiley Smile*) and a silly gospel song for the Maharishi. **C+**

The Beach Boys: *15 Big Ones* (Brother/Reprise '76). This is their best album since *Sunflower*, which is their best of this decade. Brian is aboard, if not in charge. But *Sunflower* or *Wild Honey* it's not. The oldies idea isn't itself the problem. But except for "Palisades Park" and "A Casual Look" the choices might have been more inspired, and the playful, goofy vocal intensity of the black music covers of their youth is often missing. I can deal with the Maharishi stuff by now — it simply underlines the group's public transformation from super-normals into harmless eccentrics — but never again should they commit an I-love-music song. In the current example, rock evolves from the Gregorian chant, an idea I do not consider a harmless eccentricity. Original grade: B plus. **B**

The Beach Boys: *Love You* (Brother/Reprise '77). Painfully crackpot and painfully sung, but also inspired, not least because it calls forth forbidden emotions. For a surrogate teenager to bare his growing pains so guilelessly was exciting, or at least charming; for an avowed adult to expose an almost childish naivete is embarrassing, but also cathartic; and for a rock and roll hero to compose a verbally and musically irresistible paean to Johnny Carson is an act of shamanism pure and simple. As with *Wild Honey,* the music sounds wrong in contradictory ways at first — both arty and cute, spare and smarmy — but on almost every cut it comes together soon enough; I am especially partial to the organ textures, and I find the absurd little astrology ditty, "Solar System," impossible to shake. As for the words, well, they're often pretty silly, but even (especially) when they're designed to appeal to whatever Brian imagines to be the rock audience they reveal a lot more about the artist than most lyrics do. And this artist is a very interesting case. Original grade: A minus. **A**

The Beach Boys: *M.I.U. Album* (Brother/Reprise '78). On *The Beach Boys Love You,* lyrics like those of "Solar System" may have been a little embarrassing, but basically their silliness registered as charming. "Match Point of Our Love" ("Early in the game when you broke me/Just like a serve") and "Belles of Paris" ("There's a chapel 'Sacre Coeur' in quaint Montmarte [sic]/In the open air the painters show their art") are just dumb, and despite a lot of fairly pleasant music and a few passable songs, so is this. **C**

The Beach Boys: *L.A. (Light Album)* (Caribou '79). I quite like the electronic disco extension of "Here Comes the Night," but more as an oddity than a pleasure. The chief pleasure — Brian's "Good Timin' " — is not a new song. What is new is the pop orchestration on "Lady Lynda." **C+**

The Beat: *The Beat* (Columbia '79). In which the Ramones clean up their act and/or the Knack stop smirking.

Very nice boys, very intense, twelve songs in half an hour, never stop, drive all over the place, aren't coming home tonight, wanna find a rock and roll girl, don't fit in (but will). Original grade: B plus.　　　　　　　　　　**B**

The Beatles: *Hey Jude* (Apple '70). A commercial ripoff it is, pastiching together singles separated by over five years. And I could care less. Show me an album featuring songs as good as "Can't Buy Me Love" and "I Should Have Known Better" and "Paperback Writer" and "Rain" and "Don't Let Me Down" and I'll show you *The Beatles — Yesterday and Today.*　　**A**

The Beatles: *Let It Be* (Apple '70). "I hope we passed the audition," says the leader as the record ends, and they do. Their assurance and wit would be the envy of veteran rock and rollers, and though this is a little light-weight, it makes up in charm what it lacks in dramatic brilliance. Even when the arrangements get tricky — "Let It Be" is a touch too ornate in this version — their spontaneity of impulse comes through. And while fave rave "One After 909" is pure teen simplicity, it sounds no fresher than "Two of Us," an adult song about couple bonding that I hope applies to their songwriting duo. The one mistake is "The Long and Winding Road," sunk in a slush of strings worthy of its shapeless philosophizing. But even the great are allowed to falter now and then.　　　　　　　**A−**

The Beatles: *The Beatles at the Hollywood Bowl* (Capitol '77). A tribute not only to the Beatles (which figured) but to George Martin and Capitol (which didn't necessarily figure at all). The sound rings clearly and powerfully through the shrieking; the segues are brisk and the punch-ins imperceptible; and the songs capture our heroes at their highest. Furthermore, though the musicianship is raw, the arrangements are tighter (faster, actually) than on record; Ramones-haters should note that the thirteen tunes take less than twenty-nine minutes, including patter.　　　　　　　　　　　**A**

The Beatles: *Live! at the Star-Club in Hamburg, Germany; 1962* (Lingasong '77). I don't know exactly how you rate documentary value, especially with a subject as interesting as this one, but I do know that nothing I had read prepared me for the abysmal sound quality of this record, especially how far down (and away) the voices are. Nor for the occasional listlessness of the performances themselves.　**B−**

Be-Bop Deluxe: *The Best and the Rest of Be-Bop Deluxe* (Harvest '79). The best-of sounds like Roxy Music gone heavy art-rock and makes a case for their cult reputation. Bill Nelson's guitar tone is pretty remarkable — thick yet ductile, by Phil Manzanera out of Randy California — and here he makes up for empty-headed improvisations with a career's worth of ID riffs. But he sings like someone who regards himself as an "axe victim" and thanks a seagull for enabling him to "survive." The rest-of didn't make it onto *Drastic Plastic,* and 'nuff said.　　　　　　　　　**B−**

Jeff Beck Group: *Rough and Ready* (Epic '71). Both Bob Tench's mannered-frantic vocals and Beck's conventional-maiden compositions are less interesting than their counterparts on *Truth* and *Beck-Ola* but perfectly suitable for an ordinary post-Led Zeppelin group with some nice textures and extra technique. Granted, the jazzy Latin touches (this is also a post-Santana group) are an improvement — after all, Beck is a guitarist who once rendered Rod Stewart unlistenable and believed that teaming up with Vanilla Fudge would be, er, cool.　　　**C+**

Jeff Beck Group: *Jeff Beck Group* (Epic '72). These tales of egomania (the only story he knows) reemphasize blooze roots (or is that routes?). Big deal. I agree that Beck's choppy chops occasionally surprise, but that's only because he wastes so much time refining heavy (not blues or even blooze) clichés.　　　　　　　**C+**

Beck, Bogert and Appice: *Beck, Bogert and Appice* (Epic '73). He couldn't get it on with Vanilla Fudge, so now he goes himself one better and gets it on with Cactus. Talk about yer wealth and taste. **C**

Jeff Beck: *Blow by Blow* (Epic '75). Never before have I been fully convinced that Beck could improvise long lines, or jazz it up with a modicum of delicacy, or for that matter get funky. But he still has absolutely nothing to say. It's not that he's jettisoned the vocalist — lots of jazzmen say plenty without words. It's that he's a technician and nothing more, making music guaranteed to excite only one group of listeners — those who respond to complaints about content the way atheists respond to visions of the Most High. **B−**

Jeff Beck: *Wired* (Epic '76). This continuation of *Blow by Blow*'s mindless trickery — bye-bye George Martin and Stevie Wonder (guess which one is missed), hiya Charles Mingus (an adequate "Pork Pie Hat") — is supposed to make Jeff a "jazz" musician. In fact it certifies Jan Hammer and Narada Michael Walden as "rock" musicians (retain quotes please). Best: "Come Dancing," a jumpy little Walden novelty that would make a nice B side for the Meters. **B−**

The Beckies: *The Beckies* (Sire '76). Michael Brown (the Left Banke, Stories) keeps getting better. The weld between his snazzy European colors and textures and the concise, kinetic pop structures of his American rock and roll is by now totally invisible, and the playing is energetic and expert. But these songs might as well have no words at all — not just that the lyrics don't reward careful attention, but that the singing is valiantly serviceable and that is all. Original grade: B. **B−**

The Bee Gees: *Two Years On* (Atco '71). This is a little better than the LPs the Gibb brothers came up with during their separation — *Cucumber Castle*, which at least sold some, and the solo flop *Robin's Reign*. It does include a bizarre juxtaposition of Jerry Reed imitation and singing strings. But

"Lonely Days" sounded more distinctive on the radio than it does among its epigones here — the collective vibrato is turning into a grating affectation. Presumably they broke up because they sensed that the formula was getting stale. To try to re-create it yet again is to guarantee the transformation from good commercial group to bad one. **C−**

The Bee Gees: *Best of Bee Gees Vol. 2* (RSO '73). What a pathetic comedown — the melodies soggy, the harmonies strained, the lyrics deadly dull. Fifteen songs plus lyric sheet means they're really trying to sell it, too. It'd be a better deal if as many had been hits as the notes imply. I count four top-twenty in four years, which oddly enough is also how many good songs I count, and I'm being lenient. **C+**

Bee Gees: *Main Course* (RSO '75). At first I was put off by the commercial desperation that induced these chronic fatuosos to turn out their brightest album in many years. But commercial success validated it: "Nights on Broadway" and "Jive Talkin' " turned out to be the kind of fluff that sticks. Sad to say, an unpleasant tension between feigned soulfulness and transparent insincerity still mars most of side two, which does, however, lead off with an undiscovered gem: "All This Making Love," a baroque, frantically mechanical evocation of compulsive sex. Original grade: C plus. **B+**

Bee Gees: *Children of the World* (RSO '76). Their closed-system commitment to a robot aura renders embarrassing questions about whether they mean what they're singing irrelevant, which is good. Too often, though, their pleasure in artifice doesn't wholly irradiate the rather patchy material. Best hook: Blue Weaver's organ part on "Subway." **B**

Bee Gees: *Spirits Having Flown* (RSO '79). I admire the perverse riskiness of this music, which neglects disco bounce in favor of demented falsetto abstraction, less love-man than newborn-kitten. And I'm genuinely fond of many small moments of madness here, like the way the three separate multitracked voices echo the phrase "living together." But obsessive ornamentation can't transform a curiosity into inhabitable music, and there's not one song here that equals any on the first side of *Saturday Night Fever*. **B−**

Bee Gees: *Bee Gees Greatest* (RSO '79). Not that I don't think "Jive Talkin' " and "Stayin' Alive" are "great," but it's hard to trust a group that leaves such monuments of masterschlock as "To Love Somebody" and "How Can You Mend a Broken Heart" out of its own pantheon. This is a solid sampler of twenty late-'70s hits and oddities. But I remember. **B+**

David Behrman: *On the Other Ocean/Figure in a Clearing* (Lovely '78). On *Discreet Music* and the Fripp collaborations, Eno taught me to appreciate this kind of semiimprovised, semielectric, semiminimal trance and/or background music, but I think Behrman, a Soho/California composer who uses computers for chance input and builds his own synthesizers, does it better. Certainly his textures are more interesting, without any hint of unseemly lushness — or of Glass-type climaxes, for that matter. Steady as she goes. **A−**

Maggie Bell: *Queen of the Night* (Atlantic '74). The comparison floating about is Janis Joplin, natch, but a cross between Bonnie Bramlett and Maria Muldaur — with an unfortunate soupçon of Sophie Tucker providing the Joplin — is more like it. Unlike Janis, and like most singers, Bell doesn't take hold of a song merely by breathing on it — she has to interpret. Which means she has to interact with her material. Get it, Maggie? I thought not. Original grade: B minus. **C+**

Belle Epoque: *Miss Broadway* (Big Tree '77). The 7:25 title cut features a simple and familiar bass hook together with a refreshingly harsh female vocal hook, which, added to the sour gypsy strings, make for a piece of disco this rock and roller likes as much as just about anything on *Saturday Night Fever*. I like it so much, in fact, that I find the 4:10 single version a little scant — not enough strings, fancy that — and I'm sorry to report that the specially mixed disco disc is a promotion only item. Oh well — the rest of the first side is OK, which is more than I can say for the second. **B−**

The Belmonts: *Cigars, Acappella, Candy* (Buddah '72). Can white boys sing on a street corner? Of course they can, especially if they're Italian. And especially especially if they used to pal around with Dion DiMucci. But not like the Persuasions. **B+**

Pat Benatar: *In the Heat of the Night* (Chrysalis '79). Where some "eclectic" rock and rollers brim with sheer experimental joy, Benatar is sodden with try-anything-once ambition. From showbiz "hard rock" ("Heartbreaker") to big-beat "cabaret" ("Don't Let It Show") to received "futurism" ("My Clone Sleeps Alone") to fake-Blondie "Eurodisco" ("We Live for Love"), she shows about as much aesthetic principle as Don Kirshner. Though she does have a better voice than Kirshner. **C+**

Marc Benno: *Ambush* (A&M '72). In a lot of ways, this is a perfect record — easy studio funk unmarred by a single error of commission. Benno does Boz Scaggs a lot looser and happier than Boz Scaggs has for a while, and Bobby Keys stands out among the sidemen (Radle, Keltner, Utley) only because he's never sounded better. It's divided into an irresistible dance side and a decent enough listening side. Yet I no longer trust such basically unthinking supercompetence to provide lasting pleasure. Anyone who doesn't share my reservations should probably buy this, and even if you do — well, I keep playing it. **B+**

George Benson: *Breezin'* (Warner Bros. '76). Just in case you're beguiled by his Stevie Wonder imitation (I prefer Carl Carlton's, Chaka Khan's, even Buddy Miles's) on "Masquerade" (I prefer Helen Reddy's, Aretha Franklin's, even Leon Russell's), be hereby informed that Benson is not primarily a singer, but rather a jazz guitarist of the tasty variety. And that most of what he spices up here is mush.   **C**

George Benson: *In Flight* (Warner Bros. '77). Upon reflection, it seems to me that what Benson does these days isn't a sellout but an apotheosis — this kind of palaver has been the soul of jazz guitar since the '50s. Turn those amps *up!* Let's hear some *distortion!*   **C+**

Chuck Berry: *Back Home* (Chess '70). Like the reconstructed "Reelin' and Rockin' " that opens side two, most of Berry's return to the label of his glory days is tasty, real rockin', and inessential. Also included, however, are two of his greatest songs ever: "Tulane," as canny a take on hippiedom (which Chuck has been struggling to comprehend since he first played the Fillmore) as "Sweet Little Sixteen" is on high school, and its sequel, "Have Mercy Judge," the first major blues this supposed bluesman has ever written. History, anyone? **B**

Chuck Berry: *San Francisco Dues* (Chess '71). Chuck isn't specializing in filler this time out, but the memorable cuts aren't exactly models of craftsmanship. "Festival" is the man at his most endearingly crass, envisioning a rock and roll circus featuring "bad Bo Diddley and the Beatles and the Mothers" in one line and the Woolies (his Detroit backup band) and the Loading Zone (San Fran backup, rhymes with Stones) elsewhere. The other is six minutes of doggerel over bass-and-piano accompaniment that is a good bad poem the way *Husbands* is a good bad movie.   **B−**

Chuck Berry: *The London Chuck Berry Sessions* (Chess '72). Though his backup for this promotion was less than stellar, Chuck Berry finally has an LP on the charts, which is certainly overdue recognition for the number one genius in rock and roll history. Only trouble is, the record is lousy. The live side is Chuck at his hoarsest, and "My Ding-a-Ling" isn't even funny the first time. The studio side is pure filler. Buy *Chuck Berry's Golden Decade, More Chuck Berry, Chuck Berry's on Top, St. Louis to Liverpool,* even *Back Home.* This doesn't do him justice.   **C−**

Chuck Berry: *Bio* (Chess '73). Willie Mays was the greatest baseball player who ever lived, but he just can't cut it anymore. He reminds me more of Chuck Berry every time out.   **D+**

Chuck Berry: *Chuck Berry* (Chess '75). His style has always been undeniable, but not irresistible — cf. *Bio.* Here at least its entertainment value is reconfirmed, whether he's remaking "Hi Heel Sneakers" or "You Are My Sunshine," adding blue (notes and lyrics) to "South of the Border," duetting with his daughter, or writin' and rollin' his own.   **B−**

Chuck Berry: *Rockit* (Atco '79). Well I'll be. The inventor of rock and roll hasn't made an album this listenable in fifteen years — no great new songs, but he's never written better throwaways (or covered "Ozymandias," either). Both Berry and Johnny Johnson — the piano half of his sound for a quarter of a century — have tricked up their styles without vitiating or cheapening them, and the result is a groove for all decades. Minor for sure, but what a surprise.   **B+**

Beserkley Charbusters Volume 1 (Beserkley '75). The Berkeley rock underground? Featuring Earth Quake, a failed heavy boogie band from A&M, and Jonathan Richman, reputed to have squandered numerous Warner Comm bucks studioing with the Modern Lovers yet here sounding as if he prefers to record in the WC? I played this sampler twice and shelved it. But a more sympathetic listening suggests that maybe rock and roll undergrounds are the same everywhere — tough-minded, spare and loud, and committed to an eloquent simplicity of form no matter what the embroidering tastemakers in the biz consider art. This shared commitment makes the four artists exhibited here sound as if they're all on one album, instead of a bunch of cuts, and the album is a good one.   **A−**

Charles Bevel: *Meet "Mississippi Charles" Bevel* (A&M '73). Black, thirty-four, the fourteenth of seventeen children, this upwardly mobile former civil-rights worker and self-taught musician (he never sang in church) has the surprising, unfakable attractiveness of the gifted semipro — he writes and sings as if he still revels in the rewards of getting it just . . . *right*. His songs are about black courage, hypocrisy, and ambivalence in a world shaped but not defined by racism; many of them ring like the proverbs and fables that provide him with crucial bits of language. The melodies are as sensible and eloquent as the lyrics, and Calvin Carter's production respects and augments Bevel's relaxed folk-soul voice. "Black Santa Claus" is a bathetic mistake; just about everything else gets better and better.   **A−**

The B-52's: *The B-52's* (Warner Bros. '79). Fond as I am of the pop junk they recycle — with love and panache, like the closet ecologists they are —there's something parochially suburban about turning it into the language of a world view. So I'm more delighted with their rhythms, which show off their Georgia roots by adapting the innovations of early funk (a decade late, just like the Stones and Chicago blues) to an endlessly danceable forcebeat format. Also delightful is their commitment to sexual integration — Cindy Wilson is singing more and more, although her voice occasionally gives out before her ambitions do. Major worry: only one of the copyright 1979 songs — my favorite track, "Dance This Mess

Around" — is as amazing as the 1978 stuff. Original grade: A minus   **A**

Big Brother and the Holding Company: *Be a Brother* (Columbia '70). With the obvious exception, all the original members are here, plus third guitarist David Schallock, good for both a funk-not-feedback feel and occasional psychedelic overload. Nick Gravenites is singer and auteur, and this is his message to the weary, wary, but steadfast hippies of the world — watch out for "heartache people" and "funkie Jim," but "be a brother." Bonus: Sister Janis does a bit of backup. Original grade: A.   **A−**

Big Brother and the Holding Company: *How Hard It Is* (Columbia '71). Nick Gravenites did a better job of replacing Janis than anyone could have imagined. Mike Finnegan is no substitute for Gravenites.   **C**

Big Star: *#1 Record* (Ardent '72). Alex Chilton's voice is changing. When he was a teenage Box Top, his deep, soulful, bullfrog whopper was the biggest freak of nature since Stevie Winwood sang "I'm a Man," but now that he's formed his own group he gets to be an adolescent, complete with adenoidal quaver. Appropriately, the music tends toward the teen as well, but with a tense energy in the harmonies that provides brand new thrills. Special attraction: a fantasy about India with gin-and-tonic in it.   **B+**

Big Star: *Radio City* (Ardent '74). Brilliant, addictive, definitively semi-popular, and all Alex Chilton — Chris Bell, his folkie counterpart, just couldn't take it any more. Boosters claim this is just what the AM has been waiting for, but the only pop coup I hear is a reminder of how spare, skew, and sprung the Beatles '65 were, which is a coup because they weren't. The harmonies sound like the lead sheets are upside down and backwards, the guitar solos sound like screwball readymade pastiches, and the lyrics sound like love is strange, though maybe that's just the context. Can an album be catchy and twisted at the same time? Original grade: B plus. **A**

Big Star: *Third* (PVC '78). In late 1974, Alex Chilton — already the inventor of self-conscious power pop — transmogrified himself into some hybrid of Lou Reed (circa *The Velvet Underground* and/or *Berlin*) and Michael Brown (circa "Walk Away, Renee" and "Pretty Ballerina"). This is the album that resulted — fourteen songs in all, only two or three of which wander off into the psycho ward. Halting, depressive, eccentrically shaped, it will seem completely beyond the pale to those who already find his regular stuff weird. I think it's prophetically idiosyncratic and breathtakingly lyrical. **A−**

Tony Bird: *Tony Bird* (Columbia '76). At his worst, this white Rhodesian is just a folkie — poety, sententious, and he does go on. But even when he's bad you can hear black Africa in the rhythms and intense intonations of his singing, and when he's good you can hear it in the lyrics too. I wonder how much he steals but consider him an original nevertheless. **B+**

Tony Bird: *Tony Bird of Paradise* (Columbia '78). Bird hasn't put his strongest material on this record — his debut has more knockout songs (more losers, too), and I once saw him perform a paranoid tribute to the CIA that I'd love to hear again. But he remains such an odd and abrasive singer that he has a right to go a little commercial, and producer John Lissauer knows how. Orginal grade: B plus. **B**

Birtha: *Birtha* (Dunhill '72). "Hi! I'm Chickie! Fly me to Quaalude!" In which Gabriel Mekler, sly devil, combines heavy clichés with four female musicians, none of whom seem to have last names. Although there is one enigmatic soft song, "She Was Good to Me," so maybe they're a buncha dykes or love their mothers. This could all be rationalized by some eager feminist theorist — women have never played macho rock before, and last

names are patronymics after all — but it would still be lousy music. **D**

Elvin Bishop: *Juke Joint Jump* (Capricorn '74). Elvin's sólo albums started coming out in 1969, but this is the first one this fan ever wanted to hear twice. Nothing spectacular, that would violate his sense of propriety — just rocking with a steady roll, perfect for admirers of Robert E. Lee if a mite laid-back for Broadway Bob. Nice to hear a National Merit Scholar make good. Original grade: B minus. **B**

Elvin Bishop: *The Best of Elvin Bishop: Crabshaw Rising* (Epic '75). This ain't the best — just a half-and-half selection from his CBS days, before he really had a best. The good stuff, especially "Rock My Soul," cuts a fine Saturday-night groove. The rest sounds forced, like an early show Thursday. **B−**

Elvin Bishop: *Struttin' My Stuff* (Capricorn '76). Usually, when someone tells you an album ain't nuthin' but good old rock and roll, that means it ain't nuthin'. This is the exception. After singing (and playing) the blues for ten years, Elvin makes like he was born to boogie. Completing his Marin-to-Macon switch by recording at Criteria in Miami instead of the Record Plant in Sausalito, he here provides Capricorn with enough hooks to keep the Brothers gone fishin for the next decade. All very debrained, of course, but the first side never stops, and if the title cut isn't the label's first top-ten song since "Ramblin' Man," either my name ain't Juke Box Johnny or "Fooled Around and Fell in Love" got there first. **B+**

Elvin Bishop: *Hometown Boy Makes Good* (Capricorn '77). Elvin sounds like he's on automatic, Mickey Thomas sounds like he wants to be a rock and roll star, and this album sounds like it might fly apart if you were to spin it at forty-five by mistake. It's still fun, I guess. But not *enough* fun. **C+**

Elvin Bishop: *Raisin' Hell* (Capricorn '77). This live double-LP, four sides of strong material unmarred by a single extraneous show of chops, reveals why Elvin's good-time music is actually fun. Would Charlie Daniels or Richie Furay think to rouse a crowd by announcing: "Remember, this is not a rock concert, it's a cultural event —we won't have anybody raisin' their voices and gettin' rowdy"? Uh-uh — they'd be afraid it would backfire, and with them it might. **A−**

Elvin Bishop: *Hog Heaven* (Capricorn '78). Bishop is a road musician. He doesn't knock himself out making Great Albums, but he doesn't get all twisted up racing after Breakthrough Hits, either. He doesn't even Promote Product much — on tour, he mentioned this LP only when he did a song from it, which happened once. Too bad, actually — with Amos Garrett on second lead guitar and Maria Muldaur on second lead vocal, these songs are solid boogie indeed, and I would have liked to hear an in-person version of how he outgrew his brassiere. **B+**

Stephen Bishop: *Careless* (ABC '78). Bishop ain't bad for a pop singer-songwriter — his voice is three-quarters Simon and one-quarter Garfunkel and he's got as much brains as and fewer pretensions than either. He commits no sins. Omits quite a few, though — even boasts that he's outgrown material like "I Feel So Miserable Without You, It's Almost Like Having You Here." **C+**

Bizarros/Rubber City Rebels: *From Akron* (Clone '77). There's been a Lou Reed enclave around Cleveland since the late-Velvets days, and recently it's begun to produce musicians; maybe it's the real reason the Dead Boys left for New York was to avoid comparison with bands as smart as Devo and Pere Ubu. Even so, a self-produced album showcasing ten good songs is a pleasant shock. The Bizarros' deliberate discordances (including viol, lest we forget John Cale) are carried forward on surefire junk-rock riffs; mastermind Nick Nicholis has the hang of Lou's deadpan songspeech, although some of his mannerisms are otiose and the promising lyrics aren't worked as fine as they must be to sound natural. The stoopider approach of the Rubber City Rebels — "Gotta get a brain job/Gotta get it now/Gotta get a brain job/But I don't know how" — proves more foolproof; Alice Cooper sang about dead babies, these guys claim to eat them. The album seems to be in mono, with sound presence worthy of Andy Warhol, but it hasn't quit on me yet. **A−**

The Bizarros: *The Bizarros* (Mercury '79). This catches Nick Nicholis's vocals halfway down the road to a proper stylization, and his lyrics sound like he's been reading trash rather than talking it. But he also helps shape the music here, and the music is great. Few bands demonstrate more thorough command of basic hook-and-drone, especially Velvets-like because the tempos are never breakneck. Didn't take me long to get to like every tune on the record, as well as most of Jerry Parkins's guitar parts. **B+**

Black Oak Arkansas: *High on the Hog* (Atlantic '74). For two years, BOA has toured harder than any band in history, with the biggest booking agent in the country breaking a trail of busted chops in front of them, and they still can't sell out the Academy of Music on a Saturday night. Why might that be? Because unlike most similar bands they have never achieved competence — they are actively untalented, incapable of even an interesting cop. **D**

Black Sabbath: *Black Sabbath* (Warner Bros. '70). The worst of the counterculture on a plastic platter — bullshit necromancy, drug-impaired reaction time, long solos, everything. They claim to oppose war, but if I don't believe in loving my enemies I don't believe in loving my allies either, and I've been worried something like this was going to happen since the first time I saw a numerology column in an underground newspaper. Original grade: E. **C−**

Black Sabbath: *Paranoid* (Warner Bros. '70). They do take heavy to undreamt-of extremes, and I suppose I could enjoy them as camp, like a horror movie — the title cut is definitely screamworthy. After all, their audience can't take that Lucifer bit seriously, right? Well, depends on what you mean by serious. Personally, I've always suspected that horror movies catharsized stuff I was too rational to care about in the first place. **C−**

Black Sabbath: *Master of Reality* (Warner Bros. '71). As an increasingly regretful spearhead of the great Grand Funk switch, in which critics redefined GFR as a 1971 good old-fashioned rock and roll band even though I've never met a critic (myself included) who actually played the records, I feel entitled to put this in its place. Grank Funk is like an American white blues band of three years ago — dull. Black Sabbath is English — dull and decadent. I don't care how many rebels and incipient groovies are buying. I don't even care if the band members believe in their own Christian/satanist/liberal murk. This is a dim-witted, amoral exploitation. Original grade: D. **C−**

Black Sabbath: *We Sold Our Souls for Rock 'n' Roll* (Warner Bros. '76). By omitting pro forma virtuoso moves — "Rat Salad" has vanished without a trace — this two-disc compilation makes a properly mock-nostalgic document. Only two cuts total (out of seventeen) from LPs five and six, but three from four, cleverly entitled *Black Sabbath Vol. 4,* which I never got around to putting on in 1972. And you know, I'm still not sure I've ever heard anything on it. **C**

Otis Blackwell: *These Are My Songs!* (Inner City '77). He wrote them, all right, but only once — on an amazing "All Shook Up" that ranks with Presley's — does the singer in him manage to reclaim what was long ago appropriated from the composer. His pipes could be better, and a stiff backup band doesn't help, but the basic problem is that Blackwell lacks authority as a performer — he may have invented a bag of tricks for Elvis and Jerry Lee, but he never developed enough sleight-of-manner to put them across. **B−**

Bobby Bland: *His California Album* (ABC/Dunhill '73). With Bland's old label, Duke, which ABC purchased partly to get at his contract, you cut an LP when you score a single. This is a tragically short-sighted way to treat the greatest pure singer in blues, but it does help guarantee that at least one cut will connect instantaneously, like "That Did It" on *Touch of the Blues* or "Chains of Love" on *Spotlighting the Man.* The pop moves here are no more arbitrary than the ones Bland has always gone for. But whether he's sticking to Duke material or inserting a growl into a Barry Goldberg song, he puts his stamp on nothing. **B**

Bobby Bland: *Dreamer* (ABC/Dunhill '74). On their second try, producer Steve Barri and arranger Michael Omartian pull out the pop stops, and while the result isn't too long on conviction it does have its own ersatz character. Refabricated intros worthy of Three Dog Night, prefabricated songs worthy of Bobby Bland, and a woman named Yolanda who leaves Bobby "in this wilderness with no money down" — the wilderness being Charleston, South Carolina, and Yolanda's Pygmalion being the same guy who wrote "My Maria" and "Shambala." Orginal grade: A minus. **B+**

Bobby Bland: *Get On Down with Bobby Bland* (ABC '75). Despite the funky title, this is Bland's country album, and while it won't turn him into Ray Charles, it's a modest success — he gets more suitable (even funky) arrangements from Nashvillians Don Gant and Ron Chancey than Charles gets from Sid Feller. On side one he sounds completely at (or down) home stealing songs from Merle Haggard and Charlie Rich. Overdisc he seems a little ill at ease reassuring a virgin with bom-bom-boms, but wouldn't you?   **B+**

Bobby Bland and B. B. King: *Together Again . . . Live* (ABC '76). Like they say, never again. Or anyway, live and let live. "Let the Good Times Roll" comes out of the box with notable snap, but you've heard better versions of these tunes by one B. or the other. And if you haven't, you should make it a project.   **B−**

Bobby Bland: *Reflections in Blue* (ABC '77). Blues is an art of narrow margins, and ABC's production honchos push this too far — their two songs are bores, and every time Michael Omartian touches a keyboard or a chart the record dies a little. Not a lot — I really believe he's doing his best. But though there are good moments on all of the seven remaining tracks, only "I Intend to Take Your Place" — by Jimmy Lewis, a hidden treasure of contemporary blues and soul songwriting — belongs in Bland's canon.   **B**

Bobby Bland: *I Feel Good, I Feel Fine* (MCA '79). Then you must be on something — you don't even get to sing on that track.   **C−**

Carla Bley: *Dinner Music* (Watt '77). I'm quite taken with this, which reminds me in an abstract way of *Another Green World*. Where dance jazz was unselfconsciously functional, this is art jazz that was *designed* to be functional — just as Eno designed his electronic pop-rock to fade into the background the way so much electronic pop-rock does anyway. The result is yet another of those Jazz Composer's Orchestra get-togethers between avant-gardists (JCOA stalwarts Michael Mantler and Roswell Rudd) and pop luminaries (the Stuff studio funk axis), and this time the music meshes. Unfortunately, however, I find that only two of the eight cuts — "Ida Lupino" and "Ad Infinitum" — combine mel-

ody and rigor as magically as the double-edged concept promises.   **B+**

The Carla Bley Band: *European Tour 1977* (Watt '78). Although the basic concept — Kurt Weill Meets Ornette Coleman for Indiscreet Ellingtonian Frolic — is a little abstruse, this actually does reward the sort of close listening that earns so many theoretical payoffs. Perhaps amusement is the reward a little too often, however. I like a joke as well as the next fellow, but a few emotional expositions do help assuage one's conscience.   **A−**

The Carla Bley Band: *Musique Mecanique* (Watt '79). I'm still attracted to Bley's humor, best displayed here in the title piece, a wry take on the charms and imperfections of the mechanical mode. But this is basically desultory, hinting at the feckless formalism an obsession with texture so often conceals. Beyond the jokes, and the deliberately aborted moments of lyricism, she really doesn't have much to say. Weill sure did. And so did Satie.   **B**

Blondie: *Blondie* (Private Stock '77). Ahh, New York. I remember Debbie Blondie when she was singing with nursery-rhyme breathiness for a group called the Wind in the Willows. Now she sounds flatly cynical against a very funny aural montage of girl-group and original-punk usages from the prepsychedelic era — less blithe, certainly, but more, you know, together. Which is what new-punk posturing is all about. Special award: best use of trash organ since "Light My Fire." [Later on Chrysalis.]   **B+**

Blondie: *Plastic Letters* (Chrysalis '78). Side one is everything this band is supposed to be — seven fresh, clever, evanescent songs, each with its own hip twist. Whether Deborah Harry is claiming that using telepathy to win at poker is "really not cheating" or executing a siren call for the electric age (the bell she imitates sounds like it belongs on a squad car), her vocals are on top and out front, a pop-rock delight. But side two bombs, except for "Kidnapper" and a couple of refrains, and the singing gets lost in the mud. Me, I'd buy it for side one. But I'm not sure about you.   **B+**

Blondie: *Parallel Lines* (Chrysalis '78). As unlikely as it seemed three years ago, they've actually achieved their synthesis of the Dixie Cups and the Electric Prunes — their third is as close to God as pop-rock albums ever get, or got. Closer, actually — even on side two every song generates its own unique, scintillating glitz. What seems at first like a big bright box of hard candy turns out to have guts, feeling, a chewy center, and Deborah Harry's vocal gloss reveals nooks of compassion and sheer physical give that make the protagonists of these too-too modern fragments seem as tragic (or untragic) as those of any other epoch. Plus the band really New Yawks it up — try the chorus of "Just Go Away." Original grade: A minus.   **A**

Blondie: *Eat to the Beat* (Chrysalis '79). This makes it in the end, but not by much — a tour de force like *Parallel Lines* it ain't. The soft focus of the lyrics remains more evasive than profound or mysterious, and a lot of what replaces the diminished popcraft either wanders ("Sound-A-Sleep") or repeats experiments we've heard before ("Victor"). Then again, "Sound-A-Sleep" probably ought to wander, since it's about insomnia, and the pushy organ hysterics of "Victor" are a gutsy move for a group that's supposed to have gone AOR. I don't like the overarching fatalism — me, I hope to die old and get ugly — but I do like the way the lyrics depart from pop bohemia to speak directly to the mass audience they're reaching. And Debbie just keeps getting better.   **A−**

James Blood: *Tales of Captain Black* (Artists House '79). This isn't the great Blood Ulmer record I've been waiting for. How can it be when the saxophone player is Ornette Coleman, who makes everything he plays his

own? And how can it be when the drummer is Denardo Coleman, who can't follow (let alone drive) Blood in free time *or* on the one? But it does offer the densest guitar improvisations anyone has put on record since Hendrix, and over catchy themes, too. And it does offer Ornette Coleman.   **A−**

Bloodstone: *Natural High* (London '73). Any album that includes both a hit soul-harmony ballad and "Bo Diddley" (the band's from England, natch) deserves a second listen. But believe me, the tenth is a dubious investment.   Original   grade: B minus.   **C+**

Blood, Sweat & Tears: *3* (Columbia '70). Just figured out how David Clayton-Thomas learned vocal projection: by belching. That's why when he gets really excited he sounds as if he's about to throw up. But it's only part of the reason he gets me so excited I feel like I'm about to throw up. The whole band commits "Symphony for the Devil," a pretty good rock and roll song revealed as a pseudohistorical middlebrow muddle when suite-ened. And just who added themes by Bartok, Prokofiev, Thelonious, and Fred Lewis (Fred Lewis?) to a Stevie Winwood tune? Original grade: C.   **C−**

Blood, Sweat & Tears: *Greatest Hits* (Columbia '72). As with Engelbert Humperdinck, their pop success does them more good in Vegas than on the radio, and only four of these eleven cuts made top twenty. Highlights: "Lisa, Listen to Me" and "I Can't Quit Her," neither of which made top hundred — and both of which make me   appreciate   Al   Kooper   very much.   **C**

David Blue: *Nice Baby and the Angel* (Asylum '73). Long ago, before he sought institution in David Geffen's tastefully maintained diaspora, David was a nice baby who had grown up. His songs were tortuous and somewhat arty, but they had their strengths. This one sounds like outtakes from the Eagles, all easy rhythms and ladies and outlaws in old Chevrolets. **C−**

Blue Ash: *No More, No Less* (Mercury '73). Magic for new nostalgiacs —the spirit of '66 materializes before your very ears, including "Any Time at All," a good previously unrecorded Dylan song, and an original called "Smash My Guitar." Shazam, if that's your idea of a good time. Original grade: B plus. **B**

Blue Magic: *Blue Magic* (Atco '74). The best Stylistics album since *Round Two* is a Philly Phormalist's delight. Produced by Gamble-Huff veteran Norman Harris, it features the velvety falsetto of Ted White and four hit singles (only one of which, the Tod Browning tribute "Sideshow," has broken pop). What's more, the filler includes a seven-minute "Just Don't Want to Be Lonely" that helps me understand why Ronnie Dyson and the Main Ingredient both cut the song, though not why anybody bought it when they did. **B+**

Blue Magic: *The Magic of the Blue* (Atco '74). I've never been able to go all the way with groups that specialize in repressed-backbeat falsetto ballads. The few I've liked — only the Chi-Lites and the Stylistics for more than one song at a time — barely redeemed their simpiness by sounding sincere, or do I mean dumb, and in the wake of an inspired debut these hotshots just don't. Instant professionalism, I guess, combined with the usual song fatigue. Recommended only to those who want to know what the Stylistics will sound like after Russell Thompkins gets his B.A. and learns to sing like a sane, responsible adult. **C+**

Blue Mink: *Real Mink* (Philips '71). Madeline Bell is queen of doowah in London. Roger Cook is one half of Greenaway & Cook, Britain's top commercial songwriting team, who have granted us the Fortunes' "You've Got Your Troubles" and imposed upon us White Plains' "My Baby Loves Lovin'." Their collaboration is solid white soul, marred by a couple of automatic instrumentals but graced by a charming self-consciousness as well as a few top commercial songs — oh yes, and a black singer. Original grade: B. **B−**

Blue Oyster Cult: *Blue Oyster Cult* (Columbia '72). Warning: critics' band, managed by Sandy Pearlman with occasional lyrics by R. Meltzer. Reassurance: the most musical hard rock album since *Who's Next*. (Well, that's less than six months, and this is not a great time for hard rock albums.) The style is technocratic psychedelic, a distanced, decisively post-Altamont reworking of the hallucinogenic guitar patterns of yore, with lots of heavy trappings. Not that they don't have a lyrical side. In "Then Came the Last Days of May," for instance, four young men ride out to seek their fortune in the dope biz and one makes his by wasting the other three. Original grade: A minus. **B+**

Blue Oyster Cult: *Tyranny and Mutation* (Columbia '73). Says S. Pearlman: "We want to be disgusting, not trans-repulsive." Says R. Meltzer: "This is *really* hard rock comedy." Musically, Long Island's only underground band impales the entire heavy ethos on a finely-honed guitar neck, often at high speed, which is the punch line. And the lyrics aren't inaudible, just unbelievable — a parody-surreal refraction of the abysmal "poetry" of heavy, with its evil women and gods of hellfire. Which is not to suggest that it doesn't become what it takes off from. But is that bad or good? Original grade: A minus. **B+**

Blue Oyster Cult: *Secret Treaties* (Columbia '74). Sometime over the past year, while I wasn't playing their records, I began to wonder whether a cross between the Velvet Underground and Uriah Heep was my idea of a good time. The driving, effortless wit and density of Buck Dharma's guitar flourish in this cold climate, but Eric Bloom couldn't project emotion if they let him, and I'm square enough to find his pseudo-pseudospade cynicism less than funny. Subject of "Dominance and Submission": New Year's 1964 in Times Square. Original grade: B minus. **B**

Blue Oyster Cult: *On Your Feet or on Your Knees* (Columbia '75). This live double, proof that they've earned the right to issue cheapo product, is a fitting testament. The packaging makes their ominoso joke more explicit than it's ever been, and if the music is humdrum more often than searing, maybe that means these closet intellectuals have finally achieved the transubstantiation of their most baroque fantasies. **C+**

Blue Oyster Cult: *Agents of Fortune* (Columbia '76). Just when I figured they were doomed to repeat themselves until the breakup, they come up with the *Fleetwood Mac* of heavy metal, not as fast as *Tyranny and Mutation* but longer on momentum, with MOR tongue-in-cheek replacing the black-leather posturing and future games. I wonder how long it took them to do the la-la-las on "Debbie Denise" without cracking up. **B+**

Blue Oyster Cult: *Spectres* (Columbia '77). Although Sandy Pearlman used to say the Cult's audience couldn't tolerate any suggestion that the band's laser-and-leathers fooforaw was funny, their parodic side has become progressively more overt. What do today's Cultists think of "Godzilla" ("Oh no there goes Tokyo") or the beerhall intro to "Golden Age of Leather"? I bet some of 'em like laughing at laser-and-leathers, and good. I also bet some of 'em are so zonked they wouldn't get it if John Belushi emceed, and to, er, hell with them. **B**

Blue Oyster Cult: *Mirrors* (Columbia '79). The Cult's identity has been deteriorating for years, but this is a quantum leap into anonymity — songs for slick (what happened to dense?) hard rock band by five different musicians and their numerous collaborators.

Only "In Thee," a farewell to Patti Smith by Allen Lanier that deserves to become a standard on the order of "Allison," is more than marginally interesting. **C**

The Blue Ridge Rangers: *The Blue Ridge Rangers* (Fantasy '73). If John Fogerty really wants to play all the instruments, he's wise to perform country music, because overdubbing on top of yourself is a good way to get the kind of semimechanical feel Nashville producers strive for. Although the energy rushes here (one guitar break on "Jambalaya," the no-no-nos on "Heart of Stone") are almost as rare as the new songs, the voice sounds more original than ever: Fogerty may not be Jimmie Rodgers, but he makes a damn fine Lefty Frizzell. Result: one better-than-average country (-rock) statement. **B+**

Blues Brothers: *Briefcase Full of Blues* (Atlantic '78). The studio-superstar backup band isn't exactly long on personality, but it rocks, and almost every song ranks as an underrecorded classic. John Belushi goes out of his way — earnestly, even awkwardly — to identify the original artists, which cancels out the Rasta jokes on "Groove Me." However. If Belushi told those jokes to supply his fans with their ration of dope humor, then shame on him. But if he was just nervous about treading in the voiceprints of Junior Wells and King Floyd, he had reason — he's not as convincing as most *white* blues singers, much less Junior Wells or King Floyd. Is this a top-ten album because people actually want to listen to it? Inspirational Patter: "I'd suggest you buy as many blues albums as you can." **C+**

Blues Image: *Open* (Atco '70). I love "Ride Captain Ride," really. But the only mystery ship that transports anyone from the San Francisco Bay to Parchman Farm is rock and roll — rock and roll more inspired than this. **C+**

Arthur Blythe: *Lenox Avenue Breakdown* (Columbia '79). I prefer this to, say, Blythe's more conventionally "free" *Bush Baby* (on Adelphi) because — thanks to Jack DeJohnette, Guillermo Franco, and the lilt of Blythe's theme vamps — its passion for popular rhythms enables it to say something about them. The sinuous Latin groove of "Down San Diego Way" wends through three of the four tracks. But while the California opener is unfailingly sunny, the groove runs into two-way traffic on the title tune and suffers further cross-comment on the bluesy "Slidin' Through" before disappearing into "Odessa." Just as Steely Dan's lyrics (and chord changes, I suppose) work against the surface mellowness of the music, so the strength of the groove here is challenged and transformed by solo voices and alien rhythms without ever being defeated, much less exploited for its "accessibility." And if we're interested, all this conflict helps us understand why music like *Bush Baby* exists. **A**

Hamilton Bohannon: *Bohannon's Greatest Disco Hits* (Dakar '75). I listened a lot to this record on the strength of Vince Aletti's description of Bohannon's "idiosyncratic style: long (five-to eight-minute), bottom-heavy instrumentals with minimal, chantlike or repetitive vocals framed in a nearly unvarying beat pattern so relentless that it's pushed beyond boredom to fascination. Unlike most successful disco music, Bohannon's has few peaks and almost no breaks. . . . The music's very relentlessness and lack of intensity gives it a strangely dead, 'off' quality — just as those outer-space replacements for people in science-fiction movies are always vaguely wrong, emotionless." I agree, yet somehow I'm not fascinated. On the other hand, I've never thought about it while I was dancing. **B**

Boney M.: *Take the Heat Off Me* (Atco '77). As in so much German disco, a nice tart detachment undercuts the lush vacuousness here. It's not just that the rhythms are candidly mechanical; even the stiffness of the string playing sounds calculated, as if produced by some fantastic cuckoo clock. Who else could put "No Woman, No Cry" and the Peggy Lee version of "Fever" belly-to-belly except some European who thinks that whatever crosses the Atlantic is similarly funky and exotic? **B**

Boney M.: *Nightflight to Venus* (Sire '78). I find myself amused rather than offended by tinkly-shit renditions of such sacrosanct classics as "Heart of Gold" and "King of the Road," not to mention historically relevant lyrics like "Rah rah Rasputin/Russia's greatest love machine." In fact, these folks have now surpassed Silver Connection in my Dumb (But Funny) Eurodisco competition. But the amusement palls, and it's not even all that disco. **B−**

Karla Bonoff: *Karla Bonoff* (Columbia '77). I like this woman, who strikes me as sexy and sensible and almost as wise as she wants to be. But there's something self-pitying and slightly sheeplike in her voice that turns me off. And even though I've been humming "I Can't Hold On" for three days, I suspect I'll be going to Fleetwood Mac when I want that sort of buzz in the future. **B−**

The Bonzo Dog Band: *The History of the Bonzos* (United Artists '73). I didn't like them initially because I was under the impression they were a "group" — a musical aggregation — when in fact they're a comedy troupe who play instruments. Explaining why I don't like (i.e., laugh at) them in retrospect is harder — responses to comedy are even more personal than responses to music. Just say that what they do strikes me as boarding-school humor — covertly classbound escapist silliness without Monty Python's moral underpinnings. This generous two-disc compilation, an hour and forty minutes of entertainment in all, is intelligent and imaginative. But it's also narrow for the worst reasons. **B−**

The Boomtown Rats: *The Boomtown Rats* (Mercury '78). As the clash of punk guitars battled the swelling Springsteen-cum-Lizzy pseudoclimaxes, I began to suspect a fix, especially since record-bizzers have been heard to murmur fondly about the "musical" skill of these up-and-coming Irish nasties. But throughout a first side that often shifts mood but never quits, this is the real stuff, banging home the survival value of a brain unclogged by useless feelings. Unfortunately, side two bogs down in evocations of misogyny, boredom, and the plight of the young, all surrounding an apparent throwaway called "Close as You'll Ever Be" that ought to be a single. **B+**

The Boomtown Rats: *A Tonic for the Troops* (Columbia '79). Satisfied owners of the group's Mercury debut might spring for the import (on Ensign), since this repeats two of the better tunes from that new wave no-sale. And seekers after straight-ahead cacophony might look around for the Mercury. But though this does turn rather campy at times — Bob Geldof's cheerfully narsty opportunism has lost body and focus — it will certainly do. I'll take a good calculating song about Adolf Hitler over an ordinary calculating song about the perils of romance any day, and if you're heading your music toward the rock mainstream, wit and flash don't hurt. **B+**

The Boomtown Rats: *The Fine Art of Surfacing* (Columbia '79). Bob Geldof has a journalist's gift — he'd make a terrific topical songwriter if only he believed in something. Instead, he's taken to dramatizing the usual alienation from the usual inside. Too bad. **B−**

Debby Boone: *You Light Up My Life* (Warner Bros. '77). Who cares if the single sells six million? It's only singles, y'know? Trendsetters don't buy singles. Smart people like you and me don't buy singles. But now I read that the *album* has gone platinum, too. Original grade: D minus. **D**

Debby Boone: *Midstream* (Warner Bros. '78). Does the title mean she'd rather drown than get hit by a truck in the MOR? Or that she's changing horses midrecord from Joe Brooks (get the pun?) to Brooks (get it now?) Arthur? Arthur's side offers classy material (this year Allee Willis, maybe next Janis Ian!), while Joe's is junk almost as jingly as "You Light Up My Life." I prefer Joe's. I'd also prefer to get hit by a truck. **D+**

Bootsy's Rubber Band: *Stretchin' Out in Bootsy's Rubber Band* (Warner Bros. '76). This clone of Dr. Funkenstein isn't as stoopid as he pretends to be, but he does have identity problems. Why else would he announce that "he's just another point of view," or invite us to "vanish in our sleep"? Good songs, good textures, good riffs — all ultimately undefined. **B+**

Bootsy's Rubber Band: *Ahh . . . The Name Is Bootsy, Baby!* (Warner Bros. '77). Although Bootsy's comic consciousness takes a certain toll in tightness and drive, this record does about ninety percent of what a good funk album does while offering priceless insight into obscene phone calls and cannabis cunnilingus. Free your ass and your mind can come along for a giggle. Original grade: B. **B+**

Bootsy's Rubber Band: *Bootsy? Player of the Year* (Warner Bros. '78). When I pay attention, I note that the slow stuff oozes along sexy as come-from-the-state-they're-named-after (back when they knew how to ooze) and the fast stuff gets over the hump just like rhymes-with-Podunk (long may they wave). When I think about it, I like the joke, too. So how come I'm not fucking, dancing, or laughing? Well, I suspect it has more to do with not being eleven than with not being black, and more to do with my funnybone than my booty. Schoolkids are as rich a source of jokes as Johnny Carson, but that doesn't mean I get off on *The Flintstones*. Original grade: B. **B+**

Bootsy's Rubber Band: *This Boot Is Made for Fonk-N* (Warner Bros. '79). Bootsy sounds like a kiddie-show host at the end of his tether — trotting out sound effects, Steve Martin imitations, desperate appeals to DJs, anything he can think of. Except a good riff. **C+**

Boston: *Boston* (Epic '76). When informed that someone has achieved an American synthesis of Led Zeppelin and Yes, all I can do is hold my ears and say gosh. **C**

Boston: *Don't Look Back* (Epic '78). Debut pomposities having been excised, a pure exploration of corporate rock remains. Pretty streamlined. Not only are the guitars perfectly received, but the lyrical clichés seem specially selected to make the band as credible in the arena as they are in the studio, and Brad Delp's tenor, too thin for nasty cock-rock distractions, leaves us free to contemplate unsullied form. The only thing that makes me wonder is that sometimes I catch myself enjoying it, which means some corruption is still at work here. True formalists, from Mallarme to bluegrass, leave me absolutely cold. **B—**

David Bowie: *Hunky Dory* (RCA Victor '71). After two overwrought excursions for Mercury [later released on RCA] this ambitious, brainy, imaginative singer-composer has created an album that rewards the concentration it demands instead of making you wish you'd gone on with the vacuuming. Not that he combines the passion and compassion of Dylan (subject of one song) with the full-witted vision of Warhol (subject of a better one) just yet. But he has a nice feeling for weirdos, himself included. **A—**

David Bowie: *The Rise and Fall of Ziggy Stardust and the Spiders from Mars* (RCA Victor '72). In its own way, this is audacious stuff right down to the stubborn wispiness of its sound,

and Bowie's actorly intonations add humor and shades of meaning to the words. Which are often witty and rarely precious, offering an unusually candid and detailed vantage on the rock star's world. Admittedly, for a long time I wondered who cared, besides lost kids for whom such access feels like privilege. The answer is, someone like Bowie — a middlebrow fascinated by the power of a highbrow-lowbrow form. Original grade: C plus. **B+**

David Bowie: *Aladdin Sane* (RCA Victor '73). The pubeless is-he-naked? illustration inside the doublefold suggests not bisexuality but asexuality — the affliction of a romantic for whom love turns nasty, awkward, and exploitative when touched by lust. So maybe the bleak future Bowie likes to scare his fans with is a metaphor for his own present, the American phase of which is reflected by these hard-rocking mechanisms. But the cover, "Let's Spend the Night Together," opens other possibilities; its lyric suggests an alternative to the brutality of "Cracked Actor" and its music can help you through the bitterest realities. As a result, this is more interesting thematically than *Ziggy Stardust,* and it's also better rock and roll. Original grade: A minus. **B+**

David Bowie: *Pin Ups* (RCA Victor '73). The idea of reviving these British oldies is a great one, but most of those fanatic enough to know all the originals aren't very excited. I know half and I'm not excited either. I mean, it's good to recall the screaming-frustration-on-the-nine-to-five of "Friday on My Mind," but when Bowie screams he sounds arch. And that ain't rock and roll. Yet. Original grade: C plus. **B—**

David Bowie: *Diamond Dogs* (RCA Victor '74). In which a man who has always turned his genuine if unendearing talent for image manipulation to the service of his dubious literary and theatrical gifts evolves from harmless kitsch into pernicious sensationalism. Despite two good songs and some thoughtful (if unhummable) rock sonorities, this is doomsday purveyed from a pleasure dome. Message: eat, snort, and be pervy, for tomorrow we shall be peoploids — but tonight how about buying this piece of plastic? Say nay. **C+**

David Bowie: *David Live* (RCA Victor '75). The artiste at his laryngeal nadir, mired in bullshit pessimism and arena-rock pandering — and the soul frills just make it worse. **C−**

David Bowie: *Young Americans* (RCA Victor '75). This is a failure. The tunes make (Lennon-McCartney's) "Across the Universe" sound like a melodic highlight, and although the amalgam of English hard rock and Philly soul is so thin it's interesting, it often overwhelms David's voice, which is even thinner. But after the total alienation of *Diamond Dogs* and the total ripoff of *David Live,* I'm pleased with Bowie's renewed generosity of spirit — he takes pains to simulate compassion and risks failure simply by moving on. His reward is two successes: the title tune, in which pain stimulates compassion, and (Bowie-Lennon-Alomar's) "Fame," which rhymes with pain and makes you believe it. Original grade: C plus. **B−**

David Bowie: *Changesonebowie* (RCA Victor '76). The way La Bowie's vaunted concept albums reduce to greatest hits is a revelation. Non-dross from the likes of *Diamond Dogs* and *Young Americans* holds its own with the best discrete songs from *Ziggy Stardust* and *Aladdin Sane,* and what's more, chronology resembles progress — like the Supremes regressing from "Where Did Our Love Go" to "Love Child" in reverse, although not as important aesthetically. **A**

David Bowie: *Station to Station* (RCA Victor '76). Miraculously, Bowie's attraction to black music has matured; even more miraculously, the new relationship seems to have left his hard-and-heavy side untouched. Ziggy-philes can call it robotoid if they want — I admire the mechanical,

fragmented, rather secondhand elegance of *Aladdin Sane,* and this adds soul. All of the six cuts are too long, I suppose, including the one that originated with Johnny Mathis, and David sounds like he's singing to us via satellite. But spaceyness has always been part of his shtick, and anybody who can merge Lou Reed, disco, and Huey Smith — the best I can do with the irresistible "TVC 15" — deserves to keep doing it for 5:29. Original grade: A minus. **A**

David Bowie: *Low* (RCA Victor '77). I find side one's seven "fragments" — since the two that clock in at less than 2:45 are 1:42 and 2:20, the term must refer to structure rather than length — almost as powerful as the "overlong" tracks on *Station to Station.* "Such a wonderful person/But you got problems" is definitely a love lyric for our time. But most of the movie music on side two is so far from hypnotic that I figure Bowie, rather than Eno, must deserve credit for it. I mean, is Eno really *completely* fascinated by banality? **B+**

David Bowie: *"Heroes"* (RCA Victor '77). When I first heard the Enofied instrumental textures on side two, as background music, they struck me as more complex than their counterparts on *Low,* and they are. *Low* now seems quite pop, slick and to the point even when the point is background noise; in fact, after I completed my comparison, I began to play it a lot. But what was interesting background on *"Heroes"* proved merely noteworthy as foreground, admirably rather than attractively ragged. Maybe after the next album I'll get the drift of this one. Original grade: B. **B+**

David Bowie: *Stage* (RCA Victor '78). If James Brown is the only rock and roller who deserves more than one concert album, then the Bowie to ban is *David Live. Stage* kicks off with some well-chosen Bowie oldies before moving into refreshingly one-dimensional versions of his best songs since 1975, including the key Eno collaborations, which were often oversubtle to begin with. For fans only, of course. I'm one. **B+**

David Bowie: *Lodger* (RCA Victor '79). I used to think Bowie was middlebrow, but now I'd prefer to call him post-middlebrow — a habitue of prematurely abandoned modernist space. Musically, these fragments of anomie don't seem felt, and lyrically they don't seem thought through. But that's part of their charm — the way they confound categories of sensibility and sophistication is so frustrating it's satisfying, at least if you have your doubts about the categories. Less satisfying, actually, than the impact of the record as a whole. **A−**

Boxer: *Below the Belt* (Virgin '76). What happens when an arty English keyboards-and-guitar team (Mike Patto and Ollie Halsall) decide to go accessible? Why, they take the heavy road, thus maximizing the real but limited potential of both arty and heavy. How far you go along with them depends on where you start. Original grade: B. **B+**

Randall Bramblett: *That Other Mile* (Polydor '75). A find. Transcending its well-connected professional genre, the slightly distracted passion of Bramblett's singing combines with his oblique fusion of Southern boogie, studio country-rock, and Caribbean polyrhythms to take the edge of privilege off his philosophical fatalism. His music is too warm and funny to sound self-satisfied, and the way he collects images around an aphoristic catchphrase is too open-ended to sound smug. Start with side two. Original grade: A minus. **B+**

Randall Bramblett: *Light of the Night* (Polydor '76). Bramblett is a genuinely philosophical songwriter, an A student at a first-rate modernist seminary who hasn't lost his taste for the cracker barrel. His pessimism is gentle and good-humored, just like his soulful, pleasantly aimless music. Anybody who can follow a credible song

about Karl Jung with another called "The Joke of the Coastal Plain" (that's us, fellow humans) is somebody you'll feel like listening to now and again. **B+**

Bonnie Bramlett: *Sweet Bonnie Bramlett* (Columbia '73). She tries to come on sweet, granted, but she sounds desperate. Enough to make me hope she finds peace, as if we needed another Jesus freak. **C+**

Bonnie Bramlett: *It's Time* (Capricorn '75). The first two cuts on this album are the only ones I want to hear again, and one of them was coauthored by Delaney. **C+**

Bonnie Bramlett: See also Delaney & Bonnie

Delaney Bramlett: *Some Things Coming* (Columbia '73). Either he's mad with grief or he switched to Columbia so that James William Guercio could do his horn arrangements. Too bad he didn't get him. **D+**

Delaney Bramlett: See also Delaney & Bonnie

Brass Construction: *Brass Construction* (United Artists '75). All disco bands sound alike — and if you've seen one ghetto you've seen them all, not to mention their residents, with their swarthy skin and flat (or is it hooked?) noses. Yeah sure. This specific disco band is black-identified, i.e., non-hustle/samba with lots of funk. It owes more lyrically to Gil Scott-Heron than to Barry White but evokes both and is candid to the point of wryness (and terseness) about using words primarily for musical color. I like the way the synthesized violins are timed and love the fanfare coda to "Love," my favorite cut. **B+**

Bread: *The Best of Bread* (Elektra '73). Though at times they sound like country-rock crossover of unprecedented spinelessness, this is basically prime pop — I thought "Everything I

Own'' was a better single than ''Tumbling Dice.'' I only wish they reshuffled the lyrical clichés as skillfully as the musical ones. Even in fun I can't work up much feeling for an ass man as mendacious as David Gates. **B**

Breakfast Special: *Breakfast Special* (Rounder '79). Where it survives as indigenous country music, bluegrass may well be a wondrous thing, but among citybilly archivists it only magnifies the usual folkie escapisms — purism and pastoral nostalgia — by encouraging mindless virtuosity. Which makes this virtuosic but eclectically streetwise record a small miracle that should delight anyone more spiritually attuned to the genre than a faithless wretch like me. **B+**

Brewer & Shipley: *Tarkio* (Kama Sutra '70). If these guys are Simon & Garfunkel imitators, so are Ferrante & Teicher. Take them as a country-rock band led by two guitar-playing singers with a phrasemaking knack. This is the best of three likable, unexceptional albums because it leads off with a phrase that deserves to become a cliché: ''One Toke Over the Line.'' The two other prizes here — ''Oh Mommy'' and ''Tarkio Road'' — also allude to marijuana. Original grade: B. **B−**

The Brides of Funkenstein: *Never Buy Texas from a Cowboy* (Atlantic '79). Every previous album by the Brides and Parlet has ended up pretty quickly on my reference shelves — P-Funk was obviously expending its collective energy elsewhere. But since George Clinton's current master plan involves sharpening his sidekicks' profiles, he put out on this one, and I prefer it to *Gloryhallastoopid* or *Uncle Jam Wants You*. It's gratifying to hear women asserting themselves in what has always been a sexist setup. Dawn Silva, Sheila Horn, and Jeanette McGruder generate funk power and cartoon stoopidity — next to Philippe Wynne, they're the best voices George

has. Heroine of title cut: Mother Wit. **A−**

Lonnie Brooks: *Bayou Lightning* (Alligator '79). A thoughtful guitarist, intermittently clever composer, and competent shouter, Brooks deserves to be recorded by someone as good as Bruce Iglauer. But that doesn't mean anyone who cares less about blues than Brooks and Iglauer do should buy the result. **B−**

The Brothers Johnson: *Right On Time* (A&M '77). I once tagged Earth, Wind & Fire as black MOR, but these guys straightened out my categories. EW&F is more like Elton John or early Supremes — formularized music worked out with undeniable verve. This is more in the area of Foreigner or Firefall — pop professionalism reduced to a concept in which all annoyances and other signs of life are eliminated. Funk is often automatic, but it must take some heavy discipline to make it bland. **C+**

Chuck Brown and the Soul Searchers: *Bustin' Loose* (Source '79). Toward the end of 1978, these D.C. journeymen got lucky and hit the discos with the title track, which was very funk-soul for that disco moment. The album that resulted is almost like a field recording — a completely unpretentious document of what sort of originals a modestly gifted funk-soul dance band might be doing in 1978. There's even a salsa. Very likable. **B+**

Clarence Gatemouth Brown: *Blackjack* (Music Is Medicine '77). The black musician with the unforgettable name sings like the bluesman he's thought to be, but though he plays some blues, too, more often he picks like a Nashville cat. Culturally, this is gratifying. Musically, though, it's a pleasant but by no means groundbreaking folkie jam with light jazz tendencies. Get ridda that flute, Gatemouth. **B−**

James Brown: *Sex Machine* (King '70). Some doubt the claim that this was recorded in concert in Augusta, Georgia, but everyone believes in the music. On "Get Up I Feel Like Being a Sex Machine" he creates a dance track even more compelling than the single out of the same five elements: light funk-four on the traps, syncopated bass figure, guitar scratched six beats to the bar, and two voices for call and response. When he modulates to the bridge it's like the Sprit of God moving upon the face of the waters. After that he could describe his cars for three sides and get away with it (hope this doesn't give him any bright ideas), but in fact all of what remains is prime JB except for the organ version of "Spinning Wheel" (horn bands will out) and the cover of "If I Ruled the World" (thought he already did). Side four, with its powerful "Man's World," is especially fine, closing with a soul-wrenching scream that says it all. [Later on Polydor.]   **A**

James Brown: *Super Bad* (King '70). Recorded live, it says — hmm. Were the strings that accompany "By the Time I Get to Phoenix" on stage with him, or did he borrow them from Isaac Hayes on his way to pick up the uncredited "Chain Gang" finale from Sam Cooke? But it doesn't matter. Ten minutes of super rhythm plus ten minutes of bad blues plus a surprisingly passionate "Let It Be Me" with the Jamesettes and you even forgive the bad (really bad, I mean) Albert Ayler imitation that he identifies as a tribute to 'Trane. In fact, you kind of like it.   **A−**

James Brown: *Sho Is Funky Down Here* (King '71). Brown's farewell to his own indie label is so outre purists will probably prize it. Rock-funk instrumentals dominated by (literally) anonymous electric piano and guitar, both more rock than funk, which would never be said of the rhythm section. At moments it sounds like JB Meets BB — and I don't mean the bluesman, I mean Bela Bartok — in the person of arranger Dave Matthews.

As for JB, he grunts a few times. Veddy interesting.   **C+**

James Brown: *Hot Pants* (Polydor '71). Is it rolling, James? The hit vamp (can't call it a tune, now can you?) "Escape-ism" was supposedly cut to kill time until Bobby Byrd arrived. The title track follows and it's a killer too, one of Brown's richest Afro-dances. "Blues and Pants" suggests that the title track is a mellowed-down takeoff on "Sex Machine," which is good to know. And "Can't Stand It" is not to be confused with "I Can't Stand Myself." If you say so, James. Only he doesn't. I don't think he cares. And neither do I.   **A−**

James Brown: *Revolution of the Mind* (Polydor '71). Ever the innovator, Brown here presents a live double-LP, "Recorded Live at the Apollo Vol. III." Good stuff, too — a consistent overview of his polyrhythm phase. But "Sex Machine" is sharper and "Bewildered" deeper on last year's live double. And with the medley on side three the tempo gets so hot that anybody but JB will have trouble dancing to it.   **B+**

James Brown: *Soul Classics* (Polydor '72). Brown recorded nine of these ten cuts for King; every track is good and many — "Sex Machine," "Papa's Got a Brand New Bag," "I Got You" — are great. But they're so jumbled chronologically — side two jumps from '71 to '65 back to '71 to '69 to '66 — that it's a tribute to Brown's single-minded rhythmic genius that they hold together at all. Hearing his classic '70s dance tracks in their original three-minute formats, you begin to pine for the extended album versions — devoid of verbal logic and often even chord changes, these patterns, for that's what they really are, are meant to build, not resolve. And the chief formal advantage of top-forty strictures is that they force speedy resolutions. Time: 28:25.   **A−**

James Brown: *There It Is* (Polydor '72). A generous four r&b hits here, three of them — "There It Is," "I'm a Greedy Man," and "Talkin' Loud and Sayin' Nothing'' — ace JB grooves. (Who's on congas, James?) The fourth is the "King Heroin'' sermon, which together with its ten-minute offshoot "Public Enemy #1'' is stuck cunningly — Brown has been reading his Alexander Pope — in the middle of the dance stuff on both sides. Plus an actual song, the first new one he's recorded in years, and a JB composition called "Never Can Say Goodbye'' that asks the musical question, "What's going on?'' For junkies, this is an A plus; for the rest of us, it's somewhat more marginal. **A−**

James Brown: *Get on the Good Foot* (Polydor '72). Only two hits on this studio double, though it takes Hank Ballard five minutes to describe its riches on side two — "he comes from all sides on this one.'' Lines repeat from song to song — "The long-haired hippies and the Afro blacks/All get together off behind the tracks/And they party'' — and so do riffs. The hook on the twelve-minute "Please, Please'' (not to be confused, of course, with "Please, Please, Please'') repeats one hundred forty-eight (and a half) times. I love the hook, I even like the line, and if this were the world's only James Brown album it would be priceless. But there's a lot of waste here, and Brown's voice can't carry ballads the way it used to. Original grade: B plus. **B−**

James Brown: *Black Caesar* (Polydor '73). You listen to Brown for music, not songs, but that's no reason to expect good soundtrack albums from him. He should never be allowed near a vibraphone again. **D+**

James Brown: *Slaughter's Big Rip-Off* (Polydor '73). As movie scores go, this ripoff is only medium-sized. At least it apes Oliver Nelson rather than Henry Mancini, and sometimes it even breaks away from the atmosphere into something earthier. Worth hearing: "Sexy, Sexy, Sexy.'' **C**

James Brown: *Soul Classics Volume II* (Polydor '73). In absolute terms, Brown has declined on Polydor. Even if you don't insist on great composi-

tions (never his strength) or great singing (where he's waned physically), he just hasn't matched rhythmic inventions like "Mother Popcorn'' and "Sex Machine'' for the big label. And this compilation inexplicably omits "Hot Pants,'' which comes close, in favor of his ill-advised revivals of "Think'' and "Honky Tonk.'' Still, eight of these ten tracks have made the soul top ten over the past two years, and not counting "King Heroin'' you'll shake ass to every one. **A−**

James Brown: *The Payback* (Polydor '73). Because more is often more with JB, a studio double comprising eight long songs isn't necessarily a gyp. Especially when all the songs have new titles. Not only does most of this work as dance music, but two slow ones are actually sung. "Time Is Running Out Fast,'' however, is a spectacularly inaccurate title for a horn-and-voice excursion that shambles on for 12:37. **B+**

James Brown: *Hell* (Polydor '74). Great stuff on the two good sides — tricky horn charts, "Please, Please, Please'' with a Spanish accent, law-enforcement advice. Then there's the side of ballads w/strings, which might be all right if they were also w/voice, and the side that begins "I Can't Stand It '76.' '' **B**

James Brown: *Reality* (Polydor '74). Talkin' loud and sayin' nothing, Brown's streetwise factotum intones: "He's still the baddest — always will be the baddest — that's why we give him credit for being the superstar he is.'' A bad sign (really bad, I mean). As are "Who Can I Turn To'' and "Don't Fence Me In.'' **B−**

James Brown: *Sex Machine Today* (Polydor '75). If Someone were to airlift this one tape to you in the tundra, the remakes would be godsends. But if you own another version of "Sex Machine'' you own a better one. Ditto "I Feel Good,'' ditto every aimless solo, and ditto the reading from Rand-McNally. Which leaves us with the symphosynth, the complaints that other musicians are ripping him off, and the putdowns of hairy legs. **C+**

James Brown: *Everybody's Doin' the Hustle and Dead on the Double Bump* (Polydor '75). In which JB eases the tempo and stops using his voice as a conga drum, thus fashioning a languorous funk that I guess is designed to compete with Barry White. It's not horrible, but I'd just as soon hear the competition — after all, what's JB without intensity? And then suddenly he says fuck it and closes the record with a seven minute jam on "Kansas City" so sharp it could bring back the lindy hop, at least in dreams. **B−**

James Brown: *Hot* (Polydor '75). This record has a bad rep. Most of it was reportedly cut with arranger Dave Matthews by New York studio musicians and then dubbed over by JB, and the title hit didn't do as well among blacks as David Bowie's "Fame," where its guitar lick first went public. But side one really works. If Brown did cop that lick, he certainly had it coming, and except for the sodden "So Long" everything else is touched with the extraordinary, from the cracked falsetto that climaxes "For Sentimental Reasons" to the stirring male backup on "Try Me" to "The Future Shock of the World," a high-echo rhythm track on which JB does nothing but whisper the word "disco." Unfortunately, the dance vamp and ballads overdisc are nothing new, though "Please, Please, Please" (with more male backup) sounds fine in its umpteenth version. **B**

James Brown: *Get Up Offa That Thing* (Polydor '76). "I'm Back, I'm back?" is how JB begins the commercial message on the jacket, and the title track is his biggest single in a year and a half. *"I can see the disco now,"* he emphasizes, and even the blues and the ballad cultivate a groove designed to reintroduce him to that alien world he founded. But he sounds defensive because he has a reason to be — he can't hit the soft grooves the way he can the hard ones. When he starts equating himself with Elvis Presley (just before

the fade on "I Refuse to Lose"), you know the identity problems are getting critical. **B−**

James Brown: *Bodyheat* (Polydor '76). Two or three functional dance tracks, and Brown's will always be tougher than MFSB's. But not than Brown's. "Woman" is unlistenably sanctimonious, "What the World Needs Now Is Love" is the raggedest singing I've ever heard from him, and "Kiss in 77" is "head to head and toe to toe" — in other words as "brand new" as the *"New Sound!"* he promises. **C**

James Brown: *Mutha's Nature* (Polydor '77). When they start writing songs called "People Who Criticize," you know they're *really* worried. And the anxiety always comes out in the music. **C**

James Brown: *Jam/1980's* (Polydor '78). Free of the pretentious bluster that has marred so much of his work in the disco era, this is the groove album Brown has been announcing for years. He's finally learned how to relax his rhythms without diluting his essence, and the A side is simply and superbly what the title promises, though he may have the decade wrong. The B side is less of the same, and I bet no one who buys this record ever chooses to play it. I also bet they'd get dancing if they did. **B+**

James Brown: *Take a Look at Those Cakes* (Polydor '78). The title cut is a great throwaway — an eleven-minute rumination on ass-watching, including genuinely tasteless suggestions that Ray Charles and Stevie Wonder join the fun. The rest is just throwaway — with a beat of course. **B−**

James Brown: *The Original Disco Man* (Polydor '79). In which Brown relinquishes the profit-taking ego gratification of writing and producing everything himself. Those credits go to Brad Shapiro, Millie Jackson's helpmate, who thank god is no disco man himself. Sure he likes disco tricks —synthesized sound effects, hooky female chorus, bass drum pulse — but he loves what made JB, well, the original disco man: hard-driving, slightly Latinized funk patterns against the rough rap power of that amazing voice, which may have lost expressiveness but definitely retains its sense of rhythm. Plus: disco disc of the year, "It's Too Funky in Here." And a renunciation of "It's a Man's, Man's, Man's World." Original grade: A. **A−**

Peter Brown: *Do You Wanna Get Funky with Me?* (Drive '77). The goal of Pete's bold request is of course his bedroom. That's where he keeps his synthesizers, pianos, drums, and tape machines, and what he has in mind for you is some guitar or maybe a little background singing. Who needs discos, except to finance the next one? Fantasy love affair indeed. **B**

Roy Brown: *Hard Times* (BluesWay '73). It took these five-year-old sessions, a good portion of what he's recorded since semiretiring in 1956, to open me up to the blues shouter whose crying, gospel-based style makes him a direct forerunner of both Little Richard and B. B. King. Most pre-rock 'n' roll bluesmen flounder through soulish uptempo arrangements, but Brown is so fluid he rolls along exultantly on top, proud to hold trouble to a standoff. Side one is startlingly intense, and he wrote all the songs, too — man should go on retainer with Kenny Gamble. **A−**

Shirley Brown: *Woman to Woman* (Truth '74). Not a very sisterly exchange — this is traditional woman-as-supplicant stuff, as male-identified as it gets. And the songs don't have a lot of identity either. But though most of this material wouldn't work on the radio, it comes together on album. For sheer vocal beauty, Brown is in a class with Al Green and Aretha Franklin, whose creamy natural timbres hers recalls, though it's not as rich as Aretha's nor as pure as Al's. Where Franklin and Green go for baroque rhythmic and dynamic effects, to let

you know they're in extremis, Brown's even tone suggests supernatural patience in the face of suffering. And the spare, undistracting Stax production proves that traditionalism has its uses. [Later on Stax.] **A−**

Toni Brown & Terry Garthwaite: *Cross Country* (Capitol '73). In which the spirit and guts of Joy of Cooking, united for maybe the last time (Toni has left to record solo with another label), go to Nashville for some country-fried. Needless to say, they've never enjoyed more professional backing, but especially in Nashville there is a well-known problem with professionals — they never push a song that extra notch. And at least half of these could use the help. Shouldn't be lost: "Midnight Blues." **B**

Toni Brown: *Good for You, Too* (MCA '74). I hear Brown got married and had a baby, doesn't want to disrupt her life on the pro music grind. Good for her, really — those sound like wise and even joyous decisions to me. But good for us it isn't, because somewhere along the way she lost her music. **C−**

Jackson Browne: *Jackson Browne* (Asylum '72). Many people I like like Browne. Me, I don't dislike him. The voice is pleasant, present, and unpretentious, and when I listen assiduously I perceive lyrics crafted with as much intelligence and human decency as any reasonable person could expect. Unfortunately, only critical responsibility induces me to listen assiduously. It's not just the blandness of the music, but of the ideas as well, each reinforcing the other. Even the meticulously structured requiem "Song for Adam" interests me more for the quality of Browne's concern than for its philosophical conclusions. When Bob Dylan's good, I admire him as much as I do William Carlos Williams. I admire Jackson Browne as much as, oh, John Peale Bishop, whose name hasn't entered my mind since I was an English major.   **B**

Jackson   Browne: *For   Everyman* (Asylum '73). The singer-songwriter folk are lining up behind this one as album of the year, but though I'm intrigued by Janet Maslin's suggestion that Browne fuses New York and California sensibilities, sometimes I'm afraid all she means is that he can read. Even as he lists toward the pretentious and the vague, the reflective evenness of Browne's delivery sets up an expectation of cogency that on this album is satisfied only by such relatively unambitious songs as "These Days," "Red Neck Friend," and the charming "Ready or Not." Which save it for me.   **B**

Jackson Browne: *Late for the Sky* (Asylum '74). Browne reminds me of Nixon: no matter how hard I listen to his pronouncements — important sociologically if nothing else, right? — my mind begins to wander. They're getting longer, too; the eight songs here average over five minutes. I admit that the longest is also the best, an intricate extended metaphor called "Fountain of Sorrow." But his linguistic gentility is inappropriate, his millenarianism is self-indulgent, and only if he sang as good as Dylan Thomas might I change my mind. **B−**

Jackson   Browne: *The   Pretender* (Asylum '76). This is an impressive record, but a lot of the time I hate it; my grade is an average, not a judgment. Clearly Jon Landau has gotten more out of Browne's voice than anyone knew was there, and the production jolts Ol' Brown Eyes out of his languor again and again. But languor is Browne's best mask, and what's underneath isn't always so impressive. The shallowness of his kitschy doomsaying and sentimental sexism is well-known, but I'm disappointed as well in his depth of craft. How can apparently literate people mistake a received metaphor like "sleep's dark and silent gate" for interesting poetry or gush over a versifier capable of such rhyming-dictionary pairings as "pretender"

and "ice cream vendor" (the colloquial term, JB, is "ice cream man")? Similar shortcomings flaw the production itself — the low-register horns on "Daddy's Tune" complement its somber undertone perfectly, but when the high blare kicks in at the end the song degenerates into a Honda commercial. Indeed, at times I've wondered whether some of this isn't intended as parody, but a sense of humor has never been one of Browne's virtues.   **B**

Jackson Browne: *Running on Empty* (Asylum '77). Out of the studio — this was recorded on tour — Jackson sounds relaxed verbally, vocally, even instrumentally. He cuts his own meager melodies with nice ones by Danny O'Keefe and Danny Kortchmar. He does a funny and far from uncritical version of "Cocaine" and a loving and far from unfunny version of "Stay." I consider this his most attractive album. But his devotees may consider the self-effacement a deprivation. **B+**

Jack Bruce: *Things We Like* (Atco '71). Recorded in Cream's heyday with John McLaughlin on guitar, Jon Hiseman on drums, and Dick Heckstall-Smith on saxophones, this has zip to do with rock or "jazz-rock" — it's an enjoyable contemporary jazz LP that owes more to Ornette Coleman and to bebop than to the simplistic modalism favored by most rockers. McLaughlin would be a find if Miles Davis hadn't found him in the meantime, and Bruce's playing is deft when it's solid and contained when it's stormy. His compositions are less notable — only "Hckhh Blues" stands up next to the tune borrowed from Milt Jackson and Mel Torme. But the real surprises are Hiseman and Heckstall-Smith, now kingpins of the infamous jazz-rock big band Colosseum, Hiseman because he's serviceable and Heckstall-Smith because he's a pleasure — his melodies striking, his eclecticism intelligent and strong-willed. The thinness of his tone, however, is frustrating — he is the lead voice, after all.   **B+**

Jack Bruce: *Harmony Row* (Atco '71). Contrary to rumor, this is not an Unjustly Ignored Work of Art. This is a Bad Work of Art. Bruce's music is, yes, well-made, dense and dissonant and throbbing (no one else in rock plays so much bass). But it's designed to support Pete Brown's lyrics, which are, arghh, overwrought, obscure and literary and clichéd (my favorite line, which I suppose may be a joke: "I trace your name in spinach"). I know, Brown has been disfiguring Bruce's work since Cream. But at least then he lightened up occasionally. And at least then his bad lyrics functioned mostly as vocal color for the instrumental interaction, whereas here they're enunciated in Bruce's forced art-song style and printed on a special page of the jacket. Original grade: C. **C+**

Browning Bryant: *Browning Bryant* (Reprise '74). Thought I'd slam this, the worst of the current Allen Toussaint production jobs, just to prove I was nobody's fool (see Labelle, Frankie Miller, *Highlife,* Bonnie Raitt). Actually, I find it mildly pleasant, folkie voice and all. I think I could enjoy Toussaint's songwriting, harmonies, horn voicings, and piano — and *piano* — behind George Burns, Lynn Anderson, Jack Bruce, Paul McCartney, anybody. **C+**

B. T. Express: *Do It ('Til You're Satisfied)* (Scepter/Roadshow '74). Get on the good foot, let's hear it for the Bronx, and so forth. But if the single does it 'til you're satisfied, the album does it 'til you've had it up to here. Original grade: B minus. **C+**

Tim Buckley: *Starsailor* (Straight '70). In which a man who was renowned for his Odetta impressions on Jac Holzman's folkie label switches to Frank Zappa's art-rock label, presumably so he can do Nico impressions. **C−**

Tim Buckley: *Greetings from L.A.* (Warner Bros. '72). Perverse as it may seem, Buckley's mannered, androgynous moan has real erotic appeal for some, and here it turns a trick. This is rock pornography if anything is, complete with whips, foot fetishes, meat racks, and salacious gasps, and while I wouldn't call the band hard-core, it definitely fills the groove. **B**

Jimmy Buffett: *A White Sport Coat and a Pink Crustacean* (ABC/Dunhill '73). My shit detector went crazy the moment I spied the admiring apostrophe by sports novelist Tom McGuane, and indeed, Buffett shares McGuane's sexism (he likes Key West because "the ladies aren't demanding there"), covert nostalgia, reverse preciousness, and brain-proud know-nothingism. But his good-old-boys songs are classics of sheer hair, making up for the overt "They Don't Dance Like Carmen No More" and the know-somethingish "Death of an Unpopular Poet." And a vignette called "Cuban Crime of Passion" has Dickensian heart. **B**

Jimmy Buffett: *Living and Dying in 3/4 Time* (ABC/Dunhill '74). When the best cut on a singer-songwriter's album is a tall tale, he's either Arlo Guthrie or confused about the nature of his talent. And since this tall tale is about getting drunk, he's probably not Arlo Guthrie. **B−**

Jimmy Buffett: *AIA* (ABC/Dunhill '74). On side one, apparently running out of things to say, he includes among three nondescript covers an Alex Harvey song called "Makin' Music for Money." Buffett would never do this, which is why he's recording his third album in a year and a half, right? On side two, however, he remembers his message: he's a beach bum and always will be. Let's hope so. **B−**

Jimmy Buffett: *Havana Daydreamin'* (ABC '76). Undeniably, this romantic individualist has staked out his surf; ıerhaps it is because his utopian sun- and is Florida (rooted in the South) ather than California (headed toward the Orient) that his songs are so adult, skeptical, and closely observed. He doesn't sentimentalize in any obvious sense — the outsiders he sings about (including himself) are neither pitiable victims nor heirs of unacknowledged privilege. But when he essays some lyricism (about his grandfather, say, or the "so feminine" mandolin) he becomes totally mawkish, revealing a softheadedness that in the best Hemingway tradition he is careful to conceal most of the time. And upon close analysis this softheadedness extends even to his best lyrics — he is so intent on the day-to-day that he never cultivates an overview. Buffett is singing with new lustre, and I can't bring myself to put this down. But I don't expect to be putting it on much either. Original grade: B plus.   **B**

Jimmy Buffett: *Changes in Latitudes, Changes in Attitudes* (ABC '77). Buffett's certainly more likable than the average professional rakehell — he's complex, he's honest, he takes good care of his sense of humor, and above all he doesn't come on like a hot shit. This is his most reflective album, and though I'm nothing like him — "Wonder Why We Ever Go Home" is hardly my take on aging — I find myself interested whenever he stops and thinks, which happens mostly on side one. "Banana Republics," about expatriates reaping the wages (and pleasures) of imperialism even if Buffett would never put it that way, is my favorite, but I also love this breakthrough insight from his breakthrough single: "Some people claim that there's a woman to blame/But I know it's my own damn fault."   **B+**

Jimmy Buffett: *Son of a Son of a Sailor* (ABC '78). Buffett is very good at what he does, and it says a lot for his composing that the two changes of pace by Keith Sykes are the least memorable cuts on the album. But Buffett's band can't quite cut the funny, intelligent good-time music that is his forte. Anyone who gets up and boogies to rock and roll as routine as "Livingston Saturday Night" has been shaking ass to whatever came off the bandstand since he or she reached drinking age. On record, there happens to be better

and more functional music available.   **B**

Jimmy Buffett: *Volcano* (MCA '79). In the two years since "Margaritaville" made him an "overnight sensation" — the phrase occurs in "Dreamsicle," the most confused and meaningful song here — Buffett has signed on with Irving Azoff, a manager renowned for keeping the Eagles, Steely Dan, and Boz Scaggs rich on minimal work. Whether this LP reflects a success trauma or Buffett's oft-asserted indolence I don't know. I do know that he hasn't used so many outside songwriters since *A1A*.   **B−**

Bull: *This Is Bull* (Paramount '71). Speak for yourself, Ferdinand.   **D**

Bulldog: *Bulldog* (Decca '72). Singer Billy Hocher has a little more raw energy and a lot less loving subtlety than Felix Cavaliere, but with Dino Danelli on drums and Gene Cornish on guitar this is something like what the Rascals might have become if they'd gone heavy instead of jazzy. They do well by "Too Much Monkey Business" and "Rockin' Robin" and offer at least two originals that feed my hard rock jones: "Have a Nice Day," which is sarcastic, and "No," a great single that may never get over the top. Original grade: B plus.   **B−**

Cindy Bullens: *Desire Wire* (United Artists '78). This woman sets out to prove that she can write and perform songs about the joys of rock and roll and the perils of romance that are tougher, sprightlier, and more propulsive than Eddie Money's. And does it, by George!   **B−**

The Bunch: *Rock On* (A&M '72). In which Sandy Denny, Richard Thompson, and eleven other English folkies redo twelve American songs, and I bet the Silver Beatles loved every one of them. The conjunction brings out the passionately droll in all the principals, especially Denny and Thompson, but the great moments are "The Loco-Motion,'' with Linda Peters playing Little Eva, and "Nadine,'' which Tyger Hutchings delivers deadpan, as if reading off cue cards after a quick runthrough. **B+**

Eric Burdon and War: *The Black-Man's Burdon* (MGM '71). On the front cover of this album is a black man in silhouette. On the back cover Eric, looking paunchy, rests his head in the crotch of a black woman straddled above him. He also holds her ankles. Inside the jacket, seven men, presumably the band, occupy the background of a full-length photo of a grassy field. Six of the men are black: five are bare-chested. In the foreground recline two naked blondes who obviously belong in a centerfold. The left hand of one is thrown back to reveal a clean-shaven and possibly airbrushed underarm, so that her right hand does not quite conceal her pubic hair. Her companion hides her sex with both hands. The only man who is standing appears to be walking toward the women. He has removed the belt from his pants. **D+**

Eric Burdon / Jimmy Witherspoon: *Guilty!* (MGM '71). Burdon has a clumsy knack for coming out on the other side of a bad idea — after ''Monterey,'' which was just silly, "Sky Pilot'' seemed transcendently silly. And while his stint with War symptomized his chronic racial confusion, he gets on quite well with Witherspoon — especially considering that 'Spoon is said to represent Kansas City class while Eric supposedly epitomizes Newcastle nowhere. Maybe the truth in both cases is less extreme. Anyway, neither singer comes up with anything definitive here, but both deal soulfully — sometimes almost indistinguishably — with these solid, politically tinged songs, and a sharp young guitarist named John Sterling provides a few highlights. Original grade: B plus. **B**

Eric Burdon Band: *Sun Secrets* (Capitol '74). In this age of fiberglass, Burdon's stage show appears genuinely demented — his guitar players look like head-comix versions of Chuck Berry and Panama Red, and on his second encore he holds the entire mikestand in his teeth, like a dirk. But when poor Eric was on the radio in Boston not long ago, more than one kid called in to ask how he did the guitar parts on ''Layla.'' **C**

Solomon Burke: *We're Almost Home* (MGM '72). It's the custom to blame abortive rhythm-and-blues comebacks on producers, but Burke takes onethird credit for this aimless clutter himself. The title song is acceptable, but too often the man who was once the most churchified of the Atlantic greats equates contemporaneity with a twisted shout. **C−**

J. Henry Burnett: *The B-52 Band & the Fabulous Skylarks* (Uni '72). Burnett is like the Band without self-consciousness — his vocal anguish is really moral, with a sense of history. When he opens with ''We Have All Got a Past'' he's only trying to talk someone into bed, but boy, does that title resonate. Now he should tell the B-52 Band to play less and think more and the Fabulous Skylarks to fly way. **C+**

Burning Spear: *Marcus Garvey* (Island '76). The most African (and political) sounding reggae LP yet to crease the USA. Deceptive polyrhythms and horns that hint at highlife add to the hypnotic force of Winston Rodney's eerie ululations, resulting in chants so compelling that when Rodney cries ''Give me what is mine'' you half expect Chris Blackwell to hand over the record company. Or at least to release the group's next album when this one doesn't sell. [Later on Mango.] Original grade: B plus. **A−**

Burning Spear: *Garvey's Ghost* (Mango '76). *Marcus Garvey* dub, with the instrumental tracks remixed to create illusions of depth and focus. I know two people who consider it one of the great reggae albums, and oddly enough neither is a doper. Odd because, though I'm not much of a doper myself, I find that marijuana greatly enhances appreciation of this music. Which makes sense — marijuana certainly enhanced its creation as well. But which also makes me suspicious.　　　　　　**B+**

Burning Spear: *Man in the Hills* (Island '76). The incantations are all but irresistible through most of side one — it is good when a man can think for himself, my old great-grandfather great-great-great-great-great-great-grandfather-father-father-father-father he's black, don't kill the lion. But as rituals will, this one begins to wear down before it's entirely over. [Later on Mango.]　　　　　　**B+**

Burning Spear: *Dry and Heavy* (Mango '77). The sweetness of Winston Rodney's vocals here is surprisingly acute — especially on the unselfrighteous nonviolence sermon "Throw Down Your Arms," the generalized love song "Any River," and the title cut, an impressionistically spaced-out reminiscence of his schooldays. But despite the welcome crib sheet I don't find that any of the other tracks holds my attention. That's the way it is with sweetness.　　**B**

Burning Spear: *Live* (Mango '77). Top material at Jamaican tempos for a London audience of 2000. But as usual the ceremonial extensions, while appropriate formally, call out for the physical presence of fellow worshippers. And would sound more lifelike in a studio.　　　　　　**B**

Burning Spear: *Harder Than the Best* (Mango '79). Because reggae is long on groove and short on tune, you sometimes wish you could extricate one from the other, which in a way is what this compilation does: combines the four most haunting cuts from a landmark debut with other highlights plus a dab of dub, as much as I and I need. Political and possessed, with Winston Rodney's hypnotic vocals floating, darting, and echoing over the mix, this one's a gift from the mysterious forces of commerce that shouldn't be passed up.　　　　**A**

Randy Burns and the Sky Dog Band: *Randy Burns and the Sky Dog Band* (Mercury '71). My friend from New Haven says, "Except for '17 Years on Your River,' I don't think I'd like this record if I weren't from New Haven." Exactly. This is the kind of testament every loyal local group ought to leave, with a few excellent songs (I also like "Living in the Country") and lots of memories for all the folks it's entertained. Unfortunately, few local groups ever reach this level of competence, but in any case the economics of the music industry discourage such moderate success —if your appeal isn't big-time, you're lucky to record at all, and if it is, chances are even or better that you're working a dumb variation on somebody else's gimmick. Which is not to suggest that I'd give up one great industry group like Crazy Horse for a dozen Sky Dog Bands, but merely to lament a paradox. Original grade: B.　　　　　　**B−**

Johnny Bush: *The Best of Johnny Bush* (Million '72). When Bush's hurting, almost operatic baritone strains against Tommy Hill's spare, hard, danceable arrangements, you begin to suspect that God did make honky-tonk angels after all — male ones. Now if only all of Bush's hosannas were as terse and colloquial as the three Willie Nelson songs here. Hyperbolic corn can work in country music — Bush's dramatization of Marty Robbins's "You Gave Me a Mountain" brings a catch to the throat and a tear to the eye. But too often the corn here is as commonplace as Bush's big legit move, a cover of "All in the Game."　　　　　　**B+**

Jerry Butler: *You and Me* (Mercury '70). Separated from Kenny Gamble and Leon Huff when they left Mercury, Butler Pursued His Own Artistic

Interests by working with a songwriter's workshop on the South Side of Chicago, which is a lot better than Keith Relf or Richie Furay can claim. Unfortunately, this follow-up to G&H's *The Iceman Cometh* and *Ice on Ice* is lukewarm, and a big problem is the student songs — only Terry Callier's "Ordinary Joe" is *more* than professional, which ought to be the idea. Original grade: B. **B−**

Jerry Butler: *The Best of Jerry Butler* (Mercury '70). Butler is my kind of ballad singer, not least because a lot of his material is medium uptempo. He's got a big voice — proves it once again on a live version of his 1958 breakthrough, "For Your Precious Love" — but prefers to put his soul across by the way he shifts from straight song to the throaty love sounds that are his trademark. Not surprisingly, it's the seven Gamble-Huff tracks that make this compilation — their lyrics are ordinary, but their lush cool, so well-suited to Butler's own, is anything but. **A−**

Jerry Butler: *Nothing Says I Love You Like I Love You* (Philadelphia International '78). This is indeed the Ice Man's best LP since he last recorded with Gamble-Huff in 1970 — seductive, substantial, felt. But only the dance cut, "Cooling Out," with Leon Huff heating up on piano toward the close, is really worth playing for people you don't care about going to bed with. **B**

The Butterfield Blues Band: *Sometimes I Feel Like Smilin'* (Elektra '71). Proving once again that artists who make records you admire but never play often end up making records you're not so sure you admire. These days this is a blues band only in the broadest sense — Butterfield sings infrequently if well, some if not all of the arrangements sound like Stan Kenton believing himself superior to B. B. King, and the female chorus must have wandered in from the next studio. Original grade: C. **B−**

The Paul Butterfield Blues Band: *Golden Butter: The Best of the Paul Butterfield Blues Band* (Elektra '72). Butterfield's music has held up more convincingly than it's evolved, which is why forty-five out of eighty minutes were recorded between October '65 and August '66 and why the side featuring a cut each off his last three albums is the one you can skip. What sounded like "white blues" back then sounds like "rock" now — Butterfield is so modest any label fits. Prophetic guitarists, powerful drummers, better-than-average horn men, and one heck of a great harmonica player. **A−**

Paul Butterfield: *Better Days* (Bearsville '72). Butterfield's new band —a Woodstock roots-blues supergroup of honest men singing honest songs —is his clearest concept since 1965. Unfortunately, the music is so relaxed it sounds as if they decided — collectively, of course — that laid back meant lying down. **B**

Paul Butterfield's Better Days: *It All Comes Back* (Bearsville '73). In which Butter returns to his own better days, when his miraculously unaffected but colorless singing provided pleasant valleys from which his weirdo sidemen could peak. The prize here is Geoff Muldaur's rendition of Bobby Charles's "Small Town Talk," a song about back-stabbers that sounds as if it was made for the exurban bohemian community where the music originated — probably because that's the community it was written about. Ronnie Barron's frenetic remake of his own "Louisiana Flood" comes in second. Original grade: A minus. **B+**

Paul Butterfield: *Put It in Your Ear* (Bearsville '76). The modishly far-out rhythms and textures here are so authentic they recall Jimmy Witherspoon or Bobby Bland casting desperately about for a hit. The bluesman fluffs one ballad and sounds a little strange doing romantic patter, and producer Henry Glover has for some reason set his own "Breadline" amid enough instruments to feed a family of four for six months, but once you conquer your suspicion that this is a disaster it sounds pretty good. I don't hear any hits, though. Original grade: B. **B−**

Buzzcocks: *Singles Going Steady* (I.R.S. '79). The title is the perfect conceit for this collection of eight relentless British forty-fives — arranged chronologically, the A sides on the A side and the B sides on the B — about love and lust among the unmarrieds. The Buzzcocks' knack for the title hook and the catchy backup chorus, along with their apparently asocial lyrics, tempts tastemakers in jaded olde England to dismiss them as mere pop, but over here their high-speed, high-register attack sounds powerful indeed. The best song on the record, "Orgasm Addict," is the most cynical; the second-best, "Everybody's Happy Nowadays," is the most gleeful. Good sign. **A−**

The Byrds: *(Untitled)* (Columbia '70). I'm sorry. I love them — or do I mean him? — too, but it finally seems to be ending. The new songs are unworthy except for the anomalous McGuinn showcase "Chestnut Mare," the harmonies are faint or totally absent, and the live performance that comprises half this two-record set . . . well, I'm sure you had to be there. I was, lots of times, and I guess I will be again, but mostly to demonstrate my devotion. I'm sorry. **C+**

The Byrds: *Farther Along* (Columbia '71). On that downhill road — to Kim Fowley, to songs about Antique Sandy and Precious Kate, to the day when the agent man collects what you owe him. **C**

The Byrds: *Byrdmaniax* (Columbia '71). Two good white gospel (a fundamentalist and a modernist) plus one good Roger McGuinn song (out of four, and he needed a collaborator) plus one good Skip Battin song (he needed a collaborator too — Kim Fowley). In sum, better than *Farther Along,* but if you can only tell arithmetically how much difference can it make? **B−**

The Byrds: *The Best of the Byrds: Greatest Hits Volume II* (Columbia '72). If their first greatest hits was (in Paul Williams's deathless phrase) "an essay into rediscovery," this one's a product into recouping. Thing is, a good statement could have been constructed. Let *Notorious* and *Sweetheart* stand on their own (though one song apiece is acceptable anyway), leave the anachronistic "He Was a Friend of Mine" in the dustbin of history, and tell Skip Battin to make his own album. Then pick a few more cuts — "Deportee," "Old Blue," maybe "Nashville West" or even "Child of the Universe" — from *Easy Rider* and *Dr. Byrds.* Presto: *Roger McGuinn's Greatest Quirks.* The original space cowboy deserves a testament, not an olio. **B**

The Byrds: See also Gene Clark, Chris Hillman, David Crosby, Roger McGuinn, Michael Clarke; McGuinn, Clark & Hillman

Roy C.: *Sex and Soul* (Mercury '73). Roy Hammond is a driven artist — he cut this in his garage — and his compulsiveness comes out in the lyrics; despite convincing asides about racism and Vietnam, his title ought to be *Infidelity and Suffering*. The songs are raw and outspoken, and the suffering's in the voice even more than the words — he strains its paradoxically mellow limits sometimes, so seekers after the Perfect Note should seek elsewhere. But old Swamp Dogg fans will put aside their feminist reservations and learn how the other half lives. **B+**

Roy C.: *More Sex and More Soul* (Mercury '77). Having turned soul artist just as the style was going out of fashion, he's now earned a following in Africa and the Caribbean, and more power to him. As you might have guessed from the title, this isn't up to the standard of *Sex and Soul* —strings, thinner material. But it's quirky and basic, with witty horn charts and a vocal attack that now seems pleasantly anachronistic. Killer cut: Roy shoots a friend who's in bed with Roy's wife and is inspired to the moral reflection that now he's "in a whole lot of trouble." **B**

J. J. Cale: *Naturally* (Shelter '71). After years of combatting pretentiousness we discover that unpretentiousness can be just as bad. These murmured blues meditations are so easy on the spirit that even though they have their charms they invite the mistrust of moralizers like myself — there's just too much talent here to justify such slight results. Or maybe there isn't enough talent to justify such minimal effort — only if all the songs were as absolutely beguiling as the side-openers, "Call Me the Breeze" and "Crazy Mama," would the lassitude affected by all hands be as comfortable for us as I'm sure it was for them. Push a little, fellas, it'll feel so good. Original grade: C plus. **B**

J. J. Cale: *Really* (Shelter '72). Cale outdoes such self-created white bluesmen as John Hammond by writing songs that are locked up in the conventions of the form, designed solely as carriers of pulse and mood. His slurred, whispering vocals and slurred, stuttering guitar are stylistic constants, and his lyrics aspire to the meaning-free universality of the traditional blues tropes and phrases. Mesmerizing, in its way. But the very best blues simply aren't meaning-free or locked up formally — John Hammond selects his repertoire for variety and interest, as does Lightnin' Hopkins, so why shouldn't Cale? Even if his style were as distinctive and forceful as any of dozens I could name, the fact that he consciously chooses his limits robs them of their natural aura. No surprise that the most gratifying tracks here break the mold with a little mystery — especially "Playing in the Streets," with its infusions from Vassar Clements. **B**

J. J. Cale: *Okie* (Shelter '74). For J. J., this is adventurous stuff — "I

Got the Same Old Blues" states his world view (you don't have to listen, just read the title), "Starbound" adapts his style to some (awful) space pop, and "The Old Man and Me" introduces a character whom he isn't making it with (at least he doesn't mention it).   **B−**

J. J. Cale: *Troubadour* (Shelter '76). The only time Cale ever seems to leave Tulsa is when he hies up to Nashville to cut another one of these albums. Doesn't he know that troubadours *go places?*   **B−**

John Cale: *Vintage Violence* (Columbia '70). Enigmatic lyrics had better not be attached to enigmatic melodies or nobody'll bother figuring out answers. All I want to know is: is "The journey did her well" ungrammatical, or just Welsh?   **C+**

John Cale and Terry Riley: *Church of Anthrax* (Columbia '70). I was impressed to come upon this collaboration between Riley, whose pop avant-garde meditation, *A Rainbow in Curved Air,* inspired me to concoct the term "semipopular music," and Cale, whose pop avant-garde rock group, the Velvet Underground, should have done the same. Bet the people at CBS were impressed, too. So impressed they put out an album of keyboard doodles posing as improvisations.   **C**

John Cale: *The Academy in Peril* (Reprise '72). There must be more straightforward ways of imperiling the academy than mock-classical mock-soundtracks. Granted, this sounds jake to me, and my continental friends tell me it's excellent of its sort. But I don't much care for the continent (or the sort) — that's why I had to ask them. Rock and roll: "The Philosopher," for acoustic guitar, brass, woodwinds, and (eventually) violins over strange percussion, and "Days of Steam," which reminds me of the Ernie Kovacs theme.   **B**

John Cale: *Paris 1919* (Reprise '73). In which Cale subsumes Little Feat, the academy in stasis, and other subversive elements into a form known

generically (don't tell anyone) as schlock-rock. Winsome stuff it is, too — delectable melodies, dulcet singing, and such civilized rhymes as "Andalucia" and "see ya." But when you try to get past the surface pleasure of phrases like "claim you with my iron drum" and "cows that agriculture won't allow" you realize that poets who emulate Edward Lear had better be funny about it — or else stick with Delmore Schwartz.   **B+**

John Cale: *Fear* (Island '74). With Phil Manzanera flailing his axe like rocksy music was a thing of the future and Eno doing his best Baby Cortez imitation it sounds as if somebody just played "Sister Ray" for Cale and he thought the world of it. Manzanera's feedback extravaganza on "Gun" is a landmark of six-string aleatoric, and on "The Man Who Couldn't Afford to Orgy" the entire ensemble comes up with the perfect sleazy-slick background rock for the glass-table scene in a porn flick. Concept: see title.   **A−**

John Cale: *Slow Dazzle* (Island '75). In which Cale integrates his unsingerly voice into a full-fledged rock style — kind of heavy, kind of schlocky, but done with humor and perversely appealing in its straightness. "Darling I Love You" is a tribute to his darling, "Ski Patrol" is a tribute to his ski patrol, and on "Mr. Wilson" the Velvets meet the Beach Boys for discreet, sophisticated adult enjoyment. I should also mention that the man can really scream, and (a related fact) that his version of "Heartbreak Hotel" does not make me miss Elvis. Original grade: B plus.   **A−**

John Cale: *Guts* (Island '77). This is how Island makes up for withholding U.S. release on *Helen of Troy,* and I think we're better off. As a whole, *Helen of Troy* is sodden and stylized, and while "Pablo Picasso" and "Leaving It All Up to You" are Cale at his mad best, "Mary Lou" and "Helen of Troy" itself almost drag this compilation down. They don't, though. Cale's Island music epitomizes the cold, committed dementia of the best English rock, and side two — comprising "Fear Is a Man's Best Friend," "Gun," "Dirtyass Rock 'n' Roll," and "Heartbreak Hotel" — is a hard-sell advert for the disease. **A**

John Cale: *Sabotage/Live* (Spy/I.R.S. '79). "Military intelligence isn't what it used to be," Cale intones on a title cut replete with slash and yowl. "So what — human intelligence isn't what it used to be either." Speak for yourself, John. This material, based in part on Cale's recent inquiries into foreign affairs, is fairly strong in a geocynical way that's a lot newer to rock than it is to human discourse in general. But the live recording, while no doubt economical, gets more flash than slash out of Marc Aaron's guitar and not enough singing out of Cale. And "Captain Hook," the dumbest song on the record, lasts 11:26. **B**

Randy California: *Kapt. Kopter and the (Fabulous) Twirly Birds* (Epic '72). Almost universally dismissed as a lysergic self-indulgence, the departed Spirit's tunefully distorted guitar (and vocal) showcase will grow on you if you give it half a chance — any Joe Walsh fan who lets it get by never really liked the '60s to begin with. For sheer dense weirdness it beats King Fripp, and if I had any passion for such things I'm sure I'd love it. Like most of side one a lot as it is. And where else are you going to find covers of "Rain," "Mother and Child Reunion," and current James Brown on one album? **B**

Canned Heat: *Future Blues* (Liberty '70). However much sense Alan Wilson's death meant in his life, which was never happy, it was inappropriate to his art, which until the end continued to thrive in that strange, mildly affectless, ruefully blissed-out dreamscape he discovered in country blues. On this record his creative force, never imposing but always there to be enjoyed, is at a peak, and the rest of the band finally coheres — Bob Hite sounds like himself, and Harvey Man-

del sounds like he and the rhythm section were made for each other. The first side, which runs through Wilson's "Shake It and Break It" and the painful "My Time Ain't Long" before climaxing with Wilbert Harrison's "Let's Work Together," is the prize. I'm very sorry there won't be more like it. Original grade: A. **A—**

Canned Heat: *Historical Figures and Ancient Heads* (United Artists '72). The most honest thing about this automatic boogie is the title: what can you do when Little Richard sounds as false as Bob Hite except contemplate the past? **C—**

Canyon: *High Mountain* (Columbia '70). This mysteriously uncredited white-soul-with-black-chorus-and-steel-guitar concoction apparently emanates from one Jerry Williams, who is capable of attaching solid words to solider melodies. Unfortunately, that uncredited quality extends to the gestalt, which is a little anonymous. But if "More to You" and "Please Don't Leave Me Again" sink into oblivion, no one will blame me. Original grade: B plus. **B**

The Captain and Tennille: *Love Will Keep Us Together* (A&M '75). One expected a lousy album, but not this lousy. Their good sense in appropriating Neil Sedaka's unused hit arrangement was a one-shot; the rest of the time they spread the middle of the road so thin they make "Rainy Days and Mondays" sound like "Saturday Night's Alright for Fighting." Admirers of the single should invest in a copy of *Sedaka's Back*. **D—**

Captain Beefheart and the Magic Band: *Lick My Decals Off, Baby* (Straight '70). Like *Trout Mask Replica*, this music is so jumpy and disjoint it's ominous. But after some acclimatization you can play it while doing the dishes, and good. Beefheart's famous five-octave range and covert totalitarian structures have taken on a playful undertone, repulsive and engrossing and slapstick funny. N.b.: us new dinosaurs had better kick off our "old dinosaur shoes." Or was that "Dinah Shore shoes"? Both.   **A−**

Captain Beefheart: *The Spotlight Kid* (Reprise '72). Cap's much-bruited commercial bid turns out to have all the mass appeal of *King of the Delta Blues Singers,* complete with modernized terraplane and an avowal of primitivism in which the Kid threatens to "Grow Fins." All the primordial themes are here — sex, love, poverty, destiny, ecology — and the Howlin' Wolf imitations are as dense and heartfelt as the music. Still, Robert Johnson cuts him, and primitivism is rarely better the second time around. Maybe the Stones could cover "I'm Gonna Booglarize You Baby." But if this were all it's cracked up to be, that wouldn't be the only candidate.   **B+**

Captain Beefheart and the Magic Band: *Clear Spot* (Reprise '72). This one really does rock out — it's got the Blackberries, horn charts, everything the promotion department could ask except a hummable tune. Much womanizing, of course — rather less, er, allusive than usual but laced with the unexpected, as in the title "Nowadays a Woman's Gotta Hit a Man," a prescription from which Cap exempts himself. But what makes it work is that it really rocks out.   **B+**

Captain Beefheart and the Magic Band: *Mirror Man* (Buddah '73). Recorded one night in 1965, these four pieces, which go on for more than fifty minutes, seem insultingly sloppy and thin at first — lacking Beefheart's later rhythmic assurance and aural density. But in their linear way they're pretty crazy and pretty involving. Makes you wonder why the Captain got left out of all the blues jams that followed in his wake.   **B+**

Captain Beefheart and the Magic Band: *Unconditionally Guaranteed* (Mercury '74). I've always suspected that underneath the naive surrealism the Captain might be a dumbbell, and now that he's really (really really) trying to go commercial he's providing

proof. This time he really (really) does it — writes dumb little songs with dumb little lyrics and dumb little hooks. Maybe all the dumb dumb parts can be blamed on svengali and cocomposer Andy DiMartino. And I admit that a lot of these are passable ("Magic Be") to wonderful ("Sugar Bowl") dumb little songs. But they're still dumb. Really. Original grade: C plus.   **B−**

Captain Beefheart and the Magic Band: *Bluejeans and Moonbeams* (Mercury '74). Supposedly, this album consists of outtakes from Cap's previous Andy DiMartino LP, but if anything I prefer it. "Party of Special Things to Do" (mama told him not to come) and "Observatory Crest" (Beefheart's first make-out song) surround his cover of "Same Old Blues" so cunningly that after a while you start to forget J. J. Cale, and before you know it you're at the funky harmonica feature that closes side one.   **B−**

Captain Beefheart and the Magic Band: *Shiny Beast (Bat Chain Puller)* (Warner Bros. '78). Inspired by the Captain's untoward comeback, I've dug out all his old albums and discovered that as far as I'm concerned this is better than any of them — more daring than *Safe as Milk,* fuller than *Trout Mask Replica,* more consistent than *Lick My Decals Off, Baby.* Without any loss of angularity or thickness, the new compositions achieve a flow worthy of Weill or Monk or Robert Johnson, and his lyrics aren't as willful as they used to be. Bruce Fowler's trombone is especially thaumaturgic adding an appropriately natural color to the electric atonality of the world's funnist ecology crank.   **A**

Carmen: *Fandango in Space* (ABC '74). A record so dreadful I listened to it all the way through just so I could note its passing, which I trust will be instantaneous. The worst of at least four modes: concept-rock, theater-rock, space-rock, and Anglo-Iberian, with a real live Spanish Person on castanets, vibes, and high heels. Olé. And cha-cha-cha.   **E+**

Eric Carmen: *Eric Carmen* (Arista '75). It was the theory of those who considered *Starting Over* the only good Raspberries album that the secret ingredient was new bassist Scott McCarl, who played Lennon to Carmen's McCartney. Now that the man is flying solo, you have to wonder what can be expected of one secondhand Wing. Especially one who pronounced it "rach," as in Rockmaninoff.   **C+**

Carp: *Carp* (Epic '71). For those of you who are really into Americana, here's an album with songs about Calamity Jane, a circuit preacher named Brown, and firehouse dogs. For those of you who are really into bands that have paid their dues, this one formed at the University of Oklahoma five years ago. And you won't catch Carp imitating Jefferson Airplane or Bessie Smith, either.   **C**

The Carpenters: *The Singles 1969–1973* (A&M '73). The combination of Karen Carpenter's ductile, dispassionate contralto and Richard Carpenter's meticulous studio technique is admittedly more musical than the clatter of voices and silverware in a cafeteria, but it's just as impervious to criticism. That is, the duo's success is essentially statistical: I'll tell you that I very much like "We've Only Just Begun" and detest "Sing," but those aren't so much aesthetic judgments as points on a graph.   **C+**

Joe "King" Carrasco and El Molino: *Tex-Mex Rock-Roll* (Lisa '78). Like the Western swing it rocks and rolls, Tex-Mex is an acquired taste — often a little lightweight, but say that in the wrong bar in Austin and things might get heavy. Anyway, this is the real stuff, more striking than anything on Augie Meyers's dependable Texas Re-Cord Company label mostly because Carrasco writes songs of no special significance that might

just as well have originated on the Rio Grande 100 years ago. Favorite titles: "Jalapeno con Big Red" and "Rock Esta Noche."   **B+**

The Cars: *The Cars* (Elektra '78). Ric Ocasek writes catchy, hardheaded-to-coldhearted songs eased by wryly rhapsodic touches, the playing is tight and tough, and it all sounds wonderful on the radio. But though on a cut-by-cut basis Roy Thomas Baker's production adds as much as it distracts, here's hoping the records get rawer. That accentuated detachment may feel like a Roxy Music move in the first flush of studio infatuation, but schlock it up a little and this band really could turn into an American Queen.   **B+**

The Cars: *Candy-O* (Elektra '79). Hooks are mechanical by nature, but the affectlessness of these deserves special mention; only listeners who consider "alienation is the craze" a great insight will find much meaning here. On the other hand, only listeners who demand meaning in all things will find this useless. Cold and thin, shiny and hypnotic, it's what they do best — rock and roll that is definitively pop without a hint of cuteness. Which means that for them "alienation is the craze" may be a meaningful statement after all.   **B+**

Carlene Carter: *Carlene Carter* (Warner Bros. '78). This woman has a strong voice, an assertive persona, and good taste in bands (the Rumour) and grandmothers (Maybelle C.) She's twice-divorced with two kids at twenty-two, so she Knows Life, and her songwriting definitely Shows Potential. But reach ain't grasp, strength ain't passion or style, and she could use a haircut.   **C+**

Clarence Carter: *The Best of Clarence Carter* (Atlantic '71). Carter is not a high-definition singer. His penetrating timbre, like his uvular growl and the lowdown heh-heh-heh chuckle he makes of it, is more trademark than identity. But his all-purpose preacherly delivery — the rap on "Dark End of the Street" is as good as the music — makes him a perfect conduit for the gospel-based Muscle Shoals sound, the way the low-definition Marvelettes were for Motown. The hooks are as simple as the horn charts — an organ riff, an echoed drumbeat, a heh-heh-heh. And none of the lesser hits sounds all that much like "Slip Away." **A−**

Clarence Carter: *Sixty Minutes with Clarence Carter* (Fame '73). The title has nothing to do with the record's duration — it's yet another play on this soul survivor's back-door-man routine. But thanks to Rich Hall's confident cop of the Allmans' high lick and an unusual things-ain't-getting-better lyric from George Jackson, a lot of this is more than routine. **B+**

Johnny Cash: *Greatest Hits Volume 3* (Columbia '78). In 1968, his marriage to June Carter and his Folsom Prison album made Cash look like the greatest artist in country music, but who today would think of ranking him with George Jones, Willie Nelson, or Merle Haggard? A diminished singer, writer, and public presence, he hasn't even put together enough singles for a worthwhile best-of. Here are two duets with Waylon and one with June, two decent love songs by others and three flabby ones by himself, and you know what you'll remember next day? "Oney" and "One Piece at a Time," both about working the assembly line. Somehow I don't expect him to take the hint. **B−**

Rosanne Cash: *Right or Wrong* (Columbia '79). Except for Bonnie Raitt, this is as good as the female-interpretive genre got in 1979: Cash is cool and feisty, and Rodney Crowell and Keith Sykes both find nice twists in the pains of love. But the session men sound so dead they gotta be trying. Is this some weird kind of El-Lay-goes-Nashville statement? Or just the end of an era? **B**

Shaun Cassidy: *Born Late* (Warner Bros. '78). Desperate to keep up with the younger generation (i.e. their kids), a few old Beatlemaniacs are murmuring that Shaun isn't so bad — he likes the music more than David ever did, his covers show some feeling, and "Hey Deanie" actually rocks. All of which is true. And all of which is still pretty lame. **C**

The Jimmy Castor Bunch: *E-Man Grooving* (Atlantic '76). When Castor says "that funky monster's breathin' fire down my neck," does he refer to Count Dracula, the rather cool getdown man on this LP, or is he planning a hot follow-up? **B**

Cate Bros.: *Cate Bros.* (Asylum '76). These Southern brothers relate to soul rather than boogie, with a nice gain in structure, but they could use some surface flash to highlight all that sincerity, which is a lot more profound in the vocalization than the verbalization in any case. **B−**

Felix Cavaliere: *Destiny* (Bearsville '75). The reason the *Time Peace* best-of is the Rascals album to own is the reason this runs down a groove so pleasant you often forget it's there. It's on a par with *The Island of Real,* maybe. But not *Search and Nearness.* Original grade: C plus. **B−**

Cerrone: *Love in C Minor* (Cotillion '77). Catchy tracks, a remake of "Black Is Black," and a new standard in disco porn — the protagonist brings three women to simultaneous orgasm while keeping one finger on the "Door Close" button. **B+**

Harry Chapin: *Heads and Tales* (Elektra '72). This young man takes his lost loves very seriously. Breaking up is hard to do, Neil Sedaka said that, but he didn't make a career out of it. Stash that bill in your shirt while the stashing's good, Harry. **C−**

Harry Chapin: *Short Stories* (Elektra '73). Harry had a problem. He wanted to write a song about a DJ, kind of a follow-up to "Taxi," just to prove it wasn't a fluke. Harry doesn't meet many real people, so cabbies and DJs provide that touch of social realism. He wanted to set the song in Boise, Idaho, not because he had anything to say about Boise, but because "Idaho" rhymed with "late night talk show." Unfortunately, call letters that far west start with K rather than W, which messed up his rhythm. Akron, Ohio? Wrong rhythm again. Denver, Colorado? Nope. So he called it "WOLD" and hoped no one would notice. Note: this analysis is nowhere near as long-winded as Harry's stories. **D+**

Blondie Chaplin: *Blondie Chaplin* (Asylum '77). The trick with this very attractive record is to approach it as an intense and knowing exploration of the conventions of modern rock and roll. That way you can immerse yourself in its raceless melisma, raving overdubs, and produced grooves as if engaging in a meaningful activity. But it is customary in projects of this kind to distinguish between exploration and exploitation, readymade and cliché, aural depth and aural surface, by means of a few hints in the lyrics (cf. Dave Edmunds or Dwight Twilley). Chaplin doesn't — can't bear to tamper with the purity of his vision, I suppose. **B**

Marshall Chapman: *Me, I'm Feelin' Free* (Epic '77). I can't figure out whether this tough, alert Nashville rebel fails to reach me because I'm uncomfortable with a woman who comes on like a good old boy or because I'm uncomfortable with anybody who comes on like a good old boy, but I like her enough to hope it's neither. **B**

Marshall Chapman: *Jaded Virgin* (Epic '78). Chapman's voice is even sexier than her looks, she boasts the uncompromising macho ambition of the fanatic rock and roller, and her album is graced with the subtle touches that make fanatic rock and roll come alive. Yet oddly enough it lacks momentum — which I blame not only on producer Al Kooper but on a workaday band and on Chapman's own lingering role confusion. Not one cut sustains. The Bob Seger cover never rocks out, the Hank Williams tribute gets echoed to death, "I Walk the Line" is an elegant false start, and the I-was-born-to-rock-and-roll soliloquy is one of the slow songs — as are too many of the others. **C+**

Marshall Chapman: *Marshall* (Epic '79). This "rock and roll girl" is a lot more confident, clever, and animated than such Northern counterparts as Ellen Foley and Ellen Shipley, but she's a fairly one-dimensional conservative compared to Pearl E. Gates or Chrissie Hynde. Not only does she never question what she wants, which I guess is OK, but she still equates rock and roll itself with liberation, which isn't. The reason it isn't is illustrated by her band, who reprise old boogie licks as if they're expressing themselves. **B**

Ray Charles: *Love Country Style* (ABC '70). As satisfying as Charles's first c&w records were conceptually and vocally, I was always a little turned off by his countrypolitan taste for strings and choruses, and they're still with us — more muted, but also more prosaically arranged, except on the godawful "Good Morning Dear." Still, the first side is pure Charles country — eccentric and sexy, which real country rarely is, and funny as only Charles can be. I wonder what Johnny Cash will make of the almost inaudible lowdown whisper that closes "Ring of Fire." Love it, probably. **B**

Ray Charles: *Volcanic Action of My Soul* (ABC '71). "Something," "The Long and Winding Road," "Wichita Lineman," "Down in the Valley," and "The Three Bells" on one LP? Would even Jim Reeves have the guff? Yeah, he might, which in his case is unfortunate. 'Cause Jim Reeves wouldn't syncopate that chapel bell. Or chuckle in abject lechery and infatuation on some ASCAP oldie. **A−**

Ray Charles: *A 25th Anniversary in Show Business Salute to Ray Charles*

(ABC '71). In a remarkable show of benevolent corporate cooperation, this devotes one eighteen-song disc to his work with Atlantic, when Charles was inventing soul music, and another to his work with ABC, when he was demonstrating its apparently limitless flexibility. This is the only artist in history who's moved back and forth between jazz and rock and pop without the slightest sense of strain. I find that rock — the soul style he developed, not the Beatles covers — puts useful restraints on his taste, the limitless flexibility of which hasn't always served him well. But I'll sample anything he wants to serve up.   **A+**

Ray Charles: *A Message from the People* (ABC/Tangerine '72). Beginning with "Lift Every Voice and Sing," an anthem sung by black schoolchildren, and climaxing with "America the Beautiful," ditto but with less reason, Charles says his piece. Like the ecologist he is, he extracts all remaining truth from "Abraham, Martin and John," and though he may be naive he adds a menace to "Heaven Help Us All" that Stevie Wonder wasn't genius enough to convey and turns Melanie's "What Have They Done to My Song, Ma" into the outcry of black musicians everywhere — which is probably why it rocks (and swings) like nothing he's done in years.   **B+**

Ray Charles: *Through the Eyes of Love* (ABC/Tangerine '72). He begins by transforming a tearjerker called "My First Night Alone Without You" into tragedy and climaxes by transforming a tearjerker called "Rainy Night in Georgia" into farce. In between he geniuses around.   **B**

Ray Charles: *Come Live with Me* (Crossover '74). The best songs here, one by Ray and one by Jimmy Lewis, warn the ladies about the perils of liberation, while the worst (not counting the McKuen-Brel) are by tyros named Ann Gregory and Sadye Shepard, both of whom work for his publishing company. Feminists please advise.   **B**

Ray Charles: *Renaissance* (Crossover '75). So you thought Stevie Wonder's "Living for the City" and Randy Newman's "Sail Away" were definitive, eh? Well, they are, but try these anyway. And then tell me why Little Milton's version of "We're Gonna Make It" cuts Ray's. And how the hell he found a Charles Aznavour song more mawkish than the worst McKuen-Brel. And whether he commissioned the translation himself.   **B**

Ray Charles/Cleo Laine: *Porgy and Bess* (RCA Victor '76). The problem with this Norman Granz brainstorm is Laine, a singer of formidable technique and zero soul who usually gives me tension headaches. But though she's nothing to write liner notes about, only rarely does her unnaturalness intrude — and she does do a great job with the score itself, which is no snap. Charles isn't always inspired — is he ever any more? — but the writing carries him over the smooth spots. Granz deserves credit for holding down the orchestrations and inviting Charles and his combo to improvise on the material. Of course, Granz might also unearth the *Porgy and Bess* he did twenty years ago with Ella and Louis — as might you. But this will do.   **B+**

Ray Charles: *True to Life* (Atlantic '77). Charles hasn't sung with such consistent care in years. Not that he's given up his jocund audacity — two of the best cuts here are a miraculous recasting of "Oh, What a Beautiful Mornin' " and a Bobby Charles song first recorded by, fancy that, Joe Cocker. But even on the throwaways he seems to remember the difference between goofing and goofing off. The first side is as listenable as any Charles I know, and I've learned to enjoy myself through the schmaltz of "Be My Love" and get to the easy stuff on side two. Now if only he'd let those Beatle ballads be.   **A−**

Ray Charles: *Love and Peace* (Atlantic '78). What a letdown. With covers that range from silly (is that Jack

"Riding Thumb," after he hits the road?) to obvious ("We Had It All" is quintessential Charles country adequately rendered), and with filler from his publishing subsidiary at a redundant nadir, the same old horn charts and obligatory big productions really begin to grate. Ray doesn't hit his stride until the last five words — one word, really — of the final cut, which is about poor people and addressed to the president: "Can you dig it? Amen."   **B−**

Ray Charles: *Ain't It So* (Atlantic '79). Pro forma Charles here — jazzed-up Berlin and Mercer-Allen, schlocked-up "Just Because," uninspired Manilow and McDill, original Jimmy Lewis, "Drift Away" (eat your heart out, Dobie), and "Some Enchanted Evening" (eat your heart out, Ezio). In other words, a pretty damn good record.   **B+**

Cheap Trick: *Cheap Trick* (Epic '77). I like their looks — two pretty-boys balanced off by two ugly-guys — and have no objection to their sound, which recalls the Aerosmith of *Rocks*. Nor am I shocked that they're not as powerful as the Aerosmith of *Rocks,* Jack Douglas or no Jack Douglas. But given their harmony singing you think they'd try and be more melodic. Sign of smarts: the way the phrase "any time at all" hooks "He's a Whore."   **B**

Cheap Trick: *In Color* (Epic '77). Nowadays, punk makes it possible to resist hard rock so slickly textured, but with these guys why bother? They don't waste a cut, and permit none of the stupidity or showiness or sentimentality of postheavy and/or postboogie professionalism, either. If only they seemed interested in their well-crafted say-nothing lyrics.   **B+**

Cheap Trick: *Heaven Tonight* (Epic '78). When I gave the weak side a final spin, I was quite surprised to recognize four hooks with pleasure. The strong side begins with a wonderfully funny parents song and includes a sar-

castic ditty about suicide. Am I to conclude that I'm once again seduced by this power-tooled hard rock product? Guess so.   **B+**

Cheap Trick: *Cheap Trick at Budokan* (Epic '79). The second side almost works as a best-of, but I'd wait for the studio job — despite the Japanese applause track, this was obviously recorded in the Big Room at Carlsbad Caverns. Arrangements are gratifyingly tight — ten titles on a single disc — but six of them are also available (even tighter) on *In Color*. Also: "Ain't That a Shame," the intro of which ought to give pause to those who consider Rick Nielsen an innovative guitar player as opposed to showman; a throwaway collaboration with Tom Petersson; a nice Move ripoff; and "Surrender."   **B−**

Cheap Trick: *Dream Police* (Epic '79). What's always saved this band for me was the jokes, but this time they're just not in the grooves, and there's only so much you can do with funny hats on the cover. A good heavy metal band, sure — be thankful for the fast tempos. But probably not a great heavy metal band. And you know what happens to good heavy metal bands long about the fifth album.   **B−**

Chee Chee & Peppy: *Chee Chee & Peppy* (Buddah '72). If I'm opposed to music that lays fantasy trips on the unsuspecting, then why do I dig these two prepubescents — Peaches & Herb cum Jackson 5 — singing about rings and things? Because who would believe it, that's why. The side of oldies is an expendable novelty, I admit. But producer Jesse James has come up with more good originals than Marvin & Tammi ever got. Original grade: B plus.   **B**

Clifton Chenier: *Out West* (Arhoolie '74). As the king of the accordion-based Louisiana blues known as zydeco, Chenier is revered among such patrons of the folk as Arhoolie's Chris Strachwitz, who has now recorded six albums with him. This is a good thing, I guess, but Chenier strikes me most of the time as a big frog in a small bayou — in French or English his slurs and impassioned moaning are pretty automatic, and the most distinctive thing about his accordion playing is that he plays accordion. This album adds Bay Area guitarist Elvin Bishop and pianist Steve Miller to Chenier's six-piece lineup, and I welcome the impurities — Miller is nothing special, but Bishop's solos give Chenier room to breathe and something to test his strength against. The only loss is Cleveland Chenier's counterrhythms on rubboard, which sink into the mix, but with Arhoolie that's always a danger anyway. **B**

Clifton Chenier: *Bogalusa Boogie* (Arhoolie '76). Crisp, spirited, with John Hart's tenor sax applying a crucial boot in the ass to each side and Cleveland C. rubbing his board to beat the band, this is where Clifton C. finally gets one of his famous parties onto a record. If he could keep it up he might give boogieing a good name again. **B+**

Cher: *Greatest Hits* (MCA '74). Snuff Garrett states her case more loudly than Sonny ever did, and if like me you have a soft spot in your heart for unabashed brass you find her biggest hits irresistible. The great Swarthy Trilogy — "Gypsys, Tramps and Thieves," "Half-Breed," and "Dark Lady" — is the proof of an album that cut for cut is as vulgar as any in the post-Beatles era: Grand Funk is more wholesome and more arty, Neil Diamond a rabbi by comparison. She's at least as authentic as Tammy Wynette, too. Not all of these were such big hits, but who cares when one of the ringers is "Melody," the name of an old doll to whom a just-deflowered Cher sings her proud confession. Time: 28:24. **B+**

Chic: *Chic* (Atlantic '77). I wonder about the *They Shoot Horses* reference — that is where "yowsah yow-

sah yowsah" was popularized, after all. Is this chic as anti-Depression concept? Dance as desperation? Dance as survival? Or just useful noise? **B−**

Chic: *C'est Chic* (Atlantic '78). The hooky cuts are more jingles than songs, the interludes more vamps than breaks, and I won't dance, so don't ask me. Well, maybe if you're really nice. **B**

Chic: *Risque* (Atlantic '79). Edwards and Bernard Rodgers proved on Sister Sledge's "Lost in Music" that hedonism and its discontents, the inevitable focus of disco's meaningfulness moves, is a subject worth opening up. Here, "Good Times" and "My Feet Keep Dancing" surround the sweetly romantic "Warm Summer Night" in a rueful celebration of escape that's all the more suggestive for its unquenchable good cheer. Side two's exploration of romance and its agonies also has a fatalistic tint, but in the end the asides and rhythmic shifts (as well as the lyrics themselves) give rue the edge over celebration. Subtle, intricate, kinetic, light but not mindless — in short, good to dance to. **A−**

Chic: *Les Plus Grands Succes de Chic/Chic's Greatest Hits* (Atlantic '79). Not as elegant conceptually as *Risque*, but a better party record for sure — in a music of six-minute cuts (actually, only three run over 4:42) a group this good has no trouble putting together a quality best-of after two years and three albums. Greil Marcus describes *The Motown Story* as "the history of James Jamerson's bass playing, on fifty-eight hits." This is the future of Bernard Edwards's on seven. And guess where Edwards learned his shit. **A−**

Chicago: *Chicago at Carnegie Hall* (Columbia '71). I'm not claiming actually to have listened to this four-record set — you think I'm a nut? — but the event is too overwhelming to ignore altogether, and Chicago is a C-minus group if ever I heard one. Anyway, the packaging offers textual support for my opinion. The shrink-wrap is so loose that many Christmas gift recipients are going to suspect their girlfriends of buying review copies. And the lack of paper sleeves inside the cardboard sleeves inside the big box means that the only way to avoid scratching these plastic documents is to put the whole shebang out on the coffee table and never touch it again. **C—**

The Chi-Lites: *(For God's Sake) Give More Power to the People* (Brunswick '71). The politics here are imaginatively common-sensical, from "We Are Neighbors," which adduces a racist knock-knock joke before noting that we're neighbors "whether we want to be or not," to the title cut, which owes something to both Jesse Jackson and the Esquires' "Get On' Up." And "Have You Seen Her," like "I Want to Pay You Back," is Soul Music Meets the Women's Movement, warning any man who tries "to be hip" and exploit his woman that she's strong enough to reject him for it. I suppose it's only to be expected that this guy also believes "fighting's for fools," a political notion too common-sensical to suit me. But at least he seems to have put some thought into the sentiment. **A—**

A Chi-Lites: *A Lonely Man* (Brunswick '72). It's OK that producer-singer-songwriter Eugene Record has written an entire album for the male supplicant he created. But it's not OK that except for the folk-kitsch masterpiece "Oh Girl" (a/k/a "Oh That Harmonica") not one of these songs is going to get him what he wants — true love, a roll in the hay, a hit single, anything. Nor is it okay that he bids fair to turn into the falsetto Isaac Hayes on "A Lonely Man" (a/k/a "Have You Seen Her Yet") and "The Coldest Days of My Life" (a/k/a "The Longest Song I've Ever Written"). **B**

The Chi-Lites: *Greatest Hits* (Brunswick '72). The Delfonics and the Moments may have staked first claim on Eugene Record's love man, but Record demolishes the competition, if such a macho concept is permissible in this context (and it certainly is). Not only does he outwrite the other fellas, he doesn't trip over his bassman when the tempo speeds up or make a fool of himself when analyzing the dilemmas of contemporary civilization. The fifteen-song compilation includes the entire first side (plus one) of *Give More Power to the People* and may actually be too generous — it is possible to OD on this stuff. But everything you want is here, and what you think you don't want you might. **A**

Chi-Lites: *Greatest Hits, Vol. 2* (Brunswick '76). They're still a better-than-average harmony group, but their moment is past, and although they continue to handle brisk tempos more deftly than the competition their accommodations to disco are just that — compromises, not expansions. Eugene Record's lyrics offer more than the music, which he often farms out these days: "A Letter to Myself" is classic silly self-pity, I leave it to you to imagine how "Homely Girl" turns out, and "That's How Long" (which Record didn't write) is as graphic a song about old age as has ever made 54 in *Billboard*. **B**

Chunky, Novi and Ernie: *Chunky, Novi and Ernie* (Warner Bros. '77). I had trouble placing this coolish, soulish aural cocktail until I saw the live act, which centered (at least for me) on a supernumerary conga player with the coif, sunlamp tan and Ultra-Brite grin of an airline steward. Headset Muzak. **C**

Eric Clapton: *Eric Clapton* (Atco '70). One great r&b instrumental ("Slunky"), two tracks that deserve classic status ("After Midnight" and "Let It Rain"), two that don't ("Bottle of Red Wine" and "Blues Power"), and well-played filler. I blame a conceptual error, rather than Clapton's uncertain singing, for the overall thinness. As a sideman, Clapton slipped into producer Delaney Bramlett's downhome bliss as easily as he did into Cream's blues dreamscape, but as a solo artist he can't simulate Delaney's optimism. I mean, a party song called "Blues Power" from a man with a hellhound on his trail? **B**

Eric Clapton: *History of Eric Clapton* (Atco '72). A number of worthwhile oddities on this stopgap pseudo-document: the uptempo, high-echo, Spector-produced single of "Tell the Truth," a studio jam on the same tune, and King Curtis's "Teasin'," featuring God on novelty guitar. Also some less worthwhile oddities, a lot of Cream and Delaney & Bonnie, and not enough showpieces from the Yardbirds and Bluesbreakers days (those are on other labels, which means they cost money). Yet it's gone top ten. Must be a lot of collectors out there. Or maybe just people who believe in God. **B**

Eric Clapton: *Eric Clapton's Rainbow Concert* (RSO '73). Featuring organizer Pete Townshend, affable Ronnie Wood, former bandmate Steve Winwood of Traffic, Jim Capaldi of Traffic, Rebop of Traffic, and how could I forget Jimmy Karstein? Also featuring six soggy songs that have been crisp in the past. **C−**

Eric Clapton: *461 Ocean Boulevard* (RSO '74). By opening the first side with "Motherless Children" and closing it with "I Shot the Sheriff," Clapton puts the rural repose of this laid-back-with-Leon music into a context of deprivation and conflict, adding bite to soft-spoken professions of need and faith that might otherwise smell faintly of that most rural of laid-back commodities, bullshit. And his honesty has its reward: better sex. The casual assurance you can hear now in his singing goes with the hip-twitching syncopation he brings to Robert Johnson's "Steady Rolling Man" and Elmore James's "I Can't Hold Out," and though the covers are what make this record memorable it's on "Get Ready," written and sung with Yvonne Elliman, that his voice takes on a mellow, seductive intimacy he's never come close to before. Original grade: A minus. **A**

Eric Clapton: *There's One in Every Crowd* (RSO '75). This is the J. J. Cale record we were afraid Eric was going to make (ho-hum) when he signed up those Leon Russell sidemen (yawn) for *461 Ocean Boulevard.* Only for J.J. (think I'll turn in) the nice tunes come naturally. Original grade: C. **C+**

Eric Clapton: *E.C. Was Here* (RSO '75). From Clapton a live album is welcome these days. At the very least it guarantees that his head was higher than his feet at time of recording, and live albums being what they are it also assures plenty of what he does best, which is play guitar. But though Clapton's choked lyricism can be exciting, he does have trouble breaking loose, and because George Terry's sound is so like his own their colloquies don't spark much. Besides, this is basically a blues album — four of the six cuts fit the category with varying degrees of authenticity — and I expect a blues album to be sung as well as played. **B−**

Eric Clapton: *No Reason to Cry* (RSO '76). A well-made, rather likable rock and roll LP that shows more pride and joy than the standard El Lay studio product, probably because the characters here assembled don't do this kind of thing all that much. The words are trite but the singing is eloquent and the instrumental signature an almost irresistible pleasure. But what does it all mean? **B−**

Eric Clapton: *Slowhand* (RSO '77). As MOR singles go, "Lay Down Sally" is a relief — at least it has some soul. But the album leaves the juiciest solos to George Terry, and where four years ago Eric was turning into a singer — in the manner of Pete Townshend — now he sounds like he's blown his voice. Doing what, I wonder. Original grade: C. **C+**

Eric Clapton: *Backless* (RSO '79). Whatever Eric isn't anymore — guitar genius, secret auteur, humanitarian, God — he's certainly king of the Tulsa sound, and here he contributes three new sleepy-time classics. All are listed on the cover sticker and none were written by Bob Dylan. One more and this would be creditable. **B−**

Gene Clark, Chris Hillman, David Crosby, Roger McGuinn, Michael Clarke: *Byrds* (Asylum '73). Don't believe the title, believe the artist listing. The difference is between a group, committed however fractiously to a coherent collective identity, and a bunch of stars fabricating a paper reconciliation. Maybe if Gary Usher had produced, as promised, this would be more than the country-rock supersession David Crosby has granted us — because maybe Usher would have persuaded the boys to let go of the songs they're saving for their solo albums. **C**

Guy Clark: *Old No. 1* (RCA Victor '75). I liked Clark's laconic vocal presence at first, although I eventually began to feel that, like the agreeably glopless Nashville production, it flattened this material more than it deserved. Which says good things for the material. A must for would-be Texans and other Western mythos fans. Meaningful sex fans will also dig. **B+**

The Clash: *Give 'Em Enough Rope* (Epic '78). Although in the end I find that Sandy Pearlman's production does as much justice to the power of this band as the debut does to their rough intensity, I know why some are disappointed. The band's recent strategy has been to cram their dense, hard sound so full of growls and licks and offhand remarks that it never stops exploding. Here that approach occasionally seems overworked, and so does the vision — this major (and privileged) pop group sounds as wearied by the failure of punk solidarity, the persistence of racial conflict, the facelessness of violence, and the ineluctability of capital as a bunch of tenured Marxists. But these familiar contradictions follow upon the invigorating gutter truths of the first album for a reason — they're truths as well, truths that couldn't be stated more forcefully with

any other music. Great exception: "Stay Free," Mick Jones's greeting to a mate fresh out of jail that translates the band's new political wariness into personal warmth. **A**

The Clash: *The Clash* (Epic '79). Cut for cut, this may be the greatest rock and roll album (plus limited-edition bonus single) ever manufactured in the U.S. It offers ten of the fourteen titles on the band's British debut as well as seven of the thirteen available only on forty-five. And the sequencing is anything but haphazard; the eight songs on side one divide into self-contained pairs that function as extended oxymorons on careerism, corporate power, race, and anomie. Yet the package feels misbegotten. The U.K. version of *The Clash* is the greatest rock and roll album ever manufactured anywhere partly because its innocence is of a piece — it never stops snarling, it's always threatening to blow up in your face. I'm still mad the real thing wasn't released two years ago, and I know for certain (I made a tape) that the singles would have made a dandy album by themselves. Nevertheless, a great introduction and a hell of a bargain. **A**

Merry Clayton: *Gimme Shelter* (Ode '70). Second-rate material stupidly overproduced and unreflectively emoted. Even the title song, which retains a lot of power, sounded better when she was duetting it with Mick Jagger — that is, *she* sounded better. Maybe that's what it means to be a great backup singer. **C+**

David Clayton-Thomas: *David Clayton-Thomas* (Columbia '72). Believe it or not, intol'able David has loosened up some since his big-band days, and his material is well-selected, but he still sounds as if he takes an emetic when he needs an enema, and unlike Tom Jones, whom he might emulate by losing some weight, he always compares embarrassingly to his sources. **C**

Jimmy Cliff: *Wonderful World, Beautiful People* (A&M '70). If I told you that the two other great songs here are called "Many Rivers To Cross" and "Viet Nam," would you agree that naming this album after its "hit" amounts to false advertising? Yet running through all the protest and self-help is a good cheer independent of message — partly in the headlong tempos and drum explosions, partly in Cliff's own sweet fervor.   **B+**

Jimmy Cliff et al.: *The Harder They Come* (Mango '73). The soundtrack to the greatest rock and roll movie this side of *The TAMI Show* is the greatest rock and roll compilation this side of *18 King Size Rhythm and Blues Hits*. Only it's better, because director Perry Henzell had five years of reggae to choose from, with no real label restrictions. Reggae isn't straight rock and roll, of course — its syncopation was a response to the rock that replaced shuffle r&b on U.S. radio in the early '60s. But the interplay of amped-up bass, heartbeat drums, and scratch guitar is as good a rhythm as anyone else's out right now, and though there are only two million Jamaicans, at least 50,000 of them want to be reggae stars. Among the eight who make it here are movie hero Jimmy Cliff (defiant, plaintive, inspirational) and prime minister of soul Toots Hibbert (exuberant, pressured, amused), but wonderful minor artists like the Slickers (whose "Johnny Too Bad" is a rough draft of the movie) and Scotty (whose song is a chant) are just as representative of this thriving, disorganized scene. Docked a notch for repeating two Cliff songs.   **A**

Jimmy Cliff: *Unlimited* (Reprise '73). I found this tremendously disappointing at first — not one song I could hang my head on. But the political analysis is at the very least sensible, no common thing in popular music. Cliff's singing is earnest and spirited enough to give the analysis some immediacy. And in a few cases —"Born to Win," "The Price of Peace," and

especially "Under the Sun, Moon and Stars," about his parents — it isn't just the message that puts the tune across. Original grade: C.   **B−**

Jimmy Cliff: *Music Maker* (Reprise '74). It's time we reminded ourselves that there are only three Jimmy Cliff songs on *The Harder They Come*. His other great ones are on *Wonderful World, Beautiful People*. The nearest this surprisingly ornate and dinky album comes to a good one is the indictment of Island Records' Chris Blackwell as a "No. 1 Rip-Off Man," very timely given what Island has just scrounged up for its own Jimmy Cliff album, *Struggling Man*. But both records portend a nonstar of the future — or a false one.   **C**

Jimmy Cliff: *Follow My Mind* (Reprise '75). Seekers after a reggae triumvirate insist that this album is an improvement, which is stretching the truth — the singing's a shade tougher, the writing's a shade sharper, and there are two relatively striking tracks, both of which detail Cliff's paranoia. Elsewhere he's still a victim of the folkie fallacy, in which to sing rhymed homilies clearly and sincerely is to make good music. Original grade: C.   **C+**

Jimmy Cliff: *In Concert/The Best of Jimmy Cliff* (Reprise '76). In which Cliff rerecords all the great songs he cut originally for Island and A&M — that is, all the great songs he's written, about six total — at a new royalty rate. Always a passionately soulful live performer, he puts a lot into them, but the exigencies of in-concert arrangement ake more out, and only "Viet Nam," with its litany of war-torn Third World countries, offers anything radically new. Also new are a cover of Cat Stevens's "Wild World," a singalong movie theme, and a brief sermon about the universal language.   **C+**

Jimmy Cliff: *Give Thankx* (Warner Bros. '78). Cliff hasn't evinced this much interest in years, and his female backup sounds as sisterly as Bob Marley's. But any artist whose most specific songs concern spiritual deliverance — talkin' 'bout "Bongo Man" and, yep, "Universal Love" — isn't out of the ether yet. **B−**

Clover: *Love on the Wire* (Mercury '78). Who said nobody makes fun rock and roll any more? Who said it's almost impossible to find simple rock and roll lyrics that aren't merely inane? Who said all the tasty countrified guitar licks and tasty funkified drum licks have disappeared amid the hooks, saccharin, and fustian? And who cares? **B−**

Billy Cobham: *Spectrum* (Atlantic '73). In which Mahavishnu's muscle-headed muscle man gets good reviews all for himself. Well, you know about drummers' bands. Despite a few tough minutes this is basically slick, gimmicky, one-dimensional — in a word, undemanding. All of which may make him a star. **C+**

Hank Cochran: *With a Little Help from My Friends* (Capitol '78). Another eccentric Nashville songwriter rides after gold with some famous buddies and winds up with another better-than-average country album. This one features vocals from Merle Haggard (two songs), Willie Whozit (one song), Jack Greene (who sounds like Waylon Whozit), and a dusky-voiced old favorite of mine, Jeannie Seely (Jack's singing partner and Hank's wife). Clinkerless, but way too heavy on the lighthearted throwaways. **B**

Joe Cocker: *Mad Dogs & Englishmen* (A&M '70). An impressive document, but the same overkill (eleven musicians plus nine backup singers) that was so exhilarating live wears a little thick over a double-LP, especially when you compare the four repeats from Cocker's two studio albums — he sings more accurately when nobody's rushing him. I love Leon Russell's guitar raveup on "Feelin' Alright," though. And the New Orleans horn break on "Cry Me a River." And

"The Letter." Original grade: A minus. **B+**

Joe Cocker: *Joe Cocker* (A&M '72). Not to be confused with 1969's classic *Joe Cocker!*, a distinction that gets at the difference quite nicely. It's said that Cocker's voice is gone, and I suppose that's true — it was never much less rough, but it was richer and more flexible. And the live "Do Right Woman" on side two is an overstated embarrassment. But the music on side one, with Chris Stainton providing the same old propulsion on piano as well as — hmm — collaborating with this supposed interpreter-only on some good-to-terrific songs, is as rollicking as ever, and the rest of side two is OK. The magic is gone, that's for sure, but maybe it's gone from us, not from him. **B+**

Joe Cocker: *I Can Stand a Little Rain* (A&M '74). If Jim Price were a producer worthy of the artist, or even of the artist's memory, he would have asked Jerry Lee Lewis to play piano instead of Nicky Hopkins. Not that Jerry Lee could replace Chris Stainton, who combined with Cocker last time to write more good hooks than all of Hollywood's finest coughed up for this make-work project. Original grade: C plus. **C**

Joe Cocker: *Jamaica Say You Will* (A&M '75). Think back to how drastically Cocker's early triumph — "With a Little Help From My Friends" or "Just Like a Woman" or "Darling Be Home Soon" or "Bird on the Wire" — departed from the originals; he literally forced us to rehear those songs. Then compare the strongest cut here, "Lucinda," with Randy Newman's prototype; arrangement and vocal approach are almost identical. That's the nut. Cocker and Leon Russell funkified pop so persuasively that they set up their own minitradition, and now Cocker can't imagine transcending it. **C**

Joe Cocker: *Stingray* (A&M '76). Yeah, the Stuff guys are funkier than the El Lay guys, but on side two you can hardly hear them for the backup singers (I don't mean you, Bonnie). And there are three Matthew Moore ditties, not to mention six and a half minutes of "A Song for You" (at this point I wouldn't sit still for a ninety-second punk version). Genuine high point: "Catfish," Bob Dylan's tribute to a million-dollar man Cocker still says he's never heard of.   **C+**

Joe Cocker: *Joe Cocker's Greatest Hits* (A&M '77). Cocker's seven other A&M albums are all depicted — enticingly, I guess is the idea — on the inner sleeve, and sure enough, every one is represented herein. Surprisingly, the past five years hold up pretty well — the vacuousness of "You Are So Beautiful" has always been the song's fault, and there's nothing early I like any better than "Black-Eyed Blues" or "The Jealous Kind." Ray Charles's recent cover of the latter provides some insight into Cocker's uniqueness. Sure I prefer the authentic instrument — every time Cocker hits a high note these days you're afraid it's his last — and Charles's intensity is miraculous. But the boozy, tattered quality of Cocker's voice, as well as the sense that he's about to break into tears, adds a helplessness to his version that Charles couldn't match if he wanted to.   **A−**

Joe Cocker: *Luxury You Can Afford* (Asylum '78). This begins encouragingly — Allen Toussaint's "Fun Time" is fun, "Watching the River Flow" worth watching. But neither producer Toussaint nor his Muscle Shoals henchmen can turn Phil Driscoll (who?) into Leon Russell (back when).   **C+**

Leonard Cohen: *Songs of Love and Hate* (Columbia '71). There are no bad songs on this album, and from Paul Buckmaster to acoustic strum, Bob Johnston's production fits each individually. I know, you wonder who cares. Well, I don't trust Cohen's melancholy anapests any more than I do his deadpan despair; there are plenty of songwriters both naive and arty, as

well as page poets, with a fresher sense of language. But the poets can't read like Cohen, the songwriters rarely combine his craft and his maturity, and the man can really project. His bare voice and melodies shade in his tenderness and self-mockery ("I who have no need" indeed), creating a dramatic context in which his posture becomes as credible as Denise Levertov's or Mick Jagger's. Granted, its uses are limited — best for late nights alone. Recommended to those who are turned off by Christie's opium fantasy in *McCabe and Mrs. Miller* but moved by Beatty's snow trek.   **A−**

Leonard Cohen: *Live Songs* (Columbia '73). It's strange to encounter Cohen in the company of a large group — when he leads a thirteen-minute singalong based on a blind man's placard he risks turning into the Pete Seeger of romantic existentialism. And I could do without the shaky guitar improv and the revival of "Passing Thru," though both are tolerable. But it so happens that all five of the self-covers on this album are from *Songs from a Room,* which I've always thought could use redoing. And eventually the singalong becomes a yellalong, which is much better.   **B+**

Leonard Cohen: *New Skin for the Old Ceremony* (Columbia '74). That miraculously intimate voice has become more expressive and confident over the years without losing its beguiling flat amateurishness. Some of the new songs are less than memorable, but the settings, by John Lissauer, have the bizarre feel of John Simon's "overproduction" on Cohen's first album, which I always believed suited his studied vulgarity perfectly.   **A−**

Leonard Cohen: *The Best of* (Columbia '75). I've always found "Sisters of Mercy" unnecessarily (and uncharacteristically) icky — you can read their address by the moon, eh? But if like me you admire his records more than you play them, this is the one you'll pull off the shelf.   **A−**

Leonard Cohen: *Death of a Ladies' Man* (Warner Bros. '77). The bad music here can't be blamed on Phil Spector's melodies — Cohen has never posed as a particularly tuneful guy himself. And the main thing wrong with Spector's settings, banal though they are, is that they lack doors. Ordinarily, Cohen whispers, murmurs, whines, croaks, and even screams *through* the music. Here he has to try and sing *over* it, using more or less normal volume and timbre. **B-**

Leonard Cohen: *Recent Songs* (Columbia '79). Cohen's arrangements are even more detailed and surprising than John Lissauer's, and Jennifer Warnes is the most valuable backup singer since Emmylou Harris. "The Traitor" is a minor masterpiece. And in general this record's take on courtly love in the swingers' era packs more ironic intelligence than you would have thought possible. Or necessary, unfortunately. Cohen's gift for elementary hummables seems to deteriorate as his writing evolves from the conversational toward the allegorical. Irony or no irony, "rages of fragrance" and "rags of remorse" sound suspiciously like bad poetry even when they're sung, and that's not how it's supposed to work. **B**

Natalie Cole: *Inseparable* (Capitol '75). In which the daughter of the first king of crossover pop aspires to the grandeur of Lady Soul, with results that are more Chaka than Aretha and betray a soupçon and a half of Nancy Wilson. So where's Natalie? Serving her masters, ex-Independents Chuck Jackson and Marvin Yancy. Original grade: B minus. **B**

Natalie Cole: *Natalie* (Capitol '76). I believe good singers (which Cole is) ought to sing good songs. Of these, only "Good Morning Heartache," already defined and altered by two noteworthy predecessors, and "Can We Get Together Again," which sounds suspiciously like "This Will Be," distinguish themselves. I also believe that if your producers get to write all your material, they ought to at least provide

a Sound, not the feckless eclecticism here displayed. **C+**

Natalie Cole: *Thankful* (Capitol '77). Musically, her best. She moves from style to style with passion and ease, and her svengalis are writing more crisply. But I begin to muse about Herbert Marcuse when I hear the famous daughter of a wealthy singing star belt the following Inspirational Verse: "Workin two jobs to make your livin and all you do is complain well . . . You should be thankful for what you got." Docked a notch or two for oppressive ideology. **B-**

Ornette Coleman: *Dancing in Your Head* (Horizon '77). Some may have hoped the greatest saxophone player alive would go the Weather Report route on his first small-group record since 1971, but I'm reminded more of the programmed synthesizers of Eno and Philip Glass. Basically, the record consists of charged repetitions of one motif from Coleman's symphony, *Skies of America*. The difference is that where most such music aims for a hypnotic effect, Coleman wants more: a sustained and formally satisfying version of the kind of galvanic intensity John McLaughlin used to create at climactic moments. He gets it, too. **A**

Ornette Coleman: *Body Meta* (Artists House '78). Hidden in Coleman's dense electric music are angles deep enough to dive into and sharp enough to cut your throat. This isn't quite as dense or consistent as *Dancing in Your Head* — "Fou Amour" does wander. But "Voice Poetry" is as funky as James Chance if not James Brown. And "Home Grown" is as funky as Robert Johnson. **A-**

Albert Collins: *Ice Pickin'* (Alligator '78). Like Otis Rush, Collins has always been one of those well-respected bluesmen whose records left agnostics unconvinced. But this is the most exiting blues album of 1978. Collins's guitar is clean, percussive, vehement, breaking into unlikely rivulets on the trademark shuffle climaxes, and while his voice is thin his delivery is savvy and humorous. So are his words — unlike most of his colleagues, he seems to know a lot more about sharing life with another person than "Honey Hush." **A−**

Judy Collins: *Colors of the Day: The Best of Judy Collins* (Elektra '72). "Both Sides Now" could have been designed for her rich, relaxed, rather melodramatic contralto, but elsewhere you wonder why she devoted herself to popular music rather than some genuinely meaningful lifework — decorative gardening, perhaps, or distributing alms to the needy. To hear her strew subtle melismatic decorations over "Who Knows Where the Time Goes" is to wish you could get drunk with Sandy Denny. And to hear her perambulate through "Sunny Goodge Street" is to wanna walk the dog with Donovan Leitch. **C+**

Chi Coltrane: *Chi Coltrane* (Columbia '72). A remarkable percentage of female singer-songwriters resemble movie stars, at least on their album covers, which makes me wonder whether companies sign them because they can sing and write. There's a hit single to go with the flowing blonde hair here. It's a humdrum r&b ripoff that's about as catchy as the Buffy Sainte-Marie imitation, which makes it better than the rest. **C−**

Commander Cody and His Lost Planet Airmen: *Lost in the Ozone* (Paramount '71). Cody takes the country-rock idea that good old boys form a secret counterculture to bleary new heights. Uprooted bozos who handle fast cars and hot music (or vice versa) a lot better than wimmin and booze, they're half at home in every renegade country tradition, rockabilly and Western swing and white boogie-woogie. But not one of the four vocalists achieves the hippie-redneck synthesis — they all sound like they flee to one subculture when they get kicked out of the other. And the only time the

songwriting reaches the outer atmosphere is on "Seeds and Stems (Again)," as close to pure hippie as they get. Original grade: B minus. **B**

Commander Cody and His Lost Planet Airmen: *Hot Licks, Cold Steel and Truckers Favorites* (Paramount '72). This rocks and wails with almost all the coherence and feeling of the rockabilly it takes off from, and if "Old Kentucky Hills of Tennessee" is an unabashedly oxymoronic travesty on country nostalgia (and country-rock aspiration), "Mama Hated Diesels" is so deadpan maudlin you have to check the credits to make sure they didn't cop it somewhere. Original grade: A minus **B+**

Commander Cody and His Lost Planet Airmen: *Country Casanova* (Paramount '73). Never mind howcum a loose-as-a-goose circa-1959 Texas bar band is releasing LPs for the Hip Young People's Market in 1973 — this raises a more specific question. In "Everybody's Doin' It," howcum everybody who's "truckin' " and "fuckin' " isn't also "suckin' "? Don't tell me about the good old days. **B−**

Commander Cody and His Lost Planet Airmen: *Live from Deep in the Heart of Texas* (Paramount '74). Billy C. Farlow is no more equal to "Good Rockin' Tonite" or "Cryin' Time" — Billy C. vs. Roy Brown?? Buck Owens?? — than the Airmen are equal to the Crickets or the Texas Playboys. But on this live album they come damn near to equaling themselves, and on a good night. The rockers are hot, the slow ones are soulful, and the whole thing does justice to the endearingly sloppy shuffle of a band that refuses to be pretentious about its lack of pretensions. For the young at heart and generous of spirit. **B+**

Commander Cody and the Lost Planet Airmen: *Commander Cody and His Lost Planet Airmen* (Warner Bros. '75). I don't know how you record the Airmen, whose wacked-out marginal proficiency always loses charm when etched in plastic for the ages, but it's no accident that the best thing here originated with Phil Harris. I have a couple of observations for their new producer, country-rock pro John Boylan. First, Billy C. Farlow's soul is located in his adenoids, and second, "Willin' " has already been covered by Linda Ronstadt. **C+**

Commander Cody: *Rock 'n Roll Again* (Arista '77). In which a mastermind whose own best songs were eccentric oldies and whose energy and charm were identical to his irresponsibility pens all the tunes for a slickly produced and woogieless boogie album. How the flaky have fallen. **C**

Commodores: *Machine Gun* (Motown '74). The first side is good straight hard funk, kicked off by a title instrumental that's the best thing on the record — sure sign of a good straight hard funk band. The second side is acceptable straight hard funk, with some social consciousness thrown in by corporate stablemates Pam Sawyer and Gloria Jones (they even complain that girls are banned from football and boys from sensitivity). But I'll tell you something about hard funk — I prefer mine a little crooked. **B+**

Commodores: *Caught in the Act* (Motown '75). For four songs — two hits, "Slippery When Wet" and "The Bump," surrounded by "Wide Open," which earns its reprise, and an instrumental called "I'm Ready" that's good enough for a theme —they make a case for their funk. I already believed, but the argument is a lot of fun. For the rest of the album they make a case for their soul. I'd be more inclined to believe if they hadn't bothered. **B**

Commodores: *Movin' On* (Motown '75). More — you guessed it — funk. A lot more, in fact, which I wouldn't have guessed. Sometimes anonymous, sometimes even annoying — "Cebu" 's synthesizer, "(Can I) Get a Witness" 's title. Sometimes neither — "Gimme My Mule" is country the way Otis & Carla defined

it in "Tramp," and "Mary, Mary" is funnier than Michael Nesmith's. Nonfunk: "Sweet Love." Hit: "Sweet Love." That I would have guessed. **B−**

Commodores: *Greatest Hits* (Motown '78). One thing you know about a funk band that goes number one with something as sappy as "Three Times a Lady" — they ain't as funky as they used to be. Or maybe they were never really a funk band to begin with — just potential pros who understood funk's entertainment potential the way John Denver understood folk music's. If they perceive any inflammatory potential in rhythm per se, they do what they can to dampen the fire. I love "Brick House," "Machine Gun," and "Slippery When Wet," but they're not even on the same side of this depressing compilation, half of which is devoted to Lionel Richie and his mealy mouth. **B−**

The Concert for Bangla Desh (Apple '71). The five rock sides — not counting 22:35 of Ravi Shankar, who has one-fourth of the music in this piece of rock history — average about thirteen minutes. They offer exactly what I heard at the Garden: five clear, straightforward, moving protest-era oldies from Bob Dylan, two clear, strong rock and roll oldies from Leon Russell, and Ringo singing "It Don't Come Easy." Plus eight songs by George Harrison and one by Billy Preston. And if you mail your check to the United Nations Children's Fund for Relief to Refugee Children of Bangla Desh you can avoid the middleman. Time: 89:44. **B−**

The Contortions: *Buy the Contortions* (ZE '79). Bohemias are always beset by ambitious neurotics who hawk their obnoxious afflictions as if they're the future of the species, which is why in theory James White's music is better without the words: you get the jagged rhythms and tonic off-harmonies without being distracted by his "ideas." But in fact the music is so (deliberately) stunted it needs a voice for sonic muscle, and James's lyrics do have a certain petty honesty and jerk-off humor. "I Don't Want to Be Happy" should separate the believers from the spectators quite nicely. Time: 29:47. **B+**

Ry Cooder: *Ry Cooder* (Reprise '70). According to his own complaints, which may well be warranted, the world's favorite studio bottleneck is also the man from whom Mick and Keith stole "Let It Bleed." Now if only he could sing as good as Mick and Keith maybe he'd put his own blues synthesis across. As it stands, Cooder's singing and projection are so flat they recall the folkie fantasy in which the real blues comes from toothless old men on porches — songs by Tommy Tucker and Fats Waller and even Randy Newman (who gets a lot more out of his own narrow pipes) sound as humble as those by Sleepy John Estes and Blind Willie Johnson. Cooder has two folkie virtues, though — he remembers the Depression and he finds wonderful songs. Alfred Reed's "How Can a Poor Man Stand Such Times as These" is proof of both. Time: 28:48. **B**

Ry Cooder: *Into the Purple Valley* (Reprise '71). This time Cooder's Everyman sounds homely rather than humble, with an honest wit that escapes the bankers and lawmen on his back, though the "wonderful urbanity" of F.D.R. — the phrase is calypsonian Fitz McLean's — remains an ideal. "How Can You Keep on Moving" and "Taxes on the Farmer Feed Us All," unearthed by Cooder from the public domain, are just what he's after: eloquence that's never highflown, which of course underscores the eloquence. Ditto for his guitar(s), especially on "Billy the Kid" and (Dickey Doo's!) "Teardrops Will Fall." **B+**

Ry Cooder: *Boomer's Story* (Reprise '72). Enslaved by the tradition of the new, I prefer the Cooder who rediscovers material I never dreamed ex-

isted to the Cooder who replicates Sleepy John Estes and Skip James. Especially since one of the Estes songs he's found is of even more dubious interest than Estes's singing style, while the James instrumental is a confusingly airy interlude between his two most gratifying discoveries: "Boomer's Story" and "Crow Black Chicken." Bonus: Cooder's impression of John Fahey playing "Dark End of the Street." **B**

Ry Cooder: *Paradise and Lunch* (Reprise '74). Cooder's problematic vocal authority has always made it harder for him to establish the practicability of the traditional rural values he treasures in the urban '70s. So his transformation of Bacharach-David's "Mexican Divorce" into a folk song that stands alongside Willie McTell's "Married Man's a Fool" is very encouraging. And though what impresses me about this album is its perfection of tone, what wins my love is the anomalous "Ditty Wa Ditty." Original grade: B plus. **A−**

Ry Cooder: *Chicken Skin Music* (Reprise '76). The title refers to a Hawaiian expression closely allied to "goose bumps," which has to be the most modest instance of hubris on record — I mean, does Ry really believe this is gonna make my skin prickle? Folk eclecticism is a nouveau-jug commonplace, after all, even if most nouveau jugheads do lack Ry's imagination and musicianship, not to mention the capital to dab color from Honolulu and San Antonio onto the same LP. Original grade: B minus. **B**

Ry Cooder: *Jazz* (Warner Bros. '77). Cooder's not trying to pass off this pastiche of coon songs, Jelly Roll Morton, Bix Beiderbecke, and Joseph Spence as "real jazz" — he's trying to convince us that the modest roots of "real jazz" merit revitalization. Unfortunately, the whole project is so forced that these roots — if that's what they are — show about as much life as a hat tree. **C+**

Ry Cooder: *Bop Till You Drop* (Warner Bros. '79). In which selected '60s r&b — obscure, but not totally: Howard Tate, Arthur Alexander, Ike & Tina, Fontella & Bobby — enters the folkie canon. Along with an obscure Elvis Presley song, selected older obscurities, and an original about Hollywood obvious enough for Elvin Bishop. With Ry singing as loud as he can, Bobby King chiming over him from the background, and Chaka Khan pitching in on two tracks, it even cuts a respectable groove. But drop you it won't.   **B+**

Rita Coolidge: *Rita Coolidge* (A&M '71). Despite sage advice from my female advisers, I cherished hopes that Coolidge's thick voice — which is grainy rather than gritty, like the Bramlett voice without the bravura — would grow on me the way Tracy Nelson's did. She does get more out of "Seven Bridges Road" than Tracy does by underplaying the overstatement just a little, and it's nice to hear "The Happy Song" as praise for a househusband. But in the end this is so solid that it never sparkles once. Original grade: B.   **C+**

Rita Coolidge: *The Lady's Not for Sale* (A&M '72). Cute title, but my best information is that you're still expected to pay for this in stores. And even if you weren't it would just clutter the house — from a great female hope she's developed into someone who sings "Fever" with all of the heat (and none of the charm) of Keith doin "98.6."   **C**

Rita Coolidge: *Anytime . . . Anywhere* (A&M '77). This was gonna be her annual sultry cornpone, unobjectionable except for the Neil Sedaka tune and not without its soulful moments, when A&M prexy Jerry Moss told Rita how to become worthy of Kris. You'll get more sales, Jerry opined, if people Recognize Your Material. Try a Motown revival, one of Boz's lesser songs, a Bee Gees number, maybe that wonderful Sam Cooke classic the Stones did once — and who can lose with "Higher and Higher"? It seems to have worked, too, except

that those of us with fond memories can still hear the originals. Rita is now halfway to becoming Andy Williams with cleavage. It takes a very special kind of stupidity to slow "Higher and Higher" into a down.   **C**

Alice Cooper: *Easy Action* (Straight '70). *Pretties for You* had its pseudo-decadent and -psychedelic charms, and so does this, only not as many, which makes very few indeed — "Mr. and Misdemeanor" (featuring Lucky Luciano and Kenny Passarelli) and a junkie shoe salesman to balance off all the tuneless singing, tuneless playing, tuneless tunes, and pseudo-musique concrete. [Later on Warner Bros.]   **C**

Alice Cooper: *Love It to Death* (Straight '71). Never would have figured this theatre type to come up with it, but he did — "I'm Eighteen," as archetypal a hard rock single as you're liable to hear in this flaccid year, or maybe ever. Almost as surprising, guitarist Mike Bruce surrounds it with the anthemic "Caught in a Dream" and "Long Way To Go." After which drummer Dennis Dunaway gives forth with "Black Juju," which lasts four seconds longer than all three of the above combined. [Later on Warner Bros.]   **B−**

Alice Cooper: *Killer* (Warner Bros. '71). A taste for the base usages of hard rock rarely comes with a hit attached these days, much less "surreal," "theatrical," and let us not forget "transvestite" trappings, which is why some desperate rock and rollers have convinced themselves their prayers are being answered. But while this is the band's most song-oriented LP, it falters after "Under My Wheels" and "Be My Lover," neither of them an "I'm Eighteen" in the human outreach department. And only one of the three "theatrical" extravaganzas, "Dead Babies," works on record (never mind in the theatre). Original grade: B. **B−**

Alice Cooper: *School's Out* (Warner Bros. '72). With its all-time ugly vocal, kiddie chorus turned synthesizer, and crazy, dropped-out thrust, the title hit is as raw and clever as it gets, but this album is soundtrack. Some of it's even copped — with attribution, yet — from *West Side Story*. For a while I comforted myself with the thought that *West Side Story* is more a rock musical than *Hair,* at least in spirit. But the orchestral homages to Uncle Lennie ruin the effect. Original grade: B plus. **B−**

Alice Cooper: *Billion Dollar Babies* (Warner Bros. '73). The title's as perfect as the band's latest symbol — a $, its "S" transformed into a two-headed snake. No outrage Alice has concocted equals the frank, sweaty greed of his current success. Oddly, though, this blatant profit mechanism is his most consistent album — even the song about (mercy me) necrophilia is tolerable, just like the song about tooth decay. But without a "School's Out" or an "I'm Eighteen" — neither "No More Mr. Nice Guy" nor "Elected" quite makes the grade — there's nothing to tempt anyone back to the new improved filler. Original grade: B plus. **B**

Alice Cooper: *Muscle of Love* (Warner Bros. '73). They went out on the road long enough to pick up their share of chrome (well, this sure ain't platinum), but though it must pain them to realize it, they're not machines. Or maybe it just pains them to realize that machines break down. **C**

Alice Cooper: *Alice Cooper's Greatest Hits* (Warner Bros. '74). Bet this favors passable-minus stuff from *Muscle of Love* — one cut a stiff, the other never a single — over the great stuff from *Love It to Death* because Alice-the-person had no publishing percentage on the latter. Too bad, because this is very spotty for a group that's done more than the Rolling Stones to beef up AM radio over the past few years. Nonetheless, those wise enough to have foregone album purchase up till now should stop their bucks here. **A−**

Alice Cooper: *Welcome to My Nightmare* (Atlantic '75). The solo debut actually ain't so bad — no worse than all the others. "Department of Youth" is his catchiest teen power song to date, "Cold Ethyl" his catchiest necrophilia song to date, and "Only Women Bleed" the most explicitly feminist song to hit top forty since "I Am Woman." Alice's nose for what the kids want to hear is as discriminating as it is impervious to moral suasion, so perhaps this means that the more obvious feminist truisms have become conventional wisdom among at least half our adolescents. Encouraging. **B−**

Larry Coryell: *Coryell* (Vanguard Apostolic '70). Coryell has been the jazz-rock hope since founding the Free Spirits four years ago, so it's worth noting that his best record to date sounds mostly unimprovised. The title of "Elementary Guitar Solo #5" describes it perfectly — an unsurprising, fairly deliberate progression of notes over the solid bottom of studio soul aces Chuck Rainey and Bernard Purdie, with Coryell's color, authority, and dynamics providing most of the "jazz." It's also worth noting that the most exciting track on the album does sound improvised — "The Jam with Albert" (bassist Stinson). And that he's not singing a whole lot. And that he's still singing too much. **B+**

Larry Coryell: *Spaces* (Vanguard Apostolic '70). This match-up with Coryell's British counterpart John McLaughlin — featuring a milestone rhythm section of Chick Corea, Miroslav Vitous, and Billy Cobham — spends too much time constructing tone poems for Barney Kessell and nowhere near enough playing new rock and roll. I know Coryell has lightning fingers and a brain to match and in an abstract way I admire him for it, but what's made him more than an improvising technician is a concept that includes the loud and the vulgar. Here even the inevitable raveup sounds willfully thin, as if Charlie Parker had given up saxophone for piccolo because he wanted to be respectable. **B**

Larry Coryell: *Larry Coryell at the Village Gate* (Vanguard '71). Between the first and last words of this working-trio album — "Welcome to the death of rock and roll" and "Bliss is all-eternal" — Coryell manages to play a lot of guitar, much of which (unlike the singing) sounds like rock and roll: themes over a steady beat. Even as an improvisor he's more into modal flights and electronic extravaganzas than inventing melodies off the changes. So ignore the rhetoric and face the music. **B+**

Larry Coryell: *Barefoot Boy* (Flying Dutchman '71). The closest thing to a jazz album the man has ever made is also the closest thing to an unflawed album the man has ever made. Much as I enjoy the way Coryell and Steve Marcus pass modes from axe to sax, I do prefer John Coltrane's own tributes to John Coltrane, which are numerous. But this may mean something. **B+**

Larry Coryell: *Offering* (Vanguard '72). Jazz-rock goes progressive, by which I mean cool, man. Coryell is himself, by which I mean a chameleon. But Steve Marcus sticks strictly to soprano, and Mike Mandel makes like he doesn't want anybody to know he once played piano in a (shh) rock band. Peak experience: "Scotland I," which lays out a theme worthy of Mahavishnu. In fact, I'd almost swear I'd heard it before. **C+**

Larry Coryell: *The Real Great Escape* (Vanguard '73). A last-ditch attempt at an album of rock and roll songs, including two by Jimmy Webb (one belongs to P. F. Sloan), Julie's "Are You Too Clever" (somebody'd better be), and Larry's "Makes Me Wanna Shout" (lucky it doesn't make him wanna croon). Not as bad as it might be — it has lots of rough charm and virtuosic passages, and the band sounds gutsy. But those who seek after albums of rock and roll songs will not be impressed. **B−**

Larry Coryell: *Return* (Vanguard '79). Bird lives! Oops, scuse me, I mean Byrd — Charlie Byrd. With three sons of Dave Brubeck in on the session. After all that he ends up a professional jazzman. **C+**

Larry Coryell: See also The Eleventh House Featuring Larry Coryell

Elvis Costello: *My Aim Is True* (Columbia '77). I like the nerdy way this guy comes on, I'm fascinated by his lyrics, and I approve of his rock and roll orientation; in fact, I got quite obsessive about his two cuts on the *Bunch of Stiff Records* import. Yet odd as it may seem, I find that he suffers from Jackson Browne's syndrome — that is, he's a little boring. Often this malady results from overconcentration on lyrics and can be cured by a healthy relationship with a band. Since whenever I manage to attend to a Costello song all the way through I prefer it to "The Pretender," I hope he recovers soon. **B+**

Elvis Costello: *This Year's Model* (Columbia '78). This is not punk rock. But anyone who thinks it's uninfluenced should compare the bite and drive of the backup here to the well-played studio pub-rock of his debut and ask themselves how come he now sounds as angry as he says he feels. I find his snarl more attractive musically and verbally than all his melodic and lyrical tricks, and while I still wish he liked girls more, at least I'm ready to believe he's had some bad luck. Original grade: A minus. **A**

Elvis Costello: *Armed Forces* (Columbia '79). Like his predecessor, Bob Dylan, this ambitious tunesmith offers more as a phrasemaker than as an analyst or a poet, more as a public image than as a thinking, feeling person. He needs words because they add color and detail to his music. I like the more explicitly sociopolitical tenor here. But I don't find as many memorable bits of language as I did on *This Year's Model*. And though I approve of the more intricate pop constructions of the music, I found *TYM*'s relentless nastiness of instrumental and (especially) vocal attack more compelling. A good record, to be sure, but not a great one. **A−**

Dennis Coulson: *Dennis Coulson* (Elektra '73). Coulson exploits that natural catch in his voice, a hint of vibrato that walks the line between yearning and good cheer, to bridge his Scottish loyalties and his American stylistic referents — this is genuinely mid-Atlantic singing. But if you want to be an interpreter you'd better find interpretees who give you more to say than Gallagher & Lyle. High point: "Job on the Tyne," which he cocomposed. Hope he keeps trying. **B−**

Coulson, Dean, McGuinness, Flint: *Lo and Behold* (Sire '73). Comprising ten unfamiliar-to-unheard songs written (or anyway, copyrighted) by a well-known singer-songwriter between 1963 and 1971, this organizes scraps of persona the man himself couldn't handle and might as well be called *Bob Dylan — "Yesterday" and Today*. Dennis Coulson knows Dylan's lyrics for the lazy, flirtatious embraces of perception they are, and so never sops over into literalness — Baezesque prettifying or Bandesque uglifying. And where American folk-rockers can be counted on for the just-so flourish, the swelling rhythm, these guys (aided by producer Manfred Mann, world's most sensible Dylan nut) keep it ragged — the music rocks and rolls, but it also seems to stop short every now and then, and it's catchy, hooking with a tabla here, a build arrangement there, clownish horns that signify an entire side. Cynical ("Open the Door Homer") and idealistic ("The Death of Emmett Till"), self-pitying ("Sign on the Cross") and self-reliant ("Let Me Die in My Footsteps"), but always tough and intelligent. And let us not forget funny. **A**

The Counts: *What's Up Front That— Counts* (Westbound '72). Who are these guys? Well, I presume the five on the cover are the five credited with the title track: Raoul Keith Mangrum,

Mose Davis, Demetrius Cates, Andrew Gibson, Leroy Mannuel. And that they play organ, guitar, bass, trap drums, and conga drums, with session horns. And that when they (Davis? Mannuel?) sing they favor Osibisa Afro-shout, only heavier and more soulful, to go with a basically instrumental Afro-funk that's also remarkably dense. I find most instrumental funk slick and/or contentless. This isn't. I find most multipercussion an excuse to lighten the beat. This isn't. A small find. Time:27:50. **B+**

The Counts: *Funk Pump* (Aware '74). I feared the worst when I realized the lead cut was Carole King's "Jazzman," the worst being that they'd gotten "better." More vocals, more horns, more pop moves, and when the female chorus sings "This ain't a song it's just a magic ride" you can be sure it ain't a magic ride either. The title cut is built like a fire hydrant, and I enjoy side two until "Tecalli," where their Latin accent gets suave. But jazzmen they're not. **B**

Kevin Coyne: *Marjory Razor Blade* (Virgin '74). Another British eccentric with a voice scratchy and wavery enough to make Mick Jagger sound like Anthony Newley, only this one can write songs. The annoying kid-stuff tone of the perversity here purveyed is redeemed by the fact that there isn't a chance it will sell, not even with the Brit double-LP condensed down to one. Also, "House on the Hill" is as convincing a madman's song as I know. **B+**

Kevin Coyne: *Matching Head and Feet* (Virgin '75). Coyne is the kind of minor artist whose faults—mainly an undeniable narrowness of emotional range that forces him to repeat effects—I am willing to overlook in this homogenized time. Sounding like a sly, bony, and clinically loony Joe Cocker (or a failed Deke Leonard), he here abandons quirky singer-songwriting for unkempt rock and roll. **B+**

Kevin Coyne: *In Living Black and White* (Virgin '77). Given his invisibility in this country, this may be your last chance at this gravel-gutted dwarf with his weirdo proclivities. It's also your best—the live recording is a little loose, as usual, but the voice is less panic-stricken than on his studio LPs, and the material at a peak.   **B+**

Crack the Sky: *Crack the Sky* (Lifesong '75). After too many legends of Atlantis and concept albums about the last cowboy, I was impressed to come upon John Palumbo, who can end one of his existentialist fables "Being is my . . . life" and make it sound like an aperçu. But in the end the words ("Robots for Ronnie," "A Sea Epic") are brittle, while Palumbo's dense modal structures (and Rick Witkowski's guitar inventions) have real tensile strength. Mannered, sure—so's Big Star. Slick, sure—hmm.   **B−**

Crack the Sky: *Animal Notes* (Lifesong '76). "We Want Mine," a jarring little rocker about Third World deprivation, and "Animal Skins," which quotes George Harrison as it savages every religious leader who's ever lived, convinced me for a while that the rest of this systematically disjoint music flowed and crackled appropriately. But for the most part the melodies of these art-pop set pieces don't live up to the harmonies; their premeditated shifts recall late Beatles when they work and middle Uriah Heep when they don't. I still prefer songs about Mounties to songs about centaurs. But I also prefer Mountie songs that keep galloping when the lyrical conceit gets boring, which it does. Original grade: B plus.   **B**

Crazy Horse: *Crazy Horse* (Reprise '71). The rhythms are deliberately deliberate, and maybe the reason four different guys sing lead is that they don't really trust Danny Whitten with the job. But this should throw a good scare into Neil Young even if they moved on with his blessing. It's literate both verbally (Jack Nitzsche's "Gone Dead Train" is white blues poetry) and musically (they hoe down,

they rave up, they phase out, they rock and roll). With temp worker Nils Lofgren pitching them two titles, there's not a bad song on the record. Not a bad cut, either. Original grade: A. **A−**

Crazy Horse: *Loose* (Reprise '72). Danny Whitten, Jack Nitzsche, and Nils Lofgren (remember those names) are replaced by George Whitsell, John Blanton, and Greg Leroy (forget those), leaving us (and them) with Billy Talbot and Ralph Molina. I know rhythm sections are essential, but this lifeless country-rock should teach everybody how sufficient they are. The most disappointing follow-up in memory.   **D+**

Crazy Horse: *At Crooked Lake* (Epic '72). Rick and Mike Curtis, whoever they are, replace George Whitsell and John Blanton, whoever they were, and the improvement exceeds statistical likelihood. Anybody who misses circa-1966 Byrds will be pleased to learn that this country-rock album features songs about spaceships, the brotherhood of man, and singing in a rock and roll band. And disappointed to learn that none of them sounds like a sure shot. Original grade: B.   **B−**

Crazy Horse: *Full Moon* (RCA Victor '78). I know I've called Neil Young's backup boys the greatest hard rock band in America except the Ramones, and I know Neil Young plays guitar on five cuts here. But I meant when Neil Young was *singing*. Singing Neil Young songs.   **C+**

Cream: *Live Cream* (Atco '70). Clapton, Bruce, and Baker made their money (and names) and ruined their music (and fellowship) in concert. About forty percent of what they released on record during their career was live, so this posthumous product is unnecessary by definition; it's also preferable to the live disc of *Wheels of Fire* ("Toad" and "Spoonful" are their nadir), if not to the more shapely live cuts on *Goodbye*. The intensity of side one is unmistakable and attractive, but I'll take Clapton's graceful picking on *Fresh Cream*'s "Sleepy Time

Time" over the flat-out distortions here — Hendrix has all that amp stuff locked up solid. About the strings we'll see. [Later on RSO.]   **C+**

Cream: *Live Cream Volume II* (Atco '72). Another live album, and still Atlantic withholds the legendary twenty-minute "Anyone for Tennis" they did at Ak-Sar-Ben Coliseum in Omaha on June 15, 1968! [Later on RSO.]   **C+**

Creedence   Clearwater   Revival: *Cosmo's Factory* (Fantasy '70). A lover of rock and roll, not rock, John Fogerty serves up his progress in modest and reliable doses. The songwriting's not as inspired as on *Willy and the Poorboys* — no hidden treasures like "Don't Look Now" or "It Came Out of the Sky." But the sound is fuller, the band more coherent, Fogerty's singing more subtle and assured, so that a straightforward choogle like "Ramble Tamble" holds up simply as music for seven minutes. The same goes for the most ordinary three-minute job here — finally, none of them *are* ordinary. The triumphs are "I Heard It Through the Grapevine," which consummates "Suzie Q" 's artless concept of rock improvisation, and "Lookin' Out My Back Door," in which Fogerty abandons his gritty timbre — so obviously an affectation, yet so natural-seeming — for a near-tenor that sweetly synthesizes spirituality and whimsy.   **A**

Creedence   Clearwater   Revival: *Pendulum* (Fantasy '70). "Molina" and "Pagan Baby," which make Creedence history as the first John Fogerty songs about women, are slightly subpar, "Sailor's Lament" is a little more so, and the Booker T. cum Terry Riley organ doodle on "Rude Awakening #2" is a pretentious moment I hope — and expect — he has the sense never to repeat. The rest is six songs so superpar Steve Barri or Tommy James would kill (or at least steal) for them. Ho hum, another Creedence album.   **A—**

Creedence Clearwater Revival: *Mardi Gras* (Fantasy '72). For a while I forgot my John Fogerty fixation and enjoyed side two of this country-rock debut, which is what asking Stu Cook and Doug Clifford to sing and compose transforms the seventh Creedence album into. But facts are facts. Only "Sweet Hitch-Hiker," an original as unambitious as the equally effective cover of "Hello Mary Lou," could stand on any of Creedence's great albums. "Lookin' for a Reason" and "Someday Never Comes" may be major songs, but it's hard to tell from the way Fogerty sings them. And only inspired Fogerty vocals might save C&C's competent-plus to competent-minus filler from a lifetime in Lodi. Original grade: A minus.   **B**

Creedence   Clearwater   Revival: *Creedence Gold* (Fantasy '72). Not the singles compilation they've earned, just cuts off all their gold albums — that is, a ripoff. But their style has always been more consistent than their albums (a compliment to their style, not an insult to their albums), and this is literally very playable.   **B+**

Creedence Clearwater Revival: *More Creedence Gold* (Fantasy '73). More *Creedence Gold*, or rather, less.   **B**

Creedence   Clearwater   Revival: *Chronicle* (Fantasy '76). Al Green is the only other artist of the post-*Pepper* era to make great albums while scoring consistently on the singles charts, and like Green, Creedence is worth owning in a more public and archival configuration. Fifteen of these twenty songs went top ten, and this is where anyone who snorts at the notion that Creedence was the greatest American rock and roll band should start. Then go back and catch up with the more "obscure" stuff.   **A**

Lol Creme / Kevin Godley: *Consequences* (Mercury '77). (Seven songs *plus* one piano concerto *divided by* 5cc.) *plus* (one paltry eccentric-musician-battling-ecodisaster plot *multiplied by* Peter Cook) *equals* (three good-humored, inconsequential twelve-inch discs *plus* one twelve-inch booklet *plus* one gift box). Unfortunately, it also equals something else, sure as the world ends: a list price of $20.98. For which it is docked a notch.   **C**

Jim Croce: *Photographs and Memories* (ABC '74). Death hasn't changed this engaging, rather repetitive minor artist into a genius, but it's reminded us why he was (and is) engaging. His short-haul trucker persona (world-weary machismo with a heart of gold and a soul of beaten copper) and detached lowlife portraiture (he doesn't mess around that much with Jim himself) were a relief from post-hippie confessionalism, and his music was sweet and tough, never an easy combo to bring off. But like so many tough guys, he does get mawkish — only "Operator" adds insight as well as terse melody to our romantic mythology — and though his four albums do include a few good songs that didn't make it onto this fourteen-track compilation, they're enough like those that did that you can live without them. [Later on Lifesong.]   **B+**

David Crosby: *If I Could Only Remember My Name* (Atlantic '71). This disgraceful performance inspires the first Consumer Guide Competition. The test: Rename David Crosby (he won't know the difference). The prize: One Byrds LP of your choice (he ought to know the difference). The catch: You have to beat *my* entries. Which are: Rocky Muzak, Roger Crosby, Vaughan Monroe.   **D−**

Crosby, Stills, Nash & Young: *Deja Vu* (Atlantic '70). Of the five (or seven, I forget) memorable tunes here, N's "Our House" is a charming but cloying evocation of puppy domesticity, while both N's sanctimonious "Teach Your Children" and C's tragicomic "Almost Cut My Hair" document how the hippie movement has corrupted our young people. S half-scores twice and in-law M provides the climax. Which leaves Y's "Helpless" as the group's one unequivocal success

this time out. It's also Y's guitar — with help from S and hired hands T and R — that make the music work, not those blessed harmonies. And Y wasn't even supposed to be in on this. Original grade: B plus.   **B−**

Crosby, Stills, Nash & Young: *4-Way Street* (Atlantic '71). Was it only two years ago that the formation of Crosby, Stills & Nash brought gladness to the hearts of rock and rollers who remembered that they loved tight songs rather than endless jams and believed that an ex-Hollie's pop sense would temper Byrds/Springfield folk-rock? Who would have figured that none of them would remember that rock and roll is also supposed to be funky — and fast. And that the best stuff on their live album would be the jams, dominated by the new guy, who would also write their tightest songs? And for that matter that a singalong of dig-its and right-ons by the man who wrote "For What It's Worth" and a goody-goody song about Chicago by the ex-Hollie would sound like political high points?   **B−**

Crosby, Stills, Nash & Young: *So Far* (Atlantic '75). This group might benefit from a compilation that concentrated on guitar interactions and up-tempo throwaways. Needless to say, that's not the one we get.   **B−**

Crosby, Stills & Nash: *CSN* (Atlantic '77). Wait a second — wasn't this a quartet?   **D+**

Cross Country: *Cross Country* (Atco '73). Move over, Arthur, Hurley & Gottlieb — these guys make Crosby, Stills, Nash & Young sound like Crosby & Young. Key line: "I'm just a choir boy doing what I can."   **D**

Alvin Crow and the Pleasant Valley Boys: *Alvin Crow and the Pleasant Valley Boys* (Long Neck '76). We can't be sure what it was like to hear Bob Wills's records as they came out in the '30s and '40s, but no matter what your Texas friends tell you it was a lot more exciting than this. For starters, Wills was an inventor rather than a flamekeeper, and he got clearer sound — he worked for major labels, after all. Also, Wills released singles, which means that unlike Crow he had to put out one A side for every B. Still, three or four A sides out of ten isn't bad. Just wish they were all as modern as "Nyquil Blues," in which Crow praises analgesics, decongestants, and antihistamines — by name.   **B−**

Alvin Crow and the Pleasant Valley Boys: *High Riding* (Polydor '77). The cutting nasality of Crow's vocals is revivalism at its finest — he's not an original like Ray Benson, but he's got the style down. And as a swinging eclectic he borrows anything he likes, from the Cleftones to a dope-running epic to "Turkey, Texas (Home of Bob Wills)." Stop off in Turkey first. But if you like it there, put this on your Christmas list right after Asleep at the Wheel. Original grade: B.   **B+**

Crowbar: *Bad Manors* (Paramount '71). For classicists, these guys are certainly undiscriminating — they prefer critical exuberance to critical intellect, which may be why some critics go overboard for them. Jimmie Rodgers yodel meets slide-cum-pedal-steel meets pop chorale meets folk segues, and though the originals don't match the oldies, the oldies are "House of Blue Lights" and "Let the Four Winds Blow." Original grade: B plus.   **B**

Rodney Crowell: *Ain't Living Long Like This* (Warner Bros. '78). He's smart, he's soulful, he's got that tragic sense of life — yes, folks, Gram Parsons lives on in spirit, right down to Emmylou on harmony. If only the tempos were a little snappier, there might be more than four songs on side two, and chances are that anything extra would be as good as the rest. From "California Earthquake": "You're a partner of the devil and we ain't afraid of him/We'll build ourselves another town so you can tear it down again."   **A−**

The Crusaders: *The Best of the Crusaders* (ABC/Blue Thumb '76). "A group for all seasons *and* all tastes," annotator Don Heckman proclaims, and given "Chain Reaction" and "Soul Caravan" and most of side one — especially the irresistible "Put It Where You Want It" — I guess that includes me. I resent it, though. Better Wilton Felder honking his horn and Stix Hooper laying into that beat than Tom Scott and friend, but if this is El Lay's idea of the hard stuff may Booker T. preserve us. Their basic project is soulful Muzak, Muzak with charms to soothe the complacent humanist, and there are hundreds of harder hard bop and funkier funk albums. Try Lee Morgan's *Cornbread* or James Brown's *Sex Machine*.   **B**

Culture: *International Herb* (Virgin International '79). The tunes are so cute and uncomplicated and the lyrics so basic that it's almost as if the Chi-Lites, say, had decided to sing about herb and dread instead of love and marriage. Only you never heard Eugene Record wail the way Joseph Hill does a few times on side two — probably because Record never wept about slavery in public.   **A−**

Burton Cummings: *Burton Cummings* (Portrait '76). "Stand Tall" was a deserving hit that generated a great follow-up: "I'm Scared," the uncommitted prayer for faith of a skeptic who knows the religious tensions of a materialistic epoch firsthand. But when a slickie like Cummings turns rock crooner, credibility is a continuing problem, and while everything else on this honestly crafted solo debut is passable or better, the only other cut I'd call convincing is a big-band mock-up of former small-bandmate Randy Bachman.   **B**

Burton Cummings: *My Own Way To Rock* (Portrait '77). This transparent egoist has had a way with a song ever since the Guess Who days, but the hard rock moves always seem to bring out the sexism in him — a sexism especially repellent because it serves as an outlet not for forbidden class animosities but rather for the familiar old arrogance/self-hate. So it's gratifying that his way with a song should desert him this time. **C**

Dick Curless: *Live at the Wheeling Truck Drivers Jamboree* (Capitol '73). In which a rangy baritone with a patch over one eye regales thousands of truckers with their own mythology. Sociologists will note that his rebel persona embraces lots of sex and several blues. Skeptical waitresses will guess that his "Sixty Minute Man" starts counting at coffee and ends at bye. Skeptical rock and rollers will wonder about his vocal resonance and his sense of rhythm. And Americana fans will dig it. **B**

King Curtis and Champion Jack Dupree: *Blues at Montreux* (Atlantic '73). Because great stylists aren't always great improvisers, and because great accompanists are only occasionally great leaders, even the music Curtis intended for LP release was marred by a certain marginal-differentiation monotony (his posthumous concert albums are even worse). And though Dupree, as one of Europe's resident Real Blues Singers, makes it into all kinds of collectors' series, his recent recordings have been forgettable. This LP cancels out the dross — just when Dupree's call gets redundant, Curtis responds with his saxophone. Like most live dates it lacks compression, and Dupree is old enough for his voice to be changing again, but this is a pleasant surprise. Original grade: A minus. **B+**

Cymande: *Cymande* (Janus '72). What they call Nyah-rock is African with Jamaican influences — not straight reggae so much as Rastafarian, by which I mean that a lot of the songs seem designed to give off a tribal aura. The groove is slow but very seductive, and while the improvisations aren't exciting as such, they're very satisfying rhythmically. The borrowed folk chants are exciting as such. **B+**

Cymande: *Second Time Round* (Janus '73). When you hum this music you hum Steve Scipio's bass lines — not the vocals, and not the guitar parts of Scipio's cocomposer Patrick Patterson. Which says something for the abiding flexibility that always makes it comfortable to listen to. But also helps explain why it's rarely anything more. **B**

Daddy Cool: *Daddy Cool? Daddy Cool!* (Reprise '71). OK, boys, one more time. I love '50s rock and roll too. But imitating it isn't re-creating it — it's killing it. And if you don't watch it you're all going to end up hanging from basketball stanchions by hula hoops. **C−**

Roger Daltrey: *Daltrey* (Track '73). A good-looking lad with cinematic potential, but Peter Townshend chose him as the Who's front man partly because he doesn't have the personality or the smarts to assert himself as an interpreter. That goes even when another svengali — this one a collective comprising Dave Courtney, Adam Faith, and Leo Sayer — provides him with another frame. From anybody else, this would be one more dumb concept album (about the musician's lot, woe is me), and it still is. **C**

Charlie Daniels: *Honey in the Rock* (Kama Sutra '73). For a sideman-turned-sortastar, Daniels kicks out genuine jams and takes genuine chances — the raveup on "Revelations," for instance, would sound plumb weird on an Allmans LP. Not a bad songwriter, either. But hardly a remarkable one, and he's a lousy singer — only on "Uneasy Rider," a talking blues as dry as any of Dylan's and a lot more yarnlike, does his voice serve his vision, such as it is. [Later on Epic as *Uneasy Rider*.] **B−**
The Charlie Daniels Band: *Million Mile Reflections* (Epic '79). The ad-

venturous journeyman having long since turned into a professional reactionary, he here offers nine nominally new ways to kick shit down an Interstate divider. Including a hit single lifted from Stephen Vincent Benet, rock and roll heaven south of the Mason-Dixon line, passing criticism of the Ku Klux Klan, and a sentimental reminiscence of "Mississippi," a state the adventurous journeyman fled in an uproar back when he didn't ride so easy. **C**

Rick Danko: *Rick Danko* (Arista '77). A stronger album than I'd expect from the Band at this moment in history, Danko's solo debut includes a more sharply conceived city song than Robbie Robertson has ever come up with and a more sharply conceived coffee song than . . . well, the category is admittedly less extensive. Plus the classic "Small Town Talk," one of the decade's great love songs. Plus five of the decade's ordinary ones. **B**

Johnny Darrell: *California Stop-Over* (United Artists '70). In which the first man to record "Green Green Grass of Home" and "Son of Hickory Holler's Tramp" makes something of the literate modern-country approach typified by Mickey Newbury. Among his finds: two songs by Nico's favorite Orange County poet, Jackson Browne, and "Willing," which keeps on trucking. Unfortunately, Darrell sounds too sensitive to project the kind of dumb authority that puts corny puns like

"Bed of Roses" across, and the two songs from coproducer Larry Murray are irredeemable. But old folkie away from home Dick Rosmini is Murray's better half, and Clarence White picks real good. Original grade: A minus.   **B+**

Johnny Darrell: _Water Glass Full of Whiskey_ (Capricorn '75). The five years of obscurity since _California Stop-Over_ seem to have made him permanently lachrymose. When he tries to sound bright, he also sounds clumsy, as if he hasn't stretched that particular muscle in quite a while. Q: Can a tearjerker have a formal precision of its own? A: Nope, gets too soggy   **C+**

Betty Davis: _Betty Davis_ (Just Sunshine '73). Between her connections (wife of Miles, girlfriend of Jimi) and her concept (autonomous black woman forges metal funk), Betty's got a head start in the hype department. She makes up for these advantages, however, with a forced, narrow voice and a complete absence of riff sense or melodic gift. On the other hand, she — or producer-drummer Greg Errico of the Family Stone — does know a lot about rhythm. Upshot: most overstated comic-book sex since Angelfood McSpade.   **B−**

Blind John Davis: _Stomping on a Saturday Night_ (Alligator '77). In which a sixty-three-year-old professional celebrates the ties of boogie-woogie blues with more broad-based styles of entertainment music; he makes you wish the fat-assed purveyors of such styles were as aware as he is that the difference between refreshment and escape has to do with honesty.   **B+**

Jesse Davis: _Jesse Davis_ (Atco '71). Perfunctory funk from Taj Mahal's lead guitarist, not to be confused with the downhome executive, whose first name was Jefferson. Jesse's songs are forgettable, his cover versions flat, and despite an embarrassment of studio help (Eric, Leon, Merry, Gram, etc.)

the studio is where this should have stayed. Original grade: C plus.   **C−**

Mac Davis: _Greatest Hits_ (Columbia '79). Nashville's answer to Barry Manilow is a singer (and songwriter) so smarmy he can make bringing up a son sound as unclean as finding, feeling, fucking, and forgetting.   **D**

Miles Davis: _Bitches Brew_ (Columbia '70). If this historic set is about any one thing it's electric-meets-acoustic: the theme of the twenty-seven-minute title side, in which Miles's horn combines with an electric instrument for a two-note motif that's suddenly resolved after a dozen repetitions in a single echoed trumpet blat, says it all. But it's not about any one thing — it's a brilliant wash of ideas, so many ideas that it leaves an unfocused impression. That's probably why I don't return to it as I do to the quieter electric-meets-acoustic of _In a Silent Way_, although maybe it's just that this one rocks less — three different percussionists replace Tony Williams, whose steady pulse is put aside for subtle shades of Latin and funk polyrhythm that never gather the requisite fervor. Enormously suggestive, and never less than enjoyable, but not quite compelling. Which is what rock is supposed to be.   **A−**

Miles Davis: _Miles Davis at Fillmore_ (Columbia '70). And I thought _Bitches Brew_ was unfocused. Well, it was — and it was also pretty great. This is more unfocused, and not great. Comprising four (apparently unedited) twenty-five-minute swatches entitled "Wednesday Miles," "Thursday Miles," etc., it noodles unforgivably — the electric keyboards of Chick Corea and Keith Jarrett on Wednesday provide one of the most aimless patches. Every side does offer at least one treasure — the cool atmospherics that lead off Wednesday, the hard bop in extremis toward the end of Thursday, the way Miles blows sharply lyrical over Jack DeJohnette's rock march and Airto Moreira's jungle sci-fi for the last few minutes of Friday, all the activity surrounding Steve Grossman's solo on Saturday. Just wish the damn records were banded.   **B**

Miles Davis: *Jack Johnson* (Columbia '71). In which all the flash of *Bitches Brew* coalesces into one brilliant illumination. On "Right Off" (i.e., side one) John McLaughlin begins by varying a rock riff I'll bet Miles wrote for him over Michael Henderson's blues bass line and Billy Cobham's impressively rockish pulse and then goes on to cut the leader, who's not exactly laying back himself. "Yesternow" (side two) is mellower, mood music for a vacation on the moon. A great one.   **A+**

Miles Davis: *Live-Evil* (Columbia '71). "Inamorata" wanders when Gary Bartz isn't making Coltrane noises and ends up with a recitation in which music is equated with "masculinity," but the three other long pieces are usually fascinating and often exciting: "Sivad," which begins fast and funky, then slows down drastically, and finally revs up again; "Funky Tonk," Miles's most compelling rhythmic exploration to date; and the gospel-tinged "What I Say." The four short pieces are more like impressionistic experiments. Two of them, "Selim" and "Nem Um Talvez," hark back to the late '50s. Sound quite appropriate, too.   **A−**

Miles Davis: *On the Corner* (Columbia '72). Because the tracks are very short, because Miles plays more organ than trumpet and not much of that, and because the improvisations are rhythmic rather than melodic — often on a theme from "It's Your Thing" that I'm not swearing the Isleys (much less Davis) invented — most jazzbos have thrown up their hands at this one. Well, poo on jazzbos. But that's no reason for rockbos to sing hosanna to the highest — rhythmic improvisations are hardly the equivalent of a big beat and don't guarantee a good one. I'd like to hear "Black Satin" right now. But the rest I can wait for.   **B+**

Miles Davis: *Miles Davis in Concert* (Columbia '73). Although it takes a while to get into gear, this two-record set, "recorded live at Philharmonic Hall, New York" by an unidentified six- or seven-piece band, has more going for it rhythmically than *On the Corner*. On side three, the bass throbs like jungle drums, and except for occasional guitar introjections only Miles's trumpet and organ get to work on top of the pulse. Pretty narrow in function, I admit, but what do you want from urban voodoo?   **A−**

Miles Davis: *Big Fun* (Columbia '74). Four side-long "pieces" that serve as a sampler of Davis's pre-*On the Corner* early-'70s music, with Miles playing trumpet throughout (intermittently throughout) and such luminaries as Wayne Shorter and John McLaughlin doing a lot to define their respective segments. The sitar-and-tamboura interlude that untracks the gently loping "Great Expectations" about two-thirds of the way through is typical of the album's failures — the only side that doesn't wind down prematurely is "Lonely Fire," which after meandering at the beginning develops into lyrical mood music reminiscent in spirit and fundamental intent of *Sketches of Spain*. But for the most part this is uncommonly beautiful stuff, and it gets better.   **A−**

Miles Davis: *Get Up with It* (Columbia '74). Only two of the six "short" tracks — they total about an hour — are more than good background: "Maiyisha," which recalled his most lyrical early-'60s stuff, and "Honky Tonk," a snazzy blues. Even the rocking "Red China Blues" is marred by a Wade Marcus horn chart, and "Rated X" is an experiment in organ noise that's not so great in the background either. But the two long ones — they total over an hour — are brilliant: "He Loved Him Madly," a tribute to Duke Ellington as elegant African internationalist, and "Calypso Frelimo," a Caribbean dance broken into sections that seem to follow with preordained emotional logic. Not nec-

essarily music to fill the mind — just the room. Original grade: B plus. **A—**
Miles Davis: *Water Babies* (Columbia '78). Double whammy. Not only isn't this new Miles, as people were quick to figure out despite the pseudo-streetwise *On the Corner*-style cover, but it isn't quite vintage Miles, either. Recorded in the late '60s, these were outtakes, and one of them — "Dual Mr. Tillman Anthony," a thirteen-minute piano ostinato showcase without even the justification of a heavy funk beat — should definitely have remained one. The rest is better, but I thank CBS's marketing whizzes for sending me back to Davis's great work with the same group — like *Sorcerer* and *Nefertiti*, both still in catalogue. **B+**
Miles Davis: *Agharta* (Columbia '76). This is the most commonly disparaged of Davis's many '70s double-LPs — it's said that Davis was so unhappy with his own playing that he abandoned the release to Teo Macero halfway through. But Miles isn't the hero here — he gives the album to the band, whose virtuosity is the ground of four apparently unstructured segments. Mtume, Reggie Lucas, and especially Michael Henderson provide the variable pulse, with drummer Al Foster moving from body to spirit rhythms in an effortless, guileless show of chops. Sonny Fortune triples on alto, soprano, and flute in the best reed playing on a Davis record in this decade. And guitarist Pete Cosey is simply astonishing — the noises he produces for the second half of side one comprise some of the greatest free improvisations ever heard in a "jazz"-"rock" context. Angry, dissociated, funky, and the best Davis music since *Jack Johnson*. **A**
Miles Davis: *Circle in the Round* (Columbia '79). Miles tastes better out of the can than fresh watermelon or even V.S.O.P., but these tapes, mostly from when he was working out his '70s concepts a decade or so ago, are damaged goods. Oddity: David Crosby's "Guinnevere," itself based on a three-note motif from *Sketches of Spain*. **B+**

Paul Davis: *Singer of Songs — Teller of Tales* (Bang '78). Local labels surely do a worthy work in this era of conglomerate rock. If it weren't for Atlanta-based Bang, Atlanta-based Davis might never have discovered that there's a modestly profitable audience for humorless singer-songwriters all across this land of ours. **D+**

Tyrone Davis: *Tyrone Davis' Greatest Hits* (Dakar '72). I'd be less inclined to quibble about this sixteen-song selection if the three-plus years it spans were long enough for one small factory to come up with sixteen go-rillas in a medium tempo, which is the only one Davis knows. But though there's classic stuff here, only Davis's gamely anachronistic soul style — blues crooning with touches of grit, like a less sharply defined Bobby Bland or a softer Little Milton — provides interest most of the time. And too often Willie Henderson's horns (not to mention his strings) make you yawn anyway. **B**

Cory Daye: *Cory and Me* (New York International '79). This doesn't reach like Dr. Buzzard, but it's an impressive showcase for Daye, who proves herself a much more engaging — not to mention hip — all-purpose songstress than Natalie Cole and her ilk. Sandy Linzer's material is coarser commercially than August Darnell's — the disco furbishing tackier, the nostalgia more automatic — but it fleshes out a persona that's sexy and even a little wasted without trafficking in escapist hedonism or porny impersonality. And the music really romps. **A—**

Dead Boys: *Young Loud and Snotty* (Sire '77). Despite Stiv Bators's mewl, which can get almost as annoying as Geddy Lee's falsetto, this is mostly well-crafted junk, tough and tuneful and in one case — the definitively deafening "Sonic Reducer" —

positively anthemic. But the charm of good junk has always been its innocence, and if these fellows are innocent they're pretty perverse about it —emotional incompetents out of their depth. Alternate title (stolen from Mary Harron): *Take My Life — Please*. Original grade: B minus. **B**

The Dead Boys: *We Have Come for Your Children* (Sire '78). Because they're lovable little scumbags deep down, and sincere to boot, Hilly's punk purists have dropped the heavy misogyny and recorded five cuts that laid end to end would make a listenable side. But not even the rousing "3rd Generation Nation" has the power of sexist spew like "I Need Lunch" and "Caught with the Meat in Your Mouth." Makes you wonder what 3rd generation nihilists believe deep down. **B—**

The Deadly Nightshade: *The Deadly Nightshade* (Phantom '75). Since the three women who comprise this group are avowed feminists in a time of blatant reaction, I found it hard to admit to myself how much I hated them at first. I hate them. Their music is squeaky-clean folk-rock, their humor the smug folkie sarcasm that seems to have its roots in junior high school talent shows. And they show about as much insight into the hard-earned truisms they exploit as Letty Cottin Pogrebin, author of *Getting Yours: How to Make the System Work for the Working Woman*. **C—**

Kiki Dee: *Lovin' and Free* (Rocket '74). Maybe Elton kicked off his label with this signing because he sounds demented by comparison — I mean, the excitement on this album is provided by a Jackson Browne song. Nice and even promising, but so wholesome she'll take some getting used to. **C+**

Deep Purple: *Machine Head* (Warner Bros. '72). "Smoke on the Water" is about a big fire in Montreux, obviously the most exciting thing to happen to these fellows since the London Symphony Orchestra. No jokes about who's getting burned, though — I approve of their speeding, and Ritchie Blackmore has copped some self-discipline as well as a few suspicious-sounding licks from his buddies in London. Personal to Paul Kantner: Check out "Space Truckin'." **B**

Deep Purple: *Burn* (Warner Bros. '74). The hot poop is that after ten albums the Purps have a lead singer with soulish roots who can actually write songs. The cold turd is that the music sounds the same, as ominous and Yurrupean as a vampire movie, only not as campy. **C+**

Delaney & Bonnie & Friends with Eric Clapton: *On Tour* (Atco '70). Delaney & Bonnie are what would happen to rock and roll if it were capable of growing up — maybe they're what would happen to this country if it were capable of growing up. Whites so down-home their soul inflections sound inbred, they sing of love like teens of yore, but even though their love is quite physical it's been weathered spiritually and morally. No wonder Eric Clapton found their youthful fun and mature equanimity an antidote to the formless pretensions of Cream and Blind Faith. He certainly contributes — whenever the voices don't quite carry the one-take live performances, there he is with a terse, punchy solo that adds just the right note of strength and understanding. Nice that he's got Dave Mason (and Delaney himself) to help out. And nice that they all pay their respects to Robert Johnson and Little Richard. Original grade: A. **A—**

Delaney & Bonnie & Friends: *To Bonnie from Delaney* (Atco '70). The all-their-records-sound-the-same put-downs can only mean no one is really listening. D&B's singing has always been subtler than its framework, and their framework has never been more understated than here, though a couple of mediocre songs and too many sustained-climax gimmicks do put a crimp in. Delaney sounds best when reminding us that he owes more to John Hurt than to Otis Redding, while Bonnie peaks with new humor ("Mama, He Treats Your Daughter Mean") and passion ("The Love of My Man"). **A−**

Delaney & Bonnie & Friends: *Motel Shot* (Atco '71). D&B's best since their Elektra debut in 1969 isn't what you'd call a grabber — comprising two acoustic jams of the sort that take place in motels and dressing rooms, it fulfills their most homespun-away-from-home ambitions. But though I suppose I'd prefer it if they hadn't recorded a few of the selections before, the country blues side is a seamless delight, the most unflawed listening music I've heard in a long while. And though I sometimes find the spirit-screeching on the gospel side a little painful, it sure sounds, like they say, authentic. **A**

Delaney & Bonnie: *The Best of Delaney & Bonnie* (Atco '72). Through white soul and Clapton rock and acoustic intimacy, their connubial celebration has had a steadfast sound, which means that this compilation — including cuts from the Elektra LP and put together with obvious t.l.c. —is their strongest disc. If a modicum of old marrieds is all you can take, it can displace all their albums except *Motel Shot*. And keep those divorce rumors to yourself. **A**

The Dells: *The Dells* (Cadet '73). Vocal groupies and Chicago soul loyalists believe Don Davis has revitalized the old-timers on this album and its predecessor, *Give Your Baby a Standing Ovation*. I suppose he has. But the Dells are quintessential journeymen, and when Davis made quasi-neo-Temptations out of the Dramatics he wrote the songs himself. **B−**

Dells: *New Beginnings* (ABC '78). Hard to get too interested in virtuoso harmonies expended on mediocre material, and like most vocal-group LPs, this is slow going at times. But it ends up quite impressive. Instead of resigning themselves to the oldies circuit —

four of the five Dells have been together for twenty-five years, so they sure qualify — they've sought out new songs from a variety of sources, including two George Clinton-produced Parliaments classics. Wish they didn't figure it was modern to put only four on a side, though. **B**

Sandy Denny: *Like an Old Fashioned Waltz* (Island '74). Five years ago, Denny sang lead with the progenitors of English folk-rock, Fairport Convention. Soon, however, she left-to-pursue-her-own-career. The group remained interesting enough to hold a following, but never broke through artistically or commercially, and although credible observers believed Denny had the stuff to become one of the finest women singers in the world, she didn't. One four-minute masterpiece on this otherwise sluggish album —the opening cut, written by Denny, called "Solo" — deals obliquely with these losses. Now one hears that Fairport and Denny are regrouping. And so are Steppenwolf and John Kay. **C+**

John Denver: *Poems, Prayers and Promises* (RCA Victor '71). Denver is everything an acoustic singer-songwriter might be — pretty, vapid, and commercial. "Take Me Home, Country Roads" is a genuine pop archetype, and as an inhabitant of the temperate regions of earth I find that sunshine on my shoulder makes me happy, too. But usually his voice and his songs are tepid rather than temperate, as is the mid-'60s folk sensibility and stringless/hornless instrumentation. There's more originality and spirit in Tom Jones — maybe even Engelbert Humperdinck. If James is a wimp, John is a simp, and that's even worse. **C**

John Denver: *John Denver's Greatest Hits* (RCA Victor '73). I still don't like Denver, who purveys privacy in hockey rinks and who never wonders how we are to "maintain our society" by contact with wilderness without destroying said wilderness. But except for the odious "Follow Me"—so that's why he loves his Annie so much—I find this stuff inoffensive when it's not likable. Twice it's brilliant: "Leaving, on a Jet Plane" and "Goodbye Again" are the essence of domesticus interruptus. Not that he's as talented as many of his supposed rivals. But he aims lower. **B−**

John Denver: *Windsong* (RCA Victor '75). Why haven't all those textual analysts who figured out that Paul was dead and Dylan a junkie applied themselves to the song sequence "Two Shots," "I'm Sorry," and "Fly Away," a mini-triptych that proves (rilly) that John and Annie are on the rocks!! Too morbid a thought, I bet. Upgraded for documentary interest. **C−**

John Denver: *John Denver's Greatest Hits Volume 2* (RCA Victor '77). My God, he was right about cities after all—urban blights like television and Ticketron have turned this innocent folkie into the blandest pop singer in history. Only "Annie's Song" packs any of the old simple-minded charm, and four of these ten songs are devoid of any interest whatsoever—his folksy lies about country boys and feather beds are at least upbeat by comparison. **D+**

Derek and the Dominoes: *Layla* (Atco '70). What looks at first like a slapdash studio double is in fact Eric Clapton's most carefully conceived recording. Not only did he hire Duane Allman for overdubs after basic tracks were done, but he insisted that Duane come up with just the thick, sliding phrase he (Eric) wanted before calling it a take. The resulting counterpoint is the true expression of Clapton's genius, which has always been synthetic rather than innovative, steeped in blues anti-utopianism. With Carl Radle and Jim Gordon at bottom, this album has plenty of relaxed shuffle and simple rock and roll, and Clapton's singing is generally warm rather than hot. But his meaning is realized at those searing peaks when a pained sense of limits — why does love have to be so sad, I got

the bell-bottom blues, *Lay-la* — is posed against the good times in an explosive compression of form. Original grade: A. **A+**

Derek & the Dominoes: *In Concert* (RSO '73). In a way, the absence of Duane Allman from this set is a blessing. Instead of striving fruitlessly to match the high-tension interweave of the studio versions, D&D function as the Eric Clapton Band, rolling easy the way they learned to with Delaney & Bonnie. Clapton's vocals are rough and winning, and he gets to deliver his warm, clear, rapid runs of notes and slurs, well, how to say it — in concert rather than in competition (with Duane, with Jack and Ginger, with himself). Even "Bottle of Red Wine" and "Blues Power" make sense onstage. Warning: the drum solo is on side two. **A−**

Jackie DeShannon: *To Be Free* (Imperial '70). This being 1970, DeShannon makes like the minor pop aristocrat she is with vague stabs at meaningfulness — in addition to a thickheaded "Bird on the Wire" and a cute peaceable-kingdom double-fold, there are lots of songs about her minor, aristocratic life. "What Was Your Day Like" is a sweet, factual, painfully ambiguous account of geographically unrequited love that would put me on the next plane—too late, probably. All I get from the rest is that she's been spending a lot of time in Europe. **C**

Jackie DeShannon: *Jackie* (Atlantic '72). About once a year, Jerry Wexler tries to bring a fundamentally soulful white female pop singer up to the minute. Sometimes it works (*Dusty in Memphis,* the all-time rock-era torch record), sometimes it doesn't (Cher, Lulu). This one almost works, not because DeShannon is such a terrific singer — although she's a lot more terrific with Wexler and friends pushing her from the bottom — but because for the first time in a while she's written a few terrific songs. Nothing wrong with her up-to-the-minute country-soul covers of Van Morrison, Neil Young, and their lessers, and nothing just right either. When she launches into her own "Vanilla 'Olay" or "Anna Karina," though, she sounds like time is on her side. Original grade: B plus. **B**

Jackie DeShannon: *New Arrangement* (Columbia '75). As an American songwriter who has escaped the confessional mode, and as a woman who can sing about subjects other than men, DeShannon exemplifies several healthy trends. The main thing this well-made record reveals, however, is an intelligent professionalism that matters about as much as a surge in enrollment in creative writing classes or women's liberation for female executives. **B−**

Detroit: *Detroit* (Paramount '71). Despite the old strain and stridency, the way Mitch Ryder swells with an infusion of the Host upon contact with a Wilson Pickett song is more welcome than ever. So is former Detroit Wheel Johnny Bee—these days any drummer who can play rock and roll without turning into some machine is a precious resource. And whoever told Mitch to put Ron Davies's "It Ain't Easy," Chuck Berry's "Let It Rock," and the Velvet Underground's "Rock 'n Roll" on the same album wins a James Taylor dartboard. Original grade: A minus. **B+**

Detroit Emeralds: *Do Me Right* (Westbound '71). The title tune is pure dance groove, quite distinctive; I'd compare it to a locomotive, only it's smoother, maybe a diesel. The other good stuff is less distinctive; after the "you make me wanna moan" bit I would have sworn my man Al had indulged in a little label-jumping, but the real culprit is probably coproducer W. Mitchell. **B**

Detroit Emeralds: *You Want It, You Got It* (Westbound '72). This record, which seems ordinary enough until you hear it standing up, breaks a lot of rules. The Emeralds are stay-at-home Spinners, and Abrim Tilmon, who

writes (and helps sing) their material and is credited with coarranging an album that lists no producer or personnel, is Thom Bell without an instinct for the killer hook. But side two proves that it doesn't take road dues or a surefire sales catch to make seamless, soulful dance music — I've got to move, indeed. And except for something silly about the lure of the sea, side one won't turn anybody off either. **B+**

Detroit Emeralds: *I'm in Love with You* (Westbound '73). You probably wouldn't play this one again except for "Whatcha Gonna Wear Tomorrow," but you do, and it grows on you, and you hum it sometimes, so you play it some more, and then you get tired of it and put it away and don't expect you'll ever play it again. **B**

Detroit Emeralds: *Feel the Need* (Westbound '77). If the first version of the early disco classic this album is named after, then entitled "Feel the Need in Me," moved like a crack diesel, quickening one whole side of what would have been a pretty good LP in any case, then the remade track moves more like a monorail. And while in the end I don't appreciate the streamlining (especially since the B side is quite extraneous) it still sounds pretty good. Original grade: B. **B−**

Detroit Jr.: *Chicago Urban Blues* (Antilles '77). Jr. languished in a byway of my shelves for over a year, which is the way it is with laid-back piano blues—hard to tell one record from another without trying. This broke through—insinuating, witty midnight music with loving respect for the verities, a flawless exposition of the conventions of the form. **B+**

Devo: *Q: Are We Not Men? A: We Are Devo!* (Warner Bros. '78). If this isn't Kiss for college kids, then it's Meat Loaf for college kids who are too sophisticated to like Meat Loaf. Aside from music per se, the Kiss connection is in their cartoonishness — Devo's robot moves create distance, a margin of safety, the way Kiss's makeup does. But the Meat Loaf connection is deeper, because this is real midnight-movie stuff — the antihumanist sci-fi silliness, the reveling in decay, the thrill of being in a cult that could attract millions and still seem like a cult, since 200 million others will never even get curious. (It's no surprise to be told that a lot of their ideas come from *Eraserhead,* but who wants to go see *Eraserhead* to make sure?) What makes this group worthy of attention at all — and now we're back with Kiss, though at a more complex level — is the catchy, comical, herky-jerky rock and roll they've devised out of the same old basic materials. In small doses it's as good as novelty music ever gets, and there isn't a really bad cut on this album. But it leads nowhere. **B+**

Devo: *Duty Now for the Future* (Warner Bros. '79). Side one, with its not-funny-enough instrumentals and evasive satire, was dire enough to make me suspect they'd made their arena-rock move before there was an arena in the world that would have them. But "The Day My Baby Gave Me a Surprize" and "Secret Agent Man" are as bright as anything on the debut, and the arrangements offer their share of surprizes. **B−**

Neil Diamond: *Hot August Night* (MCA '72). From the first guitar riff of this profit-taking double live showcase, it's obvious that the man is some sort of genius rock entertainer, but for the most part the great entertainer is striving for bad art and not even achieving it. The humor here is almost as sententious as the phony canta libre and the country-western parodies might get a poorer, drunker man lynched. **D+**

Neil Diamond: *Beautiful Noise* (Columbia '76). This is a monstrous record. The "rock" star who broke the Broadway barrier seems to be thinking Big Musical, in the urban sentimental mode (complete with Evil, of course) that does such small justice to

the challenge of New York. Although fellow urban sentimentalist Robbie Robertson can achieve an awesome (almost fulsome) fullness with rock instrumentation, his production is basically pop program music. Yet somewhere in my cockles I found Diamond hooking me as I listened for the last time and I had to admit that it takes a special kind of chutzpah to create a monster. **C+**

Manu Dibango: *Soul Makossa* (Atlantic '72). Melodically, Dibango's no improvisor, but the sharp cry of soprano sax against Afro-rhythms grabs ears and ass a lot quicker than the choral moves of Cymande or Osibisa. May help that these Afro-rhythmists still reside in Africa — bassist Long Manfred sounds as if he learned his stuff off literal airwaves, from the master drummer in the next village. **A−**

Manu Dibango: *Makossa Man* (Atlantic '74). Hate to say this, but what makes Dibango's African dances so much catchier than those of the competition is that he's from a French part of the continent, which means he relates to the Caribbean — all of it — rather than to rock. Let's face it, rock's catchiest beats have always come from the Caribbean. Not that catchiest is the only superlative I care about. **B+**

Manu Dibango: *Afrovision* (Island '78). Despite the title — or maybe it's what the title means — this is the most internationalist of Dibango's three U.S.-release albums, and its light funk does sound suspiciously fusionoid at first. But the cross-rhythms take over every time, so that even the jungle atmospherics of the title track breathe with a natural life far removed from the commercial exoticism toward which it may well aspire. **B+**

The Dickies: *The Incredible Shrinking Dickies* (A&M '79). You've heard of punk? Well, this is twit. **C**

The Dictators: *Go Girl Crazy!* (Epic '76). If you love the Dolls you'll like the Dictators. Maybe. New York smart-asses who have fastened on circa-1965 California teendom at its dumbest, they play punks rather than embodying punkdom, with a predictable loss of tone. But the production is three chords of pure power and the jokes are often good ones. Anyone who can make a sobersides like me laugh at a song called "Back to Africa" can't be entirely devoid of subtlety, and I love this bit of Inspirational Verse: "We knocked 'em dead in Dallas/We didn't pay our dues/We knocked 'em dead in Dallas/ They didn't know we were Jews." Original grade: B. **B+**

The Dictators: *Manifest Destiny* (Asylum '77). Their offensiveness is typified quite nicely by their name and the name of their album—anyone smart enough to fool around with such terminology ought to be decent enough not to. Their excuse is that their gallumphing beat, their ripped-off hooks, and their burlesqued melodrama are funnier than ever, and I admit that after dozens of playings I like this almost as much as I did their first. But I liked their first instantly, which is the way dumb jokes should work, and anyway, no one has answered my big question: do they play their own instruments? **B**

The Dictators: *Bloodbrothers* (Asylum '78). Because they're nice Jewish boys deep down, and sincere to boot, they offer good-humored satiric putdowns of kinky sex and teenage alienation, encouragement for R. Meltzer, and a patriotic anthem that might be scary if they were capable of sustaining the mood without cracking up. All of which is grounded, unfortunately, not in the great common store of stoopidrock readymades but in the grade-C Blue Oyster Cult moves that their gradual accumulation of instrumental competence has earned them. **B−**

Bo Diddley: *Where It All Began* (Chess '72). How bad can a Bo Diddley record be? A lot worse than this. It might have horns, or feature his versions of the latest hits, only Bo and his

producers (Pete Welding and Johnny Otis) know better than that. On the other hand, how good can a Bo Diddley record be? Unlike Chuck Berry, who must also transcend a certain musical homogeneity, Bo hasn't written a whole songbook of great lyrics, and anyway, his homogeneity is a lot more homogeneous than Chuck's. **C+**

Bo Diddley: *The London Bo Diddley Sessions* (Chess '73). This is the one the company will push, and it's his worst — give or take a joke or two, pro forma throughout. Hint: Bo's best-of is called *Got My Own Band of Tricks*. **D+**

Dion: *Sanctuary* (Reprise '71). Armed with an acoustic guitar and a wire-rimmed smile, Dion has been projecting the aura of the quintessential Bronx rocker ever since reviving his career in clubs three years ago. On this LP he applies his sweet, sliding, blues-based style to both quintessential Bronx rockers and acoustic-guitar specialties, though his good-humored stage patter seems coyer every time it repeats. Still wish he (or Warners) would put "Your Own Back Yard," his song about him and heroin, on an album. And forget "Abraham, Martin, and John." Original grade: B plus. **B−**

Dion and the Belmonts: *Reunion* (Warner Bros. '72). Most rock and roll revivals are vitiated by the suave rhythms of the singers, but not this one — probably because Dion's adult music is folk blues rather than lounge pop. Most rock and roll revivals are vitiated by sheer failure of spirit, but not this one—probably because Dion did it for fun rather than to refurbish a sagging career. **B+**

Dion and the Belmonts: See also the Belmonts

Dire Straits: *Dire Straits* (Warner Bros. '78). Despite initial misgivings, I've found this thoughtful and sexy. The decisive touch is how Mark Knopfler counterpoints his own vocals on guitar—only a musician with a real structural knack could sound like two people that way. But there's a streak of philistine ideology here that speaks for too many white r&b players these days — most of them can't be bothered articulating it, that's all. In "In the Gallery," an honest sculptor has his bareback rider, coal miner, and skating ballerina rejected by the "trendy boys," "phonies," and "fakes" who (literally) conspire together and "decide who gets the breaks." Those who find this rather simplistic should now ask themselves whether Knopfler's beloved Sultans of Swing — not to mention Dire Straits — have more in common with that sculptor than he suspects. Original grade: B plus. **B**

Dire Straits: Communique (Warner Bros. '79). Boy, people are getting bored with these guys *fast*—if they don't watch out they're gonna last about as long as Looking Glass or the Lemon Pipers. Just another case of "substance" as novelty, I guess — doesn't sound bad, but they'd better up those beats-per-minute. **B−**

Disco Party (Marlin '78). A Miami-goes-disco compilation, and why not — those Sunshine Band rhythms are a source of the style. And when a pure disco act like Eli's Second Coming fits right in with the best of George McCrae, Peter Brown, and K. C. himself, you think it may all be worth it. Though when Betty Wright wastes herself on a Gloria Gaynor imitation you wonder. **B+**

Disco-Trek (Atlantic '76). You can't deny that disco gets more music out there. If it weren't for this remixed collection of eight mostly rare "disco hits" I might never have heard Sister Sledge's "Mama Never Told Me" or the Valentinos' "I Can Understand It." And since the music isn't brand new, its tone is more soulish than is the current norm, making this a more attractive sampler than any of Motown's *Disco-Tech* collections. I'm not always crazy about its hyped-up, spliced-in feel and instrumental riff-raff, but I have to admit that they actually improve Jackie Moore's "Time," so who knows. Social note: Boers overrunning South Africa were history's most prominent trekkers. How about retitling this *Disco Tracks?* **B**

Willie Dixon: *I Am the Blues* (Columbia '70). Dixon is the first important blues composer since the classic era who isn't also an important singer. Between songwriting royalties and production income, he doesn't have to perform much — which may be why his records are so undistinguished. It's not that Dixon doesn't have a "good voice" — is it ever? But he's never developed its expressive potential. The material is classic, and the backing by an anonymous "hand-picked crew of Chicago blues veterans" adds personality (is that Otis Spann?), but this document is for collectors only. **B**

Willie Dixon: *Catalyst* (Ovation '73). Showcasing his greatest songs in front of a crack all-star band, Dixon is an adequate performer. On this album, he showcases his latest songs in front of a hack all-pro band. **C+**

Dr. Buzzard's Original Savannah Band: *Dr. Buzzard's Original Savannah Band* (RCA Victor '76). I hated this the first time I played it, which turned out to mean that I had encountered a clear, uncompromising and dangerously seductive expression of a vision of life that was foreign to me. Call it disco-sophistico: a version of post-camp nostalgia that celebrates the warmth (OK) and class (ugh) of a time irretrievably (and safely) past. Since they're not white, the Savannah Band never make you feel they love the '40s because there were no uppity muggers back then, though I still wonder about their get-thee-behind-me dismissal of hard r&b, not to mention their fashion-mag potential. But it's a pleasure to admit that their music is a fresh pop hybrid with its own rhythmic integrity, and that its sophistication is a lot brighter and more lively than most of the organic bullshit making it to the rock stage in the mid-'70s. Original grade: B plus.   **A**

Dr. Buzzard's Original Savannah Band: *Dr. Buzzard's Original Savannah Band Meets King Penett* (RCA Victor '78). A brilliant dud. The lyrics read like Ishmael Reed — soft Ishmael Reed — but for all its skillful synthesis the music just doesn't kick in. Of course, that's what I once thought about their debut. People danced to that one, though.   **B**

Dr. Buzzard's Original Savannah Band: *James Monroe H.S. Presents Dr. Buzzard's Original Savannah Band Goes to Washington* (Elektra '79). Acclimated after three and a half years, I find the music easy to love even though it's more exotic than ever — immersed in the Latin accents of '40s (and '50s) dance music, blissfully indifferent to current disco formulas. And for all the charm of Cory Daye's solo bid with Sandy Linzer, her wit and grace — that is, her chance to be remembered as the finest female vocalist to emerge in the '70s — is showcased more precisely by August Darnell's words and Stony Browder's music. I only wish I knew what the lyrics meant sometimes (especially that one about the neo-nazi). A little clarity, rather than the indulgently atmospheric Hollywood romanticism Darnell strives for, might make up for the absence of floor hits.   **A−**

Dr. Feelgood: *Malpractice* (Columbia ·'76). As with so much pub-rock, this never quite gets out of the pub. The funk quotient of bands like this one is invaluable, and their U.S. bid does offer several memorable originals ("Another Man" and "Don't Let Your Daddy Know") and worthy remakes ("I Can Tell" and "Riot in Cell Block #9"). But then there's all the OK stuff — side two is a B side indeed, if not C plus. And I can't help wondering whether a debut album that sounds like a stylized *J. Geils Band* doesn't portend death by secondhand mechanization. Original grade: B plus.   **B**

Dr. Hook: *Bankrupt* (Capitol '75). It must mean something that the only new rock record I've really enjoyed recently is a joke, but maybe it's only that their sense of humor is improving. Any band that can dress up in glitter and get booed off the stage as its own opening act is obviously delving aesthetic possibilities unknown to ordinary rock and roll hustlers. Which are here represented by the pillheads diptych, "Wups" and "Do Downs," and the dance song, "Levitate": "I want you to raise your right foot. . . Awright, now raise your left foot. . . No no no no no, don't put your right foot back down."   **B+**

Dr. Hook: *Revisited* (Columbia '76). Although his rock and roll number with this band was often forced and unfunny, you have to admire Shel Silverstein's eye for detail and ear for diction, his willingness to go for the aorta, and his did-he-mean-that? humor. This compilation includes "Cover of the Rolling Stone," still an acute account of the superstar half-life, and "Carry Me, Carrie," based on a text by Theodore Dreiser, as well as several salubriously blasé references to the dread scourge homosexuality. Docked a notch for "Penicillin Penny," who after all got *her* dose from someone with a penis.   **B−**

Dr. Hook: *Pleasure and Pain* (Capitol '78). A roguish willingness to stoop to any piece of hitbound schlock has always been part of this band's charm. But that doesn't make an album of schlock charming.   **C**

Dr. John, the Night Tripper: *Remedies* (Atco '70). Although the 17:33-minute "Angola" isn't as onerous as those oppressed by the subject of slave labor claim, I don't expect to play it again myself. But side one is addictive. "Loop Garoo" and "Mardi Gras" and the semisubliminal "dixieland" horns on "What Goes Around Comes Around" say more about this pale-faced weirdo's New Orleans roots and connections than all his gris-gris. And "Wash, Mama, Wash" is a pioneering exploration of the sexual politics of rock and roll. Needless to say, it's also very dirty.   **B+**

Dr. John, the Night Tripper: *The Sun Moon and Herbs* (Atco '71). I've never trusted his recipe for voodoo jive. So I'm not surprised that the only tasty song on this recorded-in-London supersession is about gumbo.   **C+**

Dr. John: *Gumbo* (Atco '72). Given Mac Rebennack's limitations as a songwriter, this selection of tunes that made Bourbon Street jump in the '50s is an ideal showcase for his studio-expert piano and sly, whining, raceless vocal affectations. It has its antiquarian aspect, but if Huey Smith or Allen Toussaint capture more of the spirit of New Orleans they don't do it on any album you can buy in a store. I mean, where else can you hear "Iko Iko," "Blow Wind Blow," "Big Chief," "Mess Around," and "Let the Good Times Roll" without pushing reject?   **A−**

Dr. John: *Right Place, Wrong Time* (Atco '73). A meaningful title. Fifteen years ago, sweet-and-dirty New Orleans jive conveyed the same wry rebelliousness that Dr. John's nighttripping hoodoo did ten years later. These days he's purveying fifteen-year-old New Orleans jive himself, last time with his own band and classic songs, this time with a classic band — the Meters — and his own songs. Last time worked better, but producer Allen Toussaint, whose "Life" sounds terrific b/w Dr. John's own rakish "Such a Night," gets this one over.   **B+**

Dr. John: *Desitively Bonnaroo* (Atco '74). Dr. John does enunciate more piquantly than Frankie Miller or King Biscuit Boy, but this is basically another chance for Allen Toussaint to meet up with a white blues singer and groove all the way to the bank. Not that that's bad — these days it's my favorite subgenre, and this may be the best of them all. Despite the absence of a standout song ("Mos' Scocious" is a great readymade) it's more fun than *Right Place, Wrong Time*. But it does lean toward the music-is-the-answer fallacy. Toussaint shouldn't write songs putting down those who fill their lives "with money matters" — he's too wealthy. And Dr. John shouldn't sing them — he's too hip. Original grade: B.   **B+**

Dr. John: *Hollywood Be Thy Name* (United Artists '75). In which M. Rebennack's gris-gris jive is revealed unmistakably for the schlock it's always been. Granted, it was often very good schlock, but not on this record — with its in-jokes, its cronyism, its sloppy copies, its fuzzy simulated-club sound. Nadir: the 253rd recorded version of "Yesterday."   **C−**

Dr. John: *Tango Palace* (Horizon '79). "Keep That Music Simple" is the good dr.'s prescription for cracking "the big Top 10." It was released as a single. It stiffed.   **C+**

Swamp Dogg: *Rat On!* (Elektra '71). Soul-seekers like myself are moderately mad for the obscure *Total Destruction to Your Mind*, which Mr. Dogg, formerly Atlantic producer Jerry Williams, put out on the obscure Canyon label a couple of years ago — strange, powerful, creaky voice, stranger sensibility, demented music. But the dementia on this moderately mad sequel seems laid on for appearance's sake. I'll be seeking on.   **B−**

Swamp Dogg: *Gag a Maggott* (Stone Dogg '73). Thematically, this seems to be a fairly conventional soul LP — great cover of "In the Midnight Hour" and lots of love and money in the lyrics. Granted, "Wife Sitter" is as nasty as Jody songs get, mostly because Dogg plays the cuckold-making Jody with such relish. And to call your sweetest love song "I Couldn't Pay for What I Got Last Night" is to combine the two themes more intimately than most soul men consider necessary. Nor do most soul men drive so hard — Ivan Olander's drums, Little Beaver's guitar, even the horns of the Swamp Dogg Band maintain a fierce momentum that's not conventional at all. **A−**

Swamp Dogg: *Have You Heard This Story??* (Island '75). More or less totally destructive. The one-sided concept is hypochondria — what's the last soul album to use the word "hyperventilation"? Side two leads off with the singer catching his wife in bed with another woman. By the way, I've finally figured out what his voice sounds like — an Afro-American air raid siren.   **B+**

Ned Doheny: *Ned Doheny* (Asylum '73). I don't know whether this pretty-boy singer-songwriter is a scion of the family that gave its name to the street in Beverly Hills or just thought it would be cute to call himself that. In either case it's how he got his contract.   **C**

Donovan: *Cosmic Wheels* (Epic '73). Yellow Jell-O, or: didn't you always know he'd go bananas?   **C−**

Donovan: *Slow Down World* (Epic '76). If I read my copy of *Clive* correctly, the eternally youthful Leitch received $250,000 for this LP, on which he (forthrightly) refers to himself as a "well known has-been" and (slowly) thinks up reasons why the planet should adjust to his mental reflexes, thusly: "Slow Down World — take a break for God's sake." Saith Clive: "If he's willing to make a few commercial concessions, any album of his could be a major reentry." So I guess these ain't those.   **C−**

The Doobie Brothers: *Toulouse Street* (Warner Bros. '72). The main difference between these guys and the lowest AM schlock-rock — Daniel Boone, say, or even the Grass Roots — is flashier instrumentals (a real plus) and a company that knows the value of the graven image. Nice cover, really. But the vocals and original songs (including the hit) are truly doobieous.   **C**

The Doobie Brothers: *What Were Once Vices Are Now Habits* (Reprise '74). The quotation originated with Seneca and is very impressive, though one wonders (as one is no doubt supposed to) just what vices-turned-habits are indicated. Ordinary music? Or something even more enervating? After all, boogie chillen, wouldn't it have a better beat if it were phrased "what once were vices now are habits"? Oh well — unlike Three Dog Night, who they would do well to emulate, they've never shown any flair with outside material.   **C−**

The Doobie Brothers: *Takin' It to the Streets* (Warner Bros. '76). You can lead a Doobie to the recording studio, but you can't make him think.   **C+**

The Doobie Brothers: *Best of the Doobies* (Warner Bros. '76). One reason this band epitomizes corporate rock is that it has its meager merits, and I'm ashamed to say that on this compilation I enjoy them. In fact, the bassline hooks of "China Grove" and "Long Train Comin' " move me so efficiently that by the time we get to "Listen to the Music" — which with its easy-rolling rhythms, anonymous harmonies, countrified arrangement, meticulous production, and smug message made my ten-worst list in 1972 — I'm still listening to the music.   **B+**

The Doobie Brothers: *Minute by Minute* (Warner Bros. '78). Tight playing combines with moderately intricate rhythms and harmonies for sexy, dancey pop music of undeniable craft (at least on side one). And as we all know, they could be doing a lot worse. Original grade: B minus.   **B**

The Doors: *Morrison Hotel* (Elektra '70). One side is called "Hard Rock Cafe," the other "Morrison Hotel." Guess which I prefer. Now guess which is supposed to be more "poetic." And now guess which *is* more poetic. "The future's uncertain and the end is always near" is just the Lizard King's excuse for mingling with the proles who "get on down," but it sure beats the Anais Nin tribute for originality and aptness of thought. Still, the band is rocking tighter than it ever has, Robbie Krieger's phrasing keeps things moving, and Morrison's gliding vocal presence — arty and self-absorbed though it may be — provides focus. He's not the genius he makes himself out to be, so maybe his genius is that he doesn't let his pretensions cancel out his talent. **B+**

The Doors: *Absolutely Live!* (Elektra '70). Strong performances and audio. Two previously unrecorded blues, a predictable new original called "Build Me a Woman," a surprising new original called "Universal Mind," several new fragments, and an intelligent medley. Plus "The Celebration of the Lizard" in its full theatrical glory — or rather, since this is a record, half of it. Problem is, I don't happen to be into reptiles when the music's over, much less while it's on. **B**

The Doors: *13* (Elektra '70). Greatest hits plus, and minus — album tracks that should have been singles and dud forty-fives, respectively. As for those who believe such a collection drives the final nail in the sepulchre of Jim Morrison's AM acceptance, well, I prefer his Tommy James to his Antonin Artaud. Although I admit that "Touch Me" goes too far. P.S. I know sepulchres don't have nails — that was just a test for the Artaud fans. **A−**

The Doors: *L.A. Woman* (Elektra '71). The tip-off is when in the middle of a lyric about needing someone who doesn't need etc. etc. Jim intones the line "I see the bathroom is clear." That's how you know the "raaght awn"'s in "Cars Hiss by My Window" (hiss, huh?) and the jungle talk in "The WASP (Texas Radio and the Big Beat)" (wasps, huh?) and even the cover of John Lee Hooker's "Crawling King Snake" (take that, lizard-haters) are jokes. Which is nice, because the band has never sounded better — the blues licks are sharp, the organ fills are hypnotic, and they've even hired a bass player. But if "Been Down So Long" is also a takeoff, I prefer Randy Newman's. And Newman has better ideas about "L'America," too. **A−**

The Doors: *Other Voices* (Elektra '71). Anyone can sing rock, but that doesn't mean just anyone. Richard Nixon can't, and neither can Barbra Streisand, and I bet Peter Fonda can't either. Well, neither can Ray Manzarek or Robbie Krieger, whose voices share one salient quality: uptightness. This record has some terrific moments, starting with the first hook riff, and the musicians deserve their reputations. But even a good singer couldn't do much with a line like "To roam is my infection," and this band could use a good singer. **C+**

The Doors: *Full Circle* (Elektra '72). Is this slick eclecticism what all those experts who used to claim Jim Morrison was limiting his musicians had in mind? **C**

The Doors: *Weird Scenes Inside the Gold Mine* (Elektra '72). This two-LP compendium has a theme that goes beyond "He's dead, so we'd better get in there quick." It's Morrison-as-politician, compiled by an a&r guy who took him seriously, and why not—in Morrison's politics, a&r guys were adjuncts of the prime movers of history. This includes enough solid album tracks and post-*13* hits to suck in the poppyboppers plus the best of the pretentious stuff—"Five to One," "Horse Latitudes," "When the Music's Over," and of course "The End." Which latter is the test—specifically the line "Mother I want to yeearrrgh." When I first heard it, it made me grimace; now it makes me guffaw. If it still gives you chills, you may want to buy this for your favorite niece or nephew. Inspirational Image: "mute nostril agony." **B−**

The Doors: *The Best of the Doors* (Elektra '73). Not counting the live double (from which this inexplicably includes "Who Do You Love") and the two non-Morrison albums (from which this explicably includes nothing) the Doors recorded six LPs. Now they've amassed four discs worth of reissues in addition. That's what he gets for dying on his record company. **B**

Lee Dorsey: *Yes We Can* (Polydor '70). On what is supposed to be a (if not the) classic New Orleans rock and roll album, Allen Toussaint's .500 songwriting is a little disappointing — two of the twelve cuts are self-proclaimed filler, another is Joe South's "Games People Play," another a reprise. It's really only Ziggy Modeliste's drumming that keeps side two going. But Dorsey's congenial, liquid soul-crooning style defines such great Toussaint inventions as "Riverboat," "Occapella," "Sneakin' Sally Through the Alley," and "O Me-O, My-O." Near-classic, say.   **A—**

Lee Dorsey: *Night People* (ABC '77). This record has been growing on me so slowly for so long that I wonder whether my old Allen Toussaint fixation is acting up. Then again, why shouldn't it? Dorsey's subtle, small-scale rock and roll genre statement defines songwriter-producer Toussaint better than Toussaint the performer ever has. Every cut on this astonishingly listenable album is a minor pleasure; I'm delighted by even its silliest ("God Must Have Blessed America") and simplest ("Can I Be the One") moments. Major credit goes to Dorsey's soft, snaky, infinitely good-humored and long-suffering vocal work, but Toussaint's touch is sublime throughout.   **A—**

The Dramatics: *Whatcha See Is Whatcha Get* (Stax '71). Sounds like better Motown than recently and greasier Motown than ever, and it figures — this Tempts-styled Detroit quintet, with Ron Banks in the David Ruffin role, play for the Memphis Grease Kings. "Get Up and Get Down" and "Whatcha See Is Whatcha Get" resound with uptempo bottom, and while I find the big dramatic number, "In the Rain," a little too big and too dramatic, I do prefer Don Davis's sound effects to Norman Whitfield's. Better filler than Motown, too — but not that much better.   **B**

Joe Droukas: *Shadowboxing* (Southwind '75). Not bad, very New York, almost like a horse race at OTB: Bruce Springsteen's street tough, Elliott

Murphy's media addict, and Buzzy Linhart's fuckup, with the fuckup ahead by a nose. Glorious exception: "The Sweetest One."   **B—**

Ducks Deluxe: *Ducks Deluxe* (RCA Victor '74). These swampy genre pieces, spawned in the backwaters of the English pub scene and drawled with hush-moufed abandon by Sean Tyla (spelling phonetic?), are tuneful, affectionate, raunchy, and sometimes inspired—a lick here, a yell there, a concept somewhere else. But it's a lot harder for an English band that loves America by phonograph to tell us something about ourselves in 1974 than it was for a comparable band in 1964—especially since the 1974 band loves America's rural past, just like Ry Cooder. Original grade: B.   **B+**

Ducks Deluxe: *Don't Mind Rockin' Tonite* (RCA Victor '78). Comprising six (of the seven best) tracks from the deleted *Ducks Deluxe*, three from the import-only *Taxi to the Terminal Zone*, and some singles, this candidly simplistic compilation is designed to appeal to fans of the Rumour (featuring ex-Duck Martin Belmont) and the Motors (headed by ex-Deluxe Nick Garvey and Andy McMasters). Neither of whom have all that many fans, actually. The music is pure rock and roll, maybe too pure, combining the Rumour's spirited intensity and the Motors' cheerful manipulation at a more primitive stage. Fans of the Tyla Gang will dig it.   **A—**

Dudes: *We're No Angels* (Columbia '75). The Consumer Guide Raspberry for 1975 is awarded posthumously to this Zombies tribute, which died almost immediately upon release, dismissed on name alone by everybody except diehard Wackers fans, an exclusive grouping that does not include your reviewer. Dudey it's not. There's a lovely pre-Pepper feel to it, although the bite of the Raspberries' *Starting Over* or Big Star's *Radio City* is missed, and a nice ripoff eclecticism operates as well — not so easy to evoke all the young hooples while borrowing a catch from Rod Argent. Anybody who can tell me where Brian Greenaway stole the little bit that goes "oh Lylee lady" wins a prize.   **B+**

Ian Dury: *New Boots and Panties!!* (Stiff '78). Dury is a pub rock survivor, as tough and homely as a dandelion, as English as music halls, billingsgate, and Gene Vincent. The tenacious wit and accuracy of his lyrics betray how uncommon he believes his blockheaded protagonists really are, and his music rocks out in the traditional blues-based grooves without kissing the past's ass. Tender, furious, sexy, eccentric, surprising.   **A−**

Ian Dury: *Do It Yourself* (Stiff/Epic '79). Dury's idiomatic literacy is a continuing pleasure, but only on "Quiet" (to his kids) and maybe "This Is What We Find" (comedic-philosophical) is it enough, because the music tries too bleeding hard to be ingratiating. The man is supposed to be too English for us colonials, but I feel a lot more at home with the music-hall rock of *New Boots and Panties!!* than with the fusoid pop internationalism of Chaz Jankel's arrangements here—jazz per Ramsey Lewis, reggae per Byron Lee, disco per Arthur Murray.   **B**

Dyke and the Blazers: *Dyke's Greatest Hits* (Original Sound '70). Dyke is militantly funky — the "we" in "We Got More Soul" isn't just his band but all black people, including Pearl Bailey and Nancy Wilson. On that tune, "Funky Walk," and "Funky Broadway" (and let us not forget "You Are My Sunshine"), he more than earns his hard line. But elsewhere the harsh shouting vocal rhythms just aren't funky enough to overcome all by themselves — Dyke's not James Brown yet, and the JB's play trickier, catchier patterns than the Blazers. **B+**

Bob Dylan: *Self-Portrait* (Columbia '70). Jon Landau wrote to suggest I

give this a D, but that's pique. Conceptually, this is a brilliant album which is organized, I think, by two central ideas. First, that "self" is most accurately defined (and depicted) in terms of the artifacts — in this case, pop tunes and folk songs claimed as personal property and semispontaneous renderings of past creations frozen for posterity on a piece of tape and (perhaps) even a couple of songs one has written oneself — to which one responds. Second, that the people's music is the music people like, Mantovani strings and all. But in order for a concept to work it has to be supported musically — that is, you have to listen. I don't know anyone, even vociferous supporters of this album, who plays more than one side at a time. I don't listen to it at all. The singing is not consistently good, though it has its moments, and the production — for which I blame Bob Johnston, though Dylan has to be listed as a coconspirator — ranges from indifferent to awful. It is possible to use strings and soprano choruses well, but Johnston has never demonstrated the knack. Other points: it's overpriced, the cover art is lousy, and it sounds good on WMCA.   **C+**

Bob Dylan: *New Morning* (Columbia '70). In case you were wondering how definitive that self-portrait was, here comes its mirror image four months later. Call it love on the rebound. This time he's writing the pop (and folk) genre experiments himself, and thus saying more about true romance than is the pop (or folk) norm. Two side-closing throw-ins — a sillyditty about a gal named "Winterlude" and the scatting beatnik send-up "If Dogs Run Free"— almost steal the show. And the two other side-closers, which make religion seem dumber than it already is, damn near give it back. Original grade: A.   **A−**

Bob Dylan: *Bob Dylan's Greatest Hits Volume II* (Columbia '72). Yet another self-portrait. With all of Dylan's overexposed stuff relegated to Volume

I, it unlooses one indubitable classic after another, and because it spans a decade without pretending to (or bothering with) thematic/stylistic coherence, the only overall impression it creates is a staggering, unpredictable virtuosity. Mixed into the star persona are protest ("Hard Rain") and antiprotest ("My Back Pages"), callow ass man ("All I Really Want to Do") and manly ass man ("Lay Lady Lay"). And just in case you think you already own it all, five of the twenty-two cuts are previously uncollected or unreleased. Three of them have been established as indubitable classics by other artists, and the other two begin and end the album. From "Watching the River Flow" to "Down in the Flood"— now what can that mean? **A**

Bob Dylan: *Pat Garrett and Billy the Kid* (Columbia '73). At least the strings on this soundtrack are mostly plucked and strummed, rather than bowed en masse, but it's still a soundtrack: two middling-to-excellent new Dylan songs, four good original Bobby voices, and a lot of Schmylan music. Original grade: C.   **C+**

Bob Dylan: *Dylan* (Columbia '73). Listening to this set of rejects from what used to be Dylan's worst album does have its morbid fascination — if you'll forgive the esoteric reference, it's like watching Ryne Duren pitch without glasses. Not only was the timbre and melody off — he was always wild — but he also doesn't phrase cogently, and the songs just hit the dirt. All of which is CBS's punishment after Bobby had the bad manners to sing with another label. I wonder how he could imagine that Columbia is less than benevolent.   **E**

Bob Dylan: *Planet Waves* (Asylum '74). In a time when all the most prestigious music, even what passes for funk, is coated with silicone grease, Dylan is telling us to take that grease and jam it. Sure he's domestic, but his version of conjugal love is anything but smug, and this comes through in both the lyrics and the sound of the

record itself. Blissful, sometimes, but sometimes it sounds like stray cat music — scrawny, cocky, and yowling up the stairs. Original grade: A.   **A—**

Bob Dylan/The Band: *Before the Flood* (Asylum '74). At its best, this is the craziest and strongest rock and roll ever recorded. All analogous live albums fall flat. The Rolling Stones are mechanical dolls by comparison, the Faces merely sloppy, the Dead positively quiet. The MC5 achieved something similar by ignoring musicianship altogether, but while the Band sounds undisciplined, threatening to destroy their headlong momentum by throwing out one foot or elbow too many, they never abandon their enormous technical ability. In this they follow the boss. When he sounded thin on *Planet Waves,* so did they. Now his voice settles in at a rich bellow, running over his old songs like a truck. I agree that a few of them will never walk again, but I treasure the sacrilege: Uncle Bob purveying to the sports arena masses. We may never even know whether this is a masterpiece. Original grade: A plus.   **A**

Bob Dylan: *Blood on the Tracks* (Columbia '75). The first version of this album struck me as a sellout to the memory of Dylan's pre-electric period; this remix, utilizing unknown Minneapolis studio musicians who impose nothing beyond a certain anonymous brightness on the proceedings, recapitulates the strengths of that period. Dylan's new stance is as disconcerting as all the previous ones, but the quickest and deepest surprise is in the music itself. By second hearing its loveliness is almost literally haunting, an aural déjà vu. There are moments of anger that seem callow, and the prevailing theme of interrupted love recalls adolescent woes, but on the whole this is the man's most mature and assured record.   **A**

Bob Dylan/The Band: *The Basement Tapes* (Columbia '75). These are the famous lost demos recorded at Big Pink in 1967 and later bootlegged on

The Great White Wonder and elsewhere. Of the eighteen Dylan songs, thirteen have been heard in cover versions, one by Dylan himself; the six Band songs have never even been bootlegged and are among their best. Because the Dylan is all work tape, the music is certifiably unpremeditated, lazy as a river and rarély relentless or precise — laid back without complacency or slickness. The writerly "serious" songs like "Tears of Rage" are all the richer for the company of his greatest novelties — if "Going to Acapulco" is a dirge about having fun, "Don't Ya Tell Henry" is a ditty about separation from self, and both modes are enriched by the Band's more conventional ("realistic") approach to lyrics. We needn't bow our heads in shame because this is the best album of 1975. It would have been the best album of 1967 too. And it's sure to sound great in 1983. **A+**

Bob Dylan: *Desire* (Columbia '75). In the great tradition of Grand Funk Railroad, Dylan has made an album beloved by tour devotees — including those who were shut out of Rolling Thunder's pseudo-communitarian grooviness except via the press. It is not beloved by me. Although the candid propaganda and wily musicality of "Hurricane" delighted me for a long time, the deceitful bathos of its companion piece, "Joey," tempts me to question the unsullied innocence of Rubin Carter himself. These are not protest songs, folks, not in the little-people tradition of "Hattie Carroll"; their beneficiaries are (theoretically) wronged heroes, oppressed overdogs not unlike our beleaguered superstar himself. And despite his show of openness, our superstar may be feeling oppressed. His voice sounds viscous and so do his rhymes, while sisters Ronee and Emmylou sound distinctly kid, following the leader as if they're holding onto his index finger. More genuinely fraternal (and redeeming) are the pained, passionate marital tributes, "Sara" and "Isis." Original grade: B plus. **B-**

Bob Dylan: *Hard Rain* (Columbia '76). The only reason people are disgusted with this record is that they're sick of Dylan — which is understandable, but unfair to the record. The palookas who backed him on this tour sure ain't the Band, and the music and arrangements suffer accordingly — these guys are folkies whose idea of rock and roll is rock and roll clichés. But the material is excellent, and on a few occasions—I gravitate to "Oh Sister" and "Shelter from the Storm"— Dylan sings very well indeed. **B-**

Bob Dylan: *Street-Legal* (Columbia '78). Inveterate rock and rollers learn to find charm in boastful, secretly girl-shy adolescents, but boozy-voiced misogynists in their late thirties are a straight drag. This divorcée sounds overripe, too in love with his own self-generated misery to break through the leaden tempos that oppress his melodies, devoid not just of humor but of lightness — unless, that is, he intends his Neil Diamond masquerade as a joke. Because he's too shrewd to put his heart into genuine corn, and because his idea of a tricky arrangement is to add horns or chicks to simplistic verse-and-chorus *abcb* structures, a joke is what it is. But since he still commands remnants of authority, the joke is sour indeed. **C+**

Bob Dylan: *Bob Dylan at Budokan* (Columbia '79). I believe this double-LP was made available so our hero could boast of being outclassed by Cheap Trick, who had the self-control to release but a single disc from this location. Although it's amazing how many of the twenty-two songs—twelve also available on one of the other two live albums Dylan has released since 1974 — hold up under slipshod treatment. And not only that, lyrics and poster are included. **C+**

Bob Dylan: *Slow Train Coming* (Columbia '79). The lyrics are indifferently crafted, and while their one-dimensionality is winningly perverse at a time when his old fans will take any ambiguity they can get, it does serve to flaunt their theological wrongheadedness and occasional jingoism. Nevertheless, this is his best album since *Blood on the Tracks*. The singing is passionate and detailed, and the pros behind him — especially Mark Knopfler, who has a studio career in store — play so sharply that his anger gathers general relevance at its most vindictive. And so what if he's taken up with the God of Wrath? Since when have you been so crazy about the God of Love? Or any other species of hippie bullshit? **B+**

The Dynamic Superiors: *The Dynamic Superiors* (Motown '75). The lead singer on one of the best Motown albums in years is a mascara-eyed, effeminate — gay — falsetto named Tony Washington. His devotion to group tradition has inspired Ashford & Simpson to write a more melodic bunch of songs than they've managed for any of their own albums yet. Only problem is, Washington doesn't do a very good Smokey, or Eddie Kendricks. Or Martha Reeves, or Lorraine Ellison. Sounds more like Nick Ashford. **B**

Eagles: *Eagles* (Asylum '72). These guys certainly boogie more than the bluegrass sellouts who populate the vaguely country-oriented mainstream of contemporary American rock, and they certainly write more memorable songs. But this culminates the reactionary individualism that country-rock has come to epitomize in the counterculture. What's worse, the country orientation bespeaks not roots but a lack of them, so that in the end the product is suave and synthetic — brilliant, but false. And not always all that brilliant, either. **B**

Eagles: *Desperado* (Asylum '73). With its barstool-macho equation of gunslinger and guitarschlonger, its on-the-road misogyny, its playing-card metaphors, and its paucity of decent songs, this soundtrack to an imaginary Sam Peckinpah movie is "concept" at its most mindless. I don't know, fellas, how do ya "tell the dancer from the dance"? Have to get people off their asses first. **C**

Eagles: *On the Border* (Asylum '74). The critic in me has no doubt this is their best album, although he notes that the male-bonding songs (which articulate an affirmative ethos) have more to say than the female-separation songs (which rationalize hostility into pity/contempt). And when the critic plays the record, the listener enjoys the Gram Parsons tribute "My Man," the MOR-oriented "Best of My Love," the vaguely anti-authoritarian "On the Border," the permanently star-struck "James Dean," and several others.

But the listener is too turned off by what the band represents ever to put the thing on voluntarily. **B+**

The Eagles: *One of These Nights* (Asylum '75). Put on your neckboots and wade through the slickshit and you may get a kick from the lyrics — these boys like lotsa malaise with their mayonnaise. But in rock and roll the difference between tragedy and soap opera is usually the acting, here so completely immersed in stringing sings that even the aptest phrases are reduced to the cliches they restate. **C+**

Eagles: *Their Greatest Hits 1971–75* (Asylum '76). Hum 'em high — ten poptunes from the Four Lads of I'm-okay I'm-okay are probably a must for those who've concluded they're geniuses by listening to the radio. I happen to remember that what makes *On the Border* a decent album isn't their "victory song" (over guess what kind of person) but the songs to, about, and by other men, and that the only other decent cut on last year's breakthrough was the one that told a hard truth about the artists. **B**

Eagles: *Hotel California* (Asylum '76). Speaking strictly as a nonfan, I'd grant that this is their most substantial if not their most enjoyable LP — they couldn't have written any of the songs on side one, or even the pretentious and condescending "The Last Resort," without caring about their California theme down deep. But though one strength of these lyrics is that they don't exclude the Eagles from purgatory-on-earth, Don Henley is incapable of conveying a mental state as complex as self-criticism — he'll probably sound smug croaking out his famous last words ("Where's the Coke?"). I'd also be curious to know what Mexican-Americans think of the title tune's Spanish accent.　　　　　　**B**

Eagles: *The Long Run* (Asylum '79). Not as country-rocky as you might expect — the Eagles are pros who adapt to the times, and they make the music tough. I actually enjoy maybe half of these songs until I come into contact with the conceited, sentimental woman-haters who are doing the singing. I mean, these guys think punks are cynical and antilife? Guys who put down "the king of Hollywood" because his dick isn't as big as John David Souther's?　　　　　　**C+**

Earth, Wind & Fire: *Earth, Wind & Fire* (Warner Bros. '71). This postsoul big band isn't as messy as the sum of its cross-references; on the second side especially, the heavy guitar, post-Memphis horns, and off-center 4/4 all work to similarly disquieting effect, and even the African kalimba is suitably weird. But at times the brass locks into gear just like Vegas, and the expert vocal harmonies neither fit the concept nor assert any personality of their own. Worse, even the songs that work when you're listening have a way of slipping away unnoticed once the record is over. [Later with *Need of Love* as *Another Time.*]　　**C+**

Earth, Wind & Fire: *Need of Love* (Warner Bros. '71). Busy, busy. I do admire "Energy," a jazz-rock horn experiment in the neglected tradition of Steve Marcus's *Tomorrow Never Knows* — but "Energy"'s lyrics comprise a recitation that rhymes "prana" and "nirvana." [Later with *Earth, Wind & Fire* as *Another Time.*]　　　　　　**C+**

Earth, Wind & Fire: *Last Days and Time* (Columbia '72). New label, damn near a new band, except for drummer-vocalist (-leader) Maurice White and bassist-vocalist Verdine White. Things sound a lot less confused, but EW&F centers around its rhythm section for a reason — rhythm is what they have to offer. Granted, you can hear why they signed up reed man Ronnie Laws on "Power," and you can hear why they signed up Phillip Bailey whenever he raises his voice to the highest. Maybe next time we'll figure out why their best tune is called "Mom" and their two covers are "Make It with You" and "Where Have All the Flowers Gone." Only I'm not sure we want to know.　　**C+**

Earth, Wind & Fire: *Head to the Sky* (Columbia '73). In the beginning Maurice White created Hummit Music. But not until the morning of the fourth album did he come up with a tune to match, complete with sweet clear harmonies and sinuous beat. Catchy title, too: "Evil," to be dispersed by prayer. Most of the first side keeps up the good work, although only rarely — as on the falsetto climax of "Keep Your Head to the Sky" — is it quite as transcendent physically as the lyrics would seem to demand. But the mood jazz excursion on side two exposes White's essential fatuousness. "Zanzibar," it's called, as befits a travelogue; its saxophone solo (by Ronnie Laws's replacement, Andrew Woolfolks) could make Alice Coltrane blush.　　　　　　**B−**

Earth, Wind & Fire: *Open Our Eyes* (Columbia '74). On side one the vocal systole-diastole finally comes together, with Philip Bailey definitive, as he deserves to be; Maurice White, meanwhile, provides tuneful, relatively unselfconscious songs over a light Latin-funk beat jarred by grunts, horn riffs, and keyboard squiggles. A very pleasant surprise. Side two, where they always stretch out and often make fools of themselves, is a survey of EW&F's roots, from the kalimba-hooked "Drum Song" through street rap through 1:41 of expert cocktail bebop (didn't know Maurice had that rim shot in him) through schlock scat to the devotional theme song, written in 1958 by one Leon Lumkins. A fucking tour de force.　　　　　　**A−**

Earth, Wind & Fire: *That's the Way of the World* (Columbia '75). Trailing Parliament-Funkadelic in my personal post-Sly sweepstakes, but ahead of War (bombastic), Kool & the Gang (culturally deprived), and hosts of others, this unit can do so many things it qualifies as the one-man band of black music even though it has nine members. Here ethnomusicology and colloquial homiletics are tacked onto the funk and soul and doowop and jazz, which makes for an instructive contrast — the taped-in-Africa Matepe Ensemble, whose spontaneous laughter closes out the coda, versus Maurice White, whose humorless platitudes prove there's more to roots than turning a mbira into an ersatz vibraphone. **B+**

Earth, Wind & Fire: *Gratitude* (Columbia '75). The three live sides reflect their genuine jazz orientation, flowing along enjoyably and unexcessively and offering more new material than is superstar practice. But orientation ain't chops, and despite my prejudices I'd rather hear Dvorak's *New World Symphony* than the Whites'. The four songs on the studio side are enjoyable, too — took them a while to figure out their formula, but now they've really got it down. The news that "the good Lord gonna make a way," however, is gonna come as a surprise to Him, Her, or It. **B**

Earth, Wind & Fire: *Spirit* (Columbia '76). EW&F are the real black MOR, equivalent in their catchy way to the oh-so-expert Carpenters, though of course they're much better because they're black — that is, because the post-Sly and harmony-group usages they've had to master are so rich and resilient. Most of these songs are fun to listen to. But they're still MOR — the only risk they take is running headlong into somebody coming down the middle of the road in the opposite direction. Like the Carpenters. **B**

Earth, Wind & Fire: *All 'n All* (Columbia '77). Focusing soulful horns, high-tension harmonies, and rhythms and textures from many lands onto a first side that cooks throughout. Only one element is lacking. Still, unsympathetic as I am to lyrics about conquering the universe on wings of thought, they make me shake my fundament anyway. **B+**

Earth, Wind & Fire: *The Best of Earth, Wind & Fire Vol. 1* (Columbia '78). Despite some annoying omissions, notably "Serpentine Fire," this sums them up — ten exquisitely crafted pop tunes in which all the passion and resonance of black music tradition are blended into a concoction slicker and more sumptuous than any white counterpart since Glenn Miller. **A−**

Earth, Wind & Fire: *I Am* (ARC/Columbia '79). Sexy, dancey pop music of undeniable craft, and it doesn't let up. But as we all know, they could be doing a lot better. **B**

Ecstasy, Passion & Pain: *Ecstasy, Passion & Pain* (Roulette '74). On the cover the group sits in a chain-filled basement trying sheepishly to establish an "evil" "image." They could use one — the three r&b hits are set apart only by Barbara Roy's vibrato-tinged soul shouting. I prefer "I'll Do Anything for You," a girl-groupish tune that sounds like it got misrouted to Philly when Motown moved to L.A. **C+**

Eddie and the Hot Rods: *Teenage Depression* (Island '77). This is "punk" for old-time rock and rollers frightened by the concept; these guys even claim to snort coke, and do speeded-up homages to Peter Townshend, Van Morrison, Mick Jagger, and Bob Seger. Rock on. **C+**

Eddie and the Hot Rods: *Life on the Line* (Island '77). I'm not inclined to get judgmental here. It's true that Eddie's sunlamp tan and health-club bod make him the logical successor to Shaun Cassidy. True too that the teen-militant lyrics are strictly rote, and that their hooks hardly compare with Mann & Weil's. Still, this is quite a bit solider than any album Paul Revere and the Raiders or the Dave Clark Five ever made — not counting greatest hits collections, of course.   **B—**

Edison Electric Band: *God Bless You, Dr. Woodward* (Cotillion '70). This Philadelphia group has been ignored just about everywhere but in *Rolling Stone*, where they were panned stupidly, perhaps out of geographical jealousy. All the players have the kind of blues-soul feeling that makes Nick Gravenites such a Bay Area hero, and in the best ballroom tradition the music occupies that uncharted region triangulated by rock, pop, and jazz — only it's tighter and more melodic than what you hear in the ballrooms. Original grade: B plus.   **B**

Dave Edmunds: *Rockpile* (MAM '72). A glance at the titles suggests yet another ho-hum revival — Berry 'n' blues to go with a novelty-hit remake of Smiley Lewis's (not Pat Boone's, right?) "I Hear You Knocking." But a glance at the credits establishes that Edmunds played just about everything but bass himself, even on "The Promised Land," apparently recorded in 1966. And a perusal of the titles adds Dylan twelve-bar, "It Ain't Easy," and — what's this? — Neil Young's "Dance, Dance, Dance" to The Tradition. *Sounds* pretty weird, too. **B+**

Dave Edmunds: *Subtle as a Flying Mallet* (RCA Victor '75). Only an Englishman would spend a whole album proving he had great taste in rock and roll. And he does, he does — from cock-strut to girl-group I love every one-man-Spector production. I just don't know why he took the trouble.   **B**

Dave Edmunds: *Get It* (Swan Song '77). In which Edmunds convenes the Monmouth Rockabilly Seminar, featuring source material both standard (Hank Williams, Otis Blackwell, Arthur Crudup) and arcane (Rodgers & Hart), recent research by Bob Seger and Graham Parker, and new monographs from Nicholas Lowe and Ed-

munds himself. Great stuff, although studious detachment don't necessarily do it proud. Original grade: B.   **B+**

Dave Edmunds: *Tracks on Wax 4* (Swan Song '78). Edmunds has evolved from a one-man session to the spirit of Rockpile, the hardest-driving traditional rock band in the world: Edmunds and Billy Bremner on guitar, coleader Nick Lowe on bass, and the indefatigable Terry Williams on drums. Live, everyone but Williams trades vocals, but this is Edmunds's showcase, and he sings up to the main force of a band that proves all those clichés about getting that feeling together on the road. Here to stay. **A—**

Dave Edmunds: *Repeat When Necessary* (Swan Song '79). This sounds like a Rockpile album while Nick Lowe's doesn't because Lowe loves rock and roll for everything it implies as culture while Edmunds loves it for everything it is as music. There is a richness of reference here that leaves Edmunds's rockabilly phase far behind — five of the songs are imaginative genre pieces from two pubberies that appear to specialize in pub-rock revivalism, new ones by Parker and Costello add that contemporary touch, and the zesty remake of "Home in My Hand" cuts Brinsley Schwarz's. But what defines the music is Edmunds's willingness to defer to the overdrive of the two other guys in the band, unsung guitarist Billy Bremner and pitiless drummer Terry Williams. In unity there is power.   **A—**

John Edwards: *Life Love and Living* (Cotillion '76). Soul lives, and so does David Porter — you remember, Isaac Hayes and David Porter, Sam & Dave's producers? Porter's new kid crosses Al Green and Sam Cooke as if honoring a deathbed request by his mama, Porter Inc. provides a very consistent bunch of songs, and Muscle Shoals and Malaco style the music. But only God can make a hit.   **B**

Jonathan Edwards: *Jonathan Edwards* (Capricorn '71). I too wish he'd come up with another stage name, and I deplore his reluctance to pronounce consonants. But there are worse wimp-rockers. I ask you, have Jeffrey Comanor or Pacheco & Alexander ever gotten a song about dodging the draft on the radio? Well, I think that's what it's about. In a wimpy kind of way. If you know what I mean.   **C**

Stoney Edwards: *Mississippi You're on My Mind* (Capitol '75). Scandalously underrecorded, which I'm sure has nothing to do with the fact that he's black, Edwards remains firm in his allegiances. "Hank and Lefty Raised My Country Soul," he announces, and though he sounds more like Lefty than Hank and more like Merle than either, he's got a right. The voice has Haggard's swing and melismatic burr, but it's more powerful, an advantage except when it gets too thick. And though Edwards literally can't read or write, he makes up good songs and picks better ones. Between "We Sure Danced Us Some Good Ones," a believable account of a good marriage in a music that reserves its honesty for the bad ones, to "Summer Melodies," about innocent fun, he touches all the bases without sententiousness or whoop-de-doo. Country soul indeed. Time: 26:25.   **A−**

Stoney Edwards: *Blackbird* (Capitol '76). In which well-meaning producer Chip Taylor provides Edwards with a wonderful title tune about "a couple of country niggers/Stealin' the rodeo" while nudging him in a rockish, folkish direction, probably in the belief that he has a better shot at an audience over there. The results are hardly disgraceful, though Joe Cocker didn't get away with six minutes worth of "Bird on a Wire" either. But the straight country album Edwards did last year was a lot tougher. When people in Nashville get serious, they have a tendency to fall for pretentious schmaltz — that's the story of Mickey Newbury's life. A lot of this, straight country and folkish-rockish both, is too damn close to the edge.   **B+**

The Electric Light Orchestra: *No Answer* (United Artists '72). In which Roy Wood and Jeff Lynne work out their obsession with celli, French horns, and such like. The result is crude chamber music in rock time — pretty tuneful, and sometimes pretty funny as it lumbers along. Might even get interesting if Wood and Lynne weren't also working out their obsession with suffering ladies. Though they do OK by suffering men. [Later on Jet.] Original grade: C plus.   **B−**

Electric Light Orchestra: *Electric Light Orchestra II* (United Artists '73). Roy Wood's departure leaves Jeff Lynne to re-create this band in his own image: a conventional art-rocker, less ponderous and more long-winded than previously indicated, with an uncommonly lyrical side and his own sense of humor. The symphonic "Roll Over Beethoven" has been out there waiting for a long time. [Later on Jet.]   **C+**

Electric Light Orchestra: *A New World Record* (United Artists '76). Eat your diploma, Eric Carmen —after years of floundering, they've gone all the way and made a Moody Blues album with brains, hooks, and laffs galore. My fave is "Rockaria!," about a lass who "loves the way Puccini lays down a tune." Granted, I initially thought it was strictly for those who got off on music appreciation in high school, like the lass. But now I think it's also for those who hated it, like me. [Later on Jet.] Original grade: B.   **B+**

Electric Light Orchestra: *ELO's Greatest Hits* (Jet '79). *A New World Record* aside, this is a singles band, which makes their compilation the European Tradition's answer to *Bubble Gum Music Is the Naked Truth*. I love that "Mr. Blue Sky," almost my favorite is "Turn to Stone," and how 'bout "Telephone Line"?   **B+**

Elephant's Memory: *Taking It to the Streets* (Metromedia '70). I like the way "Mongoose" grafts polyrhythms onto hard rock, and I'm pleased that they utter the word "revolution" with some notion of what it means. But like so many comrades they confuse the utterance with the fact. Propaganda requires cunning — for starters, Stan Bronstein could stop singing as if the Establishment is standing on his foot. **C+**

The Eleventh House Featuring Larry Coryell: *The Eleventh House Featuring Larry Coryell* (Vanguard '74). In person, Coryell's restless imagination has held its own against Alphonse Mouzon's cute Latin funkisms and Randy Brecker's plasma, perspiration, and lachrymal secretions. In fact, I've found the synthesis hard and multilayered — but maybe it was just loud. Here the guitarist's straining electronicism is subsumed in neat melodic contrivances. Depressing — when somebody deserves better for as long as Coryell, you begin to wonder. **B−**

Lorraine Ellison: *Lorraine Ellison* (Warner Bros. '74). Ellison's voice is so gorgeous and her spirit so possessed that it's hard to hear exactly what she's singing — you're riveted as she swoops over Ted Templeman's stark, gospel-drenched production, but nothing attaches itself permanently. Doesn't help that sometimes the swoop becomes a shriek, either. Original grade: C. **B−**

Joe Ely: *Joe Ely* (MCA '77). Ely hasn't yet learned how to disguise his rather thin timbre behind savvy phrasing, but as a result he projects an attractive openness — country singers (the men, anyway) rarely betray such innocent longing. Not that he's a country singer, exactly — this is real country-rock in a unique blend. And if Ely is only three-quarters of a singer (more like nine-tenths, actually), he's two writers — his silent partner Butch Hancock evokes the eternal cycle of good times and Tuesdays after, of connection and distance, with a delight in wordplay that complements Ely's more direct lyrical style. **A−**

Joe Ely: *Honky Tonk Masquerade* (MCA '78). You know all that brouhaha about Texas music? Here's a record that bears it out for more than two songs at a time. Ely's emotional openness seems neither sentimental nor contrived. He balls the jack with irrefutable glee and sings the lonesome ones so high and hard he makes the next room sound 500 miles away. With Butch Hancock sharing the writing, there are maybe two less-than-memorable songs on the entire album. There's great (Louisiana?) accordion, apt (Mexican?) horns, and lots of (Lubbock!) rock and roll. In short, there hasn't been anything like this since Gram Parsons was around to make *Grievous Angel*, or do I mean *Gilded Palace of Sin?* **A**

Joe Ely: *Down on the Drag* (MCA '79). Ely's songwriting pal Butch Hancock, who's beginning to sound like a great one, contributes four more; if "Fools Fall in Love" sounds like a lame title, how do you like "Wise men hit the bottom, Lord/A fool falls right on through"? But Ely himself seems to have run short of tunes, and except for "Crazy Lemon" (which gets across on the crazy force of its lyric and vocal, not on its melody), none of his songs call you back. **B+**

Emerson, Lake & Palmer: *Emerson, Lake & Palmer* (Cotillion '71). This opens with "The Barbarian," a keyboard showpiece (not to slight all the flailing and booming underneath) replete with the shifts of tempo, time, key, and dynamics beloved of these bozos. Does the title mean they see themselves as rock and roll Huns sacking nineteenth-century "classical" tradition? Or do they think they're like Verdi portraying Ethiopians in *Aida?* From such confusions flow music as clunky as these heavy-handed semi-improvisations and would-be tone poems. Not to mention word poems. **C**

Emerson, Lake & Palmer: *Pictures from an Exhibition* (Cotillion '72). This cover version of Moussorgsky's mouldy oldie does have a big new beat, but you can't dance to it, and the instrumentation seems a bit spare. Anyway, the truth is that I don't even listen to the original much. **D+**

Emerson, Lake & Palmer: *Trilogy* (Cotillion '72). The pomposities of *Tarkus* and the monstrosities of the Moussorgsky homage clinch it — these guys are as stupid as their most pretentious fans. Really, anybody who buys a record that divides a . . . composition called "The Endless Engima" into two discrete parts deserves it. **C−**

Emerson, Lake & Palmer: *Brain Salad Surgery* (Manticore '73). Is this supposed to be a rebound because Pete Sinfield wrote the lyrics? Because Certified Classical Composer Alberto Ginastera — who gets royalties, after all — attests to their sensitivity on the jacket? Because the sound is so crystalline you can hear the gism as it drips off the microphone? **C−**

Emerson Lake & Palmer: *Works: Volume 2* (Atlantic '78). When the world's most overweening "progressive" group makes an album less pretentious than its title, gallumphing respectfully through Scott Joplin and Meade Lux Lewis, that's news. But is it rock and roll? **C+**

The Emotions: *Flowers* (Columbia '76). Earth, Wind & Fire's girl group — literally. Whether it's Jeanette, Sheila, or Wanda who sounds like Diana Ross at a higher level of consciousness, the effect is exquisite. And their romantic platitudes are no worse than EW&F's universalist ones. Which is pretty bad. **B**

The Emotions: *Rejoice* (Columbia '77). They still sing real pretty, and their hit sounds pretty good on the radio, but too many of the songs that fill out this album prove how lazy you can get when you rely on how pretty you sing. **C+**

Eno: *Here Come the Warm Jets* (Island '74). The idea of this record — top of the pops from quasi-dadaist British synth wizard — may put you off, but the actuality is quite engaging in a vaguely Velvet Underground kind of way. Minimally differentiated variations on the same melody recur and recur, but it's a great melody, and not the only one, and chances are he meant it that way, as a statement, which I agree with. What's more, words take over when the music falters, and on "Cindy Tells Me" they combine for the best song ever written about middle-class feminism, a rock and roll subject if ever there was one. My major complaint is that at times the artist uses a filter that puts dust on my needle. Original grade: B plus. **A**

Eno: *Taking Tiger Mountain (By Strategy)* (Island '75). For all his synthesized, metronomic androidism, Eno is more humane than Bryan Ferry — his romanticism less strident, his oddness less devilish. It's nice, too, that in his arch, mellow way the man takes note of the real world from behind the overdubs. Every cut on this clear, consistent, elusive album affords distinct present pleasure. Admittedly, when they're over they're over — you don't flash on them the way you do on "Cindy Tells Me" and "Baby's on Fire." But that's just his way of being modest. **A−**

Eno: *Another Green World* (Island '76). Although I resisted at first, I've grown to love every minute of this arty little collection of static (i.e., nonswinging) synthesizer pieces (with vocals, percussion, and guitar). Think of it as the aural equivalent of a park on the moon — oneness with nature under conditions of artificial gravity. Played in the background, all thirteen pieces merge into a pattern that tends to calm any lurking Luddite impulses; perceived individually, each takes on an organic shape of its own. Industrialism yes. Original grade: A minus. **A+**

Brian Eno: *Discreet Music* (Antilles '77). That's discreet, not discrete — the title side comprises one quite minimal synthesizer piece more than thirty minutes long and the other three permutations of a schmaltzed-up Renaissance canon. Anybody who thought *Another Green World* sounded too much like radar blips or musical furniture should definitely avoid this. Me, I consider *Another Green World* miraculously lyrical and find that this encourages a meditative but secular mood (good for hard bits of writing) more effectively than any of the other rock-identified avant-garde music that's come our way. **A−**

Brian Eno: *Before and After Science* (Island '78). To call this album disappointing is to complain that it isn't transcendent. In fact, my objections begin only when he makes transcendence his goal: I don't like the murkiness of the quiet, largely instrumental reflections that take over side two. Dirty sound is functional in loud music, but no matter how much of a "water album" this is, the airy specificity of the *Another Green World* mix might save music like "Through Hollow Lands" from the appearance of aimlessness. None of which diminishes side one's oblique, charming tour of the popular rhythms of the day, from Phil Collins's discoid-fusion drumming on "No One Receiving" to the dense, deadpan raveup of (find the anagram) "King's Lead Hat." **A−**

Brian Eno: *Music for Films* (Antilles '78). Many of these eighteen cuts seem more like fragments than pieces, and although most of them provide subtle melodic or (especially) textural dynamics, the overall effect is a touch too willful in its impressionism for my tastes. *Another Green World* decelerating, which is a funny thing for movie music to do. Or maybe ECM with hindsight, a/k/a a tape splicer. **B+**

Brian Eno: *Music for Airports* (Ambient/PVC '79). Although I'm no frequenter of airports, I've found that these four swatches of modestly "ambient" minimalism have real charms as general-purpose calmatives. But I must also report that they've fared unevenly against specific backgrounds: sex (neutral to arid), baseball (pleas-

ant, otiose), dinner at my parents' (conversation piece), abstract writing (useful but less analgesic than *Discreet Music* or my David Behrman record). Also, I'm still waiting for "1/1" to resolve the "Three Blind Mice" theme. Original grade: B plus. **B**

John Entwistle: *Smash Your Head Against the Wall* (Decca '71). Entwistle is an important source of the fucked-up Calvinism that has always added that peculiar note of constraint to the Who—just remember where Peter Townshend turned when he needed a song about Uncle Ernie. These paeans of resentment and frustration climax thematically in songs called "Heaven and Hell" and "You're Mine" (starring John as Satan). But the music — not the melodies, the singing and playing — adds some not-so-peculiar constraints of its own. Original grade: B plus. **B**

John Entwistle: *Whistle Rymes* (Decca '72). Subjects of songs: isolation, cuckold's desertion, cuckold's rancor, cuckold's failed suicide, neurotic passivity, idiot passivity, whoring in bad faith, peeping in good faith, getting played for a fool, and nightmares. Mood of music: tuneful but stolid hard rock. Disposition of career: "interesting." **B**

John Entwistle: *John Entwistle's Rigor Mortis Sets In* (Track '73). Even in fun, Rigor Mortis is a strange name for what's supposed to be a lively rock and roll band. It may suggest why Entwistle's calling as a singer-songwriter is to provide one change-of-pace on each Who album. **C+**

The Everly Brothers: *Stories We Could Tell* (RCA Victor '72). Any dream-dream-dreamer who'll deny that this tasteful country-rock collection is unconceived, pallid, and humdrum is obliged to make the sad comparison with their autobiographical studio tour de force of 1968, *Roots,* which is thoughtful, even-tempered, and unique. **C**

The Fabulous Poodles: *Mirror Stars* (Epic '79). You've heard of punk? Well, this is twerp.　　　　　**C**

Small Faces: *The First Step* (Warner Bros. '70). One more complication in the Rod Stewart mystery. With Jeff Beck he parodies himself before he's established a self to parody. With Lou Reizner he establishes himself as a singer-songwriter of uncommon spunk and a vocal interpreter of uncommon individuality. And here he steps into the shoes of a purveyor of Humble Pie to pose as the leader of a mediocre white r&b band. Best cut: Ronnie Lane's "Stone."　　　　　**C+**

Faces: *Long Player* (Warner Bros. '71). The difference between these guys and their smaller forebears, the ones who released round-covered albums and sang "Itchycoo Park" with whine and phase, isn't just Steve Marriott vs. Rod Stewart. It's 1968 vs. 1971. Marriott was a pop craftsman with the Small Faces; with Humble Pie he's a boogie man. Stewart is a pop craftsman solo; with the Faces he's a boogie man. Boogie's not a bad idea, especially when you play it fast and loose rather than 'eavy like the 'Umbles. But as exciting as it is theoretically — and by comparison with the competition, boogieing and otherwise — it doesn't have much staying power. That's partly because they play it too loose and not quite fast enough. And partly because Stewart reserves his popcraft for solo LPs. Original grade: A minus.　　**B**

Faces: *A Nod Is as Good as a Wink . . . to a Blind Horse* (Warner Bros. '71). Rod Stewart sings lead only half of the time, which gives Ronnie Lane a chance to prove himself — his "You're So Rude" is a better (funnier and warmer) song about getting laid than "Stay with Me." Other standouts include the story of how Rod's brother became a hippie and a version of "Memphis" that's a gift from a band that has tightened up just enough. Original grade: A.　　　　　**A−**

Faces: *Ooh La La* (Warner Bros. '73). They do what they want to do very likably — this is as rowdy and friendly as rock and roll gets. But only on the title song and finale — written by the Rons (Wood and Lane) rather than the Rod — do they slap your back so's you'd still feel it five minutes later.　**B**

Faces: *Snakes and Ladders/The Best of Faces* (Warner Bros, '76). Not counting "Pineapple and the Monkey," a special for all those who believe their quintessence was sloppy instrumentals, this showcases the good stuff from *Long Player* and *Ooh La la*. Lots of fun, a solid testament to a band that was never very much into solidity — and a little more of a Rod Stewart album than is desirable for peak flavor.　　　　　**B+**

Faces:　See also Rod Stewart/Faces

Fairport Convention: *Unhalfbricking* (A&M '70). Folk-rock is a doubly willful idea in England — our bluegrass and acoustic blues are closer to

128

rock than their Child ballads. And Fairport's eleven-minute version of "A Sailor's Life" doesn't come up to the three Dylan songs (one in French) or Richard Thompson's quite un-English "Cajun Woman." But they do inject a droning energy into the material that suggests real synthesis. Thanks be to Thompson's guitar, Dave Mattacks's drums, and Sandy Denny's fondness for booze.   **A−**

Fairport Convention: *Liege and Lief* (A&M '70). Because the rhythm section has oomph and the singer soul, their pursuit of the Pentangle down the wooded path of jigs and ballads isn't entirely disastrous. But it sounds more like liege than lief to me. Traditional or original, these songs are either momentary escapes — that is, dances — or tales of common folk battling fate and the class system to something less than a standoff. Matty Groves outfucks Lord Donald, but Lord Donald kills Matty as well as his own wife; the Deserter is betrayed by comrade and sweetheart, then saved — to be a soldier — by Prince Albert. And the music, inevitably, reflects this fatalism.   **B−**

Fairport Convention: *Fairport Chronicles* (A&M '76). Stonehenge on the cover, but inside only traces of the English-folk purism that's limited the band since Dave Swarbrick began fiddling with it. Instead we get tasty Sandy Denny and Richard Thompson oddments, including Dion and Gordon Lightfoot transmuted into impure English folk. The trans-Atlantic connection dominates only one side — my favorite, needless to say. But "Tam Lin" sounds weirder in conjunction with "Percy's Song," "Walk A-while" merrier in conjunction with "Come All Ye," "Farewell, Farewell" more final at the end of four progressively doomier sides. In short, an intelligent compilation. Great notes, too.   **A−**

George Faith: *To Be a Lover* (Mango '77). I know, you love (and miss) soul music so much you don't care if it's deprived of its cultural context —when you got what it takes you hold on to what you got, right? Well, I don't know. Faith is a soft-sung reggae stylist vaguely reminiscent of early Joe Simon or some small part of David Ruffin. He writes ordinary songs and executes a delightful segue from "In the Midnight Hour" to "Ya Ya." And he let's you know why he loves "Turn Back the Hands of Time" and "So Fine" by covering Paul Anka's "Diana" along with them.   **B−**

Marianne Faithfull: *Broken English* (Island '79). A punk-disco fusion so uncompromised it will scare away fans of both genres, which share a taste for nasty girls that rarely extends to females past thirty with rat's-nest hair and last night's makeup on. The raw dance music isn't exactly original, and sometimes the offhandedness of the lyrics can be annoying, but I like this even when it's pro forma and/or sloppy, or maybe because it's pro forma and/or sloppy, like Dylan when he's good. "Why'd ya spit on my snatch?" indeed — the music's harshest account of a woman fending the world.   **A−**

The Fall: *Live at the Witch Trials* (I.R.S. '79). After dismissing this as just too tuneless and crude — wasn't even fast — I played it in tandem with Public Image Ltd. one night and for a few bars could hardly tell the difference. Of course, in this case the heavy bass and distant guitars could simply mean a bad mix, but what the hell — when they praise spastics and "the r&r dream" they're not being sarcastic (I don't think), and in this icky pop moment we could use some ugly rebellion. How about calling it punk?   **B+**

Family: *Anyway* (United Artists '71). Back before Rik Grech deserted them for (and on) Blind Faith they were a slightly demented hard rock band that made arty with a violin. Now they're a slightly demented hard rock band that makes arty with unidentifiable percussion and various croons and mumbles — at least on the studio side. On the live side they make shift. **C+**

Family: *Fearless* (United Artists '71). This hooks in on "Sat'd'y Barfly," which sets Roger Chapman to bellowing drunken boasts over dissonant piano chords. The rest is equally abrasive and eccentric, but not always so good-humored, which when it doesn't hook in can be a problem. Original grade: B plus. **B**

Family: *Bandstand* (United Artists '72). When they kick ass on "Burlesque" or "Glove" or "Broken Nose" they sound raw and abrasive in the great English hard rock tradition, but the discords are altogether more cunning, and on this album their stubborn lyricism finally finds suitable melodies on "Coronation" and "My Friend the Sun" and the bittersweet "Dark Eyes." Their sexual anger is class-conscious, always a plus, and their sadness usually a matter of time, which they get away with when the melody is very suitable. And just as they begin to get it together they break up. **B+**

Family: *It's Only a Movie* (United Artists '73). So they didn't break up after all, but the close call seems to have mellowed them — this is their funniest, funkiest, most relaxed album. I know an autumnal Roger Chapman is a little hard to imagine, but this is a man of many guises — back in the beginning he sometimes came on like an opera singer. Pick: "Leroy," inspired by "No Money Down." **B+**

Fancy: *Wild Thing* (Big Tree '74). Especially on the tour de force title track, it sounds at first as if lead singer Ann Kavanagh might be the real Suzi Quatro, but she's not, she's just the pro. You can imagine hard-core rock? Well, this is soft-core. **C+**

Fanny: *Fanny* (Reprise '70). Rather than getting all hot and heavy, Burbank's entry in the Ladies' Day Derby emulates the circa-1965 sound of groups like the Hollies and (says here) the Beatles. Execution is competent

enough — axpersonship isn't an issue with the style. But the Hollies (forget the Beatles) always had pretty good material — better than these four women can provide, although making an AM novelty out of Cream's "Badge" is a cute idea. Also, as producer Richard Perry must know, the Hollies always had amazing arrangements. **C**

Fanny: *Charity Ball* (Reprise '71). Seeing this band live was a revelation — for women, playing old-fashioned tight commercial rock and roll was a challenge rather than a self-conscious historical exercise. But that's not why there's been such improvement in the studio, although the live show held a clue — drummer Alice de Buhr was the most exciting musician on stage. This record exploits her chops and presence, sinking the pop harmonies in a harder, funkier frame. The title tune is a pure raver that oughtabeahit, but almost every song has something — or several somethings — to recommend it. Which is a lot more than I'd say of the Hollies' latest. **B+**

Fanny: *Fanny Hill* (Reprise '72). Three albums in not much over a year is two too many, and though half the new material is catchy enough, they give themselves away by opening sides with Marvin Gaye's "Ain't That Peculiar" and the Beatles' "Hey Bulldog." Several lyrics do groundwork in important women's themes (autonomy, motherhood, like that), but not one — not even "Wonderful Feeling," a disarmingly happy-sounding breakup song — offers the kind of concentrated perception that makes a song work or the kind of "Charity Ball" hook that makes you stop wondering whether a song is working. **B−**

Fanny: *Mother's Pride* (Reprise '73). In which Richard Perry bows to Todd Rundgren, June Millington aims for the balls and shoots some guy through the knee, and Alice de Buhr sings (off key) (best thing here). **C+**

Donna Fargo: *The Best of Donna Fargo* (ABC/Dot '77). Despite her fondness for rose gardens, Fargo in her prime was a lot more credible than Lynn Anderson. Her good cheer always carried real conviction, perhaps because she wrote her happiness prescriptions/descriptions herself, although that little growl she learned from Loretta didn't hurt. Only a dour young city man like me (or woman like me wife) would complain about the way hubby and Jesus combine to stop her nagging in "How Close You Came (to Being Gone)." But we also note that the happiest girl in the whole USA has a job and lets her husband make the coffee. And that a year later she allows as how she's just not up to cohabiting with Superman.   **B**

Mimi Farina and Tom Jans: *Take Heart* (A&M '71). I'm no necrologist, but the difference between Richard Farina, sharp-witted and spirited even when he was throwing himself away, and Tom Jans, often pretty and always insipid, is as telling an indictment of the acoustic singer-songwriters as I can offer. Mimi's muted burr still catches me up short sometimes, but this is what I call decadent.   **C**

Fashion: *Product Perfect* (I.R.S. '79). Order of topics on first side: consumerism, imperialism, racism, sociopathy, "rock culture," apathy (right-wing), apathy (left-wing). Sounds predictable but it isn't — all of these songs are based on post-Marcusian cliches sophisticated enough to get the average rock fan thinking hard, and some of them are based on post-Marcusian ideas sophisticated enough to get the average post-Marcusian thinking hard. Sounds unmusical but it isn't that either — the singing is clever and impassioned, the punkish, futuristic reggae-synthesizer fusion often catchy and always apt. If only I were a post-Marcusian myself I'd be in heaven. And a second side as good as the first might convert me.   **A−**

Fela and Afrika 70: *Zombie* (Mercury '77). Fela Anikulapo Kuti is a Nigerian pianist-saxophonist who makes real fusion music — if James Brown's stuff is Afro-American, his is Amer-African. No U.S. percussion ensemble would distinguish between first and second conga, but Fela's harmonic, melodic, and improvisational ideas are all adapted from Afro-American (which means part European) models. His sax style recalls the honkers, but it's more staccato, more complex rhythmically. Not only that, there are lyrics, in English, with crib sheet — very political, very associative, explicitly antibook.   **A−**

Jose Feliciano: *Encore!* (RCA Victor '71). Pretty soulful in his Castilian way, and his "Wichita Lineman" beats the Meters' (and Glen's). But the live version of "Light My Fire" mysteriously included on this best-of records for posterity one of the more obsequious band intros in entertainment history. And didn't anybody tape the scandalous "Star Spangled Banner" he did at the World Series?   **C+**

Narvel Felts: *Narvel Felts* (ABC/Dot '75). An r&b singer on the country side of the fence, Narvel recalls Roy Orbison (they both worked for Sun) or Ferlin Husky at the fountain of youth. Wotta voice — he even does "Gone." It should go without saying that I love sexy r&b covers like "Slip Away" and "Honey Love" and filthy-minded country originals like "Let My Fingers Do the Walking." But even when he's maudlin and self-involved I get off some on his naked, nasal emotion. Sometimes I like the country side of the fence myself.   **B+**

Narvel Felts: *Greatest Hits Volume I* (ABC/Dot '75). In the wake of "Reconsider Me" I consider Narvel a marvel myself, but it's hard to believe this compilation from his precrossover days hit very big anywhere. For authenticity we have four tunes from Nashville hacks Jack Foster and Bill Rice. And for eccentricity we have "Love Me Like a Rock."   **C+**

Freddy Fender: *Fuera de Alcance/ Out of Reach* (Starflite '74). Ne Baldemar Huerta, this South Texas legend is a real traditionalist, as he illustrates on the title number, a country song warbled in Spanish over a reggae backing track. Cutting that one inspired him to write a little tune called "Jamaica Farewell" twenty years *after* Harry Belafonte went pop with it. Time travel is nothing to a man who's done three years for weed, a drug commemorated — along with wine, cocaine, and morphine — on a version of "Junko Partner" that made Dr. John blush as he tickled the ivories in fond support. And "holding his hand and showing him the way is, no other than the great, incredible TV personality, Mr. Domingo Peña known from coast to coast!"   **B+**

Freddy Fender: *Rock 'n' Country* (ABC/Dot '76). Fender is a wonder of nature — I just wish one of his albums was a wonder of human devising. This is his third LP for ABC in ten months, and like the others it doesn't get the essence of a man who can follow an incandescent country version of "What'd I Say" with an incandescent country version of "How Much Is That Doggie in the Window." That's the parlay that opens side two of *Are You Ready for Freddy*, his most satisfying side for ABC to date; this is his most satisfying whole LP. His tenor is so penetrating, his Spanish lisp so guileless, that it's a pleasure to hear him sing almost anything, but he doesn't transcend himself as often as seems possible; why, for instance, should "Big Boss Man" work so much better than "Since I Met You Baby"? If only there were someone who knew.   **B+**

Freddy Fender: *Merry Christmas-Feliz Navidad from Freddy Fender* (ABC/Dot '71). A tough ex-con blissfully unembarrassed by sentimentality, and with a terrific sense of rhythm, Freddy could have made a (bilingual!) Christmas album to rank with Phil Spector's. If only Huey Meaux (producer-svengali) hadn't hogged the copyrights, thus keeping Freddy away from "Rudolph the Red-Nosed Reindeer" (his kind of song!) and — even

worse — "Feliz Navidad" itself. But I kind of love it anyway, and if it doesn't match UA's rereleased *12 Hits of Christmas* or *Rhythm and Blues Christmas*, it beats hell out of the Mormon Tabernacle Choir's *White* (get it?) (do I have to complete this title?)   **B**

Freddy Fender: *The Best of Freddy Fender* (ABC/Dot '77). Alamo diehards claim that stardom's turned Freddy into a Nashville clone, but I prefer this to the Starflite LP he cut as a local hero. It's not just that the horns no longer sound like they're coming in on another station, either — I believe in the material and I think Freddy does too. Like any overworked recordmaker, he's had his share of clinkers, but they're avoided here, and if he has to hug a stuffed (and spineless) cactus on the cover for image's sake, well, that seems authentic enough to me.   **A−**

Bryan Ferry: *"These Foolish Things"* (Atlantic '74). "A Hard Rain's Gonna Fall" defines this collection of rock classics — ranging from "It's My Party" to "Sympathy for the Devil" — as a pop statement. By transforming Dylan at his most messianic into gripping high camp complete with sound effects (when the poet dies in the gutter the chorus gives forth with a cute groan), Ferry both undercuts the inflated idealism of the original and reaffirms its essential power. Along the way, he also establishes "It's My Party" as a protest song. And just in case we're getting any highfalutin ideas, the title track reminds us that pop is only, well, foolish things, many of which predate not only Andy Warhol but rock and roll itself.   **A−**

Bryan Ferry: *Another Time, Another Place* (Atlantic '74). Comedy routines are rarely as funny the second time around, especially when you've used up your best lines — "The 'In' Crowd" is the only zinger Ferry comes up with here. Elsewhere he who plays at corruption is afflicted with disease — lead poisoning, it sounds like, affecting not only his brain but also his lungs and his pants. "You Are My Sunshine" makes "sense" slow, but too often Ferry simply indulges his taste for the lachrymose on songs that deserve better. Original grade: C plus. **B+**

Bryan Ferry: *Let's Stick Together* (Atlantic '76). A lot of people are crazy about this record, but I find its bifurcation alienating. On the one hand, we have the usual unlikely borrowings, the most effective from Wilbert Harrison and the Everlys. And as usual, these are powerful, strange, and interesting — and often quite compelling. On the other hand, we have unlikely remakes of old Roxy Music material, much of it from the groups's very first album. Although Ferry proves that he knows more about making records (and music) than he used to, the songs remain powerful, strange, and interesting — but not quite compelling. Add it all together and you get . . . two separate parts. **B**

Bryan Ferry: *In Your Mind* (Atlantic '77). Ferry has custom-designed a new line of songs for his solo concept, rather than borrowing from early Roxy or his humble forebears, and especially on side one the stuff is appealingly down-to-earth. But it doesn't go far enough. I used to think Ferry's big problem was the fruity baritone that epitomized his deliberate unnaturalness, but now I think it's the hopeless romanticism of his half-realized dreams. If he ever did convince large numbers of people to care about his obsessions, the result would be nothing more than a rather scary collective escapism. **B+**

Bryan Ferry: *The Bride Stripped Bare* (Atlantic '78). Maybe the smoke in Bryan's eyes has finally reached his heart; the apparent sincerity of some of the singing here makes those five-minute moments when he lingers ponderously over a key lyric easier to take. The Los Angeles musicians don't hurt either — the conjunction of his style of stylization (feigned detachment) with theirs (feigned naturalness) makes for interesting expressive tension. And

Waddy Wachtel is as apt a sound-effects man as Phil Manzanera ever was. **B+**

15-60-75 the Numbers Band: *Jimmy Bell's Still in Town* (Water Bros. '76). What is this I hear? Some kind of weird cross between the Grateful Dead and the Velvet Underground making its own record in Cuyahoga Falls, Ohio? No, that's not what I hear, but the description will have to do until the group comes up with another album — which I hope will feature more public lyrics and a drummer who can propagate the polyrhythms. **B−**

The 5th Dimension: *Greatest Hits* (Soul City '70). Strange that a black pop chorale should break at the same time as soul and psychedelica — even with a far-out name and black-identified label. I don't know which is worse — straight slick Jim Webb or stoned slick Laura Nyro. (Answer: *Hair*.) But I still get off on Webb's "Paper Cup," which I always regarded as the authentic alienation song ("Dangling Conversation" was the phony). And get with Nyro's "Wedding Bell Blues." **C+**

Firefall: *Luna Sea* (Atlantic '77). In which Rick Roberts allows as how he's "gonna quit that crazy runaround" — cross your heart, Rick? — and the whole band muses about how nice it would be if things never "changed for the better/But never got no worse." Such dreamers! Alternate title: *Compa Tents*. **C**

Firefall: *Elan* (Atlantic '78). I do too pay attention to mainstream rock product; in fact, I listened to this five or six times without a trace of stomach upset. The group achieves more of that old CSN(Y) feel than any of the decade's country-rock spinoffs; the album achieves more of that old rock and roll feel than any of the decade's CSN(Y) records. Commendable if not quite recommendable — didn't think they had it in them. **B−**

The First Choice: *"Armed and Extremely Dangerous"* (Philly Groove '73). The only musicians not named on the back cover are the three women depicted on the front, the ones with the voices, including a satiny lead (Rochelle Fleming, according to informed sources) who shouldn't do songs about lovable polio victims and suicidal feelings — at least not these songs. I don't expect feminist anthems against the girl-group undertow, and these people have a lot more spunk than the Three Degrees or Love Unlimited. But I do insist on high-quality schlock, and beyond the pleasant-plus hits and a memorable cover of "Love and Happiness" this isn't it. I know, the Shirelles and the Chiffons never made great albums either. So buy the singles. Original grade: B minus.   **B**

Roberta Flack: *Quiet Fire* (Atlantic '71). Flack is generally regarded as the most significant new black woman singer since Aretha Franklin, and at moments she sounds kind, intelligent, and very likable. But she often exhibits the gratuitous gentility you'd expect of someone who says "between you and I." Until she crackles a bit, forget about significance and listen to Ann Peebles.   **C**

Flamin Groovies: *Flamingo* (Kama Sutra '70). The mix and the groove are fierce enough to accommodate "Keep a Knockin'," "Comin After Me" is worthy of Chuck Berry, and "Second Cousin" could have been written for Jerry Lee Lewis, which makes a trinity. I do miss the wacked-out head of such *Supersnazz* classics as "Laurie Did It" and "The First One's Free," but the fifteen minutes expended on the last three cuts are a bigger problem — even the fast one drags. Sophisticated r&r primitivists are supposed to know about that stuff.   **B+**

Flamin Groovies: *Teenage Head* (Kama Sutra '71). Suprisingly bluesy, with a good Robert Johnson cover, a great John Lee Hooker rip, and lots of slide guitar. Plus the title track, an inspired articulation/sendup of "California born and bred" youth rebellion. But "High Flyin Baby," "Evil Hearted Ada," and "Whiskey Woman" fall into the blues-rock trap — not surprising at all.   **B**

Flamin' Groovies: *Shake Some Action* (Sire '76). So authentic that producer Dave Edmunds has reverted to the muddy mix — kinda like the Beatles or the Byrds or the Flamin Groovies. Actually, what it sounds like is mono electrically rechanneled for stereo. The Flamin Groovies were Haight-Ashbury enough to exploit aural distance in the service of a sly, spaced-out obliqueness, but these guys, deprived of singer-composer Roy A. Loney and making their way as an English pop-revival band, get their kicks by playing dumb. This compiles their best recent work and includes some good songs. But only cultists will ever hear them.   **B**

Flamin Groovies: *Still Shakin* (Kama Sutra '76). The back cover of this compilation excerpts ten favorable reviews of *Flamingo* and one of *Teenage Head*. The first side features two songs from *Flamingo* and four from *Teenage Head* plus an oldie of the latter vintage. The second side features a live-in-the-studio set of six more oldies from the same sessions. Howcum? Ask Richard Robinson, who produced all three albums. Or your collector friends.   **C+**

Flamin' Groovies: *Now* (Sire '78). In the late '60s they harked back to the late '50s; now, to borrow their title, they hark back to the middle '60s. Pretty hookily, too, though I don't get why the vocals are so ragged. And where (or when) will they be in 2001? Now?   **B−**

Flash: *Flash* (Capitol '72). People who lóve Yes will probably like this spinoff and imitation. I find Yes sharp and clever at best and this shapeless and intolerably precious at all times. Nor do I believe music gains body (or sexuality) by capillary action from its cover — the "advance" from Yes's psychedoodles to Flash's rear-view crotch shot only makes me wonder whether this band comes by its name lysergically. Original grade: C. **C−**

Flash & the Pan: *Flash & the Pan* (Epic '79). In which Australian power-pop producers Harry Vanda and George Young choose a nom de studio and turn into an instant cult item. Since the singing makes Rex Harrison sound like Mario Lanza, it's tuneful in only the most abstract sense. (Already the fanzines are paying attention.) Without the usual vocal surges it's also quite static. (Veddy interesting.) What hooks there are inhere in the chord changes. (Sounds more like art all the time.) And V&Y's ruminations on sociopolitical realities are worthy of a second-rate caper movie. (Bingo.) **C+**

Flash Cadillac and the Continental Kids: *There's No Face Like Chrome* (Epic '74). Unlike Sha Na Na, who are forced to rediscover how great oldies are every time they write an original, this isn't strictly a copy band, and on their follow-up album they prove it. Despite their unnecessarily stupid appearance, duh guys do not revert to the '50s solely for hard grit and axle grease, either, focusing instead on the sweet and funny part of pre-Beatles rock and roll. Tunes like "Dancin' (on a Saturday Night)" and "Standin' on the Corner" are impressive exercises. But only "First Girl" has a shot at entering the after-the-manner-of-Leiber-&-Stoller canon, and they didn't write it. Also, Jerry Leiber produced it, which must have helped quite a bit. Original grade: B plus. **B**

Fleetwood Mac: *Fleetwood Mac in Chicago* (Blue Horizon '70). Combining the recently released Vols. 1 and 2, this two-LP set lets five sincere but never sedulously irrelevant (cf. John Mayall) English lads explore their branches. It almost brings you back to those distant days when "white blues" was more than code for "heavy."

Knowledgeable song selection, expressive playing — especially by Peter Green, who filters B. B. King through Santo & Johnny with a saxophonist's sense of line — and lots of help from Otis Spann, Willie Dixon, Shakey Horton, and others makes the thinness of the singing seem like a tribute to a new tradition. (Later on Sire.) **B+**

Fleetwood Mac: *Kiln House* (Reprise '70). Despite the departure of the miraculously fluent Peter Green, the mansions in their jazzy blues/rock and roll guitar heaven are spacier than ever. A country parody called "Blood on the Floor" — a clumsily convoluted "Dear Doctor" — is less charitable than one would hope, but it's more than balanced off by Jeremy Spencer's membership pledge to the rockabilly auxiliary, "This Is the Rock." And somebody up there loves Buddy Holly so much he unearthed "Buddy's Song," by Buddy's mother. **A−**

Fleetwood Mac: *Future Games* (Reprise '71). These white blues (and hippie rockabilly) veterans shouldn't have to depend on new recruit Bob Welch's deftly metallized r&b extrapolation for rock and roll, but unless you count the studio jam, they do. And if the best song on the album isn't the slowest, that's only because Welch also has mystagogic tendencies. It's the simplest in any case: Christine Perfect's "Show Me a Smile." **B**

Fleetwood Mac: *Bare Trees* (Reprise '72). Their new identity is ominously mellow, but at least this time it's recognizable, and they've upped the speed a little. A lot less muddled than *Future Games* and occasionally as rich as *Kiln House,* but so thoroughly homogenized that it's hard to remember exactly how the cream tasted once it's gone down. **B+**

Fleetwood Mac: *Penguin* (Reprise '73). Those who complain about the remake of "(I'm a) Road Runner," with Mick Fleetwood smashing past the cymbals while Dave Walker shouts, probably think these studio craftspeople were slumming when they jammed with Otis Spann. I love it. I also like all of Christine McVie's husky laments. But could rilly do without Bob Welch's ever-mellower musings. **B**

Fleetwood Mac: *Mystery to Me* (Reprise '73). I downgraded this at first because I doubted the continuing usefulness (much less creativity) of such smooth-rocking expertise. And I still do — when they achieve the contained, "Layla"-like freneticism of "The City," their professed distaste for urban "darkness" insures that the breakout will be a one-shot. But this album epitomizes what they've come to be, setting a gentle but ever more technological spaceyness over a bottom that, while never explosive, does drive the music with flair and economy, the least you can expect of a band named after its rhythm section. Even Bob Welch does himself proud. Original grade: B. **B+**

Fleetwood Mac: *Heros Are Hard To Find* (Reprise '74). The proof that their formula has finally trapped them is the pitifulness of their attempts to escape — with string synthesizer, pedal steel, half-assed horns, and other catch-22s of the International Pop Music Community. Bob Welch sounds bored, which is certainly poetic justice, and even Christine McVie is less than perfect this time out. Their worst. **B−**

Fleetwood Mac: *Fleetwood Mac* (Reprise '75). Why is this Fleetwood Mac album different from all other Fleetwood Mac albums? The answer is supergroup fragmentation in reverse: the addition of two singer-songwriters who as Buckingham Nicks were good enough — or so somebody thought — to do their own LP for Polydor a while back. And so, after five years of struggling for a consistency that became their hob globin, they make it sound easy. In fact, they come up with this year's easy listening classic. Roll on. **A−**

Fleetwood Mac: *Rumours* (Warner Bros. '77). Why is this easy-listening rock different from all other easy-lis-tening rock, give or take an ancient harmony or two? Because myths of love lost and found are less invidious (at least in rock and roll) than myths of the road? Because the cute-voiced woman writes and sings the tough lyrics and the husky-voiced woman the vulnerable ones? Because they've got three melodist-vocalists on the job? Because Mick Fleetwood and John McVie learned their rhythm licks playing blues? Because they stuck to this beguiling formula when it barely broke even? Because this album is both more consistent and more eccentric than its blockbuster predecessor? Plus it jumps right out of the speakers at you? Because Otis Spann must be happy for them? Because Peter Green is in heaven? Original grade: A minus. **A**

Fleetwood Mac: *Tusk* (Warner Bros. '79). A million bucks is what I call obsessive production, but for once it means something. This is like reggae, or Eno — not only don't Lindsey Buckingham's swelling edges and dynamic separations get in the way of the music, they're inextricable from the music, or maybe they *are* the music. The passionate dissociation of the mix is entirely appropriate to an ensemble in which the three principals have all but disappeared (vocally) from each other's work. But only Buckingham is attuned enough to get exciting music out of a sound so spare and subtle it reveals the limits of Christine McVie's simplicity and shows Stevie Nicks up for the mooncalf she's always been. Also, it doesn't make for very good background noise. **B+**

The Flying Burrito Bros.: *Burrito Deluxe* (A&M '70). *The Gilded Palace of Sin* was an ominous, obsessive, tongue-in-cheek country-rock synthesis, absorbing rural and urban, traditional and contemporary, at point of impact. This is a skillful, lightweight folk-rock blend, enlivening the tempos and themes of the country music whose usages it honors. Its high point is called "Older Guys," a rock (as opposed to rock and roll) idea by definition, and though songs like "Cody, Cody" and "Man in the Fog" — as well as Jagger-Richard's previously unrecorded "Wild Horses" — obviously speak from Gram Parsons's Waycross soul, they're vague enough for Chris Hillman's folkie harmonies to take them over.   **B+**

The Flying Burrito Bros.: *The Flying Burrito Bros.* (A&M '71). Gram Parsons having gone off to follow whatever it is he follows, the Burritos are a solid, plaintive country band with rock influences. Realer than average, and nicer, but just as easy to ignore. **C+**

The Flying Burrito Bros.: *Last of the Red Hot Burritos* (A&M '72). With Chris Hillman rocking through previously unrecorded covers from "Orange Blossom Special" to "Don't Fight It," Gram Parsons's original country-soul concept for this band lives again. Unfortunately, it lives best on the previously recorded Parsons originals. And it lived better when he was singing them. Original grade: A minus.   **B**

The Flying Burrito Bros.: *Close Up the Honky Tonks* (A&M '74). This repackaged best-of-Gram is baited with five previously unreleased Parsons vocals. These are nice, but since even an unreconstructed Parsons nut like me can reel off more interesting cover versions of "Sing Me Back Home" (the Everlys), "Break My Mind" (the Box Tops), and "To Love Somebody" (initials: JJ), maybe they were unreleased for a reason. It also puts the six greatest cuts off *Gilded Palace of Sin* on one side, a convenience I'd appreciate more if *Gilded Palace of Sin,* the only full-fledged country-rock masterpiece, weren't still in the catalogue. Your local record retailer will no doubt order you one if you take the trouble of kidnapping his children.   **B−**

The Flying Burrito Brothers: See also Gram Parsons

FM (MCA '78). An AOR wish fulfillment — Superstar top twenty. I mean, the most mechanistic radio offers an occasional ear-opener, but even though all twenty songs on this soundtrack-compilation are pretty good, including Foreigner's, they're as predictable as cuts on a disc, and (worse still) diminished by their mutual proximity. This is frequency modulation at its blandest, with specific content subjugated to "sound"; it cries out for deprogramming. Typically, Steely Dan contributes a title tune that elucidates this dilemma while reveling in it. Atypically, Linda Ronstadt's live "Tumbling Dice" is so passionate and revelatory that it leaps out of its context and stomps all over the Rolling Stones.   **B−**

Dan Fogelberg: *Souvenirs* (Epic '74). It took the poor fellow three years to write these songs — why, just the title of "Changing Horses" represents weeks of thought — but in a heart-warming show of togetherness his friends helped with the record. Joe Walsh produced, Don Henley played some drums, and Graham Nash sang a few harmonies, though in the spirit of his overarching vision Fogelberg prefers to tape those on himself. Inspirational Verse: ". . . you wish someone/Would   buy   your   confessions."   **C−**

Dan Fogelberg: *Captured Angel* (Epic '75). Such kind folks at Epic Records and Full Moon Productions — not only have they let Fogelberg record nine more songs, and taken down something he hummed in the rec room for Glen Spreen to orchestrate, but they've let him put some of his art therapy on the cover. Dimensionality is beyond him (or else he doesn't know much about breasts), and it does look as if somebody put out the angel's eyes with a poker, but after all, it's the spirit that counts.   **D+**

John Fogerty: *John Fogerty* (Asylum '75). The best singing here is at medium tempos — Fogerty sounds distraught for no reason when he rocks out, and the revved-up horns just push him harder. But the best songwriting is on the fast side-openers — "Rockin' All Over the World" and "Almost Saturday Night," neither of which could be called an illumination. This is what happens when rock devolves from a calling into an idea — you can't even be absolutely certain it's him rather than you, but you know he'll never get away with it twice. **B**

Foghat: *Energized* (Bearsville '74). Conceived in memory of Chuck Berry when Kim Simmonds began handing out Kenny Burrell chord books to his Savoy Brown cohorts in 1970, this band has taken a good idea way too far. Rod Price's ubiquitous slide and Dave Peverett's iniquitous rave are decent trademarks, but energized becomes enervating in the absence of dynamic changes. Is good competent rock really good and competent if its excitement never transcends the mechanical? Is that what getting off means? So maybe they're not good and competent. **B−**

Fools Gold: *Fools Gold* (Morning Sky '76). Should this become a million seller, it will provide the most pungent do-it-yourself review since the classic *This Is Bull*. But it won't be worth it. **C−**

Steve Forbert: *Steve Forbert* (Nemporer '78). I thought this kid's folk songs were promising the first time I saw him — which was before I knew he was destined to share management with the Ramones — and I still do. **B**
Steve Forbert: *Jackrabbit Slim* (Nemporer '79). John Simon's settings go every which way — from Muscle Shoals to Kingston, from country to folk to r&b — but always seem to come up pop. Then again, what else do you do with Forbert? He's as all-American as the Band, but beyond that catchy young heartland-soulful voice he has no musical identity; his lyrics are omniverously observant, but beyond an attractive all-purpose compassion they never reveal a point of view

either. *Steve Forbert Reporting,* that's all. Which means you have to care about him as much as he does — "Make It All So Real" is as shameless as the suffering-artist theme gets — to care about his songs. And the voice doesn't do that for me. **B−**

Foreigner: *Foreigner* (Atlantic '77). You've heard of Beatlemania? I propose Xenophobia. **C**
Foreigner: *Double Vision* (Atlantic '78). I like rock and roll so much that I catch myself getting off on "Hot Blooded," a typical piece of cock-rock nookie-hating carried along on a riff-with-chord-change that's pure (gad) second-generation Bad Company. Fortunately, nothing else here threatens their status as world's dullest group. Inspirational Verse: "She backhanded me 'cross my face." **C−**
Foreigner: *Head Games* (Atlantic '79). This isn't as sodden as you might expect — these are pros who adapt to the times, and they speed the music up. I actually enjoy a few of these songs until I come into contact with the dumb woman-haters who are doing the singing. I mean, these guys think punks are cynical and anti-life? Guys who complain that the world is all madness and lies and then rhyme "science" and "appliance" without intending a joke? **C**

David Forman: *David Forman* (Arista '76). Comparisons are odiferous, and this one — David Forman/Randy Newman — is commonplace as well. Sorry. At least I don't mean the words; except for the unconvincing "Rosalie" and one or two others, these employ evocative metaphor, in the manner of Jackson Browne, rather than evocative social detail. It's the r&b-based singing and precise, manneristic arrangements, both (unintentionally?) redolent of Newman, that bother me. Even Jackson Browne knows that groupings of associative metaphors hold together best along a groove, and since Forman, unlike Newman, has the pipes to bring off the sweeter soul modulations, you'd figure he'd go that way. Instead, he *sets* each song — like a jewel, or a loose tooth in a denture. Many-faceted though they may be, these songs are neither gemlike nor biting, and the settings, unlike Newman's, too often sound readymade. **B**

Fotomaker: *Fotomaker* (Atlantic '78). In which the label that has already brought us Firefall, Festival, Foreigner, Funkpot, Fishwife, Failure, and Fuckall sponsors yet another dupergroup made up of yet another batch of craft-obsessed rock dues-payers. Unfortunately, this one is faceless even by low-profile dupergroup standards. (Say, there's a name for a band — Faceless.) After all, Firefall did blend second-line graduates of Spirit and the Flying Burrito Brothers into their distinctively unexciting rock country-pop. And Fuckall did fuse second-line graduates of Chelsea and the Harlots of 42nd Street into their harmlessly obscene rock punk-pop. But second-line graduates of the Rascals and the Raspberries make only for depressingly mediocre rock abcxyz-pop. This is formally appropriate — titles like "Where Have You Been All My Life" and "Two Can Make It Work" would be altogether overwhelmed by hooks, melodies, or singing of the slightest originality or enthusiasm. Beat the rush — boycott now, before anyone has even heard of them.   **D+**

Four Tops: *Greatest Hits Vol. 2* (Motown '71). If Levi Stubbs is one of the definitive soul men, as some believe, then what he defines is the pitfalls of the style. He's a singer who's more interested in impressing the deacons (and their wives) than feeling the spirit — overripe, self-involved, and in the end pretentious. And this material is far from his best — stuck with the low-grade rock gentility of "Walk Away Renee" and "If I Were a Carpenter" and the sermonizing of "What Is Man" and "In These Changing Times," he's a typical victim of Motown's decadence. Despite some good rhythm tracks — they always seem to get good rhythm tracks out there — the only one of these songs you'll remember fondly is "Just Seven Numbers," a simple-minded throwaway about swallowing your pride and making that call.   **C+**

Four Tops: *Keeper of the Castle* (Dunhill '72). The contrast of Levi Stubbs's self-indulgence against Motown's economical bottom worked sometimes, although toward the end the breast-beating began to sound like an Olatunji imitation. But when superschlockers Lambert, Potter, and Barri meet force with force, the results are too overbearing to interest anyone but professional theorists of camp. Original grade: D plus.   **C−**

Kim Fowley: *I'm Bad* (Capitol '72). I've nothing against hype, but it's a little low to distribute snazzy jackets containing blank discs. Caveat emptor.   **E−**

Peter Frampton: *Wind of Change* (A&M '72). Not hard to hear why he wanted out of Humble Pie — with his pretty guitar and air of abstracted yearning, the boy's almost a ringer for Dave Mason. He's equally tuneful, vague, and confused about women ("I wasn't made to do no cooking"?). The difference is that Mason would never cover "Jumping Jack Flash." But if he did he'd take it at the same insipidly insinuating tempo.   **B−**

Frampton's Camel: *Frampton's Camel* (A&M '73). Peter F. is rocking harder, probably because the above-mentioned Camel is a regular touring unit. He's writing fewer catchy tunes, probably because the abovementioned Camel is a regular touring unit. He dedicates a song to his manager, probably because the abovementioned Camel is a regular touring unit. He identifies white sugar as evil, probably because he's into health food.   **B−**

Peter Frampton: *Frampton Comes Alive!* (A&M '76). All right, Peter, you've made your point — tour enough and smile enough and the tunes sink in. I'll rate your fucking album — it's been in the top five all year. Now will you please leave? **B—**

Peter Frampton: *I'm in You* (A&M) '77). Like Steve Miller, Frampton is a medium-snazzy guitarist taking no chances on an absurdly salable formula this time out; the only development from his first (and best) two albums is that this one has a kinda "live" feel, and the material is very thin. But at least Frampton sounds completely unsmug, an achievement in a star of his magnitude.   **C—**

Aretha Franklin: *This Girl's in Love with You* (Atlantic '70). Although *Soul '69* didn't convince me she was made for pop standards, this (basically appealing) mish-mash suggests that she's better suited to pop disposables like the title track and "Son of a Preacher Man" than to rock statements like "Eleanor Rigby" and "The Weight." I admit that when she sings "The Weight" it sounds as if she knows what it means. But I still don't. Original grade: A minus.   **B+**

Aretha Franklin: *Spirit in the Dark* (Atlantic '70). At first this may sound unnaturally even — jazzy in its pleasantness, pleasant in its jazziness — but that's just because no Aretha album has ever generated such a consistent groove. Four different bands, notably the Dixie Flyers and the Muscle Shoals Rhythm Section, keep things rocking at a medium-fast tempo, and what's lost in soul intensity is more than made up for in a kind of dusky barroom aura — if you can imagine walking into some funky cocktail lounge and finding the greatest singer in the world at the piano. Infinitely playable. Powerful song for song. Classic in its casualness. Original grade: B plus.   **A**

Aretha Franklin: *Aretha's Greatest Hits* (Atlantic '71). Great stuff, but not the greatest — and not as consistent stylistically as 1969's *Aretha's Gold*, which it duplicates on eight out of fourteen cuts. As for the latest hits, well, Aretha's done better recently

than the contrived humankindness of "Bridge over Troubled Water," the contrived religiosity of "Let It Be," and the contrived black consciousness of "Spanish Harlem."   **B+**

Aretha Franklin: *Aretha Live at Fillmore West* (Atlantic '71). This record almost gets over on sheer vocal excess. Neither *Aretha in Paris* nor any of her studio albums has ever caught her in such an explosive mood, and the result is a "Dr. Feelgood" that could heal the halt and versions of "Eleanor Rigby" and "Bridge over Troubled Water" that sound like Sunday morning. But though the speedy tempos help vitalize those last two songs as well, they do less than nothing for "Respect" and "Don't Play That Song" and can't save "Love the One You're With" or "Make It with You" (did she have to do 'em both?). And while in theory nothing could be more exciting than an eight-minute duet with Ray Charles on "Spirit in the Dark," in practice I'd rather hear Ray sing "The Three Bells" and Aretha go it alone.   **B**

Aretha Franklin: *Young, Gifted and Black* (Atlantic '72). This plays straight to the nouveau-bourgeois black album audience, with all the self-consciousness and instrumentation that implies, but though it's genteel it's never bloodless: Aretha's free-flight improvisations are vehicles of a romanticism extreme and even unhinged enough to soar from the Afro-American experience right into the blithe fantasies of pop. She makes "Long and Winding Road" rock and turns the programmatic title anthem into a hymn. She proves herself a fond observer of everyday life on her own "First Snow in Kokomo." And on "Day Dreaming" she provides a metaphor her American-dreaming sisters and brothers can relate to: the song is wishful thinking, but the man it's about may just be real anyway, and that's the way America is sometimes.   **A**

Aretha Franklin: *Amazing Grace* (Atlantic '72). Because I don't think

God's grace is amazing or believe that Jesus Christ is his son, I find it hard to relate to gospel groups as seminal as the Swan Silvertones and the Dixie Hummingbirds and have even more trouble with James Cleveland's institutional choral style. There's a purity and a passion to this church-recorded double-LP that I've missed in Aretha, but I still find that the subdued rhythm section and pervasive call-and-response conveys more aimlessness than inspiration. Or maybe I just trust her gift of faith more readily when it's transposed to the secular realm.   **B+**

Aretha Franklin: *Hey Now Hey (the Other Side of the Sky)* (Atlantic '73). In which she rejects the producers who made her career for Quincy Jones and drifts off into the hey now hey with rudder trailing. "So Swell When You're Well" and "Sister from Texas" might sneak onto *Spirit in the Dark* with a little more funk, and "Just Right Tonight" busies itself nicely, but too much of this is pretentious baloney, and "Somewhere" and "Mister Spain" are horrid. Original grade: C plus.   **B−**

Aretha Franklin: *Let Me in Your Life* (Atlantic '74). Welcome Tom and Jerry (Dowd and Wexler) back — this isn't great Aretha, but it rocks steady even on the ballads. If she doesn't get away with "The Masquerade Is Over," she does renew "A Song for You" with a fresh electric piano part and a good helping of indiscreet interpretation. Guided indiscretion, that's the key — her great gift is her voice, but her genius is her bad taste. Original grade: A minus.   **B+**

Aretha Franklin: *With Everything I Feel in Me* (Atlantic '74). Aretha has established herself as such a solid property — certain to hold onto a good-sized audience for years to come, but unlikely to expand any further — that it's getting hard to resist thinking of her as a cross between Frank Sinatra and Nancy Wilson, turning out collections as custom-designed as next year's Oldsmobile. This one's more ethereal styling — less bottom, more la-la

scatting — is presaged by *Young, Gifted and Black*'s exploration of the spirituality of black pop rather than *Hey Now Hey*'s spindrift, and I like it fine. But it's hard to get excited about an album that puts so much of its soul into the codas.   **B+**

Aretha Franklin: *You* (Atlantic '75). Does the curiously unfocused effect of this album reflect Aretha's inability to direct her own career? Or is it just the way the bass is mixed? Or are the two the same?   **B−**

Aretha Franklin: *Sparkle* (Atlantic '76). Aretha vamping over competent-plus Curtis Mayfield tracks is sexy at worst, mixing rhythmic and emotional frisson, soul product as it should be, albeit deplorably post-verbal. Good late-night listening, I suppose — but not as good as *Spirit in the Dark*, or *Super Fly*.   **B**

Aretha Franklin: *Sweet Passion,* (Atlantic '77). When I work at listening, I can tell that she still sings real good.   **C+**

Aretha Franklin: *Almighty Fire* (Atlantic '78). Well, she did call the last one *Sweet Passion,* and if she calls the next one *Transcendent Glory* it won't bring the spirit back.   **C+**

Aretha Franklin: *La Diva* (Atlantic '79). Blame what's wrong with this record on the late trite Van McCoy, one of the most tasteless arrangers ever to produce an LP. What saves it is that McCoy didn't control half of these songs — arrangements by Richard Gibbs and Arthur Jenkins (rhythm only) and Zulema Cusseaux and Skip Scarborough (rhythm plus orchestration) provide frequent relief. Aretha contributes two sisterly originals, which are really fine, and one loverly original, which isn't. Because McCoy keeps intruding she never gets a flow going. But there haven't been this many good cuts on an Aretha album in five years.   **B**

Michael Franks: *Sleeping Gypsy* (Warner Bros. '77). I don't trust Franks's sambas to drowse by, but when he mentioned that he heard from his ex on the back of his checks he woke me up long enough to make me believe he had some smarts. Quite a lot of smarts, actually. Then I dozed off again. **B**

John Fred and His Playboy Band: *Love My Soul* (Uni '70). With his sharp, nasal drawl, Fred was born to pop, and though he's lost collaborator Andrew Bernard, he's keeping Shreveport's Sgt. Pepper's Lonely Hearts Club Fan Club going all by himself. Would anyone but a genuine eccentric rewrite "Sweet Soul Music" as a tribute to Johnny Winter, Pete Townshend, and Nilsson? "Agnes in Disguise (With Blanket)": "Sadie Trout." **B−**

Jeffrey Fredericks & the Clamtones: *Spiders in the Moonlight* (Rounder '77). Fredericks is the secret hero of my beloved *Have Moicy!*, but I had to penetrate a whole lot of received music before I could be sure that his own album was more than hippie cute. What it is instead is insanely funny. Dedication: "We would like to apologize to our mothers." **B+**

Free: *Fire and Water* (A&M '70). From sodden blooze to steady, unpretentious rock and roll in three progressively simpler — as opposed to easier — albums, climaxing with "All Right Now," a bone-crunching single you can groan along with. Recommended follow-up: a shortened "Mr. Big." Predicted follow-up: the already shortened "Fire and Water." **B**

Free: *Highway* (A&M '71). I know you think they're dumb, but they're not, they're just slow, and this intelligent noise proves it. Every instrument in what is basically a trio format must make a solo-quality contribution, yet every one is held in check, by the tempos and by structures in which flash is strictly discouraged. The tension that results is more gripping here than on *Fire and Water* because vocalist Paul Rodgers and guitarist Paul Kossoff have mastered the reined-in expres-

siveness that comes naturally to drummer Simon Kirke and (especially) bassist Andy Fraser — last time they showed off, but this time you can hear them trying not to. Equally important, the tracks average 3:48 instead of 5:02. But though there are hints of melodic and verbal facility as well, there aren't enough. **B**

Free: *Heartbreaker* (Island '73). "I was walking in the rain with my shoes untied," a line from newcomer Rabbit Bundrick, sums them up — I don't know myself whether it's a cleverly modified cliche or an overgrown one. But I do know that if *Free at Last* was simply listless this is actively deficient in formal acuteness. Andy Fraser has been replaced by both Bundrick's generally unnecessary keyboards (check out his organ on the otherwise engaging "Travellin in Style") and Tetsu Yamauchi's more stolid bass. Paul Kossoff, replaced by other guitarists on half the tracks, sounds like he's pursuing a solo career when he's on. And Paul Rodgers sounds more full of himself than his songs or his guitar warrant. **C+**

Free: *The Best of Free* (A&M '75). I could complain that the format automatically glosses over their austerity with an uncharacteristic catchiness, but in fact it sounds better and says more about them than *Highway*. Just as annotator Jim Bickhart claims, the band wasn't "only effective at gut-level; it was effective as *music*." But often the gutty moves — Rodgers's or Kossoff's crowd-pleasing flourishes — weren't musical, while the arty touches — the deliberate pace and general sense of containment —socked you right in the cerebrum. Which is why Bad Company grandstands, and why I'm on the critical fence. **B+**

Fresh: *Fresh Out of Borstal* (RCA Victor '70). This candidly Stonesish studio quasi-hype is dutifully class-conscious, but it bears about as much relation to the prison homosexuality alluded to in the ads as an aspirin dramatization does to open heart surgery.

That is, lest my rhetoric confuse you: this is not a record about bugger-rape. Docked two notches for misrepresenting itself.   **D+**

Dean Friedman: *Dean Friedman* (Lifesong '77). He tells us right off that he's got "a rich man's dream" and "a poor man's needs"; in other words, he's got the soul of a middle-class kid who hopes he's hitbound and doesn't have the faintest idea what rich men dream about. Hitbound he may be — this is replete with nice reflections nicely melodized. But only once, on the transcendent "Ariel," does he sound as cute as he wants to.   **B−**

Kinky Friedman: *Sold American* (Vanguard '73). Too bad Kinky's unique cross between Don Rickles and Woody Guthrie extends to his singing. Doesn't matter on the lip-smackingly tasteless "Ballad of Charles Whitman" or the foolproof "We Reserve the Right to Refuse Service." But when he gets a leetle serious, as on the title song or the signature "Ride 'Em Jewboy," you wish his voice could convey something of what he means.   **B**

Kinky Friedman: *Lasso from El Paso* (Epic '76). The clue to whether this guy deserves his reputation as a wit is that Joe Cocker, who doesn't even know what the words *mean,* does a funnier version of "Catfish." The clue to whether he deserves his ambitions as a romantic figure is "Lady Yesterday."   **C**

Robert Fripp: *Exposure* (Polydor '79). Fripp has always been a bit of a jerk, but over the years he's figured out what to do with the talent that goes along with his affliction. This concept album earns its conceit, orchestrating bits and pieces of art-rock wisdom — from punk to Frippertronics, from King Crimson to singer-songwriter — into a fluent whole. Maybe soon he'll get smart enough to forget about J. G. Bennett. "It is impossible to achieve the aim without suffering" isn't exactly big news, and old Crimson fans will swallow side two without the caveat.   **B+**

Fripp & Eno: *No Pussyfooting* (Antilles '75). Although art-rockers praise Fripp's undulating phased guitar and Eno's mood-enhancing synthesizer drones, they also complain that it all gets a little, well, monotonous after a while. That's the problem with art-rockers — they don't know much about art. I think these two twenty-minute duets, recorded more than two years ago, are the most enjoyable pop electronics since Terry Riley's *A Rainbow in Curved Air,* achieving their goal with admirable formal concision. What do the bored ones want? Can't have meter shifts 'cause there's no beat, can't have bad poetry because there's no vocalist, can't have fancy chord changes 'cause there's no key center. What's left is tranquility amid the machines, more visionary and more romantic than James Taylor could dream of being. Highlight: the unrestrained snake guitar on the unfortunately titled "Swastika Girls." [Later on Editions E.G.]   **B+**

Fripp & Eno: *Evening Star* (Antilles '76). This time F&E take dead aim at the hit single they so manifestly deserve by breaking their magic music into four distinct pieces on side one, but as a result I find the total effect more static — the endings are disconcertingly arbitrary, while *No Pussyfooting*'s full sides just keep on moving. Special award for the simulated scratch that decorates "An Index of Metals" — one of the most reassuringly fallible moments ever recorded.   **B+**

The Fugs: *Golden Filth* (Reprise '70). Not enough Tuli and a touch too much Ed, but this LP — recorded June 1, 1968, at one of their last shows — is their scush-slurfing testament. The best tune was written by William Blake under the romantic sway of a lesbian troll, but you can tell the other composers are poets too — listen to the similes break down in "Supergirl," or tell me that Jim Morrison knows somebody who "humps like a wildcat" (or anyway, knows enough to laugh about it). The music is, well, a mess, but a purposeful mess, and Ed Sanders's proems are dirty jokes at their most divine. Original grade: A minus. **B+**

Fugs 4, Rounders Score (ESP-Disk' '75). Previously unreleased (Holy Modal) Rounders oldies (the original "Romping Through the Swamp") plus a mid-'60s best-of on the original rockpoets, with ample room for the musical genius of Tuli Kupferberg — including "Morning, Morning" in a version far lovelier than Spyder Turner's and the peristaltic "Caca Rocka," a/k/a "Pay Toilet Blues." The musicianship will offend the fastidious and loses even me at times. But there's a sense in which the halting drone of these sessions, vaguely reminiscent of the early Velvets, is more appropriate to the Fugs' secondhand rock than all the classy folkies they later patched on. **B+**

Funkadelic: *Funkadelic* (Westbound '70). Q (side one, cut one): "Mommy, What's a Funkadelic?" A: Someone from Carolina who encountered eternity on LSD and vowed to contain it in a groove. Q (side two, cut four): "What Is Soul?" A: A ham hock in your corn flakes. You get high marks for your questions, guys. **C+**

Funkadelic: *Free Your Mind and Your Ass Will Follow* (Westbound '70). This is as confusing and promising and ultimately ambiguous as the catchy (and rhythmic) title slogan. Is that ass as in "shake your ass" or ass as in "save your ass"? And does one escape/transcend the dollar by renouncing the material world or by accepting one's lot? Similarly, are the scratchy organ timbres and disorienting separations fuckups or deliberate alienation effects? Is this music to stand to or music to get wasted by? In short, is this band (this black band, I should add, since it's black people who are most victimized by antimaterialist rhetoric) promulgating escapist idealism or psychic liberation? Or do all these antinomies merely precede some aesthetic synthesis? One thing is certain — the only place that synthesis might occur here is on "Funky Dollar Bill." **B−**

Funkadelic: *Maggot Brain* (Westbound '71). Children, this is a funkadelic. The title piece is ten minutes of classic Hendrix-gone-heavy guitar by one Eddie Hazel — time-warped, druggy superschlock that may falter momentarily but never lapses into meaningless showoff runs. After which comes 2:45 of post-classic soulgroup harmonizing — two altos against a bass man, all three driven by the funk, a rhythm so pronounced and eccentric it could make Berry Gordy twitch to death. The funk pervades the rest of the album, but not to the detriment of other peculiarities. Additional highlight: "Super Stupid." **B+**

Funkadelic: *America Eats Its Young* (Westbound '72). Their racial hostility is much preferable to the brotherhood bromides of that other Detroit label, but their taste in white people is suspect; it's one thing to put down those who "picket this and protest that" from their "semi-first-class seat," another to let the Process Church of the Final Judgment provide liner notes on two successive albums. I overlooked it on *Maggot Brain* because the music was so difficult to resist, but here the strings (told you about their taste in white people), long-windedness (another double-LP that should be a single), and programmatic lyrics ("Miss Lucifer's Love" inspires me to mention that while satanism is a great antinomian metaphor it often leads to murder, rape, etc.) leave me free to exercise my prejudices. Primary exception: "Biological Speculation," a cautionary parable about the laws of nature/the jungle. Secondary exception: "Loose Booty." Remember what Hank Ballard says, you guys: how you gonna get respect if you haven't cut your process yet? Original grade: C minus. **C+**

Funkadelic: *Cosmic Slop* (Westbound '73). Thank, well, Whomever, the "maladroited message of doom" inside the doublefold comes not from Brother Malachi but from Sir Lleb, and Whomever has rewarded the band with two definitively scary takes on sex and life in the future present — "Cosmic Slop" and "No Compute," both of which combine humor, pessimism, incantation, and baloney in convincing and unprecedented amalgams. Unfortunately, most of the rest is "interesting," including one profundo Vietnam monologue and many parodies of harmony-group usage. **B**

Funkadelic: *Standing on the Verge of Getting It On* (Westbound '74). Although too often it lives up to its title, this is the solidest record this restless group has ever made (under its own name — cf. Parliament) and offers such goodies as Alvin Chipmunk saying "gross motherfucker" and a stanza that takes on both Iggy Stooge and Frank Zappa with its tongue tied. It also offers this Inspirational Homily: "Good thoughts bring forth good fruit. Bullshit thoughts rot your needs. Think right and you can fly." **B+**

Funkadelic: *Let's Take It to the Stage* (Westbound '75). The group that makes the Ohio Players sound like the Mike Curb Congregation still has a disturbingly occultish bent — "free from the need to be free," indeed. But at this point I'm inclined to trust the music, which is tough-minded, outlandish, very danceable, and finally, I think (and hope), liberating. Including a Stevie Wonder ripoff and a Jimi Hendrix impression and a Black Sabbath love song and a long Bach organ coda ("Atmosphere," by Clinton-Shider-Worrell) over a rap that begins: "I hate the word pussy, it sounds awful squishy, so I guess I'll call it clit." Original grade: B plus. **A−**

Funkadelic: *Funkadelic's Greatest Hits* (Westbound '75). After "Can You Get to That," "Loose Booty," and "Funky Dollar Bill," which really are great, I'm ready to believe that "A Joyful Process" is balanced on an El-lingtonian paradox rather than immersed in schlocky pretensions. But the selection could be even better, and because Funkadelic is a groove band rather than a song band it's not very well-served by the "hit" format. In short, this is hardly the perfect Funkadelic LP. And in truth, neither are any of the others. **A−**

Funkadelic: *Tales of Kidd Funkadelic* (Westbound '76). As with James Brown, whose circa-1971 J.B.'s provided this band with its horns and rhythm section, there always seem to be waste cuts on George Clinton's albums. The difference is that Brown's are intended as filler even when they come out inspired, whereas Clinton's feel like scientific experiments even when they're entirely off-the-cuff. The title cut here, a thirteen-minute congas-and-keyboard reconnaissance decorated with a few chants, turns out to be fairly listenable. Which I noticed because it's preceded by a catchy march called "I'm Never Gonna Tell It," their greatest post-doowop experiment yet. Also out there: "Take Your Dead Ass Home!" Not to mention the horns and rhythm section. **B+**

Funkadelic: *Hardcore Jollies* (Warner Bros. '76). A good sample of their surrealistic black vaudeville, this offers none of the great climaxes of their Westbound albums — no come shots, you might say — but an abundance of good old-fashioned raunch. As consistent as any album they've made, it's dense with ensemble funk and catchy riffsongs, post-heavy Mike Hampton guitar and post-backlash soul voicings. And it rescues from the public domain not only middle-period Jimmy Page but "Comin' 'Round the Mountain" and "They Don't Wear Pants on the Sunny Side of France." **A−**

Funkadelic: *The Best of the Early Years Volume One* (Westbound '77). By cutting down to one track each from the first two albums, this upgrades Westbound's (now deleted) 1975 compilation. The only essential addition is "No Compute," but most of the six substitutions are improvements. And the one regrettable deletion, "Standing on the Verge of Getting It On," serves a rough concept: to present a very strange vocal group rather than a funk or psychedelic band.   **A**

Funkadelic: *One Nation Under a Groove* (Warner Bros. '78). I can't figure out why some Funkateers profess themselves unmoved by this one. The twelve-incher does come up a little short on guitar, but a generous Hendrix fix is thoughtfully provided on a seventeen minute, seven-inch third side, and the title cut is as tough and intricate as goodfooting ever gets. Plus: "Who Says a Funk Band Can't Play Rock?" and "Into You," two manifestos that bite close to the bone, and

"The Doo Doo Chasers," a scatalogical call-and-response cum responsive-reading whose shameless obviousness doesn't detract from fun or funk. Fried ice cream is a reality! Or: Think! It ain't illegal yet!   **A**

Funkadelic: *Uncle Jam Wants You* (Warner Bros. '79). This is fairly wonderful through the first cut on side two, but in a fairly redundant way. Bernie Worrell's high synthesizer vamps sometimes seem like annoying cliches these days, and not even Philippe Wynne can provide the marginal variety that puts good groove music over the top — maybe because he sounds like a high synthesizer himself.   **B+**

Peter Gabriel: *Peter Gabriel* (Atco '77). Even when he was Genesis, Gabriel seemed smarter than your average art-rocker. Though the music was mannered, there was substance beneath its intricacy; however received the lyrical ideas, they were easier to test empirically than evocations of spaceships on Atlantis. This solo album seems a lot smarter than that. But every time I delve beneath its challenging textures to decipher a line or two I come up a little short. **B+**

Peter Gabriel: *Peter Gabriel* (Atlantic '78). One of those records that is diminished by the printed lyrics that are its reason for being. Musically, Gabriel combines with producer Robert Fripp for alert art-rock that gets down around atonality rather than jumping into the astral-noodle soup, with Roy Bittan's romantic flourishes as welcome as "D.I.Y.," a hard-rock landmark in a hard-rock year. But even though it makes you sit up when it comes on the radio, it's basically program music, designed to support words as elitist (and programmatic) as the social commentary Gabriel used to essay in his Genesis days. Remember the immortal words of Chuck Berry: beware of middlebrows bearing electric guitars. **B−**

Chris Gantry: *Motormouth* (Magic Carpet '70). Ever wonder what the writer of a song like "Dreams of the Everyday Housewife" does when he gets home from work? Strums his guitar (like sixty), writes tuneless ditties about junkies and *Easy Rider* (sample line, if I can believe my ears: "Exileless victims of to some ungodly season"), and reads Gurdjieff (for liner notes). **C−**

Jerry Garcia: *Garcia* (Warner Bros. '72). Side one sounds almost too pleasant and catchy, as if Garcia and Robert Hunter — the most consistent songwriters anywhere over the past couple of years — had settled a little too comfortably into the slow, traditional, blues-tinged country-rock groove the Dead have been digging recently. The payoff is "Sugaree" and "Deal," classics no future-rocker could come up with. And then — surprise!— the second side balances (surprisingly unpretentious) musique concrete experimentation against the groove. **B+**

Jerry Garcia: *Garcia* (Round '74). Garcia's willingness to strain his stringy pipes on muscular material may be a function of karmic complacency, but that doesn't mean he can't sing. His voice is as expressive as Lou Reed's or Donald Fagen's and more credible than Ry Cooder's or Robert Hunter's. The first side of this plumbs lyrics by Chuck Berry, Smokey Robinson, and Irving Berlin that you may never have noticed before, and Garcia's guitar spruces up the somewhat limp backing of the Marin County All-Stars. On side two, unfortunately, some other Marin County all-stars contribute songs that need another kind of plumbing. Original grade: B plus. **B−**

Jerry Garcia: *Reflections* (Round '76). Though it's slow going, this is the first sign in years that Jerry and Robert can still write songs. I said songs, Robert, not lyrics. But sometimes, as Allen Toussaint might put it (and Jerry does), I'll take a melody. **B**

Jerry Garcia Band: *Cats Under the Stars* (Arista '78). There seem to be three good songs here until you listen to the lyric of "Rubin and Cherise." The other two, "Cats Under the Stars" and "Rhapsody in Red," are both about music. Come to think of it, so is "Rubin and Cherise." **C+**

Jerry Garcia: See also Howard Wales and Jerry Garcia

Taana Gardner: *Taana Gardner* (West End '79). If Diana Ross wants to go disco, here's how — wholeheartedly, a good way to go anywhere. Mixing Diana's knowingly sexy little-girl soprano with a touch of Shirley Goodman party novelty, Gardner shrills and coos and cools through a total of five cuts on this two-disco disc album, and even the slow dances are worthy of use. "Work That Body" works that idea, "When You Touch Me" is what it's working toward, and "Paradise Express" is recommended to Merle Haggard, who's always ready to learn something new (and funky) about trains. **A−**

Garfunkel: *Angel Clare* (Columbia '73). In case you had any lingering doubts about why you hated Simon & Garfunkel, you should hear what this castrato manque does to Randy Newman's "Old Man." Is all that sweet stuff supposed to be ironic or something? Bet Randy doesn't think so. Point of information: his first name is Art. **C**

Terry Garthwaite: *Terry* (Arista '75). Anyone who can trace the genealogy of a "Rock & Roller" "from Bessie to Billie to B.B. to Boz"— that would appear to mean Boz Scaggs, folks — obviously has eccentric ideas about rock and roll. This turns out to be a virtue. Moving Joy of Cooking's folk-jazz fusion much closer to jazz, Garthwaite emerges as a kind of white, upbeat Esther Phillips, applying a gritty Dinah Washington cast to post-rock lyrics both metaphorical and incantatory. But she's more flexible, happier — her delight in pure sound suggests both scat improvisation and novelty nonsense — and if the long-windedness of the cuts here must be blamed on a singer who's worked too long outside the studio, we can credit their occasional stiffness to producer David Rubinson, who deserves to be trapped in an elevator with the Tower of Power. **A−**

Terry Garthwaite: *Hand in Glove* (Fantasy '78). I complained about production clutter on her quickly deleted Arista album, but I must admit that David Rubinson injected a brightness that I miss in El Lay jazzman John Guerin's more tasteful work here. That could even be why the songs seem a shade duller this time. But Garthwaite's rhythmic and timbral adeptness remain unique in rock, and I'm grateful these days for any explicitly feminist analysis that is also both heterosexual and antipuritanical. Anyway, the songs are still a lot brighter than most. **B+**

Gasolin': *Gasolin'* (Epic '76). This wonderfully improbable record may signal a new movement — here comes the Copenhagen Sound. Would it were true. The LP compiles the best material from three Danish albums — which means not only released in Denmark, but sung in the native language of that funky land, with translations provided in part by an Epic PR man who deserves a new job. Gasolin''s music miraculously overwhelms the musicianship and symphonic textures of Yurrupean technopomp with the raucous good humor of genuine rock and roll, and their epithet for the U.S. —

"the redskin land," they call it — should make any American chauvinist swell with irony. Just when you're afraid they're indulging in a little Guess Who-style sexism, "It's all the same to an American dame," you figure out that what they're really saying is, "It's all the same to an American Dane." Must be. **A—**

Marvin Gaye: What's Going On (Tamla '71). This may be a groundbreaking personal statement, but like any Berry Gordy quickie it's baited skimpily: only three great tunes. "What's Going On," "Inner City Blues," and "Mercy, Mercy Me (the Ecology)" are so original they reveal ordinary Motown-political as the benign market manipulation it is. And Gaye keeps getting more subtle vocally and rhythmically. But the rest is pretty murky even when the lyrical ideas are good — I like the words on "What's Happenin' Brother" and "Flyin' High (in the Friendly Sky)" quite a bit — and the religious songs that bear Gaye's real message are suitably shapeless. Worst of all, because they're used a lot, are David Van De Pitte's strings, the lowest kind of movie-background dreck. Original grade: B. **B+**

Marvin Gaye: Trouble Man (Tamla '72). Buy the single unless you like soundtrack albums. This ain't no super-fly shit. **C**

Marvin Gaye: Let's Get It On (Tamla '73). Post-Al Green *What's Going On,* which means it's about fucking rather than the human condition, thank the wholly holey. Gaye is still basically a singles artist, and the title track, as much a masterpiece as "Inner City Blues," dominates in a way "I'm Still in Love with You," say, doesn't. Then again, it's an even better song, and this album prolongs its seductive groove to an appropriate thirty minutes plus. **A—**

Marvin Gaye: Live (Tamla '74). There's inspired singing here, but even on the stupendous version of "Trouble Man" Gene Page's orchestra

intrudes — Gaye hasn't managed to mix the instruments into the unified background presence of his recent studio albums. Also: seven great oldies banished to a "Fossil Medley," and "Jan," conceivably the worst song he's ever written. **C+**

Marvin Gaye: I Want You (Tamla '76). This isn't as disgraceful as would first appear — as disco-identified mood mewzick for light necking it offers nifty engineering, pleasant harmonies, and the occasional snatch of melody. But as a Marvin Gaye record it's a Leon Ware record. Ware is the producer who cowrote every one of these . . . tunes? segments? . . . *cuts* (which is more than Marvin can claim). But was it Ware who instructed Marvin to eliminate all depth and power from his voice? I mean, if you're into insisting on sex it's in bad taste to whine about it. **C+**

Marvin Gaye: Marvin Gaye's Greatest Hits (Tamla '76). Even though it omitted "Inner City Blues" while offering "How Sweet It Is" and "Can I Get a Witness" (already included on four other Marvin Gaye compilations and who knows how many Motown anthologies), I thought this might serve a function, since I find all of Gaye's '70s albums except *Let's Get It On* distressingly uneven. But "I Want You," "After the Dance," and the live version of "Distant Lover" are embarrassed by such stellar company. I guess when I want to hear "Trouble Man" I'll put on *Anthology.* **B—**

Marvin Gaye: Marvin Gaye Live at the London Palladium (Tamla '77). Especially considering how awkward Gaye can be on stage, this isn't bad for a live Motown album — the arrangements are finky, but some of Marvin's more interesting vocal quirks seem to have survived editing. Which is not to suggest that the live stuff is worth owning. "Got To Give It Up," on the other hand, is his quadrennial studio masterpiece, and its 11:48 are cut up on the single. Still, I think the single is what I'd buy — while petitioning for a disco disc. **B—**

Marvin Gaye: *Here, My Dear* (Tamla '78). The brightness of the disco remix Motown has made available on "A Funky Space Reincarnation" is a vivid reminder of how pathologically laid back Gaye is striving to be. I mean, seventy minutes of pop music with nary a melody line almost qualifies as a tour de force, and the third side barely escapes the turntable at all. Yet this is a fascinating, playable album. Its confessional ranges from naked poetry ("Somebody tell me please/Why do I have to pay attorney fees?" is a modernist trope that ranks with any of Elvis Costello's) to rank jive, but because Gaye's self-involvement is so open and unmediated, guileless even at its most insincere, it retains unusual documentary charm. And within the sweet, quiet, seductive, and slightly boring mood Gaye is at such pains to realize, his rhythmic undulations and whisper-to-a-scream timbral shifts can engross the mind, the body, and above all the ear. Definitely a weird one. **B+**

Marvin Gaye: See also Diana Ross & Marvin Gaye

Gloria Gaynor: *Never Can Say Goodbye* (MGM '75). The disco-hit side (three multi-percussed six-minute cuts, two of them Motown remakes) is a solid, danceable B plus. The flip (five shorter songs, the most irritating written by the singer herself) punches in at C or maybe lower. That averages out to B minus or maybe lower. But albums with listenable sides are all too rare these days. [Later on Polydor.] **B**

Gloria Gaynor: *Love Tracks* (Polydor '78). Not only does this lead off with "I Will Survive" (which I — unlike most — find too long in the eight-minute version now included on the repressed album), and "Stoplight," a piece of inspired girl-group foolishness, it winds down into commendable filler-plus. Faves: "You Can Exit" ("If you don't like the size/If you don't like the fit" of *what*?) and "Anybody Wanna Party" (which for once might induce me to). A better — and cuter — Freddie Perren album than *Best of the Sylvers*. **B+**

The J. Geils Band: *The J. Geils Band* (Atlantic '70). I find this gritty Jewish r&b band from Boston fun but somewhat retrogressive, which is admittedly the way I once felt about Creedence. Side two pops out of the box with covers from Otis Rush and the Contours and then slows down in style with two originals that deserve to get covered back. But the vocals don't do much for John Lee Hooker (no surprise) and the two instrumentals hobble the album's build (also no surprise, since great r&b instrumentals are almost as hard to come by as great white blues singers). **B+**

The J. Geils Band: *The Morning After* (Atlantic '71). Tight, funky, and what else is new? Well, three good songs: "Looking for a Love," "The Usual Place," and (especially) "So Sharp." All of which are old. **B−**

The J. Geils Band: *Bloodshot* (Atlantic '73). Never has the mass audience blunted a group's fine points so quickly. Tight arrangements? They boogie endlessly through riffs they were playing three years ago. Low-profile funk? Peter Wolf now shows off every emotional inadequacy of his phony growl. Resourceful material? The borrowed songs are almost as bad as the originals. Humor? Their idea of a funny is to rhyme "shiny" and "heinie." I hope they know where to shine this one. **C+**

The J. Geils Band: *Ladies Invited* (Atlantic '73). So much better than *Bloodshot* that for a while I thought it was something special, and in a way it is — an r&b album that includes a song about wind chimes. Would they were all as tuneful. Still, a lot of the ersatz-funk macho has disappeared from the lyrics, Peter Wolf's singing has picked up several layers of sweetness and nuance, and a couple of times they even try a harmony-group move. Inspirational Title: "The Lady Makes Demands." **B**

The J. Geils Band: *Nightmares . . . and Other Tales from the Vinyl Jungle* (Atlantic '74). Sure "Must of Got Lost" sounds great on the radio. But the rest of this is more self-imitation — two shuffles, one diddy-bop, and a laugh to the bank backwards from *Ladies Invited.* **C+**

Geils: *Monkey Island* (Atlantic '77). For no good historical reason — 1977 is hardly the year of white r&b — this marginally offensive boogie cartoon has suddenly put together twenty minutes of music as consistent as side two of its 1970 debut. A hard one and a soft one and a cover and a closet-intellectual one and a pretty good one — that's their gamut, right? Overdisc, the nine-minute title track bombs and the other originals fail to take off, but the band does a number on Louis Armstrong's "I'm Not Rough," splitting the hard part between Magic Dick's harp and J.'s guitar. So give 'em a hand, folks — they earned it. **B+**

The J. Geils Band: *Sanctuary* (EMI America '78). I like the tender fatalism of "One Last Kiss" and the demented abstractions of "Sanctuary," but if they really want to be the American Stones they have to do something equally good every track. Mick Jagger would also be useful. **B−**

The J. Geils Band: *Best of the J. Geils Band* (Atlantic '79). Here's where we catch up with their good moments, right? Wrong. Between the three cuts from *Bloodshot,* where they announced their arena-rock proclivities, and the two from *Blow Your Face Out,* where they reified them, "Musta Got Lost" is as well-named as ever. **B−**

Generation X: *Generation X* (Chrysalis '78). This punk band's notorious commitment to pop is evident mostly in surprising harmonies and song structures — musically, they're not trying to be cute. And although as singles "Your Generation," "Ready Steady Go," and "Wild Youth" never knocked my socks off, they're the nucleus of a tough, consistent, inventive album. **B+**

Generation X: *Valley of the Dolls* (Chrysalis '79). Since the music itself doesn't compel close listening, a simple improvement might be a lyric sheet permitting leisurely analysis of what's transformed their belligerence into despond and slid their penchant for pop-rock amenities into the murk. **C+**

Genesis: *Nursery Cryme* (Charisma '71). God's wounds! It's a "rock" version of the myth of Hermaphroditus! In quotes cos the organist and the (mime-influenced) vocalist have the drummer a little confused! Or maybe it's just the invocation to Old King Cole! [Later as a two-LP set with *Foxtrot.*] **C−**

Genesis: *Foxtrot* (Charisma '72). This band's defenders — fans of manual dexterity, aggregate IQ, "stagecraft," etc. — claim this as an improvement. And indeed, Tony Banks's organ crescendos are less totalistic, Steve Hackett's guitar is audible, and Peter Gabriel's lyrics take on medievalism, real-estate speculators, and the history of the world. This latter is the apparent subject of the 22:57-minute "Supper's Ready," which also suggests that Gabriel has a sense of humor and knows something about rock and roll. Don't expect me to get more specific, though — I never even cared what "Gates of Eden" "really meant." [Later as a two-LP set with *Nursery Cryme.*] **C**

Genesis: *Selling England by the Pound* (Charisma '73). The best rock jolts folk-art virtues — directness, utility, natural audience — into the present with shots of modern technology and modernist dissociation; the typical "progressive" project attempts to raise the music to classical grandeur or avant-garde status. Since "raise" is usually code for "delegitimize," I'm impressed that on half of this Peter Gabriel makes the idea work: his mock-mythologized gangland epic and menacing ocean pastorale have a complexity of tone that's pretty rare in any kind of art. Even more amazing, given past performances, organist Tony Banks defines music to match, schlocky and graceful and dignified all at once — when he's got it going, which is nowhere near often enough. As for the rest, it sounds as snooty as usual. Original grade: C plus.   **B**

Genesis: *The Lamb Lies Down on Broadway* (Atco '74). I wanted to call this the most readable album since *Quadrophenia,* but it's only the wordiest — two inner sleeves covered with lyrics and a double-fold that's all small-type libretto. The apparent subject is the symbolic quest of a Puerto Rican hood/street kid/graffiti artist named Rael, but the songs neither shine by themselves nor suggest any thematic insight I'm eager to pursue. For art-rock, though, it's listenable, from Eno treatments to a hook that goes (I'm humming) ''on Braw-aw-aw-aw-aw-aw-dway.''   **B−**

Genesis: *. . . And Then There Were Three . . .* (Atlantic '78). The departure of Peter Gabriel having long since left them a quartet, what might this title indicate? Ask ex-fan Jon Pareles: ''Without lead guitarist Steve Hackett, the band loses its last remaining focal point; the rest is double-tracking. Hence a sound as mushy as the dread Moody Blues, with fewer excuses.''   **D+**

Lowell George: *Thanks I'll Eat It Here* (Warner Bros. '79). You are of course familiar with the recording industry phenomenon in which a vocalist enters the studio (or many studios) with a few (or many) well-regarded musicians and they all ''cut'' between eight and eleven songs written by the vocalist, the vocalist's friends, and some lucky black people. Here the smartest member of Little Feat does this. Unfortunately, singing has never been his strong point, and the compositions are as flaccid as any he's ever made public. Or maybe it only sounds that way because we're used to hearing him atop Little Feat's contradictory funk, not the obliging groove well-re-

garded musicians usually achieve under such circumstances.   **C+**

George Gerdes: *Obituary* (United Artists '71). Gerdes casts his jaundiced larynx upon foibles cultural and countercultural as well as the usual romantic reverses. Very waggish. But although the notion of a wag with a lyrical soft streak is always winning, I wish this particular streak didn't extend to the plight of flower ladies and the reality of rain.   **C+**

George Gerdes: *Son of Obituary* (United Artists '72). Gerdes has a weakness for the kind of high extruded wordplay that only the stoned survive, and he uses the word ''existential'' in two different songs. Of course, one time he's jesting, as is his wont; quite frequently these songs fall somewhere between the funny, the acerbic, and the wacked out, which ain't a bad place to be. But too often the joke — like the voice — wears thin.   **B**

Get Down and Boogie (Casablanca '76). Though the claim on the jacket is excessive — it's not ''38 minutes and 47 seconds of continuous play'' unless one of your eunuchs turns it over for you — this disco-oriented and -segued compilation from the premier disco label is long overdue. Two Donna Summers, two Parliaments (which way do they disco?), and good filler. Finds: Jeannie Reynold's ''The Fruit Song'' (she likes bananas) and Giorgio's ''I Wanna Funk with You Tonight'' (a/k/a ''What'd He Say?'').   **B+**

Steve Gibbons Band: *Caught in the Act* (MCA '77). Neither of Gibbons's first two albums convinced me that the world needed a young Bob Seger — which meant among other things a craftsman who hadn't yet mastered his craft. But this time he's writing 'em and picking 'em with a sharp nose for the cliche. Assholes the world over cover Berry and Dylan on the live album, but they won't risk unrecognized classics like ''Tulane'' and ''Watching the River Flow,'' which is why they're

assholes. And how many other crafts-men could imagine a mock myth called "Gave His Life to Rock 'n' Roll'"? Original grade: B minus.   **B +**
Steve Gibbons Band: *Down in the Bunker* (Polydor '78). Transvestite to Mickey: "What's it really take to turn you on?" Mickey: "It takes all sorts. . . ." Well now, I've been hearing tales of Gibbons's plainspoken work-ing-class wit for years, but that's the first time he ever zinged me good. And not the last. This postpub retrench-ment is strewn with colloquial turns — the words knowing and compassion-ate, the instrumentation rock and roll understood as a mature language. Of course, the problem with colloquialism is that when inspiration flags even slightly it sounds ordinary, and that happens here, but on the whole this is an extraordinarily inventive step forward.   **A −**

The Gibson Brothers: *Cuba* (Island '79). Though brother Chris's vocals get wearing — his hoarse shout sounds like the ideal of male soul the entire Eurodisco network tries to sim-ulate — the title track is still a killer and the rest of the side hangs tough. As does "Better Do It Salsa!" leading off side two. And then . . .   **B +**

Gichy Dan: *Gichy Dan's Beachwood #9* (RCA Victor '79). Produced, writ-ten, and directed (but not sung) by Au-gust Darnell of Dr. Buzzard, this be-gins with the seduction sequence from a fantastical '40s shipboard movie, es-tablishing a tropical mood that per-vades the record — sometimes lyri-cally, always musically — through its finale, "Winter on Riverside Drive." Like Dr. Buzzard, Gichy Dan mixes nostalgic fun and urban realism into something exotic. And though the melodies aren't always there, the life and imagination that were wrung out of Dr. Buzzard's second album have returned.   **B +**

Mickey Gilley: *Gilley's Greatest Hits Vol. 1* (Playboy '76). Gilley is Jerry

Lee Lewis's cousin and reputed imita-tor. He's also proprietor of the largest country-music club in the known world. But his semi-mythic stature is unjustified. His piano arpeggios never get mean. His voice lacks all of Jerry Lee's shrill urgency — more like Jim Reeves with a (certain) sense of rhythm, or Bob Luman without the bite, or maybe even Perry Como Ar-kansas-born and Houston-raised. And his taste is mainstream country at best. If you like songs with roses in them — three of the ten here qualify — you'll enjoy this more than I do. But expect no rock and roll nor rockabilly nor any but the tamest honky-tonk.   **C +**

Allen Ginsberg: *William Blake, Songs of Innocence and Experience* (Verve/Forecast '70). Ginsberg's singing — crude, human, touching, superb — is an antidote to the tempta-tion to transform Blake into artsong. Tricky melodies and virtuoso accom-paniment would subvert the material. And this material is too good for that.   **A −**

Philip Glass: *North Star* (Virgin '77). Rock ears take to this avant-garde composer because he understands elec-tronic sound in a melodic context and loves rhythm, a rhythm achieved — like the hypnotic/mystical mood of the music as a whole — not through per-cussion but through mechanical repe-titions cunningly modified. There is natural drama here, but Glass never in-dulges it, which is why he appeals to Eno's side of the "progressive" spec-trum rather than to Keith Emerson's. What Eno fans may find hard to take — and what I find doubly admi-rable — is that this music refuses to fade into the background; it's rich, bright, and demanding despite its aus-terity. Onward.   **A −**
Philip Glass/Robert Wilson: *Einstein on the Beach* (Tomato '79). I'd skip the Rolling Stones to witness this five-hour maximalization of minimalism again, but on record — condensed to four discs running about three hours —

I find that its operatic conceit justifies itself all too well. This is "great," all right, but without Wilson's spectacular visuals it's also, to these pop-happy ears, tedious and sometimes even pompous. In short, I'm glad to own it, but it didn't cost me twenty-five bucks, and I don't know when I'll find time to play it again now that I've done so twice. **B+**

Gary Glitter: *Glitter* (Bell '72). The hit — "Rock & Roll, Part II" — is reputed to be reggae, but I don't understand why, unless reggae has been reduced to a catchall for anything with a simple beat. As for the album, it's easy to categorize — unreconstructed rock and roll revivalism of the most reactionary sort. Dumb. Original grade: D plus. **C**

The Godz: *The Godz* (Millenium '78). "We're everything your parents ever warned you about," they warn. "We can't feel nothin', got no heart or soul," they boast. "The Godz are rock and roll machines," they admit. Talk about your throwbacks — these evolutionary mishaps are funnier than Blue Oyster Cult, and they're not trying. Don Brewer produced. **C+**

Andrew Gold: *What's Wrong with This Picture?* (Asylum '76). Well, let's see, a quick survey of the relevant ones: guitar plugged into telephone, forty-five on tape deck, calendar opened to November 31, copy of *People* with Gold on the cover, and this record, with its borrowed life — anyone can make "Doo Wah Diddy Diddy" sound OK — and authentic self-pity. Big insight: On "Lonely Boy," the source of L.A. weltschmerz is revealed to be siblings. **C−**

Andrew Gold: *All This and Heaven Too* (Asylum '78). Gold is Barry Manilow in a flannel shirt, and that the cover depicts him in white tie only compounds the offense. Who but the ultimate session man would sing such I'm-OK lyrics in a blues-country pop-slop style so unfettered by details of

personality? In early 1977, after Elektra/Asylum made music history by raising the list price of the new Queen LP 14 percent, E/A prexy Steve Wax defended the move in terms of development capital — the profits from Queen were needed to support the label's uncommercial artists. One of Wax's examples: Andrew Gold. Who do you suppose will be promoted with the profits from Gold's $7.98 LP? The fusioneers of the label's new "jazz" line? Or Warren Zevon? **C−**

Golden Earring: *Moontan* (Track '74). The single off this, "Radar Love," was voted best of 1973 in England but ran out of radio detecting and ranging waves in this country, which made Grand Funk's "The Loco-Motion" number one instead. Yah, yah, our stupid-rock is better than your stupid-rock — especially when yours comes from Holland. **C+**

Gong: *Shamal* (Virgin '76). Since the nicest melody on the second-nicest cut on this pastiche of pastiches, "Cat in Clark's Shoes," is lifted in a much inferior version from Thelonious Monk's "Brilliant Corners," I wonder where I can find the superior version of the theme of "Wingful of Eyes." **B−**

Steve Goodman: *Somebody Else's Troubles* (Buddah '72). He wrote "City of New Orleans," which is not on this album, and songs about car towing and organic food, which are. Also two consecutive songs about racing the sun, which is at least one too many. Tour de force: an a cappella ballad about a Vietnam widow. Arif Mardin found the proper setting for his young man's quaver. **B**

Steve Goodman: *Jessie's Jig & Other Favorites* (Asylum '75). Very likable, bright and open and good-humored, but like so many solo performers, folkies especially, he can't fill an album. This isn't a question of venality — Goodman is too honest to stretch himself onto a production schedule. But his talent requires mood changes more conspicuous than so subtle an instrumentalist, or so thin a vocalist, can provide. Remember groups? **B**

Steve Goodman: *Say It in Private* (Asylum '78). If a smart journeyman like Goodman were consistently great, he'd be a genius, not a smart journeyman, and on one side the smart, slick songs attract interest without commanding it. But side two is a tiny folkie tour de force, drily reworking genre expectations so that we mourn Mayor Daley, sort of, bid a jolly farewell to our century, sort of, and know that Goodman's father is dead for real. **B**

Good Rats: *Tasty* (Warner Bros. '74). What can you say about a band *admirers* claim is the best to emerge from Long Island since the Vanilla Fudge? That even counting their Vagrants phase the Fudge never had to make quite such a thing of how persevering they were? **C –**

Robert Gordon with Link Wray: *Robert Gordon with Link Wray* (Private Stock '77). I've gotten to where I enjoy almost all of this a little, even the original compositions by Wray, who on every evidence except that of his guitar ought to retire to the Fools Hall of Fame. But it's nowhere near as exciting as Gordon's Tuff Darts album would have been; it's nowhere near as exciting as "Red Hot," the only cut that jumps out at you the way this good ole rock 'n' roll is presumably supposed to; and it's nowhere near as exciting as the Gordon-Wray band on a good night, which is really the point. I've run into that confluence of events several times; if you haven't, you won't find this worth your time. **B**

Robert Gordon with Link Wray: *Fresh Fish Special* (Private Stock '78). Gordon has perfected his craft since cutting his first album, and the follow-up is less lively as a result, because the heroic stance he's homed in on is rockabilly balladeer, which is a lot harder to approximate than '50s rock and roller. After all, the credu-

lous lucidity of Presley's slow songs is beyond mortal imitation, and how much secondhand early Twitty (or Husky) does anyone need? Original grade: C. **C +**

Robert Gordon: *Rock Billy Boogie* (RCA Victor '79). Gordon's nouveau rockabilly has always been a mite slick and a mite fast, and this is his best album because he's no longer hiding it — his blown notes are just blown notes, not stigmata of authenticity. Credit Chris Spedding's unnaturally adaptable guitar, which drives the music more aptly than Link Wray's raw protohippie licks, authentic though they may have been. I mean, half the time Gordon actually sounds as though he belongs there. Blows some notes, though. **B**

GQ: *Disco Nights* (Arista '79). One great original, one good original, and well-chosen covers (from Billy Stewart and A Taste of Honey). Lots of vocal flexibility, sincerity, and spirit. In short, don't just buy the single, remember the name. **B**

Grand Funk Railroad: *Closer to Home* (Capitol '70). What's happening to me? Maybe it's that damned billboard. Or maybe I'm beginning to appreciate — I said appreciate — their straight-ahead celebration of beat, amplification, and youthful camaraderie. After all, rock and roll has always been loud, and its rhythms have always been described as "heavy." And at least Mark Farner doesn't pretend to bluesmanship. Original grade: B. **C +**

Grand Funk Railroad: *Live Album* (Capitol '70). I know they have a great — even grand — audience. But an audience and a live album aren't the same thing — not the same thing at all. **C –**

Grand Funk Railroad: *E Pluribus Funk* (Capitol '71). The usual competent loud rock with the usual paucity of drive and detail — not only does it plod, it plods crudely. Likable, in its way — I find myself touched by

"People, Let's Stop the War." But it's not telling me anything I don't already know. Original grade: B minus.　　　　　　　　　　　　**C**

Grand Funk Railroad: *Survival* (Capitol '71). For about a year I've been saying that people aren't stupid, that there has to be something new about this music, and of course there is — it Americanizes Led Zeppelin with a fervent ingenuousness that does justice to the broad gestures of mass art. But now I read where various men of taste, having reached similar conclusions, claim in addition actually to like the stuff. That's going too far.　　**C**

Grand Funk Railroad: *Phoenix* (Capitol '72). I guess I turn in my Free Grand Funk button, because I think this declaration of independence from the dastardly Terry Knight continues their two-year decline. Especially annoying is Mark Farner's singing, which combines the worst of Jack Bruce with the worst of Eddie Fisher, but the music — including Craig Frost's organ — isn't what you'd call dynamic. Sorry, really, but . . .　**C−**

Grand Funk: *We're an American Band* (Capitol '73). If it takes me three months to decide that this is a listenable hard rock record, just how listenable can it be? Well, Todd Rundgren has done remarkable things, that's for sure — the drumming has real punch, the organ fills attractively, and Don Brewer's singing is a relief. Great single, too. Original grade: B.　**B−**

Grand Funk: *Shinin' On* (Capitol '74). Now this really is an American band — confident, healthy, schlocky, uncomplicated on the surface and supporting all manner of contradictions underneath. I prefer the title cut, which bursts with a — you should pardon the expression — raw power they've never managed before, to "The Loco-Motion," where Mark sounds shaky. But how many bands get to record a ninth album, much less make it their best? Original grade: B plus.　　　　　　　　　　　　**B**

Grand Funk: *Grand Funk Hits* (Capitol '76). This strictly post-Terry Knight compilation confirms my belief that they did most of their worthwhile recording with Todd Rundgren, although "Bad Time" and "Some Kind of Wonderful," from their first collaboration with Jimmy Ienner, are definite plusses. The strategy is clear in retrospect — back to their junk-rock roots with ? and the Mysterians and maybe even Terry Knight & the Pack. Recycling riffs, upping the tempos, shuffling their limited vocal resources, and projecting the same populist sincerity that always made them more than a hype, they fuse their heavy beginnings with the hooks they were originally too mythic to bother with on this creditable testament.　　　　　　　　　**B+**

Eddy Grant: *Walking on Sunshine* (Epic '79). A Guyanese producer and one-man band, Grant gets an almost calypsonian, steel-drum feel out of his synthesizer, as well as some nice orchestral stuff. The first side is dancey and more. But the second side is thrown away. And the lyrics are quite uncalypsonian.　　　　　　　　　**B−**

The Grateful Dead: *Workingman's Dead* (Warner Bros. '70). Of course they don't sing as pretty as CSNY — prettiness would trivialize these songs. The sparse harmonies and hard-won melodies go with lyrics that make all the American connections claimed by San Francisco's counterculture; there's a naturally stoned bemusement in their good times, hard times, high times, and lost times that joins the fatalism of the physical frontier with the wonder of the psychedelic one. And the changeable rhythms hold out the promise of Uncle John's Band, who might just save us if we'll only call the tune. Inspirational Verse: "Think this through with me."　　　　　　**A**

The Grateful Dead: *American Beauty* (Warner Bros.'70). This is the simplistic folk-rock album *Workingman's Dead* is supposed to be — sweeter vocally and more direct instrumentally, with words to match. Robert Hunter is better at parsing American conundrums than at picking American beauties, so too many of the lyrics revolve around love, dreams, etc. But only "Attics of My Life" has nothing upstairs.   **A−**

The Grateful Dead: *Grateful Dead* (Warner Bros. '71). I wish some of this live double had been done in the studio — might have saved Bob Weir's faint "Playing in the Band" if not his "Me and Bobby McGee" — and the drum-and-guitar interlude isn't going to inspire anybody to toke up, much less see visions. But even there they gather some of that old Dead magic. And it's about time they documented their taste in covers — I've craved their "Not Fade Away" for years. Original grade: A minus. **B+**

The Grateful Dead: *Europe '72* (Warner Bros. '72). This live triple is where everybody except certified Grateful Dead freaks gets off the bus, but I've still got my card and it ain't a joker. Sure they're beginning to sound very complacent — the whole "Morning Dew" side could be scratched, and the long version of "Truckin' " proves conclusively that the song doesn't truck much. But the best stuff here — the ensemble playing on "Sugar Magnolia," the movement of "China Cat Sunflower," Garcia's "It Hurts Me Too" solo, the lyric to "Ramble On Rose" — is a lot more than laid-back good. It's laid-back brilliant. Most of the rest, patchy though it may be, is laid-back good. Also, I like the way they sing. (And write.)   **B+**

The Grateful Dead: *Bear's Choice: History of the Grateful Dead (Vol. 1)* (Warner Bros. '73). Really a Pigpen memorial album, although the Dead would never be so mundane as to put it that way. Recorded Fillmore East, February 1970, and you had to be there.   **C+**

The Grateful Dead: *Wake of the Flood* (Grateful Dead '73). Capturing that ruminative, seemingly aimless part of the concert when the boogiers nod out, which doesn't mean nothing is going on — what do the boogiers know by now? Musically, this is a deceptively demanding combination of *American Beauty* and *Aoxomoxoa,* sweet tunes mined for structure and texture — including good fiddle, which figures, and good horns, which doesn't. But the lyrics are more of the old karma-go-round, with barely a hook phrase to come away with. I remember Robert Hunter when he was making up American myths. Original grade: B plus.   **B−**

The Grateful Dead: *At the Mars Hotel* (Grateful Dead '74). Brighter and more uptempo than *Wake of the Flood* (which is not to claim it's "high energy"), with almost as many memorable tunes as *American Beauty.* Robert Hunter is not progressing, however — even "U.S. Blues," an entertaining collection of conceits, seems received rather than found. And a Weir-Barlow song about money is just one more way for rich Marin hippies to put women down. Original grade: B plus.   **B−**

The Grateful Dead: *Blues for Allah* (Grateful Dead '75). I've been hypersensitive to this band's virtues for years. This time I find the arch aimlessness of their musical approach neurasthenic and their general muddle-headedness worthy of Yes or the Strawbs.   **C−**

The Grateful Dead: *Steal Your Face* (Grateful Dead '76). Their fifth live double (or triple) of the decade is the first with the sorry earmarks of the genre — namely, lots of stretched-out remakes. And believe me, the Dead can rilly stretch 'em out.   **C−**

The Grateful Dead: *Terrapin Station* (Arista '77). Although this may be the Dead's best studio album since *American Beauty,* it runs a distant second, just nosing out the likes of *Wake of the Flood,* and will convert no one. In fact, it's a good thing Weir-Barlow's "Estimated Prophet" and Lesh-Monk's "Passenger" are the band's best originals in years, because Donna Godchaux's singer-songwriting debut is a disgrace; similarly, it takes a terse, jumping arrangement of "Samson and Delilah" to cancel out (and then some) a questionable "Dancing in the Streets." A confusion of quality also pervades the Garcia-Hunter title suite on side two. It works pretty well musically; for a while, I was ready to turn in the kazoo on "Alligator" for Paul Buckmaster. Then I listened to the lyric, a fable so polite it sent me hustling back to the verbal, vocal, and musical crudities of *Anthem of the Sun*, which "Terrapin Station" recalls formally. Amazing how all the hard-won professionalism of a decade disintegrates in the face of the sporadic, irresistible inspiration of their lysergic youth.   **B**

The Grateful Dead: *What a Long Strange Trip It's Been: The Best of the Grateful Dead* (Warner Bros. '77). In this uncommonly loving compilation, Dead head Paul Wexler does what he can to eliminate the fecklessly smug and the recklessly experimental. It coheres as well as Dead albums usually do, and offers two nice singles, which is nice. But "Me and My Uncle," which hardly counts, is the only cover, a questionable decision. Plus — here's the real catch — four (out of eight) songs from *Workingman's Dead*, which coheres a good deal better.   **B**

The Grateful Dead: *Shakedown Street* (Arista '78). "I Need a Miracle" is the first anthem any of these rabble-rousing necromancers has written in years. On the title tune, however, Jerry once again warns against "too much too fast," and this album definitely ain't the miracle they need.   **C**

Dobie Gray: *Drift Away* (Decca '73). At times this long-lost '60s one-shot sounds like a black Joe Cocker — with the strain removed, naturally. His frank, unchurchy baritone works material from Nashville producer Mentor Williams for a universal country-rock whose racelessness is a real relief in a world of drawlers and twangers. But though the title hit sticks, I find its central conceit — rock and roll to soothe the soul — ultimately enervating.

Enough to make me wish he'd rejoin the in crowd, which after all is out by now. Original grade: B plus.   **B −**

Grease (RSO '78). The Sha Na Na cuts document the group's deterioration from an affectionate, phonographically ineffective bunch of copycats into a repellent Vegas oldies act. The Casey-Jacobs stage songs are entertaining and condescending takeoffs on '50s ready-mades, a little too good for Manhattan Transfer. And the updates provided for the movie by the Stigwood combine — Valli's "Grease" (written by Barry Gibb) and Travolta and Newton-John's "You're the One That I Want" — are two of 1978's better hit singles. That's probably how they should be bought, too, but this is far from a disgrace.   **C +**

The Grease Band: *The Grease Band* (Shelter '70). Can these be the same guys who backed Joe Cocker? From producer and pseudonymous pianist Chris Stainton I expected better — but not, I guess, from vocalist-composer (formerly just guitarist) Henry McCullough. The Band gets away with putting a nonsinger up front by shuffling five of them, and all five nonsing with more passion and style than Henry. And though like Henry they construct their songs out of used materials, they do that with passion and style too. Original grade: B.   **C +**

The Great Tompall and His Outlaw Band: *The Great Tompall and His Outlaw Band* (MGM '76). Tompall Glaser's slurred, soft-focus baritone might grow on me, I suppose, but as of now he's one more singing legend I'd rather hear about than hear. A touch too sentimental, a touch too nasty underneath, and whether he's playing Stills to Waylon's Young or Nash to Waylon's Crosby, it's all sour goop to me.   **C +**

Al Green: *Al Green Gets Next to You* (Hi '70). With Willie Mitchell performing the Booker T. function, Hi of

Memphis has turned into a pocket of naivete (or reaction) (or traditionalism) on the confused black pop scene. Green plays the boyish Sam Cooke supplicant — or maybe a smooth Otis Redding, or an assertive Smokey Robinson — with the startling is-that-a-synthesizer? high note that climaxes "Tired of Being Alone" serving as a trademark. He also covers the Doors, the Temptations, Roosevelt Sykes, and the gospel-phase Johnnie Taylor. And closes out side two with some greasy hard funk like you just don't hear anymore.   **A**

Al Green: *Let's Stay Together* (Hi '72). Maybe it's just that I'm so tired of the title single, but this is disappointing. *Al Green Gets Next to You* shows real emotional range — like Marvin Gaye, Green comes on both passive and active. The popularity of his romantic disappointment, however, has induced him to narrow his persona. Item: The most impressive cut on the LP is "How Can You Mend a Broken Heart?" Green's version is far superior to the Bee Gees' original, but the original is pure glop. Item: The album doesn't include one piece of real funk. Green is still the most intelligent male soul singer to emerge in years, and in the context of three or four more albums this one may sound fine. Right now, it's much too much of a good thing. Original grade: B.   **A −**

Al Green: *I'm Still in Love With You* (Hi '72). Easily the most consistent soft-soul LP of the year, anchored in with an impressive collection of unforgettable background themes. I'm happy to own it. But I still remember that less than a year ago Green looked like he might turn into the Compleat Soul Man rather than Black Smoothie of the Year, and I make the following request: Remember Otis Redding. OK, Al?   **A −**

Al Green: *Call Me* (Hi '73). I originally believed people would buy this only so they wouldn't have to get up and flip *I'm Still in Love with You,* and I was probably right. But no other album documents Green's genius for the daring nuance so thrillingly. "Stand Up" is the subtlest black identity song ever, "Jesus Is Waiting" a profession of faith you can believe in, and "Here I Am" an uptempo vehicle that sneaks up from in front of you. The interpretations of country weepers by Hank Williams and Willie Nelson are definitive. The vocals are tougher than on the two "classic" Green LPs that preceded it. And the rhythms are irresistible. Al Jackson's (and Henry Grimes's) thick third-beat 4/4 kicks in with all kinds of extra surprises, and as always it's only a frame for a music that moves as one sinuous body, with Green dodging and weaving at the head. Original grade: B plus.   **A +**

Al Green: *Livin' for You* (Hi '73). Green puts the finishing touch on his New Sexiness — non-macho but not long-suffering (Smokey Robinson), vague (Curtis Mayfield), button-down (Bill Withers), or wimpy (Russell Thompkins) — with "Let's Get Married," a promise of post-nuptial love and happiness that seems to presage small but engrossing orgasms stretching into an infinite future. And then, on a second side that opens with a stolen hymn to jailbait and continues through "Unchained Melody" and "My God Is Real" to a slow, sensuous eight-minute vamp tune called "Beware," he steps out.   **A**

Al Green: *Al Green Explores Your Mind* (Hi '74). At first I found this a depressing combination of trivial ambitions and simple greed — the hit, "Sha-La-La," is his slightest to date, and side two might easily have been unflattened with a cover. But I kept playing "Sha-La-La" to reach "Take Me to the River," a synthesis of the spiritual root of Green's music (call it God) and its emotional referent (by which I mean sex) that may be his greatest song. And in the end I loved "Sha-La-La" too. Original grade: B.   **B +**

Al Green: *Al Green's Greatest Hits* (Hi '75). Green is less open and imaginative than Sam Cooke and less painfully word-wise than Smokey

Robinson, but he belongs in their company, that of two of the half dozen prime geniuses of soul. His musical monomania substitutes Memphis for James Brown's Macon, and the consistency of his albums is matched only by Otis Redding, Aretha Franklin, and Ray Charles. But because he spins his music out over an area not much larger than a hankie, the albums also translate beautifully to a greatest hits format, and this is flawless. For those who refuse to believe the LPs contain hidden treasure and don't care that the singles "all sound the same." And for those, like me, who can go both ways with him. **A**

Al Green: *Al Green Is Love* (Hi '75). It's probably too late anyway, but you can be sure that this won't convert anybody. It's Green at his most extreme — washed with strings, more scatted than composed, occasionally almost incoherent, half concept album and half throwaway. Nevertheless, if my man wants to roll around in his own vocal tics and rhythmic nuances, I'll roll with him. And I've stopped worrying about the lyrics. Where I once found Green's reliance on romantic overstatement amusing, I can now perceive it as a symptom of a fascinating and pervasive craziness that has never been better documented than on this defenseless album. Original grade: A minus. **B+**

Al Green: *Full of Fire* (Hi '76). Although the Buck Owens cover isn't up to the Willies and Krisses of yore and the hook riffs remain in slight decline, there are definitely more good songs here than on *Al Green Is Love*. They repay textual analysis, too. Last time the mind-boggler had Green improvising nonsense verse at robbers and other interlopers; this time he assumes the persona of God the Son ("I can see you but you can't see me") and makes you love it. After all, visionaries are supposed to be far out, and this is one of the few we've got. **A−**

Al Green: *Have a Good Time* (Hi '76). Green's recent instability is usually blamed on hot grits and the short half-life of formula soul, but I'm beginning to wonder whether drummer Al Jackson, who died in 1975, wouldn't have steadied the last two albums, and I expect that this is an attempt to compensate. Wilson Pickett it ain't, but it is the straightest (and hardest) soul Green has put out since his breakthrough — the horns way up, the vocals shouting confidence and technique. Problem is, it's forced — the Hi folks (like most of their peers) can't turn out songs distinctive enough to hold up under the treatment. It's still full of fire, though, and Green is still the finest popular singer of the decade, and I'm still gratified to see him on his feet. Original grade: A minus. **B+**

Al Green: *Al Green's Greatest Hits Volume II* (Hi '77). I welcome this proof of the greatness of Green's lesser and later hits, but I'd prefer a more eccentric (hence accurate) and equally impressive selection — one that replaced the two non-singles from *I'm Still in Love with You* (a lengthened "Love and Happiness" and "For the Good Times," live staples that typify his pop mode) with, for instance, "There's No Way," "That's the Way It Is," and "Love Ritual." **A−**

Al Green: *The Belle Album* (Hi '77). Since 1975 Green has been making albums on which two or three real songs were supplemented by material so vague and unpredictable it almost announced itself as filler improvised in the studio — which is not to say I didn't find much of it hypnotic. Now, on a self-produced album focused around his own (frequently acoustic) guitar, the filler comes front and center with new assurance and perhaps even its own formal identity; the real songs themselves — his best in years — sound improvised in the studio. And more than ever, it all holds together around Green's agile rhythm, dynamics, and coloration and his obsession with the soul-body dualism at the heart of the genre he now rules unchallenged. **A**

Al Green: *Love Ritual* (Hi '78). The only thing this product — compiled from his radically uneven later albums — teaches us about Green is why London left the title tune off *Greatest Hits Volume II*. Needed it for corporate revenge after Hi deserted the sinking ship.   **B−**

Al Green: *Truth n' Time* (Hi '79). Reports that Green was no longer writing all his own material worried some supporters, but in fact composition has counted for very little in Green's recent work and is generally improved here. This is his most careful and concise music since *Livin' for You;* in fact, it's too damn concise, clocking in at 26:39 for eight cuts, although the sustaining 6:07-minute disco disc version of "Wait Here" would have put it over half an hour. None of the originals are quite up to "Belle" or "I Feel Good," but every song is solid, and two audacious covers of songs heretofore recorded exclusively by women are his best in five years. The intensity of the 2:12-minute "I Say a Little Prayer" (dig that male chorus) is precious in a time of dance-length cuts, and although I know Green devotes "To Sir with Love" to his dad, I'm glad Proposition 6 was defeated before its release. Original grade: A minus. **B+**

Peter Green: *The End of the Game* (Reprise '71). The brains behind Fleetwood Mac has always been a double threat because he's also the fingers — I've heard him keep up with Jerry Garcia on a good night. Here he lags behind Garcia on a bad jag, say side four of *Live/Dead*. Note title — maybe he's lost his marbles.   **D**

Peter Green: *In the Skies* (Sail '79). For a supposed resident of Cloud-Cuckoo Land, Fleetwood Mac's original hitmaker is doing all right — this solo comeback is a lot solider than number three from Bob Welch (featuring "Future Games" as blast from the past), number two from Danny Kirwan (blonde on the cover), or number one from Jeremy Spencer (now apparently unborn-again, though six out of seven songs pivot on the word "love" and the eternal one is graced with syn-

drums). Green's new music goes back even before *Then Play On*, but it's a lot more confident — simple guitar excursions with a Latin lilt, like Carlos Santana with a sense of form (or limits).   **B+**

Norman Greenbaum: *Petaluma* (Reprise '72). In 1966, practicing as Dr. West, he hit with "The Eggplant That Ate Chicago." In 1969, his jug-rock album *Spirit in the Sky* fermented until it produced the 1970 AM longshot of the same name. So take last year's bland *Back Home Again* as premature product and enjoy this right-on-schedule one-of-a-kind all-acoustic project — a record about living in the country rather than escaping to it by a man who's taking his "royalties/And puttin them into this goat dairy." That's from "Grade A Barn," but rest assured that this is a singer-songwriter whose knowledge of pastorale transcends the technical — as in "I'm Campin'," about how goat farmers get nature, and "Dairy Queen," about a baton-twirling miss who longs to get the hell away from Petaluma. Time: 25:13.   **B+**

Grin: *Grin* (Spindizzy '71). In which Crazy Horse phenom Nils Lofgren comes up with his own little group on producer David Briggs's own little Epic subsidiary. Choruses of children mix with gospel-cum-Robert-Plant high counterpoint; future folk tunes like "Everybody's Missing the Sun" and "If I Were a Song" vie for the lad's soul with soulful ravers like "Direction" and "18 Faced Lover." Watch him.   **B+**

Nils Lofgren/Grin: *1 + 1* (Spindizzy '71). This is what Paul McCartney might be like if he were a wunderkind: romantic balladeer on the "dreamy side," raucous yowler on the "rockin' side," with both halves miraculously innocent instead of alternately cloying and hyper. Lofgren has a lot to learn about life and love and such, but the guitar macho of "Slippery Fingers" is so dirty and so cute, the soap opera of

"Lost a Number" so fantastic, that watching him learn is sure to be a pleasure. Original grade: A minus. **A**

Grin: *All Out* (Spindizzy '72). This record speaks to my peculiar sensibility. It even includes a song that begins in a house in the country and includes the line: "Life has been kinda easy on me." Nils Lofgren is everything I think a rock and roller should be — pugnacious, explosive, cheerful, loving. But I'm not sure my taste is any more universal than someone else's for, I don't know, some minor song poet, David Blue, say, or George Gerdes. **A−**

Grin: *Gone Crazy* (A&M '73). Didn't "Beggar's Day" sound better on *Crazy Horse,* and haven't we heard those girl-world boy-toy rhymes before? You bet. This is where Nils starts to repeat himself. Not only does the lack of a moderately interesting new lyric close off a source of pleasure, it also leaves Lofgren with nothing to sing about. Let's hope this was a rush job for his new label and warn him not to rush the next. **B−**

Grin: *The Best of Grin Featuring Nils Lofgren* (Epic '76). In which CBS replaces three terrific flawed albums with a single very nice unflawed one. In other words, this does avoid clinkers, but it also avoids Nils the Eloquent Weirdo ("Slippery Fingers," "All Out") in favor of Nils the Accomplished Simp ("Like Rain," "We All Sing Together"). **A−**

Grin: See also Nils Lofgren

Grinder's Switch Featuring Garland Jeffreys: *Grinder's Switch Featuring Garland Jeffreys* (Vanguard '70). When the music's density and country-soul accent surround an obscurantist lyric like "Seven Sleepers' Den" you'd swear you were listening to the Band. But· at times Jeffreys also achieves uncanny resemblances to M. Jagger and B. Dylan, which must be how he got to write "They Call Me Fortune and Fame." And he says more with good-time rockers like "Sister Divine" and "Won't Ya Come Back Home" than with "Seven Sleepers' Den" or "An Imaginary Invalid." Molière, eh? Original grade: C plus. **B**

The David Grisman Quintet: *The David Grisman Quintet* (Kaleidoscope '77). Initially, I took this jazzy Western bluegrass concoction for an acoustic variant on one of those session superstar instrumental LPs. But where it's the tendency of a band like the Section, for instance, to sound self-satisfied, as if getting stuck that deep in a groove were a spiritual achievement, this music is always sprightly, inquisitive, and surprising. Lightweight stuff, you say — I say it's airy. **B+**

Larry Groce: *Junkfood Junkie* (Warner Bros. '76). The single was a nourishing tidbit, but consumers had better beware of filler and artificial ingredients in the large economy size. **C−**

Henry Gross: *Henry Gross* (A&M '74). Unlike the hebephrenic country-rock clowns he superficially resembles — you know, the guys who make you want to run out and buy the complete works of Black Sabbath — Henry is really fun, dedicating one song to a porn-star friend of his and wooing Sweet Sassafrass on Eastern Parkway. Brooklyn — Borough of Songwriters. Original grade: B plus. **B**

Steven Grossman: *Caravan Tonight* (Mercury '74). If I were gay, I imagine I'd love this record, because it would be about me, which would certainly be a relief, but even so I'd complain about the husky forced sensitivity of the folkie voice and the now-and-again sugar of the string arrangements. As things stand I find myself touched by his slight lisp, engaged by his melodies, enlightened by his intelligence, and (sugar will out) moved almost to tears by the title song. **B**

The Guess Who: *American Woman* (RCA Victor '70). As a Canadian,

Burton Cummings is no doubt aiming his "symbolic" rage more at the "American" than at the "woman," but his choice of "symbol" is no less despicable for its putative naivete. I like the riff that goes with it, though, and except for the poetasting "Talisman" can find it in me to enjoy every cut on this record. The beat is unyielding as well as wooden, Randy Bachman's square yet jazzy guitar style is one of a kind, and the lyrics usually give up a phrase or two worth humming. AM fans should be proud. Original grade: B plus. **B**

The Guess Who: *Share the Land* (RCA Victor '70). Somebody asked the band how they knew the Indian on the cover and they answered central casting. That must also be where they found guitarist Kurt Winter and Greg Leskiw, both of whom play ringing heavy cliches in all the proper places. Randy Bachman's clichés were altogether subtler. Original grade: C. **C+**

The Guess Who: *The Best of the Guess Who* (RCA Victor '71). What do people gain by resisting all this pop-craft? Is AM acceptance so tainted that these proven riffs and melodies shrivel the soul on contact? Or does the way Burton Cummings shifts from rock to swing to croon to growl without any show of strain or even technique just make him "slick," as they say? Granted, when I hear all the singles together like this I notice that since the romantic loss recorded in "These Eyes" Cummings has become unnecessarily spiteful. But songs that put down women and people who work for a living have never bothered AM-haters before. **B+**

The Guess Who: *Flavours* (RCA Victor '74). The Burton Cummings part of this group always wanted it to be the Doors, Santana, and Gary Puckett and the Union Gap all rolled into one. This rather monstrous goal has finally been realized. Personally, I always preferred the part that wanted to be Bachman-Turner Overdrive. **C**

The Guess Who: *The Greatest of the Guess Who* (RCA Victor '77). Unbe-

knownst to anyone but their record company, the Guess Who staged a mild comeback in 1974 and 1975 — their next-to-last official LP, *Flavours,* charted higher than anything they'd released since 1971. What this meant was that they'd gone top ten on the AM again, with the inspired "Clap for the Wolfman" — Burton Cummings quickly mastered the music-life song once somebody else thought of it. The second side of this ultimate compilation showcases their late period, which means a decrease in misogyny (and the elimination of such dubious hits as "Share the Land" and "Bus Rider") from *Best of.* Tuneful, hard-driving commercial rock and roll with some lilts for variety. What more do you want? **A−**

Arlo Guthrie: *Washington County* (Warner Bros. '70). Basically, *Running Down the Road* was about what it said it was about. As such, it was a little scary, which I liked but Arlo apparently didn't, because now he's busy finding "a place to dwell" and learning about Jesus. Or, to turn his only joke on this record around, putting his foot in his mouth and telling it where he wants to go. The Woody cover exposes the dark underside of cattle drives, but mostly it's roots and fenceposts — in short, the good earth. Which may be why he sounds sodden. **B−**

Arlo Guthrie: *Hobo's Lullabye* (Reprise '72). If somebody's gotta make exploring-the-folkie-mind-set records, oh Lord let it be somebody with a strong sense of history as well as a weakness for nostalgia. "Ukelele Lady" sounds positively intelligent backing one of Woody's heaviest anti-scab ballads, and if the new ones about trains and booze seem slightly outmoded, well, that's part of the point, right? **B+**

Arlo Guthrie: *Last of the Brooklyn Cowboys* (Reprise '73). That the folkie mind set dwells in the recording studio these days is a truth only new folk-rock songs as original as "City of

New Orleans'' can make me like. Instead, the best new tune here, Arlo's celebration of the Guthries' fiddling tradition, sounds supiciously like a traditional fiddle tune. And I never had much use for "Gates of Eden" in its, er, authentic version. **B**

Arlo Guthrie: *Arlo Guthrie* (Reprise '74). This odd little record comes on like *Arlo VII,* which might rightfully excite semi-coma among the unconverted, but it's not. For once, Lenny Waronker's expertise produces music — playing and especially singing, not aural quality — that flirts (a little coyly) with amateurishness. Plus the record is political in a consciously oblique and sometimes fuzzy smart-hippie way. Arlo's Watergate song does justice to Tom T. Hall. And the two spirituals that make you wonder why he's fooling around with the Southern California Community Choir turn out to be about Israel. **B+**

Arlo Guthrie: *Amigo* (Reprise '76). When you wrap one good-but-not-great album a year around a voice so frail and a sensibility so quirky, you're liable to find yourself pigeonholed — as a miniaturist, an odd duck if not a small fry. On the other hand, if just a few of those LPs are a little better than anyone has a right to expect, people might start thinking you're an auteur or something. I don't go for that frog talk myself, but this release has me pulling out my old Arlo albums and discovering how ideally the limitations of his voice have always suited his wry and complex understanding of things. Especially recommended: "Guabi Guabi," an absurdly cheerful African ditty that ought to be a novelty hit, and "Victor Jara," the most painful protest song in recent memory (including "Hurricane"). **A−**

Arlo Guthrie: *The Best of Arlo Guthrie* (Warner Bros. '77). A best-of with a theme: The Rehabilitation of a Smart-Ass. Side one leads with "Alice's Restaurant Massacre," retrieved from Arlo's otherwise amateurish debut, and then reprises two tuneful if soggy religious numbers. Side two leads with "Motorcycle (Significance of the Pickle) Song," rescued from Arlo's unnecessary live collaboration with Uncle Pete, follows with the hippie-desperado anthem "Coming into Los Angeles," and then "progresses" into the reconciliation and nostalgia of Arlo's mature period. I have nothing against his mature period, but it's represented more cogently and unpredictably on *Arlo Guthrie* and *Amigo*. This would be more listenable, albeit less educational, if all the folk-punk stuff were on the same side. **B**

Arlo Guthrie: *One Night* (Warner Bros. '78). Sick of going into debt to make exquisitely conceived studio albums that don't sell, Arlo here delivers a mostly live LP — with undistinguished folkie-rockie added by his road band, Shenandoah — that strings together pointless Elvis and Beatles covers, one-dimensional folk songs, and a tall tale that would have trouble making first string guard on a high school basketball team. **C+**

Arlo Guthrie: *Outlasting the Blues* (Warner Bros. '79). These reflections on God, love, and death are substantial and obviously earned, but too often they're just not acute. The problem isn't his religious overview, either — think of T-Bone Burnett. Guthrie simply goes soft aesthetically at crucial moments, and although most of the material is creditable enough, only once — on "Epilogue," Guthrie's "Under Ben Bulben" — is the enormous emotional potential of the project realized. **B**

Buddy Guy & Junior Wells: *Buddy Guy & Junior Wells Play the Blues* (Atco '72). Most attempts to broaden the blues audience fail in every way, as Wells's r&b albums for Blue Rock attest, but this one's at least a musical triumph, as relaxed and intense and authentic as any of Wells's work for Vanguard or Delmark. The sales gimmicks are tastefully hyped-up production and such participants as Eric Clapton (backup and bottleneck), Dr. John, and the J. Geils Band (on two change-of-pace Guy vocals, including "This Old Fool," which is going to be the single and ought to be). Wells has softened his spitting style with a few soul mannerisms and his harmonica has lost none of its verve; Guy's flash and facility are ideal in this context. Hurray. **A−**

Hackamore Brick: *One Kiss Leads to Another* (Kama Sutra '70). This audition tape by the Venus in Furs Society — a record collectors club whose firsthand contact with "decadence" consists of one DMT experience and moderate quantities of oral sex — bears a spooky resemblance to *The Velvet Underground* (LP number three, the lyrical one). Chick Newman's sour pitch has the deadpan emotional resonance of Lou Reed's, only folkier and more sanguine. The flat, droning beat is pure Maureen Tucker. And the organ solos are obviously an hommage to John Payne of the Serpent Power. **B**

Merle Haggard and the Strangers: *Okie from Muskogee* (Capitol '70). Despite some slack performances, this album — recorded live during Haggard's first appearance in the city he made famous and vice versa, and the only LP to date to include any version of the title song —is a passable sampler. The wild crowd and predictable fooforaw — he gets an official Okie pin and the key to the city — give it documentary value. But *The Best of Merle Haggard* is a lot more representative of a great iconoclast who's keeping it under wraps these days. Tell us, Merle, just which college dean do *you* respect? **B**

Merle Haggard and the Strangers: *The Fightin' Side of Me* (Capitol '70). This is turning into a cartoon — once again a jingoistic anthem sells a live album. Don't hippie-haters worry that hippies might have more in common with Merle than they do? After all, he does boast about "living off the fat of our great land." **C+**

Merle Haggard and the Strangers: *A Tribute to the Best Damn Fiddle Player in the World* (Capitol '70). An album of Bob Wills songs, featuring genuine Wills sidemen with Johnny Gimble (as well as Haggard himself) on fiddle? Now that's the Merle I trust. His uncountrypolitan formal sense has always gone along with a reverence for history, and his subtle, surprisingly tranquil, yet passionate singing style — all that yodel and straining head voice — was made for Wills's pop-jazz-country amalgam. **B+**

Merle Haggard and the Strangers: *Hag* (Capitol '71). Four country hits on Haggard's first straight studio album in a year and a half, but only the simple goodbye song "I Can't Be Myself" escapes bathos. "The Farmer's Daughter," "I'm a Good Loser," and "I've Done It All" have an acceptably archetypal ring. Forget the rest — Hag already has. **C+**

Merle Haggard and the Strangers: *Someday We'll Look Back* (Capitol '71). An honest two days' work, but don't let the keynote tune fool you into expecting a lot of class-conscious reminiscences. "California Cottonfields" and "Tulare Dust" are welcome, but this has its share of romantic pap, and the nostalgia of the title bubbles too close to the surface. Surprise: "Big

Time Annie's Square," Hag's peace with the hippies. **B+**

Merle Haggard and the Strangers: Let Me Tell You About a Song (Capitol '72). I object in principle to music-with-commentary albums, and Haggard is hardly as forthcoming with his "inner thoughts" as the notes promise. But despite its mawkish moments — especially Tommy Collins's dead-mommy song — the material defines Haggard's sensibility in a winning way, and since not one of the songs is great in itself I guess the commentary must do it. For controversy, there's interracial love. **B+**

Merle Haggard: The Best of the Best of Merle Haggard (Capitol '72). A misnomer — they mean *The Safest of the Best,* or *Something for Everybody.* No "Lonesome Fugitive" or "Sing Me Back Home" or "Branded Man," but both of his patriotic chores, "The Fightin' Side of Me" studio and "Okie from Muskogee" live (for the third time out of three on LP). Also: "Every Fool Has a String Section," I mean "Rainbow," and "No Reason To Quit," where his timbre, which has been softening perceptibly over the years, breaks definitively into self-pity. Plus lots of good stuff, of course, but still. . . . **B+**

Merle Haggard and the Strangers: I Love Dixie Blues (Capitol '73). The care Haggard put into his Jimmie Rodgers and Bob Wills tributes was palpable; this live-in-New-Orleans-with-horns affair is slovenly. The two great moments are covers — "Big Bad Bill (Is Sweet William Now)" and "Lovesick Blues," both originated by the legendary (blackface?) yodeler Emmett Miller. The lousy moments include current hits, overstated polyphony, and (how did we stand the wait?) a third live version of "Okie from Muskogee," this one a failed singalong. **C**

Merle Haggard and the Strangers: It's Not Love (But It's Not Bad) (Capitol '73). Merle hasn't played the poor boy or the ex-con in quite some time, but as he's turned into a legend he's all too often turned to gimmicky pseudo-concepts. This mainstream country album — his first since *Hag* — does more justice to its title than many of his more pretentious efforts. Nothing special, just marriage and its travails, but play it twice and you'll remember most of it. Original grade: B plus. **B**

Merle Haggard and the Strangers: If We Make It Through December (Capitol '74). Last time it was good to hear him go contemporary again. This time one of the two contemporary standouts sounds mysteriously like Bob Wills. The Lefty Frizzell and Floyd Tillman remakes come across fresh and clean. The Ink Spots remake doesn't. **B**

Merle Haggard: Presents His 30th Album Capitol '74). The man has been making them for less than a decade, and thirty is too damn many. But this is clearly where Haggard wants to show off his range, and the display, featuring more original songs than he's put in one place for a long time, is pretty impressive. There's a rip-roaring infidelity lyric that's definitely one of his genius pieces —"Old Man from the Mountain," it's called, complete with bluegrass shading. And though after that only "Honky Tonk Nighttime Man" and the Bob Wills/Lefty Frizzell cover are liable to be remembered, just about everything else is liable to be enjoyed. Time: 28:24. **B+**

Merle Haggard and the Strangers: A Working Man Can't Get Nowhere Today (Capitol '77). The album opens with the title song, about a Good Redneck, a class-conscious guy who pays his child support and wonders skeptically why he doesn't get ahead. It closes with "I'm a White Boy," about a Bad Redneck, a race-conscious guy who's too proud for welfare but would settle for a rich woman and/or an easy job. These are powerful pieces whether you like them or not, rendered with passionate sympathy and a touch of distance — his strongest in years. The "filler" includes covers from old standbys Williams and Wills and new favorites Delmore and Wells and an envoi to Lefty Frizzell as well as a gospel song and a running song and a sentimental standard that works (for once). Not a bad cut, and Capitol assembled it from the vaults after Haggard bolted for MCA. Why then did Hag himself put out such crap for three years? Time: 25:07. **A −**

Merle Haggard and the Strangers: *Songs I'll Always Sing* (Capitol '77). God damn it — I could put together *four* discs of Hag that would never go below A minus, but Capitol hasn't offered me the job, so this two-disc mishmash will have to do. Dreck among the gems (Haggard has small knack for heart songs), muddled chronologically and thematically (a real waste with an artist so prolific and varied), and the *fifth* album to include a live version of "Okie from Muskogee." But at least it offers all four of his great outside-the-law songs, one per side. And it's budget-priced. Time: 54:16. **A −**

Merle Haggard and the Strangers: *The Way It Was in '51* (Capitol '78). Because Haggard's singing gained resonance and flexibility as his songwriting flattened out, this factitious compilation cum concept album, one side devoted to Hank and one to Lefty, works better than his self-designed Bob Wills tribute. Time: 27:26. **A −**

Merle Haggard and the Strangers: *Eleven Winners* (Capitol '78). Continuing Capitol's reclamation/exploitation of his last five or six years with the label, this compiles his best originals from the period. Pretty conventional — when he does try to add a little something (I like the play on "grind" in the trucking song), it's rarely quite enough. **B**

Merle Haggard: *Serving 190 Proof* (MCA '79). Its impeccable simplicity and sensitivity gives Haggard's fourth and best album for MCA an autumnal feel reminiscent of recent comebacks by Chuck Berry and Jerry Lee Lewis. Granted, autumnal country music is easier to come by than autumnal rock and roll. But for Haggard, a mere

forty-one but feeling it, the effect has thematic repercussions — and he's written a batch of wise songs to flesh it out. **B +**

Tom T. Hall: *I Witness Life* (Mercury '70). I'm a fan of this Nashville original's most famous song, "Harper Valley P.T.A.," because like all his best work it combines pithy narrative with pithy ethics. Its flaw is that its truth is metaphorical — it sounds made up. The two greatest songs here — "Salute to a Switchblade" and "The Ballad of Bill Crump," one an autobiographical tale of barroom violence (and discretion) abroad, the other a biographical tale about the death of a carpenter — are documentaries in rhyme. The method isn't original, foolproof, or the only one in his kit. But boy, is he good at it. Original grade: B. **B +**

Tom T. Hall: *In Search of a Song* (Mercury '71). Forget arty pontificators like Kris Kristofferson and Mickey Newbury — wouldn't you rather have Woody Guthrie? Hall's politics are only liberal, his ironies sometimes pro forma, but like Guthrie's his observations and presentation are direct and unpretentious in a way that can't be faked or even imitated — he has a few things to say, he says them, and that's that. While in the past the dull sentimentality that is the downfall of so much country music has flawed his albums, here even the worst song, "Second Handed Flowers," qualifies as bright sentimentality (with a twist). The best is "Kentucky Feb. 27, '71," hidden away on the second side because it's too subtle to make its impact broadside. Simple as death, it recounts Hall's pilgrimage to see an old mountain man, who explains why kids move to the city — "They want to see the things they've heard about" — and apologizes for not providing Hall with a song. Original grade: A minus. **A**

Tom T. Hall: *Tom T. Hall's Greatest Hits* (Mercury '72). Except for "Ballad of Forty Dollars," a dispassionate account of a day in his life as a gravedigger, and "Homecoming," a melodramatic account of a day in his life as a star, all the zingers here compiled are also available on better albums — albums that don't include songs of inspirational tolerance like "I Washed My Face in the Morning Dew" and "One Hundred Children," which Hall executes no more wisely than any other mortal.   **B**

Tom T. Hall: *The Storyteller* (Mercury '72). Counting *Greatest Hits* this is the fourth LP from Hall in about a year, and while it's better than the last one the workload still shows. The title isn't quite a misnomer, but he does seem to be cranking out them yarns instead of looking for his own truth within them, and for the second straight album the most impressive cut is a straight love song — "Souvenirs" on *We All Got Together*, "When Nobody Wants Your Body Anymore" here. How about picking up some new material on a long vacation, T?   **B**

Tom T. Hall: *The Rhymer and Other Five and Dimers* (Mercury '73). One reason Merle Haggard's thought of as the Poet of the Common Man is that he's also in the running for Voice of the Comman Man; even with Jerry Kennedy's genius assembly line behind him, Hall's monotone isn't liable to shiver your short hairs unless he gets the words just right. Here he comes close. He honors Ravishing Ruby and remembers his own younger brother, hitching into town for medicine and coffee in the bad winter of 1949. He gets stuck in a motel in Spokane and comes back to Olive Hill with all his faults intact. And he yokes his best political song, about the man who hated freckles and Martin Luther Queen, with one of his worst slow ones, designed for those who find "candy in the windows of my mind" a poignant trope. Time: 28:35.   **A−**

Tom T. Hall: *Greatest Hits Volume 2* (Mercury '75). From the received novelty melodies of "That Song Is Driving Me Crazy" and "I Like Beer" to the prefab lyrics of "Country Is" and the odious "I Love" — a list of things people get sentimental about!

and the list gets them sentimental all over again! — this should convince any doubters in Nashville that T is just another professional manipulator, with all that liberal stuff just another marketing ploy. It damn near convinces me. And that's not even counting the two kiddie songs. Time: 27:25.   **D+**

Tom T. Hall: *Faster Horses* (Mercury '76). The first decent record by my former favorite country singer-songwriter in over three years. High point: "Big Motel on the Mountain." Rock stars are forever reviling motels, their readymade symbol of the impersonal rootlessness of life on the road; Hall obviously tore himself away from the soaps and game shows one day and deduced that the premises supported a life of their own. You think that says anything about the relationship between perceived impersonality and egocentricity? I do.   **B+**

Tom T. Hall: *Greatest Hits — Volume III* (Mercury '78). In which Hall goes to work for RCA and Mercury mops together some final product. Three of the four great songs — "I Can't Dance," "She Gave Her Heart to Jethro," and the mind-boggling "Turn It On, Turn It On, Turn It On," about the electrocution of a mass-murdering 4-F in 1944 — date from 1972 or before, when it seemed he'd never run out of stories.   **B+**

Daryl Hall/John Oates: *Abandoned Luncheonette* (Atlantic '73). This comes down to a nice equation of folk duo and soul falsetto group, brought together with the best vocal and production pyrotechnics a studio can afford. The music rocks with a smooth sophistication, although it can get sententious as well as popsy cute; the lyrics diagnose romantic malaise with clinical expertise and occasional acuity — "Everybody's high on consolation," perfect. If not too perfect. **B−**

Daryl Hall & John Oates: *Bigger Than Both of Us* (RCA Victor '76). Now they're rich boys, and they've gone too far, 'cause they don't know what matters anyway.   **C+**

Daryl Hall/John Oates: *No Goodbyes* (Atlantic '77). The three previously unreleased songs on this compilation — especially "Love You Like a Brother," an ironic double or triple whammy — define worldly, media-saturated, serially monogamous singles (as in singles bar, though I'm sure they wouldn't stoop so low) as well as the best cuts on the well-represented *Abandoned Luncheonette*. The three songs from *War Babies* take on larger issues of concern to singles — destruction by stardom, etc. **B+**

Daryl Hall & John Oates: *Along the Red Ledge* (RCA Victor '78). Do these guys still worry about being mistaken for the O'Jays? I suppose you could call them soulful, but in the style of one of those hairdressers (no imputation of sexual preference intended) who doubles as an unlicensed therapist. I admit that cut by cut and counting this is their most impressive album. Hall gets two tart ain't-love-a-bitch songs out of a broken romance that seems to have touched his "heart," while Oates puts his name on homages to Aerosmith and Talking Heads. But it's docked a notch because after all these years I still don't know which one's the blond. **B**

Dirk Hamilton: *You Can Sing on the Left or Bark on the Right* (ABC '76). This is one of those records that makes me wish I wasn't in the grading business. I really like it a lot, to the point of positively loving one song, "She Don't Squash Bugs," and getting a nice buzz every time I hear the opening lines of cut one. And while good words are the point, the good words are expressly musical; that is, they are designed for Hamilton's plosive drawl, a delivery in the general tradition of Van Morrison. Hamilton's earth mysticism recalls Morrison, too, and unlike Morrison he has a sense of humor. But also unlike Morrison, he has zilch gift for the hook; he's repetitive in the folk rather than the rock manner. So, all you subtlety fans (you know who you are) might take a chance. **B**

Herbie Hancock: *The Best of Herbie Hancock* (Columbia '79). In which the erstwhile watermelon man heats up a frozen quiche in his microwave. A/k/a *Funk Goes to Colege*. **C+**

Emmylou Harris: *Pieces of the Sky* (Reprise '74). Abetted by Brian Ahern, who would have been wise to add some Anne Murray schlock, Harris shows off a pristine earnestness that has nothing to do with what is most likable about country music and everything to do with what is most suspect in "folk." Presumably, Gram Parsons was tough enough to discourage this tendency or play against it, but as a solo mannerism it doesn't even ensure clear enunciation: I swear the chorus of the best song here sounds like it begins: "I will rub my asshole/In the bosom of Abraham." **C+**

Emmylou Harris: *Elite Hotel* (Reprise '75). This flows better than the first, but it also makes clear that Emmylou is just another pretty voice, a country singer by accident. I mean, Linda Ronstadt has the best female voice in country music, and even she doesn't satisfy the way an original like Dolly Parton or Loretta Lynn does. And since there's not a cover version here that equals its prototype, all she accomplishes with her good taste in material is to send you scurrying for the sources. I prefer Donna Fargo. Not Lynn Anderson, though. **C+**

Emmylou Harris: *Luxury Liner* (Reprise '76). Not content with her corner on the wraith-with-a-twang market, some folk's favorite folkie manque has added funk and raunch and echo and overdub to her voice. The result is a record I play some, perhaps out of sheer surprise. Song selection also helps — an unforgettable Townes Van Zandt melody is unearthed, and the two Gram Parsons selections don't automatically shame themselves by recalling the originals. Original grade: B plus. **B**

Emmylou Harris: *Profile/Best of Emmylou Harris* (Warner Bros. '78). Lucky for Emmylou I don't know as much about country music as she does — the Louvin Brothers' "If I Could Only Win Your Love" and the Carter Family's "Hello Stranger" may well render her versions forgettable. But as it is, hers sure are pretty, like almost everything here, sung with undeniable care and charm. She also defines Dolly Parton's previously unrecorded "To Daddy," as great a song as that great songwriter has ever come up with. And does all right by Chuck Berry. **B+**

George Harrison: *All Things Must Pass* (Apple '70). As a slave of the very "MAYA" (pidgin Hindi for the concrete world) Harrison warns against, I am obliged to point out that playing headsie with the Universal Mind is not introspection and that the International Pop Music Community is not a group. Presumably, the featurelessness of these three discs — right down to the anonymity of the multitracked vocals — reflects Harrison's notion of Truth, and he's welcome to it. But he's never been good for more than two songs per album, and after "My Sweet Lord" I start to get stuck. **C**

George Harrison: *Living in the Material World* (Apple '73). If you call this living. Harrison sings as if he's doing sitar impressions, and four different people, including a little man in my head who I never noticed before, have expressed intense gratitude when I turned the damned thing off during "Be Here Now." Inspirational sentiment: "the leaders of nations/They're acting like big girls." **C**

George Harrison: *Dark Horse* (Apple '74). Such transubstantiations. In which "Bye Bye Love" becomes "Maya Love," in which "windowpane" becomes "window brain." Can this mean that pain (pane, get it?) is the same as brain? For all this hoarse dork knows . . . Original grade: C. **C−**

George Harrison: *Extra Texture* (Apple '75). When they said he had a good sense of humor did they mean he was willing to grin like a Monty Python choirboy over a caption that said "OHNOTHIMAGEN"? **C−**

George Harrison: *The Best of George Harrison* (Capitol '76). Seven of George's Beatle songs on the A side, and while the titles are impressive — "Something" and "Here Comes the Sun" no more than "If I Needed Someone" and "Think for Yourself" — the voice begins to betray its weaknesses after a while, like a borderline hitter they can pitch around after the sluggers are traded away. The solo "bests" on the B are remarkably shoddy — if this is all he can manage over four LPs you wonder why he has a contract at all. (Wait, let me guess.) **B−**

George Harrison: *Thirty-three & 1/3* (Dark Horse '76). This isn't as worldly as George wants you to think — or as he thinks himself, for all I know — but it ain't fulla shit either. "Crackerbox Palace" is the best thing he's written since "Here Comes the Sun" (not counting "Deep Blue," hidden away on the B side of "Bangla-Desh," or — naughty, naughty — "My Sweet Lord"), and if "This Song" were on side two I might actually play the record again. **B−**

George Harrison: *George Harrison* (Dark Horse '79). In which Harrison returns to good old commercial rock and roll, he says, presumably because he shared songwriting on one track with Gary "Sure Shot" Wright and let Russ Titelman produce. Well, there is a good song here — "Faster," about a kind of stardom. He remembers! **C**

Wilbert Harrison: *Anything You Want* (Wet Soul '70). *Let's Work Together* was an anachronistic, even primitive r&b album based on the fluke hit of the same name, which makes this the follow-up. Side one consists entirely of roll and rock songs you'd swear you've heard before — "Your Three Letters," eh, and what's this "Let's Stick Together," and why not bring out "Kansas City" again? Very unprepossessing, very charming. In fact, if the second side weren't all standards and uncharming filler — only "Sentimental Journey" is even funny — I wouldn't be recommending this to r&b diehards only. **B**

Mickey Hart: *Rolling Thunder* (Warner Bros. '72). In which the ex-Dead drummer compounds Alla Rakha, Shosone chants, a water pump, big band jazz, and electronic music, not to mention Paul and Gracie and Jerry and other Our Gang regulars. Much more original than your typical Marin County special, but almost as forgettable. **C+**

John Hartford: *Aereo-Plain* (Warner Bros. '71). Insensitive though I am to tales of them thar pickers, I must admit that Norman Blake's guitar, Tut Taylor's dobro, and Vassar Clements's fiddle complement Hartford with tact, wit, and sly razzmatazz. But I insist that it's Hartford's funny, quirkish songs, rather than his banjo, that save me from continued boorishness. And warn that the songs are so grass-meets-bluegrass that remembering them sometimes gives me whimsy megrims and nostalgia headaches. **B+**

John Hartford: *Mark Twang* (Flying Fish '76). Hartford's come a long way from "Gentle on My Mind" and eccentric bids for stardom. These days he sings mostly about the mighty Mississip (too thick to navigate, too thin to plow) and records eccentric river music for a folk label. He's slightly the better for it, on the whole — but I wouldn't say his living sounds so secure that he should turn down a gig on the Proud Mary. A gig playing, or a gig navigating. **B**

Dan Hartman: *Instant Replay* (Blue Sky '78). Too bad one of the few disco albums that out-dollar-for-dollars the corresponding disco single is this super-efficient piece of rock funk, but deserving souls who dally with mechanization can't complain when bested by a real machine. Sole monkey wrench: the slow one, "Time and Space," on which Hartman breaks his

own rule by trying to write a meaningful lyric and then triples the misdemeanor by running it through his own larynx. Who does he think he is, Robert Plant? Machines can't sing. **B**

Fuzzy Haskins: *A Whole Nother Thang* (Westbound '76). "Which Way Do I Disco" and "Sometimes I Rock and Roll" set up an antinomy that George Clinton's second-favorite guitarist doesn't do much with. Both would have fit nicely onto *Tales of Kidd Funkadelic*, too — as would one (though not all three) of the love songs. Half a thang is the way I reckon it — or too many thangs. **B**

Ronnie Hawkins: *Rock and Roll Resurrection* (Monument '72). If all he had had were memories, Ronnie would rather drive a truck, but he also has a little extra cachet as an ex-Bandleader. The third in a series of recorded throwbacks is imbued with just enough fun to appeal to nostalgiacs. Me, I'll stick with the originals, as usual. **C+**

Hawkwind: *Quark Strangeness and Charm* (Sire '76). In the old days, this likable British band played more benefits than Joan Baez and helped give psychedelic rock its bad name — when you repeat three chords in 4/4 for forty-five minutes, it's politic to change riffs once in a while. Yet they're still around, and good for them. Here they manage to spread six songs over eight cuts — a trick accomplished by granting two rather ponderous jams names and numbers of their own — as well as introducing more substantial innovations: for every song there's a good new riff, and by now the old sci-fi/counterculture themes mean something, probably because lyricist Robert Calvert has gained wit and wisdom since the time of zonk. Irresistible: the title cut, which suggests that Einstein had trouble with girls because he didn't dig subatomic physics. **B+**

Isaac Hayes: *The Isaac Hayes Movement* (Enterprise '70). I admit that his arrangements can be "interesting" — my my my, a gypsy fiddle on "Something" — but they'd be more so at a less stately pace than four songs per LP. And if his voice is best displayed when he talks, why doesn't he do a whole album of raps like the one preceding "I Stand Accused"? Might be pretty funny.   **C**

Isaac Hayes: *Shaft* (Enterprise '71). Pretty rhythmic for a soundtrack — if a backup band played this stuff before the star-of-our-show came on you wouldn't get bored until midway into the second number. Proving that not only do black people make better pop-schlock movies than white people, they also make better pop-schlock music. As if we didn't know.   **C+**

Isaac Hayes: *Live at the Sahara Tahoe* (Enterprise '73). I like Ike live because he makes fun of himself, but though I hear the patrons laughing I miss his turquoise tights. Can't even say I wish I'd been there — not in Tahoe, thanks. But the band is crisp and funky, and he does talk more on stage than on record if you can believe that, and I even find "Rock Me Baby" sexy myself. Not "First Time Ever I Saw Your Face," though.   **B−**

Eddie Hazel: *Game, Dames and Guitar Thangs* (Warner Bros. '77). Hazel can really flick his pick, and maybe that's the problem: despite a welcome but misleading cover of "I Want You (She's So Heavy)" and the assistance of his cohorts in the Funkadelic rhythm brigade, most of the time you'd think this was a David Spinozza record. Heavy it ain't.   **B−**

Murray Head: *Say It Ain't So* (A&M '76). If mindless pap is your thing, this sure beats Eric Carmen. It's even slightly psychedoolic, and includes not a single Rachmaninoff cop. Hit single: "Say It Ain't So Joe."   **B**

Heart: *Dreamboat Annie* (Mushroom '76). As apparently spontaneous pop phenomena go, a hardish folk-rock group led by two women is a moder-ately interesting one, especially when their composing beats that of the twixt-Balin Starplane, whom they otherwise recall. I said moderately.   **C+**

Heart: *Dog and Butterfly* (Portrait '78). Georgia Christgau: "Robert Plant understands his place as second-string guitar posing as lead singer. He should — he thought it up. But this idea is belittling to Ann Wilson. 'I have a great voice!' her songs seem to say, and so she may — but what is it doing preening here among all these seamy heavy metal types?"   **C**

Heartbreakers: *Live at Max's Kansas City* (Max's Kansas City '79). Of the five titles not on *L.A.M.F.*, only the scabrous answer song "London" is even in a league with "Born Too Loose" and "It's Not Enough," both among the missing, and (believe it or not) replacement drummer Ty Stix is less subtle than Jerry Nolan. But the sound is brighter here, and the Heartbreakers' "final shows" at Max's are an institution that has earned the permanence of plastic. This captures the boys in all their rowdy, rabble-rousing abandon, and I know that when I feel like hearing them I'll be pulling it off the shelf.   **A−**

Heatwave: *Central Heating* (Epic '78). Personally, I've always thought sucking was fun, but I know people intend an insult when they say disco sucks, and this is the kind of preprogrammed pap they're thinking of. Most of it has as much emotional substance as the soundtrack to *Integrated Beach Party* — here the background music for the boisterous-barbecue sequence, there the accompaniment for the gentle-fuck scene. This does feature a nice post-doowop vocal on "Happiness Togetherness" (what am I supposed to call it, fifth cut first side?), and "The Groove Line" does its filthy work as fast as a Dr. Pepper jingle, but only on the title cut do the layered rhythms and harmonies get interesting, the way good disco should.

And surprise: this is not a hit on the disco circuit.   **C−**

Richard Hell and the Voidoids: *Blank Generation* (Sire '77). Like all the best CBGB bands, the Voidoids make unique music from a reputedly immutable formula, with jagged, shifting rhythms accentuated by Hell's indifference to vocal amenities like key and timbre. I'm no great devotee of this approach, which harks back to Captain Beefheart. So when I say that Hell's songs get through to me, that's a compliment; I intend to save this record for those very special occasions when I feel like turning into a nervous wreck. Original grade: B plus.   **A−**

Levon Helm and the RCO All-Stars: *Levon Helm and the RCO All-Stars* (ABC '78). Boogie.   **C+**

Hendrix: *Band of Gypsys* (Capitol '70). Because Billy Cox and Buddy Miles are committed (not to say limited) to a straight 4/4 with a slight funk bump, Hendrix has never sounded more earthbound. "Who Knows," based on a blues elemental, and "Machine Gun," a peacemonger's long-overdue declaration of war, are as powerful if not as complex as anything he's ever put on record. But except on the rapid-fire "Message to Love" he just plays simple wah-wah patterns for a lot of side two. Not bad for a live rock album, because Hendrix is the music's nonpareil improvisor. But for a Hendrix album, not great.   **B+**

Jimi Hendrix: *The Cry of Love* (Reprise '71). At first I responded to this by feel. It seemed loose, free of mannerisms, warmer than the three Experience LPs, as if by dying before it was finished Hendrix left all the sweet lyricism of his cockeyed mystical brotherhood jive unguarded. But it isn't just the flow — these tracks work as individual compositions, from offhand rhapsodies like "Angel" and "Night Bird Flying" through primal riffsongs like "Ezy Ryder" and "Astro Man" to inspired goofs like "My Friend"

and "Belly Button Window." What a testament. Original grade: A minus.   **A**

Jimi Hendrix: *Rainbow Bridge* (Reprise '71). Given that Hendrix is always a guitarist first, *The Cry of Love* seems like the verbal/vocal half of the double-LP he was planning when he died. Except for "Dolly Dagger," now the single and a pretty conventional Hendrix song, what you notice here is the playing — the delicate "Pali Gap," the relatively dignified (and pre-Woodstock) "Star Spangled Banner," and the amazing blues jams of side two, especially the live "Hear My Train a Coming." Rich stuff, exploring territory that as always with Hendrix consists not merely of notes but of undifferentiated sound, a sound he shapes with a virtuosity no one else has ever achieved on an electric instrument.   **A−**

Jimi Hendrix: *Hendrix in the West* (Reprise '72). Despite the introductory mini-medley of "God Save the Queen" and "Sgt. Pepper's Lonely Hearts Club Band" from Isle of Wight — a great in-concert idea that doesn't have any business on a record — these San Diego (with the Experience) and Berkeley (with Cox and Mitchell) performances make a better live album than *Band of Gypsys*. Not all of it is historic, but "Red House," done as a long blues jam marred briefly by a lazy unaccompanied passage, and "Little Wing," stronger and freer than on *Axis: Bold as Love* (or *Layla*), are definitive. And so, heh heh, is "Johnny B. Goode."   **A−**

Jimi Hendrix: *War Heroes* (Reprise '72). It figures you'd find the heavy metal down toward the bottom of the barrel — still strong stuff, but except maybe for the "Highway Chile" riff and the sheer speed of "Steppin' Stone," nothing springs out. And novelties like "Peter Gunn" and "3 Little Bears," biographically touching though they are, really do sound like filler.   **B**

Jimi Hendrix: *Sound Track Recordings from the Film* **Jimi Hendrix** (Reprise '73). "Johnny B. Goode" has about two-thirds the volume and brightness of the original, and the stuff from *Band of Gypsys* has lost clarity. None of the previously unreleased music is exceptional, although all of it is interesting, especially an early twelve-string blues. The interviews aren't bad, and at least they're at the end of each side. I wouldn't, and didn't, throw away a free copy — just filed it where the sun don't shine.   **C+**

Jimi Hendrix: *Crash Landing* (Reprise '75). The studio guys producer-curator Alan Douglas assigned to provide proper tracks (he claims the originals were unreleasable, though one must wonder whether he could have grabbed all that composition credit if he'd put 'em out untouched) do a surprisingly competent job. In fact, I don't even blame them for the competent lifelessness of side one — Jimi was a pretty fair city songwriter (cf. such guitar whizzes as Clapton, Garcia, Page, Trower, Marino, Beck), but his legacy can't be infinite. Side two, however, includes the best hook here — a soul consciousness chant called "With the Power" that features Buddy Miles and Billy Cox — as well as two astonishing instrumental showpieces, "Peace in Mississippi" (feedback heaven) and "Captain Coconut" (studio space).   **B+**

Jimi Hendrix: *Midnight Lightning* (Reprise '76). With posthumous Hendrix it's best to concentrate on the improvisations as if he were a jazz musician, and heard this way Alan Douglas's second attempt at creative tampering beats the first. Once again the standouts are instrumentals — a Mitch Mitchell vamp called "Beginnings" and especially "Trash Man," reminiscent of McLaughlin's *Devotion* only grander, more passionate, and more anarchic. Guitarist Jeff Mironov actually enriches that cut, just as guitarist Lance Quinn does "Machine Gun," which due to the stiffness of the rhythm section is less funky than either live version but smashes through as a raveup. And beyond that the blues

playing — as opposed to singing or writing — carries the album.   **B+**

Jimi Hendrix: *The Essential Jimi Hendrix* (Reprise '78). The essential Jimi Hendrix is to be found on *Are You Experienced?*, *Axis: Bold as Love*, *Electric Ladyland*, and *The Cry of Love*, from which most of the great music on this two-LP compilation was rather eccentrically excerpted. *Smash Hits* is a worthy song compilation. And if this is why *Rainbow Bridge* (two cuts), *War Heroes* (two cuts), and *Hendrix in the West* (none) were deleted from the catalogue, Alan Douglas ought to be put in escrow until they're restored.   **C+**

Jimi Hendrix: *The Essential Jimi Hendrix Volume Two* (Reprise '79). This one-LP follow-up surrounds the *Band of Gypsys* "Machine Gun" with the Monterey "Wild Thing" and the Woodstock "Star Spangled Banner," a worthy conceit, and includes a seven-inch "Gloria" that lasts 8:47 and is spectacular for about a third of that. It also includes five whole tracks from *Are You Experienced?*   **B−**

Jimi Hendrix: See also Otis Redding/The Jimi Hendrix Experience

Henry Cow: *The Henry Cow Legend* (Virgin '73). Composed to encourage improvisation, influenced by jazz yet identifying with Europe, and categorizable only as rock (although calling one cut "Teenbeat" is stretching things), the music of these Cambridge progressives is more flexible than King Crimson's and more stringently conceived than Soft Machine's. As is usual in this style, not everything works. As is also usual, the guitar (Fred Frith) carries more clout than the saxophone (Geoff Leigh). As is not usual, you can listen to what few lyrics there are without getting sick.   **B**

Henry Cow: *Unrest* (Red '79). Finally released in the States five years after it came out in Britain, this demanding music shows up such superstar "progressives'' as Yes for the weak-minded reactionaries they are. The integrity of Cow's synthesis is clearest in ''Bittern Storm over Ulm,'' based on the Yardbirds' ''Got to Hurry'' — instead of quoting sixteen bars with two or three instruments, thus insuring their listeners another lazy identification, they break the piece down, almost like beboppers. Though the saxophone is still second-rate and the more lyrical rhythms flirt with a cheap swing, the band is worthy of its classical correlatives — Bartok, Stockhausen, and Varese rather than Tchaikovsky and predigested Bach.   **A−**

Henry Cow/Slapp Happy: *In Praise of Learning* (Red '79). This 1975 U.K. release was Cow's second collaboration with guitarist-composer Peter Blegvad, pianist-composer Anthony Moore, and vocalist Dagmar, and if it's less successful than the earlier *Desperate Straights* (still an import here), that's not the new guys' fault. Dagmar's abrasively arty, Weill-derived style, as bluesless and European as any ''rock'' singing ever recorded, does manage to find a context for words that seem literary if not pompous in print; in fact, between Dagmar and the Weillish Moore-Blegvad and Tim Hodgkinson music on side one, the lyrics seem almost as astute politically as the title. But except for some atonal Fred Frith piano, the music on side two is dominated by less than winning musique concrete experiments that make such injunctions as ''Arise Work Men and seize/the Future'' seem completely academic.   **B**

The Heptones: *Night Food* (Island '76). This reminds me that British skinheads were reggae fans — it shares its sexual brutality and rhythmic monotonousness with the most desperate and overbearing heavy rock. Saved by admirably intense and cogent vocal stylings and (I count) three good songs — not enough to really give such styling someplace to go.   **B**

John Herald: *John Herald* (Paramount '73). This casually joyous solo debut by the former Greenbriar Boy gives in at times to such folky vices as mere flash, mere lyricism, and mere whimsy. But ''Fire Song,'' a casually joyous ditty about how his house burned down, and ''Brother Sam,'' unpresumptuous compassion for a returned Vietnam vet, should inspire Paul Simon to work real hard on the follow-up. And his high notes should inspire Art Garfunkel to go back to architecture school.   **B+**

The John Herald Band: *The John Herald Band* (Bay '78). I was about to note bemusedly that Herald's best songs on this album — ''Wiggle Worm Wiggle'' and ''I'm Getting Ready to Go'' — could have been written fifty years ago. Indeed they could have, because both are old bluegrass tunes. ''Slightly Blind'' and ''With Every Month'' are quite up-to-date. After that, details get hazy.   **B**

John Hiatt: *Hangin' Around the Observatory* (Epic '74). Hiatt is a Midwestern boy who wrings off-center rock and roll out of a voice with lots of range, none of it homey. Reassuring to hear the heartland Americana of the Band actually inspire a heartlander. Reassuring too that one of the resulting songs can be released as a single by Three Dog Night.   **B**

John Hiatt: *Overcoats* (Epic '75). I admit to a weakness for loony lyrical surrealist protest rockers. And I admit that this one tends to go soft when he tries to go poetic. I even admit that he has a voice many would consider worse than no voice at all (although that's one of the charms of the type). But I insist that anyone who can declaim about killing an ant with his guitar ''underneath romantic Indiana stars'' deserves a shot at leading-man status in Fort Wayne.   **B**

John Hiatt: *Slug Line* (MCA '79). This hard-working young pro may yet turn into an all-American Elvis C. He's focused his changeable voice up around the high end and straightened out his always impressive melodies, but he has a weakness for the shallow (if sincere) putdown, e.g.: ''You're too dumb to have a choice.'' Or else he'd get chosen, do you think he means? Lene Lovich: should cover "You're My Love Interest." **B+**

Dan Hicks and His Hot Licks: Where's the Money? (Blue Thumb '71). If Hicks's acoustic stylings react against the excesses of counterculture futurists, then the key moment on this live album comes when he corrects "his wife" with "I should say old lady" and no one laughs. Hicks is delicate, tuneful, and droll, with an ear for colloquial history in words and music both, but he's so diffident about focus that his mock nostalgia is too easy to mistake for the right thing. **B**

Dan Hicks and His Hot Licks: Striking It Rich! (Blue Thumb '72). This isn't as long on ambient whimsy as *Where's the Money?*, but that's OK — makes a less distracting showcase for an artist who's much better at writing songs than at contextualizing them. I count seven I'd be delighted to hear somebody cover, and it's fun to hear Hicks's own outfit go after them. Best contextualization: Maryann Price's interpretation of "I'm an Old Cowhand." **B+**

Dan Hicks and His Hot Licks: Last Train to Hicksville (Blue Thumb '73). On *Where's the Money?* I had to work to figure out why I wasn't responding; on this one I have to think to figure out why I am. Well, dozens of touches — Hicks's musical wit is undiminished, with John Girton's acoustic plectra especially charming. But the words aren't sharp enough to cut the band's chronic cuteness. **B**

Dan Hicks: It Happened One Bite (Warner Bros. '78). Hicks's songwriting is somewhat straightened (Joan Baez could do "Cloud My Sunny Mood" or "Garden in the Rain") but only slightly diminished on this 1975 soundtrack for an unreleased Ralph Bakshi movie (he sez). But for some reason it sounds a little . . . loud, even forceful. I should applaud this modernistic development, but instead I'm thinking that I'd rather hear Peter Stampfel (or R. Crumb) cover "Mama, I'm an Outlaw." **B−**

Justin Hines & the Dominoes: Jezebel (Island '76). Homey lyrics ("Jah-jah will spank you") and artful instrumental touches — I like the gentle calypso-styled horns and decorative guitar licks — may mean this is a great reggae album. But they may mean it's only a subtle one, and in such an understated genre subtlety risks extinction. **B+**

Eddie Hinton: Very Extremely Dangerous (Capricorn '78). Hinton's Otis Redding tribute goes far beyond anything ever attempted by Frankie Miller or Toots Hibbert — it's almost like one of those Elvis re-creations. The Muscle Shoals boys put out on backup, Hinton's songs are pretty good, and the man has the phrasing and the guttural inflections down pat. So what's missing is instructive: first, the richness of timbre that made Otis sound soft even at his raspiest, and second, good will so enormous that it overflowed naturally into a humor that hurt no one. **B−**

Hi Rhythm: On the Loose (Hi '76). In which Al Green's sidemen, perhaps disgruntled at Al's unwillingness to record their material, get together and cut it. Some stickler for detail is sure to point out that the singing on side two is completely out of tune, but that's OK — so is most of the singing on side one, which I prefer to *Full of Fire*. One of the more carefully thought out tracks features a mildly malicious lyric about Green himself, but it's the eccentricity of the music, which sounds as if it includes a banjo, that does him in. Loose indeed. **A−**

Tommy Hoehn: Losing You to Sleep (Power Play '78). In which the concentrated energy of Memphis power pop — the upside-down *Beatles VI* style pioneered by Alex Chilton's Big Star — defines itself as a regional sound, albeit one that has been confined almost entirely to the studio.

This romantically inclined sample includes a Chilton-Hoehn song, but it sounds feckless played back-to-back with the Scruffs. [Later on London.]   **B**

Bill Holland & Rent's Due: *If It Ain't One Thing . . .* (Adelphi '75). Despite the decline of the genre, I still hear a lot of singer-songwriter records, most of which sound smoother than this — both Holland and his band lack polish in the vaguely jazzy style mature folkies fall into. They have plenty of bounce, though, and something about the tender yet skeptical common sense of Holland's lyrics suggests that he doesn't much care for smooth stuff anyway. Not that his raggedness is a plus. But if I were an a&r man and heard some unknown put across songs as out-of-the-ordinary as "This Fourth Year" and "Do the Mambo" I'd say the hell with the cracked voice and sign him.   **B+**

The Hollies: *He Ain't Heavy, He's My Brother* (Epic '70). Despite one soupy instrumental, one soupy hit, and one soupy song of putative faith, the general air of unrelieved vapidity here only enhances yet another bright, slick, well-crafted album by our own Five Lads. Funniest conceit: "Please Sign Your Letters." Best readymade: Booker T. bottom on "Do You Believe in Love?" Original grade: B plus.   **B**

The Hollies: *Moving Finger* (Epic '70). Suddenly, for no discernible reason, the Hollies seem to be aiming their schlock at the housewife market. The nadir, an attempted artsong called "Marigold Gloria Swansong," is as aimless as bad (i.e. current) Bee Gees; usually they come on like the Sonny and Cher of slick harmony. The music hasn't lost its iridescence, but though they do generate one great soap opera — "Too Young to Be Married" — most of this is too crass for giggles. Original grade: C.   **C+**

The Hollies: *Distant Light* (Epic '72). Old rock and rollers are doing somersaults over the hit, "Long Cool Woman in a Black Dress," one of the catchier items on the recent AM. But that's all it is, and that's all this album's got. The likable songs are cancelled out by a couple of real dummies, and the musical substance is more a function of Allan Clarke's late-blooming soulfulness — pop groups have to do *something* as they push thirty — than in the long cool harmonies of yesteryear.   **C+**

The Hollies: *Romany* (Epic '72). You had your doubts about the Hollies without Graham Nash, right? How about without Graham Nash and Allan Clarke?   **C−**

The Hollies: *The Hollies' Greatest Hits* (Epic '73). Ignoring their barren stint with Mikael "Swedish Invasion" Rikfors, they add "Bus Stop," "On a Carousel," and four other Imperial sillyditties to six Epic tracks, including their three American successes of the '70s. This has the effect of underplaying their most durable froth, the early Epic music with Graham Nash — the ersatz Pepperpomp of "King Midas in Reverse" is a lot closer to their essence than the "sincerity" of "He Ain't Heavy." The programming is a mess, too. But it's the one Hollies album to own if one etc., as well as a decent LP with "Long Cool Woman" on it.   **A−**

Hollies: *Hollies* (Epic '74). Hollies scholars herald Allan Clarke's homecoming as a return to form, but though the material is their most playful in years — the slyly circular "Love Makes the World Go Round," the slyly hyperbolic "Out on the Road" — the old lightness is gone, probably forever. I mean, soul is soul — at times the sham intensity here is almost baroque. We are not charmed.   **B−**

Loleatta Holloway: *Loleatta* (Gold Mind '77). Those craving a big-voiced r&b singer should probably grab this rough-edged Philadelphia-type production. Those in control of their urges should note that nothing else on the album matches the lead cuts on each side, "Hit and Run" and "Ripped Off."   **B−**

Loleatta Holloway: *Queen of the Night* (Gold Mind '78). In an era when Donna and Diana and Natalie aim (truly) to reintroduce Josephine Baker to the great American public, this black woman extends the sexy mama tradition of rhythm and blues. Her sweet grit and tough wit are alternately abusive and forgiving, coy and defenseless, and she's got some voice. "I May Not Be There When You Want Me," a Bunny Sigler song that rocks as hard as any black music I've heard this year, is also available as a disco disc, but even the few mediocre cuts on this album are of interest, and it includes a version of "You Light Up My Life" that beats Patti Smith's all to hell.   **A −**

Rupert Holmes: *Rupert Holmes* (Epic '75). In another time this guy would be writing short stories for *Collier's;* if he really is a civilized Randy Newman, as some seem to feel, then the emphasis is on the civilized. The giveaway is the voice, devoid of feeling or even eccentricity, and hence inoffensive. Randy Newman is never inoffensive. That so many putative rock critics mistake Holmes's deftness for the real thing only proves how desperate we have become for original intelligence, no matter how shallow.   **B −**
Rupert Holmes: *Pursuit of Happiness* (Private Stock '78). As a much-covered pop singer-songwriter who narrated well-crafted musical soap operas, Holmes earned neither popular nor critical status. So now he's pursued fame by moving to an avowed singles label, jettisoning the narrative and steering between Jimmy Webb literacy at his best ("Less Is More") and Paul Williams pap at his worst ("Speechless").   **C**

The Holy Modal Rounders: *Good Taste Is Timeless* (Metromedia '71). A sextet who put the communal principle into practice — five of them sing lead, four write. They celebrate meat ("Pork liver, lambies tongues, vienna sausage"), boobs ("They're big they're round they're all around"), and

a bunch of farmers who danced till dawn one night in the spring of '65. They're not crazy about horoscopes, "cute antics," or city wimmin who live with dogs. Except for the timeless reel of "Spring of '65," their great moments are fast and relatively loud, probably because projecting soft and sweet isn't something any old communard can do. But their collective spirit is touched with poetry nonetheless.   **B +**
The Holy Modal Rounders: *Alleged in Their Own Time* (Rounder '75). I love the Rounders chronicle and the theory of Western civ and the pornographic reminiscence but I wish there were times and credits in the liner notes too because I don't feel like putting a watch on what I estimate as fifty-plus minutes of random canon and also because I wonder whether Steve Weber and maybe Luke Faust and Robin Remailly are putting out and in addition I prefer Dave Van Ronk's "Random Canyon" to Peter Stampfel's and would just as soon Peter recut "Nova" and "Synergy" as well but he probably designed the album to sound like a field recording which I'm sure is just what the Folks-with-a-capital-F at the Rounder collective wanted since this isn't traditional enough for them and maybe it's also too traditional for me but I doubt it.   **B**
Holy Modal Rounders: *Last Round* (Adelphi '79). In which Peter Stampfel and friends — including veteran Rounders Steve Weber and Robin Remailly, many Clamtones, and Antonia, composer of "That Belly I Idolize" and "God, What Am I Doing Here" (with "Fucking Sailors in Chinatown" yet to come) — prove that the counterculture still exists. Strange drug experiences are detailed, ooze is embraced, girls without underwear consume hoagies and juice. In short, Head Comix live.   **B +**

Honey Cone: *Sweet Replies* (Hot Wax '71). I know "Want Ads" is pure Jackson 5, but most of this is pure Vandellas. Producer-songwriter Ronald Dunbar must have had lots of advice from label owners Holland-Dozier-Holland — he uses every H-D-H trick and comes up with a few electronic effects of his own on this sturdy LP. Highlights: "Are You Man Enough, Are You Strong Enough" (to raise another man's child), "The Day I Found Myself" (was the day I left you). **B+**

Honey Cone: *Soulful Tapestry* (Hot Wax '71). Just as *Sweet Replies* repeated two cuts from the dud debut *Take Me with You,* this one repeats two from *Sweet Replies* — only not verbatim, which must make it all right. Wish they'd improved "The Day I Found Myself," rearranged and lengthened at a slower tempo, and "Want Ads," dulled with a bassier mix and stretched with orchestral break and vocal coda. I do like "Stick-Up," by "ABC" out of "Want Ads," and "One Monkey Don't Stop No Show," by "La Bamba" out of "Come a Little Bit Closer." But I don't like "Monkey" so much I want the encore. And filler is filler, even Dozier's and Holland's. **B−**

Honk: *Honk* (Epic '74). Funky California eclecticism in the grateful tradition of Stoneground, with the difference in names indicating a gain in irony and the forced jollity of "Gimme That Wine" exemplifying the limitations of the style. Bonnie Koloc award for authenticity through cleanliness: Beth Fitchet, "Oh Daddy Blues." Jack Tempchin award for outwriting the principals: Mark Turnbull, "Mademoiselle." Original grade: B. **B−**

The Hoodoo Rhythm Devils: *Rack Jobbers Rule* (Capitol '72). How can I say they sound like a cross between Hamilton, Joe Frank & Reynolds and the Mississippi Sheiks when I've never even *heard* the Mississippi Sheiks? I think what it means is that as much as I admire some of their original material I'd rather hear the Mississippi Sheiks sing it. Since they bring up the subject of devilish rhythms, I'll add that I'd rather hear the Mississippi Sheiks

drum it as well — and I'm not sure the Mississippi Sheiks had a drummer. Original grade: B. **C+**

Mary Hopkin: *Earth Song/Ocean Song* (Apple '71). My taste for Hopkin's limpid prettiness may be eccentric, but there it is. She sings like the demure, starstruck adolescent she was until very recently, which lends her straightforward role-playing a revelatory poignancy lacking in the genteel atavism of the folkie madonnas she superficially resembles. Recommended: "International." **B+**

Horslips: *The Man Who Built America* (DJM '79). In the past these rock pros from the Emerald Isle specialized in Gaelic folk motifs — pretty awful, but awful in their own way. This time they go for more generalized shamrock: organ doodles and half-baked harmonies haunt a concept album about Irish (note roots) immigrants who think quite a lot about the colleens (not called that, of course) left behind. **D+**

Bill Horwitz: *Lies, Lies, Lies* (ESP Disk' '75). Like most topical singer-songwriters, Horwitz succumbs to the obvious (calling him Henry Kiss-of-Death isn't much of a punch line), the rhetorical (the word "bosses" in "Father," which almost manages to bridge the generation gap through class feeling, suggests the *Daily Worker* rather than a daily worker), and the simplistic (equating the Army Corps of Engineers with the Czar's cossacks does injustice to both). But unlike most topical songwriters, Horwitz also has brushed with wisdom (the post-utopian revolutionary commitment of "Sadness"); he sounds fresh because he is. As an anticapitalist, Horwitz figured taking his tapes to the big record companies would be a waste of time, so I can't fulminate about why this is on ESP Disk' while Richie Lecea is with RCA and Myles & Lenny record for CBS. But given the courage of the record companies in these ledger-conscious times, he was probably right. **B −**

Larry Hosford: *Cross Words* (Shelter '76). A funny country singer-songwriter with complicated emotions and an elusive, strangely ageless vocal persona — mellowed-out Homer and/or Jethro, perhaps, or comic-relief L.A. cowboy gone crackerbarrel, or crackers. His wife calls him Daddy, calls his bluff, and then just calls a cab, but don't worry — here's a man who knows that love gets easier when you own a blanket with a switch on it. **B +**

Hot: *Hot* (Big Tree '77). Vocally, this group can't match the Emotions, and the music for some of these songs is undistinguished, but I'll take their hit ("Angel in Your Arms," not to be confused with "Undercover Angel") for its modestly articulate modern moralism, a virtue many of the lyrics here share. Recommended: "Mama's Girl," "You Can Do It." **B**

Hot Chocolate: *Cicero Park* (Big Tree '74). From the black-and-white London group that originated "Brother Louie" comes an album that might sound startling in retrospect and is impressive now. At the very least, its insightful confusions over class and race locate the honest roots of one kind of black conservatism. Both Mickie Most's precise, almost formal framing (pop hard rock veering toward disco) and the elocution of singer-composers Errol Brown (hard) and Tony Wilson (soft) make for an overall detachment unbroken by the passion of individual cuts. Strange to hear soul with a British accent. Original grade: B. **B +**

Hot Chocolate: *Hot Chocolate* (Big Tree '75). Not quite as substantial as *Cicero Park,* but more startling, thanks to "You Sexy Thing," the eccentrically wild-and-proper English-soul supersmash included hereupon. Original grade: B. **B +**

Hot Chocolate: *Man to Man* (Big Tree '76). OK, I do believe in miracles. Left with a two-man job by the solo flight of Tony Wilson, Errol Brown just gets on up and does it and does it. The lyrics are transparent sexist jive from "Heaven Is in the Back Seat of My Cadillac" to "Seventeen Years of Age," but Brown's dignified, cocksure vocals are so credulous that the effect is like Bryan Ferry irony divested of self-consciousness. Maybe the mannered romanticism Ferry has striven for comes naturally to an upwardly mobile West Indian like Brown. The hooks and tempos sure do. And Brown is right — "You Sexy Thing" is good enough to cop almost note for note. **A −**

Hot Chocolate: *10 Greatest Hits* (Big Tree '77). Two of these excellent songs — "So You Win Again" and "Rumours" — have never been available on a U.S. album, and there's only one cop from the highly recommended A side of *Cicero Park.* So although this steers clear of everything that's most problematic about a group that frequently essays themes a little beyond its grasp and becomes more interesting as a result, it's also an ideal introduction. Question: Is that low-register electric timbre they hold so dear really somebody's guitar? **A**

Hot Chocolate: *Every 1's a Winner* (Infinity '78). Errol Brown used to pose interesting questions, mostly about race, and though his conclusions were often quizzical or incoherent, they tended to be more provocative (if no more militant) than "Love Is the Answer One More Time." There are four good songs here and no utter losers, but one of the good ones is already on *10 Greatest Hits,* and only "Confetti Day," another installment in this strange group's family series, is up to the title chartbuster. Maybe that's because the question that really interests Brown these days is how to integrate synthesized percussion into English soul-pop. **B**

Hot Chocolate: *Going Through the Motions* (Infinity '79). For years I've resisted the idiot notion that this was a "disco" group because Errol Brown is black. So did the discos. The discos are still resisting. But I think this is the best disco parody since Silver Convention's *Madhouse.* Keynote: "Mindless Boogie." **B+**

Hot Tuna: *Hot Tuna* (RCA Victor '70). Didn't figure I'd ever put on this country blues extrapolation by Jorma and Jack's Airplane spinoff while John Hurt and Gary Davis were at hand. But the shameful fact is that between the delicate guitar play and Jorma's unpretentious vocals and unexceptionable taste, I do. Original grade: B minus. **B+**

Hot Tuna: *Yellow Fever* (Grunt '75). When this band went pro — and electric — my initial reaction was annoyance. I figured that at least when they were doing country blues the material justified their deliberate pace. But that soon passed, and for years now I've been shelving their records without comment not out of anger or even dislike but in the simple absence of anything interesting to say. When a group maintains such a level for five years, however, its uninterestingness becomes noteworthy in itself. Think of it — kozmic blooze and negative vocals boogieing on into a countercultural time that knows no past or future, outracing the Starship on automatic pilot. Quite impressive, actually. **B−**

Cissy Houston: *Cissy Houston* (Janus '71). The sharpest pleasure afforded by the Sweet Inspirations was the juxtaposition of Cissy's rather vulgar pull-out-the-stops melodrama against genteel if kinetic arrangements and material. The voice is almost as interesting as it used to be, but the juxtaposition no longer works, perhaps because new producers Koppelman and Rubin don't know the difference between gentility and complacent meaninglessness. **C**

Hudson-Ford: *Nickelodeon* (A&M '74). "Complain about pollution, the downfall of man/And half-grown humans may be your fans/Add your shit to the pile while you still can/Cause it's hell on earth." Hudson-Ford, "Burn Baby Burn" (Slick Cynic Music, ASCRAP; additional lyric by R. Christgau, Two Minute Songs, LAMF). **C**

The Hues Corporation: *Freedom for the Stallion* (RCA Victor '74). There's no way "Rock the Boat" could prepare you for the studied lameness of this LP unless you believe, as I do, that ersatz gospel liveliness doesn't validate the hit of 1974 any more than ersatz gospel beautifulness validated the hit of 1969. (That's a quiz.) Exception: "The Family," which studies hard. (Answer to quiz: "Oh Happy Day.") **C**

Humble Pie: *Performance: Rockin' the Fillmore* (A&M '71). It may seem unfair to judge a band on a live double, but they go out of their way to define themselves with this seven-song job, which celebrates the ascendancy of ruff 'n' tuff Steve Marriott over wan 'n' gone Peter Frampton by raunching up blues and soul titles too magnificent to mention in such company. Lotsa getdown vocals, lotsa getdown guitar, and an important political message, which is that short guys get laid more than normal people. A lie. **C−**

Helen Humes: *The Talk of the Town* (Columbia '75). Humes's skill is manifest, but her aesthetic assumptions don't connect for me. The Afro-American forms from which rock and roll derived acknowledged their class (not race) origins, either directly (the plain-spokenness of r&b) or by outright avoidance (doowop's go-for-broke-fantasy). White kids may have identified with ghetto blacks out of the most abject simplemindedness, but they got candor (r&b) or spiritual intensity (doowop) in the bargain. The adult nightclubbers for whom a jazz-blues stylist like Humes performed, on the other hand, related to the subtle twists of emotion implied by her intricate vocal inventions only because such intricacy takes for granted the protective veneer of culture, which is sophistication's bottom line. The hidden message of Humes's music is a ruling-class myth: that the most horrible suffering (catch the lyric of "Good for Nothin' Joe") is of manageable consequence. She denies the out-of-control. And I miss it. **B +**

Ian Hunter: *Ian Hunter* (Columbia '75). "Once Bitten Twice Shy" and "I Get So Excited" are rockers as primo as any but the greatest Mott the Hoople songs, and as a bonus the latter is about something besides rock and roll. Hunter and coproducer Mick Ronson's passion for that subject is justified by the rest of the music, even the poetry-with-rock episode. But Ian should remember that it's a mighty long way down rock and roll, because as your name gets hot your heart gets cold. Then your name gets cold. Original grade: B minus. **B**

Ian Hunter: *All-American Alien Boy* (Columbia '76). The concept fails. Hunter isn't even a one-star generalizer, and he obviously lacks that rare knack for the political song, though the bit about needing both the left wing and the right to fly is sharp (and scary). Yet the attempt at protest is gratifying, at least as honest as it is confused. At odd moments the music kicks a line like "Justice would seem to be bored" all the way home; "Irene Wilde," a throw-in about young love, is a small treasure; and "God (Take 1)" is nice Ferlinghetti-style doggerel. So while I can't recommend, I kind of like. **B –**

Ian Hunter: *You're Never Alone with a Schizophrenic* (Chrysalis '79). Six winners out of nine on this mini-comeback, and he doesn't seem to be straining, either. But that's not entirely a blessing — the musical territory is conventionally good-rockin', and only on the gnomic "Life After Death" and the second verse of "When the Morning Comes" does he reconnoiter lyrically. The titles of the bad songs — "Bastard," "The Outsider," and "Ships" (in the guess what) — are warning enough. **B**

Ian Hunter: *Shades of Ian Hunter: The Ballad of Ian Hunter and Mott the Hoople* (Columbia '79). Exemplary discophilia. The Mott 45s on side one are all the young stiffs — great album tracks edited down for an AM exposure that was rarely forthcoming, they race along with an almost punky punch on LP. The B sides and miscellaneous on side two are uneven, natch, but worth getting to know (as owners of *Greatest Hits* have already learned with two of them). Those circumspect enough to have passed up Ian's two solo albums are now rewarded with side three's best-of. And side four excerpts the solo Ian that was never released here to impressive effect. A genuinely obsessive compilation. **A –**

Kay Huntington: *What's Happening to Our World?* (United Artists '70). This is either a hilarious takeoff on circa-1964 folk music, complete with sensitive vibrato, hard little guitar parts, and very moderate good intentions, or — more likely, unlikely as it may seem — one of the most atrocious records ever made. Perfectly awful, right down to liner notes and cover portrait — Huntington, a dyed-looking Minnesotan blonde who appears very reluctant to celebrate birthdays, is wearing a red minidress. Noted primarily as a Remarkable Occurrence, which I trust someone at United Artists is already investigating. Pick: the apparently unsarcastic "Right to Poverty." **E**

Michael Hurley & Pals: *Armchair Boogie* (Raccoon '71). The man is seductive. His fast songs aren't steady enough to win any races, and when he gets to wandering I often get lost — only to notice him dying or offending Shulamith Firestone out of the corner of my ear. I don't believe the werewolf loves the maid as he tears off her clothes. But Hurley makes me want to hear his side of the story, lupine high notes and all. **A –**

Michael Hurley: *Hi-Fi Snock Uptown* (Raccoon '72). When Hurley is good, his tunes snake up on you. When he's not, they snail right past, disappearing forever behind that cabbage leaf there.   **B−**

Michael Hurley/The Unholy Modal Rounders/Jeffrey Fredericks & the Clamtones: *Have Moicy!* (Rounder '76). A dynamic trio. Hurley's sleepy LPs for Raccoon flaunted their home-made triviality, while the work of Peter Stampfel (and Steve Weber and the other Rounders) for Prestige and Metromedia and Rounder managed to make music out of chalk scraping a blackboard, or a needle scraping an old 78 — quite a feat, but not one I ever wanted to witness daily. This time, however, both forces combine with Fredericks for thirteen homemade, chalky, fit-for-78 songs that renew the concept of American folk music as a bizarre apotheosis of the post-hippie estate. No losers, though — just loadsa laffs, a few tears, some death, some shit, a hamburger, spaghetti, world travel, crime, etc. Original grade: A.   **A+**

Michael Hurley: *Long Journey* (Rounder '77). Fingers trembling, the oft-cynical critic opened the new LP by the playful, sardonic folkie recluse. Without the Rounders or Jeffrey Fredericks to change paces, there was no way it could be another *Have Moicy!*. (Aw.) But it might be woozy and charming, like *Armchair Boogie*. (Hey!) Or cute and dull, like *Hi-Fi Snock Uptown*. (Duh.) Also, the critic might fall asleep before finding out. Four months and many snoozes later, he arrived at a verdict: sardonic, charming, playful, cute, woozy, and only rarely dull. Highly recommended to *Have Moicy!* cultists. Hitbound: "Hog of the Forsaken." Whoopee.   **B+**

Mississippi John Hurt: *Last Sessions* (Vanguard '72). For some reason folk specialists hold these clear if casual tapes in low esteem, but I think they stand with his other Vanguard music. Recorded in a Manhattan hotel in February and July 1966, shortly before he died, they capture the same playful warmth and quiet rhythmic assurance that marked all his work. These aren't qualities especially well-served by youth, which is one reason Hurt exerted instant artistic authority when he was rediscovered in 1963 at age seventy-one. From "Funky Butt" to "Shortnin' Bread," this is a man who was always ready to meet his maker.   **A**

J. B. Hutto & the Hawks: *Slidewinder* (Delmark '73). Hutto boogies easy as falling off a barstool — he's kept my body interested in a slide solo for fifteen minutes at a time. So I had hopes he'd be one artist who'd thrive in a four-songs-per-side format. But compared to 1968's six-songs-per-side *Hawk Squat!* — with Sunnyland Slim's keyboards and Maurice McIntyre's sax filling in the sound — this is pretty slack.   **B−**

Janis Ian: *Between the Lines* (Columbia '75). In this time of dearth, it's probably improvident to laugh at someone so talented — good melodies abound here, and I can't think of a rock singer who has made more unaffected and pleasurable use of her or his voice lessons. But this woman's humorlessness demands snickers. It was one thing for society's teenager to pity herself because she didn't have the integrity to stick with her black boyfriend. It's another thing for a grown-up to pity her teenaged self because she was always picked last in basketball. I mean, face it, Ms. Ian — you're *short.* **B−**

Janis Ian: *Aftertones* (Columbia '76). Ian here establishes herself as the most technically accomplished popular vocalist of her (post-rock? post-folkie? pre-Vegas?) generation. She's even managing to curb the melodrama, as well as permitting herself unaccustomed glints of humor. But if you want to glimpse the crippling intellectual limitations of this sort of accomplishment, just get a load of her library, thoughtfully depicted on a cover that also features an open aerogram and an enigmatic mirror-as-window through which peers the artiste. There they stand, all her sources: a Modern Library Camus, *The Second Sex, The Greenwich Village Bluebook, How to Survive in the Woods,* and that encyclopedia of secondhand angst, Colin Wilson's *The Outsider.* How existential. One thing, though — mirrors are good windows only when surviving in the woods isn't something you ever have to think about. **B−**

The Ides of March: *Vehicle* (Warner Bros. '70). The title of a mildly enjoyable schlock single — which somehow got little FM play even though Jim Peterik does an amazing David Clayton-Thomas imitation — is also the title of a properly schlocky follow-up LP. Twelve inches is more schlock than anyone needs. Quiz: Who composed "Symphony for Eleanor"? **C−**

Iggy and the Stooges: See also the Stooges, Iggy Pop

Ijahman: *Haile I Hymn (Chapter 1)* (Mango '78). I like the sweet sobbing gasp of the singing, but as a sympathizer with the reggae-all-sounds-the-same heresy I wish there were more than four tunes. Nor do I believe that Steve Winwood transforms the groove. In fact, his presence may indicate what's wrong. **B**

Ijahman: *Are We a Warrior* (Mango '79). Still wish there were some rudimentary verbality here, but the music has won me over — the title track is the most gorgeous reggae crooning I've ever heard, and the rest of the album follows in its sweet wake like one of those half-remembered dreams that makes you glow the next day. **B+**

The Incredible String Band: *Relics* (Elektra '71). Way back in the 1960s I tried to figure out whether these acoustic Scots were magic or bullshit and concluded that they were both. But lately they've lost something. Only two of the eighteen songs on this compilation postdate March 1968. Which seems fitting — they recorded "Way Back in the 1960s" in 1967.   **B+**

The Independents: *Discs of Gold* (Wand '74). Although they've never broken top twenty, this quartet has scored eight r&b hits since 1972, four of them top ten and every one included on this efficient long player. The mode is post-Smokey with Claudette reinstated — three men and one woman who excel in the contained "love" vocal style, with Chuck Jackson adding his gift for recitative (a truly great ironic chuckle). I like the songs, too — but admit that they're not bright enough for pop.   **B+**

The Insect Trust: *Hoboken Saturday Night* (Atco '70). Thomas Pynchon, Louis "Moondog" Hardin, and an unidentified child (who else would say "busketty" for "spaghetti"?) are among the guest composers, Elvin Jones and an unidentified child among the guest musicians. Former president James Garfield makes a cameo appearance. Vocalist Nancy Jeffries applies her tobacco voice to a feminist lyric called "Trip on Me" that I recommend to Janis Joplin. The blues scholars in the group have been listening to a lot of Arabic and Eastern European music lately, but this doesn't stop Elvin Jones from sounding just like Elvin Jones. In short, these passionate humanists also sound friendly and have come up with a charming, joyous, irrepressibly experimental record. And every experiment works.   **A**

The Intruders: *Intruders Super Hits* (Gamble '73). Part of the distinction of Little Sonny Brown's throaty tenor is its built-in boyish catch, but what makes the boyishness so poignant is that it's definitely connected to a man's voice. Which means he deserves better

than the teen and teen-manqué lyrics Kenny Gamble has provided him.   **B**

Irakere: *Irakere* (Columbia '79). Latin jazz-rock for real, from Cuba. They're hot, they have amazing chops, and they've absorbed four continents' worth of music — who else would back an African "mass" (explosive) with a Mozart adagio (unintegrated)? Next time I hope they get to record in a studio rather than a concert.   **A−**

Iron City Houserockers: *Love's So Tough* (MCA '79). "Turn It Up" is one of those self-transcending cliches — a song about rock and roll escape that reveals how the truism became one. Most of the others are honorable cliches — working-class angst played for tragedy rather than irony or analysis in the great tradition of B. Springsteen. Or is it T. Lizzy?   **B**

Isis: *Ain't No Backin' Up Now* (Buddah '75). On their Shadow Morton-produced debut this brassy ten-woman ensemble sounded like a cross between Vanilla Fudge and the Mount St. Mary's College Lab Band, but here Allen Toussaint's horn arrangements cut a channel for their melodrama. As is usual on Toussaint albums, the side that features his songs is a lot stronger than the side that features the band's. Now if only he could describe lesbian life as knowledgeably as Carol Mac-Donald in "Bobbie and Maria" or Jeanie Fineberger in "Eat the Root." But that would be a lot to ask.   **B**

The Isley Brothers: *Get Into Something* (T-Neck '70). Five of the ten tracks on this album were r&b hits, and even "Girls Will Be Girls," a silly song that does not reflect "Take Inventory" 's astonishing views on the subjection of women, has its pleasures. But none of them went pop — or tore up the r&b charts — because none of them was more than a serviceable rehash. The first side rocks, the second side fluctuates, and let's hope they get into something else soon. **B**

The Isley Brothers & Jimi Hendrix: *In the Beginning* . . . (T-Neck '71). Cut around 1965, while Hendrix was still part of the Isleys' band, these casual sessions, remixed to push his guitar up with the voices, are far superior to Curtis Knight's Hendrix tapes. Make you wonder what would have happened if they'd been released at the time. Especially on "Move Over Let Me Dance," Hendrix anticipates effects Clapton introduced on "Sunshine of My Love," but in a less inflated context — could have blown some minds in Harlem. Not all of the music is don't-miss great. But it's all historic — and you can dance to it. Time: 26:49. **B+**

The Isley Brothers: *Givin' It Back* (T-Neck '71). An exciting album in theory — cover versions by a genuinely "progressive" (at least self-contained) soul act of eight (mostly) excellent (mostly) rock songs. But only "Spill the Wine" (previously a progressive r&b hit), "Love the One You're With" (previously a regressive rock hit), and "Ohio" (no complaints) are exciting in practice. Ernie Isley just can't match Jimi's "Machine Gun," and soul is wasted on "Fire and Rain" and "Lay Lady Lay," which are more powerful in their understated originals. **B**

The Isleys: *Brother, Brother, Brother* (T-Neck '72). Although the three Carole King songs seem a little tame after "Ohio" and "Cold Baloney," her simple messages fit the Isleys' lyrical-to-smarmy gospel credulousness quite neatly. But it's only on the three Isley originals that top off side one that this album makes itself felt, and interestingly enough none of them could be called "progressive": "Lay Away" and "Pop That Thang" are infectious groove tunes, while "Work to Do" is a compelling assertion of male prerogatives whose dire potential was presaged in 1969, when R. B. Greaves found himself forced to swap his wife

for his secretary. Love and money, love and money — it's a polarity that tears you apart even more when they give you a (long) shot at both. **B**

The Isley Brothers: *The Isleys Live* (T-Neck '73). "Featuring: Ernest Isley on Lead Guitar," says a sticker on the back, and that's the pitch for these (slightly) extended remakes, their last album before moving to CBS. Problem is, all that makes Little Brother a Hendrix heir is that unlike most soul-trained guitarists he doesn't merely support the vocalist — he's loud, slow, dramatic. I prefer him to Robin Trower, say — fewer chops, apter context. But they really ought to let him do his thing in the studio. Time: 55:13. **B−**

The Isley Brothers: *3 +3* (T-Neck '73). I know the singing siblings have soft tastes in "rock," but where this side of a Warners promo could you expect to find "Summer Breeze," "Don't Let Me Be Lonely Tonight," and "Listen to the Music" on the same album? Still, with "That Lady" their most original original in years, Ernie soaring around thrillingly on his magic guitar, and the others popping their various things in ever more winning combinations, this is their sexiest music in years. Just because they manhandled "Fire and Rain" doesn't mean they can't improve on James's schlock. In fact, between their sense of rhythm and their knee-jerk sincerity they make all three covers work — except for the mental jasmine part, of course. Original grade: B. **B+**

The Isley Brothers: *Live It Up* (T-Neck '74). In which Ernie finally gets to make his studio album. What sound effects — the most technosoulful around. I mean, this guy isn't just whistling wah-wah. I do believe he likes Stevie's synthesizer more than Jimi's guitar, though. **B**

The Isley Brothers: *The Heat Is On* (T-Neck '75). This is well-nigh flawless Isleys — the rockish electric textures are muted nicely on side two, "Fight the Power" does its bit to politicize the radio, and Seals & Crofts won't steal any lyrics. But Ronnie Isley isn't getting any less unctuous — when he tries to talk someone into bed he recalls one of those guys who started wearing love beads to singles bars in 1968 or 1969. Progress requires ambition, but the two aren't identical. **B**

The Isley Brothers: *Harvest for the World* (T-Neck '76). Ronnie croons, Ernie zooms, and if you suspect you've heard it all before, trust your instincts. **B −**

The Isley Brothers: *Go for Your Guns* (T-Neck '77). By the time the competent enough first side was over, I felt completely fed up with their mellifluous bullshit, especially since I'd noticed the title "Voyage to Atlantis" on side two. But that disaster excepted side two is the most hard-edged they've recorded since moving T-Neck to CBS in 1973. Needless to say, the one about "Climbin' Up the Ladder" is even more passionate than the one about "Livin' the Life." Nor is it surprising that the title tune has no lyrics at all. There's no riot goin' on. **B**

The Isley Brothers: *Forever Gold* (T-Neck '77). Best-ofs shouldn't have A and B sides, but that's how this one works for me — would have been stronger if they'd pulled something from *Go for Your Guns,* still on the charts when this was released. You want rock and roll, they'll give you rock and roll — when they want. You want insipid — well, millions do. Most Wishy-Washy Title of All Time: "(At Your Best) You Are Love." **B +**

The Isley Brothers: *Showdown* (T-Neck '78). Disco has been good for this band musically: the chic guitar-and-chant of the title tune, the slow, sensuous funk of "Groove with You," and the enigmatic air of "Ain't Givin' Up No Love" are refreshing variants on their basic moon-and-vroom, and both "Rockin' the Fire" and "Take Me to the Next Phase" are pure dance-peak ideology. Doesn't do much for their politics, though. **B**

The Isley Brothers: *Timeless* (T-Neck '78). The Isleys are one of the great music-business success stories — in a decade when the artists were supposed to take over the industry, they're one of the few (along with Jefferson Lear Jet) to make a go of their own label. But though T-Neck puts out excellent product, product is all it is. This two-LP compilation, in which their Buddah-distributed material reverts to the Isleys' company (it's virtually identical to Buddah's 1976 *The Best . . .* package), reminds us that even back when they were inventing their shtick they were also victims of it. The only great songs are "It's Your Thing" and "Work to Do"; they reuse the same harmonies and dynamics again and again. The Isleys to own, probably — but there's no doubt you can live without it. **B +**

The Isley Brothers: *Winner Take All* (T-Neck '79). What's wrong with your clockwork, guys? The two-record set is supposed to be a reissue or an in-concert. And the studio job is supposed to be one disc only. **C +**

The Isley Brothers: *Go All the Way* (T-Neck '79). Except on the title cut, a rocking Rodgers & Edwards rip, the formula here is more exact than the best formulas should have to be. And if "The Belly Dancer" is their idea of specificity, I'd just as soon they keep it vague. Cher finds better lyrics. **C +**

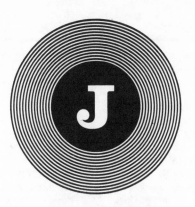

The Jackson 5: *ABC* (Motown '70). Admittedly, the charm of hearing an eleven-year-old cover Smokey, Stevie, and the Delfonics may not be enduring. And admittedly, some of the filler — "The Young Folks," for instance — is embarrassing even by Motown standards. But in fact the eleven-year-old doesn't disgrace himself against Smokey and Stevie and beats the Delfonics going away. And some of the filler — "ABC" you know, but how about "2-4-6-8"? — recalls the days of great B sides. **B+**

Jackson 5: *Third Album* (Motown '70). The first bad sign is that the best cut on the album is a ballad. The second is that the best fast one is the tossed-off "How Funky Is Your Chicken" rather than a Corporation special like "Goin' Back to Indiana" or "Mama's Pearl." The third is the worst "Bridge Over Troubled Water" I ever want to hear. Is that Jermaine or Jackie? Are we supposed to care? **B−**

Jackson 5: *Maybe Tomorrow* (Motown '71). It's getting serious when the only discernible appeal of the title hit is that Michael is singing. The follow-up, "Never Can Say Goodbye," has more going for it. As do "Sixteen Candles," originated by the Crests, and "Honey Chile," originated by Martha & the Vandellas. **C+**

Jackson 5: *Greatest Hits* (Motown '71). Surprisingly resistible for a record that offers "I Want You Back," "ABC," and "The Love You Save," three of the greatest radio ups ever. I wish they were on the same side along with the second-line fast ones so the hits could just keep on coming, you know? Admittedly, the boys do have a cute, astute way with a ballad, too. Just thank Berry that "Never Can Say Goodbye" and "I'll Be There" are good ones. **A−**

Jackson 5: *Lookin' Through the Windows* (Motown '72). They're wonders of nature no longer, but they're still a good group, and this snaps back toward the usual marvelous Motown multiplex. Jackson Browne's specifically late-adolescent "Doctor My Eyes" brings Michael along too fast, but it sounds good on the radio. And Jermaine (I think) proves equal to Ashford & Simpson's specifically adult "Ain't Nothing Like the Real Thing." Recommended ballad: "If I Could Move a Mountain." Continuing a great tradition: "E-Ne-Me-Ne-Mi-Ne-Moe." Original grade: B plus. **B**

Jackson 5: *Dancing Machine* (Motown '74). My friend who goes to discos tells me the Jacksons are the first major artists to put out a real disco album — designed for dancers, and listeners be damned. This may well be true — certainly the guitars and electric keyboards are more noteworthy than the singing. He also tells me it's the Jacksons' best album since who knows when, and what's surprising is that he's right again. This is a tribute to the aforementioned instruments, but the singing is fine, and if a lot of the songs live up to the album title, that ain't necessarily bad. For listeners (dancers too): "What You Don't Know." **B+**

The Jacksons: _The Jacksons_ (Epic '76). Sorry — Michael and his brothers just aren't high-powered enough to rev up Gamble & Huff's faltering music machine. Or is it vice versa? **C+**

Jackson 5: _Anthology_ (Motown '76). The only one of Motown's triple-LP retrospectives to concentrate on (or even include much) '70s music documents an institution in decline. Initially, the company marshalls everything it's got for one final push — not for nothing was the group's songwriting-production combine called The Corporation, and it's a measure of their seriousness that they asked the Crusaders to help with the tracks. But within two years they'd run out of gas — all the mini-comebacks after that, even the dancing-machine coup, were flukes. The proof is that the old-formula filler often surpasses the desperate imitations that became minor hits — better "E-Ne-Me-Ne-Mi-Ne-Moe" than "Skywriter" or "A Little Bit of You." The selection includes Michael's hits, Jermaine's hit, the works, and as the other albums disappear it will become essential in its way. But not to listen to, much. **B+**

The Jacksons: _Destiny_ (Epic '78). They wrote all the songs, but it's the debut self-production — after a second stiff in Philadelphia — that puts their best regular-release album since the beginning across. Specifically, it's the production on the dance tracks — the lyrics are best when you can blame them on the boogie. **B+**

Joe Jackson: _Look Sharp!_ (A&M '79). In which an up-and-coming professional entertainer tricks up Britain's latest rock and roll fashion with some fancy chords and gets real intense abut the perils of romance. Well, better "Is She Really Going Out with Him?" than "Sunday Papers," the social-criticism interlude, which inspires

fond memories of "Pleasant Valley Sunday." **B**

Joe Jackson: _I'm the Man_ (A&M '79). Oh yeah? Then get the knack back. **C+**

John Jackson: _Step It Up and Go_ (Rounder '79). Jackson is a fifty-six-year-old gravedigger who's been on the folk blues circuit since 1964 and has three albums on Arhoolie, though I'd never heard of him till this one. His guitar style is eclectic, as befits a man who got his best songs from Blind Boy Fuller and Blind Blake 78s but who also played in a country band in the early '40s. His voice is guttural yet well-defined. No innovator, and not as arresting through a whole side as he is at the outset, he's nevertheless responsible for the most pleasing (and well-recorded) new country blues record I've heard in years. **B+**

Michael Jackson: _The Best of Michael Jackson_ (Motown '75). Because you can believe that their sincerity is neither feigned nor foolish, it's good in theory for children to sing romantic ballads. But in the end only pederasts, parents, and horny little girls can get off consistently on the interpretive nuances of a boy whose voice hasn't changed — the manipulation from above is simply too transparent. I love "Rockin' Robin" and hate "Ben" and find most of the rest in between. The most interesting exception is "One Day in Your Life," a first-rate tearjerker that achieves just the right mix of autonomy and helpless innocence — probably because Michael cut it about a year ago, when he was sixteen. **B−**

Michael Jackson: _Off the Wall_ (Epic '79). In which fast-stepping Michael J. and quick-witted Quincy J. fashion the dance groove of the year. Michael's vocabulary of grunts, squeals, hiccups, moans, and asides is a vivid reminder that he's grown up, and the title tune suggests that maybe what makes Stevie Wonder (who contributes a good ballad) such an oddball isn't his genius or even his blindness so much as the fact that since childhood his main contact with the real world has been on stage and in bed. Original grade: A minus. **A**

Millie Jackson: *Millie Jackson* (Spring '72). Producer Raeford Gerald's "My Man, a Sweet Man" and "I Miss You Baby" are as melodically upbeat as Jackson's own "Ask Me What You Want," and she delivers a ghetto sermon so unfashionably judgmental it makes me want to shout amen just to be contrary. But most of the rest is so nondescript that even Jackson's big, rough, tremendously vital voice can't bring it to life. Marginal. **B+**

Millie Jackson: *It Hurts So Good* (Spring '73). A hint of concept brings the tracks on this album together — on side one she's playing up to her man, while on side two she's playing around — and the production mixes (alternates, really) Holland-Dozier-Holland and Norman Whitfield, with guest Brad Shapiro adding the occasional modernism, all of which makes for instructive contrasts with Jackson's definitively unsubtle attack. But if there isn't a bad track on the record, there isn't a compelling one either, and in pop that's the kiss of obscurity if anything is. **B**

Millie Jackson: *Millie* (Spring '74). On stage, her dress, demeanor, and delivery put across a hooker's street toughness a lot more daring than the stage toughness of Tina Turner or Laura Lee. On record, though, she remains one more funkier-than-average but basically anonymous mama. She doesn't even know what to call this album — it's *Millie* in the notes, (big caps) *Millie* (small caps) *Jackson* on the cover, *Millie Jackson* on the spine, and *I Got to Try It One More Time* on the label. I guess I'd prefer she try it one more time myself. **B-**

Millie Jackson: *Caught Up* (Spring '74). Jackson rights the flaws of a promising career with this concept album about infidelity. The other woman starts an eleven-minute version of "If Loving You Is Wrong" by talking big, briefly allows herself some typical other-woman complaints, reasserts her independence, then suddenly finds her predicament untenable. She gets better lines than the wife's, which are on side two, but any artist sharp enough to cut through the overstatement of Brad Shapiro (production) and Bobby Goldsboro (one lyric) won't let that ruin her record. If you liked *Quadrophenia* (or still recall "A Quick One"), you have no excuse for not liking this. **A-**

Millie Jackson: *Still Caught Up* (Spring '75). Jackson's specialty — the funky truth about husbands, wives, and other women — is worth this sequel. As with *Caught Up*, she has her theme in control about eighty percent of the time, and her tone has become even nastier. But since she no longer has the advantage of surprise, her stridency is beginning to seem a little forced. **B+**

Millie Jackson: *Free and in Love* (Spring '76). The songs aren't getting any stronger, bad news for a concept artist who's slowly running out of concept. But "Feel Like Making Love" (Bad Company's, not Roberta Flack's — score one for Millie), "A House for Sale," and Clarence Reid's super-funky "Do What Makes the World Go Round" combine with a terrific dramatic monologue about scoring at a party and a tour de force demonstration of sexual noises to push this one over the line. Original grade: B. **B+**

Millie Jackson: *Feelin' Bitchy* (Spring '77). Fuck this ten-pop-tunes shit, Millie says. Almost literally — the FCC will not approve. She's appealing more explicitly to her black audience, too, and has apparently returned to concepts — or rather, messages, two of them. The second side says "Don't cheat" and the first side says "Eat pussy." The first side is definitely more fun. **B**

Millie Jackson: *Lovingly Yours* (Spring '77). Her third consecutive nasty album having stiffed, she makes nice, and boy does she sound bored — a song called "Body Movements" and she barely raises an eyebrow.   **C+**

Millie Jackson: *Get It Out'cha System* (Spring '78). As a convinced monogamist, I've always approved of Millie's no-shit shtick — there's a lot more commitment to love and marriage in her acerbic skepticism-going-on-cynicism than in the old escapist fantasies or the new therapeutic bromides. Still, shtick does wear out, so I'm happy to report that "Why Say You're Sorry" is her sharpest lyric in years and "Logs and Thangs" her funkiest monologue. Also, the title tune has a line about bosses that should raise class consciousness a notch.   **B+**

Millie Jackson: *A Moment's Pleasure* (Spring '79). If only because it's so patently unlikely to result in dancefloor hits, the arrant discofication is annoying at first — these songs don't need David Van De Pitte's clamorous strings and horns or bass lines that pine for a kick-drum. But Brandye's backups add extra nuance to Jackson's ever subtler singing, and Clayton Ivy's guitar obbligatos insure a flow her declamatory approach often lacks. What's more, the disco touches lend Millie's bawdy moralism special relevance to the latest arena of modern hedonism. If only her lyric on "Seeing You Again" didn't sound like an ad for Eastern Airlines I'd be convinced she was above gross hedonism herself.   **B+**

Millie Jackson: *Live and Uncensored* (Spring '79). Millie was made for live albums, as the rap-and-belt format of her studio work suggests, and the drama here, with its raunchy audience interplay, is at least as natural as anything she's ever devised for vinyl. Her timing keeps getting sharper, her voice keeps getting bigger, the songs amount to a best-of, and you also get a monologue about soap operas and the "Phuck U Symphony." Certainly her best since the *Caught Up* diptych, and probably definitive.   **A−**

Millie Jackson & Isaac Hayes: *Royal Rappin's* (Polydor '79). The title is misleading — this meeting of the bullshitters is more groove than rap. Not that it's devoid of spoken vamps or pointed byplay — the joyful havoc they wreak on "Do You Wanna Make Love" transforms it from pap to aphrodisiac. But mostly it gives Millie a chance to get out of her bag and really sing, with Isaac playing the likable foil and the Muscle Shoals boys making it sexy.   **B+**

Jade and Sarsparilla: *Jade and Sarsparilla* (Submaureen '76). If this record weren't by two women who sing love songs to each other, I'd quickly dismiss it as long on melodrama and short on melody. But the built-in societal conflict faced by two women who sing love songs to each other not only makes the melodrama more credible — conflict is the stuff of drama, right? — but is also interesting in itself, and if I were a woman who loved women I'm quite sure I'd be playing it all the time.   **B−**

The Jaggerz: *We Went to Different Schools Together* (Kama Sutra '70). I must have gone to a different school, too — I never seem to learn that a great pop single like "The Rapper" rarely has a half-decent album attached. Well, AM fans, let this be a lesson to you.   **C−**

The Jam: *In the City* (Polydor '77). Here we find an English hard-rock trio who wear short hair and dark suits, say "fuck" a lot, and sound rather like *The Who Sing My Generation,* even mentioning James Brown in one song. They also claim a positive social attitude — no police state in the U.K., but no anarchy either. Is this some kind of put-up job, pseudo-punk with respect for the verities? Could be, but it doesn't matter. When they complain that Uncle Jimmy the "red balloon" (or is it "revoloo"?) never walks home at night, they've got his number, but when they accuse him of sleeping between silk sheets they're just blowing someone else's hot air. In the end, they could go either way — or both. In the meantime, though, they blow me out. These boys can put a song together; they're both powerful enough to subsume their sources and fresh enough to keep me coming back for more. **A −**

The Jam: *This Is the Modern World* (Polydor '77). The naive, out-of-the-mouths-of-careerists clumsiness is endearing partly because it gets at truths too obvious to interest the sophisticated; the assumption that the word modern has sociopolitical import, for instance, is laughably autodidactic at one level and yet not without resonance when pounded out over and over. Would that the pounding were a little more flexible — this might rock as invitingly as their first if only it were varied with some appropriate covers. How about "Kicks"? **B +**

The Jam: *All Mod Cons* (Polydor '79). Far from the posers cynics believe them to be, these guys are almost painfully sincere, and on this album their desire to write commercial songs that say something is palpable and winning. Unfortunately, their success is mixed at best, and the music is so tentative that I was surprised by how hard they made a set of new material rock in concert. But last year's set rocked even harder. And though I can overlook the record's gaffes and forced lines and faint playing in the aftermath of the show, I'm too much of a cynic to believe the glow will last. **B**

Etta James: *Etta James Sings Funk* (Cadet '70). As you can read on the back, funk isn't a style or something like that — it's just, well, Etta. Etta with chorus, Etta with full brass, Etta with strings even. Etta singing a Gershwin song, Etta singing a Bee Gees song, Etta singing three Acuff-Rose songs, Etta singing four Pearl Woods songs. (Pearl Woods?) Highlights: the Acuff-Rose songs. **B**

Etta James: *Losers Weepers* (Cadet '71). Kittenish one moment and cathouse the next, James offers disappointingly subtle pleasures for such a big singer — except for two ASCAP standards, the title song is the only one I'd care to hear from someone else, and not even James's foxy delight in her own moods can salvage some of them. Nor will the orchestrations — conventional in blues, soul, and big-band modes — draw anyone in. But these days only Tina Turner (who couldn't provide subtle pleasures if she wanted to) seems to get much of a kick out of the down and dirty, and James's uninhibited sense of humor and fondness for sexual combat finally jollies this album over the line. **B +**

Etta James: *Etta James* (Chess '73). Gabriel Mekler (of Steppenwolf, Kozmic Janis, Nolan Porter) introduces Etta to the rock audience with three Randy Newman covers plus, and it almost works. To hear this gospel-trained ex-junkie turn "God's Song" into a jubilantly sarcastic antihymn is to know why pious blacks consider blues devil music, and Tracy Nelson fans should hear how low "Down So Low" can get. James is full-bodied, bitter, hip without sounding educated about it. But she has trouble finding a female persona for "Sail Away" and "Leave Your Hat On." And she has trouble making anything at all out of Mekler's own stuff. **B**

Etta James: *Come a Little Closer* (Chess '74). Last time Gabriel Mekler went one for three as a songwriter and half-ruined his producee's album. This time he goes two for six. A "Mekler" tune on which Etta does nothing but moan is one of the good ones, which will give you an idea of whose contribution matters. "St. Louis Blues" is also a winner. **B −**

Etta James: *Etta Is Betta Than Evvah!* (Chess '76). What a mess. The side-openers — "Woman (Shake Your Booty)" (she's dirty and she's proud) and "Jump into Love" ("You gotta wallow in it," opines a lowdown male chorus) — promise an album of raunch after all that classy stuff. But except for a literal version of King Floyd's "Groove Me," the only other raunch here is Randy Newman's "Leave Your Hat On," which Mekler originally produced. Makes a lot more sense in this context. **B**

Etta James: *Deep in the Night* (Warner Bros. '78). Most of James's albums suffer from radical unevenness; this one is marred by its consistency. Producer Jerry Wexler's song choices are as tastefully imaginative as his arrangements, but James has never had much midrange, and her versions of (good) material from such luminaries as Kiki Dee, the Eagles, and Alice Cooper are inferior to the originals. She doesn't get much out of "Piece of My Heart," either. That said, I'll admit to enjoying side two — opening with a jaunty "Lovesick Blues" and touching base at gospel (Dorothy Love Coates), soul (Allen Toussaint), and r&b (revamping her own "I'd Rather Go Blind"). But it's still a little boring. Which means it's not the real Etta. **B**

Freddie James: *Get Up and Boogie* (Warner Bros. '79). Just what you've been waiting for, I'm sure — another soprano crooning over another cleverly entitled dance track. And coming up next, oh my god, it's "Crazy Disco Music." Think it might help if the singer were male? Well, it does, quite a bit — very cute, very unusual. In fact, since he's already fourteen, very very unusual — his soprano days are numbered. Next step, he says, is to go to "Hollywood," where they'll tell him to "Dance Little Boy Blue." Don't put your advance on it, kid. **B−**

Rick James: *Bustin' Out of L Seven* (Gordy '79). Funky, sure — he's fairly funky, although not on the slow ones. But if this is 'delic, so was the Strawberry Alarm Clock. **B−**

James Gang: *James Gang Rides Again* (ABC '70). I grant that Joe Walsh's band is more interesting than the usual power trio — because it isn't a power trio, just a trio. Walsh's guitar dominates, as is customary, but by stealth, by which I guess I mean style —rather than blasting fast he goes for country-spacey glisses that are all slide and sustain. Just wish he didn't sing that way — makes it sound like his songs are (is it possible?) guitar showcases. When's the last time my fave cut on anything was an instrumental? "Asshtonpark," it's called, and it's funkier than "Funk #49." **B−**

James Gang: *Passin' Thru* (ABC '72). Okay, boys, just as long as you're out of town by sundown. And Troiano, leave your guitar with me. That Walsh feller, he was a gentleman, but there's no tellin' what you'll be shootin' off next. **C**

Jamming with Edward (Rolling Stones '72). Given OK playing, lousy vocal mix, and all but nonexistent composition, the only virtue bestowed upon this circa-1970 Jagger/Hopkins/Cooder/Wyman/Watts jam by the attendant supergroup is a discount list price. Which only a collector would be fool enough to pay. Original grade: B minus. **C**

Al Jarreau: *Glow* (Reprise '76). This man has the looks and voice and technique and support of an instant superstar. So why isn't he? Maybe because he neither writes nor interprets songs with the soul to match his freeze-dried facility. **C+**

JB's: *Food for Thought* (People '72). On "Pass the Peas," "Gimme Some More," and an ensemble showpiece called "The Grunt," JB is conspicuous by his conceptual presence even when he's not passing, giving, or grunting. On "Escape-ism" he's conspicuous by his spiritual absence even though he raps through most of the track. Elsewhere he's just missed. **B−**

The J.B.'s: *Doing It to Death* (People '73). The consumerist-conservationist in me is appalled by the whole idea of J.B.'s records, which are basically another way for James Brown to spread himself thin. The title riff is the best he's come up with since *There It Is* — two soundtracks, a compilation, a studio double, and another J.B.'s album ago — and might have been put to better use elsewhere. On the other hand, the whole first side is adequate James Brown — that is, pretty damn good. The second side stretches Brown out on organ, never my favorite vehicle for his talent. Theme scng: "You Can Have Watergate Just Gimme Some Bucks and I'll Be Straight." Lot of different ways to take that.   **B**

Fred Wesley and the J.B.'s: *Damn Right I Am Somebody* (People '74). Significance of title designation: album masquerades intermittently as funk opera about black identity. Significance of artist designation: bandleader Wesley plays his trombone about fifty times as much as bandleader Brown sings.   **C+**

Jebadiah: *Rock 'n' Soul* (Epic '78). At last, a record designed to end those party-pooping disputes over whether to dance to disco or the Stones. Yes, record-buyers, Michael Zager has discofied six Stones classics, and I beg him to check with Santa Esmeralda (or hire the Hollyridge Strings) before trying anything like it again. Advice to partygivers: settle those arguments with the "Miss You" disco disc. Personal to Ralph Abernathy: Boycott "Brown Sugar."   **E**

Jefferson Airplane: *The Worst of Jefferson Airplane* (RCA Victor '70). For someone who enjoys their albums, like me, this factitious compilation — fifteen cuts is a lot, but though it includes all (two) of their AM smashes it doesn't even pretend to be a singles anthology — is a waste. But for someone who finds their albums wanting, like me, it has its uses, especially as overview. These folks are literate both verbally and musically. Their chops don't quite equal their tastes — "White Rabbit," with its bolero build and librarian's-eye view of lysergic acid, is perfect, but "Chushingura" is almost as sloppy in the picking as "Today" is in the sentiment. They were hippies when becoming a hippie took beatnik initiative and psychedelic imagination. And when they're good they make the for-better-or-worse evolution of rock and roll into rock seem both appropriate and inevitable.   **B+**

Jefferson Airplane: *Bark* (Grunt '71). This isn't as bad as the faithless claim (a lot better than *Bite,* for instance), but it's definitely a collection of weirdnesses rather than an album: duh boys in duh band sing a capella, Grace sings German, Grace defies cop, Hot Tuna outtake, fiddle feature, and so forth. And so on.   **C+**

Jefferson Airplane: *Long John Silver* (Grunt '72). Easily the most coherent album to come from Airplane Associates since *Volunteers* — the music is muscular, the hole left by Marty Balin finally covered over. But the printed lyrics are catchier than the tunes, Grace sings like she's facing Mecca, and Paul sings like an automatic pilot. Which suggests that maybe the hole is still there.   **C+**

Jefferson Airplane: *Early Flight* (Grunt '74). Artists are always claiming embarrassment at the unauthorized release of their early work, but this group owns the company, so I guess they know no shame. They ought to — not about these nine cuts, six recorded in 1965–66 and three in 1970, but at how played out the band has become. The two originals with Signe Anderson are early Airplane at their folkie-trippy worst, although "High Flying Bird" is fine, but even the six-minute blues jams, one with Jorma and one with Marty, sound more alive than all their space operas. The 1970 single "Mexico," about Nixon's dope crackdown, is their finest recording of the decade. And "Have You Seen the Saucers," the B side, sounds more alive than all their space operas too.   **B**

Jefferson Starship: *Dragon Fly* (Grunt '74). The key cut here is Grace Slick's gnomic "Hyperdrive," in which supertechnology (spirit-powered, perhaps?) cuts through "corners in time." If in 1973 you'd been responsible for *Baron von Tollbooth and the Chrome Nun* (Jefferson Jitney), *Thirty Seconds over Winterland* (dead live), and *Bodacious D. F.* (Marty's party), you'd want to think you'd turned a corner in 1974 yourself. But though this does achieve a slick modernization of their polyvocal sound (Barbata-powered, definitely), with Papa John Creach's fiddle and Craig Chaquico's guitar synthesizing past and future for purposes of metaphor and stage presentation as Marty Balin's cameo contribution links them audibly to their own history, it also proves that you can't get along forever on generalized imprecations against the powerful and invidious oriental-occidental comparisons.   **C+**

Jefferson Starship: *Red Octopus* (Grunt '75). This is indeed their most significant record of the decade, but what does it signify? It's their first number-one album, but it sells to an audience that refuses to distinguish between production values and musical ideas. While the returned Marty Balin is the most soulful folkie ever to set voice to plastic, he remains a mush-brain — the paragon to whom he addresses "Miracles" is actually compared to both a river and a stringed instrument. And to call "I Want to See Another World" and "There Will Be Love" jive-ass would be to imply that standard-brand American bullshit has style.   **B−**

Jefferson Starship: *Spitfire* (Grunt '76). I still respect this group, I really do. Their apparently random yet inexorable evolution as a collective entity (not just Grace & Paul Plus) resonates in their deepening textures. They seem to have ideals. You might even say they keep '60s notions of communality alive. Or are they just accommodating '70s notions of corporate identity? They're so vague — they meaning the

people, the ideals, and on this album even the textures — that it's hard to tell. Or care. Original grade: C plus.   **C**

Jefferson Airplane: *Flight Log* (Grunt '77). The truism is that their history matched the counterculture's from optimism to visions to anger to dissolution, and this compilation devotes more than a disc to phase four. I really tried to pin down some overarching theme I'd missed at the time, but dissolution seems to be it — not only did they have nothing to say, they didn't have much to say it with. The three Hot Tuna cuts sound fresh and intelligent by comparison, and the '60s stuff — only two repeats from *Worst* plus a live "Somebody to Love" — is, well, optimistic and visionary and angry.   **C+**

Jefferson Starship: *Earth* (Grunt '78). This is slightly better than *Spitfire* (not to mention *Baron von Tollbooth*) and rather worse than *Red Octopus* (not to mention *Crown of Creation*). Its only ambitious lyric seems to equate skateboarding with sex with (male) hubris; its expertness conceals neither schlock nor shtick nor strain of ego. It is leading the nation in FM airplay.   **C**

Jefferson Starship: *Gold* (Grunt '79). Though their biographies suggest no special expertise in the subject, these aging romantics sing only about love. To put their generation in kinder perspective they encourage young Craig Chaquico to play his stupid guitar. Perenially poignant Marty Balin, now departed once again, dominates this compilation like a matinee idol squeezing another year out of his profile; perenially unpredictable Grace Slick, now also departed, sounds less and less interested in providing point or counterpoint. The music isn't utterly formulaic — from their tight folkie harmonies to their John Creach phase through various oriental mysteries they've cultivated an agreeable exoticism. But it goes nowhere except the bank.   **B−**

Jefferson Starship: *Freedom at Point Zero* (Grunt '79). Hawkwind-goes-commercial leads off one side, Foreigner-hurries-home the other; both cuts are catchy, both sexist tripe. The rest of the album is a familiar muddle of fixations: space travel, good-time, the deluge, the possession of pretty girls. Personal to Mickey Thomas: ain't nobody gonna boogie on the moons of Saturn. **C−**

Garland Jeffreys: *Garland Jeffreys* (Atlantic '73). A classy singer-songwriter with staying power; a classless singer-songwriter with at least two bags of tricks. "Black and white as can be" right down to his vocals, he's a living breathing advertisement for the mongrelization of the races, and it's his existential dilemma that permits Michael Cuscuna a gourmet coproduction in which Stonesy blues shuffles rub elbows with reggae from Kingston and a song about the zoo that makes Paul Simon sound like Marlin Parkins. Is he streetwise? Damn right — wise enough to find the streets a little scary. **B+**

Garland Jeffreys: *Ghost Writer* (A&M '77). Four years is a long time between LPs; if Jeffreys sounded like a talented cult artist on Atlantic in 1973, by now he's collected so much material he sounds like the most fecund singer-songwriter since whoever. Well, save that for the next time. Meanwhile, the racial paradox is dramatized audaciously, the dreams of showbiz glory rendered with an uncommon knowing subtlety, the reggae natural-born, the voice fuller and more passionate, and the album a great buy. Original grade: A. **A−**

Garland Jeffreys: *One-Eyed Jack* (A&M '78). If this were a "sellout" it would be mottled with slavish attempts at a catchiness inimical to the reggaefied groove Jeffreys explores so deliberately. Take it as Product Due from an artist who for some reason hasn't written any of his best songs in the past year, and hope his muse returns. **C+**

Garland Jeffreys: *American Boy and Girl* (A&M '79). Jeffreys has never shown much knack for love songs, and he's not getting any better with melodies either, which means that half of this encouraging comeback gets by on his acumen as a singer and bandleader. But as you might expect from somebody who rhymes "you know what it's like" with "Wilhelm Reich," he retains his feeling for cafe society and his sense of the street, which synthesize into his eternal theme of making it. And while you might suspect him of sentimentalizing the street kids on the cover, he doesn't — he just cares about them, that's all. Original grade: B plus. **B**

Garland Jeffreys: See also Grinders Switch Featuring Garland Jeffreys

Johnny Jenkins: *Ton-Ton Macoute!* (Atco '70). The former Pinetopper got upstaged by stablemate Otis Redding at his big recording opportunity many years ago, so now, in the spirit of fair's fair, the Allman Brothers Band (sans Gregg) give him another chance by backing him with some rock and roll (not "rock"). They sound great, too. Only problem is, Jenkins got upstaged for a reason — he doesn't have much of a voice. **B−**

Waylon Jennings and Willie Nelson: *Waylon and Willie* (RCA Victor '78). Commercially, this collaboration was a sure shot. They could have hammed it up or run through on automatic; they could even have avoided connecting altogether. But as it happens, this is the strongest album either has made in a while, as full of enthusiasm and devoid of posturing as a dressing-room singout. As in most dressing-room singouts, though, things get a little too loose at times — sometimes it's hard to tell whether they remember the words. **B+**

Jesus Christ Superstar (Decca '70). Outsiders since Pat Boone have had the dumb idea that rock and roll means projecting the kind of sham intensity that the worst kind of opera lover is a sucker for, and here's more — "rock musical" is too kind. *Tommy*, in which real rock and rollers pursued a grandiose dramatic concept, was risky enough. But set semiclassical-twice-removed melodies amid received, overrehearsed rock instrumentation and all the verve and spontaneous power which is the music's birthright gets crucified.   **C−**

Jethro Tull: *Benefit* (Reprise '70). Ian Anderson is one of those people who attracts admirers by means of a principled arrogance that has no relation to his actual talents or accomplishments. He does have one undeniable gift, though — he knows how to deploy riffs. Nearly every track on this album is constructed around a good one, sometimes two; play it twice and you'll have the thing memorized. But I defy you to recall any lyrics. For all his e-nun-ci-a-tion and attention to word-craft, Anderson can't or won't create the impression that he really cares about love/friendship/privacy, which I take to be his chief theme — the verbiage isn't obscure, but he really does make it hard to concentrate. I'm sure I hear one satirical exegesis on the generation gap, though. [Later on Chrysalis.]   **B−**

Jethro Tull: *Aqualung* (Reprise '71). Ian Anderson is like the town free thinker. As long as you're stuck in the same town yourself, his inchoate cultural interests and skeptical views on religion and human behavior are refreshing, but meet up with him in the city and he can turn out to be a real bore. Of course, he can also turn out to be Bob Dylan — it all depends on whether he rejected provincial values out of a thirst for more or out of a reflexive (maybe even somatic) negativism. And on whether he was pretentious only because he didn't know any better. [Later on Chrysalis.]   **C+**

Jethro Tull: *Thick as a Brick* (Reprise '72). Ian Anderson is the type of guy who'll tell you on one album that a whole side is one theme and then tell you on the next that a whole album is

one song. The usual shit — rock (getting heavier), folk (getting feyer), classical (getting schlockier), flute (getting better because it had no choice), words. [Later on Chrysalis.]   **C−**

Billy Joel: *Piano Man* (Columbia '73). In 1971, Joel's *Cold Spring Harbor* was recorded in the vicinity of 38-rpm to fit all the material on — he's one of these eternal teenagers who doesn't know how to shut up. Stubborn little bastard, too — after his bid stiffed, he worked a Los Angeles cocktail lounge soaking up Experience. Here he poses as the Irving Berlin of narcissistic alienation, puffing up and condescending to the fantasies of fans who spend their lives by the stereo feeling sensitive. And just to remind them who's boss, he hits them with a ballad after the manner of Aaron Copland.   **C**

Billy Joel: *Streetlife Serenade* (Columbia '74). Boy, these piano boys — on "Root Beer Rag" and "The Mexican Connection" Joel abandons Irving Berlin for George Gershwin, or do I mean Roger Williams? Granted, "The Entertainer" is so nasty it's witty — so nasty it may be about Joel himself. But why does it include a Rick Wakeman imitation?   **C**

Billy Joel: *Turnstiles* (Columbia '76). As Joel's craft improves — I can recall four of these songs merely by glancing at titles — he becomes more obnoxious: the anti-idealism of "Angry Young Man" isn't any more appealing in tandem with the pseudo-ironic sybaritism of "I've Loved These Days." But I do catch myself in moments of identification with the three place-name songs on side one — "Say Goodbye to Hollywood" more than the overrated "New York State of Mind."   **C+**

Billy Joel: *The Stranger* (Columbia '77). Having concealed his egotism in metaphor as a young songpoet, he achieved success when he uncloseted the spoiled brat behind those bulging eyes. But here the brat appears only once, in the nominally metaphorical guise of "the stranger." The rest of

Billy has more or less grown up. He's now as likable as your once-rebellious and still-tolerant uncle who has the quirk of believing that OPEC was designed to ruin his air-conditioning business. **B−**

Billy Joel: *52nd Street* (Columbia '78). Despite the Chapinesque turns his voice takes when he tries to get raucous, he makes a better Elton John than Leo Sayer — he's got that same omniverous hummability. But when he is (was) good, Elton balances(d) off the smarm with camp, while Billy makes as if he really wants people to believe the words. Yuck. **B−**

David Johansen: *David Johansen* (Blue Sky '77). Balancing the unrecorded classics of the Dolls' rent-party phase — "Girls" ("I love 'em seizin' the power"), "Funky but Chic" ("Mama thinks I look pretty fruity but in jeans I feel rotten"), and "Frenchette" (as in launderette) — against ground-breaking love/heartbreak songs like "Donna" and "Pain in My Heart," this is in many ways a "better" record than either Dolls LP. Sound quality is fuller, the rhythm section funks and flows, the guitarists play genuine solos and respond to the call, and Johansen's voice is as open and direct as his new songs, finding an almost soulful musical and emotional range. Conceptually, though, it's singer-with-backup in a post-garage mode, packing no distinctive structural or sonic kick, pretty conventional for the pied piper of outrageousness. **A−**

David Johansen: *In Style* (Blue Sky '79). Johansen is equal to his more soulish musical concept — no "disco," just slower tempos, subtle be-yoo-ty, and some reggae — but he doesn't have the chops to get on top of it, and while this is solid stuff, the best of it tends to thin out a little. Although the problem isn't how often you think "that's bad" but how often you don't think "that's great," the record is summed up for me by "Big City," the most banal lyric he's ever written. Until now, you see, he'd never written

any banal lyrics at all. Now he's got three or four. **B+**

Elton John: *Elton John* (Uni '70). A lot of people consider John a future superstar, and they may be right; I find this overweening (semi-classical ponderousness) and a touch precious (sensitivity on parade). It offers at least one great lyric (about a newborn baby brother), several nice romantic ballads (I don't like its affected offhandedness, but "Your Song" is an instant standard), and a surprising complement of memorable tracks. But their general lack of focus, whether due to histrionic overload or sheer verbal laziness, is a persistent turnoff. **B**

Elton John: *Tumbleweed Connection* (Uni '71). Between the cardboard leatherette jacket and the cold-type rotogravure souvenir booklet is a piece of plastic with good melodies and bad Westerns on it. Why do people believe that these latter qualify as songpoems? Must be that magic word "connection," so redolent of trains, illegal substances, and I-and-thou. Did somebody say Grand Funk Railroad was a hype? What about this puling phony? Original grade: C plus. **B−**

Elton John: *Madman Across the Water* (Uni '71). The two decent songs here — I refer primarily to the melodies of "Tiny Dancer" (just how small is she, anyway?) and "Levon" — clock in (with lots and lots of help from Paul Buckmaster) at 6:12 and 5:37 respectively. In other words, they meander. The others maunder as well. Ugh. **C**

Elton John: *Honky Chateau* (Uni '72). John is here transmuted from dangerous poseur to likable pro. Paul Buckmaster and his sobbing strings are gone. Bernie Taupin has settled into some comprehensible (even sharp and surprising) lyrics, and John's piano, tinged with the music hall, is a rocker's delight. Also, he does have a knack for the hook. If like me you love "Rocket Man" despite all your initial misgivings, try "I Think I'm Gonna Kill Myself," about the state of teenage blues, or "Slave," about slavery. **A—**

Elton John: *Don't Shoot Me, I'm Only the Piano Player* (MCA '72). Dear Elton: If you're trying to claim it's all Bernie's fault, just hold on. One half of a songwriting team can always bail the other out of rock and roll as competent and (not counting that new sexist streak) unexcessive as this, as each of you proved on *Honky Chateau*. Maybe Bernie refuses to outgrow his pistol envy. But that's no reason for you to make the music notwith-a-bang-but-a-whimper. **C+**

Elton John: *Goodbye Yellow Brick Road* (MCA '73). Two LPs ago, Bernie Taupin passed on his way from obscure banality to clean, well-lighted banality to write a batch of imaginative lyrics, and set to those lyrics John's music sounded eclectic but not confused. Too often now it seems to chatter on anonymously. The title cut is good, "Bennie and the Jets" is great, side four is good-to-great, and a few other songs here would probably benefit from more exclusive company, but this is one more double album that would make a nifty single. Original grade: C plus. **B**

Elton John: *Caribou* (MCA '74). I give up. Of course he's a machine, but haven't you ever loved a machine so much it took on its own personality? I was reminded of my first car, a '50 Plymouth. Then I decided Elton was more like a brand-new Impala I once rented on a magazine's money. Then I remembered that I ended up paying for that car myself. Yes, I hate the way he says "don't diszgard me" too, but "The Bitch Is Back" is my most favorite song. **B+**

Elton John: *Greatest Hits* (MCA '74). I don't agree that singles are Elton's metier — his method is too hit-or-miss to permit such a surefire formula, and some of his best stuff ("Your Sister Can't Twist," "Solar Prestige a Gammon") has proven too wild or weird for a&r/p.d. consciousness. There are no clinkers here, and I suppose if you only want one of his albums this is it.

But it's stylistically ragged, two of its four great cuts are also on *Honky Chateau*, and I'd just as soon hear the first side of *Caribou*. **B+**

Elton John: *Captain Fantastic and the Brown Dirt Cowboy* (MCA '75). Says B.T. as E.J.: "I once wrote such childish words for you." Do they feel guilty about it? Have they put away childish things? What's happening to our children when a concept album about the hard times of a songwriting team hits number one on all charts the week it's released? Does it matter that the five good songs on this one aren't as catchy as the five good songs on the last one? Probably not. **B**

Elton John: *Rock of the Westies* (MCA '75). First time I read the lyrics I got angry, but not at the lyrics, which are Bernie's best; I thought the new band's machine-tooled hard rock and Elton's automatic good cheer was negating their toughness and clarity and complexity. But I was wrong. Intentionally or not, the marimba accents of "Grow Some Funk of Your Own" and the faked-up Caribbean inflections of "Island Girl" elaborate the songs' racial ironies, while the band's fiery temper on "Street Kids" and "Hard Luck Story" cuts through John's arbitrary ebullience. Now if only Bernie furnished every song with a perfect out like this one, from "I Feel Like a Bullet": "You know I can't think straight no more." Original grade: A. **A—**

Elton John: *Here and There* (MCA '76). I had a syllogism worked out on this one. Went something like a) all boogie concerts rock on out, b) Elton is best when he rocks on out, c) therefore Elton's concert LP will rank with his best. So if this sounds like slop (concert-slop and Elton-slop both), blame Socrates — or find the false premise. **C**

Elton John: *Blue Moves* (MCA '76). None of the few rockers on this impossibly weepy and excessive double-LP match anything on *Rock of the Westies*. Or, as my wife commented in all innocence of who was on: "What is this tripe?" **C**

Elton John: *Greatest Hits Volume II* (MCA '77). The two previously-un-available-on-LP originals here are peaks, but the two covers are dippy. Plus the lead cut from *Caribou* and two hits from *Rock of the Westies* and left-overs from 1971 and 1976 and the climax of *Captain Fantastic.* Is this product necessary? Depends on who's doing the needing. **B+**

Elton John: *A Single Man* (MCA '78). Like the homophilophile I am, I'm rooting for Elton, but though this isn't as lugubrious as *Blue Moves,* it comes close, and the flat banalities of new lyricist Gary Osborne make Bernie Taupin's intricate ones sound like Cole Porter. Personal to Reg Dwight: Rock and roll those blues away. **C**

Elton John: *Victim of Love* (MCA '79). What's most depressing about this incredibly drab disc is that Elton's flirtation with Eurodisco comes a year too late. Even at his smarmiest, the man always used to be on top of the zeitgeist. Original grade: D plus. **C−**

The Jimmy Johnson Band: *Johnson's Whacks* (Delmark '79). Syl's cousin performed better on Alligator's *Living Chicago Blues Volume I,* but only marginally, and he compensates by showing unexpected chops as a writer. Whether hoping to make the cover of *Living Blues* magazine or complaining that women aren't loyal any more, he comes across as a bold-faced contemporary. But his basic wail starts to sound thin after a while, his band is only solid, and his guitar can't carry the extra load. **B+**

Linton Kwesi Johnson: *Forces of Victory* (Mango '79). You have every right to be suspicious of a Jamaican-English intellectual who writes message poems in patois and then sing-speaks them with the support of top reggae professionals. But you're wrong. Politics aside, Johnson has fresh musical gifts — an inside-outside awareness of the inherent musicality of Caribbean English and a rhythmic touch as uncanny as his

band's. On this album they're enhanced by insinuating horn charts, even melodies. While some prefer his debut, the bloody *Dread Beat an' Blood* (Virgin Front Line import), for striking closer to the broken bone of British racism, I actually like the abstractions here better, especially on "Reality Poem." Also, it's a relief to encounter a reggae album that doesn't once refer to Jah. **A−**

Syl Johnson: *Back for a Taste of Your Love* (Hi '73). Note label, imagine formula. A good one, of course — as the horns ascend over bass and drums you half expect him to break into "You Ought to Be with Me" or "Here I Am." Unfortunately, the voice is too narrow and nasal to take full advantage of such a smooth approach — good thing he gets gritty now and then. Mistake: Jerry Vale's (and Ray Charles's) "You Don't Know Me," which sounds like something Al thought better of. **B**

Syl Johnson: *Diamond in the Rough* (Hi '74). At its best this is competent-plus Memphis uptempo. Which is fine, but it's no accident that the best tune is the only one that didn't come out of Hi. It's the Cate Brothers' "Stuck in Chicago," and maybe he should have stayed there. **B−**

Syl Johnson: *Total Explosion* (Hi '76). Johnson has tended to disappear in between Willie Mitchell and Al Green, but on this LP he takes his harmonica up to the microphone and stands clear as a lapsed bluesman. Good move. His voice is still shriller and more strained than Green's, but that can be a satisfying distinction in the right context. A comparison of his unexceptionably dynamic rendition of "Take Me to the River" to Green's sublime original, however, renews one's understanding of what divine spark might be. Although I wish the folks at Hi would let him sing just one Junior Wells song, say, they've done him proud. **B+**

Syl Johnson: *Uptown Shakedown* (Hi '79). Some worthy soul veterans turn disco into commercial or even artistic regeneration. Others don't. For Johnson, who here abandons the rough, bluesy intensity of *Total Explosion,* disco means compromised semi-contemporaneity. "Mystery Lady" (she wears a mask) and "Let's Dance for Love" affect post-hustle hipness but don't achieve it, lyrically or musically, which may be why the Otis Redding medley and the Brenton Wood cover sound so half-assed.   **C**

Jo Jo Gunne: *Jumpin' the Gunne* (Asylum '73). For three straight albums this second-generation band, named after a Chuck Berry song by Spirit keyboard man and hard rock stalwart Jay Ferguson, has hung tough enough to attract my attention, but despite their high-speed, cross-riffing structural facility they haven't played smart enough to hold it. "At the Spa," a nasty metaphor about the limits of entertainment, almost changed that. But in the end I find their oddly un-Californian rock cynicism almost as wearying as the other kinds.   **B−**

Jo Mama: *J Is for Jump* (Atlantic '71). A weird one. This is one of those bands that wants to shove its idea of "good music" down the audience's collective throat, and I think most rock and rollers will find the style cute and constricted. But me, I enjoy it, on this album. Danny Kootch's songs are wry, just the way I like 'em, and even the phony cocktail jazz ditty framed by the pseudo-Chick Corea piano excavations sounds good. And though the subtle sexuality that pervades the record is hardly original — vocalist Abigale Haness's stuff goes back to June Christie at least — it still turns me on. So this is recommended to my soul/brain/gonad siblings, with the added warning that it doesn't jump much.   **B+**

George Jones: *The Best of George Jones* (Musicor '70). Don't take the title too seriously — the clenched jaw and rubberband larynx of honky-tonk's greatest honky have graced more albums than he can count (seventy, eighty, like that), and only the Lord knows how many singles he's put out. This is a fairly nondescript selection of ten of them, including one B side and two I can't trace. As usual, the highest-charted are the blandest, and neither of my faves — the hyperextended deception trope "Tell Me My Lying Eyes Are Wrong" and the poor white "Where Grass Won't Grow" — made top ten country. Time: 25:43.   **B+**

George Jones: *The Best of George Jones, Vol. 1* (RCA Victor '72). "White Lightnin' " isn't the only white lightnin' Jones's longtime but no-more producer "Pappy" Daily passes around — to commemorate Jones's desertion to Epic, Daily has sold all the George he owns to RCA, and the initial result is a hither-and-yon compilation that skips from the high purity of his work with Mercury and United Artists (no Starday stuff) to the tortured midrange of the recent "I'll Follow You" and "A Day in the Life of a Fool." Much too brief, but not a bad introduction. Time: 23:05.   **A−**

George Jones: *The Best of George Jones* (Epic '75). You can hear why people say Billy Sherrill has compromised Jones on this compilation's only great song, "The Door"; Bergen White's strings begin tersely enough, but by the end the usual army of interlopers is sawing away, so that you barely notice how Jones lowers the boom on the two "the"'s in the song's final line. Ultimately, though, it isn't the production that makes this acceptable but less than scintillating — it's the conception. Too many of these songs lay out the conventional romantic themes with a slight twist, and there's virtually no room for Jones the honky-tonk crazy, the one who sang "The Race Is On" and "No Money in This Deal." One Epic cut that would help on both counts is the unsarcastic "You're Looking at a Happy Man," in which his wife leaves him.   **B+**

George Jones: *The Battle* (Epic '76). One of the artiest cover illustrations ever to come out of Nashville has misled casual observers into the belief that this is a concept album about George and Tammy's marital problems. What it is is a slightly better-than-average George Jones LP marred by a surfeit of conjugal-bliss·songs. First by a country mile: "Billy Ray Wrote a Song," about two up-and-coming Nashville professionals, both male. **B**

George Jones: *Alone Again* (Epic '76). Although it sticks too close to heart songs, this comeback-to-basics statement is the best country album of the year and far surpasses the rest of Jones's recent work. I'm getting to like the over-forty Jones as much as the rawboned honky-tonker anyway — what's amazing about him is that by refusing the release of honky-tonking he holds all that pain in, audibly. The result, expressed in one homely extended metaphor per song (the only one that's too commonplace is "diary of my life"), is a sense of constriction that says as much about the spiritual locus of country music as anything I've heard in quite a while. **A −**

George Jones: *All-Time Greatest Hits: Volume 1* (Epic '77). Jones aficionados may well object to his re-recording his old standards, especially while some of the prototypes remain in catalogue on RCA and Musicor. But though I miss the revved-up boy-man lightness of some of the originals, these are much brighter and more passionate than most remakes, and I welcome the improved sound quality and relatively schlock-free arrangements. Likable at worst, revelatory at best, and recommended. **A −**

George Jones: *I Wanta Sing* (Epic '77). The vocals aren't as intense here as on *Alone Again,* so the tomfoolery seems a little forced, though I hope he keeps trying. But as long as he's not buried in strings, soul choruses, and Peter Allen songs, I don't think he can make a bad album. Will somebody tell Billy Sherrill to withdraw that call to Australia? **B**

George Jones: *My Very Special Guests* (Epic '79). This collection of ten collaborations with outlaw old-timers, country-rock phenoms, Sta-ples, Tammy, and someone named Elvis has low points, as you might expect. But its quality has more to do with what's being sung than with who's singing it where. James Taylor, harmonizing from New York on his neo-classic "Bartender's Blues," sounds fine; Emmylou Harris, chiming in from El Lay on the lame "Here We Are," fares only slightly worse than Johnny Paycheck does on poor old "Proud Mary," which comes complete with made-in-Nashville interaction. Must-hears: "I Gotta Get Drunk," with Willie Nelson, and the amazing "Stranger in the House," which gives an unexpected clue about who taught Mr. Costello to sing. **A −**

George Jones & Tammy Wynette: *Greatest Hits* (Epic '77). If rock and roll plunges forward like young love, then country music partakes of the passionate stability of a good marriage, and here's one couple who know for damn sure that the wedding doesn't end the story. Their hits are alternately tender and recriminatory, funny and fucked up, but they're always felt and they're always interesting. And even though George and Tammy eventually succumbed to d-i-v-o-r-c-e, they don't give you the feeling that that's the way it has to come out. **A −**

Grace Jones: *Portfolio* (Island '77). This disco queen sings flat enough to make Andrea True sound like Linda Ronstadt and Tom Verlaine like Art Garfunkel, which is nice — very liberated, very punky. But it's less than ironic that a woman who demands an end to jealousy — that is, who demands the same license to fuck around that male rock stars claim as their due — should (as a fashion model) occupy a similar power position. And while I prefer her version of "Send in the Clowns" to Judy Collins's, I'd just as soon she cover "Pretty Vacant" or something. **C +**

Linda Jones: *Your Precious Love* (Turbo '72). Jones isn't too long on artistry — she likes to dispense with formality and just start at the climax, throwing her emotions and her high notes all over material like "Dancing in the Street" and "I Can't Make It Alone." Pretty amazing, in its way, and definitely recommended to people who always get out of their cars to look at waterfalls and strange rock formations. **B+**

Rickie Lee Jones: *Rickie Lee Jones* (Warner Bros. '79). It isn't just the skeptic in me who suspects that, despite the critical brouhaha, this young singer-songwriter's attractions are more sexual than musical or literary. It's also the male — "Stick It into Coolsville," eh? But the critic knows that there are only three or four of her songs — including "Coolsville" — that I'd enjoy hearing again. **B−**

Janis Joplin: *Pearl* (Columbia '70). Full Tilt Boogie prove themselves the most musicianly of her three backup bands — there's not a track where they don't help her grab the moment by the seat of the pants. Nevertheless, they and their soul/blues do her a disservice. I miss Big Brother, whose bizarre lumpenhippie "acid rock," when combined with her too frequently ignored country roots and her blues allegiances, made for an underclass triple-header altogether too threatening and unkempt to suit the kind of professional advisors who help singers assemble backup bands. No accident that the only transcendent tracks here are "Me and Bobby McGee," a country song, and "Mercedes Benz," an impromptu (or simulated impromptu) hippie goof. **A−**

Janis Joplin: *Joplin in Concert* (Columbia '72). Sure would be nice if there were more new material on this double-LP — all the Full Tilt cuts and over half the Big Brothers are available in earlier renditions. But given how little studio time she clocked, I treasure it, especially "Ego Rock," a screaming, joking blues duet with Nick Gravenites, and the expansive concert versions of three neglected classics from Big Brother's Mainstream album.

Sound quality: vibrant. Stage patter: poignant. **A−**

Janis Joplin: *Janis Joplin's Greatest Hits* (Columbia '73). I was disheartened to learn that five of these ten tracks were cut with Full Tilt Boogie, but one of them is a live "Ball and Chain," and I'm delighted to report that such competent classics as "Cry Baby" and "Move Over" sound a lot more raucous following "Try" and "Bye Bye Baby" than they did on *Pearl*. In short, this blatant piece of product represents her more fully than any other disc: spontaneity as rebellion, tied to the will, the major mode of the late '60s, preserved — imperfectly, of course — forever on a piece of plastic. **A**

Janis Joplin: *Janis Joplin* (Columbia '75). Because it captures such subtle yet essential virtues as intelligence, humor, and compassion as well as the big stuff she was famous for, film may have been Janis's real medium, and I recommend the documentary to which this double-LP is the putative soundtrack. But it ought to be seen and not heard — most of these cuts are available elsewhere, and the newly compiled early tapes are the rather tinny record of a singer who hasn't found her music or her band. **C+**

Joy of Cooking: *Joy of Cooking* (Capitol '71). Led by ex-folkie Toni Brown (the principal composer) and ex-blueswoman Terry Garthwaite (whose three rhythm songs sizzle joyously), this may not be your idea of rock and roll. The music revolves around Brown's piano, which rolls more than it rocks, and the band goes for multi-percussion rather than the old in-out. I find it relaxing and exciting and amazingly durable; I can dance to it, and I can also fuck to it. The musical dynamic pits Brown's collegiate contralto against Garthwaite's sandpaper soul, and the lyrics are feminist breakthroughs. "Too Late, but Not Forgotten" remembers a trailer camp while "Red Wine at Noon" touches international finance, but the two protagonists are

united by one overriding fact —
they're victimized as wives. And it's
about time somebody in rock and roll
said so.   **A**

Joy of Cooking: *Closer to the Ground*
(Capitol '71). I knew Toni Brown was
a folkie, so it shouldn't surprise me
that a lot of this is organic bullshit gone
to rhythm school — the title of the title
cut speaks for itself, and "Sometimes
Like a River" might also be like a
"Rainbow," "Mountain," or "New
Wind" (adjectival scansion, they call
that trick in rhythm school). Depressing to hear somebody who knows as
much abòut male-female as "The Way
You Left" and "First Time, Last
Time" apply her creative-writing skills
to anti-urban bromides. Graded leniently because I like the way (and how
much) Terry Garthwaite sings (and
writes).   **B+**

Joy of Cooking: *Castles* (Capitol '72).
If last time Toni Brown was betrayed
by her folkie upbringing, this time she
makes something of it, leading off el-
egantly with a modernized blues,
"Don't the Moon Look Fat and Lonesome," and following up quickly
enough with "Lady Called Love," a
modernized heroic ballad. Both the in-
citements to independence and the love
advisories are more general than need
be, but the music has grown crisper
and fuller while continuing to flow as
swimmingly as you'd hope.   **A−**

The Joy: *The Joy* (Fantasy '77). Maybe freedom from preconceptions has
enabled this group, which never
achieved its proper impact to begin
with, to make the best comeback LP in
memory, but more likely it's the quality of the competition. Because basically this is just a good Joy of Cooking
album. It probably helps that Terry
Garthwaite and Toni Brown now work
with black studio musicians — the
white ones on *Cross-Country* did nothing for them, and neither did the hassle
of maintaining a band. But this music
is about sure-brained songs and an ever
richer vocal interplay, just like always,
and if Toni's "You Don't Owe Me
Spring" reminds me never to forget
her penchant for limpid soppiness,
everything else makes clear that once
a rock band defines itself as adult it
need never grow old. Original grade:
A minus.   **B+**

Jules and the Polar Bears: *Got No
Breeding* (Columbia '78). Jules Shear
is an engaging singer who is no stupe
and has a way with a hook. At least
half of these songs provide mild pleasure. But Jules Shear is also a limited
singer who has nothing special to say
and no special way to say it. Los Angeles's version of Steve Forbert?   **B**

June 1, 1974 (Island '74). The highlights of a concert organized by genial
eccentric Kevin Ayers (ex-Soft Machine, but he got out when the getting
was good), this offers one side of Ayers's genially eccentric songs and one
of Eno singing Eno songs at full volume (note demonic cackle) and John
Cale singing an Elvis Presley song at
full volume (note lupine howl). And
also, oh well, Nico singing "The
End." But if there's gotta be art-rock,
Lord, let it be like this.   **B+**

Tonio K.: *Life in the Foodchain* (Full Moon/Epic '79). Tonio shouts numerous humorous words — his evolution jokes are funnier than Devo's — over the noise made by crack El Lay session men as they revisit Highway 61 at 110 miles an hour. Personal to Warren Zevon: note new speed limit. Inspirational Verse: "Yes I wish I was as mellow/As for instance Jackson Browne/But 'Fountain of Sorrow' my ass motherfucker/I hope you wind up in the ground." **B+**

Si Kahn: *New Wood* (June Appal '75). I was put off at first by the indifference to sales claimed in the booklet that accompanies this. Such smug anticommercialism usually betrays mixed motives in a purportedly political artist, and I associated this smugness with Kahn's willfully austere Appalachian music. But the songs soon shone through, correctives every one (despite an occasional baldness of instructional intent) to the romanticizations of Southern pastoral individualism that are currently so profitable. Kahn is an aficionado of poor-white virtues, but not at the expense of his vivid understanding of the labor, sadness, frustration, and small-mindedness that go along with them. **B+**

Si Kahn: *Home* (Flying Fish '79). This Carolina-based union organizer — who dedicates his second album to his father, Rabbi Benjamin M. Kahn — is the most gifted songwriter to come out of the folkie tradition since John Prine. His overview is political and his songs personal, their overriding theme the emotional dislocations of working far from home. No doubt part of his secret is that he lives among folk rather than folkies, but his understated colloquial precision is sheer talent. Some will consider the all-acoustic music thin (it's often solo or duet, twice a cappella) and the voice quavery. I find that both evoke the mountain music of the '20s in a way that makes me long for home myself, and I'm from Queens. **A−**

Madleen Kane: *Rough Diamond* (Warner Bros. '78). The perfect punk rock ashtray. Madleen looks like a *Penthouse* blonde with a camera-shy vulva and sings the same way — Andrea True telling little white lies. Promo copies of her LP come with a promo booklet featuring lotsa pix (dig those leg warmers) and text in six languages, including the original Japanese: "She chooses to sing. With her own voice. . . . The wildest words grow tame. . . ." **D+**

Madleen Kane: *Cheri* (Warner Bros. '79). On one side you can't even dance to it — it's like if Cheryl Ladd recorded Edith Piaf tributes, which she might yet, all topped off with a paean to "retro," which in case you didn't know means nostalgia with a will to power. **C−**

Kansas: *Leftoverture* Kirshner '76). Q: How do you tell American art-rock-

206

ers from their European forebears? A: They sound dumber, they don't play as fast, and their fatalism lacks conviction. The question of humor remains open: Impressed as I am with titles like "Father Padilla Meets the Perfect Gnat" and *Leftoverture* itself, I find no parallels in the music. **D+**

Paul Kantner / Jefferson Starship: *Blows Against the Empire* (RCA Victor '70). Not counting friendly neighbors, there are only two changes from the usual Airplane lineup on this "solo" venture: Jerry Garcia replaces Jorma Kaukonen for reasons of interstellar propulsion, and Paul Kantner replaces Marty Balin for reasons of ego. As much Marty's ego as Paul's, probably — I wouldn't want my name on this thing either. Kantner's singing is as murky as his melodies (there's a connection there somewhere) and for all the record's sci-fi pretensions (does Philip K. Dick actually *like* this stuff?) it never even gets off the ground. **C+**

Paul Kantner/Grace Slick: *Sunfighter* (Grunt '71). More sci-fi rev and Tamalpaian grandeur from Frisco's royal family. I dig the cover and the two Grace Slick songs, though not the way she keens them, but the rest of this is Paulie II picking his nose. **C**

Thomas Jefferson Kaye: *First Grade* (ABC/Dunhill '74). Like the *Triumvirate* album he produced for John Hammond, Mike Bloomfield, and Dr. John, Kaye's debut was sensually laid-back, with a sly intelligence he hoped to pass off as an active relationship with his environment. But this one stands beside Eric Clapton's *461 Ocean Boulevard* as a critique of the laid-back mode. The secret is the covers, which I bet producer Gary Katz (also of Steely Dan) had something to do with — especially since the whole album centers around Fagen & Becker's bitter, poignant farewell to the counterculture, "American Lovers." Together with Loudon Wainwright's painful "Say That You Love Me" and natural boogies from Link

Wray and Dr. John, it puts such Kaye titles as "Northern California" and "Easy Kind of Feeling" into the ironic perspective the artist intends. Maybe this is Katz rather than Kaye — but when you hear Kaye describe a "new religion/Called everything's gonna be all right," you won't think so. **A**

K.C. & the Sunshine Band: *Do It Good* (T.K. '74). Keyboard player (and now vocalist) H. W. Casey and bassman Richard Finch made so much moolah for T.K. prexy Henry Stone that he told them they could spend as much as $3150 on their own LP. What they come up with is the real Miami sound — the sensual Latin accents that really are sensual in New Orleans sound altogether more hyped-up here. "Queen of Clubs" was a smash in the Queen's clubs, while "Sound Your Funky Horn" and "I'm a Pushover" have creased America's soul charts, which makes three hooks right there. A weirdo and a sleeper. Time: 27:44. **B+**

K.C. & the Sunshine Band: *K.C. & the Sunshine Band* (T.K. '75). No matter what you label them, these otherwise meaningless dance tunes are as bright and distinct as the run of disco mush is dull — when it comes to formula, always opt for top forty, which compels innovation, over Muzak, which forbids it. The horns and vocals are less candidly soulful here than on their debut, and the result is an album that's poppier, lighter — almost airy. And though the songs do all sound alike, that doesn't mean they are. Far from it. Original grade: B plus. **A−**

K.C. & the Sunshine Band: *Part 3* (T.K. '76). I don't know how many KC albums the record lover need own. One may well be enough, but zero is certainly too few. This is less consistent than the second and more predictable than the first, but it's a close question: Casey and Finch are remarkably inventive within their unique little ambit. Like the others, this sounds so samey you think the riffs will never kick in — and then they do. **B+**

KC and the Sunshine Band: *Who Do Ya* (*Love*) (T.K. '78). They lead off side two with a cover of "It's the Same Old Song," and given the new ones it's a shame it isn't. **C+**

KC and the Sunshine Band: *Do You Wanna Go Party* (T.K. '79). The slight shifts in rhythmic and compositional strategy are dubious. But this band is like the Ramones — the hooks sneak up on you. What can I say? Not only do I love the title cut, but I find myself humming everything else on the record — the slow one, the cover version, the one in Spanish. **B+**

Roberta Kelly: *Gettin' the Spirit* (Casablanca '78). One good thing about disco manufacturers is that they'll try anything. Here the gimmick is Jesus, invoked by name over unusually bright, bouncy, and consistent dance tracks flavored with gospel piano and some Jerry Jumonville saxophone. For me, this conjunction adds a perverse fillip to an already attractive record — I'm sure the folks at Studio 54 can use any kind of salvation that comes their way. Mary Magdalene would approve. **B+**

Eddie Kendricks: *At His Best* (Tamla '78). Rarely has a talented singer been so ill-served by his corporate connections without failing altogether. Kendricks doesn't have the depth of a natural solo performer — the sweet clarity of his falsetto rang nice spiritual overtones against his more earthbound fellow Temptations, but it gets thin all by itself — and he needs good material to compensate. This ain't it. Most of these songs were hits, but the two uptempo smashes, "Keep On Truckin' " and "Boogie Down," are proto-disco at its most ominously one-dimensional, and except for the Tempts' "Just My Imagination" and the never-a-hit "Skippin' Work Today," the rest range from passable ("He's a Friend") to deplorable ("Shoeshine Boy"). **C+**

Doug Kershaw: *Ragin' Cajun* (Warner Bros. '76). Warner Bros. has been betting for years that "Diggy Liggy Lo" and "Louisiana Man" were the mark of a classic songwriter and borderline insanity the mark of a star. But his two '60s hits proved novelty one-shots (or two-shots) and his manic intensity proved impossible to sell. Here they finally let him do a rocking country album that may or may not appeal to the rocking country market, by which I do not mean the outlaw market — I'm talking about a market too small to make him a star. "It Takes All Day" is a minor hit, "Blow Your Horn" and "I'm Not Strong Enough" deserve to follow, and the filler is inoffensive, proving only (outlaws take note) that those who act macho are more appealing if they also act a little nuts. **B**

KGB: *KGB* (MCA '76). Heavy horseshit. Carmine Appice, Rick Grech, Barry Goldberg, and Ray (the K) Kennedy don't make a supergroup any more than Jim Price (last espied trying to bury Joe Cocker) makes a superproducer (overproducer, maybe). As for Mike Bloomfield — well, he's deserved better ever since he left Butterfield, and there's absolutely no reason to believe he'll ever go out and get it. **D+**

Chaka Khan: *Chaka* (Warner Bros. '78). Arif Mardin and the usual En Why studio funkies lay down a heavier bottom for Ms. Rufus than her El Lay street players have in years. She's expressing herself by looking for songs, too, but while every one gives her something to say, only Ashford & Simpson's "I'm Every Woman" is up to her human potential. **B**

B. B. King: *Indianola Mississippi Seeds* (ABC '70). I hate to sound like a fuddy-duddy, but the best moment here is unaccompanied — "Nobody Loves Me but My Mother," all 1:26 of it, with King singing and playing piano. B. B. King, that is — most of the piano here is by *Carole* King, who sounds fine, as do Leon Russell and Paul Harris. Even the strings and horns avoid disaster — B. B. goes pop with real dignity. But he's rarely brilliant, and the only songs on this record with a chance of being in his show a year from now are "Chains and Things" and Leon Russell's "Hummingbird," hooked on the deathless line "She's little and she loves me." I mean, what good does it do to perform that kind of tripe with dignity? **B**

B. B. King: *Live in Cook County Jail* (ABC '71). This begins inauspiciously, with introductions and a thrown-away "Every Day I Have the Blues" (compare *Live at the Regal* and weep), and ends dubiously, with the sappy show-closer "Please Accept My Love." In between B. B. socks home old hits as familiar as "Sweet Sixteen" and as worthy as "Darlin' You Know I Love You" with a tough intensity he rarely brings to the studio. I prefer the horn arrangements on the Kent originals, but the unpredictable grit with which he snaps off the guitar parts makes up for any lost subtlety. **A−**

B. B. King: *B. B. King in London* (ABC '71). Overlooking Alexis Korner's acoustic boogie, this encounter with Brit second-liners (famed blues devotee Ringo Starr is the big catch) and L.A. session stars is substantial stuff. "Caldonia" and "Ain't Nobody Home" are more than that. But rock with a steady roll it doesn't. Maybe Klaus Voorman, listed on bass, knows why. **B**

B. B. King: *L.A. Midnight* (ABC '72). Hey, I've got an idea — how about sending B. into the studio to do a *blues* album? We could bring in a tuba like Taj Mahal, hire some decent rhythm players this time, call up a coupla good white guitarists — B.'ll cut the shit out of them, of course, but it can't hurt. He's got a great new iceman-cometh song, he's always good for a jam or two, and if we have to we can always do "Sweet Sixteen" again. Roots, get back, it's a take. **B+**

B. B. King: *Guess Who* (ABC '72). Bluesy soul records aren't getting any easier to come by, and who am I to complain about one with the great B. B. King contributing guitar parts? "It

Takes a Young Girl" and "Better Lovin' Man," which sound like standards that somehow passed me by, more than make up for the clumsy "Summer in the City" and the reremade "Five Long Years." But the singer obviously isn't getting any younger, and when he begs comparison with Lorraine Ellison and Howard Tate on "You Don't Know Nothing About Love" he's risking more than he ought to. Which is admirable, in a way. **B+**

B. B. King: *The Best of B. B. King* (ABC '73). King is human and then some — never less than intelligent but often less than inspired, especially with words. So I'm delighted at how many high points this captures — "Caldonia" and "Ain't Nobody Home" from *London,* "Nobody Loves Me but My Mother" (marred by unfortunate engineering tricks) from *Indianola,* two classic blues, and "The Thrill Is Gone," one of his greatest ballads. And though I still find "Why I Sing the Blues" self-serving and "Hummingbird" silly, they sure make classy filler. **A−**

B. B. King: *To Know You Is to Love You* (ABC '73). The Stevie Wonder-composed title track isn't blues or even soul — it's one of those slow, funky grooves that smolders along for minutes before you notice you're dripping from the heat, and it almost justifies the lame idea of sending King into Sigma Sound with Dave Crawford. Elsewhere King sings indifferent songs sincerely, recites a poem he wrote, and plays his guitar when he gets the chance. **B−**

B. B. King: *Friends* (ABC '74). If Dave Crawford really wants to turn B.B. into a major "contemporary" soul singer, he shouldn't make him sing Dave Crawford's songs. Best cut: the instrumental. Time: 26:06. Original grade: D plus. **C**

B. B. King & Bobby Bland: *Together for the First Time . . . Live* (ABC/Dunhill '74). This is my kind of exploitation — a commercial gimmick that gets two masters back to their form. An honorable document it is, too, especially Bland's part. King's voice and guitar have both been more searing, the latter within recent memory, and though I'd rather hear him singing familiar old blues than mediocre new pop, the classic material does resist renewal, which is why he and Bland do so much pop these days. Sometimes, too, the joking interaction sounds a little uncomfortable — almost as if they're rivals or something. Original grade: A minus. **B+**

B. B. King: *Lucille Talks Back* (ABC '75). In which King expresses himself by (a) following "Have Faith" with "Everybody Lies a Little" (b) covering Lowell Fulson, Z. Z. Hill, and Ann Peebles (c) conversing with his guitar and (d) producing himself. Personal to Dave Crawford: listen hard to those horns. **B+**

B. B. King: *King Size* (ABC '77). Old Chess man Esmond Edwards acquits himself with honor — the charts are sharp, the sidemen prime, and most of the songs good ones. But the mildness of the two Muddy Waters covers reminds us that King conceived his style as progressive from Muddy's Delta-Chicago gutbucket, and the segue from "Mother Fuyer," the dirtiest traditional blues in the repertoire, to Bill Withers and Brook Benton is disorienting rather than revelatory. **B−**

B. B. King: *Midnight Believer* (ABC '78). In which B. B. and the Crusaders cut room for a party between sincere schlock and pseudo purism. The King's voice hasn't regained its edge and his guitar is used mostly to decorate Joe Sample's tunes, but this would rate as a mini-comeback if it included another song as good as "Never Make a Move Too Soon," the only one on the album that Sample didn't help write. **B**

B. B. King: *Take It Home* (MCA '79). The Crusaders' songwriting doesn't peak the way it did on B.B.'s 1978 collaboration with the L.A. topcats, but that's OK because it doesn't dip either. The Crusaders jam, B.B. jives and raps, and the result — give or take some background vocals and a few

overworked horn charts — is the topcat equivalent of the kind of wonderful blues-bar album Bruce Iglauer of Alligator has been getting out of less accomplished musicians throughout the '70s. A small delight. **B+**

Carole King: *Carole King: Writer* (Ode '70). I liked these musicians better when they called themselves the City — seemed to protect them against string arrangements, folkie jazz, and other exurban excrescences. Must admit, though, that the first side is a lot more eloquent, confident, and tuneful than the nice little album the City put out in 1968. Now if only the Drifters cover on the second side had some company — the reason I'm listening, after all, is that she also wrote hits for the Chiffons, the Shirelles, Little Eva. . . . **B**

Carole King: *Tapestry* (Ode '71). Pacific rock, sure, but with a sharpness worthy of a Brooklyn girl — if there's a truer song about breaking up than "It's Too Late," the world (or at least AM radio) isn't ready for it. Not that lyrics are the point on an album whose title cut compares life to a you-know-what — the point is a woman singing. King has done for the female voice what countless singer-composers achieved years ago for the male: liberated it from technical decorum. She insists on being heard as she is — not raunchy and hot-to-trot or sweet and be-yoo-ti-ful, just human, with all the cracks and imperfections that implies. And for the first time she has found the music — not just the melodies, but the studio support — to put her point across as cleanly and subtly as it deserves. **A−**

Carole King: *Music* (Ode '71). Initially this record sounds like a mechanical follow-up to *Tapestry*. Then you begin to notice the subtle musical advances and the ever more assured backup, especially from guitarists Danny Kootch and James Taylor and saxophonist Curtis Amy, and start humming "Sweet Seasons" or "Song of Long Ago." Then you realize it's really just a mechanical follow-up to *Tapestry*. I love Carole King, but her value is as limited as it is intense, and her lyrics are banal even when she doesn't write them. Original grade: B.   **C+**

Carole King: *Rhymes and Reasons* (Ode '72). The melodies retain their overall charm, but because the lyrics continue their retreat, the hooks, such as they are, never jolt the expectations. Original grade. B minus.   **C**

Carole King: *Fantasy* (Ode '73). The title means she's decided to step outside herself and write songs about imaginary situations, just like some Brill Building hack. A decision which seems to have brightened her music considerably. As for the situations themselves, well, what hath Walter Lippmann wrought? But the odd thing is that in the context of her junkie and housewife soap operas, her quest for "Directions" and "A Quiet Place to Live" could almost make you "Believe in Humanity." I said almost. Original grade: B plus.   **B**

Carole King: *Wrap Around Joy* (Ode '74). The good news is that Carole's new lyricist used to work with Steely Dan. The bad news is that in Steely Dan he was a vocalist.   **C**

Carole King: *Really Rosie* (Ode '75). I've been saying she needed a new lyricist, and here he is — Maurice Sendak, a writer of children's books favored by adults, which makes him a rock (not rock and roll) natural. By side two you begin to resent the repetitiousness of some of King's devices, but since side one comprises her most exciting music since *Tapestry* you're already converted and it doesn't matter.   **B+**

Carole King: *Simple Things* (Capitol/Avatar '77). Inspirational Verse: ". . . it's not for me to understand/Maybe destruction is part of the plan." *Maybe?* Worth millions and she doesn't know how to make an omelet.   **C−**

Carole King: *Her Greatest Hits* (Ode '78). Cut for cut this compilation is probably as strong as *Tapestry,* from which it appropriates four excellent tracks. "Believe in Humanity" is no worse than "Tapestry" itself, and it's nice to have the nicest tunes from all the dud albums that followed it in one place — especially "Corazon," "Brother, Brother," and "Been to Canaan." But it's docked a notch for lacking mythic significance.   **B+**

Clydie King: *Direct Me* (Lizard '71). Clydie has a voice that's more sly Diana than robust Martha and addresses the title plea to Gabriel Mekler, who (this time, anyway) proves neither as sly nor as robust as Berry Gordy. Luckily for her, Clydie also has a studio job with a backup trio called the Blackberries. I wonder when solo LPs from Venetta Fields and Shirley Matthews are expected. Not too soon, I hope.   **C+**

Freddie King: *The Best of Freddie King* (Shelter '75). Although Freddie's renown as the inventor of electric blues guitar is a reward for his shameless Anglophilia (here documented on "Palace of the King"), he did cut some acute r&b sides for (of all labels) King in the '50s. Forget what the Anglophiles claim for his recent work — he's been coasting for years. Here he makes do with a bunch of Leon Russell and Don Nix boogies, his voice blurred, his guitar all fake and roll.   **C+**

King Biscuit Boy: *King Biscuit Boy* (Epic '74). King Biscuit Boy/Richard Newell is a Canadian Paul Butterfield, which I mean as a compliment, and when he sings lead with producer Allen Toussaint doing backups it's the ultimate white blues fantasy. In reality, though, Newell's high-strung earnestness and virtuoso harmonica can't take this album away from Toussaint, and like so many of Toussaint's albums it's only half great. But since it divides neatly into a side of Toussaint songs (great) and a side of Newell's (passable), this time you can't blame that on the auteur.   **B+**

King Crimson: *In the Wake of Poseidon* (Atlantic '70). For a long time I thought this was the worst rock band in history simply because it was the most pretentious, but sometimes pretensions are (at least partially) earned. Their second album is more muddled conceptually than *In the Court of the Crimson King,* quite a feat. But they're not afraid to be harsh, they command a range of styles, and their dynamics jolt rather than sledgehammer (properly electric, that). Also, they can play: kudos to drummer Michael Giles and guitarist Robert Fripp, who also illustrates the old adage, "Better a Mellotron than real strings." Original grade: D plus.   **C+**

King Crimson: *Lizard* (Atlantic '71). To call this progressive rock is only to prove the term an oxymoron. But if you don't insist on snappy tunes with a good beat there are quite a few textural and technical attractions here, and the cold (not cool) jazziness of their compositions does project a certain cerebral majesty — third stream that deigns (rather than fails) to swing. Unfortunately, neither Gordon Haskell nor (keep off the weeds) Jon Anderson delivers Pete Sinfield's overwrought lyrics with the sarcasm they deserve.   **B−**

King Crimson: *Islands* (Atlantic '72). Just as I was learning to hear past the bullshit they upped the ante, so fuck 'em. When I feel the need for contemporary chamber music or sexist japes, *jazz libre* or *vers ordinaire,* I'll go to the source(s).   **C**

King Crimson: *Larks' Tongues in Aspic* (Atlantic '73). More appetizing than you'd expect — new lyricist Robert W. Palmer-Jones and new vocalist John Wetton add roughage to the recipe. But it's still the instrumental stuff that's worth savoring, and not only doesn't it cook, which figures, it doesn't quite jell either.   **B−**

King Crimson: *Starless and Bible Black* (Atlantic '74). This is as close as this chronically interesting group has ever come to a good album, or maybe it's as close as Robert Fripp has ever come to dominating this chronically interesting group. As usual, things improve markedly when nobody's singing. The lyrics are relatively sharp, but there must be better ways of proving you're not a wimp than casting invective at a "health-food faggot." Unless you *are* a wimp, that is.   **B**

King Crimson: *Red* (Atlantic '74). Grand, powerful, grating, and surprisingly lyrical, with words that cast aspersions on NYC (violence you know) and make me like it, or at least not hate it (virtually a first for the Crims), this does for classical-rock fusion what John McLaughlin's *Devotion* did for jazz-rock fusion. The secret as usual is that Robert Fripp is playing more — he does remind me of McLaughlin, too, though he prefers to glide where McLaughlin beats his wings. In compensation, Bill Bruford supplies more action than Buddy Miles. Less soul, though — which is why the jazz-rock fusion is more exciting.   **A−**

King Crimson: *USA* (Atlantic '75). Since the nearness of death was good for this band, I figured a posthumous live album might be even better, and though lyrics and vocals are still pompous annoyances, these musical themes (including the off-the-cuff "Asbury Park") are among their best. In Central Park they have no choice but to skip the subtlety and turn it up. The excitement thus generated is more Wagner than Little Richard — this record is a case study in the Europeanness of English heavy metal. But that doesn't mean it's not classic.   **B+**

King Floyd: *Well Done* (Chimneyville '75). Floyd's quiet, chocolatey voice — cf. Lee Dorsey, Aaron Neville — is prized by seekers after the New Orleans dispensation, but he's never grooved me without skipping like a cheap bootleg. So I'm pleased to report that side one of his fourth LP, climaxing with the neglected regional hit "I Feel Like Dynamite," provides songs as winsome as the straight-ahead Caribbeanisms (even some reggae) of the New Orleans r&b behind. Location of studio: Jackson, Mississippi. **B**

The Kinks: *Lola Versus Powerman and the Moneygoround* (Reprise '70). Although "Lola" was an astounding single, the only astounding thing about this album is its relentless self-pity. The evolution of Ray Davies's singing from raunch to whine is now complete; the melodies are still there, but in this context they sound corny rather than plaintive. It's one thing to indulge your nostalgia re village greens, another to succumb to it all over a concept album about modern media. N.b.: bookkeepers, song publishers, union reps, and musimoguls aren't all like rats. Key line, from "Got To Be Free": "We've got to get out of this world somehow." Original grade; C plus. **B −**

The Kinks: *Muswell Hillbillies* (RCA Victor '71). Because the Kinks Klaque hyped this as a great album when a simple perusal of the lyrics revealed more of the same olde alienation, I overreacted violently, but in unsentimental retrospect I can hear it, and I do mean hear. Most of its charms are in the casual-to-messy eclecticism with which it revives time-honored effects from the music hall and the mod era and even the mountains, and in the dotty good humor of Ray Davies's singing, which makes you think that maybe — just maybe — he doesn't take the "Acute Schizophrenia Paranoia Blues" of the "20th Century Man" at face value. But combine those two titles circa 2001 and you're in the court of the Crimson King. Original grade: C minus. **B +**

The Kinks: *The Kink Kronikles* (Reprise '72). Self-konfessed kultist John Mendelsohn has kreated an inkomparable kompilation. Great hits are few — the Kinks have made U.S. top forty only twice since their first best-of, with "Lola" and "Sunny Afternoon." But great songs abound, assembled with a konnoisseur's kraft (all right, I'll stop) from available (and deleted) LPs, uncollected singles (told

you I'd stop), and the vaults. Mendelsohn has little use for Ray Davies the would-be satirist ("Well-Respected Man," etc.), apologizing even for such marginally "boorish" efforts as "King Kong" and "Mr. Pleasant." So we get twenty-eight tracks that concentrate on Davies the lyric realist, the poet of pathos and aspiration, at his tuneful, readymade best. Definitely the world's most charming (and untidy) ripoff artist. And he wrote "Waterloo Sunset," the most beautiful song in the English language. **A**

The Kinks: *Everybody's in Showbiz* (RCA Victor '72). A few of the new songs here are as strident as anything Ray Davies has done since before he started playing the recluse in London in the late '60s. They're tight; they have a firm beat; they're, you know, rock and roll. Unfortunately, they're still self-pitying — the reformed recluse doth reflect overmuch these days on the travails of the touring superstar. But for only an extra dollar you get a live album worth at least that, featuring the antics of a reborn showman who has turned stage fright into a way of life and thus rendered his self-pity somewhat more palatable. **B +**

The Kinks: *The Great Lost Kinks Album* (Reprise '73). It says something about the limitations of the Kinks' professional renaissance that this belated compilation of B sides and outtakes, most of them recorded pre-renaissance, at around the time of *Village Green Preservation Society,* stands as the group's best album of the decade. Fragile, unkempt, whimsical, sometimes thrown away, with brother Dave left room for a cinematic fantasy of his own, it sticks close to the harmless eccentrics who comprise the only socially significant subculture about which Ray has ever had anything interesting to say. **A −**

The Kinks: *Preservation Act 1* (RCA Victor '73). Ray Davies is a sensitive artist, but he's never had an idea worth reducing to prose in his life. When he tosses off music toward no grand purpose his satire takes on a charity that justifies its shallowness. But when he gets serious he always skirts the edge of small-mindedness. This time he falls in.   **C+**

The Kinks: *Preservation Act II* (RCA Victor '74). Many are impressed by the fact that Davies's characters (yes, folks, another dramatic work here) have taken on an extra dimension, but I say that only makes two. He's finally figured out a way to integrate the horns and the girlies — sloppy Weill and sloppy madrigal on top of the sloppy rock and roll, all very lovable — but that's not enough.   **B−**

The Kinks: *Soap Opera* (RCA Victor '75). Maybe because it works so perfectly in the theater, this doesn't seem to work too well anywhere else. If you want a memento of the show, so be it. Otherwise avoid.   **C+**

The Kinks: *The Kinks Present Schoolboys in Disgrace* (RCA Victor '75). Yet another original cast recording — in the big production number, Ray Davies indicts "Education" for its failure to teach Ultimate Cause. Go get 'em, Ray.   **C+**

The Kinks: *Celluloid Heroes* (RCA Victor '76). Them as wants an overview of Ray Davies's RCA period are referred to this upstanding compilation, with eight cuts from the first two RCA albums and four from the four others. Although such unlikely gems as "Have a Cuppa Tea" and "Look a Little on the Sunny Side" are overlooked for the more obvious staples of the Kinks' road-band phase, none of the selections is bad. But they're all, well, obvious — devoid of Davies's saving grace, which is subtlety, eccentricity, some combination in there. Overview: the knack remains and the craft may actually have increased, but the gift has flown.   **B+**

The Kinks: *Sleepwalker* (Arista '77). Ray Davies's temporary abandonment of theatrical concepts may have ruined his show, but it's freed him to write individually inspired songs again. It's also freed his band to play up to its capacity, which unfortunately falls midway between professional virtuosity

and amateur fun. Doubly unfortunate, at least half the songs are in a similar range. Recommended: "Jukebox Music" and "Full Moon."   **B−**

The Kinks: *Misfits* (Arista '78). Ray Davies hasn't put so many hummable melodies in one place since *Everybody's in Showbiz* (just to make sure, he's put a couple of them both places), and the lyrics evince renewed thought and craft. All of which makes his congenital parochialism and ressentiment seem surprisingly fresh and vivid. Dismaying: "Black Messiah — Enoch Powell would be proud.   **B**

The Kinks: *Low Budget* (Arista '79). Ray Davies hasn't rocked so hard since his power-chord days in the mid-'60s, and often he shores up sloppy burlesques like the title cut just by trying harder. But I don't find his poormouthing crassness — the fusion of syndrum and macho-flash guitar on "Superman" or the schlock hooks from "Jumping Jack Flash" and "Jesus Christ Superstar" — at all charming, and anyone who detects irony in "Catch Me Now I'm Falling," his threnody for "Captain America," is too worried about the ayatollah or the Russkies to think straight. With his ceaseless whining about strikes and shortages, the plight of millionaires and the cruelty of prostitutes, Davies has turned into the voice of the middle-class ressentiment he's always been a sucker for. No, Ray, you don't have to be a superman just to "survive." Especially if you've got a song catalogue.   **B−**

Kiss: *Dressed to Kill* (Casablanca '75). I feel schizy about this record. It rocks with a brutal, uncompromising force that's very impressive — sort of a slicked-down, tightened-up, heavied-out MC5 — and the songwriting is much improved from albums one and two. But the lyrics recall the liberal fantasy of rock concert as Nuremberg rally, equating sex with victimization in a display of male supremacism that glints with humor only at its cruelest — song titles like "Room

Service'' and ''Ladies in Waiting.'' In this context, the band's refusal to bare the faces that lie beneath the clown makeup becomes ominous, which may be just what they intend, though for the worst of reasons. You know damn well that if they didn't have both eyes on maximum commerciality they'd call themselves Blow Job. **B**

Kiss: *Alive* (Casablanca '75). There are those who regard this concert double as a de facto best-of that rescues such unacknowledged hard rock classics as ''Deuce'' and ''Strutter'' from the sludge. There are also those who regard it as the sludge. I fall into neither category — regret the drum solo, applaud ''Rock and Roll All Nite,'' and absorb the thunderousness of it all with bemused curiosity. The multimillion kids who are buying it don't fall into either category either. **B−**

Kiss: *Destroyer* (Casablanca '76). Like most hard (not heavy) groups wildly favored by young teens (cf. Alice Cooper, BTO), these guys have always rocked better than adults were willing to enjoy, but pro producer Bob Ezrin adds only bombast and melodrama. Their least interesting record. **C+**

Kiss: *Rock and Roll Over* (Casablanca '77). Those who dismiss them as unlistenable are still evading the issue: they write tough, catchy songs, and if they had a sly, Jagger-style singer they'd be a menace. But they aren't a menace, my wife and my sister assure me; the kids get off on the burlesque. Does this mean that when the cartoon hero in the platform shoes bellows an order to grab the rocket in his pocket all the twelve-year-olds are aware that this is a caricature of sex, and macho sex at that? Really, I'd like to know. But I'm not getting down on my knees to find out. **B−**

The Knack: *Get the Knack* (Capitol '79). Cognoscenti I know tend to couch their belief that this is the Anticlash in purely technical terms — harmonies treacly, production punched up, and so forth. Bullshit. I too find

them unattractive; if they felt this way about girls when they were unknowns, I shudder to think how they're reacting to groupies. But if they're less engaging musically than, say, the Scruffs, they have a lot more pop and power going for them than, say, the Real Kids. In other words, ''My Sharona'' is pretty good radio fare and let's hope ''She's So Selfish'' isn't the next single. Face it, this is a nasty time, and if the Stranglers are (or were, I hope) Sgt. Barry Sadler, these guys are only Freddie and the Dreamers. Docked a notch for clothes sense. **B−**

Gladys Knight & the Pips: *Greatest Hits* (Soul '70). Reviving ''The Nitty Gritty'' isn't a very good way of getting down there — nothing else here matches the shouting funk of ''Grapevine'' or ''End of Our Road,'' and her penchant for solid schmaltz obviously goes way back. But so does her genius for it. Annoyance: the tasteful but extraneous strings on the remakes of ''Every Beat of My Heart'' and ''Letter Full of Tears.'' **A−**

Gladys Knight & the Pips: *Neither One of Us* (Soul '72). If Knight is the golden mean of female soul, here she could use some burnishing. From the hits through the covers to the fillers she turns in a more than creditable job, but only on a slow version of ''For Once in My Life'' do you feel she couldn't go a little deeper. You'd think she was planning to leave her label. **B**

Gladys Knight & the Pips: *Imagination* (Buddah '73). Damn right ''Midnight Train to Georgia'' is a great single, but that's no reason to devote an album to the wit and wisdom of Jim Weatherly. Weatherly's stuff does beat out the two Pips showcases, though — a transparently hokey ''I Can See Clearly Now'' and a song about Granny's window designed to recall the one about Daddy's mouth. **B**

Gladys Knight & the Pips: *Claudine* (Buddah '74). Gladys Knight, always in thrall to her material, meets Curtis Mayfield, always a more undisciplined composer than is safe for such an undisciplined singer. Object: soundtrack. Result: Knight's most satisfying regular-release LP. It's a little skimpy (six songs plus one instrumental for just over thirty minutes), but given Mayfield's discursive propensities I'll withhold my complaints. **A−**

Gladys Knight & the Pips: *Knight Time* (Soul '74). Or does she transcend her material after all? This is a typical Motown exploitation, comprising two strong songs that should have been on *Neither One of Us* plus manufacturer's seconds. Yet her moral seriousness loses none of its weight, and there's something in her voice, a hurtful rough place the honey missed, that makes me want to listen through the humdrum dynamics of the tracks. **B−**

Gladys Knights & the Pips: *I Feel a Song* (Buddah '74). Compared to sisters like Aretha Franklin or Tina Turner, Knight is a moderate. Her way with a ballad is suspiciously smooth and direct, and her demeanor flirts with the respectable. But she always radiates a great singer's luminous conviction, and beneath the moderation she's very comfortable with her emotional extremities. When she adds a squeal or a grunt or a growl on this album, or holds back a tear, or turns a song into a trembling sigh, you know she means exactly what she isn't saying, and I've never heard her in better voice. The material is still a little flat, but it does take in uptempo soul and Dionne Warwick pop and Bill Withers funk and Bill Withers sentiment. Plus a version of "The Way We Were" that establishes her claim to a middle-class veneer in perpetuity. **B+**

Gladys Knight & the Pips: *Second Anniversary* (Buddah '75). Success of the Vegas/television sort does more than pollute the sensibility — it diverts one's attention from the grubby business of making records. It took two production teams to turn out this arrant product, a sure sign she knows something's wrong. Strongest cut: the Pips' (and Eugene McDaniels's) "Street Brother." **C+**

Gladys Knight & the Pips: *The Best of Gladys Knight & the Pips* (Buddah '76). The second disappointing album to include both "Midnight Train" and "Imagination" isn't at all bad, but it isn't what it says it is, either. **B+**

Gladys Knight: *Miss Gladys Knight* (Buddah '78). The most inconsistent of Gladys's albums with the Pips offered frequent glimmers of the soul in the middle of the road, but this solo shot is dreary. Not only is it markedly duller than *The One and Only . . . ,* supposedly her farewell to the Pips, but it's also less interesting than *Callin',* the second album by the Pips alone together. I assume producer Gary Klein arranged the switch from New York soul session guys, who have their moments, to El Lay schlock-pop session guys, who don't. So he and second-stringer Tony Macaulay (why he have three songs on this album? why he produce them?) will do as scapegoats. But is it their fault she says "little one" instead of "little wog" on a version of "Sail Away" in which the slave trader's gently humorous persona recalls the narrator of "Try to Remember"? And was it they who saddled her with the Jim Gilstrap Singers, soon to change their name to the Paps? Even her summer TV show was more fun than this. **C−**

Reggie Knighton: *Reggie Knighton* (Columbia '75). People who still believe Randy Newman's *Little Criminals* is a great record may be silly enough to think this is a good one. **C+**

Kokomo: *Kokomo* (Columbia '75). OK for a buncha Britons, sort of like the Hues Corporation grown nostalgic for its roots. How impressive you find that depends on what you think of the Hues Corporation. **C+**

Bonnie Koloc: *After All This Time* (Ovation '71). On the first side she wishes to combine Grace Slick's priestess with Joan Baez's bowdlerizing aesthete, and the strain is gruesome, especially on the high notes. On the second side she shows the makings of a likable folkie, especially on a blues she wrote herself. But the high notes are still a strain.   **C**

Bonnie Koloc: *Bonnie Koloc* (Ovation '73). After a bland follow-up complete with standard singer-songwriter covers, this fulfills perhaps half the promise of her more attractive pretensions. Her songs drift off into their own imagery, and I've caught her rhyming "warm" and "morn," but she has more to say about her father than Judy Collins and more to say about snakes than Alice Cooper. Her melodies are durable. And the cleanliness of her voice is saved from antisepsis by a cornfed openness that has Waterloo, Iowa, written all over it.   **B –**

Bonnie Koloc: *At Her Best* (Ovation '76). Her most consistent album to date is marred by chummy material (who is David Van Delinder and why did she release his "Roslyn" once much less twice?), half-assed commerciality (two is one too many Jim Croce songs), and dumb experiments (arting up Jackson Browne is carrying grass to Topanga). Fortunately, it's also marked by a goodly selection of her more consistent originals — the eighty-percenters is how I think of them — as well as the definitive version of "You're Gonna Love Yourself in the Morning" (not to mention Jim Croce's "Hard Way to Go"). But the real reason I continue to listen through the bad tries is that she sings the way Lily Tomlin has always wished she could.   **B –**

Bonnie Koloc: *Close-Up* (Epic '77). This is where Koloc's modest, unmistakable intelligence — and voice — finally make a record work. Not that the old problems don't persist — I disapprove of songs about silver stallions, I'm sick of "We Had It All," and I guarantee that Koloc's own unaccompanied "I'll Still Be Loving You" requires more camouflage than her Marxophone (?) coda. But the two Lil Green compositions that kick off side two vie with the originals and would

set the right tone even if they didn't. She does all right by Hank Snow's "Rhumba Boogie," too.   **B +**

Bonnie Koloc: *Wild and Recluse* (Epic '78). I still like Koloc's individualism — anybody who can sing Willie Dixon's "I Need More" like a B-movie schoolmarm who's sexy when she takes off her glasses is jake with me. But despite her ear for songs and her willingness to experiment (a wino provides running commentary on side two) she still gets boring. Maybe she should try contact lenses.   **B –**

Kongas: *Africanism* (Polydor '77). This Cerrone-Don Ray concept group is the most convincing rock-disco fusion to date. The 15:21-minute A side sustains the propulsion of "Gimme Some Lovin'" for twelve-and-a-half minutes longer than Spencer Davis and Stevie Winwood did, proving (despite one dumb pseudo-seduction interlude) that Stevie's organ roll did more to keep the song going than his famous vocal.   **B +**

Kongas: *Anikana-o* (Salsoul '78). Here we have the best tracks by a 1974 version of Kongas remixed and lengthened according to current disco usages. As any good Africanist would hope, the music depends more on congas and less on traps — the A side comprises some sixteen minutes of multipercussive dance music that moves steadily after a slow start. The B side is marred by a silly Eurorock voice going on about what ever happened to his world. Africanism, that's what.   **B**

Al Kooper: *A Possible Projection of the Future/Childhood's End* (Columbia '72). I know, what could be worse than a sci-fi concept album by Al Kooper, who hasn't been good for a whole LP since early electric Dylan? Only it's really solid, without one bad cut. Kooper's melodies stick to the ribs, and his lyrics are adequate or better, and does he do a job on some oldies from Curtis Mayfield and Smokey Robinson. Recommended.   **B +**

Alexis Korner: *Bootleg Him!* (Warner Bros. '72). The most authentic English blues rediscovery since Long John Baldry.   **C−**

Kraftwerk: *Autobahn* (Vertigo '75). The Iron Butterfly of uberrock —Mike Oldfield for unmitigated simpletons, sort of, and yet in my mitigated way I don't entirely disapprove. A melody or two worth hearing twice emanates from a machine determined to rule all music with a steel hand and some mylar, and the title track is longer than "In-a-Gadda-da-Vida" sans drum solo, with a lyric (trot provided) that should become the "What's Life? A magazine" of high school German classes all over America. Original grade: C plus   **B−**

Kraftwerk: *Trans-Europe Express* (Capitol '77). No, I have not shorted out or fallen in love with a cyborg. No, I do not like Kraftwerk's previous craft-work, *Radio-Activity,* which consists mostly of bleeps. But this shares with *Autobahn* a simple-minded air of mock-serious fascination with melody and repetition. Plus its textural effects sound like parodies by some cosmic schoolboy of every lush synthesizer surge that's ever stuck in your gullet — yet also work the way those surges are supposed to work. Plus the cover and sleeve photos are suitable for framing.   **A−**

Kraftwerk: *The Man-Machine* (Capitol '78). Only a curmudgeon could reject a group that synthesizes the innovations of *Environments* and David Seville & the Chipmunks, not to mention that it's better make-out (and dance) music.   **B+**

Kris   Kristofferson: *Kristofferson* (Monument '70). "Me and Bobby McGee" is only the beginning — this former Rhodes scholar is as deft and common as any songwriter in Nashville, though he's better off keeping it personal with a heartbreak song like "For the Good Times" than justifying his scruffy appearance with penny-ante satire like "Blame It on the Stones."

But he's the worst singer I've ever heard. It's not that he's off key — he has no relation to key. He also has no phrasing, no dynamics, no energy, no authority, no dramatic ability, and no control of the top two-thirds of his six-note range. Recommended to demo collectors. [Later on Columbia as *Me and Bobby McGee.*] Original grade: B minus.   **C**

Kris   Kristofferson: *The Silver Tongued Devil and I* (Monument '71). People say Kris is ruined by producer Fred Foster. Note, however, that the ruin isn't commercial but artistic — the man sells a lot better than Randy Newman. That's because Kris's pet paradox — hobo intellectual as Music Row hit man — almost demands extraneous strings. Ungainly, not to say dishonest.   **C−**

Kris Kristofferson: *Songs of Kristofferson* (Columbia '77). Over the years, Kristofferson has learned enough about acting to challenge George Burns as a crooner, although the veteran is stronger in the rebop department. It's conceivable he might even do somewhat better now on some of his great early songs. But not on this glorified repackage.   **C**

Kris Kristofferson and Rita Coolidge: *Breakaway* (Monument '74). The least embarrassing LP either has made in years is the testament of what just might be a fairly interesting marriage. The way you can tell is that the love songs about separation and temptation and compulsion and good-timing work out, while the ode to romantic serenity (could it be by the same Sherman brothers who occasionally soundtrack a Disney movie?) sounds like it was recorded at gunpoint.   **B−**

Kris & Rita: *Natural Act* (A&M '79). Before the days of Oscar nominations and Jackie Wilson atrocities, when these married hippies were striving to gain acceptance as a mainstream country duo, they actually went out of their way to be boring — the material on *Full Moon* was so damn acceptable you almost didn't notice it was there.

So I guess *Breakaway* was "transitional," because this time the outlaw superstar duo work with much sharper songs, including three from T-Bone Burnett and two (good ones) from Billy Swan. Unfortunately, K&R don't go out of their way to be interesting, and when you're as somnambulant as this pair, sharp songs aren't enough. **B**

Jim Kweskin: *Richard D. Herbruck Presents Jim Kweskin's America* (Reprise '71). I approve of any revitalization of American-democratic myth, but life in the Lyman Family must not be very good-timey. Though these great traditional songs sound undeniably idiosyncratic, they're idiosyncratic with the kind of ol'-folks-at-bay decrepitude you might expect fom people who believe God is a harmonica player. **B –**

Labelle: *Labelle* (Warner Bros. '71). I find this group's mystique mysterious. Unlike most girl groups they boast a lady-soul front woman, but so do the Sweet Inspirations. They can trade leads like the Temptations, but rarely bother. They have their own songwriter, but she hasn't written any good songs. And though I too prefer their style of upward mobility to the Supremes', it's mostly aura — a matter of costuming and melodrama. I like what they do with "Wild Horses" — maybe the way to save that overstated metaphor is to overstate it some more. But too often they change the beauty of the melody until it sounds just like an op-e-ra. Original grade: C minus. **C**

Labelle: *Moon Shadow* (Warner Bros. '72). Nine songs — six by Nona Hendryx, one by Sarah Dash, and one each by Peter Townshend and Cat Stevens. The latter two lead off each side. And are easily the pick of the record. Cat Stevens. **C**

Labelle: *Pressure Cookin'* (RCA Victor '73). This certainly is a drastic improvement, although because Nona Hendryx still has trouble writing discernible melodies it demands more concentration than it's worth. What's changed is the arrangements — the backing musicians, especially keyboard honcho Andre Lewis (although each of the others puts a mark on at least one cut), achieve a jazzy r&b that gives the voices (all of them) room to groove. Patti LaBelle pulls out all the stops dynamically, but she also puts

them back in — there's drama as well as declamation here — and on "Hollywood" and "Let Me See You in the Light" Hendryx gives her some lines. The covers don't hurt either — whoever had the idea of segueing from Thunderclap Newman to Gil Scott-Heron did justice to this noble group concept, and Stevie Wonder proved himself a true friend. **B**

Labelle: *Nightbirds* (Epic '74). Not all pretentious records are even difficult and many fewer are worth the trouble. This is both. In the past I've found myself unmoved by Patti LaBelle's high-nosed histrionics, but Allen Toussaint grounds her (and Nona and Sarah) in a funk that's just right, more modernistic and mechanical than he usually favors. And for once there are songs. Three of Nona Hendryx's four could be called tunes, Bob Crewe and Kenny Nolan's "Lady Marmalade" is great synthetic French-quarter raunch, and Toussaint's own "All Girl Band" is unautobiographical and more charming for it. **A−**

Labelle: *Chameleon* (Epic '76). Patti emotes from up on the roof, David Rubinson masterminds some heavy funk, and Nona climaxes each side with a motto — "Nobody seems to care when they've got their share of the pie" and "Going down to your river." You guess whether "pie" or "river" refers to pussy. **B−**

Ronnie Lane's Slim Chance: *Ronnie Lane's Slim Chance* (A&M '75). Whether moved by the propinquity of their own folk tradition or by some general attraction to the eccentric, English rockers are at ease with a sprightly sloppiness that is usually left to folkies in the U.S. — they know it's rarely enough to be "tight." On this solo debut Lane takes the Faces — not the Faces themselves, but their hang-loose playfulness — into the English countryside with saxophone, tambourines, an accordion, and a choir of communards. Whether undergoing his own reincarnation on "Stone" or coming on randy and rude in "Ain't No Lady," he sounds sweet and independent; he covers Fats Domino and Chuck Berry and "Brother Can You Spare a Dime." Luverly. **B+**

Nicolette Larson: *Nicolette* (Warner Bros. '78). I've liked this woman on record with Neil Young and on stage with Commander Cody, but her solo debut is the worst kind of backup-chick garbage, pure El Lay from its folk-pop production to its Sam Cooke desecration and J. D. Souther capper. Even the jumping Marvin Gaye remake fits the pattern — Angelenos in need of a little mobility always import it from Detroit. **C−**

Denise LaSalle: *Trapped by a Thing Called Love* (Westbound '72). LaSalle seems to be a songwriter first and a singer second, which may be why there's a certain professional anonymity about her soulful moods. But the voice is there — sensual, warm, even wise, ideal for Willie Mitchell's meditative Memphis funk. And because she's a pretty good songwriter, just about every one of these twelve tracks offers its professional pleasures. **B+**

Denise LaSalle: *On the Loose* (Westbound '73). This leads with the proud, ebullient, raunchy "A Man Size Job," which outromps even "Run and Tell That" on her debut, but after that things get quite nondescript — enjoyable except for the silly cover of "Harper Valley P.T.A.," but nothing for Aretha to get nervous about. And Aretha could use a good case of nerves. **B**

Denise LaSalle: *Here I Am Again* (Westbound '75). Not many country albums are crafted so carefully — LaSalle does one a year instead of two or three — but the similarities between Memphis and Nashville are striking here. I prefer her musical formula (despite strings from the accursed David Van De Pitte) to Billy Sherrill's, but she's not singer enough to make much of it. Her songs run the gamut from loss to infidelity to less complex sexual situations while Nashville's run the gamut from loss to infidelity to less complex emotional involvements. So what's the difference? It's that when LaSalle invites her lover to let his "imagination run wild," I believe he might think of something I wouldn't. **B**

Denise LaSalle: *Under the Influence* (ABC '78). In the wake of two bad tries for the big label, this perpetually promising, perpetually frustrating singer-songwriter rebounds a little, flattering Millie Jackson sincerely every step of the way. The bleh ballad is more than overbalanced by "Feet Don't Fail Me," a sorrowful, tellingly specific cheating song. But the self-production never finds a groove. Recommended to stubborn old souls. **B**

Latimore: *More More More Latimore* (Glades '74). After last year's covers of "Take Me to the Pilot," "So Much Love," and "For What It's Worth" I hoped I'd never run into the fellow again, but here he gets basic. His voice is too ordinary to put any of the three blues up with the Bland, King, or Mabon original. But he likes what he's singing so much that he doesn't have to go for the simulated high emotion of some fancy vocal embellishment — he just puts those lyrics across, intelligent and matter-of-fact, as if you've never heard them before, which maybe you haven't. **B+**

Latimore: *Latimore III* (Glades '75). Mixing Lou Rawls and Swamp Dogg in a soul-stud groove that climaxes on the fast side with his sympathetic impression of "a redneck in a soul band" and is softened on the (less impressive) slow side by a spirited but thoughtful rendition of "Ladies' Man," a song about not getting it up that's probably the best thing Oscar Brown Jr. ever wrote. Original grade: B. **B+**

Latimore: *It Ain't Where You Been* (Glades '76). Like Barry White, Latimore is the strong talkative type — never jabbering, never letting up on the line. Unlike Barry White, he sings with enough variety to keep the backing to five basic pieces. Like Barry White, he tends to repeat himself. **B−**

Latimore: *Dig a Little Deeper* (Glades '78). In seven solid, funk-rooted tunes this obdurate soul holdout portrays, in order, a long-suffering on-the-road monogamist, a stud on the prowl, a reluctant lay ("We got to hit it off before we get it on," he tells a "liberated woman"), a sentimental monogamist, a sex slave, a good lover (title tune), and a seducer of virgins (courtesy Rod Stewart). And convinces in all seven roles. Very impressive. But I don't believe I'll introduce him to my wife. **B+**

Led Zeppelin: *Led Zeppelin III* (Atlantic '70). If the great blues guitarists can make their instruments cry out like human voices, it's only fitting that Robert Plant should make his voice galvanize like an electric guitar. I've always approved theoretically of the formula that pits the untiring freak intensity of that voice against Jimmy Page's repeated low-register fuzz riffs, and here they really whip it into shape. Plant is overpowering even when Page goes to his acoustic, as he does to great effect on several surprisingly folky (not to mention folk bluesy) cuts. No drum solos, either. Heavy. Original grade: A minus. **B+**

Led Zeppelin: *Led Zeppelin IV* (Atlantic '71). More even than "Rock and Roll," which led me into the rest of the record (whose real title, as all adepts know, is signified by runes no Underwood can reproduce) months after I'd stupidly dismissed it, or "Stairway to Heaven," the platinum-plated album cut, I think the triumph here is "When the Levee Breaks." As if by sorcery, the quasi-parodic overstatement and oddly cerebral mood of Led Zep's blues recastings is at once transcended (that is, this really sounds like a blues), and apotheosized (that is, it has the grandeur of a symphonic crescendo) while John Bonham, as ham-handed as ever, pounds out a contrapuntal tattoo of heavy rhythm. As always, the band's medievalisms have their limits, but this is the definitive Led Zeppelin and hence heavy metal album. It proves that both are — or can be — very much a part of "Rock and Roll." Original grade: B. **A**

Led Zeppelin: *Houses of the Holy* (Atlantic '73). I could do without "No Quarter," a death march for a select troop of messenger-warriors, perhaps the band's road crew, that you can tell is serious because of the snow (when they're working up to big statements it only rains) and scary sound effects. But side two begins with two amazing, well, dance tracks — the transmogrified shuffle is actually called "Dancing Days," while "D'Yer Mak'er" is a reggae, or "reggae" — that go nicely with the James Brown tribute/parody/ripoff at the close of side one. Which is solid led, lurching in sprung rhythm through four tracks that might have been on *II*, *III*, or *IV*, or might not have been, as the case may be. **A−**

Led Zeppelin: *Physical Graffiti* (Swan Song '75). I suppose a group whose specialty is excess should be proud to emerge from a double-LP in one piece. But except on side one — comprising three-only-three Zep classics: "Houses of the Holy," "Trampled Under Foot," and the exotic "Kashmir" — they do disperse quite a bit, not into filler and throwaway ("Boogie with Stu" and "Black Country Woman" on side four are fab prefabs) but into wide tracks, misconceived opi, and so forth. Jimmy Page cuts it throughout, but after a while Robert Plant begins to grate — and I *like* him. Original grade: B. **B+**

Led Zeppelin: *Presence* (Swan Song '76). Originals and influentials they obviously are, but too often individual pieces of their unprecedented music aren't *necessary*. They didn't have time to get really silly here, so this is unusually consistent, but "Hots on for Nowhere" is as close as it comes to a commanding cut, and I prefer "Whole Lotta Love" and "Rock and Roll" and "Dancing Days." Nu? **B**

Led Zeppelin: *The Song Remains the Same* (Swan Song '76). List price: $11.98. Category: live double-LP masquerading as soundtrack album or vice versa. Full title: *The Song Goes on Forever but the Road Remains the Same.* **C+**

Led Zeppelin: *In Through the Out Door* (Swan Song '79). The tuneful synthesizer pomp on side two confirms my long-held belief that this is a real good art-rock band, and their title for the first ten minutes or so, "Carouselambra," suggests that they find this as humorous as I do. The lollapalooza hooks on the first side confirms the world's long-held belief that this is a real good hard rock band. Lax in the lyrics department, as usual, but their best since *Houses of the Holy*. **B+**

Arthur Lee: *Vindicator* (A&M '72). As the brains behind Love, the Los Angeles equivalent of the Velvet Underground in both critical and commercial clout, Lee majored in popsong and minored in instrumental excursions of unusual long-windedness. On this record his brush with Jimi at the time of *False Start* seems to have fused these two interests. At its worst — which is nowhere near as bad as the second side of *Da Capo* — Lee elaborates Jimi's vocal style while Charles Karp strives fruitlessly to keep up on guitar. At its best — which is nowhere near as amazing as the first side of *False Start* — he offers readymade blues-based popsongs of undeniable drive and charm. What tips the balance for me is the only phrase that stays in my mind: "Ooh what a dish, she smelled just like a fish." Jimi was too sweet ever to make his sexism that nasty. **B−**

Laura Lee: *Women's Love Rights* (Hot Wax '72). The title hit actually mentions "women's liberators and men sympathizers," a black-music first, and unlike "Respect," say, it lays out a critical analysis as well as asserting a prerogative. But the underlying if-you-can't-beat-'em passivity of this analysis comes clear in an amazing eight-minute version of "Since I Fell for You" ("You made me leave my happy home" and so forth) that says a lot more about Lee's real power than "Wedlock Is a Padlock." It's also worth noting that many of her most militant songs were written by one William Weatherspoon. How about a chorus of "You Don't Own Me," Ms. Lee? Original grade: B plus. **B**

Laura Lee: *Laura Lee* (Hot Wax '72). The original title was *Two Sides of Laura Lee*, which went the way of the "Empty Bed Blues" promised on the jacket but still sums up the idea: soften up that man-hating persona. It succeeds, too, with songs from the Honey Cone's production team that give Lee, a gritty singer who can't match the power of a Millie Jackson or the spunk of an Ann Peebles, a chance to show off the recitatives at which she excels — I'm especially fond of "At Last," where Lee falls for a nice boy. But the prize is on the "other" side — "Rip Off," the real follow-up to "Women's Love Rights," which I'll bet was boycotted by male program directors because it was about property as well as sex. **B+**

Laura Lee: *Love More Than Pride* (Chess '72). The title of this belated but opportune package from Lee's old label says it all — in her previous incarnation, she was a not-quite-great voice without a gimmick, just like so many of her sisters. For some reason, two minor hits from 1967 —"Wanted:

Lover, No Experience Necessary'' and ''Up Tight Good Man''— aren't included. Might give it a little more flair. Might push it over thirty minutes, too. Time: 27:30. **C+**

Laura Lee: *The Best of Laura Lee* (Hot Wax '73). Millie Jackson is touted as Lady Funk, but as of now she hasn't come up with an album nearly as satisfying as this unorthodox compilation, constructed on short notice from just two LPs, the second of which never charted. Lee's voice isn't as big as Jackson's, but she's got comparable breadth emotionally and timbrally as well as stronger material. Hard-assed on one side, winsome on the other, and let's hope she doesn't fall through the cracks. **A—**

Laura Lee: *I Can't Make It Alone* (Invictus '74). Lee shows a lot of singing skill here — without downplaying her natural rasp she achieves a gratifying fullness (even softness), and she knows how to put her range at the service of a song's drama. Now if only these songs had some drama — the best moment is a whispered ad lib in which Lee describes a seduction play-by-play. And the title concept is a disgrace — 180 degrees is too damn far to turn even if that is the way life comes out sometimes. **B—**

John Lennon: *Plastic Ono Band* (Apple '70). Of course the lyrics are often crude psychotherapeutic cliches. That's just the point, because they're also true, and John wants to make clear that right now truth is far more important than subtlety, taste, art, or anything else. At first the music sounds crude, too, stark and even perfunctory after the Beatles' free harmonies and double guitars. But the real music of the album inheres in the way John's greatest vocal performance, a complete tour of rock timbre from scream to whine, is modulated electronically — echoed, filtered, double-tracked, with two vocals sometimes emanating in a synthesis from between the speakers and sometimes dialectically separated. Which means that John is such a media

artist that even when he's fervently shedding personas and eschewing metaphor he knows, perhaps instinctively, that he communicates most effectively through technological masks and prisms. Original grade: A plus. **A**

John Lennon: *Imagine* (Apple '71). Primal goes pop — personal and useful. The title cut is both a hymn for the Movement and a love song for his wife, celebrating a Yokoism and a Marcusianism simultaneously, and ''Gimme Some Truth'' unites Lennon unmasked with the Lennon of Blunderland wordplay as it provides a rationale for ''Jealous Guy,'' which doesn't need one, and ''How Do You Sleep?,'' which may. ''Oh Yoko!'' is an instant folk song worthy of Rosie & the Originals and ''I Don't Want to Be a Soldier'' an instant folk extravaganza worthy of Phil Spector. ''It's So Hard'' is a blues. ''Crippled Inside,'' with its ''ironic'' good-time ricky-tick, is folk-rock in disguise. And the psychotherapeutically lugubrious ''How?'' is a question mark. **A**

John & Yoko/Plastic Ono Band: *Some Time in New York City* (Apple '72). Half caterwauling live weirdness with the Mothers of Invention, half tuneless topical rock songs with Elephant's Memory, this is where Lennon risks his charisma instead of investing it. I like its rawness and its basic goodheartedness, though J&Y's politics are frequently condescending. But if agitprop is one thing and wrong-headed agitprop another, agitprop that doesn't reach its intended audience is hardly a thing at all. **C**

John Lennon: *Mind Games* (Apple '73). A step in the right direction, but only a step. It sounds like outtakes from *Plastic Ono Band* and *Imagine,* which may not seem so bad but means that Lennon is falling back on ideas that have lost their freshness for him. Still, the single works and I hope he keeps on stepping. Favorite *Plastic Ono Band* outtake: ''One Day (at a Time).'' Favorite *Imagine* outtake: ''You Are Here.'' Original grade: B. **C+**

John Lennon: *Walls and Bridges* (Apple '74). These songs seem more felt than those on *Mind Games,* probably because they express personal pain rather than generalized optimism — "Bless You," to Yoko in someone else's arms, is a real leap. But the melodies are received, the accompaniment ordinary, and the singing disoriented. What can it be like for this ex-Beatle to trade harmonies with Elton John (who sings backup on "Surprise, Surprise," just as Lennon does on Elton's new single) in the inescapable knowledge that it's Elton who's doing *him* the favor? Original grade: C.   **B—**

John Lennon: *Rock 'n' Roll* (Apple '75). No doubt mysteries of emotional and rhythmic commitment (soul and groove) determine why this runs out of gas after "Be-Bop-a-Lula" and "Stand by Me." But it's also true that covering Gene Vincent and Ben E. King is considerably less perilous than covering Chuck Berry, Little Richard, and Fats Domino, whose songs follow. Which may be why "Ya Ya" (Lee Dorsey) and "Just Because" (Lloyd Price) work. Too bad he didn't go for more esoterica — this could have been another *Moondog Matinee.*   **B—**

John Lennon: *Shaved Fish* (Apple '75). Eleven shots in the dark from the weirdest major rock and roller of the early '70s. All the hits are here, many of them misses, with the number-one single as out of place as "Happy Xmas" and "Woman Is the Nigger of the World." Not just because it's bad, either — in retrospect, "Whatever Gets You Through the Night" and "Power to the People" sound equally bald, equally stupid. Not counting the two available on must-own albums, the only great cuts are "Instant Karma" (Lennon's best political song) and "#9 Dream" (catchier nonsense pop than McCartney's ever managed). So I don't play it much. But I'm sure glad it's on the shelf.   **B+**

Deke Leonard: *Iceberg* (United Artists '74). Released a year ago in England by this once and future Man, Leon-ard's solo debut is as raw as the folk-rock fairytales of ex-Man Malcolm Morley are tame, which is no doubt why UA put out Help Yourself and not Leonard here. Welsh metal, Dave Edmunds influence, with slide and echo and a nice colloquial terseness applied to such traditional Llanellian themes as agro and looking for a woman — but not quite songful enough, or cool enough, to get the hots for.   **B**

Deke Leonard: *Kamikaze* (United Artists '74). Man's main man has optimistic ideas about kamikaze — on the cover he's wearing a parachute in a tree. Almost like recording solo albums while you're in a group — nice to have a cushion.   **B—**

Jerry Lee Lewis: *The Best of Jerry Lee Lewis* (Smash '70). His drive, his timing, his offhand vocal power, his unmistakable boogie-plus piano, and his absolute confidence in the face of the void make Jerry Lee the quintessential rock and roller. He's a country artist out of geography and simple pique at rock's scared-shitless powers-that-be — it was the inadequacy of country's moralism, after all, that drove him to rockabilly. So though sheer talent insures that his readings of such great songs as "Another Place Another Time" and "She Even Woke Me Up to Say Goodbye" will be definitive, he doesn't sound at home goody-goodying "To Make Love Sweeter for You." Nor are all of his throwaways as startlingly on top of it as "One Has My Name (The Other Has My Heart)." And it's only when he can repent of his sins from the luxurious slime of the pit — on "What Made Milwaukee Famous" and "She Still Comes Around"— that he comes completely into his own. Time: 25:43.   **A—**

Jerry Lee Lewis: *Live at the International, Las Vegas* (Smash '70). Unlike *The Greatest Live Show on Earth,* a rock and roll set, this concentrates on "the country and western field of music." Jerry Lee runs through a few hits, calls upon Linda Gail for a couple of numbers, barely notices Tom T. Hall's "Ballad of Forty Dollars," and climaxes with "Flip, Flop, and Fly," originated by Joe Turner in the rhythm and blues field of music. Very fast, very arrogant, and I suppose very dispensable. But Jerry Lee throws Jerry Lee away a lot easier than I do. **B**

Jerry Lee Lewis: *The "Killer" Rocks On* (Mercury '72). Is Jerry Lee essaying a rock and roll revival because the country market is drying up for him or because he's never abandoned his dreams of world conquest? Only on "Don't Be Cruel" and "Chantilly Lace" does he sound triumphant, so it must be the former, which would be the only reason for him to cut this in Nashville anyway. Consequences of cutting in Nashville include a dippy chorus and the most egocentric version of "Walk a Mile in My Shoes" since the world began. Original grade: B plus. **B**

Jerry Lee Lewis: *The Session* (Mercury '73). The hardest-rocking Lewis album in years and the best London-meets-the-legend promotion since Howlin' Wolf's is amazingly consistent and authoritative — Lewis's patented hick cool always provides its satisfactions. But the impersonality of the no-gaffes two-disc supersession encourages his habit of expressing compassion and pain without any show of conviction. Of course, that's part of his charm. And you've gotta hear Rory Gallagher take Elmore James's part on "Whole Lotta Shakin'." **B+**

Jerry Lee Lewis: *The Best of Jerry Lee Lewis Volume II* (Mercury '76). Decadence, decadence. Even at his so-called best he parodies himself, and his delight in his own insincerity seems narrow, joyless. Jerry Kennedy, formerly a model of restraint, throws on choruses, strings, horns, flutes. The nadir is the lachrymose "Middle Age Crazy," about a forty-year-old "trying to prove that he still can." Forty-year-old Jerry Lee takes that one at about half the tempo of his manic "Sweet Georgia Brown," which together with

"Chantilly Lace" proves that he still can. **B−**

Jerry Lee Lewis: *Jerry Lee Lewis* (Elektra '79). In which Bones Howe and some crack studio pros (Hal Blaine, Charlie Burton) spend four days getting a hot album out of the Killer, his first since the 1973 London sessions (and more consistent, too). Think of it as autumnal rock and roll — undiminished tempos under fadeaway phrasing. Best tune: Bob Dylan's "Rita Mae," the simple rock and roll ditty Dylan's always wanted to write. **B+**

Jimmy Lewis: *Totally Involved* (Hotlanta '74). Fans of monopoly capital will please explain how this belated subclassic of hortatory soul could happen anywhere but on a Southern indie label. Lewis, a former Ray Charles factotum, sounds a lot like Joe Tex, and like both Tex and the Genius he has little use for "good taste." Especially historic is the opening track, in praise of women who are not fine. **B+**

Linda Lewis: *Lark* (Reprise '73). This convent-educated West Indian Londoner has a cute voice, all blithe and flighty, but she also wrote all twelve of these songs and produced herself at age twenty-two — beneath the little girl who likes the flowers in your toes there's a hard-headed woman who wouldn't care if your moon was in the dustbin. How hard you're willing to look for the woman — and thus enjoy the girl's deft, sprightly, folkish music — depends on your tolerance for or attraction to cute facades. Mine decreases every time I listen. Original grade: B plus. **B−**

Gordon Lightfoot: *Sundown* (Reprise '74). If Gordon had dyed his hair and taken a short course at the local car wash — you think he would have lasted a week? — he might have found a new career as Jim Croce II. Instead, he scored one of his periodic hit singles, thus securing his status as a weird new kind of purist: uncompromising proponent of commercial folk music. Two songs about the lure of the sea and one about urban despair go down as easy as the usual plaints about female perfidy. Chad lives? **B −**

Dennis Linde: *Under the Eye* (Monument '78). If Linde showed a shred of personality, this studio rockabilly put-together might be the catchy sleeper of the year. As it is, control-board adepts will no doubt find his triple-filtered singing and multitracked musicianship appropriate to his occasionally spacey themes. And I'll just reply that if either side lived up to its first two songs I wouldn't be niggling. **B +**

Lindisfarne: *Fog on the Tyne* (Elektra '72). This went number one in England — they're getting so stuck up over there they're even growing their own simpletons. The melodies throw a hook now and again, and the harmonies are tarter than CSNY's — that deep-seated modal tradition, y'know. But though they complain in "City Song" that "your music" — by which they mean our music, fellow urbanites — "it doesn't speak, it swears," their own lyrics aren't worth mumbling. Original grade: B minus. **C +**

Little Beaver: *Party Down* (Cat '74). The great T.K. guitarist (ne Willie Hale) has a problem when he sings, which is that he can't. Ruined last year's blues album, but somehow it doesn't get in the way of this dance-groove item. The lyrics sound as if they were made up on the spot by somebody with a lot of common sense, and Beaver talks that talk as he goes about his work, which is seeing to the aforementioned groove. **B +**

Little Feat: *Little Feat* (Warner Bros. '70). Lots of "tight" groups are influenced by the Band these days, but these guys could almost pass for them.

The sensibility is freakier ("Strawberry Flats" is a weary state-of-the-counterculture song, like Mother Earth's "Then I'll Be Moving On"), and there are shades of the country Stones ("Truck Stop Girl" is a more empathetic "Dead Flowers") as well as a convincing Howlin' Wolf imitation. But the dark instrumental interweave and pained vocals are right off *Music from Big Pink*. And I've always admired that album from a distance. Original grade: B plus. **B**

Little Feat: *Sailin' Shoes* (Warner Bros. '72). The first song on side one is about memory loss through marijuana, the first song on side two about cocaine cruising. I mention this because there must be some reason why this substantial but quite mortal American-mythos band hasn't changed my life when they inspire so many others to John-the-Baptist imitations, and dope may be it. They get over on "Teenage Nervous Breakdown," which lives up to my odd belief that rock and roll ought to be fast. Favorite line: "I'm gonna boogie my scruples away." **B +**

Little Feat: *Dixie Chicken* (Warner Bros. '73). The problem with Lowell George isn't so much that he doesn't write good songs as that he doesn't write great ones. He's immersed in blues — it's his idiom. But his own boast to the contrary, "eloquent profanity" doesn't come easy to him, and it should — in a real blues artist, the secret of a simple trope like "Two Trains" is that it seems spontaneous and conventional both at once, while George's clenched throat and staggering slide bear witness to his creative effort. None of which is to say that these aren't *good* songs — when George finds the right trope (or when Bill Payne finds a piano part like the one that hooks the title cut) the strain is part of the fun. **B +**

Little Feat: *Feats Don't Fail Me Now* (Warner Bros. '74). So immersed are they in boogie tradition that they wrote a bunch of touring songs while breaking up. Good ones, of course, but I expect more of the thinking man's bar band than rock and roll doctors, American cities, and the lure of the road. Extra added distraction: a remake of "Tripe Face Boogie" designed for Sam Clayton's pulsating congas and Bill Payne's distended organ. Original grade: B minus. **B**

Little Feat: *The Last Record Album* (Warner Bros. '75). It's no surprise that as they run out of things to say — all this adds to our insight into interpersonals is a few turns of phrase — they figure out artier ways of saying them. In fact, it's a bore. I'd recommend "Long Distance Love" to Wilson Pickett, though. **B –**

Little Feat: *Time Loves a Hero* (Warner Bros. '77). Okay, so they're not a rock band or even a boogie band anymore — they're a funk band, praising the gods of rhythm for their black bassist and conga player. But neither Ken Gradney nor Sam Clayton could make the grade in P-Funk or the Crusaders or the Meters, and that's not even mentioning Bill Payne's synthesizers, which recall bad Rufus. And they still go through the motions of writing songs, the wordy kind that get in the way of the beat. In the end, though, that's what saves this — "Old Folks Boogie" beats anything on the last two albums, "Time Loves a Hero" tries, and "Rocket in My Pocket" is a Lowell George readymade like you didn't think he had in him anymore. **B**

Little Feat: *Down on the Farm* (Warner Bros. '79). Not a bad Doobie Brothers parody, but the harmonies were better last time and the laugh lines are in short supply. Might be funnier if they targeted the Doobies '79 rather than the Doobies '75. **C +**

Little Richard: *The Rill Thing* (Reprise '70). Little Richard produced this alleged comeback in Muscle Shoals. He also wrote most of the songs, including the "hit," "Freedom Blues" ("Tutti Frutti" it ain't), and the title track, a slow ten-minute funk instrumental on which he doesn't even

seem to play piano (very rill). I continue to value his singing. Best compositions:"Lovesick Blues" and "I Saw Her Standing There." **C +**

Little River Band: *Sleeper Catcher* (Harvest '78). From most rock bands I'd welcome a song like "Reminiscing," written from the vantage of an old Glenn Miller fan. It would be a sign of outreach. But from these adult contemporaries it's just an attempt to broaden their demographic. **C –**

Live at CBGB's (Atlantic '76). I know these are Our Bands (all eight of them?) and that none of them has ever recorded before. This collection still ain't *Beserkley Chartbusters*. It's still a live double-LP; the arrangements and recording still tend toward the half-assed; the programming is still so erratic that only side one is wholly tolerable; the groups are still so erratic that only Tuff Darts can advance to Studio without pausing at Stop and paying dues well in excess of $200. **B –**

Live at the Rat (Rat '77). Boston's answer to *Live at CBGB's* continues the traditionalism of a folkie bastion whose hit rock acts — Geils, Aerosmith, Eponym — have been positively proud of their unoriginality. From Susan and Thundertrain, ready to go heavy if somebody'll buy them the amps, to the British-invasion tributes of Sass, the Boize, and (the sassiest boize in the bunch) the Real Kids, this wave isn't new. And nobody's gonna catch it. Faves: Willie Alexander's "Pop Tune," Third Rail's "Bad Ass Bruce," and two two-minute ravers by DMZ that ought to be covered by the Radiators from Space. **C +**

Living Chicago Blues Volume I (Alligator '79). A problem with the three-artists-per-disc, four-cuts-per-artist format of this estimable series is that it splits one artist per disc between two sides, requiring him to meld with both of the others. Fortunately, the great dirty mean of Eddie Shaw seems made for such journeywork, linking the gutbucket soul of Jimmy Johnson, certainly the most exciting singer of the nine, and Left-Hand Frank's righthand-in-the-Delta primitivism. Which suggests that the distance between Johnson's pop ambitions (Bette Midler beat him to one of these songs) and Frank's rural idiosyncrasy isn't as great as might appear, because both are irreducibly sexual and Southern. An advantage of the format is that you can buy one disc at a time. Get my drift? **A−**

Living Chicago Blues Volume II Alligator '79). Sad to say, the music that gets split up here is the sharp spillover guitar and tongue-twisted projection of double-threat Magic Slim. Carey Bell may be a fine harp player (with harp players I find it difficult to care), but vocally he's even more undistinguished than his mentor, Little Walter. And none of the rowdy hyperactivity of Big Moose Walker's piano carries over to his singing. **B**

Living Chicago Blues Volume III (Alligator '79). Since Alligator has just released a whole album of Lonnie Brooks, I'm sure the volumes aren't supposed to be numbered in order of quality. But they might as well be. Brooks does a lot less for Texas-Louisiana than Jimmy Johnson does for Memphis, Pinetop Perkins is a Muddy Waters sideman for good reason, and despite "Berlin Wall" I'll wait a year or two on the Sons of the Blues. **B−**

Richard Lloyd: *Alchemy* (Elektra '79). Lloyd really has his pop down, and this record never fails to cheer me when it comes on — the songwriting and guitar textures are consistently tuneful and affecting. I don't mind that he always sings off-key, either — part of the charm of his pop is how loose it is. But the voice is so wacked-out that even if you'd never seen Lloyd lurching around a stage or matching magic with Tom Verlaine you'd sense that where for the Shoes or the Beat teen romance is a formal stricture, for him

it's an evasion — he's just not telling us what he knows. **B+**

Meat Loaf: *Bat Out of Hell* (Epic '78). Here's where the pimple comes to a head — if this isn't adolescent angst in its death throes, then Buddy Holly lived his sweet, unselfconscious life in vain. The lyrics offer wit amid the overblown pop-myth images of heat and power (will "lyric-sheet verse" soon turn into the macho converse of "greeting-card verse"?) and the music pulls out the stops quite knowingly (will Phil Spector soon be remembered as the Rachmaninoff of rock and roll?). Occasionally it seems that horrified, contemptuous laughter is exactly the reaction this production team intends, and it's even possible that two percent of the audience will get the joke. But the basic effect is grotesquely grandiose. Bruce Springsteen, beware — this is what you've wrought, and it could happen to you. **C−**

Robert Jr. Lockwood: *Does 12* (Trix '77). Lovers of urban blues will cherish this record by Robert Johnson's self-designated heir. It even boasts some adventurously progressive saxophone and twelve-string stylings that do no violence to a notoriously intransigent genre. But Lockwood is an undistinguished vocal interpreter, and only one of his originals — the imperturbable "Selfish Ways" — is worthy of interpretation itself. **B**

Nils Lofgren: *Nils Lofgren* (A&M '75). Lofgren has apparently regained his prodigious gift for the hook, and most of these songs catch and hold. But his visionary flash has dimmed. Somehow I expect more of this always-the-best-man never-the-popstar than a concept which demands devotion from his various women on one side while declaring devotion to his career on the other. **B+**

Nils Lofgren: *Cry Tough* (A&M '76). This one makes me feel shitty. Epic could never break his best stuff and has now topped off the disservice by discontinuing his albums. Meanwhile, over at A&M, Nils begins to sound like a professional next-big-thing, the surprise of his lyrics reduced to a turn or two and his gift for pop melody subsumed by his gift for the one-man raveup. Crying tough is playing tough, not being tough, and there was always more than toughness to Nils anyway. **B−**

Nils Lofgren: *I Came to Dance* (A&M '77). In which the aging prodigy flirts with hackdom and almost scores. He still makes killer licks sound easy, although the melodies are drying up fast, and despite an ominous piece of Inspirational Verse — "I'll play guitar all night and day, just don't ask me to think" — and a road song that sounds like the first of a series, there's more ambitious lyric-writing here than on either of the two previous A&M LPs. Thing is, except for "Happy Ending Kids" and a sly ditty about eating pussy, the lyrics don't work; whether "Jealous Gun" is straight anti-hunting propaganda or an allegory about who knows what, its language is stillborn and its pretensions annoying. **C**

Nils Lofgren: *Nils* (A&M '79). If Lofgren's early mini-Western, "Rusty Gun," was the modestly laconic offering of an up-and-comer who remembered, then "No Mercy," the boxing melodrama now getting airplay, is the rodomontade of a shoulda-been-a-contender. I bet cocomposer Lou Reed wrote the best line, but Nils sings it with indubitable bitterness: "I thought you were being ironic when you ripped your jeans." **C+**

Kenny Loggins: *Keep the Fire* (Columbia '79). I used to think Kenny had no sense of rhythm, but his problems were actually less severe — he just couldn't rock. This Tom Dowd-produced Doobie-disco job swings just like Jesse Colin Young. And if you think it isn't Doobie-disco, tell me why the one great song on the record was written with Michael McDonald. "This Is It," it's called, and it is. **C+**

Kenny Loggins with Jim Messina: *Sittin' In* (Columbia '71). This session is where engineer-producer Messina was supposed to escape group life, but no such luck. Despite the transcendent melody of "Danny's Song," Loggins makes like Richie Furay only squarer, and this sounds like more Poco-style happy-happy. Even when it's "serious." Original grade: C plus. **C**

Loggins & Messina: *The Best of Friends* (Columbia '76). I suppose this compilation deserves points for hummability and getting it over with — eight of the ten songs are from the first two albums, so it's about time — but there's just too much to forgive. The memory of K. clapping his hands like a seal while exhorting a Cheech & Chong crowd to "boogie." The memory of FM programmers offering up "Your Mama Don't Dance" as a tribute to the uptempo demons. The note that compares that song to "Wilbur Harrison's version of 'Kansas City'" (it's Wilbert, you ignorami, and it sure ain't "Kansas City"). And especially the note that connects the even limper "My Music" to "the simplicity of the early Chuck Berry days." The nerve. Chuck Berry had genius, energy, soul, spunk, wit, irreverence, brains, urgency, a good beat, a criminal record, a number-one record, brown skin, a pompadour, and a duckwalk. All they've got is a million dollars — or less, I hope. **C+**

Roy Loney & the Phantom Movers: *Roy Loney & the Phantom Movers* (Solid Smoke '79). Loney still writes fun songs, but he forces the music, which is no fun at all. The Flamin' Groovies, meanwhile, play it so loose they damn near fall apart. Ahh, synthesis. **B−**

The Lost Gonzo Band: *The Lost Gonzo Band* (MCA '75). Jerry Jeff Walker's backup band transcends its own roots to offer the best evidence to date for Austin's rep as the last refuge of the hippie visionary. The record will probably stand as the best by a new group this year; side one is virtually unflawed; and Gary Nunn's "Money" reminds me of Peter Townshend's "Tattoo" in its understated rock and roll eloquence.   **B+**

Louie and the Lovers: *Rise* (Epic '70). Doug Sahm produced these four young Chicanos from Salinas, and they share his uncomplicated commitment to the pleasure of making music with a good beat. Even more than Sahm, though, they're influenced by the ballroom — leader Louis Ortega's sincere, one-dimensional lyricism harks back to early Airplane and Dead, as does the band's flowing, literally laid-back 4/4. Good lyrics, too. Inspirational Verse: "Once you said you loved me baby/Now I cry for that one time."   **B+**

Love: *False Start* (Blue Thumb '70). Fired on the opening cut by some lead guitar from special guest Jimi Hendrix, the first side is new funk at its best: complex, carnal, and crazy. Arthur Lee has never sung so soulfully, and while new guitarist Gary Rowles ain't Hendrix, he's willing to fake it. Side two gets poppier, with fey moments that aren't up to what Lee has accomplished in that mode before. But since that's as much as anybody, big deal. Original grade: B plus.   **A−**

Love: *Reel to Real* (RSO '74). On side one the Jimi Hendrix tribute of (Arthur Lee's) *Vindicator* gives way to an Otis Redding, from simple songs to rhythmic gutturals, although Lee the ironic popmeister sticks his head in twice, which makes the naive optimism of "With a Little Energy" seem a little less one-dimensional. Different Lees contend for side two — Otis, Jimi, Arthur, the weirdo who thought of "Singing Cowboy," and sewer designer William DeVaughn, whose top-five hit from earlier this year Lee has the audacity to cover. Be thankful for what you've got indeed.   **B+**

Love Unlimited: *In Heat* (20th Century '74). Lush, charming, and powerful, this is the most tuneful way to feed a Barry White jones. I admit that the titles on side two go "I Needed You — You Were There," "I Belong to You," "I Love You So, Never Gonna Let You Go," and "Love's Theme," but Jerry Ragovoy's "Move Me No Mountain" sums up White's basic pitch better than White ever has (read that title again), and anyway, lyrics aren't the point. The point is the voices, which have taken on enough personality to be called archetypal as opposed to anonymous — sensitive, willing, and a little more credulous than is good for them. Time: 29:07.   **B+**

Lene Lovich: *Stateless* (Stiff/Epic '79). It took me half a year to get through my head what an original Lovich is. Women who know how to say when, while not unheard of in rock, tend to come on macho — tough mamas with hearts (and heads) as soft as Papa Hemingway's. But Lovich's goofy energy doesn't distract her from her feelings or damage her sex appeal or conceal a mawkish underside. And although it took an outsider to define her in a ditty ("Say When," which isn't on the import), Lovich does provide her own love song, which has integers in it.   **A−**

Andy Fairweather Low: *Spider Jiving* (A&M '74). In which the voice of (ta-ra) the Amen Corner rocks more convincingly than he ever did as an English-r&b teen throb and still somehow sounds laid-back. The secret is a rough-hewn spontaneity in which the guitar and bass that meet the Memphis Horns over an insistent but very unfunky 4/4 are both acoustic, in which Charlie McCoy plays hornpipe harp over oompah drums. The lean, direct, catchy, introspective lyrics work the same way; their substance — that is, their obsessive but unassuming speculation about man's fate — is bound up in their free use of verbatim borrowings from a common language. Apotheosis: the slyly hermeneutic "Dancing in the Dark,'' in which a discreet fatalism is shaped by courtly music-hall tune and elegant soft-shoe timing. Original grade: B plus. **A**

Andy Fairweather Low: *La Booga Rooga* (A&M '75). Low may be wide-eyed and legless, but I wouldn't compete with him over the long haul — he's got staying power. What he sees is often connected to the downs and ups of the biz, but because his metaphors are vernacular and his attack allusive his songs sound like the outcries of anyone who's ever felt outclassed, outcast, outranked, or outraged by the money boys. And although he's halfway to everything, he never whines or comes on as a misunderstood artist — just swallows it all but his pride. And then jumps up and turns around. Original grade: B plus. **A−**

Andy Fairweather Low: *Be Bop 'n' Holla* (A&M '77). Andy's up to his old tricks. With the help of some lilting Caribbean-style percussion, as infectious as Victoria II, he abandons the attack that's always put a hard edge on his cheerful rock and roll. The result is a tuneful, sexy album, and oh so frivolous — "Lighten Up" sounds like a theme song. But frivolity turns desperate when you listen hard; in the theme song, for instance, Andy identifies himself as a stranger, a slave, and a prisoner to his lonely grave. Such a joker, this boy — makes it sound like Rocky Raccoon had it coming to him. Original grade: A minus. **A**

Nick Lowe: *Pure Pop for Now People* (Columbia '78). This is an amazing pop tour-de-force demonstrating that if the music is cute enough the words can be any old non-cliche. Lowe's people cut off their right arms, castrate Castro, love the sound of breaking glass, roam with alligators in the heart of the city, and go to see the Bay City Rollers. But because the hooks cascade so deftly, I care about every one of them. As for Lowe, this Inspirational Verse: "She was a winner/Who became a doggie's dinner/She never meant that much to me." **A**

Nick Lowe: *Labour of Lust* (Columbia '79). The title is more than a (great) joke — this album is consciously carnal, replete with girls who come in doses, tits that won't quit, lumps in the pocket, and extensions that aren't Alexander Bell's invention. With Rockpile backing, it's also more straight-ahead than *Pure Pop*. This is nice — my favourite line is "I don't think it's funny no more" — but it does nothing to stop Lowe from falling into cliches like "Without Love," which ought to be funny and isn't. But then again on the other hand that's probably the point. **A**

L.T.D.: *Togetherness* (A&M '78). One thing you can figure about a funk band that gets me jiggling up and down to a song called "It's Time to Be Real": They must be real funky. Another thing you can figure is that their slow ones are unlikely to bring a tear to the eye or a chuckle to the lips. **B−**

Loretta Lynn: *Loretta Lynn Writes 'Em and Sings 'Em* (Decca '70). Owen Bradley steals a trick from Andrew Loog Oldham here even if he never heard of the fella — like *Flowers,* this is a "concept album" conceived largely to recycle old material, and like *Flowers* it works anyway. No cover filler or publishing tie-ins, just the continuing saga of a strong-willed woman committed to a male-defined world. In most of these pungently colloquial songs (punch line of "You Wanna Give Me a Lift": "But this ole gal ain't goin' that far"), Lynn is either boasting or telling somebody off, and even when she's addressing herself to a woman, what's got her excited is a man — *her* man, for better or (usually) worse. **A−**

Loretta Lynn: *I Wanna Be Free* (Decca '71). Like any country workhorse, Lynn customarily pads her three or four albums a year with the popular songs of the day. Here the unadorned sexuality of "Help Me Make It Through the Night" and the white gospel roots of "Put Your Hand in the

Hand" prove that for a great natural singer remakes needn't be a waste. But then there's "Rose Garden." And "Me and Bobby McGee." **B**

Loretta Lynn: *One's on the Way* (Decca '72). Lynn projects total empathy for the protagonist of the title song, a Topeka housewife who knows about women's oppression firsthand but regards "women's lib" as a glamorous media event, as distant as Liz's "million-dollar pact." An epochal two-and-a-half minutes, class-conscious in the great country tradition, and I don't care if it was written by a man (Shel Silverstein) who also works for Johnny Cash, Dr. Hook, and *Playboy*. What follows is an ordinary country album done right, avoiding banal covers and providing auxiliary songs of consistent interest. Lynn's "L-O-V-E, Love," about talking dirty, is among the best, and there's not a bummer in the bunch. How many works of rock can you say that about these days? **B+**

Loretta Lynn: *Loretta Lynn's Greatest Hits Vol. II* (MCA '74). Each (short) side closes off with the obligatory domestic bromide. But the other nine songs — including six by the singer and two by Shel Silverstein — embody Lynn's notion of female liberation. This notion isn't very sisterly — the only other woman who appears here is headed for Fist City —but does break through the male-identified dead ends of a Tammy Wynette. If Loretta doesn't get her love rights, then she's gonna declare her independence, and even scarier for her man, she sounds like she's itching for an excuse. You know about funky? Well, then, call this spunky. Time: 26:29. **A−**

Loretta Lynn: *When the Tingle Becomes a Chill* (MCA '76). Lola Jean Dillon's title hit is the best song about frigidity, as we once called it, since the Velvet Underground's "Here She Comes Now," and gets Lynn's most listenable side in years off with a bang. Too bad "Daydreams About Night Things," the best song about having

the hots for your spouse since "Behind Closed Doors," wasn't chosen to soften the impact of "You Love You" and "All I Want from You (Is Away)" — "Leaning on Your Love," which got the nod instead, belongs on side two, which you needn't bother with, since nobody else did. **B**

Loretta Lynn: *I Remember Patsy* (MCA '77). I had hopes this might take its place beside one of my favorite country albums, *Lefty Frizzell Sings the Songs of Jimmie Rodgers*, but Patsy Cline's legacy is a lot narrower than Jimmie's, and Loretta's not quite the singer Frizzell was, either. At forty-one, her voice is thicker than Patsy's was when she died at thirty, and she's a lot more country, especially in her pronunciation — that slight lisp, and the way she distorts the vowels around "r" sounds. On the other hand, she has decent material to work with for once, and her "Why Can't He Be You" is a breathtaking object lesson in the connections between suffering and exaltation. Annoyance: the seven-minute spoken reminiscence that closes the album. Original grade: B. **B+**

Loretta Lynn and Conway Twitty: *The Very Best of Loretta and Conway* (MCA '79). While the midrange emotions here are projected likably enough, they're nowhere near as powerful as on George and Tammy's best-of, perhaps because L&C have never been a real-life couple. But this does offer fourteen virtually dudless tracks and includes four great ones — two blatantly comedic ("Spiders and Snakes" and the classic "You're the Reason Our Kids Are Ugly") and two shamelessly bathetic ("The Letter" and "As Soon as I Hang Up the Phone," both graced by long passages of recitative). Note billing order. **B+**

Lynyrd Skynyrd: *Pronounced Leh'-nerd Skin'-nerd* (Sounds of the South/MCA '73). Lacking both hippie roots and virtuosos, post-Allmanites like ZZ Top, Marshall Tucker, and Wet Willie become transcendently boring except when they get off a good song. But in this staunchly untranscendent band, lack of virtuosos is a virtue, because it inspires good songs, songs that often debunk good-old-boy shibboleths. Examples: "Poison Whiskey," "Mississippi Kid," and "Gimme Three Steps," where Ronnie Van Zant, instead of outwitting the dumb redneck the way onetime Dylan sideman Charlie Daniels does in "Uneasy Rider," just hightails it out of there. Savvy production from onetime Dylan sideman Al Kooper. Original grade: B plus.   **A**

Lynyrd Skynyrd: Second Helping (Sounds of the South/MCA '74). Great formula here. When it rocks, three guitarists and a keyboard player pile elementary riffs and feedback noises into dense combinations broken by preplanned solos, while at quieter moments the spare vocabulary of the best Southern folk music is evoked or just plain duplicated. And any suspicions that this substantial, tasteful band blew their best stuff on the first platter should fall in the wake of the first state song ever to make top ten, which will expose you to their infectious putdowns of rock businessmen, rock journalists, and heroin. Original grade: B minus.   **A −**

Lynyrd Skynyrd: Nuthin' Fancy (MCA '75). On the one hand, two or three cuts here sound like heavy-metal-under-funk — check out "Saturday Night Special," a real killer. But on the other, Ronnie Van Zant has never deployed his limited, husky baritone with such subtlety. Where Gregg Allman (to choose a purely random example) is always straight, shuttling his voice between languor and high emotion, Van Zant feints and dodges, sly one moment and sleepy the next, turning boastful or indignant or admonitory with the barest shifts in timbre. I mean, dumb he ain't.   **A −**

Lynyrd Skynyrd: Gimme Back My Bullets (MCA '76). Ronnie Van Zant may intend those bullets for "pencil pushers" (which means not only me but you, I'll bet) but that's no reason

to shoot him down. In fact, it's just the opposite — his attraction has always been the way he gets his unreconstructed say. Unfortunately, the music could use some Yankee calculation — from Al Kooper of Forest Hills, who I figure was good for two hooks per album, and Ed King of New Jersey, the guitarist turned born-againer whose guitar fills carried a lot more zing than three doodooing Honnicutts.   **B +**

Lynyrd Skynyrd: One More from the Road (MCA '76). Like I always say, live doubles function mostly as aural souvenirs for benighted concertgoers, and here's a band I never miss. Their hits rock, their covers sidle, and yahoo.   **A −**

Lynyrd Skynyrd: Street Survivors (MCA '77). Some rock deaths are irrelevant, while others make a kind of sense because the artists involved so obviously long to transcend (or escape) their own mortality. But for Ronnie Van Zant, life and mortality were the same thing — there was no way to embrace one without at least keeping company with the other. So it makes sense that "That Smell" is the smell of death, or that in "You Got That Right" Van Zant boasts that he'll never be found in an old folks' home. As with too many LPs by good road bands, each side here begins with two strong cuts and then winds down. The difference is that the two strong cuts are very strong and the weak ones gain presence with each listen. I'm not just being sentimental. I know road bands never make their best album the sixth time out, and I know Van Zant had his limits. But I mourn him not least because I suspect that he had more good music left in him than Bing and Elvis put together.   **A**

Lynyrd Skynyrd: Skynyrd's First and . . . Last (MCA '78). I'm glad to own this album, cut at Muscle Shoals in the pre-MCA days and overdubbed for possible release before the plane crash ended their career. I'm impressed by both the packaging (forty-four photos, many terrific) and John Swenson's notes (extensive, acute), and I like the music fine. But I don't think this is where I'll go to hear Skynyrd. Even if I wanted to disregard the two song-poems by long-departed drummer-vocalist Ricky Medlocke and the less than essential alternate version of "Things Goin' On," I expect more from Skynyrd than good white funk and second-rate message songs. And "Was I Right or Wrong" ain't it.   **B**

Lynyrd Skynyrd Band: *Gold and Platinum* (MCA '79). Because Ronnie Van Zant wasn't quite an infallible songwriter, Lynyrd Skynyrd was a great band that never made a wholly undeniable album, but try saying no to this compilation and it'll loosen your bicuspids. It's not fair, really — everybody who was dumb enough to dismiss them as another pack of redneck boogie freaks now gets to catch up. Though I can hope that when they do they'll be consumed with regret at what they missed. And I can't deny that when I want to hear Skynyrd this is what I'll put on.   **A**

M: *Pop Muzik* (Sire '79). Not only did the single break the new wave/disco barrier, it packed an instant wallop worthy of its title — you could hear it explode up the charts from moment of impact. All that's audible here is Robin Scott straining to duplicate his own lighthearted, worldly-wise electicism and exposing himself as a hopeless dilettante in the process. **C**

Mary Macgregor: *Torn Between Two Lovers* (Ariola America '77). I consider it significant that Peter Yarrow's first commercial success of the decade is an Olivia Newton-John substitute, albeit one who's willing to admit she fucks around. **C**

Machine: *Machine* (RCA Victor '79). "There but for the Grace of God Go I," with lyric entirely by August Darnell, is irresistible musically — still the disco disc of the year. The two tracks with lyrics partly by August Darnell are mildly arresting musically. And the other four are ordinary Isleys-influenced black pop/funk/rock. **B−**

Magazine: *Secondhand Daylight* (Virgin International '79). If it weren't for the two great singles — "Shot by Both Sides" (available on *Real Life,* now also released domestically) and "I Love You You Big Dummy" (a B-side Beefheart cover) — I'd be certain this was the most overrated band in new-wave Britain. And given the grandiose arrangements, ululating vocals, and published-poet lyrics, I'm pretty sure anyway. Back in the good old days we had a word for this kind of thing — pretentious. **C**

Cledus Maggard & the Citizen's Band: *The White Knight* (Mercury '76). Negatory, C. W. McCall. And back it down, Firesign Theatre. This tribute to the aural graffiti of the trucker's South is surrealism in everyday life for sure. **B+**

Taj Mahal: *The Real Thing* (Columbia '71). Taj's second straight two-album set is a live one, featuring sidemen from John Simon and John Hall to Kwasi DziDournu, four count-'em four tubas, and ten count-'em ten titles. Lots of fun, but as you might expect, things get very loose, especially when the tubists lay their burdens down. Time: 59:43. **B**

Taj Mahal: *Happy Just to Be Like I Am* (Columbia '71). This relaxed, witty survey of musical Afro-America is strongest when its compositions verge on interpretations. You hear the steel drums on "West Indian Revelation" and realize that the foreign lilt of "Chevrolet" is Caribbean. You hear "Black Spirit Boogie" and realize how many ways there are to keep an acoustic guitar solo interesting once you've acquired a natural sense of rhythm. And you hear "Oh Susanna" and realize it's back to where it once belonged. **B+**

Taj Mahal: *Sounder* (Columbia '72). The first soundtrack ever patterned after a field recording, this suite/

montage/succession of hums, moans, claps, and plucked fragments, all keyed to Lightnin' Hopkins's gorgeous gospel blues "Needed Time," is regarded by one trustworthy observer, Greil Marcus, as Taj's most eloquent music. But even Greil doesn't know anybody who agrees. I've always regarded field recordings as study aids myself. **C+**

Taj Mahal: *Recycling the Blues and Other Related Stuff* (Columbia '72). Heard in the wake of one of Taj's magic shows, the live side seemed an amusing simulation, but no more — the call-and-response goes on too long at 3:40. This might also be said of the 8:40 Spanish guitar (banjo?) solo on side two. The record earns its title, though — the Smithsonian ought to hire this man. Latest instrument: the Pointer Sisters. Original grade: A minus. **B**

Taj Mahal: *Ooh So Good 'n Blues* (Columbia '73). Taj hasn't used drums on a record since *Happy Just to Be Like I Am,* but he rocks so easy it took me till now to notice. On "Little Red Hen" he matches the Pointer Sisters strut for strut, and though that's the only great one he also renews "Dust My Broom" and "Frankie and Albert," earns a medal from fat liberation by reviving "Built for Comfort," and picks two time-honored tunes out of his National steel-bodied. In short, his best in years, only what experimental genie drives him to flaw every one of his albums? Here it's "Teacup's Jazzy Blues Tune," named after his jazz-loving brother-manager and featuring a virtually inaudible upright bass solo. Original grade: B plus. **A−**

Taj Mahal: *Mo' Roots* (Columbia '74). Taj hies to the West Indies, singing part of "Cajun Waltz" in French and part of "Why Did You Have to Desert Me?" in Spanish and translating "Blackjack Davy" into reggae. Reggae predominates, a natural extension of his sleepy, sun-warmed blues. But that doesn't mean you wouldn't rather hear the Slickers do "Johnny Too Bad." Original grade: B. **B+**

Taj Mahal: *Music Keeps Me Together* (Columbia '75). In which Taj doffs the mask of folklorist and reveals himself as a pop singer in a vaguely Caribbean-Brazilian mode. Vagueness — and worse, cuteness (what they do to Joseph Spence's "Roll, Turn, Spin") — provided by the Intergalactic Soul Messengers Band. Best cut: a folkloric Caribbeanizing of "Brown-Eyed Handsome Man." **C+**

Taj Mahal: *Satisfied 'n Tickled Too* (Columbia '76). Better the Intergalactic Soul Messengers Band, who improvise less and back more (though unfortunately they compose more too), than the East-West Connection Orchestra, who root Taj in Philadelphia on "Baby Love" (no, not that "Baby Love"). And better John Hurt's title tune and Taj's "Ain't Nobody's Business" than either. **B−**

Taj Mahal: *Music fuh Ya (Musica para Tu)* (Warner Bros. '76). This time the Caribbeanization adds steel drums and a pervasive calypso beat to the country-blues vocal phrasing and jazz-voiced horns, and finally an appropriate smoothness is achieved. The songs aren't much, but "Sailin' into Walker's Cay" cancels out his bass player's tedious "Curry," and if you have to listen easy you might as well relax with this. **B**

Taj Mahal: *Brothers* (Warner Bros. '77). Movie music for a film about George Jackson. It's even got a whole side of new songs. George Jackson would have seen through it. **C−**

Taj Mahal: *The Taj Mahal Anthology: Volume 1* (Columbia '77). About time somebody whittled Taj's experiments down to a few classics, and nice to hear a blues album by him, even one from '66–'71. He sure is more idiomatic than any of the white guys who were doing revivals back then. Though he uses drums and electric guitars most of the time, he doesn't pattern himself on the hard, shouting Chicago style of Muddy Waters and such intense Delta forebears as Robert Johnson — his singing is assertive yet relaxed, like an unmenacing Lightnin'

Hopkins with a healthy admixture of John Hurt. He does get too relaxed at times, even with "Six Days on the Road" to keep him alert. But this is where to begin. **A –**

Taj Mahal: *Evolution (the Most Recent)* (Warner Bros. '78). Things finally get going toward the end of side two with an insane Howlin' Wolf imitation and a calypso-blues trucking song complete with CB. But by then the flaccid fusions and anonymous collective compositions have turned the same steel drums which sounded so fresh on *Music fuh Ya* into an annoyance, like a combination cymbal wash and synthesizer on a bad disco record. **C+**

The Mahavishnu Orchestra with John McLaughlin: *The Inner Mounting Flame* (Columbia '71). He couldn't very well call it the John McLaughlin Lifetime, but that's what it is — with Billy Cobham a somewhat heavier Tony Williams, Rick Laird subbing for fellow Scot Jack Bruce, violinist Jerry Goodman and keyboard man Jan Hammer vainly filling in Khalid Yasin's organ textures, and McLaughlin back on electric guitar. The raveups aren't quite as intense as "Right On," though "Awakening" and "The Noonward Race" come close, but McLaughlin has a much clearer idea of how to make a rock band work than Williams. No vocals is the right idea — imagine what claptrap he'd come up with putting the beyond into words. To change pace he provides more of the noble, elemental themes he introduced on *Devotion* — my favorite is "The Dance of Maya," which breaks into a blues about halfway through. Mistake: "A Lotus on Irish Streams," a lyrical digression featuring Goodman, who ought to be watched closely at all times. **A**

Mahavishnu Orchestra: *Birds of Fire* (Columbia '73). In which the inner mounting flame is made flesh? Something like that. The celestial raveups are more self-possessed, the lyrical interludes less swoony, and the modal themes are as grand as ever. **A –**

Mahavishnu Orchestra: *Between Nothingness and Eternity* (Columbia '73). This live album is as rough as they're liable to get on record — I even hear a quote from "Sunshine of My Love," and the raveup on Jan Hammer's simple rock tune "Sister Andrea" is a ballbuster. Empty patches are inevitable but remarkably few. I'm beginning to wonder, though, how long McLaughlin can make his fusion work. Because this is jazz, McLaughlin and Cobham really do improvise (about the others I sometimes have my doubts). But because it's rock the notes and accents they play don't matter all that much — what communicates is the concept, which is mostly a matter of dynamics and which hasn't changed at all over three albums. Not that the improvisations count for nothing, or that striking new melodies — which are in short supply here — couldn't keep things interesting for quite a while. But it's not going to be automatic. Original grade: A minus. **B+**

Mahavishnu Orchestra: *Apocalypse* (Columbia '74). McLaughlin was right to decide to revamp. But hiring a vocalist, a string section, Michael Tilson-Thomas, and the London Symphony Orchestra isn't revamping. It's spiritual pride pure and simple — or else impure and complicated. **C**

Mahavishnu Orchestra: *Visions of the Emerald Beyond* (Columbia '75). Well, it's surprisingly funky, though not dirty-funky — dinky-funky, sort of. Michael Tilson-Thomas is nowhere to be perceived. It's got the usual words of wisdom and choirs of angels. But mostly it's just, er, green — electric green. **C+**

Mahavishnu Orchestra/John McLaughlin: *Inner Worlds* (Columbia '76). McLaughlin's return to a small group would seem overdue, but in fact he's right on time — trapped in the dead end he saw looming ahead of him way back in 1973, which is why he resorted to orchestrations in the first place. Yup, John's got himself a funk fusion group just like Jan Hammer and Billy Cobham. Stu Goldberg (come back, Jan) and Ralphe Armstrong (composer of "Planetary Citizen") are the sidemen, Narada Michael Walden the coauthor. Walden has better technical control of funk rhythms than a lot of jazz-oriented players, but he's squeamish about grease, and as a result his tunes tend to be cute even when they're good. McLaughlin, meanwhile, tends to be impressive even when he's repeating himself. But not that impressive.   **B−**

The Main Ingredient: *Greatest Hits* (RCA Victor '73). The Moments with class and/or a sense of moderation, which goes to show what's important in life. "Everybody Plays the Fool" is catchy black pop. Everything else they play isn't.   **C**

Mallard: *In a Different Climate* (Virgin '77). In case you ever wonder what happened to Captain Beefheart's Magic Band, a few of them joined up here, playing an electric music that recalls country blues (not to mention the Captain himself) in both the guttural density of its sound and the downhome surrealism of its lyrics. Hard to tell it's them only because Beefheart, that lovable eccentric, retains legal rights to their lovable stage names, thus compelling musicians he once induced to remain anonymous to revert to their unknown monikers.   **B**

Mama Lion: *Mama Lion* (Family Productions '72). Lynn Carey, who fronts this outfit, makes speed-screamers like Lydia Pense sound like the demi-Janises they wish they could be. Together with her producer, her bassist, and her guitarist, she has written the first rock song I've heard about sex between women, but if Lynn really dug her sisters so much she'd hire some female musicians. It would help. Continual intensity is supposed to communicate passion, but this doesn't even convey

lust, except for something boring, like success.   **D−**

The Mamas & the Papas: *People Like Us* (Dunhill '71). You can blame this on the march of history, stylistic evolution, what have you, but it's not just that we've changed — so have they. John Phillips now reserves his inspiration for his solo LP, where his heart is, and overall the level of simple effort is so sappy it's startling.   **C−**

Man: *Be Good to Yourself at Least Once a Day* (United Artists '72). Authenticated by one Jones (guitarist Micky) and one Williams (drummer Terry), this collective hails from Wales, where human life as we know it began eons ago. No great songs or great solos among these four tracks, but plenty of audible camaraderie — sounds like a cross between the Grateful Dead and the Quicksilver Messenger Service of eons ago, albeit steadier than either, which is too bad in the former case and a good thing in the latter. Upped a notch for historicity.   **B**

Man: *Slow Motion* (United Artists '74). Micky Jones's trebly runs against Deke Leonard's slashing slides are what twin guitar was invented for, and the band keeps getting tougher and catchier. Bet I know where their name originated, though — in an unusually oppressive sense of Woman-as-Other. One of 'Em even steals Deke's Fender. But there's hope — on the last song he blames himself for Her perfidy.   **B+**

Man: *Rhinos, Winos and Lunatics* (United Artists '74). Compounding once and future Iceberg Deke Leonard with two Help Yourselfers and the minimum quota of Williamses and Joneses, this is the best record to come out of San Francisco in quite a while, pretty impressive for a band that never saw the Golden Gate till after the thing was released. The chemistry's right, that's all — Leonard's eccentric dissonances and gullet-model wah-wah are sweetened by the Help Yourselfers and rolled with a steady rock by Williams and Jones. Unphilosophical but trenchant, short on tunes but chocked with riffs. Original grade: B minus. **B+**

Man: *The Welsh Connection* (MCA '76). In which the loose but significant jams of yore are transmuted into the sinuous but banal instrumentals of our own day. New keyboardist Phil Ryan doubles on philosopher's stone. **C+**

Melissa Manchester: *Melissa* (Arista '75). Manchester is very sexy in a barely disciplined, almost blowzy way — maybe a touch overexpressive, a little too liberal with her emotions. "I Got Eyes" is nice juicy fuck music and "Stevie's Wonder" the ultimate fan letter from someone who's found a new model of overexpressiveness. Both transcend the rest of the album, which in turn transcends the popped seams and middling Midlerizations of her first two LPs. **B+**

Melissa Manchester: *Better Days and Happy Endings* (Arista '76). The lyric zaniness that justified her defensive overstatement and good cheer last time proves a flimsy virtue, collapsing beneath the weight of her own success. Maybe she only does want to make us happy, but that should make us sad. **C−**

Melissa Manchester: *Melissa Manchester* (Arista '79). For a flukey moment there she was Bette Midler turning into Stevie Wonder, but that was long before her discovery by the Motion Picture Academy of Arts and Sciences. Now she's Shirley Bassey turning into Debby Boone. **C−**

The Mandrake Memorial: *Puzzle* (Poppy '70). This may just be one of those Complete Works that couldn't possibly be worse than any of its parts, like the Moody Blues' whatchamacallit, but just think — it might be another rock opera. Like Nirvana's *Amazing Story of Simon Simopath*. Or *The Moth Confesses*, by the Neon Philharmonic. **D**

Barbara Mandrell: *The Best of Barbara Mandrell* (Columbia '77). These minor early-'70s hits aren't what her admirers consider the best (that's coming out right now on Dot), but they do foreshadow her concept, in which she applies her limpid center and soft edges to such soul classics as "Show Me" and "Do Right Woman" and then sells them to the country audience — by upping the tempos, oddly enough. Hard to figure what's so innovative — didn't that Presley guy do something similar? And when he went to Vegas, he went on his own terms. **C+**

Barbara Mandrell: *The Best of Barbara Mandrell* (ABC '79). Barbara's real secret isn't that she's a country singer who listens to Shirley Brown. It's that she's a country singer who reads Helen Gurley Brown. **C+**

Mandrill: *The Best of Mandrill* (Polydor '75). I approve of their Latin-funk concept and I'm struck by their name — a mandrill is one mother of a baboon, and what do you think a mandrill might be? But their music has proven disappointingly tame. Even the big hit sequence on side one — "Fencewalk" to "Git It All" to "Hang Loose" — isn't exactly a rampage. Which is probably why the hits weren't go-rillas. **C+**

The Manhattan Transfer: *Coming Out* (Atlantic '76). As the memory of the way they demean their material onstage fades, I find I can admire and even enjoy their second album. The scatter-shot eclecticism of the first LP has been aimed — especially on side one, which I much prefer — at the kind of novelty tunes, rock and nonrock, that everyone who listened to pre-Beatles radio loved. The anonymity of the oldies Tim Hauser here unearths — it took me weeks to remember that Roy Hamilton (he of "Unchained Melody") came back with "Don't Let Go," I still can't place "Zindy Lou," and even the Motown remake is from Kim Weston — makes a case for the theory that pop music is a delightful but essentially inexpressive industrial product. But the newer songs, several of which are inexpressive only in spite of themselves, destroy the illusion.   **B**

Barry Manilow: *Live* (Arista '77). So rock and rollers can't stand him and what else is new? Well, two apercus. One, he is beyond the pale of New York chauvinism. And two, all the best commercials in his notorious "Very Strange Medley" were written by other composers, just like his hits.   **C−**

Herbie Mann: *Discotheque* (Atlantic '75). "You know what that is?" said Carola, looking up from her book in astonishment. "That's an easy-listening version of 'Pick Up the Pieces.' " Almost. The disco people seem to like this, but what do they know? After all, if the Chinese hordes were to overrun our nation, Herbie would be on the racks in a month with an LP called *Little Red Book,* and Chou might well like that one.   **D+**

Manfred Mann: *Chapter 3* (Polydor '70). This horn-dominated no-guitar band succumbs to the chief pitfall of the approach, achieving fullness by sacrificing spontaneity — or rather, the appearance of spontaneity. And Mike Hugg never seems to go above a whisper. Which may be why the songs he sings come back to haunt me sometimes.   **C+**

Manfred Mann's Earth Band: *Manfred Mann's Earth Band* (Polydor '72). Mann has always embraced rock and roll's art-commerce dichotomy with uncommon passion — he used to rave on about jazz to the fanmags in the "Doo Wah Diddy Diddy" days. This extraordinary cult record achieves the synthesis. Almost every song is defined by a hook that repeats over and over — the phrase "down on my knees" in "Please Mrs. Henry," the galvanizing guitar riff that runs through the almost-hit "Living Without You." But the doo-wah-diddy is continually threatened by an undercur-

rent of jazzy disintegration — the Cecil Taylor piano jangles that close "Jump Sturdy" or the discords that dominate the closing instrumental. The deliberately characterless vocal ensembles and square rhythms defy today's pseudo-soul norm, and Mann's songs — especially the brilliant "Part Time Man," about not getting a job after World War III — are indecisive and a little down. In short, the perfect corrective to the willful brightness of boogie optimism.   **A+**

Manfred Mann's Earth Band: *Glorified Magnified* (Polydor '72). Somebody here has been contemplating Mahavishnu — not just Manfred himself, but guitarist Mick Rogers, who generates transcendental density with more rockish ideas than any would-be jazzman would deem mete. More cerebral, more electronic, and more improvisational than the first Earth Band album — but without its pop or literary gratifications.   **B+**

Manfred Mann's Earth Band: *Get Your Rocks Off* (Polydor '73). In which my favorite cult band returns to the mordant good sense of its debut album and gives guitarist Mick Rogers room to make some unsynthesized noise. John Prine's "Pretty Good" is pretty great, and "Buddah" is the devotional song of the year, which is why it's spelled like the record label rather than the wise personage.   **A−**

Manfred Mann's Earth Band: *Solar Fire* (Polydor '74). As this group moves closer to the jazzy style it no doubt covets, it begins to show the corners of its rhythmic box. As well as minimal self-knowledge — . Mann's strength has always been song interpretation, after all. You think that's why this album has no writer's credits, not even for a familiar-sounding extravaganza called (here) "Father of Day, Father of Night"? I bet they wrote this silly stuff themselves. Ah, self-expression.   **C+**

Manfred Mann's Earth Band: *The Good Earth* (Warner Bros. '74). Manfred has learned just enough about the synthesizer to be dangerous, as his previous album proved, but at least this one, intended to be "more accessible," improves with listening. Two songs are homely enough to justify the name of this progressive-identified intragalactic conspiracy: "I'll Be There" and "Be Not Too Hard." **B−**

Manfred Mann's Earth Band: *Nightingales and Bombers* (Warner Bros. '75). Space doodlers at their worst, these guys bristle with intellectual energy at their best, setting the self-conscious funkiness of songwriters like Dr. John and Randy Newman in a formalistic, futuristic rock context. This time Bruce Springsteen and Joan Armatrading get the treatment, and the result is a surprisingly songful album, their most gratifying in two or three years. Just in time for Mick Rogers to take his guitar and go home. Guess he prefers doodling. Original grade: A minus.   **B+**

Manfred Mann's Earth Band: *The Roaring Silence* (Warner Bros. '76). Side two is so slavish in its heavy-metal pretensions that it sounds like a parody that doesn't come off. Which is why I'm inclined to give up on this band and describe side one as two worthy songs stretched out of shape on a synthesizer. If this is what the audience Mann has found on tour wants, he should retreat to the studio.   **C**

Michael Mantler: *Movies* (Watt '78). Great title for the ultimate soundtrack demo, utilizing the chops and sound of Larry Coryell, Tony Williams, Steve Swallow, and Carla Bley on bracing (if rather detached) compositions that unite the conventions of jazz group writing with those of twentieth-century European music. Sticks to the ribs.   **A−**

Diana Marcovitz: *Joie de Vivre!* (Kama Sutra '76). This woman suffers from Don Rickles's syndrome — when she gets serious, watch out for flying horseshit. But "The Colorado of Your Mind" ("Go shove it up, the toochas of your mind!") and "Drop Dead" are nasty and hilarious, the kind of songs

that are adjudged "offensive to our listeners" by sensitive (male) program directors. Martin Mull should have a tenth of her spirit.   **B−**

Mark-Almond: *Mark-Almond* (Blue Thumb '71). Despite a few jarringly saccharine choral bits and some dumb screeching, this mostly instrumental enterprise by John Mayall grads Jon Mark and Johnny Almond is indeed relaxing — so relaxing people are getting excited about it. That's what happens when you confuse enlightenment with more mundane contemplative states. Miles Davis's *In a Silent Way* on the one hand and Booker T.'s *Melting Pot* on the other are just as pleasant and offer both thrills and substance underneath. This offers neither. Original grade: B minus.   **C+**

John Mark: *Songs for a Friend* (Columbia '75). In which jazz-rock (what? you don't remember Mark-Almond, the supergroup?) expresses its deepest yearnings. The inner sleeve lists the names of forty-one string players and eleven businessmen, but the first side ends with the singer threatening to quit on his boss, a Mr. Rosenfeld. Mark's business manager is named Michael Rosenfeld. Subtitle: "Bird with a Broken Wing Suite."   **D−**

Bob Marley & the Wailers: *Natty Dread* (Island '75). You'd figure the loss of vocal and songwriting input from Peter Tosh and Bunny Livingston would be crippling, and reggae melodies being what they are that's the way I heard it at first. But the I-Threes pitch in like comrades rather than backup (can the Blackberries or the Sweet Inspirations claim the same?), and while the material has thinned out slightly I'm sure there are guys in Kingston who would kill for Marley's rejects. "No Woman, No Cry," a masterpiece on the order of "Trench Town Rock" or "I Shot the Sheriff," encourages him to bend and burr his sharp timbre until it's lyrical and incisive both at once. Lyrical and incisive — that's the combo. Original grade: B.   **A**

Bob Marley & the Wailers: *Rastaman Vibration* (Island '76). If side one makes it seem that reggae has turned into the rasta word for boogie — even to a Trenchtown tragedy recited with all the toughness of an imprecation against litter — the unimpassioned sweetness of most of side two sounds like a function of reflective distance, assured in its hard-won calm. Some of it's even better. The Haile Selassie speech recreated here as "War" is stump statesmanship renewed by a believer, and if the screams that open the second side don't curdle the corpuscles of the baldheads who are being screamed at, then dread is gone from the world.   **B+**

Bob Marley & the Wailers: *Live!* (Island '76). The rushed tempos take their toll in aura; "Trenchtown Rock" can be far more precise, painful, and ecstatic; like most live albums this relies on obvious material. But the material is also choice, unlike most live albums it's graced by distinct sound and economical arrangements, and the tempos force both singer and the band into moments of wild, unexpected intensity. I used to think *Natty Dread*'s "No Woman, No Cry" was definitive. Original grade: B.   **A−**

Bob Marley & the Wailers: *Exodus* (Island '77). As with so many black artists from this country, Marley's latest lyrics seem a little perfunctory, mixing vague politics of dubious depth with hackneyed romantic sentiments of dubious depth, and so what? Marley is not obliged to devote himself to propaganda. As with so many black artists from this country, the music is primary here, a message appropriate to his condition is conveyed by the unrushed rhythms and the way the sopranos share equally with the instruments and the new wariness of his phrasing and dynamics. Some of the cuts are flat, but if the O'Jays were to put five or six good ones on an LP — including two as striking as "Jam-

ming" and "So Much Things To Say" — we'd call it solid and enjoyable at least. That's what this is.   **B+**

Bob Marley & the Wailers: *Kaya* (Island '78). If this is MOR, it's MOR like good Steely Dan — MOR with a difference. Marley has sung with more apparent passion, it's true, but never more subtly, and his control of the shift in conception that began with *Exodus* is now absolute. He hasn't abandoned his apocalyptic vision — just found a day-to-day context for it, that's all. Original grade: B plus.   **A−**

Bob Marley & the Wailers: *Babylon by Bus* (Island '78). Here's another one of those live doubles I'd love to love — because I still think they're a great band when it's customary to put them down, and because the night I caught was magnificent. But I prefer the studio versions of every one of these songs (including "Punky Reggae Party," available as an import single). In other words, here's another one of those live doubles.   **B−**

Bob Marley & the Wailers: *Survival* (Island '79). It's great in theory that Marley is once again singing about oppression rather than escape, but in practice the album's most powerful political statement is the diagram of the slave ship on the cover and inner sleeve. There's a world of difference between songs of experience like "No Woman, No Cry" and songs of generalization like "So Much Trouble." And it's a difference that Marley and his musicians are too damn sophisticated to make the most of.   **B**

Bob Marley & the Wailers: See also the Wailers

The Marshall Tucker Band: *A New Life* (Capricorn '74). If I were from the South, I imagine I'd love this record, because it would be about me, which would be some kind of relief. Since I'm from New York, I have to complain about the almost complacent evenness of the band's aural landscape even as I take off from an occasional rill and dig into their heimische rural mysticism. **B**

The Marshall Tucker Band: *Greatest Hits* (Capricorn '78). I can distinguish Tucker from the other boogie bands because they favor cowboy hats, but danged if I can tell their albums apart. Country people know one cow from the next, too, but poor deracinated souls like me refuse to be bothered until A&P runs out of milk and r&r runs out of gimmicks. Toy Caldwell does write pretty good songs for a boogie man, though, about one a year to go with the album, and it's nice to have them all in one place. Pure boogie mythos, with lots of "Ramblin' " and "Searchin' for a Rainbow," though I'm pleased to report that there are more miners and, yes, cowboys here than gamblers, a reassuring token of social responsibility. I recommend this album. It's as near as you can get these days to hearing that old steam whistle blow. **A−**

Moon Martin: *Shots from a Cold Nightmare* (Capitol '78). Hook fiends will love these ten catchy little numbers, but me, I'm put off by Martin's pop drawl — "tender" or "excited," he's dispassionate in a way that doesn't suit his musical or lyrical directness. Or maybe it's just that eight songs about treacherous girls are four or five too many. **B**

Hirth Martinez: *Hirth from Earth* (Warner Bros. '75). Martinez sings like Dr. John out of breath from doing the samba; he is interested in UFOs, not really as stars to guide us but as occasions for metaphorical speculation. Unclassifiable funky objects of this sort used to appear at a rate of about a dozen a year; now they're down to three or four. Thank Robbie Robertson, who produced. **B+**

Hirth Martinez: *Big Bright Street* (Warner Bros. '77). I like a man whose dream of utopia goes "And they never grew old/And they never caught a cold," and I like this record. Hirth has learned to use his wizened voice

more forcefully without relinquishing any of the amateurism that is his special charm, and since John Simon is a relatively reticent and eccentric producer, the funky gloss that so often accrues to El Lay favorites never turns to glitz. **B+**

Carolyne Mas: *Carolyne Mas* (Mercury '79). Mas is one of those folksingers who likes "good" rock and roll so much that she feels honored to contribute kitsch poetry like "Snow" and kitsch pop like "Do You Believe I Love You" to the genre. So I was surprised to find myself enjoying four of these songs and getting off on two, "Sadie Says" and "Quote Goodbye Quote." Only you know what? Her guitarist, David Landau, turns out to have cocomposing credits on three songs here, and they just happen to be my three favorites. Wonder how he sings. **B−**

Mashmakhan: *Mashmakhan* (Epic '71). Gene Lees says: "I like Mashmakhan first of all because it swings. There is an enormous difference between swinging and pounding. Most rock music does the latter: it just jumps up and down in one place, with no sense of rhythmic propulsion. Sadly, people who dig it are incapable of hearing real swing when it occurs." And on and on, every word bought by Epic, concluding: "This is a hell of a good group." I dare you to spend money to decide which of us is right. **D**

Barbara Mason: *Love's the Thing* (Buddah '75). Not all soul singers bloom with age; some of them just get older. Ten years ago, young and foolish Barbara was cooing "Yes I'm Ready" as if the male seduction fantasy were her own, and it probably was. Now she sounds petulant, calculating, self-centered, not brave or sensitive enough to have a go at sisterhood nor bright enough to risk autonomy. Her sole commitment: fighting over men with other women. And she doesn't even have the guile to sheathe her whine.   **D+**

Dave Mason: *Alone Together* (Blue Thumb '70). I know, the real heavy in Traffic, great songwriter, poor Stevie is lost without him, Delaney & Bonnie on tour, rakka-rakka-rakka. I love "Feelin' Alright" myself. But I've never wondered for a second what it means, and only when the music is as elemental as "Feelin' Alright" can such questions be overlooked. I mean, songs have words. This is both complex and likable-to-catchy, with a unique light feel that begins with the way Mason doubles on acoustic and electric. But he doesn't have the poetic gift that might justify his withdrawal from "games of reason" in the immodestly entitled "Just a Song." Songs have words.   **B**

Dave Mason: *Headkeeper* (Blue Thumb '72). A year and a half and three abortive collaborations later — this guy is a love expert? — he's back on the market with five new studio songs and five old live ones, two from Traffic and three from *Alone Together*. He claims this is his label's idea. Should have stayed with Mama Cass. Or better still, brother Derek.   **C**

Dave Mason: *Dave Mason Is Alive* (Blue Thumb '73). The playing is predictable, the discography incredible: one new song, five from *Alone Together* (one also available in yet another live version on *Headkeeper*), and one from the Traffic days (ditto). With love from Blue Thumb Records, or so they claim.   **C−**

Dave Mason: *It's Like You Never Left* (Columbia '73). Once again Mason, whose music has all but disappeared amid corporate machinations over the past few years, can offer new material in finished studio versions, and I bet he's genuinely happy about it. The vague romantic dolor of his songs, after all, is a professional gimmick rather than a personal commitment, and the welcome-back-folks title probably expresses his very deepest feelings. But

for me it's like I was never here in the first place.   **C**

Dave Mason: *The Best of Dave Mason* (Blue Thumb '74). Pretty hard to do a nine-song compilation on a guy who recorded only sixteen songs for you, especially when the eight best — not counting two live remakes of old hits — are already on one album. Valiantly, Blue Thumb has selected one tune from *Dave Mason Is Alive* and four from *Headkeeper* in addition to the four good ones from guess where. And I bet it'll fool some people.   **C−**

Dave Mason: *Dave Mason at His Best* (ABC '75). Q: Given ABC/Blue Thumb's limited options, how much can this best-of differ from last year's? A: Well, it replaces "Walk to the Point" with the title tune from *Headkeeper*. Q: Why?   **D+**

Dave Mason: *Very Best of Dave Mason* (ABC '78). ABC has finally compiled a Dave Mason album as good as *Alone Together* by the simple expedient of omitting only the worst and longest of *Alone Together*'s eight songs (two of which have now appeared on five of Mason's six ABC/Blue Thumb albums), adding the two live Traffic-originated tracks, and sticking on one from *Headkeeper*. Engaging throughout, especially compared to his Columbia stuff, and true to Mason's place in history. With his gentle, multipercussive impetus, warm but basically characterless vocals, skillful hooks, and dippy lyrics, the man is the father of California rock-pop. Loggins & Messina, the Doobie Brothers, Pablo Cruise, every folkie who ever tried to swing a little, where would any of them be without Dave? Docked for wellspringing.   **B−**

Matching Mole: *Matching Mole's Little Red Record* (Columbia '73). On the band's debut LP, never released in the U.S., Robert Wyatt proved his right to transliterate the French *machine molle* with the quavery, exquisite "O Caroline," then guided the mostly instrumental album through what sounded in turn like Mahavishnu with a sense of humor, gently chaotic musique concrete, and the folk-rock of inspired amateurs. But here, in another installment of that endless soup opera *The Curse of the Art Rockers,* he changes keyboard players. The villain's name is Dave McRae, and I grant you he's not as highfalutin as Keith Emerson and Rick Wakeman — this is avant-garde fatuity, very modular and/or atmospheric. Guitarist Phil Miller tries his best with songs about God and the initiation of a lesbian virgin, and Wyatt plays mouth and drums. But both of them let McRae take the album away. **C+**

Matthews' Southern Comfort: *Matthews' Southern Comfort* (Decca '70). In which Ian Matthews splits from Fairport Convention, hires a (good) pedal steel player, and sings like an angel. As you know, angels keep their intelligence discreetly concealed — no one would suspect that the song that goes "Alright, everything's alright" bears the title "A Commercial Proposition," or that the drip who begs "Please Be My Friend" is off his rocker. The sobbing overlaid on Steve Barlby's "The Watch" does hint openly at irony. But what can the man who wrote "Colorado Springs Eternal" know from irony? **C+**

Matthews' Southern Comfort: *Second Spring* (Decca '70). Disappointed though I am by the folky localism cum chauvinism of recent Pentangle and Fairport, Matthews's mid-Atlantic compromise is worse. Basically, he's James Taylor — without the whine, which I'd consider a real improvement if I could imagine Taylor "interpreting" the bitter "Jinkson Johnson" so bright and upbeat it sounded like Poco. **C**

Matthews' Southern Comfort: *Later That Same Year* (Decca '71). This one really is pretty — except when guitarist Carl Barnwell gives him love letters to read (long-winded, too: "Sylvie" runs 6:08 and "For Melanie" 6:50), he selects very lissome

melodies. And no dumb lyrics, either. But when you're so single-minded about singing pretty it's hard to convince anyone you care what the words mean. **B−**

Ian Matthews: *Some Days You Eat the Bear, and Some Days the Bear Eats You* (Elektra '74). This is Matthews's eighth album of the decade (fifth solo), and though people still tell me he's deserving, I think he epitomizes the homogeneity of the new (country-rock) schlock. If the proof of his acuity is his covers of such songs as "Propinquity" and "Blue Blue Day" and "Da Doo Ron Ron" and (on this LP) "Ol' 55" and "Dirty Work" and "Do I Still Figure in Your Life" and "I Don't Wanna Talk About It," the proof of his soft edges is that the originals are always more idiosyncratic. **C+**

Max's Kansas City 1976 (Ram '76). If the musicians at CBGB like to pose as punks, then those at Max's wish they smelled like flowers of evil. This smells like week-old all-you-can-eat instead. Emcee Wayne County begins by naming seven mythic (or at least recognizable) New York bands on the title cut, but they're not the seven who follow. In ascending order: Cherry Vanilla (pickles and ice milk), Harry Toledo (Bert Cincinnati), Suicide (the two stooges), the John Collins Band (terrific name), Wayne County (cute lisp), the Fast (good for a laugh), and Pere Ubu. Pere Ubu actually evoke the Velvets, and I'd like to see them sometime. Unfortunately, they live in Cleveland. **C**

John Mayall: *Notice to Appear* (ABC '76). What a title — is that how he knew his trial by studio was due? Granted, the first side did almost convince me that Allen Toussaint could produce a seductive rock and roll album for *anybody* (except maybe James Cotton) (and Allen Toussaint). But then I listened to side two. **C+**

Curtis Mayfield: *Curtis* (Curtom '70). Initially, I distrusted these putatively middlebrow guides to black pride — "Miss Black America" indeed. But a lot of black people found them estimable, so I listened some more, and I'm glad. Since Mayfield is a more trustworthy talent than Isaac Hayes, I wasn't too surprised at the durability of the two long cuts — the percussion jam is as natural an extension of soul music (those Sunday handclaps) as the jazzish solo. What did surprise me was that the whole project seemed less and less middlebrow as I got to know it. Forget the harps — "Move On Up" is Mayfield's most explicit political song, "If There's a Hell Below We're All Gonna Go" revises the usual gospel pieties, and "Miss Black America" has its charms, too. Original grade: B. **B+**

Curtis Mayfield: *Roots* (Curtom '71). Last time he announced his lack of "concern or interest in astrology," so when the zodiac showed up as a packaging motif I began to get nostalgic for the Impressions. But though the vagueness that was *Curtis*'s chief flaw runs rampant musically ("Love to Keep You in My Mind" goes nowhere slowly) and lyrically ("Underground" is one long mixed metaphor), it's not all that bad — the relaxed, natural groove of Mayfield's falsetto and his rhythm section are both seductive. Only on the lead cuts, however — especially the heavy-breathing sex opus "Get Down"— does he sweep you off your feet. **B−**

Curtis Mayfield: *Super Fly* (Curtom '72). I'm no respecter of soundtracks, but I can count — this offers seven new songs (as many as his previous LP) plus two self-sustaining instrumentals. It's not epochal, but it comes close — maybe Mayfield writes tougher when the subject is imposed from outside than when he's free to work out of his own spacious head. Like the standard-setting "Freddie's Dead," these songs speak for (and to) the ghetto's victims rather than its achievers (cf. "The Other Side of Town," on *Curtis*), transmitting bleak lyrics through uncompromisingly vi-

vacious music. Message: both candor and rhythm are essential to our survival. **A−**

Curtis Mayfield: *Back to the World* (Curtom '73). It grieves me to report that I've listened to this ten times and can't remember a riff — except for the one that goes *soo*-perfly, I mean *few*-churshock **C**

Curtis Mayfield: *Sweet Exorcist* (Curtom '74). No, Curtis has not latched onto another lucrative soundtrack. In fact, he claims to have written his exorcist song (about a female sexorcist) before there was an exorcist movie. He could have avoided this confusion by calling the album "To Be Invisible" after its only interesting song, from the less lucrative *Claudine* soundtrack, where Gladys Knight sings it better than him. Mayfield's next lp: *The Great Ratsby*. **C**

Curtis Mayfield: *America Today* (Curtom '75). I had hoped the featureless doodling of his post- *Super Fly* albums just meant he was treading water while transferring from Viewlex to Warner Comm. Instead it appears that he was seeking new standards of incoherence. **D+**

Curtis Mayfield: *Give, Get, Take and Have* (Curtom '76). This meanders more than is conscionable, though Curtis has been drifting through the ozone for so long that you don't notice at first. (For orientation purposes, compare Gladys Knight's "Mr. Welfare Man.") But I am most pleased to report that the opener, "In My Arms Again," is the first top-notch song he's written for himself since "Super Fly," (somebody bad riffing on guitar — sounds like . . . Curtis Mayfield), and that the three that follow rock and roll. Original grade: B plus. **B**

Mac McAnally: *Mac McAnnally* (Ariola America '77). Although it does often sound pat, as folk stoicism will in a post-folk context, the first side comes across pretty outspoken for a Mississippi singer-songwriter with royalties in the bank — the heroine of one song is a rape victim who murders both assailant and judge after the latter lets off the former. Side two is Joe South. **B −**

Paul McCartney: *McCartney* (Apple '70). As self-indulgent as *Two Virgins* or *Music for the Lions,* yet marketed as pop, this struck me as a real cheat at first. But I find myself won over by its simulated offhandedness. Paul is so charming a melodist (and singer) that even though many of the songs are no more than snatches, fragments, ditties, they get across, like "Her Majesty" extended to two minutes. And though Paul's do-it-yourself instrumentals stumble now and then, the only one that winds up on its fundament is the percussion-based "Kreen-Akrore." Maybe Linda should take up the drums. She wouldn't be starting from any further back than hubby. Original grade: B plus. **B**

Paul and Linda McCartney: *Ram* (Apple '71). "Uncle Albert/Admiral Halsey" is a major annoyance. I tolerated McCartney's crotchets with the Beatles because his mates balanced them out; I enjoyed them mildly on *McCartney* because their scale was so modest; I enjoy them actively on "Monkberry Moon Delight" because it rocks and on "Smile Away" because it's vulgar and funny. But though nothing else here approaches the willful rhythm shifts and above-it-all silliness of the single, most of the songs are so lightweight they float away even as Paulie layers them down with caprices. If you're going to be eccentric, for goodness sake don't be pretentious about it. **C +**

Paul McCartney & Wings: *Red Rose Speedway* (Apple '73). Having decided that rock and roll was fun, a good enough idea within reason, he then decided that fun wasn't so much sex and humor and high spirits as aimless whimsy, and here he finally achieves disaster with that idea. His new love ballad meanders hopelessly where "Yesterday" shifted enticingly, and his screaming Little Richard tribute now sounds like Dicky Do and the Don'ts. Quite possibly the worst album ever made by a rock and roller of the first rank — unless David Crosby counts. **D +**

Paul McCartney: *Band on the Run* (Apple '73). I originally underrated what many consider McCartney's definitive post-Beatles statement, but not as much as its admirers overrate it. Pop masterpiece? This? Sure it's a relief after the vagaries of *Wild Life* and *Red Rose Speedway,* and most of side one passes tunefully enough — "Let Me Roll It" might be an answer to "I Want You (She's So Heavy)" and "Jet" is indeed more "fun" than "Uncle Albert/Admiral Halsey." But beyond those two the *high points* are the title track, about the oppression of rock musicians by cannabis-crazed bureaucrats, and the Afro-soul intro to "Mamunia," appropriated from relatives of the Nigerian children who posed for the inner sleeve with Sah and helpmates. Original grade: C minus. **C +**

Paul McCartney: See also Wings

Mary McCaslin: *Way Out West* (Philo '74). Without self-dramatization — she favors plain melodies and commonplace imagery and her singing is gamely unhistrionic — this woman explores Joni Mitchell's territory with equal intelligence, more charm, and no drums. Her album is a rough song cycle in which she responds to the footloose incorrigibility of the musicians she loves by getting in a car with a guitar herself — without romanticizing the process. **A −**

Mary McCaslin: *Prairie in the Sky* (Philo '76). I consider it just that the most convincing cowboy-based music in years should come from a woman who starts off with this request: "Pass me by if you're only passing through." The voice is high and lonesome, not given to gush; the instrumentation is built around an acoustic guitar, but accommodates a single French horn, a drumset, or both, when appropriate; the songs — both borrowed and original — are a lesson to L.A. cowboys everywhere from an L.A. cowgirl who makes her records in Vermont. **B+**

Mary McCaslin: *Old Friends* (Philo '77). Side two begins brilliantly, seguing from "My World Is Empty Without You" to "The Wayward Wind," two unjustly forgotten chestnuts from disparate traditions that are freshened immeasurably by McCaslin's eccentric, exacting mountain style. But "Blackbird," which leads to a charming "Don't Fence Me In," has been overrecorded, and the finale — the title cut and sole original — is flat. Side one's three highlights are nice enough, but "Oklahoma Hills" doesn't live up to Arlo's, much less Woody's, and "Pinball Wizard" is a weird, brave mistake. In short, the interpreter's dilemma — attagirl, but no cigar. **B+**

Mary McCaslin & Jim Ringer: *The Bramble and the Rose* (Philo '78). On record as much as live, two folkies whose solo work runs from pleasant (Ringer) to special-if-flawed (McCaslin) make up a whole equal to the sum of its parts, which is quite enough — her precise, slightly astringent soprano is the other half of his offhand baritone. In addition to the only version of "Geronimo's Cadillac" you need own, this revives traditional mountain songs so matter-of-fact and out-of-this-world that you can understand why folklorists devote their lives to the stuff. And on the finale, "Hit the Road Jack," the dry, intelligent humor they share — hers mock-prim, his nice-gruff — finally reaches the surface. **A−**

Mary McCaslin: *Sunny California* (Mercury '79). I could warn ya that Linda and Nicolette's prior claim on all early-'60s revivals is established conclusively by the lacklustre arrangements on "Cupid" and "Save the Last Dance for Me." But would Linda or Nicolette risk putting five of their own songs on a major-label debut? They don't even have five of their own songs. **B−**

Delbert McClinton: *Victim of Life's Circumstances* (ABC '75). Any old boy who can get arrested for "cuttin' up some honky with that bone-handled knife" has earned this perfect new-rockabilly title. But as you might expect, he has more to say in the action-packed tales of adventure ("Honky Tonkin'," "Morgan City Fool") than when he's trying to prove he's a grownup ("Lesson in the Pain of Love," "Troubled Woman"). **B+**

Delbert McClinton: *Genuine Cowhide* (ABC '76). Texas partisans tout this whoopersnapper as God's own leather-lunged, bicentennial, rockabilly truth, but I can't hear it. He's not ravaged enough; his crazy enthusiasm sounds too professional, too glib; there are none of those spaced-out moments that lend such vulnerability, and credibility, to a Billy Swan. Does this mean I'm complaining that Delbert sings too good? Could be. **B**

Delbert McClinton: *Keeper of the Flame* (Capricorn '79). McClinton's cult sentimentalizes bar music — having established that a saloon is as fruitful a nexus for music as a studio, they go on to claim that it's better ("more authentic"). But despite his superior sense of rhythm, Delbert's basically a male Texas Linda Ronstadt — a strong-voiced, versatile performer who doesn't come across on record as an especially interesting person. This not only puts him at the mercy of songwriters and arrangements but limits his taste in both. Album number five, his second for Johnny Sandlin and Capricorn, is probably his best since number one — funkier but less directly dependent on r&b, longer on originals than his last two for ABC, and opening with great readings from Chuck Berry and Randall Bramblett. In short, as enjoyable and forgettable as a Friday night out. **B**

Jimmy McCracklin: *High on the Blues* (Stax '71). Some think McCracklin's faintly plosive moan is distinctive. I think it's a type — ideal for outposts of deep soul, but only serviceable (or a little more) as pure instrument. And you know what? The deep soul drumming of coproducer Al Jackson almost puts it across. **B**

George McCrae: *Rock Your Baby* (T.K. '74). The folks in Miami liked the single so much that they extended it through an entire album — literally for eight minutes, then figuratively over long stretches of closely related rhythm track, with McCrae's serviceable but emotionally limited falsetto on top. Funny thing is, the single is so durable they almost got away with it. **B**

Gwen McCrae: *Rockin' Chair* (Cat '75). I was relieved to be left tepid by this LP's original release, since it was getting embarrassing to wax warm over Miami every time out. But the newly added title hit, almost as irresistibly Memphis-cum-disco-with-a-hook as hubby's "Rock Your Baby," transforms it into more warm wax, tuff enuff to make you wonder what ever happened to soul music. Time: 28:25. **B**

Gene McDaniels: *Outlaw* (Atlantic '70). Vaguely left doggerel plus a few jazzy harmonies do a cultural ripoff make. Of course, it's true that as a token of his honesty he wanted to call it *A Hundred Pounds of Horseshit*. But the rack jobbers wouldn't let him. **C−**

Chuck McDermott and Wheatstraw: *Last Straw* (Back Door '76). As befits a Yale dropout, McDermott makes country music with an edge of educated subtlety — the comic sendups of cars and compulsive consumption sound quite a bit more political than Jerry Reed's, the forlorn laments a whole lot more existentialist than George Jones's. Yet Jerry Reed and George Jones are definitely the comparison; McDermott may sound a little like Phil Ochs or Keith Carradine in their country personas, but his voice is stronger and more country. The drawback is the ragged backup from Boston's finest, who sound like folkies

who have not yet developed any viable equivalent for slickness. **B+**

Megan McDonough: *Megan Music* (Wooden Nickel '72). A male pianist cowrote a few of these songs, presumably concentrating on the melodies, since the lyrics run the gamut from rock music to rock bands to failed love affairs, most of them with rock musicians. Maybe she should find another scene. But then maybe she couldn't be a singer-songwriter. Best line: "But babe I get lost taking off my sweater." **C**

McFadden & Whitehead: *McFadden & Whitehead* (Philadelphia International '79). The anthemic power of "Ain't No Stoppin' Us Now" made me think these guys were ready to take over, but all it meant was that every year or two they write a great song. The disco disc has gone gold, and is recommended. **B−**

MC5: *Back in the USA* (Atlantic '70). A severe disappointment at first — a rather obvious and awkward attempt, I thought, to tailor a record to some dimly conceived high school "underground," with titles like "Teenage Lust" and lines like *"Young people everywhere are gonna cook their goose/ Lots of kids are working to get rid of these blues"* (political italics mine). But the music had its way with me. Under Jon Landau, the 5's style has become choppier, harder, and more concise; when his discipline is imposed on the soaring Sinclair-meets-Coltrane expansionism of their Elektra album, as on "Looking at You," the tension is pyrotechnic. The only failure is the ballad, "Let Me Try." But all that will make this album an undeniable success is for it to sell — with propaganda, that's the test. Which means it will probably remain an ambiguous experiment. Time: 27:41. Original grade: B plus. **A−**

MC5: *High Time* (Atlantic '71). At its best, this combines the anarchic energy of John Sinclair's album with the pop control of Jon Landau's album. "Sister Anne" is a passionate farewell to a Catholic boyhood, and the jazz climax, however ill-conceived sonically (the horns sound funny after all those guitars), gets where it's going, fast. Mistake: "Miss X,''. an atrocious fuck-me-babe ballad. Some things they'll never learn. **B+**

Kate & Anna McGarrigle: *Kate & Anna McGarrigle* (Warner Bros. '76). A folkie apotheosis — dry and droll, tender, sweetly mocking its own sentiment, unfailingly intelligent. With melodies that are fetching rather than pretty (cf. Jean Ritchie) and lyrics that are not above a certain charming, even calculating, vulgarity (cf. Loudon Wainwright III). Original grade: A minus. **A**

Kate & Anna McGarrigle: *Dancer with Bruised Knees* (Warner Bros. '77). Not as tuneful as some might wish, but even a bright melody must strike artists this subtle as unseemly, rather obvious. Rarely has the homely been rendered with such delicate sophistication; these women spend sixty or seventy grand trying to make a studio approximate a living room, or maybe a church basement on production numbers, and succeed! They are prim, wry, and sexy all at once, with a fondness for family life as it is actually lived — a repository of strength, surely, but also a repository of horrors — that is reflected in their version of folk instrumentation. Rather than on-the-road guitars (with their attendant corn about the wimmin at home) they rely on accordion, piano, organ; once when they need a drum they get the kind of oompah beat you still hear in parades. Even better than the debut, albeit harder. **A**

Kate & Anna McGarrigle: *Pronto Monto* (Warner Bros. '78). The bland-out of this quiet but piquant duo is being blamed on producer David Nichtern's all-too-steady hand. And sure, I'd prefer tempos that deviated more than five degrees from dead ahead and tasty licks that didn't whis-per monosodium glutamate. But I also expect that these tough, smart women consented readily enough to his devices, especially as their own songwriting now aspires to a sweet directness that Nichtern himself is better at (compare his "Just Another Broken Heart" to Anna's "Oh My Heart" or Kate's "Come Back Baby"). And I'll trade you Ann's "Bundle of Sorrow, Bundle of Joy" for the next Maria Muldaur album sound unheard. **B+**

Bat McGrath: *From the Blue Eagle* (Amherst '76). Unlike so many singer-songwriters, McGrath sounds like he comes from somewhere — upstate New York, as it happens. Instead of attaching generalized reflections to the most surefire melodies available, he writes lyrics that evoke specific locales and situations — like Jimmy Buffett when he's good, or Tom T. Hall with a more literary flair. Granted, anyone who believes a wino is "free" should check in his thesaurus under "nothin' left to lose," but the abundant compassion, humor, and detail of these brief ballads make you want to hear them again. A small find. **B+**

Bat McGrath: *The Spy* (Amherst '78). Although he's a nice singer, McGrath is bound in by the mildly jazzy conventions of contemporary folk music. But his songs still say more about how it is for all those formerly young guys with beards who chose to live in the country back around 1970 than all the paeans to homemade bread coming out of Vermont, Colorado, and Marin. **B**

Jimmy McGriff and Junior Parker: *The Dudes Doin' Business* (Capitol '70). A waste. Vocalist Parker, an underrated blues pro, and organist McGriff, who has a name as a soloist but is better off accompanying, should produce a more than passable record almost automatically. But not when they're burdened with strings, insipid soprano choruses, and hopelessly inappropriate material. Is a bluesman singing "The Inner Light" supposed to make contact — and money — in

St. Albans? Sonny Lester — remember that name — produced.   **C+**

Roger McGuinn: *Roger McGuinn* (Columbia '73). From L.A. session men to Charles Lloyd eight-miles-high to Bruce Johnston ooh-ooh to Clark, Clarke, Crosby, Hillman & McGuinn, Roger's solo debut sounds more coherent than any Byrds album since *Sweetheart of the Rodeo,* which must prove he's an auteur. Jacques Levy plays the Gram Parsons catalyst, but since Levy only writes lyrics the chemistry is a good deal less powerful. And it does worry me that Levy worked on all the good cuts: the ones about highjacking, love in Vietnam and "my new woman," and especially "I'm So Restless," the best state-of-the-music song since "All the Young Dudes." Original grade: B plus.   **B**

Roger McGuinn: *Peace on You* (Columbia '74). McGuinn seems to have done a whole album about breaking up with his wife or somebody. Which is fine, no law against it. But real country singers have more of a knack for such things. When Charlie Rich sings "God ain't gonna love you" (in the title tune, which Rich wrote), the blasphemy comes as a shock. McGuinn just sounds churlish.   **C+**

Roger McGuinn & Band: *Roger McGuinn & Band* (Columbia '75). And band's songs.   **C**

Roger McGuinn: *Cardiff Rose* (Columbia '76). I'd written him off before Rolling Thunder, too, but this record, produced by fellow Roller Ronson and featuring various tour buddies, rocks wilder than anything he ever did with the Byrds. Unfortunately, it's more confusing than astonishing. The factitious folk songs about piracy and the Holy Grail make fewer contemporary connections than the real folk song "Pretty Polly." Ditto the previously unrecorded donations from fellow Rollers Mitchell and Dylan. Imagining how Dylan might sing "Up to Me," which sounds like a forerunner of "Simple Twist of Fate," you begin to miss the quavery McGuinn of yore. And the song that's actually about

Rolling Thunder is pretty sickening.   **B-**

Roger McGuinn: *Thunderbyrd* (Columbia '77). I hate the name-dropping title, but this is McGuinn's best since his solo debut, including a tongue-in-cheek version of Dylan's mystical-romantic "Golden Loom," a psychedelic reminiscence, and good-to-great covers from George Jones, Tom Petty, and — the conceptual triumph — Peter Frampton.   **B**

McGuinn, Clark & Hillman: *McGuinn, Clark & Hillman* (Capitol '79). Despite the occasional Byrdsy guitar run, this is pure supersession, a purposeful AOR move by pros out for a quick killing, anonymously accomplished in the music and contentless in the lyrics. Granted, McGuinn's vocals are outstanding — look at the company he's keeping — and his "Don't You Write Her Off " is a genuine grabber. But it's also the simplest thing on the record. Moral: at least you can make having nothing to say sound like fun.   **C**

McGuinness Flint: *McGuinness Flint* (Capitol '70). Benny Gallagher and Graham Lyle's consistently tuneful tributes to America and other romances derive most of their character from the jolly-English quirkishness of the band's folk-rock. Only "International," one of their two attempts at a weightier lyric, is anywhere near as irresistible as "When I'm Dead and Gone," and "Brother Psyche" indicates why they usually play it safe.   **B**

McGuinness Flint: See also Coulson, Dean, McGuinness, Flint

Ellen McIlwaine: *Honky Tonk Angel* (Polydor '72). McIlwaine falls into all the overambitious traps — she dramatizes, she vaunts her range, she improvises when she should just sing — and yet she gets away with it, because enough of her grand attempts work. It's good to hear a woman play bottleneck guitar (in an appropriate context, too) and the two times she goes up an octave on "God" in "It Wasn't God Who Made Honky Tonk Angels" almost justify a whole side. Original grade: B plus.   **B**

Ian McLagan: *Troublemaker* (Mercury '79). In which the fifth Face, his mates dispersed to the Stones, the Who, Meher Baba, and Hollywood, makes a Faces album as good 'n' raucous as, oh, *Long Player*. He's more convincing taking a pot shot at the Hollywood Face than movin' out (on guess what kind of person) or seducing a virgin (that's the Hollywood Face's specialty). But if men will be boys, this is how they should go about it.   **B**

John McLaughlin: *Devotion* (Douglas '70). McLaughlin reminds me as much of Duane Eddy as of John Coltrane — he loves electric noise for its own sake and rocks more naturally than he swings. Here Buddy Miles provides his usual ham-handed thump, a universe away from Tony Williams's sallies, and McLaughlin just marches along on top, his tone supremely heavy by choice. But like Coltrane, though in a much more detached way, he can get enormous mileage out of harmonic ideas whose simplicity is probably one source of the spirituality he generates. Rarely has a rock improvisation been more basic or more thoughtfully conceived than on the little track, where he and Larry Young trade the same elemental motif for so long it turns into an electric mantra. Original grade: A minus.   **A**

Mahavishnu John McLaughlin: *My Goal's Beyond* (Douglas '71). What a mind-fuck! Just when I have him pegged as the Duane Eddy of the Aquarian Age he goes acoustic on me! "Peace One," "Peace Two," yeah yeah yeah — it's easy when you don't plug in. Conjuring peace out of chaos the way *Devotion* does is the real trick. And while like most white people I've failed to develop my taste in sitar music, I don't like the looks of this Mahalakshmi on the cover — she's white too, and I'll bet she got on the record the same way Sri Chinmoy got to write

the notes. Sitar sound effects from George Harrison are one thing —that's just rock and roll. John's goal is supposed to be beyond.   **B**

John McLaughlin, Dave Holland, John Surman, Stu Martin, Karl Berger: *Where Fortune Smiles* (Pye '75). Recorded in New York in 1969, when McLaughlin's studio appearances were amazing everyone from Jimi to Buddy to Miles, this prefigures Mahavishnu's fusion at an earlier, jazzier stage. Pretty intense. The rock guy (drummer Martin) sounds a lot more original than the jazz guys (keyboard player Berger and — especially — saxophonist Surman), but only the justifiably ubiquitous Holland (on bass) can keep up with McLaughlin. And believe me, even if in historical fact it's McLaughlin who's trying to keep up, that's how it sounds.   **B+**

Johnny McLaughlin: *Electric Guitarist* (Columbia '78). In which the top musicians in fusion are gathered by the man who made it all possible to show the genre off aesthetically — no funk vamps, no one-run solos, no twaddle about the harmony of the universe. The project has a certain stillborn aura — it doesn't swing a lot, there is a reliance on Speedy Gonzalez climaxes, and snatches of such deathless melodies as "Holiday for Strings" and "Mohammed's Radio" are audible. Still, repetitiousness is minimized, and there are good ideas and lots of sensitive interaction. And it didn't sell diddley.   **B+**

John McLaughlin with the One Truth Band: *Electric Dreams* (Columbia '79). Indicating that when fusion grows up it may achieve the artistic significance of the "cool" jazz of the '50s. Personally, I never had much use for Barney Kessel in the first place. I grant you that Kessel never had a drummer who could roil it up like Tony Smith. But he also never had a drummer who helped sing "Love and Understanding." Ugh.   **B−**

Don McLean: *American Pie* (United Artists '71). The title cut is the great novelty song that may be about the death of rock and roll or may be about its refusal to die. The other material here indicates that McLean himself believes the former, but since it also indicates that he couldn't have composed "American Pie" — he just took dictation from the shade of Buddy Holly, who must be taking some pretty strong drugs up there to make such a mistake — you might as well judge for yourself. And do so like a real novelty-lover, by buying the single — unless you're in the market for a song about how nobody understood Van Gogh. Original grade: D plus.   **C−**

Don McLean: *Don McLean* (United Artists '72). More dreck from your unfriendly doomsaying hitmaker. Question: Why does he say "I feel like a spinnin' top or a dreidel" without explaining how a dreidel differs from a spinning top? Point of information: McLean's pubbery is called Yaweh Tunes, Inc. Point of order: No one who has sailed with Pete Seeger should put this much production into an album.   **C−**

Ralph McTell: *You Well-Meaning Brought Me Here* (Paramount '71). "Streets of London," a gentle attack on folkie self-pity, is one of several appealingly melodic urban miniatures, and it doesn't stop there. McTell is so softhearted he ought to check in with a cardiologist (maybe that's why he sounds so sad all the time), but he's not empty-headed; he knows what his world-view portends. Hence, "First and Last Man," a celebration of a real primitive — the epoch isn't identified, but I'd guess Neanderthal. So why is he in the studio with Gus Dudgeon? Beats me, but it doesn't hurt.   **B+**

The Meditations: *Message from the Meditations* (United Artists '78). A new group has to score singles often in Jamaica before getting an album, and with three singers — including two distinctive high tenors — sharing writing and lead vocals, this is a nice one. Just wish it featured more island chau-

vinism — if I'm not mistaken, "Running from Jamaica" gets on those who emigrate to Canada, Britain, the States, and *Africa* — and less of the male kind.   **B**

Melanie: *Gather Me* (Neighborhood '71). Unlike my straitlaced friends, I've always dug the idea of Melanie — Edith Piaf as Brooklyn waif, preaching the hippie gospel in that absurdly flexible and resonant alto. But I've found the reality cloying. Here she grows up just enough. "Brand New Key" is one of those impossible celebrations of teen libido that renew one's faith in AM radio, "Steppin' " is the best breakup song since "It's Too Late," and though side two slips badly toward the end, she's rarely a simp this time out.   **B+**

Melanie: *Four Sides of Melanie* (Buddah '72). Two of which you can skip: the formless formative stuff (she's eternally callow so who needs it, though "I Really Loved Harold" and "Somebody Loves Me" are nice) and the unspeakable contemporary covers (Dylan, Taylor, and Jagger as Blake, Keats, and Coleridge). But even without "Brand New Key" her hits have their charms — "What Have They Done to My Song Ma" and "Nickel Song" on one theme and "Lay Down" and "Peace Will Come" on the other. And except for the labored "Psychotherapy" the weird stuff is quite amusing. She ought to ask herself, though, why the two best cuts on her best-of are the aforementioned "Somebody Loves Me," a Gershwin tune, and "Christopher Robin," by A. A. Milne. [Reissued as *The Best of . . . Melanie.*]   **B−**

Melanie: *Photograph* (Atlantic '76). When she was a twenty-four-year-old child-woman she got points for her changeable voice and naive candor. But as she pushes thirty the voice is a given and the naivete an embarrassment.   **C+**

Melanie: *The Best of Melanie* (Buddah '77). In which Arista buys Buddah and perpetrates a literal corporate ripoff, yanking ten songs from Buddah's thoughtful if flawed twenty-three-cut Melanie compilation — including her epochal misreadings of "Mr. Tambourine Man" and "Ruby Tuesday." Title recognition, you know. **C —**

Terry Melcher: *Terry Melcher* (Reprise '74). Most will find this producer's daydream sterile at best and noxious at worst, but I like the song about his shrink and am fascinated by his compulsion to defend his Manson connections. With the requisite show of wealth and taste, he insists that he's only a spectator — why, he wouldn't even know about the hand jive if it weren't for *Soul Train*. Alternate title: *It's Alright, Ma, I'm Only Watching.* Original grade: B. **B —**

Harold Melvin & the Blue Notes: *I Miss You* (Philadelphia International '72). For most of the eight-and-a-half minutes of the title cut, one Blue Note attempts a calm rapprochement with his estranged wife over the telephone while the others shout, moan, and sob his unspoken feelings — summed up by the title, which must repeat a hundred times. But not even their topforty breakthrough, "If You Don't Know Me by Now," matches up. Gamble, Huff & Co. show off their skill at instrumental deployment and Melvin provides gorgeous vocal arrangements, but too often it all adds up to noble banalities sententiously expressed. And sometimes the banalities aren't so noble. **B**

Harold Melvin & the Blue Notes: *Black and Blue* (Philadelphia International '73). The lead singer's name is Theodore Pendergrass, not Harold Melvin, which you'd only know by reading *Soul* or *Jet* — he's not mentioned anywhere on the record or double-fold jacket. Pendergrass boasts just about the most powerful voice ever to hit soul music, though not the richest or most overwhelming. Although his smashes are dance tunes like "The Love I Lost" and "Satisfaction Guaranteed," his real calling is big ballads,

especially ones that assert dependence — "Is There a Place for Me," "I'm Weak for You." But did they have to kick things off with "Cabaret"? **B +**

Harold Melvin & the Blue Notes Featuring Theodore Pendergrass: *To Be True* (Philadelphia International '75). Black suffering above the poverty level is the lyrical twist of "Bad Luck" and "Where Are All My Friends" (written not by Gamble-Huff but by Carstarphen-McFadden-Whitehead), and to Pendergrass's credit he seems to get it—even makes a few asides. He also generates tremendous romantic authority—you really believe he wants to meet up with her "Somewhere Down the Line." He doesn't do the impossible for "Pretty Flower," though, and given the credibility of most of what remains — not to mention the intrusion of the mysterious Sharon Paige — the impossible is all that would push this over the line for me. **B +**

Harold Melvin & the Blue Notes: *Wake Up Everybody* (Philadelphia International '75). The sustained dynamics of the title track get me past its muddle-headed lyrics — Gamble-Huff sometimes act as if "hatred, war an' poverty" came along just as they were running out of subjects. And I can still go along with Teddy Pendergrass's tender strength. But sometimes he sounds a little more insecure than I think he intends — he's prone to bluster and chest-pounding, and some of his grunts are almost coughs. Anyway, he's gone. **B +**

Harold Melvin & the Blue Notes: *Collectors' Item* (Philadelphia International '76). Harold Melvin could no more give Teddy his due than he could sing lead himself, so he includes a Sharon Paige feature instead of another slow, vulnerable one — if not "To Be True" or "I'm Weak for You," then why not "Yesterday I Had the Blues," which was a hit? And Kenny Gamble could no more get off his high horse than he could do the dishes, so he includes the inevitable piece of male-chauvinism-as-moral-posture, "Be for Real," instead of "Satisfaction Guaranteed," which was a hit. And for all that this compilation is the best Teddy Pendergrass record you can buy. **A —**

The Members: *At the Chelsea Nightclub* (Virgin International '79). The inheritors of English punk haven't turned to power pop; they're putting their energies into reggae, Britain's own indigenous black music, with the r&b syntheses of the Stones rather than the blues imitations of the Savoy Browns serving as precedent. The crude feel and committed socioeconomic awareness of this album recall 1977, but the rhythms and tempos leave room for their rebellious-suburban-lad-escaped-to-the-city to give forth with a slyer kind of humor. **B +**

Eric Mercury: *Electric Black Man* (Avco Embassy '70). All things considered — tasteless hype, demeaning concept, kudos from David Clayton-Thomas, violins-and-wah-wah production, oh, the exploitative stupidity of it all — this isn't a complete disaster, because Mercury is a fairly strong singer. Maybe some day he'll put out a fairly strong album. **C**

Mer-Da: *Long Burn the Fire* (Janus '72). A follow-up to *There's a Riot Goin' On* by a group identified as "Black Mer-Da" on the disc itself, before someone at Janus got cold feet. No more riots here than with Sly, of course — just self-hate, misogyny, desperate poverty, and senseless violence, as out-of-tune voices declaim strangely catchy tunes over loitering funk patterns and jagged guitar. "Sometimes I wish I'd never been born," they announce flatly, and they can really get flat. But the most surreal passage comes toward the close of "My Mistake," when "I should have killed her instead" (author's note: of the friend he caught fucking her), horrifying enough as a surprise endline, is transformed into a little piece of artfunk, repeated amid various instru-

mental configurations by an off-key chorale that sounds positively transported. **B +**

The Meters: *Struttin'* (Josie '70). The New Orleans M.G.'s swing, but not smoothly, the way a big band does — their Caribbean lilt is pure second-line, as elliptical as a saint's march. They're the secret of Allen Toussaint-produced hits by Lee Dorsey, Aaron Neville, and Ernie K-Doe, and because they put out riffs rather than songs their own LPs are consistently danceable and listenable. Of course, to do better than that the band would have to come up with more good riffs in a year than most rhythm sections manage in a decade, and usually they compromise a little — only two r&b hits here, plus several other tracks that might have been, "Wichita Lineman" not among them. **B +**

The Meters: *Cabbage Alley* (Reprise '72). Just what do these people want? They're still making up titles like "Gettin' Funkier All the Time," even singing one called "Do the Dirt." But they're also stretching out a catchy little number called "Stay Away" with what annotator Barry Hansen refers to gingerly as "some most unusual electronic adventures" and putting voice to Neil Young's "Birds" and their own "Lonesome and Unwanted People." And what can it mean that the catchiest little number of all has no words and two titles — "You've Got to Change (You've Got to Reform)"? **B**

The Meters: *Rejuvenation* (Reprise '74). Although it's worth noting that their first hit for Warners, "Hey Pocky A-Way," is as old as the second line, it's also worth noting that they're getting results from their experiments — namely, the twelve-minute funk fusion "It Ain't No Use." And if most of the time the vocals are neutral at best, what this bunch of amateurs makes of "Just Kissed My Baby" isn't dreamed of in Three Dog Night's philosophy. **B +**

The Meters: *Cissy Strut* (Island '75). Unless you happen to be dancing, it takes a slightly inappropriate aesthetic concentration to, er, appreciate a whole album of party instrumentals. But this compilation of thirteen turn-of-the-decade r&b hits (plus album tracks) the Meters cut for Josie is worth the strain. The secret: listen to Ziggy Modeliste. He plays more off-beats and eccentric patterns than any soul drummer you ever heard, yet never breaks up the band's spare, clever riff structures; it's almost as if he's the lead. These cuts are short and catchy. Not one of them is as amazing as *Rejuvenation*'s "It Ain't No Use." But every one works. **A −**

The Meters: *Fire on the Bayou* (Reprise '75). Thanks to new conga player Cyril Neville, the singing has gotten better, but no matter how much I love "They All Ask'd for You," I'm not sure that's good. Distracts us from the drummer. And maybe it distracts the drummer, too. **B**

The Meters: *Trick Bag* (Reprise '76). Doing James Taylor and the Rolling Stones. Writing a song about pollution solutions, and one called "Find Yourself" that's more embarrassing than the one called "Disco Is the Thing Today." And covering Earl King's title tune magnificently. Why, oh Lord, why? **C +**

The Meters: *New Directions* (Warner Bros. '77). Outside of New Orleans the Meters are a cult band. All they accomplish by going pop/disco is the loss of their critical rep (whatever that's worth) and the erosion of their sales base. Yet leaving Allen Toussaint for David Rubinson was evidently the right move — he respected them so much he was even sparing with the Tower of Power. A very good commercial funk record, right down to covers that go with their natural beat — one from Peter Tosh and one from Allen Toussaint. **B +**

Metro: *Metro* (Sire '78). Chansons de l'amour esquinté — très chic, très sophistiqué, et plutôt ennuyeux. Un Alpha Band Européen avec sexe, peut-être, ou un Roxy Music pour le caba-

ret. A propos en Anglais, et tant pis. **C +**

Augie Meyers: *You Ain't Rollin Your Roll Rite* (Paramount '73). Doug Sahm's faithful organist has a rather shallow voice, but he knows good material and occasionally writes some — "Sugar Blu" is the way Doug ought to be opening his sets these days, and the title song sounds like advice to rock and rollers who get lost on their way to legendhood. Straightforward Tex-Mex like they don't hardly make no more. **B**

Augie Meyers: *Finally in Lights* (Texas Re-Cord '77). The jazzy coda doesn't ruin "Sky High," "Deed to Texas" is chauvinism at its most forgivable, and in general this is good fun. But though Meyers has grown as a singer he has nothing to add to "Release Me," and though he half-earns the right to contribute seven of his own songs I bet he knows "Baby, Baby" is sheer filler. **B −**

Lee Michaels: *Tailface* (Columbia '73). In which a self-proclaimed "Garbage Gourmet" makes up a joke so dumb that it took me four months to get it. Setup: Michaels, an organ player by trade, switches to guitar. Punch line: A cross between "Louie Louie" and "Do You Know What I Mean" that occupies an entire album. All reet! **B +**

Bette Midler: *The Divine Miss M* (Atlantic '72). Midler thinks "cabaret" encompasses every emotion and aspiration ever transfixed by pop music. People who've seen her like this record more than people who haven't, which isn't good. But as someone who's been entranced by her show many times I'm grateful for a production that suggests its nutty quality without distracting from her voice, a rich instrument of surprising precision, simultaneously delicate and vulgar. I'd ease up on the '60s nostalgia by replacing "Chapel of Love" with "Empty Bed Blues," but anybody who can expose

"Leader of the Pack"'s exploration of the conflict between love and authority has a right.   **A −**

Bette Midler: *Bette Midler* (Atlantic '73). Side two does seven great songs with umpteen instruments in just over fifteen minutes, a perfectly amazing miracle of concision. But side one is less than hot. Two (why two?) just-wrong Johnny Mercer songs lead into a properly excessive intro to Ann Peebles's "Breaking Up Somebody's Home" that is destroyed inside of two minutes by an improperly excessive, funkless production. Bette's overstatement works on "Surabaya Johnny" and "I Shall Be Released," but I've heard better. Most important, why isn't there one song by a contemporary composer here? Dylan doesn't count — I'm talking about Randy Newman, Gilbert O'Sullivan, Joni Mitchell, maybe James Taylor or Cat Stevens, she's always made me believe in miracles. As it stands, this record is perilously close to the ostrich nostalgia of her dumbest fans. Original grade: A minus.   **B +**

Bette Midler: *Songs for a New Depression* (Atlantic '76). It's going too far to claim that she's taken on a corporate personality — a very unusual individual does definitely peek out through the curtain of groupthink that hides these songs from the singer and from us. But that individual seems to have taken on so many advisers because she's afraid of herself, and such fear is not attractive in an artist of Bette Midler's power. No matter what your voice teachers tell you, wackiness is not something to modulate.   **C +**

Bette Midler: *Broken Blossom* (Atlantic '77). So she can translate Billy Joel into Phil Spector — she has nevertheless become, at least on record, just another pop singer, albeit with a few interesting ideas. I ask you, is the redemption of Billy Joel fit work for a culture heroine?   **C**

Bette Midler: *Live at Last* (Atlantic '77). Her fans may find some of the material on this live double-LP repetitious — I could do without five minutes of "Delta Dawn" myself — and her overripe singing will offend those she offends anyway. But she's never recorded fifteen of these twenty-five songs, a few repeats are enhanced by the particulars of this performance, and others gather meaning in theatrical context. A typical stroke: prefacing the glorious tearjerker "Hello in There" with campy, occasionally unkind patter about ladies with fried eggs on their heads, so that the song's romanticized heroine and the weird and depressing fried egg ladies both seem to have something in common with Bette, and therefore with each other.   **A −**

Bette Midler: *Thighs and Whispers* (Atlantic '79). The songs are pretty good, and when you listen up they get better, their apparent flatness undercut by little touches of drama, comedy, or musicianship. But the songs aren't that good. And they don't get that much better.   **C +**

Midnight Rhythm: *Midnight Rhythm* (Atlantic '79). At last a whole disco album that actually brings off all the disco tricks — exploding out of the speakers, washing over the room, and so forth. The thump of the bass drum never dominates the rhythmic pulse, and the lyrical tag lines avoid the words "dance," "dancer," "dancing," "dancin'," and "disco" — until an orgasmic break (repeated once) that goes "Dancin', dancin', dancin', dancin'." Monofunctional but potent.   **A −**

The Mighty Clouds of Joy: *It's Time* (Dunhill '74). You'd figure the showiest of all gospel groups would sell out with some flair, but the vocal transfigurations — that old Wilson Pickett (and Julius Cheeks) unhh born again — aren't the only reason this is one of the best LPs ever to come out of Philadelphia. For once, the songs — many of them from producer Dave Crawford, whose spirit must have been moved — include virtually no filler, not even (especially not even) the one that takes off from the group's name. Nicest conceit: how hard it is to be soft in a "Stoned World." **A−**

The Mighty Clouds of Joy: *Kickin'* (ABC '75). Dave Crawford, whose debut production with this group explored the spiritual affinities between showbiz gospel and studio soul, here returns to form by exploiting shared commercial asininities. Don't be fooled if they get the great exception, "Mighty High," onto DJ turntables; Joe Ligon singing "You Are So Beautiful" is even more depressing than Billy Preston. Original grade: C plus. **B−**

The Mighty Clouds of Joy: *The Very Best of the Mighty Clouds of Joy* (ABC '78). This two-disc set presents the pre-crossover Peacock-label gospel and the "appeal to Pop/R&B audiences" as a continuum, and while I'm still a fan of the Clouds' first Dave Crawford LP, guess which period sounds better. Is it the formal purity of the Peacock stuff, leaving the excitement to Joe Ligon's falsetto-piercing shouts, that makes their sermonizing seem so unpresumptuous? Or does the music just go with the message, as in the overbearing orchestrations of the more recent "God Is Not Dead" and "Look on the Bright Side"? One thing I know — gospel songs are written by mortals, too, and all the faith in the world isn't going to make a good one out of a bad one. An acceptable one, maybe. **B +**

The Mighty Diamonds: *Right Time* (Virgin '76). On the purely aural, preverbal evidence — the sweet, precise harmonies and arrangements, the intent beat — you'd figure they were singing songs of love, or at least sexual mastery. Ditto from their foolish stage act. But in fact there are no broken hearts in these lyrics, only broken bodies, and the exultation is the exultation of oppression defied. In other words, this follows reggae convention as Americans know it, and on a few cuts conventional is how it sounds. Usually, though, lead singer Donald

Sharpe sounds as if he's learned all this more recently than the Bob Marley of *Rastaman Vibration*. Original grade: B plus. **A−**

Mighty Diamonds: *Ice on Fire* (Virgin '77). Just as an assassination attempt doesn't commit Bob Marley to propaganda, so the best reggae album of 1976 doesn't commit the Mighty Diamonds to the music of Jamaica. Here they bid to become just another black harmony group, yoking Allen Toussaint's production to the Kingston beat and covering "Tracks of My Tears" (well). We could use another black harmony group, but unfortunately, Toussaint isn't noted for his work with groups, and like most harmony-group albums (not to mention reggae albums) this sounds samey even as it switches unpredictably from Toussaint songs to Mighty Diamonds originals. **B**

Mighty Diamonds: *Deeper Roots (Back to the Channel)* (Virgin International '79). Most of these songs confidently cross jingle and chant, and Donald Shaw sings in his chains like a true son of Smokey. But never once do the riddims become anthemic. For advanced reggae students only. **B**

Buddy Miles: *Them Changes* (Mercury '70). His work on *Band of Gypsys* and *Devotion* surpasses anything he ever did with the Electric Flag, but that's due to the artistic maturity of Hendrix and McLaughlin, not of Buddy Miles. His singing is too thin to carry two consecutive cuts, his drumming has to be exploited by subtler musicians, and the title cut is the only decent song he ever wrote. **C**

Frankie Miller: *Frankie Miller's Highlife* (Chrysalis '74). Macon meets New Orleans in Glasgow for a lesson in Scots soul, historical division. Allen Toussaint provides the New Orleans, but though his songs ("Brickyard Blues," yeah) certainly stand out, he doesn't hog the stage — Miller's rough warmth and knowledge of literature keep the album in play. **B+**

Frankie Miller: *The Rock* (Chrysalis '75). If like me you have a taste for English soul singers who have taste in American soul exemplars, you will be pleased to learn that Henry McCulloch does a hell of a Steve Cropper imitation. But Miller is no Joe Cocker (not to mention Toots Hibbert) (not to mention . . .) and he was better off writing fewer songs. **B**

Jacob Miller: *Dread, Dread* (United Artists '78). Miller had never impressed me with Inner Circle on Capitol, so I put aside this solo effort without much pain. Then an adept suggested I flip the loudness switch and turn up the bass and treble — advice that applies to all of Tom Moulton's reggae remixes for U.S. UA. Boom — different music. The Rasta homilies are a little thin and the remakes of "Why Can't We Be Friends" and "Dock of the Bay" unnecessary, but "Tenement Yard" is neither, and I love Miller's basic vocal trick, which makes him sound like a kid imitating a machine gun. The adept tells me Inner Circle sounds better in Jamaican too. **B+**

Steve Miller: *Number 5* (Capitol '70). The songs about going to the country, going to Mexico, and eating chili are more substantial than those about Vietnam, Jackson-Kent, and the military-industrial complex. Fortunately, all three of the latter are supposed to bring the album to a rousing (*zzzzz*) climax, which leaves side one free to bring you back humming. **B**

Steve Miller: *Rock Love* (Capitol '71). Those who deemed *Number 5* a throwaway should find number six instructive: one side of live "blues," one of dead "rock." **C−**

Steve Miller Band: *Recall the Beginning . . . A Journey from Eden* (Capitol '72). I think this is a concept album in which Miller's rejection by a female drummer named Kim symbolizes "all the pointless suf-

fering/Humanity." But I don't intend to make sure. **C−**

Steve Miller Band: *Anthology* (Capitol '72). Says Miller in the notes: "Always before, you know, people more or less needed to be fans to like the albums. Oh, I mean there'd be some good cuts and a couple of not-so-good cuts, and then some cuts I don't even like to remember. But *Anthology* is what I always wanted to make — two good LPs that'll hold up." And you know what? That's so accurate I won't bother quibbling about "Motherless Children" or "Baby's House." But what can it mean that thirteen of the sixteen survivors were recorded three years ago? **B+**

Steve Miller Band: *The Joker* (Capitol '73). As a spacey rock prophet he's terrible (who isn't?). As a blues singer he's incompetent (I wouldn't come on in his kitchen for a glass of water). But as a purveyor of spacey pop-rock blues, he has his virtues. Question: what the hell is "the pompitous of love"? The Medallions wouldn't tell me. **B−**

Steve Miller Band: *Fly Like an Eagle* (Capitol '76). Miller's eccentricity — James Cotton harp amid the Sam Cooke amid the technologized ditties — has no center or even epicenter except for the pastoral antimaterialism so common among exurbanite rock tycoons. But in the end his borrowed hooks and woozy vocal charm are an irresistible formula. Finds good covers, too — "Mercury Blues" (copyright 1970 by K. C. Douglas, whoever he is) fits right in. Original grade: B minus. **B+**

The Steve Miller Band: *Book of Dreams* (Capitol '77). This one avoids significance as aggressively as a Coca-Cola commercial (unless "My Own Space" counts). And thanks to the sidemen's songs, it isn't as catchy as a Coca-Cola commercial. Not to mention *Fly Like an Eagle*. Original grade: C. **B−**

The Steve Miller Band: *Greatest Hits 1974–78* (Capitol '78). In which Miller selects seven tracks from *Book* *of Dreams* (I'd omit the garbled non-original "Jungle Love" and the long synthesizer intro to "Jet Airliner," but he did bag every good one), six from *Fly Like an Eagle* (an easier job), and one from *The Joker* (ditto), revealing a California singles artist as likably lightweight as Jan & Dean. This music may recycle blues riffs, but its spirit is pure escapist pop; country living replaces surf and cars as utopian metaphor and Miller's voice, always too slight for real blues, sounds suitably out-of-it. As philosophy it's venal, but as unabashed diversion it's pretty nice. After all, was he ever good for anything else? **A −**

Mink DeVille: *Mink DeVille* (Capitol '77). Those who believe "underground" rock means a return to basics and nothing more will cheer this sleek, friendly white r&b record, because they'll understand it. Those who insist on learning something new about the basics will continue to prefer the Ramones and Blondie, or Springsteen and J. Geils. Original grade: B minus. **B**
Mink DeVille: *Return to Magenta* (Capitol '78). The main thing wrong with Willie DeVille is that he hasn't had a new idea since he decided he didn't like acid in 1970. Even as the songpoet of greaser nostalgia he's got nothing to say — the most interesting writing on this record is an old David Forman tune — and the romanticism of his vocal style makes me appreciate George Thorogood. **C +**

Sugar Minott: *Black Roots* (Mango '79). This is Jamaican pop, by which I mean modestly tuneful Rasta talk mellifluously sung. Pleasant, but nothing to base a canon on — only "Oppressors Oppression" (makes a wise man mad) and "Two Time Loser" (in love careless love) will do more than make you hum along. **B**

The Miracles: *City of Angels* (Tamla '75). Tom Smucker, explaining why this was included in his annual top ten: "Motown moves to L.A. and likes what it finds. It's very important that in an era when people don't like cities some people can still find them romantic. And that L.A. is the city. And that Motown are the people." This is sweet and true, but it ignores the point, which is that this record is a riot. In fact, its achievement is so complete, so true to itself, that the lurking possibility of a put-on can't be dismissed. Space makes it impossible to reprint Inspirational Verse (Q: If the first line is "Homosexuality" and the rhyming word is "society," what's the third line? A: "Well I guess they need more variety"), but print doesn't do it justice anyway. You have to hear the intonations, the falsettos, the backups, the orchestration, some of which can be credited to producer Freddie Perren. All this plus: the first soul song about an underground newspaper. **B**
The Miracles: *Greatest Hits* (Tamla '77). No one could replace that rich falsetto anyway, but there are less squeaky ones around than Billy Griffin's. I blame Freddie Perren for bringing out the worst in him, though — Griffin wrote "Love Machine," the only positive pleasure here. **C +**

Joni Mitchell: *Ladies of the Canyon* (Reprise '70). Joni's new dependence on piano implies a move from the open air to the drawing room — or at least living area — that's reflected in richer, more sophisticated songs. Sometimes the wordplay is still laughably high school — "lookout thru the pain" my eye. But "Both Sides Now" was only the beginning, and this album offers at least half a dozen continuations, all in different directions. Side two leads off with songs to a (real) FM DJ and a (figurative?) priest and includes her versions of "Woodstock" and "The Circle Game" as well as my own favorite, "Big Yellow Taxi," an ecology song with a trick ending. Original grade: B plus. **A −**

Joni Mitchell: *Blue* (Reprise '71). As Joni grooves with the easy-swinging elite-rock sound of California's pop aristocrats, her relation to their (and her own) easy-swinging sexual ethic becomes more probing. But thoughtfulness isn't exactly making her sisterly — I've even heard one woman complain that she can't sing Joni's melodies any more. Well, too bad — they're getting stronger all the time, just like the lyrics. From the eternal ebullience of "All I Want" to the month-after melancholy of "Blue," this battlefront report on the fitful joys of buy-now pay-later love offers an exciting, scary glimpse of a woman in a man's world. Original grade: A minus.   **A**

Joni Mitchell: *For the Roses* (Asylum '72). Sometimes her complaints about the men who have failed her sound petulant, but the appearance of petulance is one of the prices of liberation. If this has none of the ingratiating ease of *Blue,* that's because Mitchell has smartened up — she's more wary, more cynical. Perhaps as a result, the music, which takes on classical colors from Tom Scott's woodwinds and Bobby Notkoff's chamber strings, is more calculated. Where the pretty swoops of her voice used to sound like a semiconscious parody of the demands placed on all female voices and all females, these sinuous, complex melodies have been composed to her vocal contours with palpable forethought. They reward stubborn attention with almost hypnotic appeal.   **A**

Joni Mitchell: *Court and Spark* (Asylum '74). The first album she's ever made that doesn't sound like a musical departure — it's almost standard rock, *For the Roses* gone mainstream. But the relative smoothness is a respite rather than a copout, the cover version of "Twisted" suggests a brave future, and she's the best singer-songwriter there is right now. Even the decrease in verbal daring — the lyrics are quite personal and literal — makes for a winning directness in songs like "Help Me" and "Raised on Robbery." Now all I want to know is whether "Free Man in Paris" is about David Geffen.   **A**

Joni Mitchell: *Miles of Aisles* (Asylum '74). The two Joni-with-guitar/piano/dulcimer sides of this live double are impossibly tedious even though she's learned to sing songs that were beyond her half a decade ago — if she was so crazy about folkie-purist records she would have gone that way in the studio originally. The two new songs are mere bait — they wouldn't be on the album if she'd recorded them before. And the two sides with the L.A. Express establish her as the most gifted of the new folky-jazzy singers — I mean, Kenny Rankin should just *forget it.*   **B –**

Joni Mitchell: *The Hissing of Summer Lawns* (Asylum '75). Mitchell's transition from great songwriter to not-bad poet is meeting resistance from her talent and good sense, but I guess you can't fight "progress." Not that she's abandoned music — the supple accompaniment here is the most ambitious of her career. But if she wants jazz she could do better than Tom Scott's El Lay coolcats, and the sad truth is that only on a couple of cuts — "The Jungle Line" and "Don't Interrupt the Sorrow" — do these skillful sound effects strengthen the lyrics. The result is that Mitchell's words must stand pretty much on their own, and while she can be rewarding to read — "The Boho Dance" is a lot sharper than most I'm-proud-to-be-a-star songs — she's basically a West Coast Erica Jong. If that sounds peachy to you, enjoy. Original grade: B minus.   **B**

Joni Mitchell: *Hejira* (Asylum '76). Album eight is most impressive for the cunning with which Mitchell subjugates melody to the natural music of language itself. Whereas in the past only her naive intensity has made it possible to overlook her old-fashioned prosody, here she achieves a sinuous lyricism that is genuinely innovative. Unfortunately, the chief satisfaction of Mitchell's words — the way they map a woman's reality — seems to diminish as her autonomy increases. The reflections of a rich, faithless, compulsively mobile, and compulsively romantic female are only marginally more valuable than those of her marginally more privileged male counterparts, especially the third or fourth time around. It ain't her, bub, it ain't her you're lookin' for. **B+**

Joni Mitchell: _Don Juan's Reckless Daughter_ (Asylum '77). This double album presents a real critic's dilemma — I'm sure it's boring, but I'm not sure how boring. Insofar as it isn't, Jaco Pastorius deserves as much credit as the artiste. Just the way it did on _Hejira,_ his bass enables her to deal with the syntheses that obsess her — melody and rhythm, form and anima. But only on the title cut does he enable her to realize them. Time: 59:30. **B−**

Joni Mitchell: _Mingus_ (Asylum '79). Okay, okay, a brave experiment, but lots of times experiments fail. There's more spontaneity, wisdom, and humor in the 2:25 of Mingus "raps" than in all her hand-tooled lyrics, and her voice isn't rich or graceful enough to flesh out music that gains no swing from a backing band a/k/a Weather Report. **C+**

McKinley Mitchell: _McKinley Mitchell_ (Chimneyville '78). A small miracle: Bobby Bland meets Brook Benton in the timeless realm of the not-quite-folkloric, where soul and blues sound precisely contemporary and strings voice old horn riffs with no suggestion of sellout. Mitchell's seven tunes don't measure up to the other three — "Dream Lover," "You're So Fine," and a classic blues from the early '70s called "Open House at My House." But it doesn't matter, because this is one of those groove records on which ordinary songwriting is transmuted by perfect pacing and unshakable stylistic conviction. **A−**

Moby Grape: _20 Granite Creek_ (Reprise '71). At first I thought this reunion album lacked magic, but these guys sound remarkably whole for a band that failed to take over the world in 1967. You can hear the country undertone now, but you can also hear why you missed it — at their most lyrical these guys never lay back, and lyricism is something they're usually rocking too hard to bother with, though their compact forms guarantee poetic justice. Full of hope as they foresee their doom, stoned and drunk and on the move and yet always together, and above all intense, they should have at least taken over the country. All they really lacked was a boss, and what could be more American than that? Original grade: B minus. **B+**

The Modern Lovers: _The Modern Lovers_ (Home of the Hits '76). These legendary sessions, produced by John Cale for Warners in the early '70s but never released, still sound ahead of their time. Jonathan Richman's gift is to make explicit that love for "the modern world" that is the truth of so much of the best rock and roll; by cutting through the vaguely protesty ambience of so-called rock culture he opens the way for a worldiness that is specific, realistic, and genuinely critical. Not that he tries to achieve this himself — he's much too childlike. Sometimes his unmusicianship adds a catch to a three-chord melody and his off-key singing unlocks doors you didn't know were there. But other times he sounds like his allowance is too big, as worldly as Holden Caulfield with no '50s for excuse — the first rock hero who could use a spanking. Original grade: A minus. **A**

Essra Mohawk: _Essra Mohawk_ (Asylum '74). Here is a vocalist who should throw away all her Leon Russell records. When she calls herself a "full-fledged woman," it sounds like "pool player's" woman, which given her persona makes more sense. **D**

Molly Hatchet: _Flirtin' with Disaster_ (Epic '79). Some doctrinaire new wavers see the rapid success of this

Jacksonville sextet as a reactionary portent, but as an old Skynyrd fan I can't get upset. They do boogie better than, let's see here, Missouri, Bama, Crimson Tide, .38 Special, Wet Willie, Atlanta Rhythm Section, or (mercy sakes) the Charlie Daniels Band. Really, they sound pretty good. Only one thing missing: content. **C+**

The Moments: *The Moments Greatest Hits* (Stang '77). "Love on a Two Way Street" is this classic falsetto group's only pop breakthrough because it's their only pop tune — Sylvia Robinson gets lots of mileage out of Harry Ray's tenor, but she's not Thom Bell or Eugene Record. For that matter, Ray isn't Russell Thompkins or Eddie Kendricks — I love the proto-disco moans on "Sexy Mama" and the overarching agony of "I Do," but for the most part he projects a romanticism so transparent that its artificiality shows through. A one-disc selection might work, but two means twenty certified r&b hits that never venture five miles over the speed limit. **B**

The Moments: See also Ray, Goodman & Brown

Eddie Money: *Eddie Money* (Columbia '78). Sorry, girls (and guys) — live inspection reveals that the sleek stud on the cover (and in the ads) is as pudgy and sloppy as his voice. He even has jowls. Watch those cheeseburgers, Eddie boy, or you'll never get to the caviar. **C−**

Keith Moon: *Two Sides of the Moon* (Track '75). It's hard to imagine the auteur of this alternately vulgar, silly, and tender travesty/tour de force as anyone but Keith Moon; his madness translates not only to film (*Stardust, Tommy*) but even to the supersolo studio jobs that this parodies so deliciously. I presume they thought it was funny to mix the backup singers (Nilsson, Nelson, Flo & Eddie) up in front of the guy with his name on the cover. And it was. Time: 25:42. **B**

The Moonglows: *Return of the Moonglows* (RCA Victor '72). On the one hand, this revival of the great '50s group is obviously a money-making scheme. On the other hand, ex-Moonglow and -Motown producer Harvey Fuqua has done a serious updating job — strings, after all, are the correct studio equivalent of the group's smooth polyphonous style, and "I Was Wrong" fuses the two periods beautifully. But there were strings in the '50s, too, and it meant something for the Moonglows to replace them with voices. On both hands, I'd rather listen to the real stuff. **C+**

Jackie Moore: *Sweet Charlie Babe* (Atlantic '73). Figures that this should fall somewhere between state-of-the-art and great-mean soul: the five hits go back to "Precious, Precious" in the winter of '71, with the two latest cut at a funkier-than-usual Sigma in Philadelphia and the others by a simpler-than-usual Crawford-Shapiro team at Criteria in Miami. Moore's voice is simultaneously sweet and rough, an unusual combination in a woman, and the songs are pretty consistent. But she lacks not only persona but personality, so that what in technical terms is pretty impressive stuff never goes over the top. Original grade: B. **B+**

Jim Morrison: *An American Prayer* (Elektra '78). Subtitle: "Music by the Doors." Auxiliary subtitle: "Poems, Lyrics and Stories by James Douglas Morrison." Like every Morrison exploitation, this one is done with love — the Doors play like they've never been away. What it exploits, however, is a bad poet who got a chance to jack off with both hands when he didn't have to carry a tune. If you think lines like "Large buxom obese queens" or "We need great golden copulations" or "To propagate our lust for life" or "Death and my cock are the world" read bad, you should hear him recite them. **C**

Van Morrison: *Moondance* (Warner Bros. '70). An album worthy of an

Irish r&b singer who wrote a teen hit called "Mystic Eyes" (not to mention a Brill Building smash called "Brown Eyed Girl"), adding punchy brass (including pennywhistles and foghorn) and a solid backbeat (including congas) to his folk-jazz swing, and a popwise formal control to his Gaelic poetry. Morrison's soul, like that of the black music he loves, is mortal and immortal simultaneously; this is a man who gets stoned on a drink of water and urges us to turn up our radios all the way into (that word again) the mystic. Visionary hooks his specialty. Original grade: A. **A+**

Van Morrison: *His Band and the Street Choir* (Warner Bros. '70). Morrison is still a brooder — "Why did you leave America?" he asks over and over on the final cut, and though I'm not exactly sure what he's talking about, that sounds like a good all-purpose question/accusation to me — but not an obsessive one, and this is another half-step away from the acoustic late-night misery of *Astral Weeks*. As befits hits, "Domino" and especially "Blue Money" are more celebratory if no more joyous than anything on *Moondance,* showing off his loose, allusive white r&b at its most immediate. And while half of side two is comparatively humdrum, I play it anyway. Original grade: A minus. **A**

Van Morrison: *Tupelo Honey* (Warner Bros. '71). Van seems to be turning into a machine and a natural man simultaneously. I like the machine a whole lot — this super-bouncy product is almost as rich in cute tunes as *The Shirelles' Greatest Hits.* But I worry that domestic bliss with Janet Planet — who here abandons liner notes to pose with hubby fore, aft, and centerfold — has been softening Van's noodle more than the joy of cooking requires. **A−**

Van Morrison: *Saint Dominic's Preview* (Warner Bros. '72). "Jackie Wilson said it was reet petite," he shouts for openers, and soon has me believing that "I'm in heaven when you smile" says as much about the temporal and the eternal as anything in Yeats. "Listen to the lion," he advises later, referring to that lovely frightening beast inside each of us, and midway through the eleven-minute cut he lets the lion out, moaning and roaring and growling and stuttering in a scat extension that would do Leon Thomas proud. The point being that words — which on this album are as uneven as the tunes — sometimes say less than voices. Amen. **A−**

Van Morrison: *Hard Nose the Highway* (Warner Bros. '73). The relaxed rhythms are just lax most of the time, the vocal surprises mild after *St. Dominic's Preview,* the lyrics dumbest when they're more than mood pieces, and the song construction offhand except on "Warm Love." Original grade: C plus. **B−**

Van Morrison: *It's Too Late To Stop Now* (Warner Bros. '74). Songs that wore poorly or were just lame in the first place have more force and rightness on this exemplary live album than in their studio versions, and "Here Comes the Night" sounds fresher than it did in 1965. In addition, Morrison documents his debt to blues and r&b definitively — you can hear Bobby Bland all over the record, and cover tributes are paid as well to Ray Charles, John Lee Hooker, Sonny Boy Williamson, Muddy Waters, and Sam Cooke. Original grade: A minus. **A**

Van Morrison: *Veedon Fleece* (Warner Bros. '74). I count it as progress that his muse is feeding him baseball metaphors, but Morrison hasn't vented his Gaelic soul so unabashedly since *Astral Weeks.* He'd get away with it if there were more than one decent song on side two. Soothing, evocative late-night music that indulges his discursive side. Favorite title: "You Don't Pull No Punches but You Don't Push the River." **B+**

Van Morrison: *A Period of Transition* (Warner Bros. '77). "It Fills You Up" and "Heavy Connection" work on chant power alone, but even they go on a little too long, and in general this is an unexciting record — but not definitively. It's full of the surprising touches — the (borrowed) instrumental intros to the blues that opens side one and the jump tune that opens side two, a throw-in couplet about Amsterdam that might as well have Van's fingerprints on it, and even the can't-always-get-what-you-need chorus on "Eternal Kansas City" — that signify talent putting out. I don't know; maybe that's depressing proof that this isn't just a warmup. But after three years, let's say it is. **B**

Van Morrison: *Wavelength* (Warner Bros. '78). Unlike *A Period of Transition,* this is a good Van Morrison record, as up as any he's ever made, but it's certainly not a great one. You might pay attention to side two, an evocative reinterpretation of Van's America fixation, but side one is nothing more (and nothing less) than class programming. **B +**

Van Morrison: *Into the Music* (Warner Bros. '79). The rockers are a little lightweight, the final cut drags halfway through, and that's all that's wrong with this record, including its tributes to "the Lord." You might get religion yourself if all of your old powers returned after years of failed experiments, half-assed compromises, and onstage crack-ups. Like that other godfearing singer-songwriter, Morrison has abandoned metaphorical pretensions, but only because he loves the world. His straightforward celebrations of town and country are colored and deepened by his musicians — especially sprightly violinist Toni Marcus (feh on Scarlet Rivera) — and by his own excursions into a vocalise that has never been more various or apt. The only great song on this record is "It's All in the Game," written by Calvin Coolidge's future vice-president in 1912. But I suspect it's Van's best album since *Moondance.* **A**

Pablo Moses: *I Love I Bring* (United Artists '78). A lot of these charming, moralistic reggae ditties have the lyrical and melodic simplicity of Sunday School hymns — "Be Not a Dread"

could almost be a roots "Jesus Loves the Little Children." And whoever devised the synthesizer riffs that set off Moses's spacey singsong deserves a gold star. **A —**

Mother Earth: *Satisfied* (Mercury '70). Tracy Nelson doesn't touch everyone, but once she does she carries you away. She can be sexual and spiritual not successively but on the same note and breath; she seems to suffer and to transcend suffering simultaneously. Vocally, Mother Earth is now Tracy Nelson, and although in theory I miss the male voices — especially that of Robert St. John, whose songwriting always added something too — I'm not really complaining. Yet this record is a slight disappointment. I love it, but I know that my prejudices are strong and that only once — on her own composition, "Andy's Song" — does Tracy burst calmly into free space as she does so often on the two previous Mother Earth lps and on *Tracy Nelson Country.* Recommended unequivocally to her cadre and equivocally to the benighted. **A —**

Mother Earth: *Bring Me Home* (Reprise '71). On the face of it this is a slight improvement, introducing three major songs — the Eric Kaz side-openers and Steve Young's "Seven Bridges Road." And if the powerful, arresting arrangement of Kaz's "Temptation Took Control of Me and I Fell" isn't as far out as what the original band used to try in San Francisco, it's certainly played with more assurance. Still, when you've boiled it down to backing up the singer and the songs, both had better be special all the time. And they ain't. Original grade: A. **B +**

Mother Mallard's Portable Masterpiece Co.: *Like a Duck to Water* (Earthquack '76). Synthesizer mantras recommended to those exploring the space between Eno and Philip Glass, with the warning that they're more sober than the lighthearted name-title-label might make you hope. Original grade: B plus.   **B**

Mothers, Mothers of Invention: See Frank Zappa

The Motors: *The Motors* (Virgin '77). Good label, good name, good image, even a reference from Ducks Deluxe, but beware — this is your basic homogenized bombast. The giveaway is the logo. Remember the Consumer Guide rule: never trust a group with a logo.   **C**

The Motors: *Approved by the Motors* (Virgin '78). Last time, they essayed a commercial takeoff on punk, which they traced back to Grand Funk Railroad rather than the Stooges; this time (punk having been declared economically unsound by English bizzers), they have a go at power pop and come out sounding like the Foundations rather than the Small Faces. Since reformed pub rockers are more comfortable with cuteness than with power, this is an enormous improvement — "Airport" is as funny as any Nick Lowe genre piece and catchy enough to do jingle duty at Gatwick. Unfortunately, just to keep up their pseudopunk credibility, they also include an equivocal celebration of sadism. I mean, fun is fun.   **B +**

Mott the Hoople: *Mott the Hoople* (Atlantic '70). Despite the hype, these guys strike me as an ordinary hard rock combo. Their sameyness is not disguised by the melange of influences on side one — early Kinks, Bob Dylan, Sir Douglas, Bob Dylan, Sonny Bono, Bob Dylan, and Bob Dylan — and on side two this melange is quickly boiled down to its medium: sloppy hard rock with heavy leanings, big on post-Kingsmen instrumentals. Original grade: C.   **C +**

Mott the Hoople: *Brain Capers* (Atlantic '72). After a debut album that pitted imaginative borrowing against imitative self-expression, *Mad Shadows* and *Wild Life* descended thrashing and caterwauling into the depths of rock and roll psychodrama — what could one expect of "improvisations" based on such faceless "originals"? So this is a heartening reverse — not only do they unearth Dion's suppressed farewell to junkiedom, "Your Own Back Yard," and a good old Youngbloods number, but they provide originals that can stand behind them. Unfortunately, the two exceptions take up more than twelve minutes.   **B**

Mott the Hoople: *All the Young Dudes* (Columbia '72). Those enamored of the dirty sound Guy Stevens got out of (or imposed on) this band complain that David Bowie's production is thin and antiseptic, but I always found their Atlantic albums fuzzy, and anyway, the material is powerful enough to overwhelm such quibbles. Mick Ralphs and Verden Allen make catchy. Bowie's title tune captures the spirit of a dispossessed younger (than me, Bowie, or Mott the Hoople) generation united by a style against time. The Velvet Underground cover is definitive. And Ian Hunter does more than get away with a long, slow, pretentious one at the close — "Sea Diver" is a triumph. Original grade: A.   **A −**

Mott the Hoople: *Mott* (Columbia '73). Ian and the boys are definitely too self-referential, and they don't entirely convince me that they've earned our credence as the great failed band of the new loser mythology. But as rock and roll this is damn near irresistible, sure to stand as a textbook of killer riffs 'n' hooks. Even the throwaways are ace, except maybe for Mick Ralphs's Spanish guitar showcase. And not only has Ian's Dylan fixation become funny, but Ian knows it. Original grade: B plus.   **A −**

Mott the Hoople: *The Hoople* (Columbia '74). "Roll Away the Stone" and maybe "Golden Age of Rock 'n' Roll" are classics in their neoclassical mode, which is also to say that they're nothing new, and the marginal stuff is quite undifferentiated. I suspect that Ian Hunter's ego, which he deserves, is crowding out the others. And I know for sure that Ariel Bender flashes more ego than Mick Ralphs ever did, and that he deserves none of it.   **B**

Mott the Hoople: _Rock and Roll Queen_ (Atlantic '74). Mick Ralphs's title tune — which is to "Starfucker" as Bad Company is to the Rolling Stones — defines the virtues and limitations of this raucous compilation. Rescuing serviceable rockers from all of their Atlantic albums and utilizing only the most simple-minded covers ("You Really Got Me" and "Keep a Knockin' "), it presents pre-Bowie Mott as an endearingly crude touring band, with enough hooks to keep things going. And it draws on only five minutes of _Brain Capers._   **B +**

Mott the Hoople: _Greatest Hits_ (Columbia '76). Hits my ass. Never heard "Foxy Foxy" on the radio, and never want to. But the other new one, "Saturday Gigs," recapitulates quite movingly a banal theme this collection fleshes out with real wallop: a band and its fans. Four songs is too much overlap with _Mott,_ but this is the essence of Mott the Hoople as a group, which always needed Ian Hunter and always did more than back him up.   **A −**

Mountain: _Mountain Climbing_ (Windfall '70). We all know they're the original Cremora — what this makes clearer is that they're Jack Bruce's third of the jar. On "For Yasgur's Farm" Felix Pappalardi emulates JB's self-dramatizing vocal propriety as well as his bass lines, but when Leslie West runs an acoustic guitar solo from raga to flamenco without ever touching the blues you know he's not doing an Eric Clapton tribute. Can't fit the humongous "Mississippi Queen" into this theory, but I can tell you who wrote "Theme for an Imaginary Western": Jack Bruce and Pete Brown.   **C +**

Mountain: _Flowers of Evil_ (Windfall '71). You can't deny these boys are pros — they know how to pace an album, hard ones and soft ones and golden oldies and rhinestone originals,

and I still love their famous fat-skinny counterpoint on stage. But any group that can attach a line like "Proud and gentle was the loving of the last two island swans" to a great hard rock tune has got to be doing something wrong.   **C**

Mountain: _The Best of Mountain_ (Windfall '73). _Mountain Climbing_ is the only album of theirs I've ever enjoyed even momentarily. This selects all of its enjoyable tracks and adds relatively classy filler like "Nantucket Sleighride" (heavy-metal myth discovers America) and "The Animal Trainer and the Toad" (one of two songs on this record to mention Beethoven). So I guess it's better. But it's not that much better. [Later on Columbia.]   **C +**

The Move: _Shazam_ (A&M '70). Its enthusiasts to the contrary, this is hardly the greatest rock and roll record ever to thump down the pike. It's just an artier version of the overly self-conscious mode I call stupid-rock, simultaneously gargantuan and prissy, like dinosaurs gallumphing through the tulips. It would be a lot worse if it weren't so funny, but it would also be a lot less funny if it were a little better. Recommended to Stooges fans who just found a five-dollar bill.   **B −**

The Move: _Looking On_ (Capitol '71). Anyone who doesn't believe heavy metal is a Yurrupean plot will kindly inform me which B the countermelodies on this one were stolen from. Not Berry or the Beatles, believe me.   **C +**

The Move: _Message from the Country_ (Capitol '71). I have reservations about any record that falls into the dubious category of hard rock for critics, but am willing to grant that to climax a side of music from Brobdingnag with a Johnny Cash imitation is to show truly transcendent chutzpah. In fact, after brief acclimatization I like every cut. What seemed forced on _Looking On_ now seems comic — there are parodies here of everything from weedy Yes-style vocals and wimpy Baby-style acoustics to rockabilly and music hall. And melodic moves that sounded glued on now seem integral. Recommended to those who like the idea of Grand Funk Railroad better than the reality. **A −**

The Move: *Split Ends* (United Artists '73). "Do Ya" — rated single of the year in the rock press, apparently the only place it was distributed — signals a phase in the Move's career that comprises four songs, three uncharacteristically rock-and-rolly and all prime. Most of what remains here was first released on the more exotic *Message from the Country* (already a cut-out), which I also admire. Consistently good stuff, although the styles do grate. Original grade: B plus. **A −**

The Move: *The Best of the Move* (A&M '74). I could trot out the complaint that this double-LP would make a good single, but why bother? Comprising the band's 1967 U.K. debut LP and a lot of uncollected forty-fives, with two sets of notes and detailed discographical data, this is a labor of love that lists at only a buck over the one-record price. Anyway, they wouldn't pick the same cuts I would: my fave is "Wave Your Flag and Stop the Train," which they regard as a Monkees imitation — not a very exact one, I'd say, but close enough to the pop at which they supposedly excelled. I love rock and roll — I just want it to be better. Bands like the Move feel hemmed in by rock and roll — they want it to be different, or more. When they succeed, as the Move finally did, it's often better too. But usually it's less. **B**

Geoff & Maria Muldaur: *Pottery Pie* (Reprise '70). On side one, the nice tunes from the predictable variety of traditional and contemporary sources are too unfocused to be more than pleasant, but the flip is a modest post-folkie treat. "Me and My Chauffeur Blues" shows off Maria's sexiest moods — coy, melancholy, swoony, demanding, and at the end she and her chauffeur come together — while "Death Letter Blues" shows off

Geoff's most haunted blues voice. In between he camps up "Brazil," she strolls through "Georgia on My Mind," and Jim Kweskin asks Mel Lyman for further instructions. **B**

Geoff & Maria Muldaur: *Sweet Potatoes* (Reprise '72). I really like this album, especially when Geoff gets nasty on "I'm Rich" and the sophomoric cheap shot "Kneein' Me," both of which he wrote. But Chuck Berry's "Havana Moon" gives away his limitations. "Havana Moon" simply isn't a very good song — it's only "interesting," as a pop aberration that has nothing to do with the thrust of Berry's music. Muldaur's version works quite well only because it singles out how "interesting" (and obscure) the song is. And too often "interesting" is all he wants to be. **B +**

Geoff Muldaur and Amos Garrett: *Geoff Muldaur and Amos Garrett* (Flying Fish '78). Because Garrett's amiable baritone and astringent guitar tend toward blues, this is more coherent Muldaur than either of his Warner solos. And I assume a limited budget curbed some of his sillier experimental fancies, which couldn't have hurt. But his fondness for genteel schlock — tunes by Chopin and Tchaikovsky, a rancid chestnut called "Beautiful Isle of Somewhere" — still grates. **B**

Maria Muldaur: *Maria Muldaur* (Reprise '73). Cut by cut, this bid to contemporize Maria's nouveau-jug music (two songs each from Wendy Waldman and David Nichtern, one each from Dr. John and Kate McGarrigle) is intelligent and attractive. But the overall effect is just slightly aimless and sterile. Maybe it's Muldaur's quavery voice, which only rarely has driven me to attention, or the low-risk flawlessness of the Lenny Waronker/Joe Boyd production. Or maybe it's just the curse of the jugheads — not knowing how to make good on your flirtations with nostalgia. **B +**

Maria Muldaur: *Waitress in a Donut Shop* (Reprise '74). In which a new

'50s nostalgia, beatnikism, is manipulated to exploit reasonable doubts and fears about sex-role redefinition. No woman hip (or even tasteful) enough to love Skip James has the right to pretend there's such a thing as an earth mother. And if the production last time was too safe, this is what it was guarding against — ecch-lectic cliches. **C+**

Martin Mull: *Martin Mull* (Capricorn '72). Firesign Theater/Cheech & Chong equals Randy Newman/Martin Mull. **B—**

Mungo Jerry: *Mungo Jerry* (Janus '70). One accidental if inevitable hit reveals this English jug band as the best novelty group since the Coasters, though the Royal Guardsmen and the Chipmunks aren't what I'd call heavy competition. Great hostling noises, an echo-chamber parody that could make Stan Freberg turn to commercials, and a fair share of dirty talk. But just as Alvin's falsetto used to wear thin after a while, so does Mungo's drawl —and kazoo. Original grade: B plus. **B**

Mungo Jerry: *Mungo Jerry* (Pye '75). Long after vanishing in the States they were making like the next Creedence over there, releasing six French singles in 1971 alone and cracking top ten in England three more times. Their mood quickly shifted from old- to good-timey, always vaguely entertaining and sometimes on target, as in the affectionate but critical getting-old song "You Better Leave That Whiskey Alone." But leader Ray Dorset never showed the kind of acuity as a singer or writer that turns bands into Creedences over here. **B**

Elliott Murphy: *Aquashow* (Polydor '73). The music here sounds so middle-Dylan that it inspired me to play *Blonde on Blonde,* after which unfair comparison I began to suspect Murphy of glibness. But although his themes aren't new and he does come at them like a know-it-all, that's not his fault — he does know quite a bit, maybe more than is good for him, and the quick phrases merely shield a plausible sincerity. Special concern: interrelations between women's self-knowledge (and lack of it) and the emotional disappointments of sexual love. None of which you're obliged to notice until you enjoy the music a dozen times. Original grade: A. **A—**

Elliott Murphy: *Lost Generation* (RCA Victor '75). The mistake is Paul Rothschild's production, too tasty and anonymous to support the innocence that made Murphy's basically tinny voice and underachieved rock and roll convincing. Deprived of the benefit of the doubt, Murphy's awkward literaryness starts to stick out. You wonder whether his lost generation was really shaped with a "technicolor carving knife." You wonder just how much he knows about Eva Braun. You wonder why the two strongest cuts on the record — the love songs on side one — are the ones you notice last. And in the end you hope the next record makes it. **B**

Elliott Murphy: *Street Lights* (RCA Victor '76). This time I can't blame the production — if anything, Steve Katz's understated hard rock and adept background voices lend emotional weight to songs that would otherwise sound hopelessly immature. Murphy's voice has always been callow, but whereas two-and-a-half years ago he came across as a compassionate kid who reached out toward the world as a natural function of his self-discovery, now he sounds like an effete young man who strikes out at the world as a natural function of his self-involvement. The distinction is less than clear-cut, and perhaps too sharp to apply to an artist of such laudable moral ambition, but anyone who praises someone whose "wounds are open for the sake of art" (ugh! what a line!) has never heard the one about the heart and the sleeve. **C+**

Elliott Murphy: *Just a Story from America* (Columbia '77). If anyone can write a rock ballad to a deposed Russian princess made famous by Ingrid Bergman it's Murphy — the image sums up the F. Scott Fitzgerald/Rhett Butler (and Eva Braun?) side of a boy-man who's also heir to the traditional reverence for Jimi Hendrix and James Dean. Instead, the song is the embarrassing epitome of a record on which Murphy sounds spoiled instead of sensitive, presumptuous instead of ambitious, and about as comfortable with rock and roll as Roderick Falconer.   **C −**

The Walter Murphy Band: *A Fifth of Beethoven* (Private Stock '77). What a ripoff. Here I am expecting disco versions of "Claire de Lune," *Carmina Burana,* and at least three Brandenburg concerti, and what do I get but eight tunes by W. Murphy? Take it from me, Walter — from Beethoven you make great schlock, transcendent schlock even, but from Murphy you just make schlock.   **D +**

Anne Murray: *Snowbird* (Capitol '70). An honest if rather clumsy pop country album from the Canadian who had a well-deserved hit with the title song. Her corny and superfluous "Get Together" is more than made up for by (believe it or not) the best cover version of "I'll Be Your Baby Tonight" I know, and if "Running" is a little stiff, you tell me how many other pop country artists sing the praises of draft dodging. Time: 24:26. Original grade: B.   **B −**

Anne Murray: *Annie* (Capitol '72). Since her first hit Murray has personified pop at its most unaffected, nice in all the obvious ways — intelligent, cheerful, warm, even wholesome. The strongest of her five albums offers ten realistic, deeply felt songs, including "You Made My Life a Song," the most unpained come-back-if-you-break-up-with-your-new-love I've ever heard. I like every cut. Just wish I loved one. Time: 28:38. Original grade: B plus.   **B**

Anne Murray: *Danny's Song* (Capitol '73). Murray's kind of pop must flirt with blandness if it is to be seductive at all, and this time she Goes Too Far. Conventional material is a big problem — even the title tune has been defined elsewhere, and by Kenny Loggins. In fact, there are a couple of live tracks here that have been defined elsewhere by Murray herself.   **C +**

Anne Murray: *Love Song* (Capitol '74). I worry that my former second-favorite clean-cut female singer will do a Helen Reddy and begin reminding me of Doris Day, but if anything this is a move toward La Vern Baker — "Just One Look" and "You Won't See Me" rock with unexpected grit. She should have left Kenny Loggins when the leaving was good, and I wish more of her MOR packed as much domestic drama and fresh-air sincerity as "Another Pot 'o Tea" or "Real Emotion," but this is her best to date.   **B**

Anne Murray: *Country* (Capitol '74). Say what you like about countrypolitan, Murray has a lot more roots than Olivia Newton-John — is Hank Snow from Melbourne or Nova Scotia? And say what you like about strings, Brian Ahern's are a lot more thoughtful than Billy Sherrill's — is a cliche only authentic when it becomes a habit? But though the country audience deserves credit for giving Murray a hearing, this compilation proves that it doesn't bring out the very best in her. Wish somebody could figure out what does.   **B**

Anne Murray: *Highly Prized Possession* (Capitol '74). This is a hair and a half from capturing her amused, husky sweetness and square-jawed sex appeal, and I'll settle. Ballads, message songs, and medium-tempo heart-tuggers have all been slightly upgraded, and the reggaefied Bobby Darin and her latest Beatles cover rock as good as Ronstadt.   **B +**

Anne Murray: *Together* (Capitol '75). Tom Smucker, who should know, says the difference between the departed Brian Ahern and Tom Catalano, the producer Murray has inherited from Helen Reddy, is the difference between Revisionist Anti Schlock and Assumed Schlock. If Schlock is "materialism in a Dionysian mode" — innocent, like Las Vegas as Tom Wolfe explains it — then Assumed Schlock "takes consumption for granted as consumption turns into smug middle-class accumulation." In other words, all the Canadian songwriters in the world can't overcome the extravagant dullness of these arrangements: the rock 'n' roll cut could be Giselle MacKenzie in 1956. Say it ain't so, Annie.   **C**

Anne Murray: *I'll Always Love You* (Capitol '79). Murray's third album with Jim Ed Norman continues her gradual revitalization. Norman does clean, honest, Nashville-quality work, Murray gives forth with the old sensible spunk, and the singles break country and cross over just like they're supposed to. But the potential a few of us perceived in her five years ago is gone. Then Murray seemed to have a shot at women's pop, in the honorific way that term was used after Warhol and the Beatles — a Canadian gym teacher who could rock and roll, a militantly ordinary audience with a lesbian fringe. Now she's just quality MOR, singing the El Lay songbook (only two Canadian composers here, one of whom is Jesse Winchester) like a down-to-earth Emmylou, or Linda without charisma. Which means that exactly how good her records come out no longer matters.   **B −**

Junior Murvin: *Police and Thieves* (Mango '77). Great rhythm tracks, better-than-average falsetto, and two compelling cuts leading into eight pleasant ones make for a more than passable and slightly less than recommended reggae LP.   **B**

Musique: *Keep on Jumpin'* (Prelude '78). Just to reassure anyone pin-headed enough to suspect that I've gone over to The Enemy, I thought I'd mention this disco cult item, one of those tragedies of amyl nitrite poisoning that so distress sympathetic observers like myself. To start with the worst, half the record is devoted to a stupefying pop melody yclept "Summer Love" for 6:17 on side one and "Summer Love Theme" for 8:00 on side two. By comparison, the serviceable dance mix of the title track shines, and the headliner would be brilliant in any company: 8:20 of spare polyrhythm that never stops jumpin' and might be mistaken for the Wild Magnolias in the age of mechanical reproduction (except that it's faster). The problem is the title, which not surprisingly dominates the lyric. I grant that ("Push, push") "In the Bush" is a phrase that sticks in the mind, but so is "sit on my face." I can imagine dancing to either in the heat of the 8:20. But would we have anything to say over coffee the next morning?   **C +**

Mutiny: *Mutiny on the Mamaship* (Columbia '79). In which former P-Funk drummer Jerome Brailey — a/k/a Him Bad, Bigfoot — leads a noisy revolt against "George Penatentiory," who stands accused of faking the funk. The charge isn't fair, but Brailey proves he's no clone (and earns his sobriquets) with a boomingly bottom-heavy LP that's more lowdown powerful than anything the muthashippas have ever tried to do. And if his lovey-dovey moves are received — unlike George, Brailey never led a great harmony group — his horn and guitar parts are far out indeed. Hope there's an answer record.   **A −**

The Naked Carmen (Mercury '70). The aptest instance of overpretension in the history of rock-is-art. It makes more sense to do a rock/pop take-off on a vulgar work in a vulgar genre than to collaborate on derivative moderne with Zubin Mehta (the Mothers) or stick your amps in front of a notoriously venal symphony orchestra (Deep Purple). The c&w version of "The Toreador Song" is perfect. Great package, too. I may even keep it. **C**

Graham Nash: *Wild Tales* (Atlantic '74). The title is as phony as the rest of the album, which despite the paid-for goodies — harmony here, intro there, even a song somewhere or other — is a tame collection of reshuffled platitudes. Especially annoying: "Oh! Camil," in which Graham lets us know that he is morally superior to a doubt-ridden Vietnam vet. **C−**

Johnny Nash: *I Can See Clearly Now* (Epic '72). Based on a simple, undemanding, slightly syncopated rhythmic figure that sounds like it was lifted from "Wimoweh" and is broken only by a chorus of angels, its unremittingly cheerful tag line redeemed by the unexpected realism of "I can see all obstacles in my way," the title song is the first true reggae ever to go top ten in the U.S. It's also the kind of single that can get you through a traffic jam. The album melds Caribbean soul — composer Bob Marley's is the best —

with Nash's diffident, church-derived, televisable vocal conception. It might get you through a day in the country if all the other available music were by Chuck Mangione. **B**

Nashville (ABC '75). The only musician of promise here, Ronee Blakley, hasn't righted any of the quirks that unfocused her solo debut three years ago, and she's no more a country singer than Wendy Waldman. If the music makes the movie, as more than one film critic has surmised, then the movie is a lie. Another possibility: the critics are fibbing a little to cover their ignorance. **C**

Rick Nelson: *In Concert* (Decca '70). Reassuring to learn there are constants in this changing world — a dozen years ago, Nelson was an inspired fake, and he still is. At worst this is a tasteful country-rock album marred by a mildness typical of the style and one too many Dylan covers. "Hello Mary Lou" far outshines any of Rick's four originals, but "Hello Mary Lou" has always been a terrific song, and I'd go see this band in a club in Denver any time. Original grade: B. **C+**
Rick Nelson and the Stone Canyon Band: *Garden Party* (Decca '72). This is the music "no one heard" at the Garden party because Rick "didn't look the same." Despite such titles as "Are You Really Real?" and "A Flower Opens Gently By" he has some

reason to pout if music rather than songs is the operative concept — the band is concentrated, jagged. Best music: Chuck Berry's "I'm Talking About You." Second-best song: Rick's own "So Long Mama." **B −**

Tracy Nelson: *Mother Earth Presents Tracy Nelson Country* (Mercury '70). Country specialists don't approve of this — seem to feel it's cheating to step lively with such undeniable material. But only an inspired cheat would feature songs by Crudup, Willis, Scaggs, and T. Nelson on her country album. And only a paragon would sing them so sweet, direct, and strong. Nor would the mix of musicians — led by original Elvis guitarist Scotty Moore — occur to your everyday Nashvillian. Country, rock, who cares — eleven beautiful songs beautifully rendered. Original grade: A minus. **A**

Tracy Nelson/Mother Earth: *Tracy Nelson/Mother Earth* (Reprise '72). Living with the animals is turning this band bovine. The big development — not counting the new billing — is a goodly helping of gospel piano, which like everything else is quite pleasant without counteracting the inevitable drags. Praise the Lord for one thing: they do admit to the "Tennessee Blues." **B**

Tracy Nelson/Mother Earth: *Poor Man's Paradise* (Columbia '73). Jack Lee's three songs include one about how California was too hectic for him, and the only tune better than that comes from Willie Dixon, a specialist in the blues music a band of more or less the same name once played. **C +**

Tracy Nelson: *Tracy Nelson* (Atlantic '74). Even at her peak, Nelson risked sluggishness; you wondered whether that was placidity or metabolic malfunction. Now her voice has thickened, its seriousness become leaden. It takes her a minute longer to finish "Down So Low" than it did six years ago. Literally tedious: "tiresome be-cause of slowness, continuance, or prolixity." **C −**

Willie Nelson: *Yesterday's Wine* (RCA Victor '71). The great Nashville songsmith has never bowled anyone over with his singing, and here he finds the concept to match. Since "perfect man" has already been and gone, he announces at the outset, "the voice of imperfect man must now be made manifest, and I have been chosen as the most likely candidate." Most of these songs — though not the two best, "Yesterday's Wine" and "Me and Paul"— are on religious themes, and on more than one he seems to be playing the part of God's messenger, which tends to limit their general relevance. But if that's how he got to "These Are Difficult Times," maybe it was worth it. Anyway, sometimes his nonsinging bowls me over. **B +**

Willie Nelson: *Shotgun Willie* (Atlantic '73). This attempt to turn Nelson into a star runs into trouble when it induces him to outshout Memphis horns or Western swing, and his unaccompanied-acoustic version of "A Song for You" takes some getting used to. After a while though, you notice that you're noticing every song. And then you realize that the two you notice most — the slyly vengeful "Sad Songs and Waltzes" and the cuckold's tragedy "She's Not for You"— are also the two oldest. A star, eh? **B +**

Willie Nelson: *Phases and Stages* (Atlantic '74). Although the musical concept-theme that pops up here and there is unnecessarily explicit, the songs more than justify it. On the woman's side of the breakup, try "Washing the Dishes" (soap gets in your eyes) or "Sister's Coming Home"/"Down at the Beer Joint" (going home to mother as non-joke); on the man's, "It's Not Supposed to Be That Way" (but it is) and "Pick Up the Tempo" (on the rebound). What's more, Nelson's combination of soft-spoken off-key and battered honky-tonk matches the bare, responsive country music Jerry Wexler has gotten out of the Muscle Shoals regulars. Payoff: the two Mike Lewis string arrangements are actually climactic. Original grade: B plus. **A −**

Willie Nelson: *Red Headed Stranger* (Columbia '75). This tale of a murdering preacher wild in his abandonment has inspired much loose talk about violence and Western myth. Ed Ward argues that the Stranger is a fantasy of vengeance rejected on side two, but all I hear is that he's redeemed by another woman there — if she leaves him, he'll kill her too. Some of the individual pieces are quite nice, but the gestalt is the concept album at its most counterproductive — the lyrics render the nostalgic instrumental parts unnecessarily ironic and lose additional charm in narrative context. Original grade: C. **B −**

Willie Nelson: *The Sound in Your Mind* (Columbia '76). "That Lucky Old Sun" sounds better than "Amazing Grace"; Steve Fromholz's "I'd Have to Be Crazy" sounds better than Willie's "The Sound in Your Mind." Willie had better watch it — Major Artists can't grind out Product the way Country Music Stars do or people'll start thinkin' they're slippin'. Original grade: C. **B −**

Willie Nelson: *To Lefty from Willie* (Columbia '77). Although Nelson earned his legend as a songwriter, he's turning into a singer now that profit-taking time has come — does broaden one. The amazing thing is that he gets away with it. On this heartfelt if opportune farewell to Lefty Frizzell, his cracks and creaks and precisely conversational timing hold their own against the more conventionally exquisite singing of Merle Haggard or Frizzell himself. Of course, the material doesn't hurt. Time: 29:36. **B +**

Willie Nelson: *Stardust* (Columbia '78). I can always do without "Unchained Melody," and at times I wish he'd pick up the tempo. Basically, though, I'm real happy this record exists, not just because Nelson can be a great interpretive singer — his "Moonlight in Vermont" is a revelation — but because he's provided me with eleven great popular songs that I've never had much emotional access to. Standards that deserve the name — felt, deliberate, schmaltz-free. **A −**

Willie Nelson: *Face of a Fighter* (Lone Star '78). It's been four years since Nelson put together an album of the mournful country love songs that earned him an outlaw's independence, and even that was a concept job. These ten slow songs — maybe six special, no clinkers — were recorded thirteen years before that, apparently as demos, and the music is wonderful. Nelson's voice has never come on more fragile or deliberate — you can almost hear him figuring out what commonplace he's going to illuminate next — and his band sounds equally sure-footed. Rarely is there a lick you haven't heard somewhere before, but the lick always seems just a leetle different, which may be because it's so exquisitely timed and may be because it's just a leetle different. **A −**

Willie Nelson and Leon Russell: *One for the Road* (Columbia '79). As the duo dueted swingingly through "I Saw the Light" and "Heartbreak Hotel" on the first of these four sides, I thought Willie had somehow gotten away with yet another triumphant nonalbum, but the slack B-Western self-parody of "Don't Fence Me In" and "Sioux City Sue" on side two set me straight. And sides three and four, where Leon accompanies Willie through another batch of stardust, are a mistake — even if the music were as good (compare this "Lucky Old Sun" to the one on *Sound in Your Mind*), it's too soon for a reprise. Frank Sinatra he's not. **B −**

Willie Nelson: *Willie Nelson Sings Kristofferson* (Columbia '79). Needless to say, he also outsings Kristofferson, and without much extra in the god-given department, though the high note that climaxes "Please Don't Tell Me How the Story Ends" is a doozy. But his inborn tact is wasted on this material. As Al Green, Janis Joplin, Elvis Presley, and even Ray Price have proven, the way to put such arrant corn across is to pull out the stops. **B −**

Willie Nelson: See also Waylon Jennings and Willie Nelson

Mike Nesmith & the First National Band: *Magnetic South* (RCA Victor '70). "I love it here on the range," the Smart Monkee yodels, but then he adds that he'd "love it more if it changed," which sums up *his* country-rock synthesis quite nicely. I don't know if he's serious about this "free from euphemisms and alive with their own emotions" stuff he writes about in the notes, but one reason I like his songs is that they never seem to mean exactly what they say — even "Joanne," which could be covered by Paul Butterfield or Linda Ronstadt or somebody, partakes of the bemused natural distance that saves his more aimless experiments from getting lost. **B**

Mike Nesmith and the First National Band: *Loose Salute* (RCA Victor '70). In which Nesmith continues his transmutation into Gram Parsons for television fans, or the Jimmie Rodgers of Sunset Strip. I'm beginning to suspect that he takes his meandering thoughts and marble columns in the sky more seriously than they deserve. But his songwriting gifts are at a peak on this amalgam of gimmicks and mannerisms, long-vowel articles and near-yodels and electronic excursions and alien rhythms. At its best, sublime schlock; at its worst, downhome kitsch. **B +**

Michael Nesmith & the First National Band: *Nevada Fighter* (RCA Victor '71). This begins perfectly, with Nes fleeing the "Grand Ennui" (which I heard as "Opry" first time). And continues honorably with "Propinquity (I've Just Begun To Care)" (the Stone Poneys tribute). And then falls flat on its face with three vacant originals and a side of moderately well-chosen but extremely unnecessary covers. Nes-

mith just isn't a strong enough singer for such stuff — makes you think he got his gig through connections. **C +**

Michael Nesmith & the Second National Band: *Tantamount to Treason Volume 1* (RCA Victor '72). The good original is willfully weird. So are the bad ones. So is the good cover. The bad covers are just bad. Volume 1, eh? **C**

Michael Nesmith: *Compilation* (Pacific Arts '77). Nesmith began his career on RCA as a crackpot inventor and ended as a bankrupt cottage industry. The title of his final RCA LP, *And the Hits Just Keep On Coming,* was more wishful than sarcastic, which is why he's seen to its reissue, as well as that of *Pretty Much Your Standard Ranch Stash,* another pretty much standard country-song sampler. Seven of the twelve cuts on this compilation (another great title) come from those two albums. The side that concentrates on earlier stuff is an amazing contraption, one piece of zonked Nashville after another. The other side is a pretty much standard-plus display case. Among the missing: "The Grand Ennui," "Calico Girlfriend," "Mama Nantucket," "The Keys to the Car." **B +**

Michael Nesmith: *Infinite Rider on the Big Dogma* (Pacific Arts '79). The Smart Monkee has turned into the Young Herb Alpert, rock's most successful artist-businessman. Pacific Arts, which he owns outright, has purchased his RCA masters for reissue and released albums by such artists as Charles Lloyd. It's also put out Nesmith's ghastly boxed audio-allegory-with-book *The Prison* his desultory reputed cult album *From a Radio Engine to the Photon Wing,* his live LP, and now this intelligent, hard-rocking item. What's not clear is whether the records make money — TV commercials are the company's staple. Though Nesmith hasn't sounded this good in years, there's a difference between the pop eccentric he's become and the country-rock eccentric he used to be — he's now a little behind the times instead of ahead of them. Still beats most of what the majors market as power pop. But the only necessity he conveys is a continuing compulsion to make music. And that's not sufficient. **B −**

Mickey Newbury: *Looks Like Rain* (Mercury '70). Sounds like rain, too — also wind, train whistles, ghosts, humming, whistling, electric sitars, and Norman Luboff. If the Mystic Moods Orchestra is Jerry Kennedy's idea of artistic production, he should stick to putting five pieces behind Jerry Lee and Tom T. But my guess is that it's Mickey's. The man is, or can be, a great songwriter, but this lady who left him because she was sad has thrown him into a depression so interesting he wants to savor every drop — almost ruins "She Even Woke Me Up to Say Goodbye" by taking it too slow. Never trust meteorological symbolism — never. [Later with *Live at Montezuma Hall* on Elektra.] **B −**

Mickey Newbury: *'Frisco Mabel Joy* (Elektra '71). Newbury has somehow attracted the meaningfulness vote by patching bits of "Dixie," "All My Trials," and "The Battle Hymn of the Republic" into a new copyright called "An American Trilogy," but don't worry, not everything here is so ponderous and thick with emotion. Not so ponderous, anyway — he's still mulling over that love affair, and he does get weepy about it. This is the new Nashville? Because his relationships break up in California? **C +**

Randy Newman: *12 Songs* (Reprise '70). As a rule, American songwriting is banal, prolix, and virtually solipsistic when it wants to be honest, merely banal when it doesn't. Newman's truisms — always concise, never confessional — are his own. Speaking through recognizable American grotesques, he comments here on the generation gap (doomed), incendiary violence (fucked up but sexy), male and female (he identifies with the males, most of whom are losers and weirdos), racism (he's against it, but he knows

its seductive power), and alienation (he's for it). Newman's music counterposes his indolent drawl — the voice of a Jewish kid from L.A. who grew up on Fats Domino — against an array of instrumental settings that on this record range from rock to bottleneck to various shades of jazz. And because his lyrics abjure metaphor and his music recalls commonplaces without repeating them, he can get away with the kind of calculated effects that destroy more straightforward meaningmongers. A perfect album. **A +**

Randy Newman: *Live* (Reprise '71). Six of these fourteen wonderful songs are on Newman's first album and four on his second, all set off by the arrangements that are the other half of his gift, none crippled by one-take vocals. Of the four new ones, "Lonely at the Top" — originally written for Frank Sinatra, who refused to have anything to do with it — is the only killer. **B**

Randy Newman: *Sail Away* (Reprise '72). Like most aesthetes, Newman is an ironist. This is fine when he's singing about human relationships, which tend to be problematic, but it's rarely sufficient morally to the big political and religious themes he favors these days. If *12 Songs* was *Winesburg, Ohio* (or even *Dubliners*) transported to 1970 Los Angeles, *Sail Away* sometimes has the tone of Tom Lehrer transported to 1972 Haiphong, where he has no more business than Bob Hope. But never before has Newman managed to yoke his orchestral command to his piano, and I hope the leap in listenability will attract some new admirers. Also, the cosmic ironies do fit the title song, in which a slave trader becomes the first advertising man, or perhaps — this is not Tom Lehrer stuff — Melville's confidence-man, for a masterpiece even stranger and more masterful than Newman's other masterpieces. **A −**

Randy Newman: *Good Old Boys* (Reprise '74). Despite my immense misgivings — Newman's political sensitivity, a useful attribute in one conceptualizing about the South, has never impressed me — I'm convinced that this is Newman's second-best album. It also rights a career that was threatening to wind down into cheap sarcasm. Contrary to published report, the white Southerners Newman sings about/from are never objects of contempt. Even Newman's psychotic and exhibitionist and moron show dignity and imagination, and the rednecks of the album's most notorious songs are imbued by the smart-ass Los Angeles Jew who created them with ironic distance, a smart-ass's kindest cut of all. There is, natcherly, a darker irony: no matter how smart they are about how dumb they are, they still can't think of anything better to do than keep the niggers down. **A**

Randy Newman: *Little Criminals* (Warner Bros. '77). Always the master craftsman, Newman doesn't waste a second here, doesn't permit an inept lyrical insight or musical fillip. But over the past three years he doesn't seem to have written one song that ranks with his best. Among all these explorations of America's dirty white underbelly, only the out-and-out jokes — the gross intolerance of "Short People" and the Eagles music on "Rider in the Rain" — distinguish themselves. Very disappointing. **B +**

Randy Newman: *Born Again* (Warner Bros. '79). This has more content and feeling than *Little Criminals*. But as with *Little Criminals* its highlight is a (great) joke — "The Story of a Rock and Roll Band," which ought to be called "E.L.O." and isn't, for the same reason supergroupie radio programmers have shied away from it. Hence, the content comprises ever more intricate convolutions of bad taste; rather than making you think about homophobes and heavy-metal toughs and me-decade assholes the way he once made you think about rednecks and slave traders and high school belles, he makes you think about how he feels about them. Which just isn't as interesting. **B +**

Tom Newman: *Fine Old Tom* (Antilles '77). Tom seems to have recorded this far across the sea in 1975, but more than that even my Anglophile sources can't tell me. Analogies: Dave Edmunds (studiomania and general non-esoteric musical orientation, although Newman isn't interested in overpowering anyone), Ray Davies (vaguely but persistently, for both eccentricity and vocal approach), Eno (more precisely, not only for eccentricity and vocal approach but also for style of smarts, although Newman isn't so blatantly avant-garde). Pretty catchy. **B +**

New Riders of the Purple Sage: *New Riders of the Purple Sage* (Columbia '71). Many find the weakness of John "Marmaduke" Dawson's singing an a priori turnoff, but I'm perversely attached to it. This diminutive, definitely mild-mannered c&w fantast betrays (I said betrays) none of the manipulative self-regard that marks the true wimp, and his voice suits the folkie-hippie casualness of the band's "country"-"rock." A feckless myth, to be sure — trucking women and heroic dopers, gentle aspiration and mysterious evil. But a charming and tuneful one. Original grade: A minus. **B +**

New Riders of the Purple Sage: *Powerglide* (Columbia '72). Last time the offhand, dreamy mythos of the originals seemed designed for the thin, dreamy pathos of the voices, and even then the combination didn't wear very well except as pastoral Muzak. This time the originals are depressingly unoriginal, and the memory of the country, Motown, and rock classics they cover renders the voices pathetic. Original grade: C. **C −**

New Riders of the Purple Sage: *The Adventures of Panama Red* (Columbia '73). If your idea of adventure is getting .wasted, you too might end up in bed with Panama Red. And if your idea of country-rock singing is drawling at medium volume in the general vicinity of the correct pitch, you might think they're improving themselves by letting Dave Nelson and Dave Torbert take their turns at the mike. **C –**

New Riders of the Purple Sage: *The Best of New Riders of the Purple Sage* (Columbia '76). Five of the six best songs here are on the debut; the other one, in case you care, is Robert Hunter's "Kick in the Head." Docked two notches for uselessness, another for the "New Riders of the Purple Sage is a registered trademark," and yet another for putting a circle-R next to the title on the spine. **D +**

The New Seekers: *We'd Like to Teach the World to Sing* (Elektra '71). This is what folk-rock really means. This is what country-rock really means. This is what pop-rock really means. This is what all theories of salvation by music really mean. They mean people paying their own money to hear a Coca-Cola commercial with new lyrics. Inspirational Bon Mot: "Can I put my guitar underneath your bed?" **D +**

Olivia Newton-John: *Have You Never Been Mellow* (MCA '75). After checking out the competition — I've given up on Helen Reddy, Anne Murray repeats herself, and Loretta Lynn's latest is a bummer — I began to entertain heathenish thoughts about this MOR nemesis, whose mid-Atlantic accent inspired Tammy Wynette to found a country music association designed to exclude her. At least this woman sounds sexy, says I to meself, but Carola soon set me straight. "A geisha," she scoffed. "She makes her voice smaller than it really is just to please men." At which point I put away my heathenish thoughts and finished the dishes. **D +**

New York Dolls: *New York Dolls* (Mercury '73). At least half the white kids who grow up in Manhattan are well off and moderately arty, like Carly Simon and John Paul Hammond. It takes brats from the outer boroughs to capture the oppressive excitement Manhattan holds for a half-formed human being the way these guys do. The careening screech of their music was first heard in the Cooper Union station of the Lexington IRT, and they don't stop there. Mixing early-'60s popsong savvy with late-'60s fast-metal anarchy, they seek love l-u-v from trash and bad girls. They go looking for a kiss among the personality crises. And they wonder whether you could make it with Frankenstein. Original grade: A. **A +**

New York Dolls: *In Too Much Too Soon* (Mercury '74). Like so many cocky songwriters, David JoHansen overloaded his debut with originals and then found that record promotion wasn't a life activity that inspired new ones. But his stock of golden oldies is so private — Leiber & Stoller's "Bad Detective" could have been written to order, and he steals "Showdown" from Archie Bell — that this expresses his innermost self and locates him in history simultaneously. It also avoids such mundane follow-up perils as excess ambition, minimal material, and instant tedium. Follow-up producer Shadow Morton has psyched him into recutting the vocals until his full talents as an impersonator shine through. He's also added gongs, gunshots, and girlie choruses to JoHansen's usual slew of sound effects. Greatest sound effect: Johnny Thunders's buzzsaw, destined to vie with heavy-metal fuzz in the hearts of rock and rollers everywhere. Greatest non-JoHansen song: Johnny Thunders's mewling "Chatterbox." **A +**

New York Shakespeare Festival: *Threepenny Opera* (Columbia '76). No matter how little use you have for musical theatre — I have very little myself — this score must be the exception. Even in translation (the only way I know them) Brecht's fifty-year-old lyrics retain an ironic fervor that makes tough-minded moderns like Randy Newman or Fagen-Becker sound attenuated and cerebral, and

Weill's discordant music carries its own charge. Without attempting to compare the accuracy of the Blitzstein and Manheim-Willett versions, I'd give Blitzstein's Theatre de Lys recording (on MGM) an edge over this one: of the current cast, only Raul Julia's Mack the Knife is clearly preferable to his predecessor, and Ellen Greene's egotistical "stylizations" — in Lotte Lenya's part! — are barely tolerable. But the new sound is better, and while Manheim and Willett don't approach Blitzstein's poetry (or prosody), their sexual and political explicitness is an attraction — when's the last time you heard the verb "to oppress" used appropriately in a song? I'm glad to own both; you should sample at least one. Docked a notch for Ellen Greene.   **A −**

Nico: *Desertshore* (Reprise '70). *The Velvet Underground and Nico* plus *Chelsea Girl* convinced me that Nico had charisma; *The Marble Index* plus *Desertshore* convince me that she's a fool. The difference is that now Nico writes the songs — songs with titles like "The Falconer" and "Abschied," songs that indulge her doleful monotone instead of playing rhythms and tempos against it. Nothing new here — bohemian hangers-on always get to publish their work while the less socially adept ("charismatic") are shafted. John Cale, with his "spare" arrangements, plays patron. Time: 29:20.   **C**

Nico: *The End* (Island '74). I don't know vy she's moaning about unved virgins and vether to betray her hate, and I don't vant to know. The Manzanera-Eno-Cale settings, which I believe is what one calls this sort of elevated sound effect, are suitably morbid and exotic. But funereal irony aside, her parlay of the Doors' "The End" and the Fuehrer's "Das Lied Der Deutschens" contextualizes both tunes more pejoratively than is intended. Nico is what happens when the bloodless wager their minds on the wisdom of the blood and the suicidal make something of their lives. If this be romanticism, give me Matthew Arnold — and gimme shelter.   **C**

A Night at Studio 54 (Casablanca '79). The ultimate disco sampler — all the AM crossovers plus major floor hits. Only sometimes AM can be gross (Cher) and sometimes floor hits are bland (or worse) away from the floor (not to mention on it) (Love and Kisses, Musique, the unspeakable Patrick Juvet). I find even the two usable sides resistible, and miss the Three Degrees' "Steve Rubell Medley": "Walk Right In," "Cocaine Blues," and "Jailhouse Rock."   **B**

Nilsson: *Nilsson Sings Newman* (RCA Victor '70). For those benighted who still believe the original can't sing, here's a sweeter version, including appropriately lovely versions of two rare urban celebrations — "Vine Street" (the one that led off Van Dyke Parks's *Song Cycle*) and "Dayton, Ohio 1903." Not so dynamic musically, though — just Nilsson singing and Newman behind on piano. Time: 25:17.   **B +**

Harry Nilsson: *Nilsson Schmilsson* (RCA Victor '71). In which the whimsy and vocal pyrotechnics of *Aerial Ballet* and *Pandemonium Shadow Show* (now cunningly collapsed into a disc called *Aerial Pandemonium Ballet*) are apotheosized under the direction of popmeister Richard Perry. The bathrobed recluse who shows his unshaven face on the cover (his well-stocked fridge is on the back) veers from kitsch fantasy both romantic ("Without You") and comic ("Coconut") to terrified evocations of everyday existence (the cockeyed antemeridian triptych — "Gotta Get Up," "Driving Along," and "Early in the Morning" — that kicks off side two). The two-and-a-half years since his last real LP, *Harry*, have been worth it — if only every artist could learn to mark time until a good one was ready. Original grade: A minus. **A**

Harry Nilsson: *Son of Schmilsson* (RCA Victor '72). Nilsson functions on the edge of parody — his best stuff succeeds simultaneously as a kind of takeoff and as a genuinely moving example of the genre that has inspired him. Unfortunately, most of this album, which follows so close on the heels of his biggest commercial success that Nilsson (natch) makes a joke of it in the title, is too often merely funny or strange. This is wonderful as far as it goes. But those three or four songs that are much better than that suffer by association. Inspirational Verse: "You're breakin' my heart/ You're tearin' it apart/ So fuck you." **B +**

Nilsson: *A Little Touch of Schmilsson in the Night* (RCA Victor '73). The "Schm" is for schmaltz, to which this is a tribute — the selections, none of which were written after 1958, include "For Me and My Gal" and "I Wonder Who's Kissing Her Now." Theoretically, this is a charming idea — who among us is better equipped to bring such music back to life? Actually, it's soporific — devoid of humor or irony but without any rediscovery of the whole-hearted emotion on which the old songs are predicated. Nilsson doesn't sing with much power and Gordon Jenkins's charts don't even qualify as period pieces. I know, I'm just a dumb rock and roll fan, so go waste your money. I wouldn't give my extra copy to my mother. **C −**

Nilsson: *Pussy Cats* (RCA Victor '74). Only the Umpteenth Beatle could juxtapose "Subterranean Homesick Blues" and "Loop de Loop" without giving off the sweet stink of a Bryan Ferry parody. With producer John Lennon keeping him honest, Harry goes raw, playing even the ballads for ugliness. But at the same time, no joke, he plays it all for laughs. **A −**

Nilsson: *Duit on Mon Dei* (RCA Victor '75). I have a weakness for sardonic nonsense, but this man is definitely running out of ideas — even his haphazardness is getting predictable. Crazy like a fox I can sit still for, but not crazy like an audio salesman. **B −**

Nilsson: *Sandman* (RCA Victor '75). Subtler than Dr. Hook, more soulful than 10cc, and sexier than Henny Youngman. Includes a new interpretation of "Jesus Christ You're Tall" and a new theme song: "Here's Why I Did Not Go to Work Today." **B −**

Nilsson: *Greatest Hits* (RCA Victor '78). Those who are taken with Nilsson the sweet, slightly kooky popmeister will approve of this reliable compilation — probably even dig Gordon Jenkins on "As Time Goes By." Those who are attracted to the popmeister by his apparent insanity will play it only in their most conservative moments. **B +**

999: *High Energy Plan* (PVC '79). A more ideologically suggestive title than the British *Separates* for a band that kicks off a very listenable (or jumpable) side by declaring "I believe in homicide" and ends it by warning "crime don't pay." In other words, all but hard-and-fast punk loyalists are liable to find this a bit thin. Clue: the substitution of two new tracks, no doubt to induce collectors to buy both the import and the domestic, has no effect on overall quality. **B**

The Nitty Gritty Dirt Band: *Will the Circle Be Unbroken* (United Artists '72). A public service by what is ordinarily a fairly weak-minded folk-rock aggregation, this three-record set unites six great traditional country singers — Mother Maybelle Carter, Earl Scruggs, Doc Watson, Roy Acuff, Merle Travis, and Jimmy Martin (of Bill Monroe's Bluegrass Boys) —with old-time material so tried and true that even this unreconstructed urbanite has heard most of it before. But rarely with such easy pleasure. All of the obvious pitfalls — uninspired performances, schlocky backup, arty or arbitrary programming, and of course folkie irrelevance — are avoided, and if the set is never definitive, it's an instant classic nevertheless, an intensely agreeable way into mountain music. As for the Dirt Band, Jimmy Martin was so impressed with their alertness that he offered to hire them, and I'm sorry they didn't take him up on it. **A −**

Don Nix: *In God We Trust* (Shelter '71). Although he's a white fella, Nix is something of a fixture on the Memphis blues-soul scene, and the music here is passable in the manner of fixtures on the Memphis blues-soul scene — despite a few bizarre and distracting insertions by septuagenarian bluesman Furry Lewis, which constitute an in-joke characteristic of fixtures etc. Its abiding interest is as an almost unfathomable example of downhome antireligious irony. At least I think it's anti. **B −**

Nolan: See Nolan Porter

No New York (Antilles '78). Especially with Adele Bertei on organ, the Contortions can be a great band, extending Ornette Coleman's *Dancing in Your Head* into real rock and roll territory, and it's exciting to be able to hear them minus James Chance's stupid stage shtick. (Maybe they'll become a studio group, like Steely Dan.) But the rest of this four-band compilation has the taint of marginal avant-gardism: interesting in occasional doses, but not as significant as it pretends to be. Arto Lindsay's hysterical blooze singing holds DNA together — wish they were on side one with the Contortions. I like the relentless music of Mars's "Helen Fordsdale" (the words are incomprehensible even with a lyric sheet, which if the lyric sheet is any indication is just as well) and the paranoid poetry of "Puerto Rican Ghost." And although in the wake of Chance's theme song, "I Can't Stand Myself," I've begun to tolerate Lydia Lunch droning "the leaves are always

dead" etc., she credits herself with too much maturity by publishing as Infantunes. Abortunes would be more like it. **B +**

No Nukes (Asylum '79). I prefer the movement to the music, but both share a woozy notion of what constitutes genuine consensus and how much it's likely to achieve. Carefully integrated both racially (Raydio, Chaka Khan, Gil Scott-Heron, Sweet Honey in the Rock, not to mention the Doobies and various backup bands) and culturally (Springsteen and Petty for the low-rent "hard rock" crowd), it's nevertheless limited by the social connections of its stalwarts. And though this three-LP set features attractive music from all but the real dips, even the best of it is almost devoid of bite, rough edges, and main force. Graded leniently for a worthy cause. **C +**

NRBQ: *Scraps* (Kama Sutra '72). I've never quite gotten with the abbreviation. New doesn't mean cute, or fancy, or at least it shouldn't, and rhythm-and-blues doesn't mean this. I don't understand why they turned the Q into Quintet by adding singer Frank Gadler, either — all he's ever added is more cuteness, even doing a John Sebastian on one cut. They're tuneful as hell, but so arch — "Who Put the Garlic in the Glue?" indeed — that the only tune I can bear to contemplate is "Magnet." Which attracts me like one. See, they've got me doing it. Yuk. [Later with *Workshop* on Annuit Coeptis.] **B**

NRBQ: *Workshop* (Kama Sutra '73). This band continues to live up to its full name (now Quartet rather than Quintet again), suggesting a cross between a chamber group (virtuosity and rhythmic decorum) and the New Lost City Ramblers (intelligent folkiness). Terry Adams plays rock and roll like a man who knows jazz wasn't invented by Chick Corea, and I do enjoy their sense of humor — the organ pumping into "C'Mon if You're Coming," or the out-of-synch, out-of-timbre Adams blues piano that undercuts "Blues Stay Away from Me." But I get no sense of why they engage in this musicianly reconstruction of r&b tradition; the jokes, none of which would make Carson, are what there is of a point. And if I'm going to listen to rock and roll without overdrive I need more reason than that. [Later with *Scraps* on Annuit Coeptis.] **B**

NRBQ: *All Hopped Up* (Red Rooster '77). OK, how about this? They're a power pop band who are too offhand about the power. A song band, you know? I like the Beatlesish "That's Alright" and the anti-dog "Call Him Off, Roger" and one or two of the covers and maybe (or maybe not) the adorable "Ridin' in My Car." And the piano player — I like the piano player. **B**

NRBQ: *At Yankee Stadium* (Mercury '78). Although I give them points for stick-to-it-iveness and good cheer, their records have always struck me as complacent because even the subtlest r&b has a more pronounced backbeat. But on his second try, drummer Tom Ardolino makes a marginal but telling difference — the performance is urgent, intense, up, so that even given their adolescent romantic preoccupations (life on the road, it keeps you young) the songs take on a complex life worthy of their chord changes. And try Terry Adams's Jimi-meets-Thelonious clavinet on "Talk to Me." **B+**

NRBQ: *Kick Me Hard* (Rounder/Red Rooster '79). I'm gratified that three out of four successive songs on side two — "Chores," "This Old House," and "Things We Like to Do" — mention problems of home maintenance, albeit invidiously (I put off the vacuuming myself). Makes you think that after ten years they're starting to grow up more than "It Was a Accident" makes you fear. **B+**

Ted Nugent: *Free-for-All* (Epic '76). Side one is well-wrought heavy metal — tensile and clever, reminiscent of Deke Leonard only clearer.

Side two is the usual frantic melodrama. **B−**

Ted Nugent: *Cat Scratch Fever* (Epic '77). Nugent may well have turned into a cartoon, but I prefer cartoon carnivores to cartoon vegetarians. And speaking of cartoons, better the Kiss imitations of today than the Robin Trowers of yesteryear — Ted is no more sexist than Kiss, and he sings better. Ten fast, simple, stupid rock and roll songs for guitar and shout, six or seven of which would keep anyone under thirty-five awake for four or five minutes on the Interstate, and from here things can only go downhill. **B**

Gary Numan & Tubeway Army: *Replicas* (Atco '79). Resistant as I am to the new strain of synthesizer punk now reaching us from England, I didn't connect to this for months — not until I listened to the singing. Numan's lyrics abound with aliens and policemen and pickups in what sounds at first like the worst sort of received decadence, but his monotone is too sweet and vulnerable for that impression to stick. To you it may be sordid sex and middlebrow sci-fi; to him it's romance and horror. The debut (*Tubeway Army,* Beggar's Banquet import) is faster, more pointed, and includes no instrumentals. This is catchier, more haunted, and includes two. Original grade: A minus. **B+**

Laura Nyro: *Christmas and the Beads of Sweat* (Columbia '70). Nyro is one of those hypersensitive types —they're usually women, which says more about women's oppression than their gifts, though it pertains to both — who can't see the condition for the nuance. There's no denying she's unique — her jazzy pop-gospel synthesis is without precedent or facsimile. No denying that she's serious, either, and probably in a good way — dedicated to her vision and her craft rather than pompous or solemn. But for an unsolemn person she cracks very few jokes, and her way with words, like everything else about her, is self-consciously romantic. She was born 150 years too late. When she's on, her music can overtake you anyway, but there's no "Wedding Bell Blues" or "Stoney End" on this album — melodically, "Up on the Roof" dwarfs her every meander. The plus is on general principles. **C+**

Laura Nyro: *Gonna Take a Miracle* (Columbia '71). In which the Bronx tearjerker reveals the source of her gloppy sensibility — good old girl-group rock and roll. Which is fine, except that glop tastes best prepared according to the traditional recipes, rather than disguised as untrammeled lyricism the way it is here. Might be different if Nyro were Aretha Franklin, as is painfully obvious every time she shows off the high part of her famous range. Still, backup singers Labelle don't screech once, Gamble & Huff control the rhythm section if not the artiste, and two of the ten remakes are ear-openers: "I Met Him on a Sunday," which begins accappella, and "Monkey Time/Dancing in the Street," which rocks. **B−**

Laura Nyro: *Smile* (Columbia '75). The momentum of the Moments' "Sexy Mama" does her nicely through "Children of the Junks," in which r&b goes to Hong Kong, and "Money," the second straight track to use the word "tax-free," although it ends ominously, with instructions to "make your vibe go round." And sure enough, this gasps on from there like a novice practicing circular breathing. I'd say that after four years she's out of training, but she's never been *in* training. **B−**

Laura Nyro: *Season of Lights: Laura Nyro in Concert* (Columbia '77). Most rock and rollers are too loose on live albums, but Nyro gets so carried away in the studio that the unerasable living band insures relatively straightforward remakes. My favorite moment, though, is when she introduces the musicians in a speaking voice nasal enough to make Dion sound Delta born-and-raised — finally I understand why Bronxites love her. I await explanations from Queens. **B−**

Phil Ochs: *Greatest Hits* (A&M '70). Sporting his gold lame suit and boasting that "50 Phil Ochs fans can't be wrong!," the Singing Yippie bids for pop power once again on this prematurely entitled work of art. Van Dyke Parks's classy, countrified production suits Phil's strange lyricism a lot better than the baroque excesses of *Pleasures of the Harbor,* but in the end Ochs's compulsive sweetness does him in anyway. It's always been one of the prime paradoxes of folkiedom that our most astringent protester should come on like Richard Dyer-Bennett gone Nashville, and the sad truth is that the lone protest number is the weakest cut on the disappointing second side. But even the first side, as strong as any pop Ochs has written to date, works in spite of his voice. Fond as I am of "James Dean of Indiana," I think it would be even more haunting done deadpan, by Arlo Guthrie or Tom T. Hall. **B−**

Odyssey: *Odyssey* (RCA Victor '77). Native New Yorkers who just can't wait anymore for the next Dr. Buzzard have turned to this, in which the Dr.'s producer once again weaves meaningful lyrics into a texture discrete enough not to digest its own strands. But the sad truth is that words and music here are much less dry, audacious, and, well, hip. For me, they evoke the Anglophile West Indies rather than the barrio. **B−**

Carl Oglesby: *Carl Oglesby* (Vanguard '70). In which the first president of SDS takes after Leonard Cohen, offering a clue as to why the framers of the Port Huron Statement didn't change the world in quite the way they envisioned. Overwritten, undermusicked, not much fun, not much enlightenment — in short, the work of someone who needs a weatherman (small "w" please) to know which way the wind blows. Original grade: C. **C+**

Ohio Players: *Skin Tight* (Mercury '74). Alternate title: *Shoogity-Boogity.* **B**

Ohio Players: *Fire* (Mercury '74). The makers of *Shoogity-Boogity* bring you: *More Shoogity-Boogity.* **B**

Ohio Players: *Greatest Hits* (Westbound '75). On Mercury the Players are a funk factory, turning out delightful but very similar hits and surrounding them with functional filler. On Westbound they were experimentalists whether copying Funkadelic or Cactus. Not that all the experiments were interesting, much less successful, or that a hit format displays them at their best — I'd welcome a second long jam in addition to the two-part "Pain." Which is one of the three successful as opposed to interesting songs on this compilation. The others are "Ecstasy," after the manner of George Clinton, and "Funky Worm," impersonated by Junie Morrison. **B**

The Ohio Players: *Honey* (Mercury '75). A/k/a *Boogity-Shoogity,* and I don't mean to be mean — I quite like

285

these guys in limited doses. There are even good slow ones here. What's more, it's their funniest album ever, and that's no typo. Only I can't quite convince myself that artistic development is even a category for a group that is clearly pure Act if not pure Product. What I can do, however, is be glad that they make Earth, Wind & Fire sound like the Herbie Mann Singers. **B+**

Ohio Players: *Contradiction* (Mercury '76). "Contradiction" and "Far East Mississippi" are in such a no-bullshit mode that they can get away with change-of-pace woo-pitchers, although they've done better than these. But, like Gerald Ford, they can't get away with "Bi-Centennial." Original grade: C. **B−**

Ohio Players: *Gold* (Mercury '76). OK, I don't approve of their album covers, although this one is relatively innocent — instead of casting the bald naked woman in molten metal they put wings on her feet and let her deliver a gold record, like an angel, or a carrier pigeon. But the visuals don't turn me off the aurals, which at their best fuse the body heat of funk with the mind games of the novelty single — that is, unite rhythmic and conceptual eccentricity. The not-on-any-album cuts are wasted —"Feel the Heat (Everybody Disco)" works just well enough to prove how mistaken they were to soften their attack for a subtitle. But four or five of these tracks are unmitigated miracles of commerce, and all of them are of a piece. **A−**

Ohio Players: *The Best of the Early Years Volume 1* (Westbound '77). A misnomer — should be *Early Year*. To be precise, 1972, when they released both *Pain* and *Pleasure*. Suggested retitle: *Half Pain and Half Pleasure*. **B−**

The Ohio Players: *Everybody Up* (Arista '79). Let's see, how did that thang go? Boogity-sheboppity? No, that's not it. Was it shoobity-boobity? *Boobity!* Shit. Hey, maybe that's it — shittiby-bittiby. Nah. Er . . . **C+**

The O'Jays: *Back Stabbers* (Philadelphia International '72). The title cut is single of the year, so I'm not surprised that it's unequaled here, but I wish something came close. Most will opt for "Love Train," a propulsive flag-waver attached to UNESCO lyrics about people all over the world joining hands, presumably so they can't stab each other in the you-know-where. Me, I prefer the follow-up, "992 Arguments," but "I'm a Man" or "Baby Love" it's not — more like "It's the Same Old Song." Original grade: B minus. **B+**

The O'Jays: *Ship Ahoy* (Philadelphia International '73). Every time side two gets rolling my ass tells my brain to go away —"For the Love of Money" is that great, although it's all (gradually) downhill from there. But when I put on side one my brain kicks back in, and my brain is right — not a song I ever want to hear again. Original grade: B plus. **B**

The O'Jays: *Survival* (Philadelphia International '75). Except for the astonishing "Rich Get Richer," based on a text by Ferdinand Lundberg, this is the drabbest studio album this group has made since joining Gamble-Huff. Unfortunately, "Rich Get Richer" is not the single. **C+**

The O'Jays: *Family Reunion* (Philadelphia International '75). In which Jesse Jackson (or is it Reverend Ike) goes disco, proving that the words do too matter. The self-serving, pseudo-political pap Kenny Gamble sets his boys to declaiming here underlines the way the overripeness of this vocal and production style can go mushy, which it does. Even the working-class party anthem "Livin' for the Weekend" is ruined by the rest of the side — some play-her-like-a-violin soft-core and the unspeakable (would it were unsingable) "I Love Music." Moral: the rich and the superrich shit — the nouveau-riche can fuck you over too. Original grade: C minus. **C**

The O'Jays: *Message in the Music* (Philadelphia International '76). The message in the message is inoffensive enough to let the message in the music come through; my favorite lines (not that I don't have unfavorites):

"Heaven is just a condition/Hell is a condition too." But the music never peaks; the songs are too medium, if you know what I mean, their pleasures bound up in performance subtleties that ought to be hooked, at least once, onto something obvious. **B –**

The O'Jays: *Collectors' Items* (Philadelphia International '77). Steadfast stylistically since "Back Stabbers" in 1972, Kenny Gamble's three-man mouthpiece ought to make an ideal best-of — if you dig Kenny Gamble. I regard him as a gifted pop demagogue — black capitalist masquerading as liberator. The oppressively patriarchal "Family Reunion" is the lead cut, setting the tone of a collection three of whose four sides are rendered unlistenable by Gamble's sermonizing and/or sentimentality. What's more, the O'Jays deserve him. Eddie Levert is the master of the soulful harangue, parading the trappings of emotional commitment with literally incredible showbiz chutzpah. When I happen to agree with what they're saying, or when an inoffensive lyric is attached to one of Leon Huff's greatest hooks, I like them fine. But I obviously can't expect Kenny to put together a compilation for me. Maybe I'll make a tape. **C +**

The O'Jays: *So Full of Love* (Philadelphia International '78). If the title's true — I've never considered Eddie Levert one of the great romantics — it's sure not all they're full of. Exception: Bunny Sigler's "Strokety Stroke." **C +**

Danny O'Keefe: *Danny O'Keefe* (Cotillion '70). Though he thinks too much about smog and winos, O'Keefe sings the blues like a good old boy and takes his "mama" with him when he leaves town — in short, handles standard new-troubadourisms with some originality. And every once in a while he writes a potential standard like "Sweet Rollin' " (femme fatale) or "Good Time Charlie's Got the Blues" (a rounder's tragedy). But producer Ahmet Ertegun stifles "Saturday Morning" in Shoals soul, arranges

"Steel Guitar" sans steel guitar, and indulges all of his boy's most misguided pretensions. **B –**

Danny O'Keefe: *O'Keefe* (Signpost '72). Arif Mardin has neutralized O'Keefe's folk-Muzak potential by embellishing it — better his studiorock "Good Time Charlie" than Ahmet's folkie-rockie-with-flute one, and not just because it got O'Keefe on the radio. In a neon romantic like O'Keefe — who sounds most at home telling junkie stories or covering "Honky Tonkin' "— spectral percussion, a steel guitar mixed for eerieness, even a clarinet function as intelligent new-schlock shading that acknowledges his fundamental commercialism. And commercial he is — just about every song has a melodic hook. Though we'd be better off without one on "Shooting Star" ("the morning is waiting for Electra"?) and "The Valentine Pieces" (don't ask). **B**

Mike Oldfield: *Tubular Bells* (Virgin '74). A musician with the technique and formal imagination of Terry Riley or Philip Glass can create electronic keyboard meditations worthy of hokey adjectives like "mysterious" or "majestic." The best I can come up with here is "pleasant" and "catchy." Oldfield isn't Richard Strauss or even Leonard Cohen — this is a soundtrack because that's the level at which he operates. **C +**

100 Proof Aged in Soul: *Somebody's Been Sleeping in My Bed* (Hot Wax '70). The unidentified lead singer admires (or envies) David Ruffin, and not since early Smokey have so many proverbs and idioms — too many cooks, Johnny comes marching home, love is sweeter the second time around — squeezed onto one album. Plus the complete text of a "sincere" champagne dinner seduction. **B +**

One Way Featuring Al Hudson: *One Way Featuring Al Hudson* (MCA '79). Disco sanity. Alternate title: *One Side Featuring Al Hudson.* **B**

The Only Ones: *Special View* (Epic '79). Dry, witty, and unassumingly polysyllabic, his sentiment sheathed in irony, Peter Perrett is a bemused/distressed/displaced romantic with an uncanny command of conventional hard rock — like a nice Lou Reed, or Ray Davies gone to college. Which means he's a new waver mostly by historical association. This selection from his first two British albums (plus one single) is an ideal introduction to an artist who may be major if he sticks at it.   **A −**

The Original Animals: *Before We Were So Rudely Interrupted* (United Artists/Jet '77). Not bad for a reunion LP — a lot more authentic sounding than the Byrds'. But then, the Animals weren't as good as the Byrds. And the only time Eric Burdon really recaptures that old white magic is on "Many Rivers to Cross," such a cliche by now that only a singer as crude as Eric, with his desperate key changes and random enthusiasm, can bring it to life. Me, I'll take "Sky Pilot."   **B −**

− **The Original Texas Playboys:** *Live and Kickin'* (Capitol '78). This is a lot more than nostalgia, granted. But it just doesn't kick.   **B**

Orleans: *Orleans* (ABC '73). In case you're interested, this band is mucho hot among Eastern rock cognoscenti (read, know-it-alls). Very pleasant, too, although John Hall doesn't sing as tasty as he plays. The only impressive song is "Half Moon." Anything Janis Joplin used to sing is impressive, so that may not mean much.   **C +**

Osibisa: *Osibisa* (Decca '71). "Crisscross rhythms that explode with happiness," promises this London-based African and West Indian troupe, but they can't leave it at that, and neither singer-guitarist Wendell Richardson nor singer-saxophonist Teddy Osei explodes with very much of anything. Which leaves it all up to an ensemble that often sounds a little muddled —

though I'll always stop and listen to the strange, sour unison horn line and unhappy lyric of "Phallus C."   **B**

Osibisa: *Woyaya* (Decca '72). I don't want to say they're hokey, but this is their second consecutive album to begin with jungle sounds, and I think we get the point. Actually, the problem is that they're not hokey enough, or not in the right way — plenty of quasi-virtuoso jams and brother-brother-brother, but nothing tricky enough to echo in your head once the drums have faded away.   **B −**

Osibisa: *Heads* (Decca '72). When it comes to lists of cities visited on tour, I'll take James Brown — he's got a better beat, maybe even a more African one. But if you happen to be in one of those cities on the appointed night, you should probably try to hear them — their records have never come up to their live notices. Original grade: B.   **B −**

The Osmonds: *Greatest Hits* (Polydor '77). Come on, they weren't so terrible. In a time when AM music was really beginning to deteriorate "Yo-Yo" and "Down by the Lazy River" and even the scandalous "One Bad Apple" rated in the upper third of the radio pleasure zone, and their "young" songs were not devoid of cuteness. But even at their best they did sound forced. And their own contribution to the deterioration of AM radio was considerable.   **C**

Gilbert O'Sullivan: *Himself* (MAM '72). I admit I ignored this until the advent of the genius single "Alone Again (Naturally)," which I like best for the way its tossed-off structure matches its casual, crucial equation of filial and romantic affection. But I insist I was always intrigued by the idea of a singer-songwriter managed by the same godfather who brings us Tom Jones and Englebert Humperdinck. He's uneven, and he may turn into a major annoyance, but before that happens we ought to acknowledge that he's also a complete original. Persona:

insecure lower middle-class Irishman with a screw loose. Message: it's normal to have a screw loose. Rhymes: "Nothing Rhymed." **B**

The Johnny Otis Show: *Live at Monterey!* (Epic '71). In-concert compilations are often incoherent, but the blues-style hard jive beloved of performer-turned-majordomo Otis has such formal integrity that this r&b spectacular moves smoothly for four sides. Some of the featured players are no more than Otis's hired hands, including guitarist Shuggie O. But (in ascending order) Roy Milton, Big Joe Turner, Ivory Joe Hunter, Little (?) Esther Phillips, Roy Brown, and Cleanhead Vinson are a cast that beats anything Richard Nader's ever put into the Garden. **B +**

The Outlaws (RCA Victor '76). No truth-in-packaging awards here — you'd never know from the label that most of this has been heard before in other configurations — but how about a cheer-and-a-half for the programming? Me, I often find Waylon and Willie (and Tompall and Jessi) a little tedious over a whole side. This never gets boring. **B +**

The Outlaws: *The Outlaws* (Arista '75). Outlaws my ass — I bet they'd punch a time clock if it'd make the tour go smoother. Combining the most digestible elements of the Eagles and the Allmans without ever hinting that there might be a teensy bit of genius or even originality beneath the surface — because there isn't — this is now the hottest new rock group in America. How depressing. **C −**

Pablo Cruise: *A Place in the Sun* (A&M '77). This mainstream synthesis is not without a certain agreeable tension — vocally and instrumentally, these boys do have their licks down. But it's also a demonstration of how today's pop exploits the rhythmic and dramatic cliches of yesterday's black music. Lyrics, too — Cory Lerios and Dave Jenkins are credited as the sole composers of "Raging Fire," in which love lifts them higher than they've ever been before. **C**

Pablo Cruise: *Worlds Away* (A&M '78). The Cruisers hit my enemies list somewhere on Interstate 95. Hook glut, it's called — hear David Jenkins sing "once you get past the pain" fifty times in a day and the pain will be permanent. Even if the next hit is the title cut, a genuine rocker, the band is the '70s Grass Roots, and if Orleans and the Doobie Brothers are the obvious forerunners, that's their cross to bear. It don't mean a thing if it's studio swing. **C**

Tom Pacheco: *Swallowed Up in the Great American Heartland* (RCA Victor '76). Harry Chapin meets Waylon Jennings and guess who cornholes who. Or: I do too love America, that's why I hate what it's become. Or: this land is your land, this land is my land, from the Armadillo to the Rikers Island. **C**

Robert Palmer: *Some People Can Do What They Like* (Island '76). My guess is that Palmer dresses classy as a subterfuge, to make people think that subdued quality is deliberate. Instead he's convinced me that I'll get off on a white r&b singer from Savile Row the same day I give up Jack Daniel's for sherry and join the Dartmouth Club. **C+**

Graham Parker: *Howlin Wind* (Mercury '76). Parker builds his white r&b of such familiar materials that it takes awhile for the songs to sort themselves out, but their fury is unmistakable — in the time-honored English manner, bass and drums play the house-rocking rhythms of Chicago and Detroit for righteous anger rather than good-time escape. Then songs come clear, marred at times by the white bluesman's chronic romanticism of the blood — "Gypsy Blood," to be precise — but so passionate that every personal animus takes dead aim at the great world. Parker's "strange religion/Without any God" may well be himself. But when he instructs the Lord not to ask him questions, he doesn't extend the prohibition to Graham Parker. Original grade: B plus. **A**

Graham Parker: *Heat Treatment* (Mercury '76). Parker doesn't just have the makings of a major artist, he is one. Because his more reflective and/or accusatory tendencies here show up his rather narrow timbral and melodic range, this isn't quite as engaging as *Howlin Wind*. Even the verve of the Rumour's arrangements and Parker's deft and pithy way with vernacular speech don't entirely redeem "Black Honey" or "Help Me Shake It." But the sound is a lot fuller, and the defiance in the face of social collapse more bracing as a result. Original grade: A minus. **A**

Graham Parker: *Stick to Me* (Mercury '77). This is indeed a disappointment. The production is muddy, the female chorus an excrescence, and "The Heat in Harlem" vapid and overblown. But it's not as depressing as the faithful believe. Sure, I'll probably put on *Howlin Wind* or *Heat Treatment* when I feel like hearing Parker — unless I just have to hear one of *these* songs, most of which eventually implanted themselves in my subconscious just like the others. **A –**

Graham Parker and the Rumour: *The Parkerilla* (Mercury '78). If you think it's a little early for a concert album by Parker, who's not exactly Peter Frampton on the rackjobber circuit, you're right, but only if you view this — three live sides plus one 33-rpm single (the fourth version of "Don't Ask Me Questions" Parker has put on disc) — as music, or product. Regard it instead as a gambit designed to terminate his contract with Mercury. The music that fleshes out the gambit has a nice intensity that gets left out of those nasty rumors. But none of the songs are new and none of the remakes revelatory. **B –**

Graham Parker and the Rumour: *Squeezing Out Sparks* (Arista '79). An amazing record. Parker's mood, which has narrowed into existential rage with a circumstantial root, makes for perfect, untamable rock and roll. Guitar, drums, vocals, lyrics, and hooks (and more hooks) mesh into ten songs so compelling that you're grateful to the relative lightweights for giving you a chance to relax. And if Graham is pissed off merely because he's not a big star yet, he translates his frustrations into credible, emotionally

healthy anger — the kind you feel when they can't fit the real news into print. Original grade: A plus. **A**

Junior Parker: *I Tell Stories Sad and True, I Sing the Blues and Play Harmonica Too, It Is Very Funky* (United Artists '72). Once a big man on the blues circuit, Parker was turning into the forgotten Beale Streeter by the time he died last year, and this is a respectful farewell — Sonny Lester, who wrecked his recent collaboration with Jimmy McGriff, keeps things simple (well, fairly simple). Never as penetrating as B.B. or Bobby, Parker smooths his way over the arrangements with the calm of a man who was mellow before the concept existed, at least in its present deracinated form. Highlight: the sad, true story that goes with "Funny How Time Slips Away." Original grade: B plus. **B**

Parliament: *Osmium* (Invictus '70). What happens when a black harmony group names an album after the heaviest metal, depluralizes its name, and pluralizes its music? It may be pretentious bullshit, but it sure is interesting pretentious bullshit — bagpipes and steel guitars, Bach and rock, Satchmo as Kingfish, work chants as dozens, all in the service of a world view in which love/sex becomes frightening, even brutal, and no less credible for that. **B**

Parliament: *Up for the Down Stroke* (Casablanca '74). What seems to distinguish this mysterious alternate version of Funkadelic (same personnel, different label) from the original is that it's more politic. Its excesses don't offend. Gone is all the scabrous talk of holes and bitches, and gone too are the politics themselves — the nearest this comes to social criticism is to praise the brain. But what's left is damn near a (musical) revolution. The material George Clinton has amassed over the years — the harmony-group vocal chops, the Jimi H. guitar, the James B. horns and rhythms — is here deployed in yet another audacious deconstruction/reconstruction of black pop traditions, and this time it works. All of the voice arrangements skew the original "I Wanna Testify" (which is reinterpreted for comparison) the way those of Big Star do, say, "Run for Your Life." The horns and guitars weave and comment and come front. And the title cut kicks and jams. One more riff like that and they'd take over the world. **A −**

Parliament: *Chocolate City* (Casablanca '75). On the first side a DJ who reminds me of original AM scatman Jocko Henderson jive-raps on the satisfactions of suffrage and then gives way to a danceable, listenable, forgettable groove. On the second side, interesting but hookless off-harmony excursions, two of them too slow and/or too long, break into some heavy funk for the ages. **B**

Parliament: *Mothership Connection* (Casablanca '76). That DJ from Chocolate City, or maybe it's the Chocolate Milky Way, keeps the beat going with nothing but his rap, some weird keyboard, and cymbals for stretches of side one. And later produces the galactic "Give Up the Funk" and a James Brown tribute that goes "gogga googa, gogga googa" — only believe me, that doesn't capture it. **A −**

Parliament: *The Clones of Dr. Funkenstein* (Casablanca '76). The message seems to be that clones are cool, and the proof seems to be the predictable yet effective funktoons that dominate the album. But I remain an unreconstructed Yurrupean rationalist/individualist, and I wish there were a few more tracks as specific as "Dr. Funkenstein" and "Sexy Body." **B +**

Parliament: *Parliament Live/P. Funk Earth Tour* (Casablanca '77). Because it mixes music from all three George Clinton creations (including a new chant) and conveys a lot of the anarchic, participatory throb of a P. Funk concert, this live double serves a real function. But the recording doesn't do much justice to the music's bottom, or its top. **B +**

Parliament: *Funkentelechy vs. the Placebo Syndrome* (Casablanca '77). This seems like your representative 'delicment LP at first, featuring one irresistible and quite eccentric dance cut, other dance cuts that are at moments even more eccentric (including one based on nursery rhymes), bits of inspired jive, bits of plain jive, and an anomalous slow one. But with familiarity the three rhythm hooks that anchor the album start sounding definitive. And never before has George Clinton dealt so coherently with his familiar message, in which the forces of life — autonomous intelligence, a childlike openness, sexual energy, and humor — defeat those of death: by seduction if possible, by force if necessary. Original grade: B plus. **A**

Parliament: *Motor-Booty Affair* (Casablanca '78). A kiddie record that features the return of the Chipmunks as "three slithering idiots" doing their thing underwater. Irresistible at its most inspired — aqua-DJ Wiggles the Worm is my favorite Clinton fantasy ever — and danceable at its most pro forma. **A −**

Parliament: *Gloryhallastoopid* (Casablanca '79). At its stoopidest ("Theme from the Black Hole," which features a "toast to the boogie" that goes — naturally — "Bottoms up!") this makes *Motor-Booty Affair* sound like *The Ring of the Nibelungenlied.* But at its dumbest ("Party People," apparently a sincere title) it makes *Motor-Booty Affair* sound like "Sex Machine" or "Get Off Your Ass and Jam." And there's too much filler. Stoopid can be fun, George — even inspirational. But mainly you sound overworked, and that's a drag for everybody. **B +**

The Alan Parsons Project: *I Robot* (Arista '77). I might agree that the way this record approximates what it (supposedly) criticizes is a species of profundity if what it (supposedly) criticized was schlock. As it is, the pseudo-disco makes Giorgio Moroder sound like Eno and the pseudo-sci-fi makes Isaac Asimov seem like a deep thinker. Back to the control board. **C**

The Alan Parsons Project: *Eve* (Arista '79). Musically, this is a step toward schlock that knows its name — a few smarmy melodies mixed in with the production values and synthesizer furbelows. Thematically, it's both sophomoric and disgusting — programmatic misogyny rooted in sexual rejections that were clearly deserved. Visually, it's sadistic — the three women on the Hipgnosis cover wear black veils that only partly conceal their scars, warts, and blotches. What is it they stencil on street corners? Castrate art-rockers? **D**

Gram Parsons: *GP* (Reprise '73). In which Parsons stakes his claim to everything he loves about country music — its bathos, its moral fervor, its sense of peril. Whether he's replicating these qualities in his own songs or finding them in the genuine article, his interpretations achieve the synthesis of skepticism and longing that drove him to devise country-rock in the first place. Physically, he isn't always up to what he knows — that's a folkie's voice cracking on "She" — but he can be proud that the only track here that beats Tompall Glaser's "Streets of Baltimore" is his own "Kiss the Children." **B +**

Gram Parsons: *Grievous Angel* (Reprise '74). On *GP*, Emmylou Harris was a backup musician; here she cuts Parsons's soulfully dilettantish quaver with dry, dulcet mountain spirituality. On *GP*, Parsons was undeviating in his dolor; here he opens up the honky tonks, if only to announce that he can't dance. The best Gram Parsons album — and hence the best country-rock album — since *Gilded Palace of Sin*, with all that irony and mystery translated from metaphor into narrative. Original grade: A minus. **A**

Gram Parsons/The Flying Burrito Bros.: *Sleepless Nights* (A&M '76). These cover versions — some cut with Emmylou, some with the Bros., all but two previously unreleased — were

outtakes for a reason (shaky vocals and/or conceptual irrelevance, usually), and they don't make him any more alive. For archivists only. Original grade: C plus. **B –**

Dolly Parton: *The Best of Dolly Parton* (RCA Victor '70). The clear little voice is camouflage, just like the big tits. When she's wronged, as she is in five of this record's six sexual encounters (four permanently premarital, one in which hubby throws her into a "mental institution"), her soprano breaks into a cracked vibrato that for me symbolizes her prefeminist pride in her human failings ("Just Because I'm a Woman") and eccentricities ("Just the Way I Am"). Not all of these minisoaps are perfectly realized and "In the Ghetto" is a mistake. But as far as I'm concerned she rescues "How Great Thou Art" from both Elvis and George Beverly Shea, maybe because a nonbeliever like me is free to note that the one who ruined her only happy love affair (with her fella Joe and her dog Gypsy, both of whom die) was the Guy in the Sky. **A**

Dolly Parton: *Coat of Many Colors* (RCA Victor '71). Beginning with two absolutely classic songs, one about a mother's love and the next about a mother's sexuality, and including country music's answers to "Triad" ("If I Lose My Mind") and "The Celebration of the Lizard" ("The Mystery of the Mystery"), side one is genius of a purity you never encounter in rock anymore. Overdisc is mere talent, except "She Never Met a Man (She Didn't Like)," which is more. Time: 26:56. **A –**

Dolly Parton: *My Tennessee Mountain Home* (RCA Victor '73). This concept album begins with the letter Dolly wrote her mom and dad when she was first pursuing her dreams on Music Row. Fortunately, its subject isn't Music Row, except by contrast. Unfortunately, its pastoral nostalgia, while always charming, is sometimes a little too pat. Sentimental masterpieces like the title track are no easier to come by than any other kind, and the slowed-down remake of "In the Good Old Days (When Times Were Bad)" — the early hit in which she declined to go back — doesn't add as much bite as this city boy needs.   **B +**

Dolly Parton: *Bubbling Over* (RCA Victor '73). A better-than-average Parton album in many ways, but beyond the usual dull spots two cuts really bother me. Often her genteel aspirations are delightful — who else would pronounce it "o'er our heads," just like in poetry books, instead of slurring "over"? But when her sentimentality becomes ideological —"Babies save marriages," or "Stop protesting and get right with God" —you remember why most great popular artists have rebelled against gentility. Time: an exceptionally scanty 24:06.   **B**

Dolly Parton: *Jolene* (RCA Victor '74). "Jolene" proves that sometimes she's a great singer-songwriter. "I Will Always Love You" proves that sometimes she's a good one. Porter Wagoner's "Lonely Comin' Down" proves that sometimes she should just sing. Her own "Highlight of My Life" proves that sometimes she should just shut up. And the rest proves nothing. Time: 24:27.   **B −**

Dolly Parton: *Love Is Like a Butterfly* (RCA Victor '74). Except for the title tune, the only really interesting songs here are two by Porter Wagoner — Dolly's already done a whole album of "Take Me Back," and "Bubbling Over" is a lot more effervescent than "Gettin' Happy." Still, she repeats herself (and apes others) nicely enough. And blues strings followed by gospel medley rescues side two at the close. Time: 26:06.   **B**

Dolly Parton: *Best of Dolly Parton* (RCA Victor '75). In her productivity and devotion to writing Parton is like a nineteenth-century woman novelist — a hillbilly Louisa May Alcott. What's best about her is her spunkiness and prettiness (Jo crossed with Amy); what's worst is her sentimentality and failures of imagination

(Beth crossed with Meg). And this is the best of her best. At least half of these songs have an imaginative power surprising even in so fecund a talent — images like the bargain store and the coat of many colors are so archetypal you wonder why no one has ever thought of them before. The psychological complexities of "Jolene" and "Traveling Man" go way beyond the winsome light melodramas that are Parton's specialty. And even when the writing gets mawkish — "I Will Always Love You" or "Love Is Like a Butterfly" — her voice is there to clear things up. Time: 26:25.   **A +**

Dolly Parton: *Dolly* (RCA Victor '75). Another concept album, this one about — uh-oh — love. All that salvages what would otherwise be atrocious greeting-card doggerel is her singing, and it's not enough. Time: 28:28. Original grade: C.   **C +**

Dolly Parton: *All I Can Do* (RCA Victor '76). Emphasizing Dolly's perky, upbeat side, this doesn't offer a single must-hear track, but it's remarkably consistent. Songs like "When the Sun Goes Down Tomorrow" (country girl goes home) and "Preacher Tom" (saving in the name of the Lord) reprise old themes with specificity and verve, and the covers from Emmylou Harris and Merle Haggard broaden her perspective without compromising it. Intensely pleasant.   **B +**

Dolly Parton: *New Harvest . . . First Gathering* (RCA Victor '77). Aficionados complain that her sellout has become audible, but while I admit that the cute squeals on "Applejack" are pure merchandising, she's always been willing to sell what she couldn't give away. I think Dolly has made the pop move a lot more naturally than, say, Tanya Tucker. The problem here afflicts every genre: material.   **B −**

Dolly Parton: *Heartbreaker* (RCA Victor '78). Her singular country treble is unsuited to rock, where little-girlishness works only as an occasional novelty. As a result, the rock part of her crossover move fails, relegating her to the mawkish pop banality that tempts almost every genius country singer. This she brings off, if you like mawkish pop banality; I prefer mawkish country banality, which is sparer. **C**

Billy Paul: *360 Degrees of Billy Paul* (Philadephia International '73). At his worst, Paul is black naturalness at its most mannered — florid, hyped up, homiletic, sort of a Les McCann of small-time jazz singers. But Gamble and Huff have been making great music out of middlebrow jazz for years, and when they give Paul a good song — several of the black-consciousness riffs, which G&H seem to turn out as if they were so many follow-ups to "Tighten Up," are better than "Me and Mrs. Jones" — his overstatement is no more offensive than Ray Charles's. On stupid, unrealistic songs (e.g. "I'm Just a Prisoner") he sounds stupid and unrealistic, which figures. **B –**

Tom Paxton: *Heroes* (Vanguard '78). As dinky musically as any other electric folk session, but most of the songs escape the sentimental self-righteousness you expect from this old-timer. They're funny when they mean to be, which is often. And two very impressive farewells, to Phil Ochs and Stephen Biko, aren't funny at all. **B**

Johnny Paycheck: *Greatest Hits* (Epic '74). The one-time rockabilly's unassuming Nashville-macho baritone proves a surprisingly ductile medium for Billy Sherrill's basic love-and-marriage exploitation — he defers so meekly to his material that he sounds more domesticated than Tanya, Tammy, or even Charlie Rich. **C +**
Johnny Paycheck: *Greatest Hits Volume II* (Epic '78). Outlaws are hardly immune to palaver, of course. But the best-of format eliminates the posturing to which this well-named entertainer resorts when the songs get thin, while his current Waylonism limits him to one pretty good romantic ballad. Almost every other selection talks funny

and sings tough — in my favorites, a drunk who picks on a Mexican has his ear surgically removed and John resigns from the I.R.S. **A –**

Freda Payne: *The Best of Frëda Payne* (Invictus '72). Recommended to those who neglected to purchase "Band of Gold" (wedding-night impotence!) and/or "Bring the Boys Home" (Vietnam with violins! a black sister calling out for peace with her brother content to exhort from the background!), which together with two familiar-sounding tunes by label-owners Holland-Dozier-Holland and two entertaining soap operas make for as nice a side of minor Motown as you're likely to get from the original these days. **B**

Peaches & Herb: *2 Hot!* (Polydor '78). Anyone who believes all black pop is "disco," nothing more and nothing less, should analyze the outfront vocals and submerged grooves of this enthusiastically lascivious Freddie Perren trifle, which broke because disco DJs are willing to program whatever's danceable, not because AM DJs are willing to program whatever's listenable. And in the end it proved so listenable that "Reunited" established itself as an anachronistic smooch classic — the counterpart of "Shake Your Groove Thing," a timely hoochycooch classic. Original grade: B. **B +**
Peaches & Herb: *Twice the Fire* (Polydor '79). There's not a bad cut on this album, and though there isn't a great one either I'll settle for "Howzabout Some Love," the Sunshine Band song of the year, "Roller-Skatin' Mate," the dance craze song of the year, and "Love Lift," the neologistic song of the year. Boogaly-boop to you. **B +**

Pearl Harbor & the Explosions: *Pearl Harbor & the Explosions* (Warner Bros. '79). A rhythm band ought to have a better rhythm section — most of this rocks OK for DOR, but the funk beneath "Get a

Grip on Yourself,'' for instance, is stiff to no purpose. The riffs are hooky, though, and Pearl E. Gates is an independent — not to say insular — woman who knows what her habits cost. There are no tears on her pillow and she doesn't care if your aim is true, but she doesn't waste her energy on macha bluster, either — prefers the cutting remark and isn't above turning her wit on herself. Which does *not* mean she has any intention of "reforming." **B+**

Ann Peebles: *Part Time Love* (Hi '70). Suggesting what we already knew: that good soul music is more a matter of faith than of fashion. Wilson Pickett may have lost his, but this twenty-three-year-old is just beginning to testify. Her background is gospel and her dynamic blues, the perfect combination, and even when the songs aren't first-rate, which they usually are, her lean, slightly burred timbre meshes with the incredibly spirited Memphis music (Memphis is where even session men believe) to intensify their meaning. Among my faves: "Give Me Some Credit" (downhome girl-group) and "It's Your Thing" (it's hers, bro). I just wish there were a dozen songs instead of ten. Time: 26:59. **A−**

Ann Peebles: *Straight from the Heart* (Hi '72). Why gritty singing like this can't be heard on "progressive" radio when a borderline hysteric like Lydia Pense is an automatic add ought to be investigated by the Civil Rights Commission. "I Feel Like Breaking Up Somebody's Home Tonight" is pre-ideological female rage, and the woman shows her sense of roots and prerogatives by coming up with competitive covers on both Bobby Bland and Sam & Dave. Time: 26:08. **A−**

Ann Peebles: *I Can't Stand the Rain* (Hi '74). After two hot albums that didn't sell and a smoldering single that did, Peebles slides into the best-selling Al Green groove and doesn't quite catch fire. Reason: neither her raw honey timbre nor her bright, direct personality give her much access to Green's incendiary guile. Salvation: the Hi rhythm team. Time: 26:54. Original grade: B. **B+**

Ann Peebles: *Tellin' It* (Hi '75). Peebles's small, rough-cut ruby of a voice can't buy her Aretha's kind of time; her hesitant pursuit of a dramatic frame, an artistic self, will never do the duty of a real persona. Which may mean that Willie Mitchell is wrong for her. Not only does his seamless funk deprive her of the sharply accentuated settings her instrument was created for, but his concentration on music to the exclusion of image leaves her singing warmed-over Millie Jackson wife-and-other-woman lyrics with the wan confusion they deserve. **B−**

Ann Peebles: *If This Is Heaven* (Hi '77). Peebles believes heaven is doing it every night after the kids have gone to bed ("I'm So Thankful"), and if only she'd work a little harder on her Mavis Staples impression ("It Must Be Love") she'd make a believer out of me. **B**

Ann Peebles: *The Handwriting Is on the Wall* (Hi '78). More tough talk about sex and love (and sex) — unfalteringly funky, consistently credible, and mildly enjoyable. Great one: "Old Man with Young Ideas." **B−**

David Peel and the Lower East Side: *The Pope Smokes Dope* (Apple '72). The hippie as hype strikes again. Not that Peel isn't a "real" hippie — on the contrary, he's a case study in the moral inadequacy of authenticity. He's real, yes — and he's also stupid and hypocritical. In 1969 Danny Fields, then "house hippie" at Elektra, got Peel's *Have a Marijuana* onto the charts; now John Lennon's doing the same thing for this tuneless doggerel. It's enough to make you miss the Maharishi. **E**

Paul Pena: *Paul Pena* (Capitol '72). Certain black bohemians — Richie Havens is the perfect example — have developed a style of humanitarianism unspecific enough to make "War" and "Ball of Confusion" sound like Frantz

Fanon. Pena's outlook is similar, but between his rolling virtuoso guitar and his abiding vocal soulfulness (the man leaves mere conviction back with Norman Vincent Peale) he moves me. Even the naivete of the lyrics makes for home truths unavailable from more sophisticated writers.   **A −**

Teddy Pendergrass: *Teddy Pendergrass* (Philadelphia International '77). In the immediate wake of Teddy's break with Harold Melvin, this sounded like pure cop-'em cut-'em con-'em and account-'em, but time quickly proved it an ordinary quickie. That is, the first two tunes on each side, estimable though they are, aren't what make you forget the last·two. It's the last two that make you forget the last two.   **B**

Teddy Pendergrass: *Life Is a Song Worth Singing* (Philadelphia International '78). Romantic schlock at its sexiest and most honest. Pendergrass is in such control of his instrument that the more commonplace of the Sigma Sound orchestrations never spoil the mood, while the good ones — let's hear it for the sax breaks on "Only You" — accent it the way they're supposed to. The key is that he's not belting much — except for one dull party number, everything is medium-tempo or slower. Pendergrass has a tendency to bluster when he belts, to come on too strong. The slow stuff — these aural seductions are hardly "ballads" — plays up his vulnerability and gives his vocal textures room to breathe a little. Original grade: A minus.   **B +**

Teddy Pendergrass: *Teddy* (Philadelphia International '79). Whether he's flexing his chest at Madison Square Garden or inviting the (presumably female) listener into his shower, Teddy has a self-deprecating sense of humor that his obsessive male posturing tends to obscure. Call him butch rather than macho and be thankful for small favors.   **B**

Teddy Pendergrass: *Teddy Live! Coast to Coast* (Philadelphia International '79). The three live sides include no new tunes and none from his first album. Many women scream, and a few sing into his hand-held mike. Both uptempo tunes on the studio side are pretty good, but they're interspersed with an exceedingly distracting interview conducted by one Mimi Brown. MB: "How *do* you like your eggs?" TP: "Hard." MB: "Out of your three albums, which is your favorite?" TP: "I'd say my first."   **C**

The Pentangle: *Cruel Sister* (Reprise '70). They still declare fealty to Transatlantic Records, but this is a retreat into pure — or impure, ask a folklorist — traditional English balladry. Gone is the jazz feeling Danny Thompson and Terry Cox can insinuate so cunningly, not to mention the American songs, and I prefer "In-a-Gadda-Da-Vida" to the eighteen-minute "Jack Orion," about a noble fiddler betrayed by his serving lad. Don't they realize that every verse of "Cruel Sister" used to end "Fa la la la la la la la la la" because in the olde days people had nothing else to do at night?   **C +**

Pere Ubu: *The Modern Dance* (Blank '78). Ubu's music is nowhere near as willful as it sounds at first. Riffs emerge from the cacophony, David Thomas's shrieking suits the heterodox passion of the lyrics, and the synthesizer noise begins to cohere after a while. So even though there's too much Radio Ethiopia and not enough Redondo Beach, I'll be listening through the failed stuff — the highs are worth it, and the failed stuff ain't bad. [Later on Rough Trade]. Original grade: B plus.   **A −**

Pere Ubu: *Dub Housing* (Chrysalis '79). Because I trust the way Ubu's visionary humor and crackpot commitment rocks out and/or hooks in for the sheer pleasure of it, I'm willing to go with their excursions into musique concrete, and on this record they get me somewhere. The death of Peter Laughner may well have deprived

America of its greatest punk band, but the subsequent ascendancy of synth wizard Allen Ravenstine has defined a survival-prone community capable of bridging the '60s and the '80s without acting as if the '70s never happened. Imitating randomness by tucking randomlike sounds into deep but tactfully casual structures, joyfully confusing organic and inorganic sounds, they teach us how to live in the industrial shit — imaginatively! **A**

Performance (Warner Bros. '70). Merry Clayton and Ry Cooder and Buffy Sainte-Marie and composer-producer Jack Nitzsche are pretty good for a soundtrack and pretty forgettable for a record album. The Last Poets are the Last Poets. Randy Newman's version of Nitzsche's metaphor to impotence, "Gone Dead Train," is a white blues landmark. And Mick Jagger's version of Jagger-Richard's scabrous, persona-twisted "Memo from Turner" is his envoi to the '60s. **B —**

Carl Perkins and NRBQ: *Carl Perkins and NRBQ* (Columbia '70). This is uniformly pleasant, but Carl can't wear those shoes no more — he's an aging country singer who sounds it. And since he wrote about half of these tunes as well as singing half of them, we might mention that for the most part he's a competent and utterly unexciting composer. As for NRBQ, their jumpy version of that blues-bopping beat merges all too well with the novelty-music aspect of rockabilly — at times this sounds an itty bit cute. Cute and I like them: Terry Adams's hippie pastorale, "On the Farm," and a Perkins guitar showpiece called "Just Coastin'." **B**

Carl Perkins: *Ol' Blue Suede's Back* (Jet '78). Perkins was never an Elvis or a Jerry Lee or even a Gene Vincent, and Ricky Nelson, for instance, put more good rock and roll on record. Young Blue Suede's *Original Golden Hits* is still in catalogue on Sun, and (for completeness freaks) his entire

Sun output is available on three Charly imports. Excepting "That's Alright Mama," nothing on this Nashville we-can-too-rock-'n'-roll session conveys the verve and discovery of even his optional '50s stuff. **C +**

Permanent Wave: A Collection of Tomorrow's Favorites by Today's Bands on Yesterday's Vinyl (Epic '79). "Television Generation" and "Just Another Teenage Anthem" never really got me as singles, and neither the Kursaal Flyers nor New Hearts proved deep enough to make good albums, but on this pop punk compilation they sound absolutely ace. Masterswitch's "Action Replay," the Cortinas' "Heartache," and the Vibrators' "Judy Says" also fit in. The Diodes' "Red Rubber Ball" is as useless as every other piece of Toronto punk I've heard. Since they also lead off the group's new collection on domestic Epic, the two nice cuts by the Only Ones are redundant. The teaser by the Spikes is good enough to make me hope they record an album. And the teaser by After the Fall is so good that I won't mind owning it twice when their album comes out. Quite snazzy, recommended to dabblers and discophiles alike. **B +**

The Persuasions: *Acappella* (Straight '70). By recording half of this live, the best way to assure that the vocal textures will be lost (they sound better in subway tunnels than on stages anyway), Frank Zappa and/or his agents reduce this group to the level of Alice Cooper, Wild Man Fischer, and the GTOs — another act in the freak show. **C +**

The Persuasions: *We Came to Play* (Capitol '71). "You should never try to put a tuxedo on the funky blues," reads Richard Penniman's epigraph, but that doesn't mean they should go naked: Jimmy Hayes's bass pulse may be a wonder, but it isn't a trap set. The studio work here captures their live blend, but that's not quite enough —

every lyric, melody, arrangement, and lead has to rank with those of "Man, Oh Man" or "Walk on the Wild Side" for an acappella album to call you back. **B+**

The Persuasions: *Street Corner Symphony* (Capitol '72). If you believe acappella is inherently superior to "commercial" rock and roll, you'll prefer the Persuasions' covers to the Sam Cooke and Impressions and Temptations originals. But if you think it's an eccentric alternative, you'll note that Jerry Lawson's style is a punchier, less delicate variation on the sweet gutturals of David Ruffin, who himself barely gets by — with skillful help from Norman Whitfield — on a grade-B ballad like "I Could Never Love Another." **B**

The Persuasions: *Spread the Word* (Capitol '72). The offhand concept announced by the title — gospel and its dissemination — doesn't come out as sentimental as you might expect. Not counting "The Lord's Prayer," the only straight gospel song here is "When Jesus Comes," a millenarian vision that seems rather vague after the more detailed (and profane) utopia described in "When I Leave These Prison Walls." "The Ten Commandments of Love," "Heaven Help Us All," and "Hymn #9" (a Vietnam junkie song recommended to John Prine) all translate church metaphor into secular maxim, while "Lean on Me" and "Without a Song" apotheosize the pious commonplace. "T. A. Thompson" reveres a rev. And Bob Dylan's "Three Angels" — one of the dopiest songs about religion ever written — is here transformed into apt intro and reprise. **B+**

The Persuasions: *We Still Ain't Got No Band* (MCA '73). On their r&b album they go head to head with Jimmy Reed and outdo Sam Cooke as well as unearthing a doowop standard that Don Robey probably doesn't remember he wrote (if he did). They also go head to head with the Impressions, the Drifters, and the Coasters. And unearth a

soul substandard by one Jimmy Hughes that will live on in the memory of Jimmy Hughes's mother. Time: 27:47. **B**

The Persuasions: *I Just Want to Sing with My Friends* (A&M '74). Most of side two works despite the horns. But producer-songwriter Jeff Barry's benign poppification sounds positively metastatic when counterposed against the arty purity of the few acappella cuts he permits. **B−**

The Persuasions: *Chirpin'* (Elektra '77). Those who agree with the group's in-it-for-love producer David Dashev that this disc is "definitive" find Jerry Lawson's deadpan interpretation of Tony Joe White's "Willie and Laura Mae Jones" and Joe Russell's solo claim on "To Be Loved" more resonant than I do. But I am impressed by the acapella anthem "Lookin' for an Echo" and the way they sustain "Women and Drinkin' " for seven minutes, and I really like the easy stuff: "Papa Oom Mow Mow" and "Sixty Minute Man." **B+**

The Persuasions: *Comin' at Ya* (Flying Fish '79). The least "contemporary" record they've ever essayed — except for "Love Me Like a Rock," all the material dates back to when their acapella style was a genuine urban folk response to what was on the radio — is uniformly listenable. It's also their first for this bluegrass-centered Chicago label, and thanks — here's what folkies are for. **B+**

Peter, Paul & Mary: *Reunion* (Warner Bros. '78). To turn "Forever Young" into the post-hippie "My Way," the way Dylan does, just means you've become a showbiz reprobate. To turn it into a rinky-dink reggae like these three geezers means you've been middle-aged and liberal since you were fifteen. **D+**

Tom Petty and the Heartbreakers: *Tom Petty and the Heartbreakers* (Shelter '76.) Addicts of updated nostalgia and rock and roll readymades should find this a sly and authentic commentary on the evolving dilemma of Harold Teen. The songs are cute, the riffs executed with more dynamism than usual, and the singing attractively phlegmy. And like they say at the end of other cartoons, that's all, folks. **B +**

Tom Petty and the Heartbreakers: *You're Gonna Get It!* (ABC/Shelter '78). ". . . might sound strange/Might seem dumb," Tom warns at the outset, and unfortunately he only gets it right the second time: despite his Southern roots and '60s pop-rock proclivities, he comes on like a real made-in-L.A. jerk. Onstage, he acts like he wants to be Ted Nugent when he grows up, pulling out the cornball arena-rock moves as if they had something to do with the kind of music he makes; after all, one thing that made the Byrds and their contemporaries great was that they just got up there and played. Thank God you don't have to look at a record, or read its interviews. Tuneful, straight-ahead rock and roll dominates the disc, and "I Need to Know," which kicks off side two, is as peachy-tough as power pop gets. There are even times when Tom's drawl has the impact of a soulful moan rather than a brainless whine. But you need a lot of hooks to get away with being full of shit, and Tom doesn't come up with them. **B**

Tom Petty and the Heartbreakers: *Damn the Torpedoes* (Backstreet/MCA '79). This is a breakthrough for Petty because for the first time the Heartbreakers (his Heartbreakers, this *L.A.M.F.* fan should specify) are rocking as powerfully as he's writing. But whether Petty has any need to rock out beyond the sheer doing of it — whether he has anything to say — remains shrouded in banality. Thus he establishes himself as the perfect rock and roller for those who want good — very good, because Petty really knows his stuff — rock and roll that can be forgotten as soon as the record or the concert is over, rock and roll that won't disturb your sleep, your conscience, or your precious bodily rhythms. **B +**

P.F.M.: *Cook* (Manticore '74). I've always wondered what it stood for, and this title gives me a clue: Pasta Fazool Machine. Somebody ought to tell them about red pepper. **C −**

PG&E: *The Best of PG&E* (Columbia '73). You have to sympathize with a band whose tragic history includes the theft of their name — a name greater than Tongue & Groove or Nova Local — by a power monopoly. But this boasts as many moments as they deserve. Charlie Allen synthesizes Taj Mahal and Otis Redding (more Arthur Conley, actually) over a blues-soul ensemble without the chops or drive of the similar bands led by Delaney Bramlett, one of Pacific Gas & Electric's producers. The highlight is their only hit, the rousing "Are You Ready?" Added attractions include "Rock and Roller's Lament," which is autobiographical, and "Staggolee," which isn't. **B −**

Phillip & Lloyd (the Blues Busters): *Phillip & Lloyd (the Blues Busters)* (Scepter '75). Anybody who thinks Jamaican music is all ganja and so-Jahseh should check out this not-bad collection of soul remakes, produced by Kingston's answer to Herb Alpert, Byron Lee (whose own American LP, *Disco Reggae,* includes a slinky version of "Shaving Cream"), and showcasing an accomplished duo of long popularity. Not bad, like I say, but nothing to make you jot down WLIB's Caribbean hours on the door of your refrigerator. Exceptions: "Baby I'm Sorry" and (especially) "Keep on Doing It," both of them, oddly enough, reggae originals. **C +**

Esther Phillips: *Burnin'* (Atlantic '70). With her lubricious, naturally sardonic high vibrato, this modern blues singer is well equipped to carry Dinah Washington's torch, and a club date with the likes of Chuck Rainey and Cornell Dupree is the perfect place for her to shine her light — even the horn overdubs sound hot. But there are only three blues, and she doesn't bring quite enough to either the standards ("Shangri-La" is the most regrettable) or the "contemporary material" (one Aretha, one Beatles) with which a nightclub pro fills out her act. **B+**

Esther Phillips: *From a Whisper to a Scream* (Kudu '72). The idea is for her to go pop in two opposite directions — (black) rock material, which is good, and slick arrangements, which aren't. So while it's gratifying to hear her tackle Allen Toussaint, Marvin Gaye, and Gil Scott-Heron, whose song about a junkie with no reason to kick is her tour de force, Creed Taylor proves a thankless producer. It's not just the strings, but the way their simple syrup is played against climaxes that pack all the excitement of an escalator. **B**

Esther Phillips: *Alone Again, Naturally* (Kudu '72). Here Phillips gets too cocky with her song choices. By eschewing the piano hook, she covers "Use Me" without making you fantasize about Bill Withers. But Gladys Knight still owns "I Don't Want to Do Wrong." And Gilbert O'Sullivan still owns "Alone Again, Naturally." **B**

Esther Phillips: *Black-Eyed Blues* (Kudu '73). Because the excess instruments support a funkier groove (not to mention that they support a groove at all), the six songs on this album convey more of her smarts and soul than the ten on its predecessor — she really gets to signify, even on the two ballads. High point: a straight Dinah Washington blues. **A−**

Esther Phillips: *Performance* (Kudu '74). Phillips's adventurous material is one reason her jazzy pop blues are so lively, but here she's bested by Eugene McDaniels's "Disposable Society" ("They've thrown away sincerity, the keystone of integrity") and Allen Toussaint's title tune ("I'm a thing that makes music they don't understand"). On the other hand, eight minutes of

Chris Smithers's "I Feel the Same" seems just about right. Original grade: A minus. **B+**

Esther Phillips w/Beck: *What a Diff'rence a Day Makes* (Kudu '75). When it works, Phillips's music balances good songs and a good beat. This time her new arranger tries to push her over into a disco groove, so it's not surprising that some of this sounds a little untracked. **B**

Esther Phillips with Beck: *For All We Know* (Kudu '76). Well, "What a Diff'rence a Day Makes" was a hit. So it follows that "For All We Know" will be a hit too. Right? **B−**

Esther Phillips: *Confessin' the Blues* (Atlantic '76). Consistent material (lots of twelve-bar) and the complete absence of violins make these sessions — recorded in the mid-to-late '60s, half with big band and half with combo — preferable to the run of her Kudu albums. But that's not to make the purist assumption that the settings are ideal — the combo is a bit too elegant, the charting ordinary. Compare "Cherry Red" on *Alone Again, Naturally,* where modernistic blues from Stuff inspires a funny, pained intimacy, to this one, which begins with Sonny Criss blowing some real blues out from between his colleagues but ends with a climax that compels Phillips to belt for no dramatic reason. **A−**

Esther Phillips: *Capricorn Princess* (Kudu '76). In which Creed Taylor rescues her from Joe Beck and then immediately swamps her in mush yet again, so that her Janis Ian cover doesn't match the original and her bitter "All the Way Down" almost sounds out of place. Q: And what's *your* sign, Creed? A: $ **B−**

Esther Phillips: *You've Come a Long Way, Baby* (Mercury '77). Anyone who believes Creed Taylor is a neutral presence should check out Phillips on her own: using Kudu producer Pee Wee Ellis and the basic Kudu formula — mixing blues and standards and rock with MOR and disco crossovers — she comes up with her most consistent album of the '70s. She divvies up the sides, putting mostly crossover stuff on the B, where it holds its own. She takes on someone named Mischa Siegal to help Ellis with the string arrangements, which are discreet, more trim than wallpaper. And she does an extra blues. Not to mention "Into the Mystic." **B +**

Esther Phillips: *All About Esther Phillips* (Mercury '78). I thank Esther for making me hear that "Native New Yorker" is about danger and selfishness. But not for the discobeisance and inbred songwriting. **B −**

Esther Phillips: *Here's Esther . . . Are You Ready* (Mercury '79). Proving her resilience once again, this thirty-year-woman skates over "Philadelphia Freedom" with a lot more cool than Aretha managed on "The Weight," explores her blues roots with a Ruby & the Romantics cover, and gets good material out of what still looks suspiciously like a stable. Special plaudits to producer Harvey Mason, who reminds us that disco horns and strings are supposed to push push. Fave: the danceable get-down parody, "Oo Oop Oo Oop." **B +**

John Phillips: *John Phillips* (Dunhill '70). Phillips doesn't have a beautiful voice — that was Denny Doherty — but he can project as well as write, and most of these murmured reports from Topanga and Malibu are tossed off with a not unattractive noblesse oblige. Lou Adler's unhurried, witty, soul- and country-tinged production suits them perfectly. Elitist, perhaps, but more about leisure enjoyed in the wake of accomplishment than about the perquisites of money and power. **B +**

Wilson Pickett: *Right On* (Atlantic '70). It's good that Pickett is tempering his pricky masculinity with gospel compassion, but not so good that he's softening his edge. "Sugar Sugar" (which is fun) plus "Hey Joe" (which is I'm not sure) do not equal "Hey Jude." Original grade: B plus. **B**

Wilson Pickett: *In Philadelphia* (Atlantic '70). What the Gamble-Huff band does for Pickett, Pickett does for the Gamble-Huff songwriters. The way the horns mix Southern drawl and Northern speed-rap makes me nervous, and I wish side two slowed down with the oblique "Help the Needy" instead of the all-over-the-place "Days Go By," but overall the musicians make the singer go and the singer makes the songs go. Time: 26:34. **B +**

Wilson Pickett: *The Best of Wilson Pickett Vol. II* (Atlantic '71). "A Man and a Half" is the quintessential Pickett title from this period — he's always striving to become more than he has any reason to expect to be. Yet for all the overstatement of "Born to Be Wild" or "You Keep Me Hangin' On" (the Box Tops did a better job on that one) he got there pretty often — in screaming tandem with Duane Allman on "Hey Jude," in voluble tandem with Gamble-Huff on "Engine Number 9," in can-you-top-this tandem with his own greatest hit on "I'm a Midnight Mover." And on "She's Lookin' Good" he matched the ease of "Don't Fight It," which was probably hardest of all. **A**

Wilson Pickett: *Don't Knock My Love* (Atlantic '71). Pickett's variation on the New Pretentiousness in Black Music is to progress beyond simple horn riffs into the busy little world of producers Brad Shapiro and Dave Crawford. As an idea, it's better than most — Duke Ellington did a lot with something similar — but in practice it's just about unlistenable. The nadir is "Don't Knock My Love — Pt. 2," a fantasia for brass on which Pickett doesn't sing at all. But Wade Marcus's strings can make anything worse, and Pickett sounds as desperate when his interpretations are spiritless as when they're frantic. Best cut: a cover of Free's • "Fire and Water." Hmm. Original grade: C. **C +**

Wilson Pickett: *Wilson Pickett's Greatest Hits* (Atlantic '73). Packaging the magnificent *Best of* (still using fake stereo on ten cuts) with a modification of the excellent *Best of Vol. II* (trading "Hey Joe," "Cole, Cooke and Redding," and "Born To Be Wild" for "Don't Knock My Love — Pt. I" and "Mama Told Me Not To Come" even up). A must-own for the benighted.   **A**

Wilson Pickett: *Join Me and Let's Be Free* (RCA Victor '75). As a respecter of history, I want to note that this is the Wicked's best since he stopped being bad, kicking off with a likable groove that I began to find tedious well before Carola stopped dancing.   **C+**

Wilson Pickett: *A Funky Situation* (Big Tree '78). Pickett's halfhearted disco move won't go over at the Loft, but it sure beats anything he did for RCA. "Changed my clothes, but I didn't change my soul," he assures us, and that's it exactly. The production (by Rick Hall and Don Daily) and especially the horn arrangements (by Harrison Calloway, Jr.) are dense and eventful rather than overblown and crowded, and unlike so much disco they're designed only to kick ass, never to engulf and wash over. What's more, Pickett is singing again — rarely does he resort to the random scream. His own "Lay Me Like You Hate Me" is a startling distillation of what he's always really been about, and though most of the other songs are just ordinary-plus, they've been chosen with obvious care — no song-factory seconds here. Original grade: B plus. **B**

Wilson Pickett: *I Want You* (EMI America '79). I'd like him back too, but wishing won't make it so. Half straight disco, half soft — for Pickett — soul, this is a mildly enjoyable album that hasn't broken pop or disco or added a "Lay Me Like You Hate Me" to his legend. N.b.: the four (out of seven) best songs are the ones he helped write. Also n.b.: the best of them all is on the disco side.   **B−**

Pilot: *Pilot* (EMI '75). All those nostalgic for Hollies harmonies about the girl next door line up here. Will it bother you if the recording is as slick

as tomorrow's oil spill? Somehow I thought not.   **C+**

Pink Floyd: *Atom Heart Mother* (Harvest '70). Believe it or not, the, er, suite on the first side is easier to take than the, gawd, songs on the second. Yeah, they do leave the singing to an anonymous semi-classical chorus, and yeah, they probably did get the horns for the fanfares at the same hiring hall. But at least the suite provides a few of the hypnotic melodies that made *Ummagumma* such an admirable record to fall asleep to.   **D+**

Pink Floyd: *Meddle* (Harvest '71). Not bad. "Echoes" moves through 23:21 of "Across the Universe" cop with the timeless calm of interstellar overdrive, and the acoustic-type folk songs boast their very own melodies (as well as a real dog, rather than electronic seagulls, for sound effect). The word "behold" should never cross their filters again, but this is definitely an improvement: one eensy-weensy step for humanity, one giant step for Pink Floyd.   **B−**

Pink Floyd: *Obscured by Clouds* (Harvest '72). (Very) occasional songs from the Barbet Schroeder film *La Vallee.* The movie got buried, now skip the soundtrack.   **C**

Pink Floyd: *The Dark Side of the Moon* (Harvest '73). With its technological mastery and its conventional wisdom once-removed, this is a kitsch masterpiece — taken too seriously by definition, but not without charm. It may sell on sheer aural sensationalism, but the studio effects do transmute David Gilmour's guitar solos into something more than they were when he played them. Its taped speech fragments may be old hat, but for once they cohere musically. And if its pessimism is received, that doesn't make the ideas untrue — there are even times, especially when Dick Parry's saxophone undercuts the electronic pomp, when this record brings its cliches to life, which is what pop is supposed to do, even the kind with delusions of grandeur.   **B**

Pink Floyd: *Wish You Were Here* (Columbia '75). No dumb tribulations-of-a-rock-star epic here — the dedication to long-departed crazy Syd Barrett gives it an emotional resolve that mitigates what little self-pity lyricist Roger Waters allows himself. Even more remarkable, the music is not only simple and attractive, with the synthesizer used mostly for texture and the guitar breaks for comment, but it actually achieves some of the symphonic dignity (and cross-referencing) that *The Dark Side of the Moon* simulated so ponderously. And the cover/liner art is worthy of all the stoned raps it has no doubt already inspired. **A −**

Pink Floyd: *Animals* (Columbia '77). This has its share of obvious moments. But I can only assume that those who accuse this band of repetitious cynicism are stuck in such a cynical rut themselves that a piece of well-constructed political program music — how did we used to say it? — puts them uptight. Lyrical, ugly, and rousing, all in the right places. **B +**

Pink Floyd: *The Wall* (Columbia '79). For a dumb tribulations-of-a-rock-star epic, this isn't bad — unlikely to arouse much pity or envy, anyway. The music is all right, too — kitschy minimal maximalism with sound effects and speech fragments. But the story is confused, "mother" and "modern life" make unconvincing villains, and if the recontextualization of "up against the wall" is intended ironically, I don't get it. **B −**

Plastic Bertrand: *Ca Plane Pour Moi* (Sire '78). French rock and roll is French rock and roll — good for a novelty, maybe, but that's it. Ditto for Belgian, wise guy. Anyway, I can't understand the words. **C**

Platinum Hook: *Platinum Hook* (Motown '79). Taken though I am with the nominal ingenuity of such pomp-rock tyros as Trillion and Tycoon, this disco concoction wins first prize in the latest name-that-band sweepstakes. Talk about your money and your mouth. But in the future perhaps an even more direct approach is indicated. Possibilities: Rack Jobber, Airplay, AOR, A&R, Executive Vice-President for Promotion and Marketing. **D +**

Poco: *Poco* (Epic '70). The most overrated underrated group in America. All of CSNY's preciosity with none of the inspiration, all of bluegrass's ramifications with none of its roots. In short, the perfect commentary on the vacuity of competence. Q: Is that useless long instrumental rock or jazz or country or bluegrass? A: If it's useless, it's none of the four. And if it's all of the four it's none of the four. **C +**

The Pointer Sisters: *The Pointer Sisters* (Blue Thumb '73). "All this rock and roll you hear don't mean a thing to me," they admit, although in other respects they seem like young women of superior intelligence. Really, sisters, we let rock and rollers redo Lambert, Hendricks & Ross and sing Barbara Mauritz songs (good ones, anyway) and mention Volvos. Not to mention cover Lee Dorsey. Although encouraging the Hoodoo Rhythm Devils to play "Wang Dang Doodle" for seven minutes is a no-no. Original grade: C plus. **B**

The Pointer Sisters: *The Best of the Pointer Sisters* (ABC/Blue Thumb '76). I realize in retrospect that I didn't like how they sounded mostly because I didn't like what they portended — camp-elegant escapist nostalgia. But in truth they're not bad at it — less liberating than Bette or Dr. Buzzard, but less reactionary than Manhattan Transfer or whoever's breaking out of the boites this month. Church roots help, and not just vocally — their superb taste (from Dizzy Gillespie to Allen Toussaint) has a moral center expressed in songs of their own like "Jada," a generation-gap lyric that ranks with "Handbags and Gladrags," and "Shakey Flat," about moving to the country from an actual city.

What's more, someone seems to know when they're good — with David Rubinson putting his twenty grand in, they've committed a lot of excesses and banalities, but not too many survive on this compilation.   **B +**

The Pointer Sisters: *Energy* (Planet '78). With Richard Perry at the helm and the hyperactivity of sister Bonnie channeled into a socially useful project, they reappear here as Linda Ronstadt, in triplicate and with a beat. In other words, these are excellent songs rockingly performed. But there's something overly temperate about the music, and most of the songs have been interpreted more smartly by artists who care as much about words as they do about notes. Original grade: B.   **B −**

Bonnie Pointer: *Bonnie Pointer* (Motown '78). Thanks to (coproducer) Berry Gordy and the miracle of modern multitracking, Bonnie makes like the Marvelettes of your dreams for an entire side. People didn't conceive vocals this intricate and funky back in Motown's prime, much less overdub them single-larynxed, and the result is remakes that outdo the originals — by Brenda Holloway and the Elgins — and originals that stand alongside. The other side comprises originals of more diminutive stature cowritten by (coproducer) Jeffrey Bowen. (Catalogue number: M7-911R1).   **B +**

The Police: *Outlandos d'Amour* (A&M '79). Tuneful, straight-ahead rock and roll is my favorite form of mindlessness, and almost all of these songs — riffs-with-lyrics, really — make the cretin in me hop. But only "Can't Stand Losing You" makes him jump up and down. And the "satiric" soliloquy to an inflatable bedmate makes him push reject.   **B +**

The Police: *Reggatta de Blanc* (A&M '79). The idea is to fuse Sting's ringing rock voice and the trio's aggressive, hard-edged rock attack with a less eccentric version of reggae's groove and a saner version of reggae's mix. To me the result sounds half-assed. And though I suppose I might find the "synthesis" innovative if I heard as much reggae as they do in England, it's more likely I'd find it infuriating.   **B −**

The Pop: *The Pop* (Automatic '77). Jesus, another one of those self-motivated hard rock bands putting out its own album. These guys are from L.A., with OK lyrics and better everything else; little things like breaks and bridges mean a lot to them, and so do big things like guitars. Intense (rather than inflated) and understated (rather than wimpy) at the same time.   **B +**

The Pop: *Go!* (Arista '79). Amid the sludge of Yew Ess Ay 1977, the chiming, slightly tinny British Invasion tributes of these pioneering L.A. power poppers were as daring formally as their self-distributed album was politically. Two years later everybody's doing it and their synthesis has become correspondingly fuller and more intricate, incorporating Anglophile moves that range from Roxy Music automation to Clashy football-cheer backup vocals. Still missing are depth of vision (these are power poppers, after all) and killer hooks (aren't they?).   **B +**

Iggy Pop: *The Idiot* (RCA Victor '77). The line on Iggy is that this comeback album with Bowie and friends proves his creative power has dissipated. I say bullshit. The Stooges recorded prophetic music, but only some of it was great: because Iggy's skill at working out his musical concept didn't match his energy and inspiration, the attempted dirges fell too flat and some of the rockers never blasted off as intended. Dissipated or not, the new record works as a record. By now, Iggy barbs his lyrics with an oldtimer's irony, which suits the reflective tone Bowie has imposed on the music just fine. In retrospect, it will appear that this was Iggy's only alternative to autodestruct. Not true, perhaps, but retrospect favors artifacts. As do I.   **A −**

Iggy Pop: *Lust for Life* (RCA Victor '77). If *The Idiot* exploits the (trance-prone) affinity for the slow rocker that Bowie evinced on *Station to Station,* this reestablishes the (apollonian) affinity for the dionysiac artist Bowie made so much of five years ago on Mott's *All the Young Dudes.* Like most rock and rollers, I prefer this to *The Idiot* because it's faster and more assertive — which means, among other things, that the nihilistic satire is counteracted by the forward motion of the music itself. **A−**

Iggy Pop and James Williamson: *Kill City* (Bomp '78). Unlike the Stooges' albums, this collection of doctored tapes from 1975 is never brought to a halt by some luded-out threnody. But it doesn't offer any necessities of life, either — no "I Wanna Be Your Dog" or "Search and Destroy," not even a "Gimme Some Skin" or "Here Comes Success" or "China Girl." And it sounds sludgy. **B**

Iggy Pop: *TV Eye* (RCA Victor '78). In the great tradition of Uncle Lou, here's a live quickie for you — four songs from the two recent RCA albums, plus a classic or two from each hard-to-find Elektra, plus the collectors' single "I Got a Right." You get to hear "Lust for Life" without the laff-a-line chorus, "Funtime" with anti-Semitic flourishes, and lots of irrelevant bombast and concert-hall echo. Much of it works anyway, but that doesn't mean I can't dock it a notch for pissing me off. **C+**

Iggy Pop: *New Values* (Arista '79). This album provides what it advertises only to those who consider Iggy a font of natural wisdom — there are such people, you know. But it does get at least partway over on the strength of a first side that has the casual, hard-assed, funny feel of a good blues session — except that it rocks harder, which ain't bad. **B+**

Nolan: *No Apologies* (Lizard '70). A black singer whose idiom is rock-influenced soul (or vice versa) turns Randy Newman's "Let's Burn Down the Cornfield" into a song about smoldering sharecropper unrest (well, sort of) and finds good ones by David Blue (well, sort of) and Booker T. Plus writing wise, witty, rocking songs of his own, songs that belong in this company, many of them about racial identity. Formally, this is the Rod Stewart strategy, and the artistic achievement is comparable. But does he have Stewart's backing on the radio or in the express? Well, no. **A−**

Nolan Porter: *Nolan* (ABC '72). Reggae-flavored originals and interpretations from a college-educated, opera-trained black cab driver who ought to put a band together. He strains Randy Newman and Van Morrison but the reggae on this record sounds better cut for cut than Johnny Nash's. Superb: "If I Could Only Be Sure," the single, with a hook that makes me talk to myself everytime I hear it. **B+**

Andy Pratt: *Andy Pratt* (Columbia '73). "Avenging Annie" is an astounding tale of feminist revenge in the twilight of the counterculture. I can't imagine how it occurred to this poor little rich boy. (Oh, all right — this poor little rich boy with the bizarre falsetto and eccentric pop sense.) (Hey, maybe his wife left him.) **C**

Andy Pratt: *Resolution* (Nemporer '76). The craft that went into this record could pass for genius, and side one includes four or five memorable songs and one moment of wit — a line about a "fuzzy-brained intellectual" that reviewers delight in quoting. I guess I just expect more than one moment of wit per side from self-described intellectuals, even fuzzy-brained ones. Sententious pop at its best, recommended only to those whose taste for such junk amounts to a jones. **B**

Andy Pratt: *Shiver in the Night* (Nemporer '77). In which Leo Sayer goes berserk. Or is it Eric Justin Kaz? A repellent image in either case. **C**

Elvis Presley: *That's the Way It Is* (RCA Victor '70). His seventh album (three admittedly reissues) and third live LP of 1970 leans toward uptempo countryish ballads rather than the usual pop-rock eclecticism and proves that he can remember the words without cue cards. I know that's the way it is — but is it the way it has to be? **C+**

Elvis Presley: *Elvis Country* (RCA Victor '71). A disastrous conceit, in which snippets of a "theme" song segue between tracks, makes it very hard to tell what happens to the Big Concept — Elvis Sings Ernest Tubb, Bill Monroe, Bob Wills, Anne Murray, etc. Most of his recordings sound suspiciously casual anyway, like preconcert runthroughs, and these segues add a rushed medley feel. "The Fool" and "It's Your Baby, You Rock It" work, and "Whole Lot-ta Shakin' " works out. But Tubb's "Tomorrow Never Comes" is a horn-fed monstrosity. And somehow I don't think Elvis had his heart in "Snowbird." **B−**

Elvis Presley: *Elvis Sings the Wonderful World of Christmas* (RCA Victor '71). I prefer the open-throated version of his awesomely pious sentimentality — "It's Now or Never," "If I Can Dream," etc. — to his more constricted attack, used here to signify high seriousness. But when he's serious about classic catchy pop like "Silver Bells" and "O Come, All Ye Faithful" it doesn't much matter, especially when you also get a transition from "I'll Be Home on Christmas Day" to "If I Get Home by Christmas Day." And here's what everyone was really waiting for — "Merry Christmas Baby," 5:45 of awesomely offhand dirt. **B+**

Elvis Presley: *Elvis as Recorded at Madison Square Garden* (RCA) Victor '72). If you want post-comeback Elvis, stick with *TV Special* and *Memphis/Vegas*. Unless your home entertainment center is equipped with a magic holograph and seats 20,000, this will not recreate the excitement of that justifiably fabled concert. In fact, it won't even come close. That's what arena gigs are about. **C**

Elvis Presley: *He Touched Me* (RCA Victor '72). As an evangelical tool, white gospel balances the sweet and the sententious the way "Reach Out to Jesus" does, but too often it topples like "An Evening Prayer," and guess in which direction. Still, Elvis doesn't toss this stuff off — he hasn't sung with such consistent care since his comeback was at stake. And just like black gospel (fancy that), "sacred" music isn't always solemn — half the time it's fast enough to pass for rock and roll. In fact, for a counterpart to the airy intensity and passionate grace of "I, John" you might have to go back to the Sun recordings. **B+**

Elvis Presley: *A Legendary Performer* (RCA Victor '73). I'm told this compilation is his best in years, but what does that mean? That people play it instead of *A Date with Elvis* or *TV Special,* from which all the "later unreleased" tracks were originally excluded? And the interviews are all right, but you can't dance to them. For collectors, historians, and popular culture majors. **B**

Elvis Presley: *Promised Land* (RCA Victor '75). Why is the new Elvis Presley album slightly better (even according to the singles charts) than, for instance, the last Elvis Presley album? Because Elvis decided to make like a big baritone? After all, he's often horrible when he chooses that move. But inspiration is funny, and on this one he'll make you care about, for instance, how a cliche like "Your Love's Been a Long Time Coming" is going to end. Time: 28:11. **B**

Elvis Presley: *Moody Blue* (RCA Victor '77). Despite his capacity for undifferentiated emotion and his utter confidence with almost every kind of American music, Presley didn't automatically impart dignity to anything he laid his voice on the way such natural singers as George Jones and Al Green and Dolly Parton do. Originally a spoiled tough of omnipresent sexual magnetism, he deteriorated into a spoiled stud past his prime, so that while he was always sexy he wasn't always seductive. Whether he's turning it on ("Unchained Melody") or playing it cool ("Little Darling"), his miscalculations can be embarrassing. But he retains so much presence that he can make two Olivia Newton-John songs sound like country classics indifferently remembered. And when he hits it right, as on the first three tracks of side two, his sincerity, vulnerability, and self-possession are as potent as ever. It seems perfectly suitable that this shoddily conceived LP, pressed on blue plastic for gimmick appeal, should turn into his biggest of the decade on the strength of the ultimate gimmick.   **B −**

Elvis Presley: *His Hand in Mine* (RCA Victor '78). With its mawkish self-righteousness, the title epitomizes why we backsliders have permanent doubts about fundamentalist culture. As do the music's secular sellouts, overblown sanctimony, and simulated heavenly hosts — and the thought of RCA making money on two dead messiahs at once.   **C**

Elvis Presley: *Our Memories of Elvis Volume 2* (RCA Victor '79). The idea is to remove the goop — strings, horns, choruses — from nondescript '70s album tracks, shuffle 'em up good, and call it "pure Elvis." But though Volume 1 was a bare-faced exploitation, this one happens to work. Maybe someone figured the potential market hated goop of any kind. In any case, the song selection is neat, including "Green Green Grass of Home," "Thinking About You," the lovely "I Can Help," and a previously unreleased "studio jam session" on Dylan's "Don't Think Twice" that is actually too long at 8:36. The mix is weird — I hear imperfectly erased goop ghosts on "Way Down," for instance — but as near as I can tell this is EP's best pop album of the decade.   **B +**

Billy Preston: *The Kids and Me* (A&M '74). True enough, his songs have become less offensive, but his instrumentals remain in the novelty phase and he still sings like Soul Synth No. 1. Take "Nothing from Nothing" as this year's "You're So Vain" — proof that a great single can come from any fool. But don't be quite so positive he won't make an album you want to hear some day.   **B −**

Pretenders: *Pretenders* (Sire '79). Tough gals, tough gals — suddenly the world is teeming with tough gals. And Chrissie Hynde is a good one. Maybe not all of her songs are championship singles, but she's got more to offer emotionally and musically (and sexually) than any of the competition, unless Patti counts. She's out for herself but she gives of herself as well; when she alternates between rapacity and tenderness you don't feel she's acting coy or fucked up, although she may be. And she conveys these changes with her voice as well as with her terse, slangy, suggestive lyrics. James Honeyman Scott's terse, slangy, suggestive guitar steals don't hurt either.   **A −**

Dory Previn: *Mary C. Brown and the Hollywood Sign* (United Artists '73). Previn doesn't just belabor a cliche, she flails it with barbed wire, and she never writes about a concrete situation when with extra words she can falsify it via abstraction. A feminist friend once persuaded me that such transparent pretension can only signal pain and bewilderment, but if I found a cat trapped in a washing machine, I wouldn't set up a recording studio there — I'd just open the door.   **D**

Alan Price: *O Lucky Man!* (Warner Bros. '73). How does an acerbic, good-humored music journeyman like Price (find *This Price Is Right,* on Parrot) fall in with a pompous, overfed con artist like Lindsay Anderson? By playing the Acerbic, Good-Humoured Music Journeyman Symbol in a pompous, overfed movie. Two or three deft political songs do not redeem an LP that runs 24:43 despite filler. It figures —the movie is an hour (or three hours) too long. **B −**

Alan Price: *Between Today and Yesterday* (Warner Bros. '74). So many tastemongers promoted this as a great one that I listened hard, which didn't work — most of it is simultaneously banal and overstated, which adds up to pretentious. Saved by the last three songs on the "Yesterday" side, which are, I admit, kind of Brechtian. But three songs do not make a great one. **B**

Charley Pride: *The Best of Charley Pride Volume 2* (RCA Victor '72). Says Paul Hemphill: "There might be something to the suspicion that he is Nashville's house nigger . . . if he didn't sing 'Kawliga' better than Hank Williams did." Wrong. First you sing *real* good, and then maybe they *let* you be house nigger. Pride's amazing baritone — it hints at twang and melisma simultaneously, and to call it warm is to slight the brightness of its heat — loses focus as he settles exclusively into "heart songs." Though these tales of married love are worthy enough, only "Is Anybody Goin' to San Antone" ranks with "Does My Ring Hurt Your Finger" or "Just Between You and Me" or "All I Have to Offer You," while "I'm Just Me" asserts an "identity" so vague it couldn't get him a tricycle license. In however irrelevant a way, "Kaw-Liga" at least acknowledged the existence of race, and "The Snakes Crawl at Night" at least casts him as a criminal. Neither was much to retreat from. But they helped round out a persona that's beginning to seem dangerously shallow. Time: 26:08. **B**

Charley Pride: *The Best of Charley Pride Vol. III* (RCA Victor '76). It's no longer so easy to hit consistently in Nashville with such MOR (MOR country, I mean) material, but Pride does it, specializing in happy-marriage songs (which I often find likable) and touching such themes as Jesus, elusive dreams, childhood home, and country-singer-on-the-road (with sex). An achievement, even though he's got a gimmick as well as a voice — which seems to be softening slightly, losing its resonant edge. But especially given how middling his MOR often is, I wish he wanted to do — or is it could do? — more. **B −**

Prince: *For You* (Warner Bros. '78). Like most in-studio one-man bands, the nineteen-year-old kid who pieced this disco-rock-pop-funk concoction together has a weakness for the programmatic — lots of chops, not much challenge. But I like "Baby," about making one, and "Soft and Wet," ditto only he doesn't know it yet. And his falsetto beats Stevie Wonder's, not to mention Emitt Rhodes's. **B −**

Prince: *Prince* (Warner Bros. '79). This boy is going to be a big star, and he deserves it — he's got a great line. "I want to come inside you" is good enough, but (in a different song) the simple "I'm physically attracted to you" sets new standards of "naive," winning candor. The vulnerable teen-macho falsetto idea is pretty good too. But he does leave something to be desired in the depth-of-feeling department — you know, soul. **B +**

John Prine: *John Prine* (Atlantic '71). You suspect at first that these standard riffs and reliable rhythms are designed to support the lyrics rather than accompany them. But the homespun sarcasm of singing that comes on as tuneless as the tunes themselves soon reveals itself as an authentic, rather catchy extension of Nashville and Appalachia — and then so do the tunes, and the riffs, and the rhythms. Anyway, the lyrics are worth accompanying — not the literary corn of the absurdly overpraised "Sam Stone," but the cross-generational empathy of "Hello in There" and "Angel from Montgomery," the heartland hippieism of "Illegal Smile" and "Spanish Pipedream." And Arif Mardin hooks up "Pretty Good" pretty good. Original grade: B. **A**

John Prine: *Diamonds in the Rough* (Atlantic '72). Not as rich as the debut, but more artlessly and confidently sung — the gruff monotone avoids melodrama in favor of Prine's own version of good-old-boy, adding a muscular good humor to throwaway gems like "Frying Pan" and "Yes I Guess They Ought to Name a Drink After You." Plus several decent lyrics about women, the Jesus song of the year, and a Vietnam tribute dedicated to Henry Clay, who helped start the (first) American Civil War.   **A −**

John Prine: *Sweet Revenge* (Atlantic '73). Prine is described as surrealistic and/or political even though the passion of his literalness is matched only by that of his detachment: inferential leaps and tall songs do not a dreamscape make, and Prine offers neither program nor protest. It's the odd accretions of everyday detail — as in the "four way stop dilemma" of "The Accident" — that heighten the reality of his songs, and his elementary insight that social circumstances do actually affect individual American lives that distinguishes him politically from his fellow workers. That's why when he finally writes his music-biz takeoff it's a beaut; that's why "Christmas in Prison" deserves to be carved on a wooden turkey.   **A**

John Prine: *Common Sense* (Atlantic '75). Despite the singer's lax manner, these songs are anything but throwaways. Nor are they self-imitations: Prine customarily strives for coherence, but this time he has purposely (and painfully) abjured it. He seems to regret this at one point — during a more or less cogent lament for a dead friend — but the decision was obviously unavoidable. It results in the most genuinely miserable album I've heard in years. Original grade: B plus.   **A −**

John Prine: *Prime Prine: The Best of John Prine* (Atlantic '76). Not as rewarding cut for cut as *John Prine* or *Sweet Revenge,* not as interesting conceptually as *Diamonds in the Rough* or *Common Sense.* Good songs, useless album.   **B −**

John Prine: *Bruised Orange* (Asylum '78). In the title tune, Prine reports that he's transcended his anger, and I'm happy for him, but a little worried about his music. *Common Sense* was agitated to the point of psychosis, but it had an obsessive logic nevertheless. Here Prine sounds like he's singing us bedtime stories, and while the gently humorous mood is attractive, at times it makes this "crooked piece of time that we live in" seem as harmless and corny as producer Steve Goodman's background moves; no accident that the closer, "The Hobo Song," is Prine's most mawkish lyric to date. Still, Edward Lear's got nothing on this boy for meaningful nonsense, and just to prove he's still got the stuff he collaborates with Phil Spector on a surefire standard: "If You Don't Want My Love," with lyrics worthy of its title. Original grade: B minus.   **B +**

John Prine: *Pink Cadillac* (Asylum '79). Weird. With production by Knox and Jerry (Sons of Sam) Phillips, Prine has never rocked harder. But he's slurring his vocals like some toothless cartoon bluesman emulating an Elvis throwaway — related to the Sun sound, I guess, but perversely. Are the new songs any good? Hard to tell.   **B −**

Procol Harum: *Home* (A&M '70). *A Salty Dog* had Matthew Fisher putting his two pence in, not that I've ever missed an organist before. And on *A Salty Dog* the Robin Trower blues was country and droll rather than technological and macho. And on *A Salty Dog* they didn't print the lyrics, which ought to end those silly rumors about Gary Brooker's intellectual attainments. Believe me, a smart singer would try and play "Whaling Stories" for laughs. Then again, a smart singer wouldn't write with Keith Reid in the first place.   **C +**

Procol Harum: *Broken Barricades* (A&M '71). Just because the resident poetaster doesn't have his own acoustic guitar, people make this out to be some kind of triumph for good old rock and roll, which is absurd. Good old rock, maybe. Pompous, muddy, indecipherable. **C –**

Procol Harum: *Live in Concert with the Edmonton Symphony Orchestra* (A&M '72). Gigging with a local band this way would be a terrible idea for more accomplished rock and rollers, but as it is, the enthusiastic provincials kick Procol's ass on "Conquistador," great meaningless fun in the tradition of "Quick Joey Small." And you have to admit that the string and horn arrangements are *different*. **B –**

Procol Harum: *Grand Hotel* (Chrysalis '73). For years these guys have vacillated between a menu of grits that certainly ain't groceries and larks' tongues in aspic. Despite their current white-tie conceit, they still haven't decided. Personally, I wish they'd pick their poison and choke on it. **C**

Procol Harum: *The Best of Procol Harum* (A&M '73). Not bad for profit taking. The melodies are at their ingratiating schlock-classical best, the tempos up enough to render the lyrics extraneous. Among the four never-on-LP inducements are "Lime Street Blues," a jolly barrelhouse that mentions underpants, and "Homburg," which introduces their "multilingual business friend." But the old stuff reminds us that Keith Reid once knew writing can be a goof — even his "commercial" lyrics from the '70s ("Simple Sister," "Whiskey Train")

are self-servingly arrogant. And the Gary-Brooker's-greatest format demonstrates conclusively that he learned his oft-praised blues mannerisms from the constipated guy in the next toilet stall. **B +**

Professor Longhair: *Live on the Queen Mary* (Harvest '78). Roy Byrd's pianistic intricacies — which inspired Fats Domino, Huey Smith, Allen Toussaint, Dr. John, and other New Orleans luminaries — come through better on this live recording than on Atlantic's '50s compilation. This I credit to the hazardously busy (and uncredited) bass-and-drums accompaniment, which provides enough movement down below to allow Prof to really get rolling up top. Blues backup isn't supposed to work that way, but these guys get away with it, and good for them. P.S. Prof sings off-key a lot. P.P.S. It doesn't matter — sometimes it's even cute. **A –**

Flora Purim: *Stories to Tell* (Milestone '74). If there were no lyrics on this revolving misnomer, I might kowtow before the kozmic ineff of its big-name jazz accomp, but I know that any musician (singer) who tells me "time is lie" ain't tellin nuthin *but* lies. **C**

Flora Purim: *Open Your Eyes You Can Fly* (Milestone '76). Shut your mouth and maybe they'll let you land. **C**

Q

Quadrophenia (Polydor '79). Confusing. This (intermittently remixed) "soundtrack" condenses the original two-LP set down to one disc plus one cut (the cut that never quite fit in anyway), and the only song I miss is "The Dirty Jobs" (maybe Pete figured the Clash had him beat on that one). But there's no libretto, and the point of *Quadrophenia*-the-album wasn't individual songs anyway. The rest comprises previously unreleased new and old Who songs of considerable interest and some quality and a side of good oldies you may or may not own (I didn't have two of them myself). **B**

Suzi Quatro: *Suzi Quatro* (Bell '74). This woman sings "I Wanna Be Your Man" and "All Shook Up" without gender changes, although she does rewrite a line of the latter so that she's "queer as a bug." But nothing in her own songwriting equals the one-riff rock of the two Chapman-Chinn singles, especially "48 Crash," and the last time I got off on someone dressed entirely in leather was before John Kay started repeating himself. **B**

Suzi Quatro: *Quatro* (Bell '74). Dumb, yes. Samey, still. Leiber-Stoller's "Trouble" sounds silly — even in that chrome sweat suit, Suzi can't convince me she's evil. And I wish her physical equipment — her medium-sized voice, her static bass playing, and her workmanlike band — were up to her concept and the likable, mostly Chapmann-Chinn mate-rial. But I do believe she's tough and independent, and I'd rather hear Quatro shouting out "Keep A Knockin' " than a whole album of Maria Muldaur stylizations. **B−**

Suzi Quatro: *Your Mama Won't Like Me* (Arista '75). The songs are a shade weaker, but the real problem — and I'm sure Clive Davis had nothing to do with it — is classier arrangements that give her more room to sing. Suzi just doesn't have the stuff to make like an interpreter, whether torching up "Fever" or doing a Janis on "Strip Me." She lives and dies as a straight-ahead rocker. **B−**

Suzi Quatro: *If You Knew Suzi . . .* (RSO '79). Just because she's with Robert Stigwood doesn't mean she's trying to sound like Andy Gibb. But she doesn't put out Blondie's snazz just because Mike Chapman is still producing, either. Yvonne Elliman's, maybe. **C+**

Queen: *Queen II* (Elektra '74). Wimpoid royaloid heavyoid android void. **C−**

Queen: *A Night at the Opera* (Elektra '75). This is near enough to the reported mishmash to make me doubt that it sells for what's good about it. Which is that it doesn't actually botch any of a half-dozen arty-to-heavy "eclectic" modes — even something called "Prophet's Song" sounds OK — and achieves a parodic tone often enough to suggest more than meets the ear. Maybe if they come up with a coherent masterwork I'll figure out what that more is. Maybe if they come up with a coherent masterwork *they'll* figure out what that more is.   **B –**

Queen: *News of the World* (Elektra '77). In which the group that last January brought us a $7.98 LP to boycott devotes one side to the wantonness of woman and the other to the futile rebelliousness of the doomed-to-life losers (those saps!) (you saps!) who buy and listen.   **C**

Queen: *Jazz* (Elektra '78). Despite the title — come back, Ry Cooder, all is forgiven — this isn't completely disgusting. "Bicycle Race" is even funny. Put them down as 10cc. with a spoke, or a pump, up their ass.   **C +**

Quicksilver Messenger Service: *Just for Love* (Capitol '70). Whether *Happy Trails* is one of the great live albums or (my theory) one of the greatly overrated ones, Quicksilver needn't have bothered — their studio LPs capture that ballroom ambience right down to the echoed vocals and the imprecise impressionistic accompaniment. And though the debut is more listenable, this beats it for sheer documentary charm. Complete with twin guitars and a "Ladies Section"

on the jacket comprising twenty-six first names, here is the quintessential Frisco band — its writing folky without the roots, its playing jazzy without the chops, its concepts unencumbered by any sense of form. The big news is the return of Dino Valenti, but the big attraction is the quintessential Quicksilver anthem, "Fresh Air," as in "Have another hit." Plus those twin guitars — John Cipollina and Gary Duncan, we salute you.   **B –**

Quicksilver Messenger Service: *What About Me* (Capitol '70). From the self-righteous "political" singalong to the putdown of New York to the phony samba to the horny production number, this is what people don't like about hippies. Another thing they don't like about hippies is that Dino Valenti is a hippie.   **C –**

Quicksilver Messenger Service: *Anthology* (Capitol '73). With nary a selection from last year's flop and four awful ones from its predecessor, this compilation is where they admit defeat, and why not? Neither Nicky Hopkins expressing himself nor Dino Valenti acting free — good thing (for him) that he was busted for dope rather than impersonating a vocalist or he'd still be up the river — could stop this band from dating in record time. **C +**

The Raes: *Dancing Up a Storm* (A&M '79). The failure of "A Little Lovin' " to crack top forty portends a duller future for AM radio than any new wave blackout. A hooky girl-group classic that broke disco when a percussion break was patched in, the tune is certifiable contemporary pop. Wish I could recommend the album, too, but you know how girl groups are. **C+**

Gerry Rafferty: *City to City* (United Artists '78). A miraculously homogeneous album — except for the breakthrough sax refrain on "Baker Street," neither voice nor instrument ruffles the flow of hard-won axioms and sensible hooks. Very nice, I mean it — if yin and yang is your meat, this beats Percy Faith a mile. But Fleetwood Mac it ain't. **B−**

Gerry Rafferty and Joe Egan: *Stuck in the Middle with You: The Best of Stealers Wheel* (A&M '78). This duo charted three singles: the title smash, its follow-up (a stiff, actually), and "Star," which was not about astronomy (or even astrology). It also released three albums, the first of which stands in relation to the others as does the first single to its fellows. Later its better half became a mystic of sorts and scored yet another fluky smash. Hence, album number four. **C+**

Bonnie Raitt: *Bonnie Raitt* (Warner Bros. '71). A singer-guitarist (and occasional composer) who renders all the Collins/Baez melodrama superfluous, Raitt is a folkie by history but not by aesthetic. She includes songs from Steve Stills, the Marvelettes, and a classic feminist blues singer named Sippie Wallace because she knows the world doesn't end with acoustic song-poems and Fred McDowell. An adult repertoire that rocks with a steady roll, and she's all of twenty-one years old. Original grade: B plus. **A−**

Bonnie Raitt: *Give It Up* (Warner Bros. '72). Raitt's laid-back style (shades of John Hurt and John Hammond, touches of Aretha Franklin and Bessie Smith) is unique in its active maturity, intelligence, and warmth. With Chris Smither's "Love Me Like a Man" ("lyrics adapted by Bonnie Raitt") and Sippie Wallace's "You Got to Know How" she dares any crotch-rocker to match her sexual expertise. On Joel Zoss's "Stayed Too Long at the Fair" and Jackson Browne's "Under the Falling Sky" she dares any sensitive type to wax lyrical without a drum kit. And on her own "You Told Me Baby" and "Nothing Seems to Matter" she invites Lenny Welch to return the favor. Original grade: A minus. **A**

Bonnie Raitt: *Takin' My Time* (Warner Bros. '73). I hear people asking when Bonnie is going to do something new, but conveying songs from Calypso Rose and Martha Reeves Vandella into the women's music of the '70s is new enough for me. I must ad-

314

mit, though, that neither statement is enhanced by association with the folkies whose ballads she favors — too pretty, too ordinary. **A −**

Bonnie Raitt: *Streetlights* (Warner Bros. '74). Best cut: Allen Toussaint's "What Is Success," about the "so necessary" spiritual expenditures entered above a record company's bottom line. Whereupon Raitt pays her tribute to schlock four times over. Typically, she can uncover a stirring moment in the most stillborn possible-single, but the limits of her integrity have already been defined by three flexible, often playful, yet obviously uncompromising albums, and when the strings and woodwinds rise up, they dispossess her. Even "What Is Success" suffers a setback when Raitt accedes to Toussaint's impersonal "he." That's no "he," Bonnie — that's you. Original grade: B minus. **B**

Bonnie Raitt: *Home Plate* (Warner Bros. '75). Produced with much tape trickery and laying on of experts by Paul Rothchild, this defeats its own gloss by refining and expanding the conventions of emotive, projective "sincerity" that have informed pop music from Al Jolson to Linda Ronstadt. By her thoughtful phrasing and gentle-to-gritty timbre, by her understated dramatic presence, by the songs she chooses to sing, Raitt makes her "compassion" seem unsentimental and even sharp-tongued without any loss of outreach. I love every cut, from John and Johanna Hall's "Good Enough," her most alluring analysis of a long-term sexual relationship yet, to John David Souther's "Run Like a Thief," which is about going to bed with your best friend's mate. **A**

Bonnie Raitt: *Sweet Forgiveness* (Warner Bros. '77). Although Paul Rothchild edited Bonnie's road band as painstakingly as he did the El Lay pros of *Home Plate,* this came out sounding unfashionably raw, almost live, because instead of punching in the perfect note and the clean tone he went for the most intense moment available

from months of takes. I don't like "Runaway," which is flat and plodding and wrong for her, and I wish there were a stunner like "Good Enough" or "Sweet and Shiny Eyes" here. But Bonnie is singing rougher than ever before. Anyone who can induce me to dance to Eric Kaz has got to be doing some kind of job. **A −**

Bonnie Raitt: *The Glow* (Warner Bros. '79). I suppose I should blame Peter Asher for how pat a few of these songs sound, but in fact I blame him only for pianist Don Grolnick, who single-handedly (well, actually I guess he used two) transforms the title cut from a cry of alcoholic despair to a self-pitying piece of hightone lounge schlock. She's never sounded better on the slow ones — Hayes-Porter's "Your Good Thing" is the killer — and her own "Standing by the Same Old Love" adds significantly to the pitiful store of rock songs about enduring sexual relationships. But I could stand some more hard raunch. **B +**

Ramatam: *Ramatam* (Atlantic '72). Like Birtha, this is a heavy group with female lead guitarist. Lester Bangs, holding forth as a connoisseur of schlock-rock, thinks this is great and Birtha is horrible. I think this is less horrible, that's all. Still the same strained, stupid lyrics with singing to match and programmed high energy to help it all go down (or past). Plus some very extraneous woodwind breaks and heavy licks hot off the lathe. Good old (or new) rock and roll it ain't. **C**

Ramones: *Ramones* (Sire '76). I love this record — love it — even though I know these boys flirt with images of brutality (Nazi especially) in much the same way "Midnight Rambler" flirts with rape. You couldn't say they condone any nasties, natch — they merely suggest that the power of their music has some fairly ominous sources and tap those sources even as they offer the suggestion. This makes me uneasy. But my theory has always been that good rock and roll should damn well make you uneasy, and the sheer pleasure of this stuff — which of course elicits howls of pain from the good old rock and roll crowd — is undeniable. For me, it blows everything else off the radio; it's clean the way the Dolls never were, sprightly the way the Velvets never were, and just plain listenable the way Black Sabbath never was. And I hear it cost $6400 to put on plastic.   **A**

Ramones: *Ramones Leave Home* (Sire '77). People who consider this a one-joke band aren't going to change their minds now. People who love the joke for its power, wit, and economy will be happy to hear it twice. Hint: read the lyrics. Original grade: A minus.   **A**

Ramones: *Rocket to Russia* (Sire '77). Having revealed how much you can take out and still have rock and roll, they now explore how much you can put back in and still have Ramones. Not that they've returned so very much — a few relatively obvious melodies, a few relatively obvious vocals. But that's enough. Yes, folks, there's something for everyone on this ready-made punk-rock classic. Stoopidity, both celebrated and satirized. Love (thwarted) and social protest (they would seem to oppose DDT). Inspired revivals (the Trashmen) and banal cover versions (Bette Midler *and* Cass Elliott beat them to "Do You Wanna Dance?"). And, for their record company and the ears of the world, an actual potential hit. If "Sheena Is a Punk Rocker" was the most significant number eighty-four record in history, what will "Rockaway Beach" do for number twenty? (Did I hear five?) **A**

Ramones: *Road to Ruin* (Sire '78). Like any great group, this one is always topping itself. Album four alternates definitive high-speed rockers — "I Wanted Everything," "I'm Against It," and "She's the One" are as good as any they've ever done — with more candidly lyrical slow ones that rank with the oldie, "Needles and Pins," as compositions. The lyrics of "I Just

Want to Have Something to Do" and "I Wanna Be Sedated" test the barrier between their Queens-geek personas and their real lives as professional musicians without a hint of rocky-road bullshit. Only the "Bad Brain" (a title) theme seems repetitious — personally, I'm glad it's fading. But the guitar breaks bring tears to my personal eyes, and I await Gary Stewart's version of "Questioningly."   **A**

The Rascals: *Search and Nearness* (Atlantic '70). Talk about acid casualties — these guys are victims of psychedelica even if they never touched the stuff. But those who ignore the atrocious title and listen to the songs are in for a surprise, because this is no *Freedom Suite*. In fact, it may be their most consistent regular-release LP — only one waste cut per side. If the Rascals are spouting universalist truisms, so is every other soul band these days — usually without coming up with anything as original or unpretentious as the warmly tongue-in-cheek "Right On." The only problem is that that's the high point — no new classics for Aretha to cover. Special surprise: Dino Danelli's modal jazz instrumental "Nama." Original grade: A minus.   **B+**

The Rascals: *Peaceful World* (Columbia '71). I was impressed at first by the effortlessness of Felix Cavaliere's evolution from white punk r&b to white cosmic jazz. Only the Beach Boys have changed so much with so little apparent strain. Yet in the end the jazz musicians he's signed on — Fathead Newman, Joe Farrell, Pepper Adams, Ron Carter — aren't especially well-suited to popularize Coltrane and Pharoah and Sun Ra. And even if Felix were singing enough, he wouldn't be singing very good stuff — composition has never been his strength, and lately he's been thinking about other things. Original grade: B plus.   **C+**

The Rascals: *The Island of Real* (Columbia '72). You can hear Felix trying to get back as side one begins — he sings "feel good to be alive" as if the phrase had just occurred to him. On "Saga of New York" he goes into high gear — catchy, funny, sexy, simple-minded — and he holds his own against "Be on the Real Side." But as Buzzy Feiten starts tricking up his own "Jungle Walk," you wonder whether jungles are coy. And then you realize that there's a pink horse on the cover for a reason. **B −**

Raspberries: *Raspberries* (Capitol '72). A clever label on the shrink-wrap smells the way people who make stickum labels think raspberries should smell, and the clever music inside sounds the way people who make stickum music think the Raspberries should sound — that is, the way people who go to music school think the Beatles should have sounded, with rough edges elided and lots of Chopin-esque white-album flourishes. Worse still, the conservatory-trained goo lovers are apparently the Raspberries themselves. "Go All the Way" does so, and better pop-tight than country-tight, but not that much better. Original grade: C. **C +**

Raspberries: *Fresh* (Capitol '72). The Nostalgia Squad loves these guys — supposedly, they reincarnate the halcyon days of the pre-psychedelic mid-'60s, when rock was simple, happy music sung by harmonizing foursomes in mod clothes. Only thing is, that music used to keep us humming all day, and after listening to this for a month all I remember is three songs: "Let's Pretend," "I Wanna Be with You," and a remarkable Beach Boys takeoff that has tape decks in it. Whatever happened to Gerry and the Pacemakers, anyway? Original grade: C. **B −**

Raspberries: *Side 3* (Capitol '73). I admit that I like all four Eric Carmen songs here, especially the atypically guitar-tough "I'm a Rocker," but I swear if there were more than four I'd like every one less. Wally Bryson's and David Smalley's more conversational timbres and subtle ruralisms provide welcome relief. Now if only

Wally and David could write good songs, too. After all, Eric had to learn. **B**

Raspberries: *Starting Over* (Capitol '74). I don't quite believe it myself, but this really does it — brings the middle '60s into the middle '70s. Full of great singles for a singular time, which obviously doesn't mean this one. Two secrets. First, Scott McCarl is the big bad John they've always needed to complement Eric Carmen's supersweet Paul. Second, a vague concept (just like *Sgt. Pepper!*) adds dimension to several otherwise minor tracks. Highlights: "All Through the Night" (Eric as Rod the Mod), "Hands on You" (drumless John-and-Paul takeout), and "Overnight Sensation" (about being in it for hit records rather than money, which is what I call a concept). **A −**

Raspberries: *Raspberries' Best Featuring Eric Carmen* (Capitol '76). Packaged with dozens of reprints and newly commissioned pieces, several of which promulgate the absurd saw that they were as good "musically" as the you-know-who — as if they ever came close to the Beatles' delicacy or insane enthusiasm or melodic inspiration — this is an Eric Carmen showcase, just like it says. Carmen's taste for mawk is documented revoltingly on his solo debut, but on this compilation it finds only one outlet, the eight-minute "I Can Remember." Otherwise, here are all his good tunes with none of Wally Bryson's or Scott McCarl's, reminding me that the silly love songs I love the most tell me something more about the artist than that he or she loves silly love songs. **A −**

Genya Ravan: *Urban Desire* (20th Century-Fox '78). She oversings, the band's ordinary, and the lyrics (both hers and those she chooses) often get blowzy; the only grade-A cuts are "Jerry's Pigeons" and (A plus) "The Sweetest One." So maybe I'm soft — maybe I just can't resist a real New York doll. In a woman who combines the hip cool of Lou Reed with the emotionality of Springsteen, a case of Joplinitis — a rare disease these days — is rather endearing. Original grade: B plus. **B**

Genya Ravan: *. . . And I Mean It!* (20th Century-Fox '79). Some find this teen-identified sexy mama — in "Roto Root Her" (her title, don't blame me) she demands an I.D. chain — embarrassing, others politically incorrect. Ian Hunter (on this album) and Lou Reed (on the last) could care less, and I prefer her to any incarnation of Suzi Quatro. Fave: "Night Owl"'s autodoowop. **B**

Lou Rawls: *She's Gone* (Bell '75). Since we've stopped resisting middle-class soul, why is Lou Rawls more objectionable than Gladys Knight? Because for Rawls, middle-class soul feels like a compromise rather than an achievement. Again and again, the sureness of his rich voice betrays a subtle disdain for what he's doing, and even worse, what he's doing often deserves it. Respectful Gladys would never settle for a song as fustian as "Hourglass" or as contrived as "Now You're Coming Back Michelle." Which is why she's irresistible. **C −**

Don Ray: *The Garden of Love* (Polydor '78). An exemplary, super-functional version of Eurodisco's electronic dream — synthesizers and power plectrums overlaid with what disco people call rock vocals. This last means you can tell it's a white man singing, and whoever emotes the uptempo stuff sure does sound like Mick Jagger alongside the gigolo imitator on "My Desire." Consistently spacey and sexy, the way this music is supposed to be, and who says it's apolitical? After all, if "It's a shame to complain but we've got to have a lot more loving" isn't a credo, what is? **B**

Raydio: *Raydio* (Arista '78). In a depressing time for readymades, here at last is a group — led by a session ace, no less — that seems delighted enough with the tricks it's stolen to put them

together with some flair. This trails off into filler on side two, but I like five of its eight songs more than the smash hit "Jack and Jill." Black pop music like they've almost stopped making. Original grade: B plus. **A −**

Raydio: *Rock On* (Arista '79). Ray Parker's idea is to synthesize the old black-music tradition of the male vocal group with the new one of the self-contained funk band, and here he proves that he has what it takes as a composer to keep the idea going. None of these songs stands out like "Is This a Love Thing" and "Me" did on the debut, but every one is danceable/listenable fun. **B +**

Ray, Goodman & Brown: *Ray, Goodman & Brown* (Polydor '79). Resistant though I am to the seductions of falsetto romanticism, the reincarnated Moments generate a Persuasions-like formal intensity with a few simple gimmicks — studio patter, apparently impromptu acappella codas, fast songs. Their thematic range is still hopelessly narrow — responsible sexual love, pedestal included. But they sing better than the Persuasions. And they're not just a falsetto group any more. **B +**

The Real Kids: *The Real Kids* (Red Star '77). These fellas worry about people thinking they're "fags" — honest, they admit it — so they reject punky posing for wholesome pro-girl rock 'n' roll, including a few good songs ("All Kindsa Girls," "Like Darts") and many banalities. **B −**

The Records: *The Records* (Virgin '79). "Starry Eyes" is a great single, but it's all hook, and hooks like that don't grow on albums. Which is why only two of the songs that fill in the blanks, "Teenarama" and "Insomnia," transcend pop professionalism. Really, it takes more than obedience to the Byrds — the foreboding cool of the Cars, the grabby propulsion of the Knack, anything. **B −**

Redbone: *Redbone* (Epic '70). This special-price two-record set has excited reviewers, all of whom get off on the group's ethnicity — Redbone (said to be a Cajun word for half-breed) comprises four honest-to-Gawd Injuns! But can a red man sing the whites? Sorry, not this time. After all, what in Native American tradition would predispose a band toward rock and roll? Much more impressive is that Pat and Lolly Vegas wrote "Niki Hokey," but except maybe for "Witch Queen of New Orleans," there are no more of these here. Better you should send your five bucks to the Piutes. Original grade: C minus. **C**

Leon Redbone: *Leon Redbone* (Warner Bros. '75). On record, he's an exemplary folkie, making up in organizational intelligence what he lacks in inventive spark. Melding antique songs of varying origin into a mature New Orleans instrumentation absent from his unaccompanied stage appearances — which are at first intriguing, then stultifying and/or annoying — he offers an alternative to the narrowness of both stylistic commitment and audio reproduction that makes the original New Orleans recordings inaccessible. Worthwhile work. Original grade: A minus. **B +**

Leon Redbone: *Double Time* (Warner Bros. '77). People who consider this a one-joke act aren't going to change their minds now. People who dismiss the joke for its lameness, torpor, and eccentricity will gloat over this disappointing second LP. I myself wonder why I liked the first one so much. Hint: compare the credits. **B –**

The Red Clay Ramblers: *Stolen Love* (Flying Fish '75). Like so many unpretentious and unheard-of string/bluegrass/jug amalgams, this one offers a pleasant but rather slight variation on a familiar musical question, to wit: "Do I really want to hear another version of 'Golden Vanity' just because this time the mate is a she?" They also do Bessie Smith, which is a mistake,

and a shape-note hymn, which isn't. Noteworthy for uncovering an antifeminist mountain song from the '20s and for reviving the joyful, rather zany emancipation celebration, "Kingdom Coming," which Peter Stampfel singles out as the first truly American melody. **B –**

Otis Redding: *Tell the Truth* (Atco '70). Atlantic is obviously scraping bottom on Otis — there's nothing here I'd play to prove he was the greatest soul singer who ever lived, and several of the performances sound exploratory. But almost every track offers some special moment — the curly little horn part on "Give Away None of My Love," Otis's offer to bet "five dollars and a quarter or even more" on "Snatch a Little Piece," his tributes to fellow Maconites James Brown and Richard Penniman. And even when he's got-ta got-ta got-ta do his shtick he's one of a kind. Original grade: B minus. **B +**

Otis Redding/The Jimi Hendrix Experience: *Historic Performances Recorded at the Monterey International Pop Festival* (Reprise '70). Historically, what's happening is two radically different black artists showboating at the nativity of the new white rock audience. Both have performed more subtly and more brilliantly, even on live albums (*Live in Europe,* the first side of *Band of Gypsys*), and maybe I'm nostalgic. But while at the time I admired Redding ("the love crowd" pegged that audience perfectly) and was appalled by Hendrix ("a psychedelic Uncle Tom," I called him, and that's one of the dozens of things he was), in retrospect they seem equally audacious and equally wonderful. As evocative a distillation of the hippie moment in all its hope and contradiction as you'll ever hear. **A –**

Helen Reddy: *I Don't Know How To Love Him* (Capitol '71). Reddy applies a lean pop voice almost devoid of grit or melisma to what are basically rock songs — that is, songs conceived grittily and melismatically. At her best, as in the unadorned interpretations of "Crazy Love" and "A Song for You," she sounds refreshingly clear-eyed. At her worst, on Mac Davis's "I Believe in Music," she sounds like a Sunday School teacher pretending to be one of the girls. And the rest of the time she's holding gentility to a draw, or vice versa, as when the cellos that set up "How Can I Be Sure" turn into the violins that schmaltz it around.   **B**

Helen Reddy: *Helen Reddy* (Capitol '71). Reddy just sings words and melody instead of dramatizing them. She prefers songs to musical doggerel (a special weakness of Judy's) and hints at jazz intonation and timing rather than trying to sound pristine (like Joanie). Although she still sounds a little awkward rocking out, the forceful, uncluttered arrangements here recapitulate the virtues of her vocal attack, and the lyrics are intelligent and outspoken. Including: a scathing death-of-a-cocksman song that Carole King somehow left off *Music,* a John Lennon autotherapy that sounds inquisitive instead of foolish, and a frolicsome sisterhood ditty that she wrote herself.   **A−**

Helen Reddy: *I Am Woman* (Capitol '72). The hit added many instruments and one conciliatory stanza to the debut-LP version, which may be the way the Grammy bounces but is also how Reddy's feeling these days. She is wife, with baby son and marital crisis behind her, and she's enjoying her success. Tom Catalano's discreet schlock is right for a celebration of connubial privacy like Kenny Rankin's "Peaceful" because it implies the affluence underlying her domestic contentment. This time, at least, the production doesn't drown out Reddy's essential intelligence, compassion, and confidence. But avoiding complacency may prove a problem. Original grade: B plus.   **B**

Helen Reddy: *Long Hard Climb* (Capitol '73). Item: "Don't Mess with a Woman," which wins this-cut-only

producer Jay Senter and arranger Jim Horn a special in-record award for vacuity through bombast, is also distinguished by its unlikely inclusion of the word "sisterhood." Item: Reddy's most effective dramatic quality used to be her unaffectedness. Now it sounds as though she learned to sound natural on the stage. Which of course she did. Item: California disc jockeys are playing Bette's version of "Delta Dawn" on top of Helen's and chortling. Item: For almost two years I've had a picture of Helen Reddy on my wall. It's coming down. And I'm sorry.   **C**

Helen Reddy: *Love Song for Jeffrey* (Capitol '74). Side two is a partial recoup — however uncool devoting songs to loved ones may appear to the Autonomous Assholes of America, it makes sense when in fact your family (mother, father, namesake aunt) is dying all around you, and what's more it sounds like it makes sense. But that's no excuse for promulgating the peculiar idea that "Songs" make better friends than people, which misses the point of why people sing in the first place.   **B−**

Helen Reddy: *Helen Reddy's Greatest Hits* (Capitol '75). I've pretty much given up on Reddy. Never again will she risk arrangements that accentuate what's most idiosyncratic about her voice, probably because the pop audience would be even more threatened by such a sharp instrument (and the sharp mind that goes with it) than the rock audience. Nevertheless, hearing all her pop favorites in one place isn't as dispiriting as I'd feared. Didn't realize she'd had three hits about women who'd probably be diagnosed as clinically insane, and am pleased to report that the intro featuring Reddy's daughter has been restored to "You and Me Against the World" — we're more in need of songs about single parents than of songs about nuclear couples.   **B−**

The Reds: *The Reds* (A&M '79). My conscience says to dock this a notch for incipient pretensions and general meaninglessness, but my memory reminds me that despite indecipherable lyrics and a few overblown instrumental passages both sides have provided me with the basic hard rock rush again and again. Signature: high hook over frantic mid-range guitar. • **B +**

Red Shadow: *Live from the Panacea Hilton* (Physical '76). When I heard that a bunch of Marxist-Leninists from Cambridge had made a satirical rock and roll record, I couldn't wait to hear it, but believe me, you can. Only Marxist-Leninists from Cambridge would spend so much time mocking elitist academics while their own distance from working-class experience, typified by the lack of conviction in their folk-rock, remained so palpable. Exceptions: "Hunger," recommended to Harry Chapin, and "Movement Lovers," which because it is about left politics qualifies as genuine socialist realism. **C**

Redwing: *Redwing* (Fantasy '71). Much return-of-good-old hoopla coming our way on this Sacramento quartet, and you can hear why —they're concise and quirkily intense in a laidback time (and place). But finally they don't do much more for Sacramento than, say, Randy Burns does for New Haven — even if they do take after the Band, to whom Ralph J. rather presumptuously compares them on the back cover, and Moby Grape. Difference is songs (and singing) that evince care and craft but no special inspiration. Isn't it always? **B −**

Jerry Reed: *The Best of Jerry Reed* (RCA Victor '72). Reed sustains three identities: redneck crazy, fancy picker, and soap idol. He's a great crazy, greater even on "Amos Moses" and "Tupelo Mississippi Flash" than on "When You're Hot, You're Hot." And he's an all right picker, if you like pickers. But he couldn't sell soap to a hippie's mother. If RCA can't put together a whole album called *The Crazy Jerry Reed*, at least they could program one side that way. **B −**

Jimmy Reed: *I Ain't from Chicago* (Bluesway '73). At his best — on Vee-Jay in the '50s — Reed sang with the languid self-assurance of a man who never ran for the bus because he wanted to spend the fare on a glass of wine, and the unindustrious shuffle rhythms of the Vee-Jay band ambled right along behind. Great stuff. Evidence: *The Ultimate Jimmy Reed,* a new Bluesway collection of his best Vee-Jay performances that sounds crisper than the competitive Buddah pressing of several years ago. This more recent material, however, is busied up with Motown bass lines and soul drumming obviously provided by upstarts who believed they could do better than back this codger. A few cuts avoid the problem, but the material is spotty anyway. **C +**

Lou Reed: *Lou Reed* (RCA Victor '72). Hard to know what to make of this. Certainly it's less committed — less rhythmically monolithic and staunchly weird — than the Velvets. Not that Reed is shying away from rock and roll or the demimonde. But when I'm feeling contrary he sounds not just "decadent" but jaded, fagged out. On the other hand, he dabbles with the best of them. "Wild Child" has the offhand, reportorial feel of a Bob Dylan dream, "Walk It and Talk It" is a "2120 South Michigan Avenue" based on "Brown Sugar," and in "I Can't Stand It" lean post-gospel harmonies and a Stonesish bass line fill out that headlong mechanical "Here She Comes Now" rush. Question: what are the guys from Yes doing on this record? I mean, talk about staunchly weird. Or are we just talking about art-rock? **B +**

Lou Reed: *Transformer* (RCA Victor '72). All that's left of this great singer and songwriter is his sly intelligence, and sometimes I'm not so sure about that. Whether this is scenemaking music or anti-scenemaking music doesn't matter — it's effete, ingrown, stripped to inessentials. First line of strongest song: "Vicious, you hit me with a flower." Original grade: C plus. **B −**

Lou Reed: *Berlin* (RCA Victor '73). I read where this song cycle about two drug addicts who fall into sadie-mazie in thrillingly decadent Berlin is a . . . what was that? artistic accomplishment, even if you don't like it much. Well, the category is real enough — it describes a lot of Ornette Coleman and even some Randy Newman, not to mention a whole lot of books — but in this case it happens to be horseshit. The story is lousy — if something similar was coughed up by some avantgarde asshole like, oh, Alfred Chester (arcane reference for all you rock folk who think you're cool cos you read half of *Nova Express*) everyone would be too bored to puke at it. The music is only competent — even Bob Ezrin can't manufacture a distance between the washed-up characters and their washed-out creator when the creator is actually singing. Also, what is this water-boy business? Is that a Buddhist cop? Gunga Din? Will Lou lick the bloomin' boots of 'im that's got it? **C**

Lou Reed: *Rock n Roll Animal* (RCA Victor '74). At its best, Reed's live music brings the Velvets into the arena in a clean redefinition of heavy, thrilling without threatening to stupefy. "Lady Day," the slow one here, would pass for uptempo at many concerts, the made-in-Detroit guitars of Steve Hunter and Dick Wagner mesh naturally with the unnatural rhythms, and Reed shouts with no sacrifice of wit. I could do without Hunter's showboating "Introduction," and I've always had my reservations about "Heroin," but this is a live album with a reason for living. **A −**

Lou Reed: *Sally Can't Dance* (RCA Victor '74). Lou sure is adept at figuring out new ways to shit on people. I mean, what else are we to make of this grotesque hodgepodge of soul horns, flash guitar, deadpan songspeech, and indifferent rhymes? I don't know, and Lou probably doesn't either — even as he shits on us he can't staunch his own cleverness. So

the hodgepodge produces juxtapositions that are funny and interesting, the title tune is as deadly accurate as it is mean-spirited, and "Billy" is simply moving, indifferent rhymes and all. **B +**

Lou Reed: *Lou Reed Live* (RCA Victor '75). This rocks almost as good as *Rock n Roll Animal*. But where that record reanimated the Velvets, the reworked solo stuff here is invested with the kind of contempt that Lou seems to think goes naturally with having a real audience. And I could do without the drumboasts on "Waiting for My Man." **B −**

Lou Reed: *Metal Machine Music* (RCA Victor '75). Lou's answer to *Environments* has certainly raised consciousness in both the journalistic and business communities. Though it is a blatant rip-off, it is not — philistine cavils to the contrary — totally unlistenable. But for white noise I'll still take "Sister Ray." **C +**

Lou Reed: *Coney Island Baby* (RCA Victor '76). At first it's gratifying to ascertain that he's trying harder, but very soon that old cheapjack ennui begins to poke through. Oddly, though, most of the cheap stuff is near the surface — the songs sound warmer when you listen close. And not even in his most lyrical moments with the Velvets has he let his soft side show as nakedly as it does on the title cut. **B +**

Lou Reed: *Rock and Roll Heart* (Arista '76). "I Believe in Love" is a fairly hilarious send-up of the let's-getdown game Lou is playing right now; I mean, could Mitch Ryder or Ian Hunter "believe in the Iron Cross" one line and "good-time music" a couple later? (Christ, I hope they don't take this as a challenge.) But the joke doesn't quite hold up, and sometimes it gets lost altogether, at which point Reed sounds like he's imitating his worst enemy, himself. Not the disgrace his followers believe, but not the bad-time music he's capable of. **B −**

Lou Reed: *Walk on the Wild Side: The Best of Lou Reed* (RCA Victor '77). Released to coincide with another label's publicity push for the new boy, this compilation may evince bad faith, but with (cocompiler) Lou that's part of the artistic statement. In fact, except for an intrusion from *Berlin,* side one epitomizes what I now think of as his "New York conversation" phase — those casual, tuneless, bitchy/ironic/tender monologues endemic to Manhattan. And while side two is less coherent, moving from live Velvets remakes to another New York conversation to a deserving b/w to the surprising sweetness of "Coney Island Baby," it's as good cut for cut as any side Lou's released on RCA. **A −**

Lou Reed: *Street Hassle* (Arista '78). I know Lou worked his ass off on this one, but he worked his ass off on *Berlin,* too — like so many of his contemporaries, maybe he's better off not aiming for masterpieces. The title sequence honors Eros as much as Thanatos, a heartening development, and I'm a belated convert to "I Wanna Be Black," which treats racism as a stupid joke and gets away with it. But the production is muddled and the self-consciousness self-serving. Original grade: B. **B +**

Lou Reed: *Lou Reed Live: Take No Prisoners* (Arista '78). Partly because your humble servant is attacked by name (along with John Rockwell) on what is essentially a comedy record, a few colleagues have rushed in with Don Rickles analogies, but that's not fair. Lenny Bruce is the obvious influence. Me, I don't play my greatest comedy albums, not even the real Lenny Bruce ones, as much as I do *Rock n Roll Animal.* I've heard Lou do two very different concerts during his Arista period that I'd love to check out again — Pàlladium November '76 and Bottom Line May '77. I'm sorry this isn't either. And I thank Lou for pronouncing my name right. **C +**

Lou Reed: *The Bells* (Arista '79). Lou is as sarcastic as ever — the lead cut is called "Stupid Man," and in a typically acid rhyme he links "capricious" and "death wish." But due in part to the music's jazzy edge and warmly tra-

ditional rock and roll base (special thanks to Marty Fogel on saxophone) he also sounds . . . *well-rounded,* more than on *Street Hassle.* The jokes seem generous, the bitterness empathetic, the pain out front, the tenderness more than a fleeting mood. And the cuts that don't work — there are at least three or four — seem like thoughtful experiments, or simple failures, rather than throwaways. I haven't found him so likable since *The Velvet Underground.* **B +**

Martha Reeves: *Martha Reeves* (MCA '74). This attempted masterpiece doesn't make it because Richard Perry has failed the fundamental test of the interpretive producer — matching performer and material. To an extent, this is Reeves's fault — her gorgeous voice has trouble gripping complicated ideas. But it's also true that the competition for undiscovered song gems has stiffened since the early days of Cocker and Three Dog Night, so that even a prospector as wily as Perry hopes to dig one out of a slag heap like Vini Poncia. The strongest cuts here ("Wild Nights," "Imagination,") have been recorded definitively elsewhere. Which makes this the modern, big-budget equivalent of a second-rate Motown album. **C +**

Steve Reich: *Music for 18 Musicians* (ECM '78). In which pulsing modules of high-register acoustic sound — the ensemble comprises violin, cello, clarinet, piano, marimbas, xylophone, metallophone, and women's voices — evolve harmonically toward themselves. Very mathematical, yet also very, well, organic — the duration of particular note-pulses is determined by the natural breath rhythms of the musicians — this sounds great in the evening near the sea. I find it uplifting at best, calming at normal, and Muzaky at worst, but as a rock and roller I often get off on repetitions that drive other people crazy. Usually, I should add, these people tend to be nervous anyway. **A −**

Clarence Reid: *Running Water* (Alston '73). This veteran writer-producer has his soul in the right place — Miami, as far south as he can get it. And though he's a/k/a Blow Fly, purveyor of parody porn, the true Reid is as unyielding a moralist as Porter Wagoner or Ernest Tubb. He cheats a lot, just like his daddy, but he also pays — in one song, his "real woman" goes off to find "a real man," while in another she simply kills herself and is he sorry. The only drawback is that Reid is a writer-producer for a reason — vocals. **B**

Clarence Reid: *On the Job* (Alston '76). Reid's strongest LP to date isn't quite strong enough. Except for "Sleep with Me," which peaks with its title, the second side works various imaginative Southern-soul grooves, climaxing with "Nappy-Haired Cowboy" (who's shot down by Reid, the nappy-haired sheriff). And it's too bad Wilson Pickett isn't singing "Come On with It" or "Baptize me." But he's not. **B**

John Renbourn: *Faro Annie* (Reprise '72). If the medieval dance tunes and Bach sarabandes on last year's *Lady and the Unicorn* were neither rock and roll nor my cup of tea, the same goes for these Child ballads and folkie blues. But anybody who can induce me to listen to something called "Willy o' Winsbury" all the way through is no ordinary folkie. I know because his mates in the Pentangle just tried it on *Solomon's Seal*. Which reminds me that Renbourn at his best is supple and modest — and bluesy — enough to remind me of the Pentangle at their best. Original grade: B. **B+**

The Residents: *Fingerprince* (Ralph '76). With its mechanized vocal sounds and displaced melodies, this is the kind of vanguardy post-pop pastiche Frank Zappa might be putting together if he hadn't left his brain at the bank in 1971. Most of my informants prefer *Meet the Residents* or (especially) *Third Reich n' Roll*, with its disrespectful but familiar quotes from the likes of "It's My Party" and "96 Tears," but I find this current album more listenable — *Another Green World* with a chip on its shoulder, sort of. Original grade: B plus. **B**

The Residents: *Duck Stab/Buster & Glen* (Ralph '78). Much to my annoyance, I not only find myself nyaahing along to these weird, misanthropic, exuberantly absurdist post-art-rock fragments, I find myself giggling. Just the thing to divert precocious but obnoxious ten-year-olds. **A−**

Return to Forever Featuring Chick Corea: *Hymn of the Seventh Galaxy* (Polydor '73). The futuristic, Mahavishnu-style jazz-rock gets hot enough at times to make you believe in spirit energy. But Corea's themes lack the grandeur of McLaughlin's, and what good is God without grandeur? Part of the problem is technical — when you articulate fast runs cleanly on an electric piano you sound precious almost automatically. Too often, though, I suspect that's what Corea wants. Better he should try for the cosmic joke — like when "Captain Senor Mouse" breaks into "La Cucaracha." **B**

Return to Forever: *Romantic Warrior* (Columbia '76). Right on schedule, two or three years behind John McLaughlin, Chick Corea tries to beat the fusion cyclotron. Where McLaughlin fell for a few silly orchestral trappings, Corea essays pompous, ersatz-classical compositions — while continuing to display Al DiMeola, Stanley Clarke, and Lenny White in all their dazzling vacuity. Jazz-rock's answer to Emerson, Lake & Palmer — the worst of both worlds. **D+**

The Rezillos: *Can't Stand the Rezillos* (Sire '78). A bright but somewhat amelodic punk novelty album that probably grows hooks on stage. Programmable: "Flying Saucer Attack" and "No," which kick things off. **B**

Emitt Rhodes: *Emitt Rhodes* (Dunhill '70). A formalist in an age of licence,

Rhodes writes very tuneful rock and roll songs and overdubs all the voices and instruments in the studio, distinguishable from Paul McCartney mostly by his compulsive precision. As a believer in pop structures I approve, but as a lover of rock and roll I'm beginning to suspect that the bouncy little beat — and probably the dinky little lyrics — come with the package. **B −**

Charlie Rich: *The Fabulous Charlie Rich* (Epic '70). I never took Charlie's coulda-been-Elvis rep very seriously until I heard the passionately confident Jimmy Reed medley that opens side two of this Nashville album. What's missing is Elvis's insolent verve — Rich is sometimes soulful to a fault, veering dangerously toward mere sincerity, a clue to his Nashville success. But there's a payback in maturity and attention to musical detail. No more blues, except for a redefinitive "Since I Met You Baby," and no rock or rockabilly. But he manages to render a piece of countrypolitan mawk like "A Picture of You" at least interesting by sheer belief, and the way he sings his wife Margaret's "Life's Little Ups and Downs" makes you know what they mean by "'til death do us part." **A −**

Charlie Rich: *Boss Man* (Epic '70). "I Do My Swingin' at Home," Billy Sherrill has him say, but what makes Charlie special is that he also swings in the studio. That's one reason this doesn't sound like a formula country album. Another is that after "Nice 'n' Easy" he and his wife take over the songwriting on side one. Best: "Memphis and Arkansas Bridge," about getting lost in the big city. **B +**

Charlie Rich: *The Best of Charlie Rich* (Epic '72). Rich's jazzy chops and heartfelt polish transform Nashville's best chicken fat into high-quality mainstream pop — Arkansas's answer to Nat Cole. Cole was better at it, but I prefer Rich's homely subject matter and rock and roll roots. Complaint: this includes four cuts from *Fabulous* but neither of the blues. **A −**

Charlie Rich: *Behind Closed Doors* (Epic '73). I welcome the title hit not just because it's richly deserved but because it makes love and marriage seem exciting enough to break out of Nashville. But the album is a typical Music Row mediocrity. Love and marriage is Rich's natural subject at this stage of his career (life, I mean), but to limit him to it is counterproductive — part of the excitement of the bond is what happens outside its circle, and I don't mean cheating. **B −**

Charlie Rich: *Very Special Love Songs* (Epic '74). If *Behind Closed Doors* compromised what Rich knew, this glop betrays it, which Charlie obviously can feel. The man sounds depressed and confused, as if he wishes Billy Sherrill's syrupy strings and sappy songs would go away but can't quite figure out why, since it was Sherrill who made him a star. Reportedly, the producer has socked a lot of Rich's blues and rock sides into the vault. Wait for them, and meanwhile thank him for these reissues: *Fully Realized* on Mercury (astringent strings), and *Tomorrow Night* on RCA ("Big Boss Man," not B.S.) **D +**

Jonathan Richman and the Modern Lovers: *Jonathan Richman and the Modern Lovers* (Beserkley '76). Well then, is this Lou Reed without chemicals or Loudon Wainwright III with a cold? If the former, he'd better renegotiate his right to be fey by balancing off each new LP with some rock 'n' roll drone ("Road Runner," say, or the Earth Quake cuts on *Beserkley Chartbusters*). And if the latter, there'd better be one funny song as astonishing as "Pablo Picasso" (or "Rufus Is a Tit Man") every time. **B +**

Jonathan Richman and the Modern Lovers: *Rock & Roll with the Modern Lovers* (Beserkley '77). This all-acoustic record is even further in general tough-mindedness from *Jonathan Richman and the Modern Lovers* than that fey testament was from *The Modern Lovers;* it defines the difference between a child who is cute and a child who knows adults think children are cute. Sometimes I think I should hate it. But in fact I don't, because its self-indulgence represents not the manipulative arrogance of a star but rather the craziness of an almost powerless case of arrested development, and you can hear that. However unattractive a child Richman may be, he does convey the fragile lyricism only children are capable of. Original grade: B.   **B+**

Jonathan Richman and the Modern Lovers: *Back in Your Life* (Beserkley '78). I'd say this is great kiddie music — lotsa innocence, lotsa animal songs, even a snot joke. But kiddies seem to prefer Donna Summer. So put him down as an original and wonder yet again just how much that counts for.   **B+**

Jonathan Richman and the Modern Lovers: See The Modern Lovers

Jeannie C. Riley: *Jeannie C. Riley's Greatest Hits* (Plantation '71). Ever since "Harper Valley P.T.A." this woman has just *known* soap operas aren't made up, and even in Nashville her accent qualifies her to play the Avenging Hick. The credibility isn't always a virtue, but I'm a sucker for the accent — especially on "The Girl Most Likely," in which poor-but-proud-and-how Jeannie gloats over the surprise marriage of that stuck-up Suzie Jane Grout (spelling phonetic).   **B**

Terry Riley: See John Cale and Terry Riley

Minnie Riperton: *Perfect Angel* (Epic '74). Our Lady of the Five Octaves, who's been working as a music teacher since the Rotary Connection passed on, improves herself here. Abandoning mannered abruptness and pseudo-psychedelic melodrama, she achieves a sensuous spirituality that may be overdomesticated but at least seems real-life.   **B**

Scarlet Rivera: *Scarlet Rivera* (Warner Bros. '77). Those who call this the worst record of the year (I've met two) must only listen to sidepeople's albums when the sidepeople are Dylan's (or "his," as the notes here would have it). In fact, many sidepeople stretch out one or two acceptable melodies and some should-be rejects into an instrumental LP. Although come to think of it most of them come up with eight cuts, not six. And most of them can improvise some. Hmm.   **D−**

Johnny Rivers: *L.A. Reggae* (United Artists '72). Thank the latest rock and roll revival — there are so many of them, you know? — for respite on the radio and another album of Rivers-a-go-go. There are modernization moves, of course — two get-out-the-vote songs (just what George needs) plus the mysterious reggae conceit plus a heartfelt if belated antiwar song — but basically this is just Johnny nasalizing on some fine old memories. "Rockin' Pneumonia" and "Knock on Wood" are especially fine.   **B**

Fenton Robinson: *Somebody Loan Me a Dime* (Alligator '74). Blues devotees wonder why Robinson, originator of what is now regarded as Boz Scaggs's classic and clearly a blues musician of courage, imagination, and skill, remains unknown off the circuit. Let me suggest some reasons. 1) He's so smart he gets a lot of mileage out of his voice, but the voice itself lacks power as an instrument and a dramatic vehicle. 2) His songs are well-written but hardly catchy; the closest this comes to a hook is the chordal ascent on "Gotta Wake Up." 3) His formal extensions are stylish and thoughtful, but he rarely lets loose and just has a good time.   **B+**

Fenton Robinson: *I Hear Some Blues Downstairs* (Alligator '77). Basically, this is an up — tempos faster, falsetto deftly and soulfully deployed, guitar unclichéed. In addition, the title song is a refreshingly matter-of-fact celebration of the form. But matter-of-factness is rarely refreshing for half an hour. **B+**

Smokey Robinson & the Miracles: *What Love Has Joined Together* (Gordy '70). At first this seems disgracefully skimpy — six romantic ballads totalling 27:36, including a slow "My Cherie Amour," a cover of Herb Alpert's vocal debut, and one count-it one (old Mary Wells) tune by Smokey himself, for title and "concept." Then you notice a gliss, a chuckle, a soulful paragraph or two, and realize that he's singing even more exquisitely than usual. Then, if you're me, you get annoyed at the Mo-on-the-town arrangements, with their full string sections and muted trumpets. And then, if you're me, you find yourself transformed by the urge to act as nice as Smokey himself. **B+**

Smokey Robinson & the Miracles: *One Dozen Roses* (Tamla '71). Twelve songs, just like in the old days, every one sweet and smooth and tinged with pain. And just like in the old days barely half of them are as vivid (musically or verbally) as hits like "The Tears of a Clown" or "I Don't Blame You at All." For your convenience, all of the good ones are listed on the cover, and all of the second-raters aren't. Original grade: A minus. **B+**

Smokey Robinson & the Miracles: *Flying High Together* (Tamla '72). A dutiful, pleasant, and very mild close-out — I enjoy "With Your Love Came," for instance, mostly because it starts out like "Loving You Is Sweeter Than Ever." Easy to imagine better versions of the nice enough Ashford-Simpson and Wonder-Wright songs, and the champ adds only a Johnny Bristol piano riff to hits by up-and-coming falsettos Record, Thompkins, and Jackson. **C+**

Smokey Robinson & the Miracles: *1957–1972* (Tamla '72). If this live-double souvenir of Smokey's farewell tour with his group were the only Miracles record I owned I'd play it a lot. It totals less than an hour including patter and offers little that's new, but the show band gets through all the oldies with a minimum of extraneous swing and only on "Shop Around" does Smokey betray the kind of embarrassment that so frequently afflicts upwardly mobile performers reprising their teen hits. Good for him — he knows these are great songs, and he sings his ass off. Time: 57:23. **B+**

Smokey Robinson: *Smokey* (Tamla '73). This is a good bad record and you'll just have to forgive Smokey in advance. It turns out that he didn't split with the Miracles for domestic reasons — somewhere in his heart, he wanted to be Isaac Hayes — and yet somehow he's beyond all his own bullshit. Listen to "Harmony," about the Miracles, or "Just My Soul Responding," a landmark of post-psychedelic soul protest, or "The Family Song," an astrology lyric that ought to be covered by Shirley Ellis, or Grace Slick. **B**

Smokey Robinson: *A Quiet Storm* (Tamla '75). Only "Virgin Man," the most audacious and appropriate song he's written in years, kept *Pure Smokey* from drifting away. The title cut here announces Robinson's intention of distilling that drift into a style — rhythmically it seems to respond more to his internal state than to any merely physical criterion. Audacious in its way, and sexy, too, I guess, but he can't be my love man until he finds a beat. Which he does — not on the number-one soul hit "Baby That's Backatcha," but as the record is drawing to a close, on "Love Letters" and the coy "Coincidentally." **B**

Smokey Robinson: *Deep in My Heart* (Tamla '77). Smokey has a right to the romanticism that has saturated his solo career — ick with kick has always been his specialty — but I get more from the *Big Time* soundtrack than from *Smokey's Family Robinson*. And then there's this, in which various Motown hacks attempt to approximate the bright, direct style of a less mature Smokey and come up with four songs (two of which begin each four-cut side) that actually do so. Whereupon Smokey, pro that he is, sings them as if he wrote them himself. **B+**

Smokey Robinson: *Where There's Smoke . . .* (Tamla'79). Most of Smokey's finest solo album is in the sexy do-the-rock mode of his biggest solo hit, "Cruisin'." Motown purists-come-lately will no doubt be miffed at the snappy discofication of "Get Ready" that opens the "Cruisin' " side. But what cavils will they level at the new songs on side one, which modernize the man's concise, smoldering romanticism with a zip and flair that seemed lost to him years ago? Never count a soul man out — never. **A−**

Tom Robinson Band: *Power in the Darkness* (Harvest '78). Musically this is fairly foursquare, not clever enough for good pop nor unrelenting enough for great rock, and the lyrics are pretty foursquare too, rarely suggesting that politics involves internal contradiction as well as oppression. But at the very least the package exemplifies Robinson's penchant for good works — in addition to a ten-song LP it includes a seven-song bonus record. More important, almost every one of these songs kicks in eventually, and four take no time at all: the instant hit "2-4-6-8 Motorway," the proud, sardonic singalong "Glad to Be Gay," a music-hall number about the rewards and ambiguities of male-to-male friendship called "Martin," and "Winter of '79," in which the epochal repression of that future season is recalled from some further future as a hard but (compare Davie Bowie, Black Sabbath) by no means apocalyptic piece of history. **A−**

Tom Robinson Band: *TRB 2* (Harvest '79). A measure of how good Robinson is at writing his rock and roll protest songs is that you often don't remember them by title — almost every one jogs the memory with an additional catchphrase. Another is that though I know a white man is making it with a black man and I know it's more than all right, I still can't suss out the details of "Sweet Black Angel." A third is that I started singing "Sweet Black Angel" to myself the first time I played the record. And the capper is that since I saw him live every other song here has been ringing in my head as well. **A−**

Vicki Sue Robinson: *Never Gonna Let You Go* (RCA Victor '76). In the great tradition of Gloria Gaynor's *Never Can Say Goodbye,* you can not only dance to one whole side of this disco album but listen to it — and in the case of the emblematic "Turn the Beat Around," bang the dashboard to it. In the same great tradition, side two is unmitigated crap. Next: Doreen Taylor's *Never Get Off Your Back.* **B**

Maggie and Terre Roche: *Seductive Reasoning* (Columbia '75). Female singing duos must function as mutual support groups; last time a women's sensibility this assured, relaxed, and reflective made it to vinyl was Joy of Cooking. These folkies manque are a little flat here, a little arch there, but in general the shoe fits: no ideological feminism, but plenty of consciousness. **B+**

The Roches: *The Roches* (Warner Bros. '79). Robert Fripp's austere production of this witty, pretty music not only abjures alien instrumentation but also plays up the quirks of the Roches' less-than-commanding voices and acoustic guitars. Thus it underscores their vulnerability and occasional desperation and counteracts their flirtations with the coy and the fey. The result is not a perfect record, but rather one whose imperfections are lovingly mitigated. Replete with memorable melodies, heartbreaking harmonies, wise words, and lotsa laffs. **A**

Rock 'n' Roll High School (Sire '79). Two excellent new Ramones songs, plus a Richie Valens cover shared by the Ramones and the Paley Brothers, plus a live medley of five familiar Ramones songs, plus P. J. Soles singing one of the new ones poorly. Plus high-quality new-wavish stuff of varying relevance, most of it off albums that people who enjoy the samples would probably enjoy owning. Plus high school songs of varying quality not including the Beach Boys' "Be True to Your School" or (for shame, it was in the movie) the MC5's "High School" **B**

Johnny Rodriguez: *The Greatest Hits of Johnny Rodriguez* (Mercury '76). Fourteen big ones from the one-time goatnapper and Chicano Charley Pride, only don't get your hopes up — he doesn't have Charley's big voice (or Freddy's big soul, either). He does sound very country, clear and nasal, but I bet he's more grateful for his good looks and would be happy to turn into the Chicano Engelbert Humperdinck if the Chicano Tom Jones were beyond his means. And doubt that Humperdinck's within his means either. **C+**

Kenny Rogers: *Ten Years of Gold* (United Artists '77). You can tell Kenny's pop rather than outlaw because his beard is neat. You can tell he's pop rather than country because his singles average over three minutes. You can tell he's country rather than pop because he sings about adultery all the time. You can tell he's country rather than outlaw because he's foursquare for virtue. And you can tell he's heavy metal because he advocates murder. **C**

The Rolling Stones: *Get Yer Ya-Yas Out!* (London '70). Yeah, I was at the Garden when this was being recorded, and I had a great time. But despite Mick Taylor's guitar on "Love in Vain" and the spruced-up "Live with Me," there's not a song here that isn't better somewhere else — including the two Chuck Berry covers and the one-act "Midnight Rambler." **B**

The Rolling Stones: *Sticky Fingers* (Rolling Stones '71). You'd think some compensation was in order a year and a half after the fact, but that old evil life's just got them in its sway. From titles like "Bitch" and "Sister Morphine" and (the one Altamont reference) "Dead Flowers" through "Brown Sugar"'s compulsively ironic and bacchanalian exploitation/expose to the almost Yeatsian "Moonlight Mile," this is unregenerate Stones. The token sincerity of "Wild Horses" drags me. But "Can't You Hear Me Knocking" and "I Got the Blues" are as soulful as "Good Times," and Fred McDowell's "You Gotta Move" stands alongside "Prodigal Son" and "Love in Vain." Original grade: A minus. **A**

The Rolling Stones: *Hot Rocks 1964–1971* (London '71). If you don't like the Stones, this might serve as a sampler — the only dubious cut is the live "Midnight Rambler." But if you don't like the Stones, why are you reading this book? Look, here's how it works. Except for *Satanic Majesties*, which isn't represented here, all of their '60s studio albums are musts. Couldn't even tell you where to start. *Now!*, maybe. Or *Let It Bleed*. *Aftermath*? *Beggars Banquet*? **B−**

The Rolling Stones: *Exile on Main St.* (Rolling Stones '72). More than anything else this fagged-out masterpiece is difficult — how else describe music that takes weeks to understand? Weary and complicated, barely afloat in its own drudgery, it rocks with extra power and concentration as a result. More indecipherable than ever, submerging Mick's voice under layers of studio murk, it piles all the old themes — sex as power, sex as love, sex as pleasure, distance, craziness, release — on top of an obsession with time more than appropriate in over-thirties committed to what was once considered a youth music. Honking around sweet Virginia country and hipping through Slim Harpo, singing their ambiguous praises of Angela Davis, Jesus Christ, and the Butter Queen, they're just war babies with the bell bottom blues. **A+**

The Rolling Stones: *More Hot Rocks* **(*Big Hits and Fazed Cookies*)** (London '72). The companion volume's for dabblers; this is for specialists. One of the two previously-unavailable-on-LP B sides, "We Love You," is the only time they ever trounced Sgt. Pepper good, and long about the middle of the early, previously-unavailable-in-U.S. r&b cuts they really get a sly groove going, upping the tempo and lagging the phrasing on "Come On" and "Fortune Teller" and "Poison Ivy" and "Bye Bye Johnnie." Sometimes specialists have more fun. **B+**

Rolling Stones: *Goats Head Soup* (Rolling Stones '73). Except for the spavined "Dancing with Mr. D." and the oxymoronic "Can You Hear the Music," these are good songs. But the execution is slovenly. I don't mean sloppy, which can be exciting — I mean arrogant and enervated all at once. Mick's phrasing is always indolent, but usually it's calculated down to the last minibeat as well; here the words sometimes catch him yawning. Without trying to be "tight" the band usually grooves into a reckless, sweaty coherence; here they hope the licks will stand on their own. Only on "Starfucker," the most outrageous Chuck Berry throwaway of the band's career, does this record really take off. **B**

The Rolling Stones: *It's Only Rock 'n Roll* (Rolling Stones '74). This is measurably stronger than *Goats Head Soup*, and I hear enough new hooks and arresting bass runs and audacious jokes to stretch over three ordinary albums — or do I mean two? I also hear lazy rhymes and a song about dancing with Father Time and two sides that begin at a peak and wind down from there and an LP title that means more than it intends — or do I mean less? Original grade: A minus. **B**

The Rolling Stones: *Made in the Shade* (Rolling Stones '75). Six tracks from two of the greatest albums of the decade and four from two of the more dubious ones. Not the four best, either. **C+**

The Rolling Stones: *Metamorphosis* (Abkco '75). *Flowers* it ain't, but *Jamming with Edward* it ain't either. The second side holds up better than the first, the sound and musicianship are rough and thin throughout, and most of the arrangements were obviously given up in the middle (remember *One Plus One*?), sometimes because the songs were worth giving up on. But Bill Wyman's "Downtown Suzie" and Oldham-Richards's "I'd Much Rather Be with the Boys," to choose two previously unheard for all too obvious reasons, rank with all but the greatest Stones originals, and at its worst this still represents the world's greatest rock and roll band during the period when they were earning the title. **B+**

The Rolling Stones: *Black and Blue* (Rolling Stones '76). More blatantly imitative of black-music rhythms and styles than any Stones album since *December's Children,* and also less original (if more humorous) in the transformation, this nevertheless takes genuine risks and suggests a way out of their groove. Lots of good stuff, but the key is "Hot Stuff," pure Ohio-Players-go-to-Kingston and very fine shit, and the high point "Fool to Cry," their best track in four years. Diagnosis: not dead by a long shot. **A−**

The Rolling Stones: *Love You Live* (Rolling Stones '77). As a Stones loyalist, I am distressed to report that this documents the Stones' suspected deterioration as a live band, a deterioration epitomized by the accelerating affectation of Mick's vocals. Once his slurs teased, made jokes, held out double meanings; now his refusal to pronounce final dentals — the "goo*d*" and "shoul*d*" of "Brown Sugar," for example — convey bored, arrogant laziness, as if he can't be bothered hoisting his tongue to the roof of his mouth. His "oo-oo-oo"'s and "awri-i"'s are self-parody without humor. This is clearly a professional entertainer doing a job that just doesn't get him off the way it once did, a job that gets harder every time out. **C+**

The Rolling Stones: *Some Girls* (Rolling Stones '78). The Stones' best album since *Exile on Main Street* is also their easiest since *Let It Bleed* or before. They haven't gone for a knockdown uptempo classic, a "Brown Sugar" or "Jumping Jack Flash" — just straight rock and roll unencumbered by horn sections or Billy Preston. Even Jagger takes a relatively direct approach, and if he retains any credibility for you after six years of dicking around, there should be no agonizing over whether you like this record, no waiting for tunes to kick in. Lyrically, there are some bad moments — especially on the title cut, which is too fucking indirect to suit me — but in general the abrasiveness seems personal, earned, unposed, and the vulnerability more genuine than ever. Also, the band is a real good one — especially the drummer. **A**

Sonny Rollins: *Nucleus* (Milestone '75). Eat your heart out, Grover Washington (Archie Shepp) (yeah King Curtis too). This is as rich an r&b saxophone record as I know, combining repetition and invention, melodies recalled and melodies unimaginable, in proportions that define the difference between selling out and reaching out. This man says more with his tone than most musicians do with a full set of chops (which he also has, of course). If you really believe you don't like "jazz," this is as good a place to start as any. **A−**

Max Romeo: *War ina Babylon* (Island '76). Romeo has long been a professional rude boy ina the Anglian outposts of Babylon, and this career training is reflected in the brightness of his reggae, refreshingly explicit and immediate (both musically and lyrically) in the wake of second-rate Toots and Marley. In fact, I find his album more attractive than all but two reggae LPs

released stateside in 1976 — the Mighty Diamonds and the first Burning Spear. But I won't argue with anyone who finds it tediously close in spirit to the foregone conclusions of Peter, Paul & Mary. **B+**

Max Romeo: *Open the Iron Gate* (United Artists '78). Unlike the lacklustre *Reconstruction*, these sweet, throbbing prophecies and jeremiads fulfill the promise of Romeo's U.S. debut. Or more likely anticipate it: the rocksteady rhythms suggest that it was cut years ago. Romeo is no innovator, though, and I think I catch a claim that Haile Selassie isn't really dead in one song, which would make it no earlier than 1975. There's a lot else to catch — Romeo remains very hooky for a Jamaican, and praise Jah for that. **A−**

Linda Ronstadt: *Silk Purse* (Capitol '70). This ought to be a good record. She's tough (and sexy) live, and she sure does pick good tunes — Mickey Newbury's new-Nashville "Are My Thoughts with You?," which in Newbury's 45-rpm version has gotten a lot of play on my bedroom jukebox, says a lot about love and its dislocations, but so does Mel Tillis's old-Nashville "Mental Revenge," which I'd never heard before. Country material over rock-flavored arrangements is the concept, and the honky vulgarity of Ronstadt's voice the reason. But only occasionally — "Lovesick Blues" and "Long Long Time" are both brilliant — does she seem to find Kitty Wells's soul as well as her timbre. Time: 28:26. Original grade: B minus. **B**

Linda Ronstadt: *Linda Ronstadt* (Capitol '72). In which she makes a silk purse out of *Silk Purse,* not such a great idea — smoother, better crafted, more beautiful, and decidedly less interesting. Hardcore country songs are down to three, and here's the giveaway: four entries from the Sensitivity Squad (Jackson Browne, Livingston Taylor, and the Erics Kaz and Andersen). **B−**

Linda Ronstadt: *Don't Cry Now* (Asylum '73). In which whatever was raunchy and country about her is laundered in David Geffen's homogenizing machine, manned this time by John David Souther, who must have told her that "Sail Away" was just another pretty song. You think she's gotten so used to playing the dumb chick that she's turned into one? **C+**

Linda Ronstadt: *Different Drum* (Capitol '74). With any suggestion that she can rock expunged from this compilation, we get five (out of ten) cuts by the Stone Poneys, the two good ones composed by none other than Michael Nesmith and the worst by Tim Buckley, who inspires her to imitate Joan Baez imitating (if that's necessary) a snooty spinster. We also get Jackson Browne and Livingston Taylor. Hey, maybe she *can't* rock. **B−**

Linda Ronstadt: *Heart Like a Wheel* (Capitol '74). For the first time, everybody's sexpot shows confidence in her own intelligence. As a result, she relates to these songs instead of just singing them. It's even possible to imagine her as a lady trucker going down on Dallas Alice — and to fault her for ignoring the metaphorical excesses of Anna McGarrigle's title lyric just so she can wrap her lungs around that sweet, decorous melody. **A−**

Linda Ronstadt: *Prisoner in Disguise* (Asylum '75). I agree that this is a letdown after *Heart Like a Wheel,* but I wish someone could tell me why. Maybe the explanations are vague — she's repeating a formula, she's not putting out, etc. — because a singer like Ronstadt, who specializes in interpreting good songs rather than projecting a strong persona, must achieve an ineffable precision to succeed. But maybe it's simpler than that. People say her versions of "Tracks of My Tears" and "Heat Wave" are weak, but they're not — they simply don't match the too familiar originals. "When Will I Be Loved?" and "You're No Good," on the other hand, were great songs half-remembered, kicking off each side of *Heart Like a Wheel* with a jolt to the memory. And this album could sure use a jolt of something. **B**

Linda Ronstadt: *Hasten Down the Wind* (Asylum '76). Linda's always wanted to be a Real Country Singer, but RCS put out two or three LPs like this every year. You know — find some good tunes, round up the gang, and apply formula. Like the great RCS she can be, she comes up with some inspired interpretations; the flair of "That'll Be the Day" and "Crazy" do justice to the originals, and her version of the title song almost makes you forget its unfortunate title. But you cover Tracy Nelson's "Down So Low" at your peril even if you believe not one in ten of your fans remembers it, and the three Karla Bonoff lyrics make her (I mean Karla, but Linda too) sound like such a born loser that I never want to hear anyone sing them again. **B−**

Linda Ronstadt: *Greatest Hits* (Asylum '76). Because it compiles work from both Capitol and Asylum, I anticipated an ideal sampler, especially when the first side induced me to enjoy "Desperado," which she sings real purty. But the second side features her inferior versions of no less than three songs, suggesting that one might be better off obtaining her best music from its corporation of origin. **B+**

Linda Ronstadt: *A Retrospective* (Capitol '77). Safe (five cuts from *Heart Like a Wheel,* worth owning itself), genteel (six from *Linda Ronstadt,* her most conventional album for the label), and occasionally tasteless ("Hobo" is pure artysong and "Will You Love Me Tomorrow" failed nostalgia), this is nevertheless a listenable compilation. "Lovesick Blues" and "Rescue Me" rock a lot better than "Heat Wave," the Stone Poneys stuff surpasses that on *Different Drum,* Capitol's 1968 "Silver Threads and Golden Needles" sounds fresher than Asylum's 1973, and the genteel stuff does mix well, as they say. **B+**

Linda Ronstadt: *Simple Dreams* (Asylum '77). In which Andrew Gold goes off and Pursues His Solo Career, enabling Ronstadt to hire herself a rock and roll band. She's still too predictable — imagine how terse and eloquent "Blue Bayou" would seem if instead of turning up the volume midway through she just hit one high note at the end — but she's also a pop eclectic for our time, as comfortable with Mick Jagger as with Dolly Parton, interpreting Roy Orbison as easily as Buddy Holly. Even her portrayal of a junkie seeking succor from Warren Zevon's "Carmelita" isn't totally ridiculous. And I admit it — she looks great in a Dodger jacket. **B+**

Linda Ronstadt: *Living in the U.S.A.* (Asylum '78). This one divides right down the middle. The last four covers on the second side are so clumsy that I may never again hear the opener, Little Feat's "All That You Dream." But I do kind of like the first side, specifically including the forced intensity of the Chuck Berry and Doris Troy remakes. Only on "Alison," though, does she enrich what she interprets. **B**

Root Boy Slim & the Sex Change Band Featuring the Rootettes: *Root Boy Slim & the Sex Change Band Featuring the Rootettes* (Warner Bros. '78). This band satisfies the first requirement of rock and roll comedy — they play their simplified Little Feat funk well enough to make fun of it. Inspirational Verse: "Hey look out buddy/Get off my wig/Oops I didn't realize/You was quite so big." **B**

The Rose (Atlantic '79). The usual soundtrack alibis don't apply to a Paul Rothchild production utilizing studio-certified musicians and a dozen tunesmiths hacking out rock songs to order. In fact, all that distinguishes this collection of nine Bette Midler performances from, say, your usual backup-goes-solo bid is that it was recorded live — for "feel," I guess. Although it is true that except for the off-color "Love Me with a Feeling" the high points are the monologue on side one and a prolonged fanfare. **C**

Diana Ross: *Diana Ross* (Motown '70). The sound of young America grows older, replacing momentum with progress and exuberance with nuanced cool. Producers Nick Ashford and Valerie Simpson provide all but one of the songs — they've written a couple of great ones for Marvin & Tammi in the past. Unfortunately, the same couple (of songs) provide two of the three high spots here. And there ain't no high spot high enough. (Catalogue number: S-711.) **C+**

Diana Ross: *Everything Is Everything* (Motown '70). If I'm not mistaken (and let's face it, that's possible) this is an answer record to Aretha's *This Girl's in Love with You*. A little heavier on the corporate consultants, granted, but she does cover Aretha's own "Call Me" as well as several Beatles numbers and Bacharach-David's Carpenters (instead of Herb Alpert) hit. Blame its inferiority on the inferiority of her corporate consultants — and on her own. **C+**

Diana Ross: *Surrender* (Motown '71). This time the hits Ashford & Simpson have written for Diana were written for Diana, which minimizes embarrassing comparisons. And the verve of side two — where Motown finally learns how to kowtow to Broadway and keep the songwriting royalties — suggests that she's learning to hold her own. **B**

Diana Ross: *Lady Sings the Blues* (Motown '72). Billie Holiday is uncoverable, possibly the greatest singer of the century, yet the fact is that Ross's versions — which occupy only two sides of this soundtrack album — are intensely listenable. That's the word I want, because it doesn't fit Holiday, who either seizes your full attention or disturbs you in the background. While copying Holiday's phrasing and intonation, Ross smooths them out, making the content easier to take without destroying it altogether. This may be a desecration and a deception, but it speaks to the condition of a ghetto child who's always had a talent for not suffering, for willing herself up and through. Not every singer turns into a junkie, after all. **B+**

Diana Ross: *Touch Me in the Morning* (Motown '73). One advantage of imitating Billie Holiday's vocal style is that you get to sing Billie Holiday's material. Another is that you get to sing like Billie Holiday. **C**

Diana Ross: *Diana Ross* (Motown '76). This is a generally catchy album by the sad standards she's settled for, but beyond Ashford & Simpson's gorgeous, mournful "Ain't Nothin' but a Maybe" and the seven intoxicating minutes of "Love Hangover" it's often catchy-annoying rather than catchy-compelling or at least catchy-fun. Major offenders: "Theme from Mahogany," the boop-nostalgia "Smile," and its clone, "Kiss Me Now," which captures her at her archest. (Catalogue number: M6-861.) Original grade: C. **B−**

Diana Ross: *Diana Ross' Greatest Hits* (Motown '76). I'd hoped this would drag me kicking and giggling to rock and roll perdition, just like the old Motown best-ofs. Instead I found I had to learn to like it. Which I did, eventually — these are good pop tunes for the most part, and her "Ain't No Mountain High Enough" sounds more valid now than it did when Marvin & Tammi were fresh in my ear. But rock and roll perdition is beside the point, because this isn't rock and roll. **B+**

Diana Ross: *Baby It's Me* (Motown '77). I've got nothing special against Richard Perry, although he used to find more interesting songs — and songwriters, which since he's now developed his own stable is more relevant. But even when he made interesting records he tended to push the epicenters of eccentric artists toward the middle of the road, and that's not what Diana needs. Her problem isn't her vocal limitations, although she's obviously no Betty Carter, but her blank taste. What if the best of the slick trivia here were combined with, I don't know, a good '30s pop tune done straight, a blues, something obscure by Al Green, something familiar by a non-Motown girl group? Might be worth hearing, and Perry could make it happen. Yeah sure. **C+**

Diana Ross: *The Boss* (Motown '79). In which La Suprema passes a crash course at the Ashford & Simpson School of Total Adult Fulfillment, although not with As. It's her house, she wants your good lovin' once in the morning and once in the evening, she'll compete and regret it, she'll cooperate and be glad, and she shall survive, because she's the boss. Quite smart, quite sexy, but sometimes dull — it doesn't do much for A&S's crash material that there's only one singer. **B**

Diana Ross & Marvin Gaye: *Diana & Marvin* (Motown '73). Motown's record division could really put out some terrific albums if the publishing division wasn't always butting in. Of the six Motown-composed tracks, only Ashford & Simpson's "Just Say, Just Say" and the hit, "My Mistake," have any charm of their own. But this girl-boy duo sound just great on two Bell-Creed songs and the follow-up single, Wilson Pickett's "Don't Knock My Love." And while I suspect it was Marvin who edged Diana into the warmest and loosest — and streetest — performance of her career, maybe it was just the proximity of "Pledging My Love." **B+**

Roxy Music: *Roxy Music* (Reprise '72). From the drag queen on the cover to the fop finery in the centerfold to the polished deformity of the music on the record, this celebrates the kind of artifice that could come to seem as unhealthy as the sheen on a piece of rotten meat. Right now, though, it's decorated with enough weird hooks to earn an A for side one. Side two leans a little too heavily on the synthesizer (played by a balding, long-haired eunuch lookalike named Eno) without the saving grace of drums and bassline. [Later on Atco.] **B+**

Roxy Music: *For Your Pleasure* (Reprise '73). These guys make no secret of having a strange idea of a good time, but this isn't decadent, it's ridiculous. Side one surrounds two pained, strained torch jobs with two classic neo-rockers and finishes with a song about an inflatable sex doll that's almost not stupid (title: "In Every Dream Home a Heartache"). Side two surrounds a fast fast one with two long mostly instrumental slow ones that are almost not boring. Verdict: almost not not bad. [Later on Atco.] **B**

Roxy Muxic: *Stranded* (Atco '74). Any artist as oblique and ambitious as Bryan Ferry deserves an oblique, ambitious review, here provided (unintentionally) by Sidney Tillem in his "Figurative Art 1969: Aspects and Prospects": "By moral in the context of art I mean a style which executes the deeper social and psychological function of form, as opposed to a particular aspect of vanity called *taste*. Pop sensibility, pop consciousness, pop sentimentality have been invaluable in clarifying the provincialism and nostalgia that actually permeate a culture that has come to pride itself on sophistication. But they have not resulted in a new art simply because the requisite idealism has been lacking." **B+**

Roxy Music: *Country Life* (Atco '74). The Teutoni-textures of this music are proof negative of Bryan Ferry's deep-seated romanticism. But what happens when romanticism goes sour? And what is Phil Manzanera doing on that Nico record that closes with her version of "Deutschland Uber Alles"? Oh well, I've always said good rock has to be dangerous. But when did I say it could be slow? **B+**

Roxy Music: *Siren* (Atco '75). Good album — a lot of fast ones and a great hook. Of course, Roxy Music albums always have hooks, but "Street Life" and "Virginia Plain" never told us as much about Roxy's less accessible music as "Love Is the Drug," an equation which represents not liberation from artificial stimulants but the breakdown of both sexual and emotional abandon into "just another high." Very appropriate to situate the song in a singles bar, for that '70s reality is the exemplary environment for Bryan Ferry's romantic pessimism. Much of what his music has to say about such environments is fascinating, even perversely

attractive — but ultimately a little off-putting, which I guess is the point. **A−**

Roxy Music: *Viva! Roxy Music* (Atco '76). This isn't bad, not for a live album issued in lieu of current studio product. Concentrating on relatively obscure material from the first two LPs, which always sounded a bit thin, it adds humor and some untrammeled Phil Manzanera to "In Every Dream Home a Heartache." But I prefer the studio "Bogus Man" and "Chance Meeting," thin and all. And that is bad. **B**

Roxy Music: *Greatest Hits* (Atco '77). I've never thought average guys were compelled to ape the ruling class, I don't believe romance is inevitably corrupted, and the collapse of European culture is long overdue. In short, what Bryan Ferry has to say has never spoken very loud to this listener no matter how you break it down. So while others may mourn the nuance and conceptual integrity of *Stranded* and *Country Life* and *Siren,* I get off on this compilation, which puts his dialectic on display in its most entertaining guises. What with all the popcraft and robot energy and campy asides — and genuine emotion and ideas — ! was even inspired to listen to "A Song for Europe" from beginning to end. Found I could translate the French part. **A**

Roxy Music: *Manifesto* (Atco '79). This isn't Roxy at its most innovative, just its most listenable — the entire "West Side" sustains the relaxed, pleasantly funky groove it intends, and the difficulties of the "East Side" are hardly prohibitive. At last Ferry's vision seems firsthand even in its distancing — he's paid enough dues to deserve to keep his distance. And the title track is well-named, apparent contradictions and all. **A−**

The Rubinoos: *Back to the Drawing Board!* (Beserkley '79). Live, this is a great '60s cover band — you should see how they choreograph "Walk Don't Run." Doing their own lame originals on record, though, they try so hard to sound fresh and appealing you get the feeling they're about to spit up on your shoulder.   **C+**

David Ruffin: *At His Best* (Motown '78). Although some blame Ruffin's very intermittent post-Tempts success on deliberate corporate neglect, I've never found even his biggest solo hits all that undeniable — ungrouped, his voice seems overly tense whether it's grinding out grit or reaching for highs. Corporate decay is another matter. The four Tempts songs on this compilation aren't necessary — Ruffin has managed to chart ten songs in the nine years he's been on his own — but they certainly show up the more recent compositions. Seems apt that the best non-Tempts cut was written by Kenny Gamble and Leon Huff, the Berry Gordy/Holland-Dozier-Holland of the '70s.   **B−**

The Ruffin Brothers: *I Am My Brother's Keeper* (Soul '70). The Mississippi-bred Ruffins are as close as Motown gets to Southern soul, so it's probably geography that makes their approach more Sam & Dave than James & Bobby Purify — all growling melismatics, with Jimmy's higher and much narrower timbre providing sweet relief from David's rough power. And for once in Motown's life there are a lot of good covers — from Ben E. King, Jerry Butler, even the Delfonics (even James Taylor).   **B**

Rufus: *Rags to Rufus* (ABC '74). With Chaka Khan pushed up front this looks like L.A.'s answer to Tower of Power — white funk players behind black singer. Chopswise neither the hornless five-piece band nor the horny three-octave voice is up to Oakland's pride, but I prefer the attitude, which is to admit your limitations and keep it simple. Maybe no one would have noticed if Stevie Wonder hadn't given them "Tell Me Something Good." But he did.   **B**

Rufus Featuring Chaka Khan: *Rufusized* (ABC '74). Chaka's got a mostly new, mostly black band, and it makes a difference, especially in the in-house songwriting, with hooks courtesy guitarist Tony Maiden. The lyrics are worth catching, too, especially the answer to "Rocket Man," in which the wife croons "The universe is calling you" without a hint of sarcasm. Guess that's what assuming the spiritual mannerisms of Stevie and Aretha — launching your voice into free fall, I mean — can bring you to. Original grade: B minus.   **B+**

Rufus Featuring Chaka Khan: *Rufus Featuring Chaka Khan* (ABC '75). No doubt they think they're getting classy, but I think they're getting cute — compare the hip-skipping "On Time" to last year's booty-bumping "Rufusized." They're also starting to keep the composing royalties in the family. Exception, Bee Gees Go Home Division: Chaka's up-and-over "Jive Talking."   **B**

Rufus Featuring Chaka Khan: *Ask Rufus* (ABC '77). So Chaka's turning into a "sophisticated song stylist." Just what we needed. What she needs is sophisticated songs. They never learn.   **C+**

Rufus & Chaka: *Masterjam* (MCA '79). Relieving me of ugly suspicions that the secret of *Off the Wall* wasn't Michael Jackson but producer Quincy Jones and songwriter Rod Temperton, the same pair pitches in here with much slighter results. In fact, they get exactly the kind of demi-jazz you'd expect Quincy Jones to substitute for funk. After all, the band has aspired to demi-jazz for years. Now what I want to know is whether the singer aspires to Flora Purim — the signs are mixed, but her sliding rhythms make me fear the worst.   **B−**

The Rumour: *Max* (Mercury '77). Because Graham Parker's songs take so long to kick in, I worried about coming down on his band too soon — until I realized that their songs already had kicked in, without my noticing or caring. The singers don't help the lyrics, the lyrics don't help the singers, and this is depressing. **C+**

The Rumour: *Frogs Clogs Krauts and Sprouts* (Arista '79). If it's true they wanna be the Band, then what's with the Donald Fagen imitations? (Bob Andrews sings!) And who's doing Walter Becker? (My guess: Brinsley Schwarz.) Expert, quirky, and arresting at first. Then expert and quirky. And do I have to tell you what comes next? **B−**

The Runaways: *The Runaways* (Mercury '76). Don't let misguided feminism, critical convolutions, or the fact that good punk transcends ordinary notions of musicality tempt you. This is Kim Fowley's project, which means that it is tuneless and wooden as well as exploitative. How anyone can hang around El Lay so long without stealing a hook or two defies understanding. Maybe it's just perversity — which would make it the only genuinely perverse thing about the man. **C−**

The Runaways: *Queens of Noise* (Mercury '77). I'll tell you what kind of street rock and roll these bimbos make — when the title cut came on I thought I was hearing *Evita* twice in a row. Only I couldn't figure out why the singer wasn't in tune. **C**

The Runaways: *Waitin' for the Night* (Mercury '77). This band surprised me live, nowhere near as willing to pander sexually as its publicity suggests, and Kim Fowley contributes his first decent tune since "Alley Oop" to the new album. I guess if somebody has to strike macho guitar poses I'd just as soon it were girls. But Joan Jett's inability to bellow through the wall of noise (she shrieks flatly instead) suggests that there are perhaps more generous musical models, for human beings of all sexes, than Aerosmith. **C+**

Runt: *Runt* (Ampex '70). If there were any justice, "We Got to Get You a Woman" would melt Ti-Grace Atkinson's heart and "I'm in the Clique" would earn the artiste a free night at the Record Plant. But they're not playing the single on WBAI, and the artiste, ex-Nazz and present whiz Todd Rundgren, already knows his way around. Takes a certain professional brass to write a song called "There Are No Words" that goes "Oh, Ah, OOOOO" — or to assume the persona of a newborn twin, especially for nine minutes. [Later on Bearsville.] **B**

Runt: *The Ballad of Todd Rundgren* (Ampex '71). If pop can be either sunny or moony, this is green cheese. And though it's less wildly uneven than its predecessor, that cuts two ways — the boyish "Be Nice to Me" and the mock-macho "Parole," while quite nice, will never call me back to the ordinary stuff the way *Runt*'s prize runts did. [Later on Bearsville.] **B**

Todd Rundgren: *Something/Anything* (Bearsville '72). I don't trust double albums, especially when all sixteen cuts on three sides were laid down by the singer-composer-producer and all seven on the fourth by a studio pickup band. But this has the feel of a pop masterpiece, and feel counts. The many good songs span styles and subjects in a virtuoso display that runs from the evanescent "I Saw the Light" to a true tale of high-school grossouts called "Piss Aaron." And the many ordinary ones are saved by Todd's confidence and verve. The studio pickup side, for instance, gains genuine meaning from his tongue-in-cheek notes ("I drafted it into some sort of operetta, that kind of thing being very popular nowadays"). Studio games that would infuriate me on somebody else's record add context here. And his perpetual adolescence is winningly lyrical and winningly snide, though rarely at the same time. Original grade: A. **A−**

Todd Rundgren: *A Wizard/A True Star* (Bearsville '73). I'm supposed to complain that for all his wizardry he's not a star yet, but just you wait, he can't miss, the Mozart of his generation, that last a direct quote from a fan who collared me at a concert once. Bushwa. His productivity is a pleasure, but it always makes for mess. Examine the enclosed fifty-odd minutes and you'll find a minor songwriter with major woman problems who's good with the board and isn't saved by his sense of humor. Original grade: B plus.   **B –**

Todd Rundgren: *Todd* (Bearsville '73). Enough already. On sides one and four of this not-too-specially-priced double-LP, the useful moments are buried in the usual aural gadgetry, and only occasionally does he pick himself up from the rubble on sides two and three. Todd has honest ambitions, and they're welcome, but his invention has worn so thin they seem delusory. Uneconomical and unecological. Original grade: C plus.   **C**

Todd Rundgren: *Faithful* (Bearsville '76). As you probably know by now, one whole side recreates six '60s studio masterpieces note-for-note, from the calculated spontaneity of Bob Dylan to the electronic perfectionism of the Beach Boys and the Beatles. This is impressive and amusing, you can fool your friends, but it's overwhelmed (once you've heard it a few times) by what might be called the Enoch Light (or *Your Hit Parade*) (or voiceprint) effect. That is, Todd's vocal imitations (a phrase that deserves one of his slurs) sound thin and forced. This is especially notable considering how well his voice works on the other side, his clearest and most interesting set of songs since *Something/Anything*. It also reinforces the unfortunate impression that even when clearly interesting, Todd is factitious and compulsively secondhand.   **B**

Todd Rundgren: *Hermit of Mink Hollow* (Bearsville '78). Only a weight as willfully light as Todd can be trusted to put his smartest song ("Onomatopeia") on "the easy side" and his dumbest ("Bag Lady") on "the difficult side."   **C +**

Todd Rundgren: See also Utopia

Rush: *A Farewell to Kings* (Mercury '77). The most obnoxious band cur-

rently making a killing on the zonked teen circuit. Not to be confused with Mahogany Rush, who at least spare us the reactionary gentility. More like Angel. Or Kansas. Or a power-trio Uriah Heep, with vocals revved up an octave. Or two.   **D**

Bobby Rush: *Rush Hour* (Philadelphia International '79). A lot of this is fun — I'm delighted to find Leon Huff collaborating with someone who's got funk in his soul, and heartened to hear a protest song about the problem of lost keys. But a lot of it — the witless "Evil Is," the characterless "Hey, Western Union Man" — is dumber than Kenny Gamble.   **B –**

Otis Rush: *So Many Roads* (Delmark '78). Rush has been the bluesfan's bluesman for years, but this album — recorded live in Hibiya Park, Tokyo, a/k/a Pepper's Lounge East — is the first time I've been able to hear why. Reason's simple — lots of room for his guitar. Rush is a "good singer" with a "good instrument" — sweet, penetrating, slurred — but the words aren't where his soul goes. It goes into the form itself. Like B. B. King's, only less predictably by now, his solos expand upon the Chicago verities in almost jazzlike flights without ever transgressing against them.   **B +**

Tom Rush: *Tom Rush* (Columbia '70). Rush was a prophet in the days of folkies rampant, working with Al Kooper and Roosevelt Gook on a side of Chess-style rock and roll in 1966 and beating the crowd to J. Mitchell, J. Taylor, and J. Browne in 1968. Nor was he limited to good ideas — his rich, clear, lithe voice broke into raunch so naturally that his up-and-bluesy "Something in the Way She Moves" cut all subsequent versions. But now that his brainstorms have become world currency he seems stuck in the latest folkie fad, high-gloss vocal decorum. And now that everyone's discovering unsung songwriters he's forced to resort to knowns like F. Neil and J. C. Young or unknowables like M. McLaughlin (McLauchlan?) and D. Whiffen (Whitten?). This could be a rut. **B−**

Brenda Russell: *Brenda Russell* (Horizon '79). If it's pop you crave, slow down a minute and check this out — eight love songs, all in sensual-to-pert medium tempos, all sweetly hooky. Russell's singing is breathy, soulish, and trickier than it seems, and though her lyrics are sometimes quite clumsy, they always sound felt and particular. Even the string arrangements avoid the vague and saccharine, especially those by David Wolfert, who produced Dusty Springfield's best album of the '70s. The material isn't as powerful, but this reminds me more than a little of Dusty's best album of the '60s, and that's high praise. **B+**

Leon Russell: *Leon Russell* (Shelter '70). This is weirder than what you'd expect from a man whose Phil Spector savvy and slick gospel piano have helped stabilize both Delaney & Bonnie and Joe Cocker. Russell has all of Mick Jagger's whine and shriek and none of his power, so while the singing is distinctive, and valid, it grates — impressive material from "Dixie Lullaby" and "Shoot Out on the Plantation" would simply be more so with other vocals. If not Delaney, Bonnie, or Joe, how about Marc Benno? **B+**

Leon Russell and the Shelter People: *Leon Russell and the Shelter People* (Shelter '71). Russell knows how to put music together, but he still has trouble putting it across. His Okie-cum-Brooklyn (ersatz Nworleans?) drawl is the outcry of a confused homeboy driven to fuse rootsy eccentricities with masscult shtick and flash, and his meaningfulness clarifies nothing. The Dylan covers here are trying to tell us something, but in the end Russell's newfound (and competent enough) zeitgeistery ("Stranger in a Strange Land") and protest ("Alcatraz") aren't as interesting as the in-

jokey "Ballad of Mad Dogs and Englishmen." Which tells us something else. **B**

Leon Russell: *Carney* (Shelter '72). Not the radical falloff some report — just slippage, the first side listenable and the second flaky. Not that I expect "Manhattan Island Serenade" or "Cajun Love Song" to get covered like "This Masquerade." And not that I enjoy anything else as much as "If the Shoe Fits," a cheap shot at hangers-on that says more about the performer's lot than "Tight Rope" and "Magic Mirror" put together. Original grade: B. **B−**

Leon Russell: *Stop All That Jazz* (Shelter '74). The bad jokes start with the cover, which depicts Leon in a cannibal stewpot, the joke being that since he's not even tasty any more why would they bother? (Oo-ee.) Leon's version of "If I Were a Carpenter" has a part about rock stars and groupies that is even dumber than the original. (Stop, my sides are splitting.) And the title is a sly reference to the horn riffs which are the only music on this record I ever want to hear again. (Stop anyway.) **D+**

Leon Russell: *Will o' the Wisp* (Shelter '75). Last time he played the arrogant layabout and pissed everyone off, so now that he's trying too hard should we feel sorry for him? He knows it's make-or-break, and he obviously wants to do new things. But he just doesn't have the chops, not even conceptually. **C−**

Leon Russell: *Best of Leon* (Shelter '76). From "Roll Away the Stone," more iconoclastic than Mott the Hoople's, to "Stranger in a Strange Land," more iconoclastic than Robert Heinlein's, the first side reminds you what an uncommon rock and roller he can be. But on side two, which yokes "A Song for You," "This Masquerade," and "Hummingbird" to three potboilers from *Will o' the Wisp*, you realize that his iconoclasm was (is?) as accidental as his standards. **B+**

Leon Russell: *Americana* (Paradise '78). I never quite got Leon's point back in the days of mad dogs and superstars, so you'll forgive me for having allowed his very first Kim Fowley collaboration to slip off the charts (from a high of 110 in *Record World*) before it reached my turntable. Turns out to be notable as a real con artists' summit — there's a tribute to "Elvis and Marilyn" that is now being distributed in verse form, a soap opera called "Housewife" that panders so ecumenically it's been covered by Wayne Newton, and a song to Leon's latest agent, Jesus. **C−**

Leon Russell & Marc Benno: *Asylum Choir II* (Shelter '71). If the first one was their acid album this 1969 session is their protest album, beginning and ending with advice to a "straight brother" and featuring a revised "Sweet Home Chicago" (for Mayor Daley and his "northern rednecks"), a soppy antiwar song, a scabrous antiwar song, and a confusing anti-smoking song. As well as four love songs that will never make Merv Griffin, one because it advocates "eating salty candy." **B**

The Rutles: *The Rutles* (Warner Bros. '78). I dream of power poppers brazen enough to apply a few rough edges to "I Must Be in Love." Could be a fave rave. Could even be fun. Unlike this limp aural satire. **C**

Mitch Ryder: *What I Did on My Vacation* (Seeds & Stems '78). What he remembers best, apparently, is sex with men, and the songs that result put across all the sin, fear, passion, love-and-hate, pleasure, and release that buggery seems to have involved for him. The lyrics sometimes lack coherence, and the music is a more sensitive version of the now outdated r&b-based guitar flash he favored with Detroit back in 1970. But the overall effect is revelatory. **B**

Frederic Rzewski: *Coming Together; Attica; Moutons de Panurge* (Opus One '73). The design of "Coming Together" is simple, even minimal: Steve ben Israel reads and rereads one of Sam Melville's letters from Attica over a jazzy, repetitious vamp. Yet the result is political art as expressive and accessible as *Guernica*. In ben Israel's interpretation, Melville's prison years have made him both visionary and mad, and the torment of his incarceration is rendered more vivid by the nagging intensity of the music. The other side features a less inspiring political piece and a percussion composition, each likable but not compelling, but that's a cavil. "Coming Together" is amazing. **A−**

Sad Cafe: *Misplaced Ideals* (A&M '78). In which the decade's most paradoxical, characteristic, and disgusting pop-music synthesis — combining hard rock's compulsive riff energy with MOR's smooth determination to displease no one — is achieved without recourse to jazzy rhythms or semiclassical decoration. Misplaced ideals my ass — they threw them down the deepest hole they could find. **C−**

Doug Sahm: See Sir Douglas

Buffy Sainte-Marie: *Moonshot* (Vanguard '72). Because there's something almost perversely machinelike about her vibrato, more Yoko Ono than Judy Collins, I've never been comfortable relegating this particular folkie to the crystal teardrop brigade. Here she finally does something overtly perverse — comes out of Nashville with what sounds in its most interesting moments like an art-pop record (with politics, of course). Those who love or even respect her are dismayed. I say her next step is to take up the Moog. Original grade: B. **B−**

The Saints: *(I'm) Stranded* (Sire '77). With its intermittent hooks, droning feedback, shouted vocals, and oldie about incest, this album from Australia achieves the great mean of punk style. Five years from now, it could sound like a classic or a naive one-shot. At the moment, it's recommended only to addicts. Original grade: B. **B+**

The Saints: *Eternally Yours* (Sire '78). "Private Affair" is the perfect punk-cum-early-Kinks song, "International Robots" invents a Jonathan Richman clone, and Chris Bailey should dub in the vocals on Seymour Stein's *Wild in the Streets* remake. But the lyrics are received protest, the tempos have slackened, and if those horns are somebody's idea of a joke I am not amused. The very idea. **C+**

Ed Sanders: *Sanders' Truck Stop* (Reprise '70). This is literally a country-rock takeoff — not a parody but a departure. But though I hesitate to criticize a man who is not only a saint and a genius but who says hello to me at the post office, I must point out that the yodeling country twang Sanders developed with the Fugs has never known the difference between parody and departure, which makes some of these songs seem crueller than they're intended to be. Of course, sometimes they're cruel on purpose — like "The Iliad," a saga of good old queer-bashing with a Greek-to-me intro. And sometimes, like "Jimmy Joe, the Hippybilly Boy," they're — snurfle — lyrical and sad. Original grade: C plus. **B**

Ed Sanders: *Beer Cans on the Moon* (Reprise '72). Sanders has never been very programmatic, and lyrics like "Nonviolent Direct Action" are why. Even the thrusts at Henry Kissinger, Melvin Laird, and Dita Beard are heavy-handed. Believe me, I don't want the best song on the record to be about a robot in love with Dolly Parton. But that's the way it is.   **C+**

Santa Esmeralda: *Don't Let Me Be Misunderstood* (Casablanca '77). I know people who think a flamencoized fifteen-minute disco version of an Eric Burdon song is some sort of sacrilege, but I just hum along. Sacrilege? Eric Burdon? Doesn't anybody remember "San Franciscan Nights"?   **B**

Santana: *Abraxas* (Columbia '70). On the debut most of the originals were credited to "Santana Band"; this time individual members claim individual compositions. Can this mean somebody thought about these melodies (and lyrics!) before they sprung from the collective unconscious? In any case, they've improved. And in any case, the best ones are by Peter Green, Gabor Szabo, and Tito Puente, none of whom is known to be a member of the Santana Band.   **C+**

Santana: *Santana III* (Columbia '71). In theory, the polyrhythms intensified the momentum while the low-definition songwriting served the freeflow gestalt. In fact, the Latin lilt lightened the beat and the flow remained muddy indeed. So the electricity generated by the percussion-heavy opening cut comes as a pleasant surprise, and the movement of what follows is a surprising pleasure. New second guitarist Neal Schon deserves special thanks for crowding out Gregg Rolie's organ. Maybe soon he'll come up with more than one idea per solo.   **B**

Santana: *Caravanserai* (Columbia '72). Some of the slower electronic stuff fails to sustain my admittedly tentative interest, and the Gillette commercial vocals take this post-hippie business altogether too far. Still, I'm happy to report that the experiment — away from Latino schlock and toward Mahavishnu you can dance to, sort of — is not only honest but successful and not only successful but appropriate. After all, improvisation has always been their "thing." Original grade: B.   **B−**

Santana: *Welcome* (Columbia '73). More confident and hence more fun than *Caravanserai*, this proves that a communion of multipercussive rock and transcendentalist jazz can move the unenlightened — me, for instance. Good themes, good playing, good beat, and let us not forget good singing — Leon Thomas's muscular spirituality grounds each side so firmly that not even Flora Purim can send it out the window. Original grade: B.   **B+**

Santana: *Santana's Greatest Hits* (Columbia '74). The problem with their albums turns out to be too complex to be solved by eliminating uninteresting tunes — which is a backhanded compliment to the complexity of their concept. In any case, this compilation reduces their music to a cross between pan-African blooze and Latin-metal pop. The fine (and, er, not so fine) cuts it showcases work better in their original contexts — as heads, lynchpins, focal points of improvisions that are not (yet?) what they should be.   **B−**

Santana: *Borboletta* (Columbia '74). Old Santana fans beware. Ad copy to the contrary, the only Latin roots here flowered in Brazil long 'round '66. Airto Moreira isn't Sergio Mendes, I admit, but Leon Patillo isn't Leon Thomas either.   **C+**

Santana: *Amigos* (Columbia '76). Bill Graham and David Rubinson augment Sri Chinmoy's everybody's-everything strategy with direct-hit tactics as Carlos resumes his attack on the rock marketplace. Greg Walker doubles credibly as soul man and sonero, and "Dance Sister Dance" is the band's all-time hottest original even if it is lifted from a universal salsa riff. As Armando Peraza proves (on "Gitano"), better salsa conservatism than samba impressionism. And as Carlos proves, better salsa than Wes Montgomery at his schlockiest or a tune called "Europa" that lives up to its name.   **B**

Santana: *Festival* (Columbia '77). As a salsa band they're still OK, but a ten-tune format and the sincere desire for AM proselytization don't make them a pop band. (Putting vocals on all the tracks might help.) It makes them a mediocre fusion band. (Is there another kind?) **C+**

Santana: *Moonflower* (Columbia '77). Mixing greatest oldies with lesser newcomers, salsa classics with rock covers, European concert hall with San Fran studio, this seamless double album should stand as the working definition of a world-class band. My objections stand, too — the improvisations sometimes divert when they should sustain, the groove is often too easy, and the vocal ensembles sound like commercials. But all these flaws, for better or worse, suit music of such global appeal. And Carlos Santana has never played so well for so long. In the rock guitar tradition he is less a man of style than of sound, a clear, loud, fluent sound that cleanses with the same motion no matter how often that motion is repeated — as long as the intensity and the context are there. On this album, the live cuts provide both. **B+**

Santana: *Inner Secrets* (Columbia '78). It's sad when one of the few megagroups with a groove powerful enough to get it out of any jam resorts to hacks like Lambert and Potter for a hit. I mean, Santana is schlocky anyway. But Santana's own schlock has some dignity. **C+**

Santana: *Marathon* (Columbia '79). In their selfless pursuit of universality they've signed on a second Eddie Money graduate and replaced Greg Walker, their finest vocalist, with a Scot named Alexander J. Ligertwood, who proves his internationalism by aping that eternal foreigner Lou Gramm. Odd, you can hardly hear the congas. **C**

Carlos Santana Mahavishnu John McLaughlin: *Love Devotion Surrender* (Columbia '73). On the back cover is a photograph of three men. Two of them are dressed in white and have their hands folded — one grinning like Alfred E. Neuman, the other looking like he's about to have a Supreme Court case named after him:

solemn, his wrists ready for the cuffs. In between, a man in an orange ski jacket and red pants with one white sock seems to have caught his tongue on his lower lip. He looks like the yoga coach at a fashionable lunatic asylum. Guess which one is Sri Chinmoy. **B−**

Devadip Carlos Santana: *Silver Dreams Golden Reality* (Columbia '79). Frustrating, especially for an earthbound churl like myself — spiritual program music that mixes genuinely celestial rock with the usual goop. The "title" song (which for some arcane reason — scansion, probably — substitutes the word "Smiles" for "Reality") is an altogether revolting string-fed banality. It's followed by an instrumental on which the guitarist attains his soaring apogee, and a Sri Chinmoy (!) tune — arranged by Narada Michael Walden (!!) — that achieves a natural impressionism Eno (!!!) couldn't hope for. See what I mean? **B−**

Saturday Night Fever (RSO '77). So you've seen the movie — pretty good movie, right? — and decided that this is the disco album you're going to try. Well, I can't blame you. The Bee Gees side is pop music at a new peak of irresistible silliness, with the former Beatle clones singing like mechanical mice with an unnatural sense of rhythm. And the album climaxes on a par-tee even non-discoids can get into, beginning with the best of David Shire's "additional music," then switching almost imperceptibly to something tolerable by MFSB and revving into all 10:52 of the Trammps' magnificent "Disco Inferno." But I find the other two sides unlistenable, mostly because the rest of Shire's additions are real soundtrack-quality stuff — he even discofies Moussorgsky (see Emerson Lake & Palmer) without making a joke of it (compare Walter Murphy on side two). And there's one more problem. While you're deciding to buy this record, so is everyone you know. You're gonna get really sick of it. Maybe you should Surprise Your Friends and seek out Casablanca's *Get Down and Boogie* instead.   **B+**

The Savage Rose: *Your Daily Gift* (Gregar '70). Also known as the Copenhagen Rhythm and Blues Ensemble, this band has a knack for combining funky riffs with persistent melodies (borrowed from where, this ignorant American wonders). But though Annisette's multi-octave Lolita voice is certainly distinctive, I find her about as sexy as Yma Sumac, and as long as she sings Anders Koppel's lyrics she won't be any font of wisdom either. Last straw: a desultory eight-minute instrumental called "Tapiola."   **C+**

The Savage Rose: *Refugee* (Gregar '71). Fast tempos, soul piano, and (I bet) Jimmy Miller's production do wonders for Anisette's come-on, and the lyrics prove that getting laid is a universal language. Death, too.   **B**

Savoy Brown: *The Best of Savoy Brown* (London '77). More even than John Mayall, this band was the great mean — that is, the mean — of the purist (as opposed to heavy) wing of what we in America once called British blues, and these eight tracks, none recorded after 1972, say it all. "Train to Nowhere" is a minor classic, "A Hard Way to Go" and maybe one or two others mildly memorable, and that's it for twelve albums. I mean, who wants to hear (third but not last vocalist) Dave Walker sing "Wang Dang Doodle" when it's on *The London Howlin' Wolf Sessions?* And who but an annotator would describe an empty-headed Kim Simmonds guitar solo (over a rhythm section that's simultaneously stolid and shaky) as "piercing and blistering"?   **B−**

Leo Sayer: *Silverbird* (Warner Bros. '73). The musical tricks repeat themselves, but they're good — the sharp, punky growl that accedes so naturally to the vulnerable falsetto, the punch of the drums against the depth of the strings. But the words fail me. Sayer makes much of his mask — a mask so enigmatic that it registers, at best, as a blank. Why then should I wonder what's behind it?   **B−**

Leo Sayer: *Just a Boy* (Warner Bros. '75). Personally, I took him more seriously in his clown suit.   **C+**

Leo Sayer: *Another Year* (Warner Bros. '75). Leo sounds so much like Elton this time that I thought I'd finally figured him out, for like Numero Uno he seems very aware that people buy hooks, not words, belting/crooning every lyric with the same synthetic intensity regardless of its worth. The switch to a social realist tack here would then be explained by the presence of new songwriting collaborator Frank Farrell. My problem: Sayer writes the words, Farrell the melodies. Sayer's problem: we love Elton for his megalomania, and megalomania is something you have to earn.   **B−**

Leo Sayer: *Endless Flight* (Warner Bros. '76). Like his great (also greater) exemplar, Leo has abandoned all pretensions mid-career (except on the title cut). And sure enough, Warners has now broken three big singles off this album, which makes 1977 the year of Leo Sayer the way 1976 was the year of Fleetwood Mac. Not quite as gratifying, is it? My pick for number four: "I Think We Fell in Love Too Fast," a natural for the young divorcee crowd.   **B**

Leo Sayer: *Thunder in My Heart* (Warner Bros. '77). That ain't thunder, Leo, it's the pitter-patter of little duds.   **C**

Leo Sayer: *Leo Sayer* (Warner Bros. '78). The wee hitmaker covers "La Booga Rooga," which means admirers of Andy Fairweather Low should be pleased. We'd be even more pleased if Leo didn't do the same favor four times over for admirers of Tom Snow.   **C+**

Boz Scaggs: *Moments* (Columbia '71). When Scaggs announces that his girl is a looker because "she looks like she's standin' right there," you believe he's got a right to sing like Neil Young wishing he were Smokey Robinson. But when he praises "Downright Women" or concocts a pop instrumental w/ strings for his rock band, you wonder. **B**

Boz Scaggs: *Boz Scaggs & Band* (Columbia '71). I oppose the nice 'n' easy school of rock 'n' roll, but this time he not only cops to his groove (last album he still had other ideas) but proves he can jump out of it. Especially on "Monkey Time," a gloss on "Mickey's Monkey" so spaced-out you hope music is his only jones. Original grade: A minus. **B+**

Boz Scaggs: *My Time* (Columbia '72). In search of the perfect makeout music for ex-hippies, Scaggs ditched his band of bohos halfway through and hied to Muscle Shoals, where the laid-back lie down with the overproduced as a regular thing. It may just be my imagination, but except for "Dinah Flo" and "Slowly in the Wind" — written by his bassist, David Brown, who's challenged Scaggs with cryptic lyrics on all of his Columbia albums — I think I like the boho stuff better. Original grade: C plus. **B**

Boz Scaggs: *Slow Dancer* (Columbia '74). Bet Boz is real proud of himself — he's landed a genu-wine Motown producer. Maybe next time he'll get one a little snazzier than Johnny Bristol. **B−**

Boz Scaggs: *Silk Degrees* (Columbia '76). Scaggs is criticized for his detachment, but I say it's subtlety and I say thank god for it. In the past, he's sometimes bought (not to mention sold) his own lushness, but this collection is cooled by droll undercurrents — white soul with a sense of humor that isn't consumed in self-parody. Inspirational Verse: "Gotta have a jones for this/Jones for that/This runnin' with the joneses, boy/Just ain't where it's at." Original grade: B plus. **A−**

Boz Scaggs: *Down Two Then Left* (Columbia '78). Scaggs obviously labored over this one, getting every second so right that there wasn't a whole lot left. After dozens of listenings I'm convinced that side one is tedious and side two quite listenable. But it wasn't worth my trouble — or his. **B**

Gunther Schuller: *Country Fiddle Band* (Columbia '76). Why do I love this semiclassicized perversion when country fiddle and bluegrass music that strives for authenticity leaves me cold? It's all in the candor of the striving; as usual, I'm put off by the way so-called folk groups formalize a tradition that had spontaneity and unselfconsciousness at the root of its attraction. This silly symphony is something else. The melodies are fetchingly tried-and-true, the (unintentional?) stateliness of the rhythms appropriately nineteenth-century, and the instrumental overkill (twenty-four instruments massed on "Flop-Eared Mule") both gorgeous and hilarious. A grand novelty. **B+**

Brinsley Schwarz: *Despite It All* (Capitol '71). In the wake of willful hype and confused debut, this follow-up has been panned or ignored, an injustice. I'm impressed that four English guys could get the Byrds' kind of bittersweet, covertly strange c&w so right, though actually it's not so different from what the Stones started doing with r&b. My favorite line is either "Why don't you financially back her" or "Because it's so important." My favorite song is "Country Girl." My favorite title is "The Slow One." **B+**

Brinsley Schwarz: *Silver Pistol* (United Artists '72). One side of quite entertaining British Americana and one of barely interesting British Americana. Inconveniently for me, the bad side includes my fave, "The Silver Surfer," which stars a deus ex machina called the Silver Surfer. That should tell you everything you need to know except who decided to drench the country-rock in Hammond organ. The organ player, I'll warrant. Marginal. **B+**

Brinsley Schwarz: *Nervous on the Road* (United Artists '72). On *Silver Pistol*, such songs as "Egypt" and "Unknown Number" rendered Gram

Parsons irony willfully opaque. Here Nick Lowe would seem at first to be overcompensating — the side-openers, one by his innocent accomplice Ian Gomm, are genre pieces that announce a disc of straightforward country-rock. But then you notice "I Like It Like That" turning into "the place of the name," or hear that Lowe is "scumbag bound." Which prepares you for the last three songs on side one, each a pleasant country-rock genre piece, each shot through with displacement and tragedy. **A−**

Tom Scott and the L.A. Express: *Tom Cat* (Ode '75). Joni Mitchell please note: this isn't jazz, it's background music without the foreground. It doesn't swing, it doesn't rock — it hops. **C−**

Gil Scott-Heron / Brian Jackson: *Winter in America* (Strata-East '74). The jazz poet turns jazz singer — good idea, only he had a better beat and just slightly less melody when he was reading. Exception: "The Bottle," which you can dance to. **C+**

Gil Scott-Heron: *The Revolution Will Not Be Televised* (Flying Dutchman '74). The "hairy-armed women's liberationists" of the title track are still with us, but at least this compilation avoids the fag-baiting that dishonored his first album, not the only sign of growth. His agitprop has lost a lot of punk arrogance over the decade without surrendering commitment, and as he learns to sing his compassion becomes palpable. **B+**

Gil Scott-Heron, Brian Jackson and the Midnight Band: *The First Minute of a New Day* (Arista '75). The improvement in this poet-turned-musician suggests that white singer-songwriters could benefit from commitment to a musically sophisticated culture. He's got it, and he flaunts it. The singing will get stronger, and maybe someday every lyric will compare with the inspiring, despondent "Winter in America." In the meantime, the free-jazz-gone-populist band generates so much rhythmic energy that it carries over the weak spots. One heartfelt suggestion: no more long poetry reading, at least on record. I laughed at "Pardon Our Analysis" the first time, but now I find myself avoiding side one. **B**

Gil Scott-Heron and Brian Jackson: *From South Africa to South Carolina* (Arista '75). This is what happened to Pharoah Sanders and I say yeah. The danceability of Jackson's music reifies the tribal aspirations of new-thing avant-gardism just as Scott-Heron's talent for modest analysis brings all that cosmic politicking down to earth. Also, I'm really getting to like Scott-Heron's singing — his instrument will never equal Leon Thomas's, or Pharoah's, but that's not what it's about. **B+**

Gil Scott-Heron and Brian Jackson: *It's Your World* (Arista '76). The original version of "The Bottle," a protest songpoem about people who live in glass containers, was a disco hit, and now Arista is trying to break the live version on the radio, but these efforts have been disdained by discriminating progressive programmers everywhere — after all, how serious can it be if people dance to it? I hope you know the answer. If anything proves how serious Scott-Heron has become, it's the infectious groove running through all four sides of this concert album. You've heard of selling out? This is selling in. **A−**

Gil Scott-Heron & Brian Jackson: *Bridges* (Arista '77). Quite rapidly, Scott-Heron has developed into a reliable pro, like some old country singer. The music and singing provide lasting service, and the words evolve with the times, which is the point. In a self-anointed aesthete, that would be tantamount to failure, but for a message artist it's high praise. As long as his eye stays fresh, I don't believe Scott-Heron can make a bad album, and his fans will like this one OK. **B**

Gil Scott-Heron and Brian Jackson: *Secrets* (Arista '78). Scott-Heron stokes the protest-music flame more generously than any son of Woody, and in sheer agitprop terms "Angel Dust," one of those black-radio hits that somehow never crossed over, is his triumph — haunting music of genuine political usefulness. Of course, it would be hard to imagine the Arista promo team busting its butt to get "Third World Revolution" on the air as a follow-up, even if it had a hook, but I'll settle for a tribulations-of-stardom song with an educational refrain: "Do you really want to be in show bizness?" **B+**

The Scruffs: *"Wanna' Meet the Scruffs?"* (Power Play '77). Only a sucker for rock and roll could love this record, and I am that sucker. A middle-period Beatles extrapolation in the manner of Big Star (another out-of-step Memphis power-pop group on a small, out-of-step Memphis label), it bursts with off harmonies, left hooks, and jolts of random energy. The trouble is, these serve a shamelessly and perhaps permanently post-adolescent vision of life's pain, most of which would appear to involve gurls. To which objection the rockin' formalist in me responds, "I wanna hear 'Revenge' again." **A−**

Gary and Randy Scruggs: *The Scruggs Brothers* (Vanguard '72). Significant that two musicians so close to the Flatt-picking roots — though it ought to be remembered that their father is an entertainer, not a mountaineer — have put together such a doleful-sounding country-rock band in the face of the good-time sippin'-that-wine stuff the more famous guys are selling. Original grade: B. **B−**

Sea Level: *Cats on the Coast* (Capricorn '78). Because he can sing and write songs, the newly acquired Randall Bramblett imparts a modicum of pop structure, a relief after the shapeless jazzy boogie of their debut. His "That's Your Secret," followed by the Allmansish "It Hurts to Want You So Bad," kicks the whole first side into tol'able playability. **B−**

Sea Level: *On the Edge* (Capricorn '78). It becomes clearer and clearer that these are Dixie dregs indeed. Ringing over the Allmans' inexorable flow, Chuck Leavell's Tyneresque piano chordings used to provide a satisfying simulation of spiritual uplift, but in a fusion I'll take Lonnie Liston Smith (if you can believe that). Nor is Randall Bramblett (even) a Joe Henderson on saxophone. Bramblett does contribute four strong songs. Unfortunately, three are available on his second solo album, *Light of the Night,* in arrangements that demonstrate conclusively the arbitrariness of these. **C−**

Seals & Crofts: *Seals & Crofts* (TA '70). In moments of self-criticism I sometimes believe I'll praise anything that's tight and tuneful. This record proves those suspicions unfounded. That'll teach 'em to print their lyrics on the inside jacket. **C−**

Seals & Crofts: *Diamond Girl* (Reprise '73). In the classic folk-schlock manner, female contributors to this album (predictable exception: Bobbye Hall, here designated Miss rather than Ms) are listed by first name. Only these women aren't groupies — they're wives, and the album is dedicated to them. Well, I'm sure it sounds better on a pedestal than on a turntable. **C−**

Seals & Crofts: *Unborn Child* (Warner Bros. '74). This may be catchy but I refuse to get caught; they may be good at what they do, but what they do is so disgusting that that only makes it worse. I would tell them to find their roots, but instead of regrouping as the Champs, they'd probably convince Warner Bros. to waste more vinyl on the Anita Kerr Singers. **D−**

The Son Seals Blues Band: *The Son Seals Blues Band* (Alligator '73). As the notes say, it's rare for a young bluesman to defy the commercial realities and try to develop his own writing and playing style. What they don't mention is that the writing has a ways to go. But I like the coarse flow of his "scuffling" guitar, especially in a distort mode — like the choked comping behind "Your Love Is Like a Cancer," which neatly enough is the album's most striking lyric.　　　　**B**

Son Seals: *Midnight Son* (Alligator '76). Were it not for the brash reentry of the Winterized Muddy Waters, I could wax superlative; as it is, let's call it the finest Chicago blues record *recorded in Chicago* (get it?) since the second Hound Dog Taylor (also on this label). Seals performs the thrillingly paradoxical trick of keeping a raw guitar style under impeccable control and sings much better than his serviceable voice would seem to permit. In other words, he really knows what he's doing, and knowing doesn't stop him from doing it to it — it helps. So vibrantly conceived that I'm not even sure I should complain about the horns.　　　　**A −**

Son Seals: *Live and Burning* (Alligator '78). Seals's club work tends to be rawer than the (genuinely) "progressive" *Midnight Son,* so this product makes sense. And nice as it is that Seals composes his own material, the numerous borrowings — my favorites are from Jimmy Reed, Elmore James, and Pinetop (I think) Perkins — are a peer's prerogative.　　　　**A −**

John B. Sebastian: *John B. Sebastian* (Reprise '70). Sebastian is as on for this solo debut as he ever was for the Lovin' Spoonful, and when he's on, the hummability quotient of his songs is dizzying — a good half of these imprint themselves upon impact. But just like Spoonful albums used to, this drags in the second half, and I feel vaguely let down. Maybe it's the gently paternalistic sexism of "She's a Lady" and "What She Thinks About." Or maybe it's his taste in T-shirts. Original grade: A minus.　　**B**

John Sebastian: *The Four of Us* (Reprise '71). Sebastian makes the mistake of beginning this with two great blues, after which his own funk and

mawk sound lifeless. This is unfair. They're really only feckless — or careless, like his love. The title suite (or whatever it is) is the tie-dyed mind at its sloppiest.　　　　**C**

John Sebastian: *The Tarzana Kid* (Reprise '74). It's nice to know California John isn't doing this for money. He's so warm he never has to sing for his supper — he can always get work as a chafing dish.　　　　**C −**

Neil Sedaka: *Sedaka's Back* (Rocket '74). In which a self-admitted mean old man approximates a cross between the young Paul Anka and the post-Bennington Reparata and the Delrons, only his voice is higher and his lyrics more considered. The whole first side, ending with the cheerfully perverse "Little Brother," is perfect pop moderne, and that's not where you'll find my own pick hit, the cheerfully normal "Love Will Keep Us Together."　**B +**

Neil Sedaka: *The Hungry Years* (Rocket '75). Modes of integrity: *Sedaka's Back,* compiled from two-plus English albums, sounded organic, while this star-time El Lay session sounds homogenized. Neil's voice has changed — the light girl-groupy moments have turned bitchy and the sentimentality is thick with incipient sobs. Figure best-ofs are his natural element and remember that only, if he goes away can he come back again.　**C +**

Mike Seeger: *Music from the True Vine* (Mercury '72). In which the great folkie socks fourteen weird old mountain songs into the archives. Seeger sings with spunk and authenticity, plays eight acoustic instruments, and taps his foot pretty good, and even if you (and I) can't dance to it, I guarantee you somebody can.　　　　**B +**

Mike Seeger: *The Second Annual Farewell Reunion* (Mercury '73). This distinguishes itself from Seeger's solo *Music from the True Vine* by gathering famous folk into makeshift supersessions, and from the Dirt Band's *Will the Circle Be Unbroken* by singling out less surefire songs and musicians. Taught me that I prefer sister Peggy's mournful harmonies ("Texas Ranger") to Maria Muldaur's dulcet ones ("Take Me Back to the Sunny South"), and Mike's acerbic baritone to brother Peter's avuncular pick-'em-up.   **A−**

Jeannie Seely: *Jeannie Seely's Greatest Hits* (Monument '72). In 1966, Seely's "Don't Touch Me" took country women's sexuality from the honky-tonk into the bedroom even though it didn't end up there, and the on-again off-again ache in her voice retained its savor afterwards. But never again did she find a song at once so moral and so febrile. Time: 26:51.   **B**

Bob Seger System: *Mongrel* (Capitol '70). Seger has a brain — you'll learn more about revolutionary youth from "Leanin on My Dream" than from John Sinclair, who has a walk-on in "Highway Child" — but you'd never guess it from his singing. He's one of these heavy guys who equates fake agony with real soul — wrote "Song for Rufus" to himself.   **C+**

Bob Seger: *Smokin' O.P.'s* (Palladium '72). Zippy title for an album of seven covers and two originals — O.P.'s is Midwestern butt-bummers' slang for Other People's. But for some reason Seger has cadged songs already covered definitively by such *other* o.p. as B. B. King, the Isley Brothers, the Grateful Dead, and the Rolling Stones. Both his band and his voice sound a lot more adroit than they did last time he was caught smokin'. But who needs 'em? [Later on Reprise, and then on Capitol.]   **C+**

Bob Seger: *Back in '72* (Palladium/Reprise '73). Much sharper covers (his "Midnight Rider" beats Cocker's) plus originals that ain't bad for tours 'n' tribulations — "Rosalie," to CKLW programmer Rosalie Twombley, is a stroke in more ways than one, and the details of a day on the road in "Turn the Page" actually make you feel sorry for the poor guy. Elsewhere he feels sorry for himself, which is not the same thing.   **B**

Bob Seger: *Seven* (Palladium/Reprise '74). Unbecoming for a seven-LP veteran to be stuck vocally at the adolescent outrage stage, midway between screech and scream, but he's learning — a high-speed Chuck Berry chant called "Get Out of Denver" kicks the whole first side into high gear. Glad too that he has his doubts about the upper-middle class, and that he's attracted to schoolteachers, including one he expects to know "20 Years from Now." He could be nicer to groupies, though. [Later on Capitol.] Original grade: B.   **B+**

Bob Seger: *Beautiful Loser* (Capitol '75). In which he redeems the over-expressionistic "River Deep, Mountain High" (on *Mongrel*) with a funny version of "Nutbush City Limits" (a better song anyway) and writes his own "Katmandu" (roll over, Cat Stevens). And beyond that there's the title tune, which seems overunsarcastic to me.   **B−**

Bob Seger & the Silver Bullet Band: *Live Bullet* (Capitol '76). The impassioned remakes from *Beautiful Loser* on side one are what live doubles are supposed to be for, and this one is sparing with the cheerleading and calisthenics. In short, it's good of its kind. But I'm from New York, I see a lot of rock concerts, and even when I'm in the room it takes more than "Ramblin' Gamblin' Man" and "Heavy Music" and refurbished songs from a guy's last album to get me excited.   **B**

Bob Seger & the Silver Bullet Band: *Night Moves* (Capitol '76). I've never had much truck with Seger's myth — he's always struck me as a worn if well-schooled rock and roll journeyman, good for one or two tracks a year. But this album is a journeyman's apotheosis. The riffs that identify each of these nine songs comprise a working lexicon of the Berry-Stones tradition, and you've heard them many times before; in fact, that may be the point, because Seger and his musicians reanimate every one with their persistence and conviction. Both virtues also come across in lyrics as hard-hitting as the melodies, every one of which asserts the continuing functionality of rock and roll for "sweet sixteens turned thirty-one." In one of them, the singer even has his American Express card stolen by a descendant of Ronnie Hawkins's Mary Lou, if not Mary Lou herself. Worrying about your credit rating — now that's what I call rock and roll realism.   **A −**

Bob Seger & the Silver Bullet Band: _Stranger in Town_ (Capitol '78). This isn't just an honest, rough-and-ready craftsman reverting to form, because he's trying to repeat an inspired, uncharacteristically precise success. So he sounds phony at times, desperate to inject drama into run-of-the-mill material that might work in a more fluid, less fraught-with-meaning live setting. Exception: "Feel Like a Number," in which the banal critique of quantification is renewed by Seger's measured intensity.   **B −**

Sid Selvidge: _The Cold of the Morning_ (Peabody '76). Selvidge's voice is so rich it's a curse, especially since it's combined with a good-humored grasp of blues tradition — all he has to do is release the notes and people tell him he's a genius. On this evidence, Selvidge is only a craftsman. His gifts as a lyricist are limited, and his guitar can't sustain a whole album. But the two lead cuts and Selvidge's own "Frank's Tune" overcome.   **B**

The Sex Pistols: _Never Mind the Bollocks, Here's the Sex Pistols_ (Warner Bros. '77). Get this straight: no matter what the chicmongers want to believe, to call this band dangerous is more than a suave existentialist compliment. They mean no good. It won't do to pass off Rotten's hatred and disgust as role-playing — the gusto of the performance is too convincing. Which is why this is such an impressive record. The forbidden ideas from which Rotten makes songs take on undeniable truth

value, whether one is sympathetic ("Holidays in the Sun" is a hysterically frightening vision of global economics) or filled with loathing ("Bodies," an indictment from which Rotten doesn't altogether exclude himself, is effectively anti-abortion, anti-woman, and anti-sex). These ideas must be dealt with, and can be expected to affect the way fans think and behave. The chief limitation on their power is the music, which can get heavy occasionally, but the only real question is how many American kids might feel the way Rotten does, and where he and they will go next. I wonder — but I also worry. Original grade: A minus.   **A**

Sgt. Pepper's Lonely Hearts Club Band (RSO '78). At first I felt relatively positive about this project. I'm not a religious man, I liked the Aerosmith and Earth, Wind & Fire cuts on the radio, and I figured the Bee Gees qualified as ersatz Beatles if anyone did. Well, let's hope clones aren't like this. From the song selection, you wouldn't even know the originals were once a rock and roll band. Most of the arrangements are lifted whole without benefit of vocal presence (maybe Maurice should try hormones) or rhythmic integrity ("Can't we get a little of that disco feel in there, George?") And what reinterpretations there are are unworthy of Mike Douglas. George Burns I can forgive, even Peter Frampton — but not Diane Steinberg, Sandy Farina, Frankie Howard. I never thought Alice Cooper would stoop to a Paul Williams imitation. I never thought Steve Martin would do a Nerd imitation. Get back, all of you. Back I say.   **D +**

The Shakers: _Yankee Reggae_ (Asylum '76). California competition for James Isaacs's 1975 discovery, _Freed at Last,_ by Ras Irwin Freed and the Tropicanas. Sounds like Steve Miller bunny-hopping with Gary Lewis & the Playboys toward the Isle of Wimp.   **D**

Sham 69: *Tell Us the Truth* (Sire '78). On the "studio side," where the marginal differentiations are nicely tricked up, Jimmy Pursey comes across as a thoughtful eccentric with his own ideas about punk dilemmas both musical and social. Turn the record over and he devolves into a passionate blur of the most faceless English punk sort. Anyone naive enough to structure a song around a repeated shout of "George Davis Is Innocent" can be charming for a while, but not for 11:31, which is how long it takes the "live side" to self-destruct. **B**

Dee Dee Sharp: *Happy 'Bout the Whole Thing* (TSOP '75). This is touted as the current Gamble-Huff sleeper, and no, that has nothing to do with her being married to one of them. It means that not only does it include two good songs, but that they come one after the other at the beginning of a side. Side two, in case you're interested. **C+**

Billie Joe Shaver: *Old Five and Dimers Like Me* (Monument '73). Kris Kristofferson produced this record because Billie Joe Shaver can really write songs. But they aren't so irresistible that Billy Joe can get away with singing them — not even (not even?) with Kris giving lessons. **B**

Cybill Shepherd: *Cybill Does It . . . to Cole Porter* (Paramount '74). Her voice is surprisingly pleasant, but you'd never know how these songs sparkle. Since Cole didn't like to . . . do it with (or "to") women very much, maybe the "do" is as hostile as it sounds. **D−**

Johnny Shines: *Johnny Shines* (Blue Horizon '72). Born in 1915, Shines is the most vigorous surviving practitioner of acoustic Delta blues. With his intense vibrato, his observant, imaginative, yet tradition-soaked lyrics, and his incomparable slide guitar, he ought to be recorded once a year by the Library of Congress. Right. He did this session for English blues fiend Mike Vernon in 1968, but only now has it been released in the States. A band featuring Willie Dixon and Shakey Horton is on half the cuts. **A−**

Johnny Shines: *Too Wet to Plow* (Blue Labor '77). Shines isn't Robert Johnson made flesh and come to walk amongst us — you should hear his Biograph stuff — but here he takes advantage of his forty-year edge to make an album that's easier to listen to — because it *sounds* better — than *King of the Delta Blues Singers*. Engineering is only a means to an end — the real secret is a devotion to the form so passionate that Shines's playing and singing are wild and brilliant as they've never been before. Guitarist and change-of-pace vocalist Louisiana Red and harpman Sugar Blue add small touches of plenty. The songwriting fades some on side two. **A−**

Shirley and Company: *Shame Shame Shame* (Vibration '75). This bargain package includes: 1) title smash and follow-up, very similar but a little slower; 2) instrumental versions of same; 3) a song that reprises the smash riff and tells what a terrific dancer Disco Shirley is; 4) a recycled "Iko Iko"-style folk song; 5) several boy-girl duets; 6) other stuff. Very slapdash, very expedient, and quite smashing. **B+**

The Shirts: *The Shirts* (Capitol '78). Driving through the Bronx on my way from South Carolina to Maine, I heard "Lonely Android" on the radio and wondered for a moment if the Ramones were making an art-rock move. This gaffe was probably a symptom of homesickness, but it does indicate that on record, where Annie Golden's Broadway proclivities are invisible, this becomes a vaguely interesting (or at least eccentric) band — Focus gone CBGB without chops, kind of. **C+**

The Shirts: *Street Light Shine* (Capitol '79). This is awful only on the big side-closers, and the occasional klutziness of the lyrics is redeemed not only by a winning sincerity but by improved (sometimes pretty) singing and composition — try "Starts with a Handshake" or "Love Is a Fiction." I might even want to play the end-of-the-world song for Chris Stein. Sincerity can be infectious. **B —**

Shoes: *Black Vinyl Shoes* (PVC '78). Recorded by elves on a TEAC four-track in a living room in Zion, Illinois, this offers fifteen hooky, bittersweet reflections on sexual strategy among the under-twenty-fives. Clever melodic contours plus vocals faded and echoed so far back they take on the mystery of synthesized guitars equal a natural for pop obsessives. **A —**

Shoes: *Present Tense* (Elektra '79). A formalist's delight — the three principals pursue their theme of Sad Love as obsessively as a cavalier writing sonnets to his lady. Their voices are interchangeably breathy, their tempos unflappably moderate, their guitar hooks unfailingly right. And when for a change of pace one of them sounds bitter the effect is as startling as a Johnny Ramone guitar solo. **A —**

The Sidewinders: *The Sidewinders* (RCA Victor '72). These snappy, hard-hitting songs are what rock and roll used to sound like back when singles were singles and boys would be boys. Except for "Slip Away" — which I bet provides the melodramatic interlude live — every cut offers its little gift. But producer Lenny Kaye knows as well as anyone that in the halcyon days of top forty real largesse was required — melodies like "Rendezvous," the only potential hit I hear here. Not that transforming "Flight of the Bumble Bee" into "Tel-Star" wasn't a fun idea. **B**

Bunny Sigler: *Keep Smilin'* (Philadelphia International '74). The Gamble-Huff producer-songwriter, whose only major hit as a performer was a Shirley & Lee revival, Phillifies himself honorably — in addition to two or three romps he sings soppy stuff like he wishes he were Smokey Robinson. Unfortunately, only "Somebody Free" comes close — closer than the romps do to Shirley & Lee. Which leave the acapella-tinged "Sweeter Than the Berry" and the oddly arresting "Love Train" (a local) to put the album across. **B**

Judee Sill: *Judee Sill* (Asylum '71). It's her devout hope that we'll "savor each word like a raspberry," and I do mean devout — Sill yearns for the day when Christ the Bridegroom will "take all the gentle away." Thank god her music is spiritually unpresumptuous — pythagorean melodies and spare, delicate chamber-folk arrangements that set off her homespun drawl (the lyric sheet favors spellings like "cuz" and "gunna"). Wish I could also say her lyrics were tart as raspberries, but they remind me more of peaches — fuzzy. **B**

Judee Sill: *Heart Food* (Asylum '73). Beneath a lusher surface, her voice enriched with overdubs and less idiosyncratically accented, Sill has become a real militant. Christ is a "Soldier of the Heart," a "Vigilante"; although "the chosen are few" we're supposed to "see how His mercy shines," presumably because he saves any of us sinners at all. Last shall be first or not, this is pretty repulsive as ideology, yet until the kyrie eleisons at the climax I find it paradoxically seductive. Say she's a mad saint instead of a sainted madwoman and make room for another rock crazy. **B +**

Silver Convention: *Save Me* (Midland International '75). All I know about this predominantly black group is that its home town is Munich, in Germany, and that its current single, "Fly, Robin, Fly," is currently, well, taking off. The style is very bare and pure, sort of minimal disco, with lyrics so simple-minded they couldn't have been devised by anyone who knows English as a native language. Like so much good disco, it's funny, and not intentionally, one of those aberrations that could be turned into a major annoyance by major popularity. For the time being, however, it's catchy yocks. Original grade: B.   **B +**

Silver Convention: *Silver Convention* (Midland International '76). I hedged last time for fear this group would turn into an annoyance if they got big, but they didn't. Instead they persist as an odd classic, instantly identifiable within a notoriously homogeneous genre, replacing soft disco's characteristic baby-oil flow with an endearingly square herky-jerk. Unfortunately, this collection necessitates a more serious hedge, on grounds of material ("songs" seems too arty a term). They should have borrowed "Lady Bump" and "Big Bad Boy" from Penny McLean, whose bland vocalizing is best buried in the mix, as it is here, rather than showcased on a "solo" album.   **B –**

Silver Convention: *Madhouse* (Midland International '76). Just what you've always wanted — protest disco, in which the philosophical evasions of disco and its lifestyle are taken on (in "oratorio" form) within the genre itself. That means it's simplistic by definition. It's also a noteworthy curio, and a listenable one. Original grade: B plus.   **B**

Stanley Silverman: *Elephant Steps* (Columbia '74). A mere Chuck Berry expert cannot judge the quality of the "classical" music herein contained, although he can mention that he does not intend to investigate it further. The "rock," however, was apparently concocted by David Clayton-Thomas's heir covert and the pit band from the Oslo production of *Hair*. And any English major can see through the "libretto."   **C –**

Simon & Garfunkel: *Bridge Over Troubled Water* (Columbia '70). Melodic.   **B**

Carly Simon: *Carly Simon* (Elektra '71). Since affluence is an American

condition, I suppose it makes sense not only for the privileged to inflict their sensibilities on us, but for many of us to dig it. Too bad, though. It's OK for "That's the Way I've Always Heard It Should Be" to voice a cliché, but not with that calculated preciosity and false air of discovery. If Carly's college friends are already old enough to have alienated their children, her self-discovery program is a little postmature anyway.   **C –**

Carly Simon: *No Secrets* (Elektra '72). If a horse could sing in a monotone, the horse would sound like Carly Simon, only a horse wouldn't rhyme "yacht," "apricot," and "gavotte." Is that some kind of joke? Why did Mick Jagger want her? Why does James Taylor want her? Come to think of it, why does she want either of them?   **B –**

Carly Simon: *Hotcakes* (Elektra '74). "You're So Vain" left a nice afterglow — as Ellen Willis says, it proves that rock and roll is so democratic that even a rich person can make a great single. But except for the startling "Mockingbird" (buy the forty-five if you must) the album's most interesting moment occurs when Simon whistles. Need I add that her whistling is flat musically and epistemologically?   **C**

Carly Simon: *The Best of Carly Simon* (Elektra '75). Given her self-knowledge and her fans' taste (they like *her*, right?), a compilation isn't going to get her at her best, though this does collect some of her more attractive melodies. Light a fart for the two big Jacob Brackman statements: "Attitude Dancing," which means exactly what it says, and "Haven't Got Time for the Pain," which doesn't, not quite — the most insidious let's-write-God-a-love-song to date.   **C +**

Carly Simon: *Boys in the Trees* (Elektra '78). Carly generally makes marriage seem both more boring and more nasty than I've found it to be, but not on this album, where matrimony is abandoned for more adolescent subjects. Even the two please-don't-cheat-oh-hubby songs — the better (and nastier) of them written by Carly's hubby — can be interpreted by her younger fans as please-don't-cheat-oh-boyfriend. In a way, this is too bad — if Carly were to come up with an interesting song about marriage, someone less conventional musically than Carly & Arif might cover it and give Carola and me something new to sing along to. John and Yoko, where are you now that we need you? **C+**

Carly Simon: *Spy* (Elektra '79). This advocate of the fuck-around-and-fib-about-it school of post-monogamy ("Morality is what I can do and still live with myself," she revealed to her publicist recently) dedicates her latest to Anais Nin, and for once I think she's selling herself short — at her best she's sharper than Anais Nin. If she'd been able to maintain the shrewd, ironic, vengeful-to-loving-to-bemused pace of the first three songs, she might actually have made a case for her ethical theories. But after that she mostly seems confused. Anais would be proud. **B−**

Joe Simon: *Drowning in the Sea of Love* (Spring '72). Strange — Simon leaves producer-mentor John Richbourg for Gamble-Huff and all of a sudden he's taking after Jerry Butler. Also strange, especially in an Ice Man, is the way his voice begins to melt when it ventures below the timbreline — how syrupy it gets at the end of "Something You Can Do Today," for instance. Strange, but nice. Now if only Gamble-Huff would write more filler like "O'le Night Owl" to go with their two hits per album. Original grade: B plus. **B**

Joe Simon: *Joe Simon's Greatest Hits* (Sound Stage 7 '72). In his Nashville phase Simon carried on for Sam Cooke with a will. For secular gospel, the rolling "It's Hard to Get Along"; for spiritual blues, his big hit version (among blacks) of Taj Mahal's "Farther On Down the Road"; for transcendent nonsense, the high-flying "Moon Walk"; and for straight soul, his specialty, the contained drama of

"Hangin' On," the Grammy-winning "Chokin' Kind," and the current "Misty Blue." **B+**

John Simon: *John Simon's Album* (Warner Bros. '70). Somewhere beyond the plaintive quaver, rootsy supersession rock is mixed with pre-WW2 touches in a series of homely sketches — many of them about outsiders trying to make something of their lives, a theme to which a plaintive quaver is well-suited. Highlight: "The Song of the Elves," in which outsiders brag about how tall they are. **B+**

Paul Simon: *Paul Simon* (Columbia '72). I've been saying nasty things about Simon since 1967, but this is the only thing in the universe to make me positively happy in the first two weeks of February 1972. I hope Art Garfunkel is gone for good — he always seemed so vestigial, but it's obvious now that two-part harmony crippled Simon's naturally agile singing and composing. And the words! This is a professional tour of Manhattan for youth culture grads, complete with Bella Abzug, hard rain, and people who steal your chow fong. The self-production is economical and lively, with the guitars of Jerry Hahn and Stefan Grossman and Airto Moreira's percussion especially inspired. William Carlos Williams after the repression: "Peace Like a River." **A+**

Paul Simon: *There Goes Rhymin' Simon* (Columbia '73). Quite consciously — why do you think the new single is so equivocal about the phony hues Kodachrome lays on reality? — Simon sacrifices the manic-depressive range of his solo debut in search of an equivalent for S&G's all-encompassing homiletic pleasantness. The vocals are softer, smoothed over with borrowed or double-tracked harmonies, and the pep shots from more specialized styles (by the Dixie Hummingbirds, the Onward Brass Band) less speedy. The lyrics celebrate domestic satisfactions and seem to find political ambiguities more curious than ominous. None of which is bad or dishonest — it suggests a new grace and flexibility for the mass-pop mode, and invests small subjects and emotions with an almost luminous wit and awareness. But I have my doubts about Kodachrome too. **B+**

Paul Simon: *Paul Simon in Concert: Live Rhymin'* (Columbia '74). You get the Jessy Dixon Singers' rendition of "Jesus Is the Answer," you get some improvised "yes I would"'s, you get several S&G songs sans G, and you get lots of inferior remakes. Not for nothing is he a studio obsessive. **C+**

Paul Simon: *Still Crazy After All These Years* (Columbia '75). I resented the patina of cheerfulness on *There Goes Rhymin' Simon* (1973) because I thought it sold out the terse, evocative candor of *Paul Simon* (1972). Now I miss its intimations of universality. I hope in 1977 I'm not moved to praise unduly the small, self-involved ironies that define this record at its best ("50 Ways to Leave Your Lover," "You're Kind") without alleviating its lugubriousness ("Night Game," "Silent Eyes"). P.S. As you probably know, Art Garfunkel is back for one number. As you may not have noticed, Simon takes this as a cue to revert to the sophomoricism of "Richard Cory" and "The Sound of Silence" — "a finger on the trigger of a gun" indeed. **B**

Paul Simon: *Greatest Hits, Etc.* (Columbia '77). Including only two cuts from the must-own *Paul Simon* plus the live version of a third, adding two quizzical new songs, and unerringly selecting the most durable tracks from *Rhymin' Simon* and *Still Crazy* — I'd replace the overly quizzical (or else arrogantly insular) "Have a Good Time" with "Was a Sunny Day" (pure bliss plus Roches) or "You're Kind" (the fifty-first way to leave your lover), but that's a matter of personal ideology, and the omission of S&G's actually-a-hit "My Little Town" more than makes up. In short, fourteen good-to-great pop tunes for our time. **A**

Nina Simone: *Baltimore* (CTI '78). Carried along on David Matthews's uncharacteristically infectious arrangement, Simone's version of one of Randy Newman's more perfunctory American-names songs is a glorious fluke on the order of Baez's "Night They Drove Old Dixie Down." I'm glad, though, that it's available as a single, because unlike owner-annotator Creed Taylor I don't find that Simone's "magnificent intensity . . . turns everything — even the most simple, mundane phrase or lyric — into a radiant, poetic message." On the contrary, her penchant for the mundane renders her intensity as bogus as her mannered melismas and pronunciation (move over, Inspector Clouseau) and the rote flatting of her vocal improvisations. There are several good cuts here; the song selection is often inspired (Hurley-Wilkins's "The Family," perfect). But a woman who not only avoids coming out with the "bitch" in "Rich Girl" but hobbles the rhythm as well has real problems. **B−**

Valerie Simpson: *Valerie Simpson* (Tamla '72). Look what Valerie has done — discovered that Motown is only plastic. I was so happy believing it was human, or something for people to dream on. The previous two sentences recycle one of Simpson's songs, called "Genius." Genius, isn't she? No. **C−**

The Sinceros: *The Sound of Sunbathing* (Columbia '79). Wayne Robins clued me in on why I wasn't connecting with these sly, solid, snappy songs when he told me they reminded him of Freddie and the Dreamers. Right — it's Freddie evolved from teen lies to pop candor, effetely nasty rather than revoltingly cute, acknowledging his own little failings and hostilities in a mildly remorseless voice. And sly, solid, and snappy for all that. **B−**

Stephen Sinclair: *A Plus* (United Artists '77). Wrong. **D+**

Siouxsie and the Banshees: *The Scream* (Polydor '78). Hippies were rainbow extremists; punks are romantics of black-and-white. Hippies forced warmth; punks cultivate cool. Hippies kidded themselves about free love; punks pretend that s&m is our condition. As symbols of protest, swastikas are no less fatuous than flowers. So it's not surprising that Siouxsie Sioux, punk's exemplary fan-turned-artist, should prove every bit as pretentious as model-turned-rocker Grace Slick or film-student manque Jim Morrison. Nor is it surprising that while the spirit is still upon her she should come up with a tunefully atonal, modestly sensationalistic album. **B +**

Sir Douglas Quintet: *Together After Five* (Smash '70). The hallmark of Doug Sahm's warm, reliable, steady-rocking Tex-Mex is that it always sounds like you've heard it before — not the lyrics, which Doug just jotted down on some rolling papers five minutes ago, but the riffs. This can drive you crazy — "Nuevo Laredo" is "Mendocino," obviously, but where the hell does "Revolutionary Ways" come from? When the mood is right, though, it gives the music a kind of folkish inevitability that doesn't get boring because Tex-Mex is such a stew of influences. This is way too loose, and forget the slow ones, but what fun. Original grade: B. **B +**

Sir Douglas Quintet: *1 +1 +1 =4* (Philips '70). "Let's [garbled] it seriously, man, get all the notes right," Doug orders his platoon before they attack an obscure Hayes-Porter song, and you can hear them trying — throughout the album, the effort gets in the way. Except for the classic "Be Real," the most striking groove is struck by guests Wayne Talbert and Martin Fierro, who impersonate McCoy and 'Trane on the coda to "Don't Bug Me!" **B −**

Sir Douglas Quintet: *The Return of Doug Saldana* (Philips '71). What makes Doug so moving is the diffidence with which he reflects on his "mellow" (and not so mellow, unless you think drought and rail monopolies are just part of the American karma) counterculture experiences; his bohemian sketches aren't any artier than "She's About a Mover." On this album the relaxed but sloppy groove of *Together After Five* meets the attempted musicianship of *1 +1 +1 =4* as Doug rejoins his "Chicano brothers" from hometown San Antonio. The result is a blues-based synthesis that's good for a lot of relatively distinctive songs, including "Stoned Faces Don't Lie," his most memorable since "Mendocino." Original grade: B plus. **A −**

Doug Sahm and Band: *Doug Sahm and Band* (Atlantic '73). Sahm may not be the only completely unselfconscious white rock and roller of the post-Beatles era, but I dare you to name the other one, and that's why Jerry Wexler's part of his cult. But Doug's a talent, not a genius, and a country-rock/country supersession posing as a "band" is only going to inhibit him. Despite (hell, including) the new Dylan song, humdrum plus. **B −**

Doug Sahm: *Rough Edges* (Mercury '73). Look at it this way — if the Atlantic genius factory hadn't tried to transform this all-time ready-steady-go into a '70s folk hero, Mercury would never have hashed together these Quintet rejects. Apparently the potential singles were already used up — covers of Ray Sharpe's "Linda Lu" and Tom T. Hall's "The Homecoming" are the standouts. But every one is as unkempt and wonderful as the rest of Doug's Mercury stuff. And somebody (compiler Paul Nelson? remix engineer Al Vanderbilt?) has insured that the sound is uncommonly bright and strong. **B +**

The Sir Douglas Band: *Texas Tornado* (Atlantic '73). Having embraced Doug's sloppiness, do we now penalize him for getting it together? It's a shock to hear him make like a big-band singer, but on the two opening cuts (both self-composed and -produced) he sounds enough like a good one to remind me that Texas was famous for "territory bands" in the '40s. And while the Quintet-style side two is never quite inspired, it's never less than competent fun. Yeah, competent — the singing especially has the kind of force and definition he's always rendered irrelevant in the past. His old fans don't need this record. But those who've always found him ragged might just go for it.   **B+**

Doug Sahm: *Groovers Paradise* (Warner Bros. '74). In which Doug Clifford and Stu Cook, the rhythm section that supposedly held Creedence in thrall, find a master whose core simplicity is completely unassailable. Those who consider him repetitious and derivative certainly won't enjoy these foolish songs of praise to the Lone Star State, his most unambitious music since the days of *Together After Five*. But they're the fools. Original grade: A minus.   **B+**

Sir Douglas & the Texas Tornados: *Texas Rock for Country Rollers* (ABC/Dot '76). The first side is just Sahm country and though I could do without the pedal steel I like it fine — "Cowboy Peyton Place" and "Texas Ranger Man" are genre songs at their overstated best. The second side is redneck hoohah and I found it easier to take him seriously as a hippie, maybe because I'm more hippie than redneck myself — "Country Groove" and "Floatway" and of course "You Can't Hide a Redneck (Under That Hippy Hair)" sound written to order, and if they did the hustle in Austin I'm sure he'd have added one of those (which might be more fun).   **B**

Siren: *Strange Locomotion* (Dandelion/Elektra '71). Like Fleetwood Mac, this is British blues that neither chokes on false roots nor enmires itself in boogie reductionism. Kevin Coyne's humorously belligerent drawl embodies the band's wit and its punk chauvinism. Mistake: "Fetch Me My Woman," which (second mistake)

goes on for 7:40. Original grade: B.   **B+**

Sister Sledge: *We Are Family* (Cotillion '79). The disco disc features identical versions (at 8:06 and 6:04) of the two side-openers — the title track, a magnificent, soul-shouting sisterhood anthem that could set straight cheerleaders and militant lesbians dancing side by side, and "He's the Greatest Dancer," a seductive tribute to a fellow who gets to doff his designer clothes in the presence of countless panting women. (I wonder if I would have been so amused by the boy from New York City in 1965 if I'd known that in 1979 he'd be taken seriously.) All that's missing from the album is "Lost in Music," that one-in-a-hundred I-love-you-know-what song that illuminates its subject. Plus a couple of useless slow ones and some chic riffs. So the d.d. would be your buy — if you could buy it.   **B+**

Slade: *Slade Alive!* (Polydor '72). More or less the nonstop raver you'd expect, only friendlier, offering a much clearer sense of a performer relating to an audience than most concert LPs. Since I've never laid eyes on loud-man Noddy Holder, maybe it's just that I'm untrammeled by preconceptions, or maybe Holder's such a simpleton he's a cinch to suss, or maybe Holder's a genius. But most likely it's a little of all three. Surprise: the (sweet) pop of "Darling Be Home Soon" works better than the (automatic) overdrive of "Born to Be Wild." Second surprise: just before the final verse, someone approaches the microphone and delivers a very articulate belch.   **B+**

Slade: *Slayed?* (Polydor '73). These guys aren't singles specialists like Gary Glitter or (I insist) T. Rex —they deliver a whole album of boot-boy anthems that are every bit as overpowering as has been reported, and also more fun (reporters panic real easy). Noddy Holder can wake up the crazee in my neighborhood any time he wants. But that doesn't mean I'm predicting Slademania — not in a nation where Loggins & Messina are encouraged to sing about rock and roll. **A −**

Slade: *Sladest* (Reprise '73). This includes "Gudbuy t' Jane" and "Mama Weer All Crazee Now," the best cuts on *Slayed?* because it compiles the English hits of these Anglopop phenoms. I take it the reason "Gudbuy" and "Crazee" are the best cuts on *Sladest* as well is that these Anglopop phenoms turned into raving maniacs only recently. Clearly, it's what they were meant to be, and although *Slayed?* is less tuneful, I prefer it. You don't ask an air raid siren to play "Stardust," or even "Glad All Over." **B +**

Slade: *Stomp Your Hands, Clap Your Feet* (Reprise '74). If this band were an established monolith in America the way it is in England, the love ballad and the music-hall sendup might sound nimble, but as it is they sound lame. Worse, only one of the clap-stompers — the defiant "Do You Still Do It" — raises the roof. Original grade: B plus. **B**

Slave: *The Concept* (Cotillion '78). While pioneering funk groups like Funkadelic and the Commodores, manned by veteran musicians, clearly evolved out of existing black-music formats, the younger ones often resemble third-generation rock groups in concept and spirit. Unless you prefer Kansas to the J.B.'s, this is not a compliment; profound thoughts like "Now will always be forever" might well grace the back of a Starcastle album. This is a Starcastle kind of band, too, right down to its general derivativeness and pretensions to content. But it doesn't make Starcastle music. Despite moderate tempos, the first side of the band's third and best LP chugs by smartly without once pausing to pose — it's fun, and it's interesting, too. Lesson: if the play of rhythms, textures, studio tricks, and vocal techniques constitutes the real content of your music, black is as beautiful as ever. **B**

Grace Slick: *Manhole* (Grunt '74). She sounds like herself on several cuts and Bette Midler on one, but she also sounds tired, and for the most part this is as inflated as the worst Airplane. I wonder too why she participates as neither writer nor vocalist on "It's Only Music" (not that I'd want to be associated with it myself). But the title demands to be committed to print. **C**

The Slits: *Cut* (Antilles '79). For once a white reggae style that rivals its models for weirdness and formal imagination. The choppy lyrics and playful, quavering, chantlike vocals are a tribute to reggae's inspired amateurism rather than a facsimile, and the spacey rhythms and recording techniques are exploited to solve the great problem of female rock bands, which is how to make yourself heard over all that noise. Arri Up's answer is to sing around it, which is lucky, because she'd be screeching for sure on top of the usual wall of chords. Some of this is thinner and more halting than it's meant to be, but I sure hope they keep it up. **B +**

Sly & the Family Stone: *Greatest Hits* (Epic '70). As someone who was converted to Sly over the radio rather than at the Fillmore, I still have my doubts about his albums — even *Stand!* falters during "Sex Machine." But this is among the greatest rock and roll LPs of all time. The rhythms, the arrangements, the singing, the playing, the production, and — can't forget this one — the rhythms are inspirational, good-humored, and trenchant throughout, and on only one cut ("Fun") are the lyrics merely competent. Sly Stone's gift for irresistible dance songs is a matter of world acclaim, but his gift for political anthems that are uplifting but never simplistic or sentimental is a gas. And oh yeah — his rhythms are amazing. **A +**

Sly & the Family Stone: *There's a Riot Goin' On* (Epic '71). Despairing, courageous, and very hard to take, this is one of those rare albums whose whole actually does exceed the sum of its parts. Bleak yet sentient songs of experience like "Runnin' Away" and "Family Affair" lend emotional and aesthetic life to the music's dead spaces; bracing alterations of vocal register, garish stereo separations, growls and shrieks and murmurs, all the stuff that made Sly's greatest hits the toughest commercial experiments in rock and roll history, are dragged over nerve-wracking rhythms of enormous musical energy. The inspiration may be Sly's discovery that the pot of gold at the end of the rainbow doesn't mean shit, but what's expressed is the bitterest ghetto pessimism. Inspirational Verse: "TIME they say is/The answer/But I don't believe it." Original title: *Africa Talks to You*. Length of title track: 0:00. **A +**

Sly & the Family Stone: *Fresh* (Epic '73). Now that the truncated rhythms of Sly's post-dance-to-the-music have become the stomping ground of War (heavy) and Stevie Wonder (bubbling over), Sly takes the lyrics into middle-Dylan territory, exploiting his own genius for hook phrases — "in time," "thankful n' thoughtful," "babies makin' babies" — only to fasten a superabundance of elusive images to a jagged groove. Many of the songs turn in on themselves — one vaguely inspirational number ends with a derisive "cha-cha-cha" — as Sly's vocals shift in tone, texture, and volume and the extra percussion and repeating horn riffs accentuate the music's brutally staccato effect. He seems willing once more to sing of love and fun, of gratitude and the great circle of life, but he also equates his legendary tardiness with his legendary self-destructiveness and comments on his inaccessibility as decisively as is appropriate. Plus a great twist in Sly's relationship with the white power structure: a cover of "Que Sera, Sera." **A**

Sly & the Family Stone: *Small Talk* (Epic '74). Although you can hear different, you'd almost think Sly's sense of rhythm had abandoned him, because his first flop is a bellywhopper — its

scant interest verbal, its only memorable song a doowop takeoff. Back to what roots? **C**

Sly & the Family Stone: *Heard Ya Missed Me, Well I'm Back* (Epic '76). The rhythms and vocals may not be compelling, but they're certainly unpredictable. The words aren't great, but they play the margins of black music's romantic-spiritual themes with some finesse. Anyone else and we'd be waiting until he fulfilled his potential. But he already has. **B −**

Sly & the Family Stone: *Back on the Right Track* (Warner Bros. '79). This really is Sly's best since *Fresh*, but the title does give it away, because Sly isn't going to progress by trying to recapture the past. *Fresh* was a great finale because it gathered five years of energy and innovation into an almost autumnal synthesis. There are cuts here — "The Same Thing," "Shine It On" — that might fit into that synthesis. But there aren't any that could define it, much less suggest a new one. Time: 27:07. **B**

Sly & the Family Stone: See also Sly Stone

Small Faces: See Faces

Patti Smith: *Horses* (Arista '75). I don't feel much intelligent sympathy for Smith's apocalyptic romanticism. Her ideas are as irrelevant to any social apocalypse I can envision as they are to my present as a well-adjusted, well-rewarded media professional. But Smith (in this manifestation) is a musician, not a philosopher. Music is different. The fact that I'm fairly obsessive about rock and roll indicates that on some sub-intellectual level I need a little apocalypse, just to keep my superego honest. That, of course, is exactly what she's trying to tell us. However questionable her apprehension of the surreal, the way she connects it with the youth cult/rock and roll nexus is revelation enough for now. This record loses her humor, but it gets the minimalist fury of her band and the revolutionary dimension of her singing just fine, and I haven't turned off any of the long arty cuts yet. Original grade: A minus. **A**

Patti Smith Group: *Radio Ethiopia* (Arista '76). It's priggish if not stupid to complain that *Radio Ethiopia*'s "four chords are not well played." If they were executed with the precise attack of an Aerosmith, *then* they would not be well played. For although there's no such thing as an unkempt heavy metal record — technocratic assurance is the soul of such music — unkempt rock and roll records have been helping people feel alive for twenty years. When it works, which is just about everywhere but the (eleven-minute) title track, this delivers the charge of heavy metal without the depressing predictability; its riff power — and the riffs are even better than the lyrics on this rockpoet experiment — has the human elan of a band that is still learning to play. **A −**

Patti Smith Group: *Easter* (Arista '78). As basic as ever in its instrumentation and rhythmic thrust, but grander, more martial. That's what she gets for starting an army and hanging out with Bruce Springsteen (not to mention lusting after Ronnie Spector), and she could have done a lot worse: the miracle is that most of these songs are rousing in the way they're meant to be. Meanwhile, for bullshit — would it be a Patti Smith album without bullshit? — there's the stuff about "niggers" and "transformation of waste," and as if to exemplify the latter there's a great song from *Privilege,* a movie I've always considered one of the worst ever. Guess I'll have to look at it again. **A −**

Patti Smith Group: *Wave* (Arista '79). A lot of folks just don't like Patti anymore, and so have taken to complaining about the pop melodicism ("AOR sellout") and shamanistic religiosity ("pretentious phony") she's always aspired toward. Me, I wish she'd forget she was such a bigshot, and I find "Seven Ways of Going" and "Broken Flag" as unlistenable as (and less interesting than) "Radio

Ethiopia." But this is an often inspired album, quirkier than the more generally satisfying *Easter* — especially on the sexual mystery song "Dancing Barefoot," quite possibly her greatest track ever, and, yes, the reading for the dead pope that she goes out on. **B +**

Chris Smither: *Don't It Drag On* (Poppy '72). Smither writes tough-minded yet numinous post-folk songs that do justice to his adventurous taste in other people's — the covers include "Friend of the Devil," "No Expectations," and "Down in the Flood." His Vaughan-Monroe-sings-the-blues baritone is both yearning and astringent, and he sounds like he wishes he were playing bottleneck even when he isn't. A smart record. Original grade: B plus. **A −**

Snail: *Snail* (Cream '78). Just what you've always wanted — a hard rock band with a name that makes Crawler sound like REO Speedwagon. **C +**

Phoebe Snow: *Phoebe Snow* (Shelter '74). This woman's languorous, swaying folk-jazz fusion is striking enough to suggest that her debut LP will become some sort of cult item. And it's better than most cult items. But her groove does not quite carry cuts as protracted as "It Must Be Sunday." Nor is it an encouraging sign that the most commercial lyric on a verbally distinguished album, "Poetry Man," is also the most fatuous. The plus is for encouragement, and for the graceful way her voice combines nasality and smoothness. **B +**

Phoebe Snow: *Second Childhood* (Columbia '76). Although the rumors of a major new artist that began after the success of "Poetry Man" — still her sappiest song, although the lyrics here aren't what they call creative writing — originated with fuzzy-minded mongers, I'm pleased to report that her trademark melismatic quaver hasn't degenerated into a gimmick, and I acknowledge that this is a good record of its type. I just have my doubts about how good a jazz-folk mood-music record can be. Money isn't all that's "worthless/When your music's mirthless" — sometimes the music is as well. Original grade: B plus. **B**

Phoebe Snow: *It Looks Like Snow* (Columbia '76). Except for "Mercy on Those," a quite remarkably tedious profession of self-righteousness that occupies the last 6:06 of side one, Snow's gifts as a singer and lyricist are finally channeled. The silly mystical ideas are way down below her overriding good sense; up above we find a fairly strong, direct, and happy woman who is by no means vegetating in her contentment, perhaps because she's too insecure ever to become complacent. She's rocking a lot more, correct practice for a content but uncomplacent person, and when her voice wavers it no longer sounds as though it wants to disappear altogether. And the three non-originals — "Teach Me Tonight," "Don't Let Me Down," and "Shakey Ground" — make quite a combo. Original grade: A minus. **B+**

Phoebe Snow: *Never Letting Go* (Columbia '77). By now Snow projects a jazz singer's assurance, and though the originals are still overshadowed by the covers I'd like to hear Tammy Wynette try "Majesty of Life," about "what can happen to a girl in her hometown." But the tempos are invariably too reflective, and the reprises invariably too much. **B**

Phoebe Snow: *Against the Grain* (Columbia '78). With Barry Beckett coproducing she speeds things up occasionally, but if the orchestrations were his idea she lost on the deal. And this time she dies on the nonoriginals. "Do Right Woman" is redundant, "The Married Men" funked up, and Patti Austin's "In My Life" just a dull song. "He's Not Just Another Man" has always been her problem. And Paul McCartney's "Every Night" shows up the hooklessness of almost everything else. **C+**

Gino Soccio: *Outline* (Warner Bros./ RFC '79). The record of the year on the disco circuit earns its title by re-

jecting the washes of strings and brass outsiders associate with the form for a consciously minimalist exploration of mechanical dance rhythm, devoid of even the appearance of melody or meaningfulness. This is great in theory, and maybe on the circuit, but it comes out of my speakers dry and cold. **B–**

Soft Machine: *Third* (Columbia '70). Robert Wyatt's light touch imbues these pleasant experiments with their own unique pulse, but only because the music is labeled rock is it hailed as a breakthrough. It does qualify as a change of pace — on the group's last album three musicians put seventeen titles on two sides, while on this one eight musicians put four on four. But though Mike Ratledge's "Out-Bloody-Rageous," to choose the most interesting example, brings together convincing approximations of Terry Riley-style modular pianistics and John Coltrane-style modal sax (Hugh Hopper has Jimmy Garrison's bass down perfect), Riley and Coltrane do it better. Only Wyatt's "Moon in June" is eccentric by the standards of its influences — which must be why it's hard to name them all. **B**

Soft Machine: *"Fourth"* (Columbia '71). Having dropped the trance-music distensions for theme-and-variation arrangements (long on the arrangement and short on the variation though they may be), does the band still call this "rock"? It's English jazz, that's all — neither as flawed as you'd fear nor as muscular as its American counterparts. Non-composing saxophonist Elton Dean is the dominant voice, as saxophonists tend to be. He's adequate or better at free blowing, no mean accomplishment, but he's also a little thin in the embouchure, as English saxophonists tend to be. **B**

Soft Machine: *Six* (Columbia '73). Karl Jenkins, whose horns and keyboards replace Elton Dean's alto, provides the band's best track since "Moon in June": "The Soft Weed Factor," in which a tiny piano riff builds through dozens (hundreds?) of repetitions into a rocking and roiling modular extravaganza. But with Robert Wyatt gone for two albums now, most of the rest is jazz of no discernible inspiration. Mike Ratledge sounds thinner every time out — I kept wondering if I'd blown a channel. Maybe he's taking a cue from Jenkins, who makes Dean sound like Gato Barbieri when he picks up his soprano.   **B** −

Soft Machine: "7" (Columbia '74). What bothered me about Mike Ratledge' thinness on *Six* was mostly a matter of physical tone, but I had his ideas in the back of my mind as well, and here's why. At least Mike Oldfield knows how to use a studio.   **C+**

Soup: *Soup* (Soup '70). Now setting up distribution with movement movers like the White Panthers, this Appleton, Wisconsin group also sells its self-produced LP for three bucks from 4411 West Broadway, 54911. Comes in a plain brown jacket, with credits on a piece of lemon-colored paper stuck inside the shrink-wrap. The music isn't overtly political, just good, which ought to be what it comes down to: simple, plaintive, midtempo rock dominated by singer-composer-guitarist Doug Yankus. Actually, Yankus is a guitarist first — his playing dominates both the serviceable songs on one side and the blues-evolving-into-jazz jam on the other, and it sure beats Richie Furay or Carmine Appice. Makes you wonder just how efficient corporate capital is, doesn't it?   **B**

The Souther, Hillman, Furay Band: *The Souther, Hillman, Furay Band* (Asylum '74). Complaining, complaining — when you're not lying, you're complaining.   **C+**

Souther-Hillman-Furay Band: *Trouble in Paradise* (Asylum '75). Country-rock apercu of the month: this band usually goes by its initials because they stand for Shit Hits the Fan. Or do I mean Fans?   **C−**

Southwind: *Ready to Ride* (Blue Thumb '70). I welcomed this group just because it existed — there ought to be a hundred warm, competent, eclectic bands putting ten rock and roll songs on albums, but there probably aren't more than twenty. Later, however, I re-examined the warm, competent songs in question and noticed that the two good ones were by Johnny Cash and Hank Williams. So say eclecticism with certain, er, tendencies, and rest assured that not a one of the guys plays pedal steel. Original grade: B.   **C**

Sparks: *Propaganda* (Island '75). Admirers of these self-made twerps certainly don't refer to them as pop because they get on the AM — for once the programmers are doing their job. So is it because they sing in a high register? Or because a good beat makes them even more uncomfortable than other accoutrements of a well-lived life? "Never turn your back on mother earth," they chant or gibber in a style unnatural enough to end your current relationship or kill your cacti, and I must be a natural man after all, because I can't endure the contradiction. Original grade: D plus.   **C−**

Sparks: *Introducing Sparks* (Columbia '77). On its five albums for Bearsville and Island, this skillful brother act compounded personal hatefulness with a deliberately tense and uninviting take on pop-rock. But with their Columbia debut, *Big Beat*, they began to loosen up, and here one cut actually makes surf music history, in the tending-to-hyperconsciousness section. This is tuneful, funny, even open. But the fear of women and the stubborn, spoiled-teenager cynicism is still there, and it's still hateful.   **B**

Sparks: *No. 1 in Heaven* (Elektra '79). Anglophilia's favorite androids were destined from day of manufacture to meet up with some rock technocrat or other, so thank Ford it was Giorgio Moroder, the most playful of the breed. They even got a minor dance hit out of it — "Beat the Clock," a good one — but that's not the point. The point is channeling all their evil genius — well, evil talent then — into magic tricks. Like the ultimate voice-box song. Or the title tune, which sounds like "Baba O'Riley" and then breaks down into Eno (or is that Gentle Giant?). Fun fun fun. **B+**

Spinners: *Spinners* (Atlantic '73). Five hits make this soul album of the year, though it took me quite a while to get past Thom Bell's need to make everything smooth as a silk suit (never bothered me with the Stylistics because they were out-and-out silly, like a silk cardigan) and the lyrics' tendency to go nowhere after the hook (two by Yvette Davis are all but incoherent). In the end, it gets over on sheer melodic appeal and vocal beauty. Oddity: an exuberant big-band version of "Don't Let the Green Grass Fool You." Original grade: B. **A−**

Spinners: *The Best of the Spinners* (Motown '73). "It's a Shame" was their big hit — for Motown, I mean. The date was 1970. Their only other chart record for the label was five years before that and didn't go pop for the best of reasons — quality. **C+**

Spinners: *Mighty Love* (Atlantic '74). If like me you're more taken with "I'm Coming Home" than you ever were with "I'll Be Around," then like me you're not a Thom Bell fan or maybe even a Spinners fan. You're a fan of the Spinners' first tenor, Felipe Wind (sp?), whose vocal improvisations, as free as Al Green's though in more of a jazz scat mode, play against the Spinners' disciplined harmonies in a virtuoso demonstration of the limits of slick. Original grade: B. **B+**

Spinners: *New and Improved* (Atlantic '74). The slow side is Dionne Warwicke in flight plus filler. The fast side is Phillipe Wynne (sp?) in flight plus good filler (good 'cause he keeps flying). The prizes are "Sadie," a mom song that should have broken pop, and "Then Came You," a love song that did. **B**

Spinners: *Pick of the Litter* (Atlantic '75). It isn't the production that puts the slow ones over, it's the Spinners proving themselves more than aides to Philippe Soul Wynn (sp?). Henry Fambrough's rich, creamy, ever-so-slightly burred tenor makes his two ballads glow. Bobbie Smith's more tightly focused timbre intensifies "You Made a Promise to Me." And Philippe's clipped, rapid-fire improvisations ride "Honest I Do" and "All That Glitters" straight into the sunset. Original grade: B. **A−**

Spinners: *Spinners Live!* (Atlantic '75). A renowned show group whose supersmooth producer inhibits improvisation would seem like a good bet for a live double. But this one opens with "Fascinating Rhythm" and includes impressions of the Supremes, Tom Jones, and Louis Armstrong. It divides the pre-climactic "Love Don't Love Nobody" between two sides and mixes the horns and strings so high you long for supersmoothing. And it doesn't let you see their feet during "Mighty Love." **B−**

Spinners: *Happiness Is Being with the Spinners* (Atlantic '76). The physical pleasure — not quite luxurious, but much more than comfortable — of hearing these five men join their voices in song is undiminished, and the complete, seven-minute "Rubberband Man" is Phil (sp?) at his most expansive. But when I try to recall the tunes here I end up humming their kinfolk from other albums. **B−**

Spinners: *Yesterday, Today and Tomorrow* (Atlantic '77). The first side would be their most featureless since they joined Thom Bell if it weren't for the asinine "Me and My Music," which I regret to report is catchy enough for a single. But the second is their most listenable since *Pick of the Litter*. Philippe Wynn (oh, the hell with it) walks away with an eight-minute fast one on top of an eight-minute slow one, but it's a disco-flavored showpiece, produced by Thom's brother Tony and featuring ringer singer John Edwards, that gets things going. Purists fear the worst from Tony's groove, and they may be right, but "Honey, I'm in Love with You" ain't it. Edwards sounds a little like Al Green, which of course has nothing to do with my enthusiasm. **B**

Spinners: *Spinners/8* (Atlantic '77). John Edwards makes quite a different impression when he replaces Philippe Solo Wynn (sp?) instead of supplementing him — his style is so mellifluous it melts right into Thom Bell's (Tony Bell's, too). In fact, without Philippe's excesses the essential blandness of the whole concept squooshes down on their collective head. I'm all for responsible love, believe me — the trick is to keep it interesting. **C+**

Spinners: *The Best of Spinners* (Atlantic '78). Good stuff — how could it not be? And hurray for "Sadie," which never crossed over. But they should have included "I'm Coming Home" and the album-length "Rubberband Man," thus giving the departed Phylyppe Win (sp?) his propers. And AM radio being what it is, the ballads are all medium-tempo, not Henry Fambrough's natural speed — he likes to mull things over. **A−**

Spinners: *Dancin' and Lovin'* (Atlantic '79). New producer Michael Zager must think three out of six ain't bad. There's the Frankie Valli one-up, the disco double-entendre, and the P-Funk clone. But what happened to the Spinners? **B−**

Spinners: *From Here to Eternally* (Atlantic '79). Signs of hope here —a Stevie Wonder tribute that's almost as loving as Melissa Manchester's, good dance tune, good pop tune, and the wonderful John Edwards soul scat on the chorus and coda of "Are You Ready for Love." But the lyrics are banal at best and the melodies often annoying — both typified, wouldn't you know, by the verse of "Are You Ready for Love." **B−**

Spirit: *The Twelve Dreams of Dr. Sardonicus* (Epic '70). Both Randy California and the band have their own cool, rich, jazzy style — a genuine achievement, but that doesn't mean you have to like it. They play better than they write, and since they still

play songs, that's a problem. A worse problem is that the lyrics are rarely as cerebral as the music. "Nature's Way," for instance, sounds as if it ought to be sardonicus, but though I'm intrigued by the suggestion that it's about death I still think it's a slightly inarticulate ecology song. Could be covered by Peter, Paul & Mary —who also have their own style. **B**

Spirit: *Feedback* (Epic '72). In a way, Al Staehely's earthy rock and roll is a relief from the California spaces of what were supposedly this band's great days — songs as hard as his fast ones aren't easy to come by these days. Unfortunately, he sounds like the kind of guy who's more likely to think of his dick than his music when you tell him he's hard. Wonder how fast he is. **B−**

Spirit: *The Best of Spirit* (Epic '73). The notes identify them as "pioneers" of "topical lyrics that were realized by the production of the song," which makes me think again about the way the first two cuts, "1984" and "Mechanical World," shift texture and tempo. By the stars, I do believe these fellows helped invent art-rock. This is not an unmixed distinction, but it could be worse: the topicality is a notch above ordinary rock sci-fi (they have a sense of humor), the derivations more jazz than classical. The big plus here, though, is that great shining 2:39 of hard rock guitar, Randy California's "I Got a Line on You." **B+**

Spooky Tooth Featuring Mike Harrison: *The Last Puff* (A&M '70). The Beatles cover is "I Am the Walrus," no doubt cos Harrison is so heavy. Well, I don't want him. With Chris Stainton playing piano and coproducing you'd figure he'd at least essay a decent Joe Cocker imitation, especially since Joe loaned him a song. Right. **C+**

Spooky Tooth: *Tobacco Road* (A&M '71). Released as *It's All About* in England in 1968, before anybody had figured out how to really exploit all these iron zeppelins and lead butterflies, this offers Beatles harmonies, a roundabout song that preceded Yes's, and a straight remake of "The Weight" in addition to the hilariously melosoulful John D. Loudermilk cover that provides its U.S. title. Ahh, the good old days. **B –**

Spooky Tooth: *You Broke My Heart So I Busted Your Jaw* (A&M '73). The title is heavy-metal logic, illustrated with a Klaus Voorman cartoon depicting a henpecking dominatrix. The songs, mostly by returned prodigal Gary Wright, depict the perils of egotism. The connection is more heavy-metal logic. **C**

Spring: *Spring* (United Artists '72). In which Brian Wilson produces his old female backup group — the Honeys, featuring his wife Marilyn — in what sounds like the best and is certainly the most charming Beach Boys album since *Sunflower*. The old combination of ingenuousness and sophistication works as well as ever, only this time the vocals rather than the lyrics are naive — direct, pretty, effortless, thoughtless. And Wilson's studio work is as precise and humorous as ever. **B +**

Dusty Springfield: *A Brand New Me* (Atlantic '70). Kenny Gamble and Leon Huff have bestowed upon Dusty — who as a singer of contemporary pop has only one peer, Dionne Warwick — the same cool-soul formula that's worked so successfully for Jerry Butler, but here it's wearing thin. The songs (every one written in part by Gamble) echo each other melodically and rhythmically, the instrumentation never varies, and neither does the vocal mood. If only Dusty could bring all her moods together — starting with her harder-driving stuff and working through the title cut here — she'd make a greater album than *Dusty in Memphis*. But that's a lot to ask. Time: 25:32. **B –**

Dusty Springfield: *Cameo* (ABC '73). Offensive as I find the notion of a "girl singer" in this year of our enlightenment, something about this thirty-four-year-old woman demands the term, because her genius is to make me believe, down beneath my rational self, that she needs me. Simultaneously gushy and ladylike, she sings like the beautiful maidservant of men's vainest and most shameful fantasies — always the supplicant, always in love. Yet at the same time she manages to elicit sisterly sympathy from other women. Lambert and Potter have mixed the orchestra way too high on this record, but for these guys, who usually write banal melodies that stick so stubbornly you hate them for it, the tunes are complex and likable. Maybe that's because L&P adjusted them for a tough human being who convinced them mid-session that she wasn't just some backup chick doing a solo spot. Recommended: "Of All the Things," "The Other Side of Life." **B**

Dusty Springfield: *It Begins Again* (United Artists '78). Roy Thomas Baker has encouraged Dusty's breathiness and then had the good manners not to suffocate it in the orchestral mix, and I'm grateful; I could listen to her sing tracking charts when she exhales that way. But the sad truth is that Baker has given her only a couple of strong ballads, the fluky treasures from Chi Coltrane and Barry Manilow that open each side, and so the fast numbers, never her forte, sound like filler. Next time, Baker should look beyond the pop pros for material like, say, "Small Town Talk," "Makin' Love Don't Always Make Love Grow," "I Can't Stand the Rain." And he should make sure there's a next time. **B**

Dusty Springfield: *Living Without Your Love* (United Artists '78). Fledgling producer David Wolfert doesn't get her voice as subtly as Roy Thomas Baker (or Jerry Wexler) did, but he gives her more good songs than she's had in a decade. Also more good sides: one, featuring a "You've Really Got a Hold on Me" that vies with Smokey's, and "Closet Man," which is about what it sounds like and nice indeed. **B +**

Rick Springfield: *Beginnings* (Capitol '72). Would you believe second-generation Emitt Rhodes? Well, this is an exemplary singles album — gimmicky, banal, full of filler, and filled out with a few more catchy little numbers to go with "Speak to the Sky." Recommended follow-ups: "Hooky Jo" to keep on rock-rock-rocking, "If I Didn't Mean to Love You" for a future in Vegas balladeering.   **C+**

Bruce Springsteen: *Greetings from Asbury Park, N.J.* (Columbia '73). "The Angel" and "Mary Queen of Arkansas" are turgid unaccompanied-acoustic horrors that could scare anybody off this particular Dylan hype. But the jokey lingo and absurdist energy of everything else are exactly the excesses that made Dylan a genius instead of a talent — it takes real conviction to save "But did not heed my urgency" with "Your life was one long emergency." Even urban-mythos rambles like "Lost in the Flood" are not without charm. And in songs like "Growin' Up" and "Blinded by the Light" there's an unguarded teen-underclass poetry that has Springsteen's name on it. Original grade: B.   **B+**

Bruce Springsteen: *The Wild, the Innocent, and the E Street Shuffle* (Columbia '73). Folkie trappings behind him, Springsteen has created a funky, vivacious rock and roll that's too eager and zany ever to be labeled tight, suggesting jazz heard through an open window with one r&b saxophone, or Latin music out in the street with zero conga drums. He celebrates youth in all its irresponsible compassion and doomed arrogance, but he's also old enough to know better — for him, the pleasures of the city are bigger and more exquisite than the defiance and escape that define most hard rock. "New York City Serenade" is as bathetic as you might fear, but "Rosalita" is more lyrical and ironic than you could have dreamed. This guy may not be God yet, but he has his sleeveless undershirt in the ring. Original grade: B plus   **A−**

Bruce Springsteen: *Born to Run* (Columbia '75). Just how much American myth can be crammed into one song, or a dozen, about asking your girl to come take a ride? A lot, but not as much as romanticists of the doomed outsider believe. Springsteen needs to learn that operettic pomposity insults the Ronettes and that pseudotragic beautiful-loser fatalism insults us all. And around now I'd better add that the man avoids these quibbles at his best and simply runs them over the rest of the time. If "She's the One" fails the memory of Phil Spector's innocent grandeur, well, the title cut is the fulfillment of everything "Be My Baby" was about and lots more. Springsteen may well turn out to be one of those rare self-conscious primitives who gets away with it. In closing, two comments from my friends the Marcuses. Jenny: "Who does he think he is, Howard Keel?" (That's a put-down.) Greil: "That is as good as 'I Think We're Alone Now.'" (That's not.)   **A**

Bruce Springsteen: *Darkness on the Edge of Town* (Columbia '78). "Promised Land," "Badlands," and "Adam Raised a Cain" are models of how an unsophisticated genre can illuminate a mature, full-bodied philosophical insight. Lyrically and vocally, they move from casual to incantatory modes with breathtaking subtlety, jolting ordinary details into meaning. But many of the other songs remain local-color pieces, and at least two — "Something in the Night" and "Streets of Fire" — are overwrought, soggy, all but unlistenable. An important minor artist or a rather flawed and inconsistent major one. Original grade: A minus.   **B+**

U.K. Squeeze: *U.K. Squeeze* (A&M '78). Musically, the instrumental is the only boring cut on the whole first side, but the record as a whole is a case study in excitingly adequate hard rock craftsmanship spoiled by trashy literature. When a band obviously influenced by *Queen*, *Rock Scene*, muscle mags, and boarding-school porn finishes off by advising their postpunk admirers to "get smart," it sounds like they want 'em to stop reading *Hustler* and start reading *Oui*. **B**

Squeeze: *Cool for Cats* (A&M '79). Power poppers (remember them?) suck this stuff up, and I understand why — not only does its songcraft surpass that of the band's debut, but it also isn't quite as sophomoric. It's sophomoric enough, though, and like so many such records makes you wonder where the power is. Not in the vision, that's for sure. And not in the beat. Great song: "Up the Junction." **B**

Stackridge: *Pinafore Days* (Sire '74). Much admired by 10cc fans, buttered scone addicts, and Sgt. Pepper's orderlies, this George Martin-produced studio artifact is notable mostly for the high quality of its in-jokes ("Los Paragayos" and "Don Juan with a shakey hand" in the same song!). It's not mean-spirited — I much prefer Stackridge's satiric tone to 10cc's — but it's so precious it's not funny either. Does it rock? Are you kidding? **C+**

Jim Stafford: *Jim Stafford* (MGM '74). This post-booze cousin of Roger Miller and Jerry Reed gave us two for the price of one with "Spiders and Snakes," a genuinely amusing novelty single about teenage sex. My only objection to his genuinely amusing novelty album is that "Mr. Bojangles" comes between "I Ain't Sharin' Sharon" and "Wildwood Weed." **B+**

Stairsteps: *Stairsteps* (Buddah '70). What's happening to traditional family values in this mixed-up world of ours? They cop the guitar lick from "Hey Jude," they cover "Dear Prudence," they cover "Getting Better" note for note and beat for beat, they drop the "The 5" from their name, they drop Cubie, and they buy Clarence an eyepatch. O-o-h child indeed. **C+**

The Staple Singers: *The Staple Swingers* (Stax '71). Don't be put off by the title. The Staples haven't been a gospel group for years, and now that they're admitting it they can build a credible pop-soul sound on their two extraordinary assets — Mavis's urgent voice and Pop's laggard lick. This has its clumsy moments, but it also has its transcendent one: "Heavy Makes You Happy," a hit single from the same pen that gave us "Sugar Sugar." And Smokey Robinson provides moral suasion. Original grade: B plus **B**

The Staple Singers: *Be Altitude: Respect Yourself* (Stax '72). Musically, this is a triumph of the Staples' evolving pop style. The arrangements fit, and Roebuck and Mavis have never sounded more at home. But despite "I'll Take You There," a lot of the material is as silly as the contorted title pun. Even "Respect Yourself," you will recall, has that line about stopping pollution by coughing into your hand. **B−**

Staple Singers: *Be What You Are* (Stax '73). This is a pleasing, consistent album — no gaffes. But no gifts either, unless you count Bettye Crutcher's apparently literal "Drown Yourself," which provides relief from a charity that's all too unremitting. In truth, the music sometimes seems a little unremitting too — bet I'd like both hit songs just as much if they didn't clock in at 5:01 and 4:27 on LP. **B**

Staple Singers: *City in the Sky* (Stax '74). For no discernible reason — when last seen (on Broadway), they appeared ready to settle for Winnemucca if Vegas didn't call — this is their toughest and best Stax LP. Once again the prime virtue is consistency, but this time they add a few lumens to the average brightness of each performance. And though their social vision may be vague, at least they were political before it was commercial, which gives them an edge. Best cut: "My Main Man," about Jesus. Worst cut: "There Is a God," an attempted a posteriori proof based on the fact that it's not raining. Original grade: B. **B+**

Staple Singers: *The Best of the Staple Singers* (Stax '75). For most of this decade, Roebuck Staples — born December 12, 1915, about two weeks after Frank Sinatra — has been the oldest performer with direct access to the hit parade by some twenty-five years, so here's your chance to mind your elders. It's Mavis's lowdown, occasionally undefined growl that dominates, of course; you should hear how secular she gets with an O. V. Wright blues that got buried on *The Staple Swingers*. But Pops's unassuming moralism sets the tone and his guitar assures the flow.   **A —**

The Staple Singers: *Let's Do It Again* (Curtom '75). If you want to buy an album just to own Mavis gasping like she does on the radio, it's your money. Be hereby informed, however, that the forty-five version is eighty-four ugly seconds skinnier than the thirty-three. Other statistics: producer Curtis Mayfield included a total of about ten minutes of instrumentals on the classic *Super Fly* and *Claudine* soundtracks. This forty-minute (eight-cut) job includes only two real songs plus a lot of doo-doo-doo, and the orchestrations — by Richard Tufo (responsible for the waste cut on *Claudine*) and Gil Askey rather than Johnny Pate (who did *Super Fly*) — are mush.   **D**

The Staples: *Unlock Your Mind* (Warner Bros. '78). For producer Jerry Wexler, this was obviously a labor of love. For the Staples likewise. Respects itself, you might say. But whether the problem is the songs or the way Mavis relates to them, only one cut, "Handwriting on the Wall," would stand tall on their Stax best-of.   **B**

Starcastle: *Real to Reel* (Epic '78). Given the fluttering keyboards, weedy vocals, and fantasy-fiction medievalism favored by these Midwestern up-and-comers, you'd figure this was just round four of dips to disc, but it's worse than that. That title means something; in the great tradition of heartland eclecticism (or is it rootlessness?) (not exploitation, surely?) they're adding power-rock and pop-melody moves to the art-rock casserole. With hooks, yet. Lord save us.   **C**

Edwin Starr: *Involved* (Gordy '71). Starr is more naturally strident than any of the Temptations, which suits both "War," a song he simply takes away from them, and "Stop the War," Barrett Strong's most strident protest yet. But he can also bring off the peaceful denouements Motown-political requires: Smokey's "Way Over There" changes the pace, and then "My Sweet Lord" helps you forgive "Stand!" Although he wastes twelve minutes on "Ball of Confusion," this is Norman Whitfield's peak production.   **B +**

Edwin Starr: *Clean* (20th Century-Fox '78). Disco! Where do its hits go? Absolutely nowhere! But they do give deserving old soul singers another moment, now don't they?   **B —**

Ringo Starr: *Sentimental Journey* (Apple '70). For over-fifties and Ringomaniacs: the reports that he did this collection of standards for his Mums are obviously true.   **C —**

Ringo Starr: *Beaucoups of Blues* (Apple '70). Finally he gets to impersonate Buck Owens for an entire record. I admit that over the distance he doesn't merely sing flat — sometimes the voice threatens to fade away altogether. But both the songs and Pete Drake's production bespeak a high-quality obsession — the music sticks. And Ringo is still Ringo, which means he's good at making himself felt.   **B**

Ringo Starr: *Ringo* (Apple '73). This is not a Beatles album but a Ringo album — a likable curiosity. Ringo's droll sincerity was always good for a change of pace; his songs were wonderful in context. Here that context is provided by an occasional harmony (especially John's on "I'm the Greatest") that makes me long for much, much more. It might be different if the songs were all as good as "Photograph," but without a real singer to work with, Richard Perry cannot transmute questionable material into magic.

And don't kid yourself — the Beatles could. **B−**

Ringo Starr: *Goodnight Vienna* (Apple '74). The title tune is great Ringo, as is "No No Song," and he does well enough with the rest of this well-chosen material, the exceptions being the three tunes he had a hand in writing himself. But the supersession form is deadening. *Beaucoups of Blues* took some initiative. **B−**

Ringo Starr: *Blast from Your Past* (Capitol '75). Though I wish John Lennon's "Goodnight Vienna" replaced "I'm the Greatest," Lennon's misbegotten attempt at a mock theme song for Ringo, basically this compilation is what might happen if you or I — or any innately unpretentious person with strong tastes in rock and roll and lots of smart pros helping out — were to spend five years putting together an album, with the false starts eliminated. It could only happen to an ex-Beatle, of course, but what the hell — it does include his great debut B side, "Early 1970," which could only have occurred to a passionate Beatle fan. **B+**

Ringo Starr: *Ringo's Rotogravure* (Atlantic '76). This fellow definitely sounds like he could use a band. You think Leon Russell might drum one up? **C**

Ringo Starr: *Ringo the 4th* (Atlantic '77). Less than three months after its release, the Ringo fan in me dutifully played this for a third and last time. Whereupon the journalist began to wonder how many people were buying such dreary music just because it was by a Beatle. And was both saddened and pleased to learn that the answer, for all practical purposes, was no one — it never got higher than 199 in *Record World*, which I'll bet was some statistician paying his respects. **D**

Status Quo: *Piledriver* (A&M '73). No more plasticene pictures for these lads — it's boogie all the way, and if only they'd go with stuff like "Don't Waste My Time" and "Big Fat Mama" for an entire side I might even wish 'em goodspeed. But of course they can't, they know boogie gets boring after a while, and so without a singer or an axeman or fancy chords they try a couple of ballads and a blues, which are also boring. **C+**

Status Quo: *Rockin' All Over the World* (Capitol '78). In which Europe's premier boogie band remembers its commercial beginnings in pop psychedelica. You've heard the riffs these twelve simple rockers are based on before, and you're almost certain to enjoy hearing them again — both the filtered ensemble vocals and the limited solo space distance and depersonalize each cut into an artifact of ass-shake. Good old rock and roll in yet another award-winning costume. **B+**

Stealers Wheel: *Stealers Wheel* (A&M '72). Skeptics said: "Producers' group." I disagreed, because Leiber & Stoller have done nothing but sit on their genius for almost a decade, and because half of this duo had a promising pre-history as half of the eccentric English-folk-rockish Humblebums. Anyway, almost every song on the album sounded substantial — until I really listened, whereupon most of them sounded, well, let's say thoughtful. Conclusion: at the very least, the kind of group producers like. **B**

Stealers Wheel: *Ferguslie Park* (A&M '73). What a clever notion, or should I say concept — a whole album about the vicissitudes of rock groupdom. On the evidence, however, Egan & Rafferty don't know much more about that than anyone else, especially the rock part. If only they'd had the guts to transform their meager experiences into an album that explored male friendship, instead of flirting with it the way this one does, there might be real reason to listen. Original grade: B minus. **C+**

Jan Steele/John Cage: *Voices and Instruments* (Antilles '77). Produced by Brian Eno for his own Obscure label, this hath charms to soothe the aging punk. It's rock only by association —

Steele is aided by a "very quiet, repetitive" rock-improvisation ensemble called F & W Hat, while Cage makes use of the voice of the pataphysical Robert Wyatt. But if the idea of devotional music for secular people appeals to you, and if you find ECM "jazz" impressionistic and unstructured, keep your ear out for this. Original grade: A minus. **B+**

Steel Pulse: *Handsworth Revolution* (Mango '78). A promising debut from the first (black) English reggae group, and I bet there'll be others. The ideology is Rastafarian, but its mood is less steamy — as cool-headed as herb permits, and righteously angry. Now let's hope the music, which is distinctive but not all the way there yet, catches up with the words. **B**

Steel Pulse: *Tribute to the Martyrs* (Mango '79). I can't tell whether the relatively clearheaded politics of these English Jamaicans detract from their ejaculatory, off-center music or make it sound more avant-garde than it is. Both, probably. If their Steve Biko song isn't as affecting as Tom Paxton's, their George Jackson song beats Dylan's, and I can't imagine anyone else, not even Tom Robinson, making a hook out of "rock against racism." One of their secrets, as you might have guessed, is a terrific beat. Another is forthright singing of a sort that — and now I'm guessing — can only grow out of unshakable conviction. **A−**

Steely Dan: *Can't Buy a Thrill* (ABC '72). How about that — a good album with two hit singles attached. And as you might expect of New York natives who reside in the City of the Angels, both brim with ambivalence: "Do It Again," a catchy modified mambo with homogenized vocals that divert one's attention from its tragic tale of a loser so compulsive he can't get himself hanged, and "Reelin' in the Years," a hate song to a professed genius. Think of the Dan as the first post-boogie band: the beat swings more

than it blasts or blisters, the chord changes defy our primitive subconscious expectations, and the lyrics underline their own difficulty — as well as the difficulty of the reality to which they refer — with arbitrary personal allusions, most of which are ruses. Original grade: B plus. **A**

Steely Dan: *Countdown to Ecstasy* (ABC '73). With the replacement of lead singer David Palmer (who fit in like a cheerleader at a crap game) by composer-pianist-conversationalist Donald Fagen (who looks like he just got dressed to go out for the paper) they achieve a deceptively agreeable studio slickness — perfect licks that crackle and buzz when you listen hard, Grass Roots harmonies applied to words that are usually twisted. Not only does "Bodhisattva" come on like a jazzed-up "Rock Around the Clock" — it shines like China and sparkles like Japan. But somehow I don't think Fagen really intends to hold hands with an Enlightened One, not even out of base curiosity. Original grade: A minus. **A**

Steely Dan: *Pretzel Logic* (ABC '74). This album sums up their chewy perversity as aptly as its title — all I could ask is a lyric sheet. "Rikki Don't Lose That Number" blends into AM radio with an intro appropriated from Horace Silver, while the other side-opener builds a joyous melody of Bird riffs underneath a lyric that invites one and all to "take a piece of Mr. Parker's band." The solos are functional rather than personal or expressive, locked into the workings of the music. And even when Donald Fagen's voice dominates as it comes out of the speakers it tends to sink into the mix in the mind's ear — recollected in tranquility, the vocals seem like the golden mean of pop ensemble singing, stripped of histrionics and displays of technique, almost . . . sincere, modest. Yeah sure. Original grade: A minus. **A+**

Steely Dan: *Katy Lied* (ABC '75). Opening with an economic crash and closing with a smacked-out rumination about succor, betrayal, and Vietnam, the first side seems surprisingly sweet and lyrical — mostly by way of the Manhattan nostalgia of "Bad Sneakers" and the faithless passion of "Rose Darling," but also, and most tellingly, in the rumination. This is a matter of rhythm and timbre rather than verbal content — the music lets us know that their cynicism is no more a celebration of cynicism than their smack references are a celebration of smack, lets us know we can break the habit. By comparison the three skillful urban miniatures on side two seem thin and tight, never quite brought around by the more expansive emotions of "Your Gold Teeth II" (throw them out and see how they roll) and "Any World (That I'm Welcome To)" ("Is better than the one I come from"). **A−**

Steely Dan: *The Royal Scam* (ABC '76). The first question is whether the melodic retreat represents a refusal to indulge the audience or a withering of invention. The second is whether the conscious choice of a jagged, pinched music is a wise one. As if in compensation, the lyrics are less involuted and personal, but in fact their objectivity intensifies Steely Dan's natural nastiness. Whether this narrowing of spiritual possibilities is willed or a symptom of the same chronic insularity that makes Fagen and Becker unwilling to tour, the result sounds a trifle arty and a trifle producty at the same time. Does it matter whether they call San Juan "the city of St. John" in reference to the apocalypse or because it scans nice? Original grade: B plus. **B**

Steely Dan: *Aja* (ABC '77). Carola suggests that by now they realize they'll never get out of El Lay, so they've elected to sing in their chains like the seà. After all, to a certain kind of reclusive aesthete, well-crafted West Coast studio jazz is as beautiful as anything else, right? Only I'm no recluse. I hated this record for quite a while before I realized that, unlike *The Royal Scam*, it was stretching me some; I still find the solo licks of Larry Carlton, Victor Feldman, et al. too fucking tasty, but at least in this con-

text they mean something. I'm also grateful to find Fagen and Becker's collegiate cynicism in decline; not only is "Deacon Blues" one of their strongest songs ever, it's also one of their warmest. Now if only they'd rhymed "I cried when I wrote this song" with "Sue me if I play it wrong," instead of "Sue me if I play too long." Preferring long to wrong could turn into their fatal flaw. **B+**

Steely Dan: *Greatest Hits* (ABC '78). This picks what's worth picking off *The Royal Scam,* adds the negligible "Here in the Western World" to their output, and leaves "FM" on *FM,* which I consider parsimonious. Essential music in a superfluous configuration. **B−**

Steppenwolf: *Steppenwolf 7* (Dunhill '70). Laying back hasn't been good for them, and neither has getting heavy. Their way lies somewhere in between — which come to think of it is also how it is for the rest of us. **C−**

Steppenwolf: *For Ladies Only* (Dunhill '71). These fellows certainly have lost their hip aura, and their bid for the feminist vote here is likely to be undercut by, let's see, titles like "Jaded Strumpet" (not to mention "For Ladies Only"), the customized Penismobile in the gatefold, and the vagina dentata — denture atop shapely gams — from which the band recoils on the enclosed poster. Too bad, since the title tune does lay out rock and roll misogyny with the kind of dumb, well-meaning insight I've always liked in John Kay. Wish he had come up with a few more dumb, well-crafted hooks as well. **C+**

Steppenwolf: *Sixteen Great Performances* (ABC '75). Comprising the same material as *Sixteen Greatest Hits* (1973), which added two cuts to the first side and three to the second of *Steppenwolf Gold* (1971), this doesn't concentrate unduly on *Steppenwolf* (1968) and/or *Steppenwolf the Second* (1968), and will probably placate the leather-clad young man whose chopper you were just so importunate as to collide with. But for yourself stick to *Steppenwolf* and *Steppenwolf the Second,* from back when Gabriel Mekler could still force John Kay to come on like a hard-rock monster.   **C+**

Steppin' Out: *Disco's Greatest Hits* (Polydor '78). Compiled by Vince Aletti and Ritchie Rivera, this deejay-blended disco-mix double-LP surpasses even such compilations as Casablanca's eclectic *Get Down and Boogie* and Marlin's funky *Disco Party.* Although local talent (Joe Simon, the Fatback Band) is represented, I find the spacey, lush-but-cool Eurodisco that predominates even more enticing, no doubt because the filler in which such music is usually swamped has been eliminated. New discoveries include the Chakachas' legendary "Jungle Fever" and "Running Away" by Roy Ayers, ordinarily the emptiest of "jazz" pianists. This is disco the way it should be heard — as pure dance music, complete with risky changes.   **A−**

Cat Stevens: *Mona Bone Jakon* (A&M '70). As an admirer of "Matthew and Son" and "I Love My Dog," two rock songs we should have heard more of in 1967, I made Cat my token singer-songwriter when this came out — the melodies were memorable, the dry intimacy of the singing had a nice post-creative-trauma feel, and I liked "Katmandu," which was about the physical (rather than spiritual) geography of a religious quest. Only later did I notice "Lady D'Arbanville" (his girlfriend), "Trouble" (too much for him), and "I Wish, I Wish" (a map of his soul). Original grade: B plus.   **B−**

Cat Stevens: *Tea for the Tillerman* (A&M '71). My big problems with this record are no doubt why it's a hit: the artificially ripened singing, which goes down like a store-bought banana daiquiri, and the insufferable sexist condescension of "Wild World." **B−**

Cat Stevens: *Catch Bull at Four* (A&M '72). Reading the lyric of "The Boy with the Moon and Star on His Head," I was impressed by how unpretentiously it simulated early English poetry. But when I listened — a widely recommended method for the perception of songs — I noticed affectations like "the naked earth beneath us and the universe above," and winced at the next-to-last couplet, which ends with a weak word for the sake of a weak rhyme. Then I browsed in Norman Ault's anthology of Elizabethan lyrics. Forget it, Cat.   **C**

Cat Stevens: *Buddha and the Chocolate Box* (A&M '74). The difference between an album you love and an album you hate is often one or two cuts. An inspired song that fulfills a fantasy you never knew you had can make you believe in a whole side, while a song that commits some deadly sin can drag innocents to perdition. In "Music," for example, Cat tells us there wouldn't be any "wars in the world/If everybody joined in the band." This kind of lie is called a tautology; it's like saying there wouldn't be any hunger if everyone became an ice cream man. And makes you wonder why a guy who loves trees so much (reference: "King of Trees") designed a double-fold cover with cardboard inner sleeve for this unlovable single LP.   **C−**

Cat Stevens: *Greatest Hits* (A&M '75). Stevens has more spunk and verve than any other singer-songwriter I dislike. He's unpretentious yet harmonically idiosyncratic, with nice dissonances and a rocking chunka beat. He can be charming about things that really are nice, like dawn, and a few of the many songs he has written about his own confusion have a winning je-ne-sais-quoi. Unfortunately for such a confused person, though, most things aren't really nice, and when "the world as it is" isn't driving him to tears ("Peace Train") he often lies about it.   **B−**

B. W. Stevenson: *My Maria* (RCA Victor '73). How does this pudgy Texas hippie come up with one great single that sounds like Jay and the Americans ("My Maria") and another that is covered by Three Dog Night ("Shambala")? Somebody named Daniel J. Moore helps him. **C+**

Al Stewart: *Love Chronicles* (Epic '70). A landmark; the first rock record to use the word "fuck" ("fucking," actually) at the end of a line, an achievement typical of its occasional flaws — the rhyming word, "plucking," is forced — and unrepresentative of its success. The eighteen-minute title cut is a decent, serious, and touching reminiscence of sexual growth that for all its male bias is recommended to songwriters reluctant to shed their adolescence. The other songs are well-observed despite their sentimental tendencies, and guest guitarist Jimmy Page proves that folk-rock is his metier. **B+**

Al Stewart: *Year of the Cat* (Janus '76). Rather than gothics or sci-fi, Stewart goes for historical novels, and as long as he shuts up about Nostradamus — who inspired last year's *Past, Present and Future,* you'll remember — I say good for him. Well, actually the historical note is limited this time out to one song about Lord Grenville and references to Leonardo, phantom harlequins, etc. The prevailing tone is more spy-novel. I ask you, did Eric Ambler have an ear for melody? **B−**

Gary Stewart: *Out of Hand* (RCA Victor '75). This is the best regular-issue country LP I've heard in about five years — which given my tastes may just mean that it's barely a country record at all. The wild urgency of Stewart's voice reminds me of both Hank Williams and Jerry Lee Lewis, communicating an unconstraint that feels genuinely liberating even when Stewart himself sounds miserable. Don't be misled by that mod look; this man has got to be a little crazy. **A−**

Gary Stewart: *You're Not the Woman You Used to Be* (MCA '75). In case it's not clear why rock and rollers are

so excited about a new country singer, it's because he really sings rockabilly, which supposedly flourished for a few years in the mid-'50s and then vanished. What I like best about this compilation of flop singles from a few years ago is the way Stewart transforms rockabilly's adolescent phobias about wimmin into unabashed burlesques involving the likes of "Big Bertha" and "The Snuff Queen." Time: 26.20. **B+**

Gary Stewart: *Steppin' Out* (RCA Victor '76). "Well-produced" for sure, more country and more rock and roll all at the same time. But it sounds as if the craziness has been rationalized right out of him. **B**

Gary Stewart: *Your Place or Mine* (RCA Victor '77). A strong comeback — Stewart's tendency to get mired in mannerism remains, but to hear him spit out "Ten Years of This" ("this" being a marriage) or change Guy Clark's "I'm looking to get silly" to "I'm looking to get sloppy drunk" is to be reminded that Jerry Lee Lewis has always lived off his mannerisms. Undomesticated hard country. Original grade: B plus. **A−**

Gary Stewart: *Little Junior* (RCA Victor '78). This is a likable album because Stewart is a likable artist, secure by now in his good-humored bad-old-boy persona. But only once — on a version of Ry Cooder's "I Got Mine" that ranks with the greatest Jerry Reed novelties — does he give that persona a shot in the arm. **B**

Gary Stewart: *Gary* (RCA Victor '79). The good sound is still there — those Jerry Lee vocals, that spare Nashville backup — but the good songs aren't. Jack Tempchin and Leroy Preston and Bill Payne try their hand, but the best thing here is by Dickey Betts, and Tanya Tucker has just covered it better. **C+**

Rod Stewart: *Gasoline Alley* (Mercury '70). I suspected Stewart of folkie leanings the first time I saw him do his broken-down bluesman imitation with Jeff Beck at the Fillmore. But his solo debut proved such a landmark that when he opened this one with a title tune about the slums featuring only mandolin and acoustic guitar I didn't even snicker. Much all-around excellence here — Stewart writes songs with almost as much imagination as he picks them, and his band is as (dare I say it?) sensitive as his voice. Nothing as revelatory as "Handbags and Gladrags" or "An Old Raincoat Won't Ever Let You Down," though. Original grade: B plus.   **A−**

Rod Stewart: *Every Picture Tells a Story* (Mercury '71). Because he's tawdry enough to revel in stellar pop-and-flash, Stewart can refine the rock sensibility without processing the life out of it. His gimmick is nuance. Rod the Wordslinger is a lot more literate than the typical English bloozeman, Rod the Singer can make words flesh, and though Rod the Bandleader's music is literally electric it's the mandolin and pedal steel that come through sharpest. A smash as huge as "Maggie May" must satisfy Rod the Mod the way a classic as undeniable as "Maggie May" does Rod the Artist. But it's "Mandolin Wind" leading into Motown leading into Tim Hardin that does justice to everything he is. Original grade: A.   **A+**

Rod Stewart: *Never a Dull Moment* (Mercruy '72). He's so in love with the run of life that it would be a contradiction for Stewart to attempt any grand aesthetic advances, so why wonder whether his art is improving until it gets boring? This doesn't peak as high as *Every Picture*. But "You Wear It Well" starts ringing in your head like "Maggie May" after a couple of plays. The three originals on the first side check in not long after. And Stewart's augury of the incipient early '60s revival, "Twistin' the Night Away," is the perfect nostalgia combo — the unimaginable twist with the irreproachable Sam Cooke. Original grade: A.   **A−**

Rod Stewart/Faces Live: *Coast to Coast/Overture and Beginners* (Mercury '73). I mention this only because it's even worse than most live albums. On the studio versions of these songs, the sloppiness is a fringe benefit, but this is so raggedy it falls apart. Do you really want to spend five bucks for a tacky guitar solo and a second-rate rendition of "Jealous Guy"?   **C−**

Rod Stewart: *Sing It Again Rod* (Mercury '73). In which Mercury bides time with a best-of while Rod makes faces. The selection is sharp until "Pinball Wizard," obviously thrown in as bait for those who already own Rod's four very sharp albums. Packaging advance: a jacket shaped like a highball glass.   **B+**

Rod Stewart: *Smiler* (Mercury '74). Except for an embarrassingly unnatural "Natural Man" (that's right, Aretha's), the failure here is elusive, but that doesn't make it any less real — spiritual tone, energy, horns, something like that. For me, the better part of valor is to give up before the Elton John track wears out the way the Sam Cooke stuff and "Dixie Toot" already have.   **B−**

Rod Stewart: *Atlantic Crossing* (Warner Bros. '75). After *Smiler* I was convinced that his talent had vanished; this makes it seem that he'll be breathing life into ten songs a year in perpetuity. The Southern session men he works with here suit his more generalized interpretive approach, on the "slow side" as well as the "fast."   **B+**

Rod Stewart: *The Best of Rod Stewart* (Mercury '76). As if to prove how arbitrary compilation albums from consistent album artists are, this omits four selections from *Sing It Again Rod*. The third side, which features both halves of a previously uncollected single and the previously unavailable-on-disc "What Made Milwaukee Famous," has its uses. And the stuff from *Smiler* should never have come out in the first place.   **B+**

Rod Stewart: *A Night on the Town* (Warner Bros. '76). This is Stewart's most ambitious record since *Never a Dull Moment* four years ago, but its ambitions are only partly fulfilled. If he's gonna start doing big message numbers, he'd better rise above the bathetic liberalism of "Tradewinds," the most overblown song he's ever recorded 'cept maybe for the symphonic version of "Pinball Wizard." And if he's gonna break new ground thematically, as on the "gay" "Killing of Georgie," he'd better come up with slightly less Dylanesque melodies — in the course of comparing Stewart's song with its fraternal twin, "Simple Twist of Fate," I was reminded of just how precise an arrangement can be. Original grade: B plus **B**

Rod Stewart: *The Best of Rod Stewart Volume II* (Mercury '76). Special price, says a simulated sticker on the jacket, but that's the only thing on this ragbag that's worth a glad hand. A fast shuffle, not a fair deal. **B –**

Rod Stewart: *Foot Loose and Fancy Free* (Warner Bros. '78). Gosh, what a terrific idea — a concept album about a cocksure rock and roller who Cannot Love. How'd all those cliches get in there, I wonder. I mean, the first side works up a very nice groove, although it'll add nothing to Rod's reputation as a composer or a humanitarian. But side two opens with a Vanilla Fudge remake and doesn't recover till the confessional finale, itself festooned midway through with a "Whoo!" so pro forma you'd think Rod had run out of steam. **B –**

Rod Stewart: *Blondes Have More Fun* (Warner Bros. '78). He used to mean to be meaningful and now he means to be trashy, but that doesn't make him decadent. Decadent is when Carol Bayer Sager writes all your songs for you. **B**

Rod Stewart: *Greatest Hits Vol. 1* (Warner Bros. '79). Cut for cut this is Stewart's most consistent Warners album, and it does rescue three tracks from *Foot Loose and Fancy Free.* But its malfeasances are so annoying — there are already three (Mercury) albums that include the anachronistic "Maggie May," and it would be nice to have the disco mix of "Do Ya Think I'm Sexy?" on an LP — that maybe you should seek out *Atlantic Crossing.*

"Tonight's the Night" you know to death, right? But when's the last time you heard his "Three Time Loser" or "This Old Heart of Mine"? **B +**

Rod Stewart: See also Faces

Stiffs Live (Stiff '78). Elvis the C provides a brand-new existentialist prounciamento, "I Just Don't Know What to Do with Myself," but the real treat here is Nick Lowe's "Let's Eat," which garnishes a hot-and-greasy Mitch Ryder organ pump with lyrics like "I wanna move move move move move my teeth" and "Let's buy two and get one for free." Filling out the good side are "I Knew the Bride" (Lowe's answer to "You Never Can Tell"), Larry Wallis's "Police Car" (grand theft automatic), and two cuts by Wreckless Eric that seem unlikely to be eclipsed by their studio versions. Unfortunately, Costello's live "Miracle Man" and the three Ian Dury performances were eclipsed before they came out. **B +**

Stephen Stills: *Stephen Stills* (Atlantic '70). Stills always projects an effortless swing, and his tradeoffs with Eric Clapton on "Go Back Home" are keen and then some. He seems too damn skillful to put down. Yet there's something terribly undefined about this record. Hmm — maybe it's the songs. Original grade: B plus. **C +**

Stephen Stills: *Stephen Stills 2* (Atlantic '71). Stills has always come on as the ultimate rich hippie — arrogant, self-pitying, sexist, shallow. Unfortunately, he's never quite fulfilled this artistic potential, but now he's approaching his true level. Flashes of brilliant ease remain — the single, "Marianne," is very nice, especially if you don't listen too hard to the lyrics — but there's also a lot of stuff on order of an all-male chorus with jazzy horns singing "It's disgusting" in perfect tuneful unison, and straight, I swear. Keep it up, SS — it'll be a pleasure to watch you fail. **C**

Steve Stills: *Manassas* (Atlantic '72). Yes, Steve has gotten it together a little, even deigning to cooperate with real musicians in a real band, and yes, some of this four-sided set echoes in your head after you play it a lot. The only problem is you're never sure where the echoes come from.   **C+**

Stephen Stills: *Stills* (Columbia '75). In which Stills recycles his "favorite set of changes/Already good for a couple of songs." His admirers might find that endearing, I know. They might even dig him copping a lick from Alice Cooper later on in the lyric. But me, I find it pathetic.   **C**

The Stills Young Band: *Long May You Run* (Reprise '76). Like the tour, the album (recorded in Miami, where many of the songs take place) is a profit-taking throwaway, but that's not necessarily a bad thing — Young is always wise to wing it, and the less Stills expresses himself the better. Also, there's an exponential advantage in hearing Steve sing lead only every other cut. His "Make Love to You" ("you're such a lady") does inspire "Midnight on the Bay," Neil's stupidest song in many a moon. But most of the time Neil's in a droll mood — title song's a riot. Not bad for California rock. Original grade: A minus.   **B**

Sly Stone: *High on You* (Epic '75). The lyrics haven't regained their punch, and neither have the melodies — when he does try to say something, you barely notice. But the old rhythmic eccentricity, both vocal and instrumental, makes this more interesting to listen to than the run of dancey goop. Let's not give up on him yet.   **B−**

Sly Stone: *Ten Years Too Soon* (Epic '79). Pieties aside, John Luongo does better with this monstrous concept — seguing "contemporary" instrumental stylings into Sly's (not the Family's) greatest dance tracks —than you'd expect, and the album is at least a listenable curiosity. I mean, it's *funny* to hear a kickdrum-syndrum break follow the familiar "for people who only need a beat." And "High on You" is actually improved. But of course, the concept failed — this got virtually no disco play. And *Greatest Hits* is still in catalogue.   **B−**

Sly Stone: See also Sly & the Family Stone

Stoneground: *Stoneground* (Warner Bros. '71). People exercise themselves calling this a hype, but I've heard a lot worse and am happy to wish them humility and dues. Certainly the aptest use of Sal Valentino since the Beau Brummels were on Autumn (the Beau Brummels on Warners were my idea of a hype). In the best moment, Valentino's fake-dirty vocals interlock with a real dirty song called "Stroke Stand."   **B−**

The Stooges: *Fun House* (Elektra '70). Now I regret all the times I've used words like "power" and "energy" to describe rock and roll, because this is what such rhetoric should have been saved for. Shall I compare it to an atom bomb? a wrecker's ball? a hydroelectric plant? Language wasn't designed for the job. Yet despite its sonic impact I find that the primary appeal of the music isn't physical — I have to be in a certain mood of desperate abandon before it reaches my body. It always interests me intellectually, though — with its repetitiveness beyond the call of incompetence and its solitary new-thing saxophone, this is genuinely "avant-garde" rock. The proof is the old avant-garde fallacy of "L.A. Blues" — trying to make art about chaos by reproducing same. Original grade: B plus.   **A−**

Iggy and the Stooges: *Raw Power* (Columbia '73). In which David Bowie remembers "the world's forgotten boy" long enough to sponsor an album — and mixes it down till it's thin as an epicure's wrist. The side-openers, "Search and Destroy" and "Raw Power," voice the Iggy Pop ethos more insanely (and aggressively) than "I Wanna Be Your Dog." But despite James Williamson's guitar, the rest disperses in their wake. **B+**

Iggy and the Stooges: *Metallic K.O.* (Import '76). Ignorami consider this dim live tape Prime Ig cos "you can actually hear the bottles flying." Also cos Ig utters the words "cunt, pricks, buttfuckers" (trying to run this world sez Ig, who'd never dream of such a thing himself). And let us not forget "Hebrew" (rhymes with "Rich Bitch"). Great "documentary" but sometimes I really dig Joni Mitchell. **C+**

The Stooges: See also Iggy Pop

Stories: *Stories* (Kama Sutra '72). The Left Banke, Mike Brown's long-ago previous group, seem a little prissy in retrospect, but they were sweet at the time, no? Well, this may seem prissy some day, too, but it'll never seem sweet — too intense. And if the other songs had the melodic sinew of "St. James" and "Step Back" it might seem quite strong now. **B**

Stories: *About Us* (Kama Sutra '73). This group tests our male-timbre chauvinism — Ian Lloyd sounds disconcertingly like a goil. Too bad he voices the same old male sentiments — don't let me down, push me 'round, or complain when I leave at the dawning — because the music is special: dense, clean, kinetic, almost mid-Beatles in spirit, but contemporary. If only they'd written one lyric as breathtaking as most of Michael Brown's melodies or as strong and as flexible as Lloyd's voice turns out to be or as commercial-meaningful as their hit remake of Hot Chocolate's "Brother Louie." **B+**

Stormin' Norman & Suzy: *Fantasy Rag* (Perfect Crime '75). This might just be another good-time band dedicated to the proposition that scuzz is cute if it weren't for Suzy Williams's natural echo, which calls up images of riverboats and cathouse pianos despite the thin recording. Unfortunately,

Norman Zamcheck's voice calls up images of an account executive fulfilling his inner nature, and while his songs really are fantasy rags — "Wealthy Philanthropist," for example, is a piquant piece of '20s camp — he captures Suzy perfectly only twice. The titles suggest her emotional range: "Rise, Angel" and "Crazy Lady." **B**

Stormin' Norman & Suzy: *Ocean of Love* (Polydor '78). If anything, this intelligent major-label debut is a half-step down. There are no disabling gaffes, and in theory it's good for Suzy to sing more and Norman less; her big, sad, cheerful voice sounds more like itself, too. But despite the ocean noises and "The Gallant Balloonist" and a coda that goes "socked right in the kisser — right in the eye," this is definitely an attempt at de-zanification. And what the world needs from Suzy Williams is not another chick — oops, woman, forgot about "You Keep Me Cryin' " — singer. It's Suzy. **B**

The Stranglers: *Rattus Norvegicus* (A&M '77). These guys combine the sensitivity and erudition of ? and the Mysterians with the street smarts of the Doors and detest the act of love with a humorless intensity worthy of Anthony Comstock. You can tell by the way they discreetly bring up subjects like musicianship and education in interviews that, just as they claim, they don't belong to anybody's new wave. Too dumb. **C**

Strawbs: *Grave New World* (A&M '72). An acoustic-gone-electric work about cosmic verities, many of them glum. It even comes with its own woodcuts . . . they're not really woodcuts, but that only goes to prove how plastic everything is these days. I should bless those who cause me pain, it says here, but that surely doesn't apply to a record that gives me the blahs. **D**

Mel Street: *Mel Street's Greatest Hits* (GRT '76). Street is sincere and rather modest; he keeps the music basic and never tries to overpower anyone with his personable baritone or unexaggerated drawl. But he sure does have a weakness for illicit love, and he ought to face up — referring to the objects of one's lust (a term he specifically disavows) as angels (in three out of ten song titles) will not fool the Lord.   **B**

Streetwalkers: *Streetwalkers* (Mercury '75). Roger Chapman, still blessed or cursed with one of those voices that can kill small game at a hundred yards, here combines the best of Family with some Jeff Beck bruisers. Object: Aerosmith for adults. But their urban nastiness doesn't seem to have earned its saturation in blues mythology.   **C+**

Streetwalkers: *Red Card* (Mercury '76). In a time of hard rock drought, this will do — the tempos are up, and such songs as "Run for Cover" and "Roll Up, Roll Up" and "Decadence Code" suggest that they're observing our famous wasteland as well as experiencing it. Ominoso with a vengeance. Original grade: B plus.   **B**

Streetwalkers: *Vicious but Fair* (Mercury '77). Artistically, this contingent of veterans is a casualty of punk; the stylized menace of their cultish, calibrated art-rock-cum-heavy-metal has been rendered obsolete by the outgoing explosiveness of the real thing. And although I've always been a nominal fan of Roger Chapman, it does serve him right — that's what you get for perfecting arrested-adolescent fantasies of sin and sexual warfare as your hairline recedes and your pot thickens. Original grade: B minus.   **C+**

Barbra Streisand: *The Way We Were* (Columbia '74). Theoretically, I am encouraged by Barbra's abandonment of Richard Perry and Contemporary Material, and in practice I love the title song, one of those beyootiful ballads that are the gift of AM programming to the reprobate rock and roller. But my big theory has always been that we like contemporary material because it is, well, contemporary, and in practice most of these performances generate a pristine, somewhat chill unreality even as they simulate warmth, maturity, all that stuff. Also, I'm not humming any of them after half a dozen plays.   **B−**

Streisand/Kristofferson: *A Star Is Born* (Columbia '77). Due largely to Kristofferson, whose recording career will soon be as vestigial as George Segal's, the movie isn't quite the ripoff you'd figure, but the album, which lists at a pricey $8.98, most certainly is. As with all soundtracks, you get the stars' voices but not their chests, and Rupert Holmes and Paul Williams have ended up with the kind of rock and roll cliches that real rockers assume. What else could I expect? Neither Barbra nor Kris has made a listenable album, much less a stellar one, in the history of Consumer Guide.   **D+**

String Driven Thing: *String Driven Thing* (Charisma '72). This English quartet features a violinist, but stay where you are — no resemblance to Ian Anderson or David LaFlamme. Well, maybe a little — I could do without the mytholyric "Jack Diamond" and find the beat stiff at times. Still, they have one, not bad for a group driven by an electric bass and such ordinarily peripheral percussion devices as congas and tambourines. In fact, they get pretty wild, with the violin exploited for dementia. Yet the lyrics are sane and well-observed. In my favorite, God doesn't play in a rock and roll band.   **B**

Alice Stuart: *Full Time Woman* (Fantasy '71). Beautiful melodies and clean, countryish, somewhat static post-folk arrangements transform these lyrics into memorable statements of feeling and principle. A bit male-identified, I admit, but the salutory synthesis of small voice and independent spirit proves that a woman doesn't have to be macho to be autonomous. Now who'll prove it for men?   **B+**

Alice Stuart and Snake: *Believing* (Fantasy '72). The winning combination of tiny voice and tough lyrics is washed out by the lyrics, and the melodies don't exactly triumph either. When the two best songs on a singer-songwriter's album are written by others, you know something's wrong. Original grade: B minus.   **C+**

The Stylistics: *The Stylistics* (Avco '71). I try to be hip and think like the crowd, but when it comes to vocal harmony I'll take a black falsetto group over some privileged anti-barbershop quartet — especially if they have songs. I'll even let them have a pastoral fantasy — seems like a fair antithesis to their urban reality, an antithesis captured neatly on "Country Living" by the clash of extreme artifice and back-to-nature rhetoric. The first side doesn't quit, and although I could do without the silly (and musically long-winded) politics of "People Make the World Go Round" on the second, I can also make do with them. Original grade: B plus.   **A−**

The Stylistics: *Round 2* (Avco '72). James Taylor is merely a wimp —Russell Thompkins, Jr. is a Wimp God. The creamy fluidity of his falsetto is miraculous, and the settings provided by composer-producer Thom Bell simply heavenly. Unfortunately, the material isn't as consistent on the group's second album in a year (three hits plus uneven filler) as on the first (five hits plus impressive filler).   **B+**

The Stylistics: *Rockin' Roll Baby* (Avco '73). Thom Bell and Linda Creed have a right to run short of tunes after two fairly amazing albums with this group. But since the title cut proves that Russell Thompkins can sing fast, the first side is hard to excuse — not only very fallible, but interminably so.   **C+**

The Stylistics: *Heavy* (Avco '74). These guys are going to miss Thom Bell, who unlike Hugo & Luigi knows how to shape songs for Russell Thompkins's falsetto and unlike Van McCoy knows the difference between strings and tomato soup. At least this album provides its own hit cut, instead of rereleasing an old Bell ringer —

"Heavy Fallin' Out" is an impressive if flukish bit of upbeat production.   **C**

The Stylistics: *The Best of the Stylistics* (Avco '75). What I love about the Stylistics is that they're so out of it. Authentic modern-day castrati, they elevate the absurd high seriousness of the love-man mode into an asexual spirituality that the Delfonics, say, only hinted at — and the country-rock harmonizers only fake and exploit. Their spirituality doesn't have much to do with real life, but it's always liberating to encounter it on the radio. *And now, with the flick of a switch, you can approximate this liberation in your home.*   **A−**

The Stylistics: *Love Spell* (Mercury '79). Their second album with Teddy Randazzo is their most generally listenable since *Round Two*. Now someone should tell them — or better still, Teddy — that general listenability is not what producing a producer's group is about. It's about go-rillas.   **C+**

Laurie Styvers: *Spilt Milk* (Warner Bros. '71). Normally, I ignore records as rightfully obscure as this one, but I thought it was time I mentioned that our hippest record company is getting more complacent all the time — just how many L.A. airheads can we stand? Styvers is the kind of person who makes me like junkies — you know, the baby you want to steal candy from, so trite and pretty-poo in her fashionably troubled adolescence that you hope she chokes on her own money. One line says it all: "There just aren't words for the songs of the people who really feel." Oh shut up, Laurie.   **E**

Suicide: *Suicide* (Red Star '77). A friend who loves this record offers the attractive theoretical defense that it unites the two strains of "new wave" rock minimalism — neoclassy synthesizer and three-chord barrage. So maybe it will prove popular among theoreticians. For the rest of us, though, there are little problems like lyrics that reduce serious politics to rhetoric, singing that makes rhetoric sound lurid, and the way the manic eccentricity of this duo's live performance turns to silliness on record. **C+**

The Suicide Commandos: *Make a Record* (Blank '78). The hooks are buried even further into the mix than the vocals and the drumming, but they're there somewhere, and I must admit that every time I hear the opening chords of either side I sit up and grin. For punk junkies only. **B−**

Donna Summer: *Love to Love You Baby* (Oasis '75). Did you come yet? Huh? Did you come yet? **B−**

Donna Summer: *A Love Trilogy* (Oasis '76). This is marred by new what's-going-*on*-in-the-next-apartment distractions; again and again. Donna bids the object of her affections "come . . . come . . . come" before adding "to my arms," so that when she cries out "don't let go" you have to wonder of what. But it does boast two otherwise uninterrupted sides of baroque German disco fluff and proves that she can carry a tune as well as a torch. I can even imagine playing it at a party. **B**

Donna Summer: *I Remember Yesterday* (Casablanca '77). Cut of the month is "Love's Unkind," a remake of "Then He Kissed Me" that I prefer to the original for the way its solo saxophone opens a window in the wall of sound. But the Supremes and Dr. Buzzard (and Natalie Cole?) takeoffs are stale if not stuffy, and when Kraftwerk goes to the disco the best you can usually hope for is air conditioning. **B−**

Donna Summer: *"Once Upon a Time . . ."* (Casablanca '77). Roll over Pete Townshend and tell Jerry Leiber the news — here's the first disco opera, a double-LP concept album with acutal lyrics that tell an actual story printed on the inner sleeves. First two sides are uniformly strong but without real peaks, and from there it's downhill to a climax indicated by the two final titles, "I Love You" and "Happily Ever After." But you *can* dance to it. **B−**

Donna Summer: *Live and More* (Casablanca '78). When a studio creation does her greatest hits on stage, she diminishes them (arrangements worthy of the Supremes at the Copa, which is more than I can say for "My Man Medley"), and when her more is "Mac Arthur Park Suite," she makes you remember what less is supposed to be (I much prefer Andy Kaufman's interpretation). **C**

Donna Summer: *Bad Girls* (Casablanca '79). You tend to suspect anyone who releases three double-LPs in eighteen months of delusions of Chicago, but Donna is here to stay and this is her best album. The first two sides, four songs per, never let up — the voice breaks and the guitars moan over a bass-drum thump in what amounts to empty-headed girl-group rock and roll brought cannily up-to-date. Moroder makes his Europercussion play on side four, which is nice too, but side three drags, suggesting that the rock and roll that surfaces here is perhaps only a stop along the way to a totally bleh total performance. Me, I still love my Marvellettes records. **A−**

Donna Summer: *On the Radio: Greatest Hits Volumes I & II* (Casablanca '79). The title tells us Summer wants to be a pop queen rather than a dance queen, and the music tells us she's got a right: almost in a class with '60s Motown. I mean, this woman will never compete for Lady Soul, but she enjoys singing as much as Diana Ross ever has, and if her timbre isn't as magical her robust technique makes up for it. Despite the repeat of the title tune (the first time is dandy), the overlap with *Bad Girls* (another must-own), and the inevitable "MacArthur Park" (almost tolerable in this non-suite version), her best-of proves that whatever the virtues of her disco extensions, she makes like a rock and roller at AM size. **A**

Lonesome Sundown: *Been Gone Too Long* (Joliet '77). A/k/a Cornelius

Green of Opelousas, Louisiana, Sundown came out of a decade's retirement to cut this modest but exemplary blues LP. With his rounded rhythms, entertaining arrangements, good-hearted vocals, and Slim Harpo guitar, he is to Johnny Shines what the bayous are to the Delta — not as deep, but more fun. [Later on Alligator.] **B+**

The Sunshine Band: *The Sound of Sunshine* (T.K. '75). You can't trust anybody anymore. Fronted by K.C., a/k/a H. W. Casey of Casey and Finch, they are the Booker T. and the MG's of the great Southern label of the '70s. But this is just the boys in the bands sans vocals, the post-soul equivalent of a Paul Kossoff or Vassar Clements LP. Wait for them to put "Miss B." on a K.C. collection. Time: 26:32. **D+**

Supa: *Homespun* (Paramount '72). Every time I think I've run up against the ultimate country-funk inanity — Hookfoot, say — I find someone even dumber. Guess what this lover of the good red Canarsie clay says money won't buy? And what rhymes with buy that he gets on his motorcycle? Gawd. **D−**

Super Black Blues Volume II (Blues-Time '70). On the first volume T-Bone Walker, Joe Turner, and Otis Spann joined an extraordinarily mellow studio jam that found all three in good humor and good voice — a unique document. This live sequel is a solid sampler, blues one step closer to jazz than Muddy Waters or B. B. King (who emcees). Turner and Cleanhead Vinson do their standards with a one-man horn section; Walker and Leon Thomas work with a combo that includes congas and bongos. Thomas is something of a ringer, but he certainly sounds a lot more earthbound here than with Pharoah Sanders. Recommended to blues fanatics, blues novices, and anyone lucky enough to find it in a bargain bin. **B+**

Supertramp: *Crime of the Century* (A&M '74). They say this is the rock and roll of the future, which I find a depressing thought even though (or because) the amalgam is a moderately smart one. Straight-ahead art-rock, sort of — Queen without preening, Yes without pianistics and meter shifts. And "Bloody Well Right" documents a gift for the killer hook. Now if only "Bloody Well Right" weren't an impassioned plea for complacency. Maybe if we close our eyes they'll go away. **C+**

Supertramp: *Even in the Quietest Moments . . .* (A&M '77). Most "progressive" rock is pretentious background schlock that's all too hard to ignore. This is modest background schlock that sounds good when it slips into the ear. I guess we should thank "Babaji," whichever one he is. **C+**

Supertramp: *Breakfast in America* (A&M '79). I like a hooky album as well as the next fellow, so when I found that this one elicited random grunts of pleasure I looked forward to listening hard. But the lyrics turned out to be glib variations on the usual *Star Romances* trash, and in the absence of vocal personality (as opposed to accurate singing) and rhythmic thrust (as opposed to a beat) I'll wait until this material is covered by artists of emotional substance — Tavares, say, or the Doobie Brothers. **C+**

The Supremes: *Floy Joy* (Motown '72). For the most part this miracle of homogeneity bounces along in the background, occasionally brightening the room with a riff or a harmony or a phrase or a touch of electricity that betokens writer-producer Smokey Robinson expressing himself. "Your Wonderful Sweet Sweet Love" and "Floy Joy" and "Automatically Sunshine" aren't prime Smokey. But they're choice, meriting my most generous Muzak rating. **B+**

The Supremes: *The Supremes* (Motown '72). Jean Tyrell Isn't Diana Ross. Here the new appointee confronts producer/arranger/songwriter Jimmy Webb, who isn't a boy genius anymore, but with a small "i." The result is, well, confusing and schlocky, but it does feature Young Jimmy doing a Sweet Baby James imitation in the background. I remember when Florence Ballard and Mary Wilson used to have that job. **C+**

The Supremes: *At Their Best* (Motown '78). In which the great pop factory of the '60s flounders around in the superstar '70s, incapable of fabricating hits around the greatest of girl-group trademarks. "Stoned Love," from 1970, is the last undeniable single Berry Gordy's depleted forces can provide their act; by the time Smokey enters the lists in 1972 he's turned into an album artist. "Love Train"? "You're My Driving Wheel"? Has it come to this? **C+**

Swampwater: *Swampwater* (RCA Victor '71). On their own Linda Ronstadt's backup boys prove honest country-rockers, which is like (and probably is) honest folkies with more chops. Very tuneful in a variety of styles, with Gib Guilbeau's fiddle pushing toward the bayous and John Beland's guitar pulling 'em back to L.A. But their best lyric is about a dancing bear, and their version of "Headed for the Country" is less bathetic than Johnny Darrell's only because they couldn't project big emotions if they wanted to. Time: 26:50. **B**

Billy Swan: *I Can Help* (Monument '74). As befits an unknown one-shot who names his album after his big single — especially a single that advances the rockabilly moment eighteen years — Swan has made an LP with a B side. Only it's one of those B sides thrown together so casually that you find yourself attracted by its elan. Programmed with "I Can Help" are four listenable examples of Swan's detached singing style, all separated from nostalgia by wacky absurdist touches. But on side two the absurdism is provided solely by Swan's willingness to waver perversely off pitch on otherwise straightforward tunes from Elvis Presley, Charlie Rich, and C. Boone,

whoever he is. It's only a sloppy quickie, but I like it. **B+**

Billy Swan: *Rock 'n' Roll Moon* (Monument '75). Any rockabilly who sings "I'm still me and you're still you" as if he's boasting, or trying to, knows the intense nervousness of good old macho in a way Carl Perkins only had nightmares about. Which is why this record is as good as it is, and also why it isn't any better. **B+**

Billy Swan: *Billy Swan* (Monument '76). Isn't it wonderful? Here's this guy who really doesn't sing very well at all and not only has he now made more good albums than Three Dog Night and the Mormon Tabernacle Choir combined, but they keep getting better. Except maybe for "Blue Suede Shoes" there are no waste cuts this time, and no mediocrities either. The well-meaning optimism and the insecure persona mesh perfectly, and the tunes are pleasurable throughout, whether he stole them from the Sun catalogue or wrote them himself. Inspirational Verse: "Am I Lucky Am I Lucky Son Of A Gun." **A−**

Billy Swan: *Four* (Columbia '77). Last year Swan made the finest rockabilly album of the current revival, songful and manic and ebulliently inadequate, and it didn't sell shit. Now someone seems to have taught him a lesson — this time we get horns and strings that show up his voice and a song about California that is no less drab than most of the others. For everybody's sake, let's hope this doesn't sell shit either. **C**

Billy Swan: *At His Best* (Monument '78). I'm still glad to own all of his first three albums (and to have filed his more recent stuff in the darkest recesses of my hall). But despite the title recognition moves — his "Don't Be Cruel" grows on me, but he should leave "Shake, Rattle and Roll" to Delbert if not Joe — this is probably the most flattering portrait of this mild-mannered wild-eyed boy you can find. **A−**

Rachel Sweet: *Fool Around* (Stiff/Columbia '79). Two compositions by (ousted?) svengali Liam Sternberg have been replaced on the U.S. release by prime, straightforward rockers. This makes sense. Like Tanya Tucker, Sweet thrives on simple material, and while I like Sternberg's catchy, thoughtful songs, their fussy, uncolloquial moments don't suit Sweet's hot-teen persona: Deborah Harry might sound charmingly klutzy on the rhythmically overwrought "Cuckoo Clock" or "Suspended Animation" ("I could wait for any duration"), but Sweet just sounds like she's following instructions. Unfortunately, both these songs were left on the LP, while natural Sweet stuff like "Just My Style" and "Truckstop Queen" (on Stiff's Akron anthology) were omitted. This doesn't make sense. **B+**

The Sweet: *The Sweet* (Bell '73). In which Phil Wainman, Mike Chapman, and Nicky Chinn ask the musical question: is heavy bubblegum bazooka-rock? Their answer: only when it goes pop. So while I'm as impressed as anyone with the success of "Little Willy," I want to know what happened to "Blockbuster." Not to mention "Wig-Wam Bam." Original grade: B. **B−**

Sweet: *Desolation Boulevard* (Capitol '75). Bazooka-rock lives, even without Chapman and Chinn. In the absence of Slade (whose failure to participate on the recent LP that bears their name must be considered disquieting), these guys play second-bill steamroller to Kiss. **B−**

The Sweet: *Give Us a Wink* (Capitol '76). An experiment that proves it is more aesthetically fruitful to veer toward Slade without a Noddy Holder than to veer toward Deep Purple without a Ritchie Blackmore. Science marches on. So does commerce. About art you can never be sure. **C+**

The Sylvers: *Best of the Sylvers* (Capitol '78). They were nice enough to program this fast-side/slow-side. Now if only the fast side didn't fade from "Boogie Fever" and "Hot Line" (by

Lewis & Perren) to "Cotton Candy" (add Yarian) to "High School Dance" (switch to four Sylvers) to "Free Style" (switch to one Sylver). **B−**

Sylvester and the Hot Band: *Sylvester and the Hot Band* (Blue Thumb '73). In which everybody's favorite black transvestite internalizes songs by Neil Young ("Southern Man"), James Taylor ("Steamroller"), and Procol Harum (guess) as well as Ray Charles (not bad, in its way) and Billie Holiday (and people complain about Diana Ross). "Southern Man" is almost unrecognizable in its rock-funk arrangement, which is interesting, and if you think Sweet Baby Wimp sounds funny invoking a "churnin' urn of burnin' funk" just imagine those words from a cartoon character who is three-fourths Tweety Bird and one-fourth — well, it is the puddy tat's name — Sylvester. Finale: a Stax-Volt "My Country 'Tis of Thee." Quite a curiosity. **B−**

Sylvester and the Hot Band: *Bazaar* (Blue Thumb '73). This opens powerfully, with a hard-rock showstopper original called "Down on Your Knees." But its overall message is confused, because just as his band seems to be going macho, Sylvester himself is emulating the gospel ladies he grew up with — and covering Gram Parsons's "She." **C**

Sylvester: *Step II* (Fantasy '78). When Harvey Fuqua brought Sylvester back to the vinyl wars last year, he was seeking a disco hit. Well, eureka — "You Make Me Feel (Mighty Real)" is a real mutha for ya, one of those surges of sustained, stylized energy that is disco's great gift to pop music. In fact, the whole first side is classic dance montage. Side two proves that Sylvester remains incapable of impersonating Cissy Houston or Eddie Kendricks, though he's getting closer, and n.b.: on the most convincing cut he strays down into his speaking voice. Original grade: B minus. **B+**

Sylvester: *Stars* (Fantasy '79). In which Mr. S. stretches his two best tricks — for thrills, a supernal burst of sound too sweet for a shriek that he un-looses well above his normal falsetto range; for romance, a transported croon — over a consistently satisfying four-cut disco album, with help from his own Martha Wash and the Labelle-without-camp of Hodges, James and Smith. The title track tinges Sly Stone with Andy Warhol, but the tour de force is a remake of Ben E. King's "I (Who Have Nothing)," and you know what? Its artificiality suits the schlocky lyric at least as well as King's virtuoso dramatics. **B+**

Sylvester: *Living Proof* (Fantasy '79). The three concert sides are what Sylvester wants — his graduation from disco into the world of Thelma Houston and the Pointer Sisters. But insofar as he succeeds artistically he does so on effort, not achievement — he simply can't generate the requisite vocal lustre so far above his speaking register. And insofar as he succeeds commercially he does so on the strength of the studio (i.e. disco) side — which succeeds pretty well artistically, too. **B−**

Sylvia: *Pillow Talk* (Vibration '73). *Let's Get It On* without production values. Call it underdeveloped if you want; I'll mention that it's unaffected. Including the best peace lyric heard lately, entitled "Had Any Lately?" **B**

Booker T: *Evergreen* (Epic '74). This laid-back folk-funk has body; it's physically attractive. And it's nice that T can put his own mild voice to his own mild lyrics like any other rock aristocrat. I might even agree that the candor of its complacency (one song puts down streetlights, another celebrates T's in-laws, the Kristoffersons) is refreshing. Actually, though, it pisses me off. **C+**

Booker T. & the M.G.'s: *Greatest Hits* (Stax '70). Because the sound of the organ invites textured vagueness as surely as that of the vibraphone does tinkly fluff, there are better ways to hear such themes as "Eleanor Rigby" and "Something" (both hits for another group, by the way) than on Booker's Hammond B-3. But when the improvs begin, we're back in riffland, where such spare, exemplary soul melodies as "Hip Hug Her" and "Time Is Tight" were born — and where Mr. T. can get back to fleshing out (and heating up) the disciplined cross-rhythms of his Memphis Group. **A−**

Booker T. & the M.G.'s: *Melting Pot* (Stax '71). Here the Memphis motorvators surpass the somewhat boxy rhythms that have limited all their albums as albums except for *Uptight*, which had vocals. Al Jackson's solidity, a linchpin of rock drumming as surely as Keith Moon's blastoffs and Charlie Watts's steady economy, is unshaken by the shifts the arrangements demand, and his deftness per-

mits a more flexible concept in which Booker lays back some on organ and Steve Cropper gets more melodic input. A Vegas-jazz ("L.A. Jazz Song" is a title) boop-de-doo chorus upsets the balance of side two pretty badly, but for the first twenty minutes this is unbelievably smooth without ever turning slick. Original grade: A minus. **B+**

Talking Heads: *Talking Heads 77* (Sire '77). A debut LP will often seem overrefined to habitues of a band's scene, so it's not surprising that many CBGBites felt betrayed when bits of this came out sounding like Sparks or Yes. Personally, I was even more put off by lyrics that fleshed out the Heads' post-Jonathan Richman, so-hip-we're-straight image; when David Byrne says "don't worry about the government," the irony is that he's not being ironic. But the more I listen the more I believe the Heads set themselves the task of hurdling such limitations, and succeed. Like Sparks, these are spoiled kids, but without the callowness or adolescent misogyny; like Yes, they are wimps, but without vagueness or cheap romanticism. Every tinkling harmony is righted with a screech, every self-help homily contextualized dramatically, so that in the end the record proves not only that the detachment of craft can coexist with a frightening intensity of feeling — something most artists know — but that the most inarticulate rage can be rationalized. Which means they're punks after all. **A—**

Talking Heads: *More Songs About Buildings and Food* (Sire '78). Here the Heads become a quintet in an ideal producer-artist collaboration — Eno contributes/interferes just enough. Not only does his synthesized lyricism provide flow and continuity, it also makes the passive, unpretentious technological mysticism he shares with the band real in the aural world. In fact, there is so much beautiful music (and so much funky music) on this album that I'll take no more complaints about David Byrne's voice. Every one of these eleven songs is a positive pleasure, and on every one the tension between Byrne's compulsive flights and the sinuous rock bottom of the music is the focus. I have more doubts than ever about Byrne's post-hippie work-ethic positivism — on one new song, he uses the phrase "wasting precious time" and means it — but if it goes with music this eccentric and compelling I'm damn sure going to hear him out. **A**

Talking Heads: *Fear of Music* (Sire '79). David Byrne's celebration of paranoia is a little obsessive, but like they say, that doesn't mean somebody isn't trying to get him. I just wish material as relatively expansive as "Found a Job" or "The Big Country" were available to open up the context a little; that way, a plausible prophecy like "Life During Wartime" might come off as cautionary realism instead of ending up in the nutball corner with self-referential fantasies like "Paper" and "Memories Can't Wait." And although I'm impressed with the gritty weirdness of the music, it is narrow — a little sweetening might help. **A—**

James Talley: *Got No Bread, No Milk, No Money, But We Sure Got a Lot of Love* (Capitol '75). The most attractive thing about this homespun Western-swing masterpiece — infusing both its sure, unassuming intelligence and its plain and lovely songs — is a mildness reminiscent of the first re-

corded string bands. Talley's careful conception and production both work to revive a playing-pretty-for-our-friends feel that most folkies would give up their rent-controlled apartments for. Despite its intense rootedness, it's neither defensive nor preachy — just lays down a way of life for all to hear. **A**

James Talley: *Tryin' Like the Devil* (Capitol '76). Something about this record as a whole is slightly off — maybe it's Talley's humorlessness, or maybe it's that his voice is much better suited to the startling talky intimacy of his first record than to the belting bravado with which he asserts his ambitions this time. But every song works individually, and an audacious concept — returning a consciously leftish analysis to the right-leaning populism of country music — is damn near realized in utterly idiomatic songs like "40 Hours" and "Are They Gonna Make Us Outlaws Again?" It belts good enough. **A—**

James Talley: *Blackjack Choir* (Capitol '77). Populism always has a sentimental side, but here the received images take over: bluesmen singin' sad songs and everybody lovin' love songs, lasses from Georgia and broken dreams from Chicago. His voice is richer, and "Magnolia Boy" and "When the Fiddler Packs His Case" are as great as anything from the first two albums, but I hope this is a lapse. **B—**

James Talley: *Ain't It Somethin'* (Capitol '77). The country populism on Talley's previous album was vague enough to suit Johnny Cash or Charley Pride (not to mention Jimmy Carter) and went with mawkish love songs and some dubious B.B. King guitar. This one is as tough culturally/politically as *Tryin' Like the Devil*, as tender romantically/domestically as *Got No Bread*, and puts in some James Brown funk where it belongs. Original grade: A minus. **B+**

Tangerine Dream: *Stratosfear* (Virgin '77). I respect their synthesizer textures in theory, but these guys should leave the accessibility to Kraftwerk. When they program in received semi-classical melodies and set the automatic drummer on "bouncy swing," the result is the soundtrack for a space travelogue you don't want to see. **C**

A Taste of Honey: *A Taste of Honey* (Capitol '78). Those who cite "Boogie Oogie Oogie" as definitive disco dumbness should reread the lyrics of "Tutti Frutti" and think about the great tradition of the left-field girl-group novelty — "Mr. Lee," "Iko Iko," "Shame, Shame, Shame." But though a couple of other songs here, notably "Distant," indicate that their pan may flash again, late converts are advised to seek out the single and wish they could buy the disco disc. **C+**

Howard Tate: *Howard Tate's Reaction* (Turntable '70). Born in Macon and resident in Philadelphia, Tate is a truly underground soul singer whose few small late-'60s hits (collected on one superb Verve LP) have earned him a rep among cognoscenti as diverse as Mike Bloomfield and Mark Farner. This album, produced by underground schlock-soul singers Lloyd Price and Johnny Nash in Jamaica, is based on even smaller hits. One of them, "These Are the Things That Make Me Know You're Gone" ("refrigerator left ajar," like that), dishonors his rep. But "My Soul's Got a Hole in It" doesn't, and Tate's voice is potent enough to activate more inert material. Cognoscenti will dig. **B**

Howard Tate: *Howard Tate* (Atlantic '72). In which Jerry Ragovoy sets out once again to prove to a callous world that the man with the high aaahh deserves better than a hack license between visits to the studio. This does almost as much for Tate's amazing vocal and emotional range — as cocksure as Wilson Pickett one moment, as sweet and hurting as B. B. King the next, and as corny as Joe Tex to top it off — as his Verve stuff with Ragovoy. Reservation: a few too many

compositions by the producer. "She's a Burglar" and "Keep Cool, Don't Be a Fool" are as memorable as "Piece of My Heart," but I don't know about the hitchhiking song. How about a little "Good Rockin' Tonight," Jerry? **A—**

Bernie Taupin: *Bernie Taupin* (Elektra '72). That's right, Elton John's lyricist — you think there were two of them? Reciting his verse to musical accompaniment, just like Rod McKuen. Who does it better. **E**

Tavares: *In the City* (Capitol '76). It's so simple even arrant schlockmeisters like Lambert and Potter can pull it off. You'll need a dynamite single to set the mood, of course, but if you're patient and work hard there'll be an "It Only Takes a Minute" every year or two. Make sure a couple of the other entries from your songwriting mill are of top quality ("Ready, Willing and Able," "In the City") and then —this is important — fill holes with outside material (Edgar Winter, George Clinton, AWB) for variety. So how come no other disco-oriented vocal group has produced a satisfying album this year? Might as well ask why money is green. **B+**

Tavares: *Sky-High!* (Capitol '76). In the tradition of the produced group, they make hit singles, not albums, and *In the City* was apparently a fluke. This time they've switched to Freddie Perren, whose affinity for the transcendantly awkward lyric, best represented on the Miracles' *City of Angels*, here produces such gems as "The mighty power of love/It's got more force than any shove" and "Son you gotta give a heck/You gotta promise to give respect.") Three fine tunes, four or five drecky ones. **B—**

Tavares: *The Best of Tavares* (Capitol '77). Anonymous vocally, the creatures of various cheerfully crass producers, these five brothers are professional entertainers without apology, and this is the cream of a lifetime of sweat. Side one crackles through their three best uptempo tracks into "Don't

Take Away the Music,'' which I find tolerable because in this song — one cliche deserves another — music equals love instead of its ever-lovin' self. Side two is silly soulish stuff highlighted by a couple of choice Lambert & Potter oxymorons: "The Love I Never Had'' and "Remember What I Told You to Forget.''   **A−**

Alex Taylor: *With Friends and Neighbors* (Capricorn '71). I figure it's time I come out with it. I hate James Taylor and I don't trust any of his damn family either. But if I had to choose I think I'd take Alex — he sounds kinda bluesy, like he's in it for the money. Original grade: B.   **B−**

Hound Dog Taylor and the House-Rockers: *Hound Dog Taylor and the HouseRockers* (Alligator '71). This had been around for a while when, in a low mood, I innocently put it on after three sides of Warner Bros. rock and roll as folk Muzak — the new Youngbloods, the new double Stoneground. Yawn, sigh, and then pow — electronic gutbucket from the Chicago blues bars, the rawest record I've heard in years. Taylor makes a neoprimitivist showboat like James Cotton sound like a cross between Don Nix and the Harmonicats, and about time. N.b.: a guitar-playing friend tells me the axe Hound Dog brandishes on the cover is the cheapest you can buy.   **A−**

Hound Dog Taylor and the House-Rockers: *Natural Boogie* (Alligator '74). Taylor is a spiritual and cultural miracle. Only John Lee Hooker is as unselfconsciously inelegant, and Hooker doesn't have Brewer Phillips's bass and Ted Harvey's drums to turn his blues into rock and roll. All three players are absolutely comfortable with their severe formal limits — their simplicity is unerring. Yet given the limits all three are virtuosic and expressive, especially Taylor, whose runs, slurs, and stutters move the groove as they personalize it. Taken together, his singing and his slide mine the guttural for all the music in it, and when he does a slow one you believe.   **A−**

Hound Dog Taylor and the House-Rockers: *Beware of the Dog* (Alligator '76). Released posthumously, this live album was in the works well before Taylor's death — it's a celebration, not an exploitation. There's no real gain in spontaneity — how could there be? But for those who like their blues on the hot side, it's where to start.   **A−**

James Taylor: *Sweet Baby James* (Warner Bros. '70). I have solved the Taylor Perplex, which seems to revolve around whether James was a verier godsend when he was gracing Macdougal Street with the Flying Machine, discovering the Beatles on Apple, or now. My answer: none of the above. Which leaves an even more perplexing question: which god is supposed to have sent him? Not the one in Rock and Roll Heaven, that's for sure. Original grade: C plus.   **B−**

James Taylor: *Mud Slide Slim and the Blue Horizon* (Warner Bros. '71). If even his admirers acknowledge that his music has lost some of its drive (*lost some of its drive?*), then even a sworn enemy can admit that he's capable of interesting songs and intricate music. Having squandered most of the songs on his big success, he's concentrating on the intricate music — the lyrics are more onanistic than ever, escapist as a matter of conscious thematic decision. From what? you well may wonder. From success, poor fella. Blues singers lived on the road out of economic necessity, although they often got into it; Taylor is an addict, pure and simple. A born-rich nouveau star who veers between a "homestead on the farm'' (what does he raise there, hopes?) and the Holiday Inn his mean old existential dilemma compels him to call home deserves the conniving, self-pitying voice that is his curse. Interesting, intricate, unlistenable. Original grade: C minus.   **C+**

James Taylor: *Gorilla* (Warner Bros. '75). This is no better than *Mud Slide Slim* (several good songs if you care about James's agonies) or *One Man Dog* (several interesting experiments if you care about James's ideas), and although it *is* better than *Walking Man,* so is *The Best of the Cowsills.* Basically a solid piece of singer-songwriter product — I might actively enjoy "Lighthouse" or "Angry Blues" if someone else sang them, and I enjoy "Gorilla" and "Mexico" now. So why do his devotees regard it as a heartening comeback? Because its desecration of Marvin Gaye has propelled it into the top ten? Or because they never cared about his agonies or ideas either? **C+**

James Taylor: *Greatest Hits* (Warner Bros. '76). As egoists go, Taylor is a talent — a gifted guitarist, a better-than-average melodist, a pithy lyricist whose feeling for Americanese is warm if corny. And his voice you can get used to — it's soulful in its way, and he can phrase. But melodies aside, he's not a star for his virtues. He's a star because he's an egoist — because he vaunts his sensitivity so expertly. So it's inevitable that this best-of should shortchange his sense of humor ("Gorilla," "Chili Dog," "Money Machine") and horror ("Knocking 'Round the Zoo," "Junkie's Lament") and preserve his disgraceful covers of "You've Got a Friend" and "How Sweet It Is." If you want "Fire and Rain," buy *Sweet Baby James.* At least it's a piece of history. **C**

James Taylor: *JT* (Columbia '77). James sounds both awake — worth a headline in itself — and in touch; maybe CBS gave him a clock radio for opening an account there. "Handy Man" is a transcendent sex ballad, while "I Was Only Telling a Lie" and "Secret o' Life" evoke comparison with betters on the order of the Stones and Randy Newman, so that the wimpy stuff — which still predominates — sounds merely laid-back in contrast. Best since *Sweet Baby James,* shit — some of this is so wry

and lively and committed his real fans may find it obtrusive. **B**

James Taylor: *Flag* (Columbia '79). What's wrong with most of these songs is that Taylor is singing them. He can sing, sure — the "Day Tripper" cover and "Is That the Way You Look" show off his amused, mildly funky self-involvement at its sharpest and sexiest. But too often the material reveals him at his sharpest and most small-minded; John Lennon might get away with "I Will Not Lie for You," but JT's whine undermines whatever honesty the sentiment may have. **C+**

Johnnie Taylor: *Johnnie Taylor's Greatest Hits* (Stax '70). Heir to Sam Cooke in the Soul Stirrers and Otis Redding at Stax, Taylor is everything you could ask of a soul singer except great. Gritty, rhythmic, and felt just aren't enough — there has to be something absolutely distinctive in the phrasing and timbre, and he's always been a little vague in both departments. But on this compilation there's plenty of definition from Don Davis, who has production and writing credit on five of the six cuts on side two, an examination of monogamy and its vicissitudes that will shortly be covered whole by none other than Charley Pride. (Just kidding.) **A−**

Johnnie Taylor: *One Step Beyond* (Stax '71). In which Taylor delivers a love sermon and works his two themes for two hits. "Jody's Got Your Girl and Gone" is a memorable addition to the mythology of infidelity, but "I Am Somebody" is at best a competent black pride riff in biracial drag — like the rest, nothing to be ashamed of rather than something to be proud of. **B−**

Johnnie Taylor: *Taylored in Silk* (Stax '73). With the aid of Wade Marcus's gloopy strings, this is where Taylor goes pop, and though he's trying for silk it sounds like the same old polyester — eight songs stretched over thirty-three minutes, including one soul-wringer hit, one blues-talking hit, and filler, much of which does have a certain reflective charm. **B−**

Johnnie Taylor: *Super Taylor* (Stax '74). Last time the best cuts took a while despite their hit history, which meant you never got to the others without working at it. Here "It's September" (a you're-due-home lyric finished off with a sharp question mark of a guitar riff) and "I've Been Born Again" (testifying so ebulliently for fidelity that it sounds like both fun and the truth) have seduced me into listening to both sides again and again. And you know, they're pretty good. Original grade: B plus. **B**

Johnnie Taylor: *Eargasm* (Columbia '76). Taylor's commitment to the traditional soul style remains unimpeachable even when he accedes to material as modish as the likable but lightweight "Disco Lady." But to call him traditional is not entirely a compliment — he still lacks the kind of aggressive originality that can take a mediocre hook-and-lyric by the ear and drag it out of oblivion. Which is where too much of this album remains. **C+**

Johnnie Taylor: *Chronicle — The Twenty Greatest Hits* (Stax '77). Despite the somewhat self-serving title — the man did record for Stax pre-Don Davis, and the final track has never been a single before and will never be called a hit again — this testifies. Only on the breakthrough "Who's Makin' Love" did he ever cut a track to equal any of dozens by Otis or Aretha, but for a journeyman he's a minor genius — who knows more about fucking around than Alfred Kinsey. **A−**

Kate Taylor: *Sister Kate* (Cotillion '71). Good song selection overproduced to conceal the basic characterlessness of the singer, who is unfortunately no relation to Hound Dog. **C−**

Koko Taylor: *Koko Taylor* (Chess '72). Taylor sounds like you always wanted those women with Big in front of their names to sound — powerful, even rough, without ever altogether

abandoning her rather feminine register. But though mentor Willie Dixon is the greatest contemporary blues composer, he's no more reliable album to album than any other song factory — the best lyric here, "Love You Like a Woman" ("But I'll also fight you like a man"), isn't his. Terrific production, though — his soul devices are so crude and obvious they're funny, amazing, or at least odd. Original grade: A minus. **B+**

Koko Taylor: *Basic Soul* (Chess '72). Apparently, what basic soul means to Willie Dixon is basic blues — the music is in the traditional Chicago style, as it should be. But the songs have lost additional wang dang doodle — the standout is "Violent Love," in which Willie and Koko try their hand at camp and don't get bitten. **B**

Koko Taylor: *I Got What It Takes* (Alligator '75). Taylor's first album in three years illustrates the difference between blues as (theoretical) pop music on Chess and blues as (theoretical) art music on Alligator. There's a certain hothouse quality to this album — it's devoid of endearing, enriching commercial vulgarities. But both band (featuring Mighty Joe Young and Sammy Lawhorn on guitar and the endearing Abb Locke on saxophone) and material (from Taylor and Dixon through Elmore James and Magic Sam and Ruth Brown to Otis Spann's unnecessarily theoretical "Blues Never Die") range beyond Chess's commercial strictures, which more than makes up. **B+**

Koko Taylor: *The Earthshaker* (Alligator '78). Considering its size, Taylor's voice has never been what you'd call rich — she flubs the pitch quite a bit, and on the slow ones she's often sounded flat emotionally as well. But it retains amazing presence — by now it's deepened and roughened so much that her late work for Chess sounds girlish by comparison. Two or three of the slow ones here really drag, always a crippling flaw in Chicago blues, but the uptempo stuff is exemplary — the songs are fun as songs, and the guitar on her latest remake of "Wang Dang Doodle" is ace. **B+**

Livingston Taylor: *Echoes* (Capricorn '79). Vocally, Liv is almost James's twin but not quite — he adds a touch of depth to the lissome drawl and subtracts all wow and flutter. Since what makes James unique is also what makes him repulsive, I find Liv more likable but less interesting — especially given his songwriting, which this best-of, drawn from his three early-'70s LPs, makes the best of. I ask you, what good is a funny voice without a sense of humor? **C+**

Bram Tchaikovsky: *Strange Man, Changed Man* (Polydor '79). Bram's multitracked, overechoed interpretations of old-wave profundities like "I'm the one that's leaving" and new wave bromides like "all these people suck" makes him sound like a power pop Crosby, Crosby & Crosby. One of these tunes is reputed to have been a hit, but damned if I can tell which one. **C+**

Television: *Marquee Moon* (Elektra '77). I know why people complain about Tom Verlaine's angst-ridden voice, but fuck that, I haven't had such intense pleasure from a new release since I got into *Layla* three months after it came out, and this took about fifteen seconds. The lyrics, which are in a demotic-philosophical mode ("I was listening/listening to the rain/I was hearing/hearing something else"), would carry this record alone; so would the guitar playing, as lyrical and piercing as Clapton or Garcia but totally unlike either. Yes, you bet it rocks. And no, I didn't believe they'd be able to do it on record because I thought this band's excitement was all in the live raveups. Turns out that's about a third of it. **A+**

Television: *Adventure* (Elektra '78). Those scandalized by *Marquee Moon's* wimpoid tendencies are gonna try to read this one out of the movement. I agree that it's not as urgent, or as satisfying, but that's only to say that *Marquee Moon* was a great album while *Adventure* is a very good one. The difference is more a function of material than of the new album's relatively clean, calm, reflective mood. The lyrics on *Marquee Moon* were shot through with visionary surprises that never let up. These are comparatively songlike, their apercus concentrated in hook lines that are surrounded by more quotidian stuff. The first side is funnier, faster, more accessible, but the second side gets there — the guitar on "The Fire" is Verlaine's most gorgeous ever. **A−**

Jack Tempchin: *Jack Tempchin* (Arista '78). In which the successful L.A. songwriter and former (putative) Funky King becomes a Schmeagle for our time — in the course of four terrific songs he loses his keys, misplaces his car, doesn't get laid, and spends fifteen days under the hood. That's the trick, Jack — tell enough jokes on yourself and your self-pity becomes tolerable. **B**

The Temptations: *Psychedelic Shack* (Gordy '70). It's no accident that the best cut here begins "Ain't no words to this song." For all the hyperactivity of his horn charts, Norman Whitfield is a lot better equipped to get funky than to lead Motown's belated raid on "relevance," and many of these lyrics are dreadful. Several of them are quite all right, though, and "War" does help mitigate the climactic wishy-wash of "Friendship Train." More to the point, the singing and playing really do fuse the production styles of Smokey and Sly, a major achievement. Why do white people challenge these songs so much quicker than they did "Lucy in the Sky" or "Happiness Is a Warm Gun"? Are friendship trains any dumber than bed-ins? **B**

The Temptations: *Greatest Hits, Volume 2* (Gordy '70). They have declined, it's true. Though my animus against "Ball of Confusion" disappeared the moment I heard four teenaged girls sing it in a doorway on Avenue B, "Psychedelic Shack" and "Don't Let the Joneses Get You Down" are worthy of the Monkees and a couple of the love songs (on the same side, I'm happy to report) are drab. But "Cloud Nine" and "Run Away Child, Running Wild" not only work as pop protest but bear witness to how funky these smoothies have become. And so do such pinnacles of harmony as "I Wish It Would Rain" and "I Can't Get Next to You."   **A−**

The Temptations: *Sky's the Limit* (Gordy '71). Greater even than "Just My Imagination" is "Smiling Faces Sometimes," in which for twelve minutes Norman Whitfield's spacey string and sound effects combine with a rhythm track that might as well be looped to transform Eddie Kendricks's soft lead into the rap of a paranoid soothsayer. But on the flip Whitfield funks up James Bond horns for nine horrible minutes and finds a Swahili title for an offensively defensive brotherhood appeal.   **B**

The Temptations: *Solid Rock* (Gordy '72). The Whitfield-Strong notes describe the Temptations as "five of the strongest individuals we've ever met," but nowhere are these individuals named. There is, however, a roll call of studio musicians.   **C**

The Temptations: *All Directions* (Gordy '72). The producer gets one side — live "funky music," a song about white people that's actually nasty, and the Franz Mesmer Memorial Version of "Papa Was a Rolling Stone," all 11:45 of it. The group gets the other — sweet ballads of varying quality plus three minutes of easy Isaac Hayes funk. The album is their best of the decade — mostly on the strength of the producer's side.   **B+**

The Temptations: *Masterpiece* (Gordy '73). One hesitates to complain about "another" tale of oppression in the ghetto, but Norman Whitfield, who dominates the tale by spacing out his few ideas over fourteen minutes, provides the temptation.   **C+**

The Temptations: *1990* (Gordy '73). Not only isn't this good Motown, it isn't good Motown psychedelic — except for some sharp strumming on the title track (a half-assed indictment of/tribute to America) it never takes off rhythmically *or* vocally.   **C−**

The Temptations: *A Song for You* (Gordy '75). "Shakey Ground" could almost be some old gospel stomper, a good thing on an album that includes a tribute to Kahlil Gibran. And though the selection *is* a bit of a cliché, it's nice to hear David Ruffin stretch out on the title tune. Only wait a second, that's obviously not David Ruffin. Paul Williams? No, he died. Norman Whitfield? No, he left, and anyway I don't think he's a singer. And Eddie Kendricks, I mean Damon Harris, a tenor. Oh yeah, Dennis Edwards.   **C**

The Temptations: *Bare Back* (Atlantic '78). In which a major club attraction, its hitmaking days apparently past, essays "A Holland Group Production Inc." in hopes of postponing the transition to oldies act.   **C**

10cc: *10cc* (UK '73). If you only know the forty-five-rpm version of "Rubber Bullets," then you missed their best rhyme: "balls and chains" with "balls and brains." A calculated, devilishly clever version of what the Beach Boys ought to be doing. Or the Bonzo Dog Band should have done. Or something.   **B+**

10cc: *Sheet Music* (UK '74). Points for studio mastery and general literacy — "Oh Effendi," about the vicissitudes of Middle Eastern trade, is Cole Porter-ishly clever — but demerits for a detachment that might seem pathological if it weren't so damned expert. Great satire communicates a feeling — most often hatred or anguish, although it can be kinder, as in "The Dean and I" on *10cc* — that is lacking from this too-too apollonian (cerebral? professional? glib?) endeavor. Though if the feeling itself is absent, a good beat will sometimes suffice in its stead.   **B**

10cc: *The Original Soundtrack* (Mercury '75). Is it supposed to be parody to make your imitation movie mush more unbearable than any real thing, or just expert musicianship? And stretching your only decent melody (a nonsatirical love song) over six tedious minutes, is that a joke? And who is the butt of "Une Nuit A Paris," the dumb yank or the greedy frog? Cor, or do I mean blimey, most of this wouldn't last long enough to close Saturday night. **D+**

10cc: *100cc* (UK '75). It can't be easy to put together a compilation album that's less listenable than either of the two regular-issue LPs to which you have access, but displaced impresario Jonathan King, trailing kisses in the direction of "I'm Not in Love" (which he doesn't control) and "Everyone's Gone to the Moon," does the trick here with the help of a few B sides. Secretly, I suspect, King still hopes to score a schlock smash like the two aforementioned, so instead of sticking to the uptempo burlesques that are 10cc's entree to the human race he gives a lot of their art-school slow stuff a second shot. And comes up with zilch. **B−**

10cc: *How Dare You!* (Mercury '76). The putrefaction isn't as extreme as on last year's hit album, but the affliction would seem permanent — they don't know whether they're supposed to be funny or pretty, and so nine times out of ten they're neither. **C**

10cc: *Greatest Hits 1972–1978* (Polydor '79). Separating the jokes from the japes, eschewing atmospheric preciosity, and climaxing with two great pieces of lovesong schmaltz that define the group's seriousness, this is as consistent a 10cc LP as you can buy. But I miss oldies like "Johnny, Don't Do It," "The Worst Band in the World," "Oh Effendi." And I still don't believe "Dreadlock Holiday" is "Safe European Home" in corporate-rock drag. **B+**

Ten Wheel Drive with Genya Ravan: *Brief Replies* (Polydor '70). This beats lighthouse (arrghh) and Blood, Sweat & Tears (urrp), but with their intricate charts and printed music

Michael Zager and Aram Schefrin make like they paid their dues in a conservatory. Which I'm sure they did. The intensity of Janis surrogate Ravan is a little less harsh and wearying on the follow-up, though. And it all comes together on "Morning Much Better," about when rather than how to make love. **C+**

Ten Years After: *Cricklewood Green* (Deram '70). Despite Leo Lyons's responsive bass and Ric Lee's reliable drums, it's obviously the speed and tensile tone of Alvin Lee's guitar that makes this music what it is — pure boogie, a style which benefits from impurities. As such, it's best experienced on *Undead*. Alvin sings pretty well, but his songwriting is barely serviceable, which puts the ordinary amenities of studio pop beyond his means. **B−**

Ten Years After: *Watt* (Deram '70). Except for "Sweet Little Sixteen" and "The Band with No Name" ("band" means "song"; I suggest "Ghost Riders on the Ground") this is distinguishable from *Cricklewood Green* primarily by its cover. Docked a notch for coming after *Cricklewood Green*. **C+**

Ten Years After: *A Space in Time* (Columbia '71). In which the rock heavy comes of age with his toughest, fullest, and most coherent album. I like it in a way, but it does lack a certain winning abandon, and I'm not crazy about the heavy's economic theories — fellow seems to believe that if you "tax the rich to feed the poor" you soon run out of rich, with dire consequences. Original grade: B plus. **B−**

Ten Years After: *Rock & Roll Music to the World* (Columbia '72). I remember when this was a promising group — that Alvin Lee, he sure could sing and play, and those other guys sure did get it together behind him. But in four years and then some, all they've accomplished is to get it together some more. As unslick as ever, they're nevertheless a lot tighter in the commercial sense, and the speed and brevity of such cuts as "Choo Choo

Mama" exemplify Alvin Lee's rockabilly approach to blues. On its own terms, this is mature, impressive work. But I suspect that the next time I feel like hearing TYA — in eight months or so — I'll put on *Undead*. It's pretty crude, but you know about old time's sake. **B**

Ten Years After: *The Classic Performances of Ten Years After* (Columbia '76). OK, so the classic performances are on Deram. Neoclassic, then. I still find that their late phase has its kinetic (as we used to say) charms. And admit that even without the regrettable "Positive Vibrations" I'd be very unlikely to play this except for historical reference. **B**

Joe Tex: *I Gotcha* (Dial '72). Joe's rhythms have gotten a lot trickier since the days of "Show Me" and "Skinny Legs," which is probably the real reason the title tune was such a smash — the story line isn't up to his vintage stuff even if Joe was moved to restate it for a finale. Granted, I did turn up the treble to find out what he was asking her to do in "You Said a Bad Word" (still don't know). But beyond that there's only — talk about common touch — "Bad Feet," which has nothing to do, narratively, with getting on the good one. **B−**

Joe Tex: *Bumps and Bruises* (Epic '77). Tex is a novelty artist whose subject is morality, so that in one song a little old lady brains a mugger with a can of sauerkraut, in another Tex advocates tolerance for "sissies," and in a third he sings a humorous chorus about having his hands cut off — all over some very punchy dance tracks by James Brown out of Stax-Volt. Amazingly rich and spirited for a comeback album off a freak hit. **B+**

Joe Tex: *Rub Down* (Epic '78). Because the jokes and grooves are mostly baldies and retreads, there's an obvious alternative title: *Let Down*. But that's only in comparison to *Bumps and Bruises*, the fruit of a layoff long enough to give this glorious bullshit

artist the chance to think up some really good cons. **B−**

Thin Lizzy: *Jailbreak* (Mercury '76). The proof of how desperate people are for new Springsteen is that they'll settle for this — even "The Boys Are Back in Town" is the sort of thing that ends up in Bruce's wastebasket. If Irish teen traumas are as boring as Phil Lynott's descriptions of them, it's no wonder they have trouble maintaining their birthrate. And if Irish teen traumas are as secondhand as Scott Gorham's guitar lines, the Irish will probably end up preferring Springsteen too. **B−**

38 Special: *38 Special* (A&M '77). For this group, booked by Ronnie Van Zant's agent, managed by his manager, and led by his kid brother, some special Inspirational Verse: "It's a Saturday night ordinary/All the pros know what dues to pay/Ain't really good for nuthin'/'Cept to take some other rocker's chance away." **D+**

B. J. Thomas: *Billy Joe Thomas* (Scepter '72). B. J. might be the Johnny Rivers of the Leon Russell generation — he was born in Texas, after all — if only he had better taste. Some pleasant stuff complements the two great ones here — "Rock and Roll Lullabye," the hit, and the suppressed Carole King nasty, "A Fine Way to Go" — but anyone who'd agree to record "We've Got to Get Our Ship Together" is in need of some brain-caulking himself. Original grade: B minus. **C+**

B. J. Thomas: *The Very Best of B. J. Thomas* (United Artist '74). I understand now that Thomas never turned rock and roller because he was, and is, a country singer. And like most he does better with the real stuff — "No Love at All" comes close for a pop song and he broke with a Hank Williams cover — than with Bacharach-David. But I still want to know who left "Rock and Roll Lullabye" off this thing. **C**

Irma Thomas: *Safe with Me* (RCS '79). I assume they reprised the title song because they thought it was a sure shot, but they miscalculated, which is too bad — this album could use a sure shot. Thomas is deep, the material intelligent, and the mix of soul and disco disarmingly offhand. I like every cut except the gris-gris-for-tourists "Princess La-La." But I don't love a one of 'em. **B+**

Marlo Thomas and Friends: *Free to Be . . . You and Me* (Bell '73). I've been giving this high-minded feminist kiddie record to various young Americans on the theory that it is not necessary, or easy, to like the New York Dolls at age five. I figured it would be good for them, like baths. Surprise number one is that they all love it, to a person. Surprise number two is that I myself would much rather listen to Carol Channing on housework than to Robert Klein on dope. **A−**

Richard Thompson: *Henry the Human Fly* (Reprise '72). From "The Old Changing Way" to "The New St. George," Thompson intensifies the common-folk sympathies of the best English folk-rockers into militant class consciousness. Not that he's into protest — just dramatization (Brecht would approve). His plain, expressive voice and plain, brilliant guitar do their work. Official title of the track I think of as "Live in Fear": "Roll Over Vaughan Williams." Inspirational Verse: "Don't expect the words to fall too sweetly on your ear." **A−**

Richard & Linda Thompson: *Hokey Pokey* (Island '74). Richard Thompson may not be quite the "refugee" he believes — folkies have a way of romanticizing anything down-and-outside — but one-eyed Smiffy, big-spending Georgie, prematurely mature Billy, and the denizens of the Egypt Room are certainly a vivid cast of outcasts. And not only does he know

about love gone wrong — "I'll Forget It All in the Morning" is as bleak as relationship songs get — he also knows about ice cream. **A**

Richard and Linda Thompson: *Pour Down Like Silver* (Island '76). I wish there were an American folk duo that combined such engaging music with such committed intelligence. (The McGarrigles don't count — they're Canadian.) But since neither pessimism nor private poetry guarantees profundity, I also wish these lyrics earned their dourness as persuasively as the music does. Irresistible: "Hard Luck Stories." **B+**

Richard Thompson: *Live (More or Less)* (Island '77). This is Linda's album too no matter what the cover says — one disc is the duo's 1974 English debut, *I Want to See the Bright Lights Tonight,* and while the collection of previously unavailable live material emphasizes Richard's modal guitar, you should hear them team up on "Dark End of the Street." Most folk-rock succeeds only in accentuating the irretrievability of the past, but the Thompsons' hard-nosed Sufi fatalism delivers them from nostalgia. When they sing about getting "to the border," they're talking about dying, not smuggling weed from Mexico, and they make the crossing sound like an earthly triumph ("drowned in a barrel of wine" indeed). Because they believe in eternity, the Thompsons don't sentimentalize about time gone — they simply encompass it in an endless present. **A−**

Richard & Linda Thompson: *First Light* (Chrysalis '78). Richard T. has always redeemed corny themes with a humor dry enough to be mistaken for nasty, as when he includes "I'll punch you in the nose" in a list of odd jobs he'll do. But nowhere else on "Restless Highway," "Sweet Surrender," and "The Choice Wife Died for Love" — the bulk of side one — do the lyrics deviate from the expectable. Just as distressing, the guitar veers away from Thompson's unique, timeless modalism toward the studio country-rock favored by new sidemen Willie Weeks and Andy Newmark. I love "Strange Affair," one of his greatest death songs yet, and still find the austere harmonies bracing. But I want the Thompsons' pervasive Anglicism straight when I want it at all. **B**

George Thorogood and the Destroyers: *George Thorogood and the Destroyers* (Rounder '77). What is it that a blues interpreter black or white is supposed to do? Something about making the song his (or hers, Bonnie) — the way Mick Jagger always does, even on his absurd version of "I Just Wanna Make Love to You." Thorogood claims only "One Bourbon, One Scotch, One Beer." And if the rest sounds good when it comes on the radio, that says more about the radio than it does about the rest. **B**

George Thorogood and the Destroyers: *Move It on Over* (Rounder '78). It's impossible not to be charmed by Thorogood's enthusiasm, and instrumentally this band is as likable as, say, Hound Dog Taylor's HouseRockers. But only closet folkies could vest hope in a noncomposer whose taste in material is markedly less interesting than the Blues Brothers' and whose only virtue as a vocalist is his complete lack of embarrassment. Harmless, but inconsequential. **B**

Three Dog Night: *It Ain't Easy* (Dunhill '70). Admitting it won't gain me any of the hip cachet I crave, but I admired and enjoyed this group's first LP. I found the second mediocre and the live job that followed it wretchedly excessive, but this one — their fourth in just fourteen months — gets back: exemplary song-finding and not too much plastic-soul melon-mouthing or preening vocal pyrotechnique. Highlights: the hit version of Randy Newman's "Mama Told Me Not to Come," with just the right admixture of high-spirited schlock to turn it into the AM giant it deserves to be, and a departure from pre-Beatles times

called "Good Feeling (1957)." Original grade: B plus. **B**

Three Dog Night: *Harmony* (Dunhill '71). Next to Grand Funk, they're the country's top touring act, and they sell singles in the multiple millions besides. They're slick as Wesson Oil. And when they choose the right material and go light on the minstrel-show theatrics, they're fine — next to "Maggie May," "Joy to the World" is the most durable single of the year. Their albums do vary — avoid the "Joy to the World" vehicle *Naturally* — but I think this is the best. Even if you're hostile, you'll have to concede that any group that can string together great-but-obscure songs from Marvin Gaye, Joni Mitchell, and Moby Grape without inspiring a rush back to the originals has something going for it. Wish they'd cut the poetry reading, though. Original grade: A. **B+**

Three Dog Night: *Seven Separate Fools* (Dunhill '72). Their worst-ever studio LP doesn't deserve to be called slick. It's professional and expensive, yes, but it's also a mess — oversung, overarranged, overpackaged. Their tasty material has turned into a mush of campaign-promise social consciousness, and the two songs I know in other versions sound bloated. This could be the beginning of the end. **C**

Three Dog Night: *Joy to the World — Their Greatest Hits* (ABC '74). Things seem to be winding up for the Kings of Oversing, but this fourteen-song compilation demonstrates that the singles, unlike the albums, didn't diminish much. It also suggests that though they're praised when at all for translating weirdos like Nilsson and Newman into AM, they also deserve credit for preserving the odd goody (two apiece) by the likes of Paul Williams and Hoyt Axton. Only Lighthouse keeper Skip Prokop proves beyond help. **B+**

Thunderclap Newman: *Hollywood Dream* (Track '70). Drums: Speedy

Keen, a Cockney who writes and sings a very creaky lead. Guitar: Jimmy McCulloch, who is sixteen and looks thirteen. Piano, surname, and miscellaneous: Andy Newman, who is in his late twenties and looks in his early forties, and who didn't want to join because it meant giving up his pension at the post office. Message of hit single: "the revolution's here." Producer and miscellaneous: Peter Townshend. Is this your idea of fun, Peter? Is this your idea of art? What ever happened to Arthur Brown, anyway? And will you pay the man his pension? Original grade: B plus.   **B −**

Tin Huey: *Contents Dislodged During Shipment* (Warner Bros. '79). They get arch at times, both lyrically (e.g. the "surreal" "Puppet Wipes") and in rhythm changes and instrumental breaks that betray an art-rock heritage. But like Pere Ubu, these Akron boys make art-rock that *rocks,* with chops you can enjoy for all the music's sake. And if their humor is collegiate, I'm a sophomore.   **B +**

Toots and the Maytals: *Funky Kingston* (Island '75). The quick way to explain the Maytals is to say that in reggae they're the Beatles to the Wailers' Rolling Stones. But how do I explain Toots himself? Well, he's the nearest thing to Otis Redding left on the planet: he transforms "do re mi fa sol la ti do" into joyful noise. I wish he had real politics — any Jamaican who can only pray to God about this time tough hasn't ever been compelled to explore all his options — and lately his arrangements have been looser than I'd like, but this is a gift. Original grade: A   **A −**

Toots and the Maytals: *Reggae Got Soul* (Island '76). In Toots the physical voice is all but equivalent to the artistic "voice," the way that term is applied to poets sometimes, and all its warmth, humor, and vivacity come through here. But what has made Toots doubly impressive is the amazing hit songs his voice was attached to.

For starters: "Sweet and Dandy," "5446 Was My Number," "Monkey Man," and "African Doctor." None of these has been released on an American Maytals album, and nothing on this album, not even "Rasta Man" or "True Love Is Hard to Find," equals any of them.   **B +**

Toots and the Maytals: *Pass the Pipe* (Mango '79). This isn't as well-crafted song for song as *Reggae Got Soul,* but because it doesn't assume that "soul" equals U.S. success it's a lot less confused, and I like it more. The music's momentum is unimpeded by bad faith, and the three compositions that do stand out — especially "Famine," as amazing a juxtaposition of horror and good cheer as Jimmy Cliff's "Viet Nam" — sound like great ones. **B +**

Peter Tosh: *Legalize It* (Columbia '76). Unlike most sidemen who go on to pursue their own artistic interests, ex-Wailer Tosh has managed to gather about half an album for his solo debut, which ain't bad. "Ketchy Shuby" even has the makings of a novelty hit. But oh, how his light heart and romantic spirit are missed among his old mates.   **B**

Peter Tosh: *Equal Rights* (Columbia '77). What's most impressive about this music is its sinew. The tracks are strong, yet although they usually include at least seven instrumental parts, they never sound lush, full, or even jubilantly multipercussive, which given Tosh's increasingly ominous lyrics is a good thing. Yet while Tosh's lyrics are more correct politically than Marley's, they're only marginally more eloquent. His singing is rather less eloquent.   **B +**

Peter Tosh: *Bush Doctor* (Rolling Stones '78). The musical surprises on Tosh's second album established his gift for dublike production depth in a song format. The instant memorability of the tunes here does the same for his melodic gift. Mick and Keith add a few ingratiating touches. Nice. **B +**

Peter Tosh: *Mystic Man* (Rolling Stones '79). Mysticism should keep its own counsel; boast about it, translate your supposed experience of the ineffable into any but the most simpleminded ideology, and ninety-five times out of a hundred you'll sound like a smug asshole. Tosh's ever more preachy vocal stance does nothing for his dopey puns ("shitty" for "city," far out), his confused political-economic theories, or his equation of hamburgers with heroin. And his musicians sound like the bored pros rockers so often turn into. **C+**

Allen Toussaint: *Toussaint* (Scepter '71). "Everything I Do Gonna Be Funky," announces the pianist-composer-producer-arranger behind dozens of New Orleans hits on a great cut that Lee Dorsey did even better, but lurking amid the ensuing instrumentals are Roger Williams (maybe somebody classier, but that's who it sounds like to me), "The Hallelujah Chorus," and Vince Guaraldi. Granted, on the A side Toussaint sings five excellent songs, four of which he wrote himself. But Joe Simon did better with "Chokin' Kind." And Lee Dorsey did better with "Working in a Coal Mine." **B**

Allen Toussaint: *Life, Love and Faith* (Warner Bros. '72). Toussaint relies on overdubbing to camouflage his often colorless delivery and occasionally colorless songwriting. But if going solo stretches him thin, it also stretches him — the phasing-and-saxophone on "Goin' Down" is a producer's dream come true, "Victims of the Darkness" is recommended to Norman Whitfield, and on "Out of the City" he reminds us that in the country "the grass is greener on every side." **B+**

Allen Toussaint: *Southern Nights* (Warner Bros. '75). Toussaint's vocals have gained confidence in a soft-sung kind of way, but I really like only two songs here, one of which has been done better by Bonnie Raitt and the other of which is called — I hesitate even to type it — "Basic Lady." You have to figure that anyone who can

write a Grammy-winner for Glen Campbell might fall victim to delusions of mediocrity. **B−**

Allen Toussaint: *Motion* (Warner Bros. '78). I've always found pleasure in Toussaint's hackwork and clucked sympathetically over his ambitious failures, but complaints about Jerry Wexler's conventional soul production here miss the point — it's Toussaint himself who aspires to conventionality. Abandoning the infectious, melody-shy chanting of his best LPs, he now sings with all the passion of James Taylor, which is probably as close to Glen Campbell as he can get. Auditioning for "Southern Nights II" there are various mild concoctions — I forget which is which, but the title tune could well be with Barry Manilow at this moment — that are not offset by several mixed successes and one reminder of eccentricities past. "Optimism Blues" indeed. **C+**

Tower of Power: *Bump City* (Warner Bros. '72). San Fran white boys replicate black style, with black singer to assure authentication? Where have we heard this before? I grant that they're really from Oakland, and that the style is a modern if dubious one — brassy Dave Crawford funk. But that doesn't help the songs, or the charts. And it doesn't turn Rick Stevens into Charlie Allen. Or Linda Tillery. Or Sly Stone. Or Freddie Stone. **C**

Tower of Power: *Tower of Power* (Warner Bros. '73). Come off it, guys. You really lucked out with Lenny Williams and you know it — when he swoops up that way he makes it sound as if Aretha herself ought to cover "This Time It's Real," which isn't likely. So get all those horns out of his face. I know there are five of you, but why not just make fancy with the Pointer Sisters and leave Lenny be? You said it yourselves, or rather, Lenny did: "Sometimes hipness is what it ain't." **B**

Tower of Power: *Back to Oakland* (Warner Bros. '74). No matter whose top forty Lenny Williams makes, this isn't a soul, funk, or r&b band — the arrangements are simply too complex. It's more a stripped-down (no trombones except for guest shots) big band in the era of Doc Severinsen. Compare to any Basie edition and you will hear written charts that sound spontaneous, not to mention estimable soloists and Basie himself. And compare to a more mortal aggregation and you'll still hear riffs somebody could write songs around — but not these guys. **C+**

Tower of Power: *Urban Renewal* (Warner Bros. '74). What softened me up was the novelty effects on baritone sax, but I've always been a sucker for songs about the energy crisis and "victimless crime" anyway, and they do all right with affairs of the heart for once — even borrow a silly one from Johnny Guitar Watson. Renewed, maybe — urban I assume. **B+**

Tower of Power: *Live and in Living Color* (Warner Bros. '76). I guess they really are hot live if it comes across on the live album — the uptempo numbers have real edge, and Lenny Pickett's long honk on the 23:40-minute "Knock Yourself Out" is such a gas it makes the ensuing organ solo endurable. But Hubert Tubbs just isn't Lenny Williams — he makes the appropriate vocal sounds at the appropriate junctures, but that's all. This ruins the ballads, never a strong point. And Lenny Pickett's tweets don't add much either. **B**

Peter Townshend: *Who Came First* (Track '72). Townshend sounds as relaxed in this rather folkish Meher Baba tribute cum "gynormouse ego trip" as Paul McCartney in his do-it-yourself studio, and a lot less self-absorbed — other musical gurumongers sound "Content" (title of worst song here), but Pete seems happy, too. So much so that some of this music is a little lightweight — expressing the kind of undiscriminating joy in the everyday one might expect from somebody who considers "You always were, you always are, and you always will be" both a profound sentiment and a

snappy way to finish off a concept album. But I'm encouraged that Ronnie Lane (singer-songwriter on "Evolution") offers to drink (alcohol, get it?) to the Master and his Truth. And in the end the homely sweetness and frailty of this music prevails. [Later on MCA.] Original grade: B. **A−**

Pete Townshend-Ronnie Lane: *Rough Mix* (MCA '77). Meher Baba inspired psalmody so plain and sharply observed, maybe he was all reet after all. Three of Townshend's contributions — "Keep Me Turning," "Misunderstood," and an unlikely song of adoration called "My Baby Gives It Away" — are his keenest in years, and while Lane's evocations of the passing scene are more poignant on his Island import, *One for the Road,* "Annie" is a suitably modest folk classic. Together, the two disciples prove that charity needn't be sentimental, detachment cold, nor peace boring. Selah. Original grade: B plus. **A−**

Traffic: *John Barleycorn Must Die* (United Artists '70). With Dave Mason gone there's not much electric guitar or songwriting, leaving the chronically indecisive Stev(i)e Winwood to his feckless improvised rock, or is it folksong-based jazz? Not much bass no matter what it is. And Chris Wood blows a lot. **C+**

Traffic: *Welcome to the Canteen* (United Artists/Island '71). Lax at times, but not bad for live jazziness — Stevie Winwood and Dave Mason play as engagingly as Mike Ratledge and Elton Dean, say, and in a genuine rock style. Praise the masses it's a lot more aggressive than their studio work, with the double percussion of Jim Gordon and Rebop Kwaku Baah driving pretty hard at times. Even the lackadaisical "Gimme Some Lovin'" doesn't seem like a desecration. **B−**

Traffic: *The Low Spark of High Heeled Boys* (Island '71). These guys waste their talent — they're devoid of intellectual thrust, they've never figured out what to do with their beloved jam form, and more often than not their lyrics are designed only to fill holes in the music or the meter. Yet they're onto something here. Their modest improvisations have a lot more force and hook appeal than the ones of *John Barleycorn*, they've figured out how to incorporate horns without compromising their electricity, and sometimes it even sounds as if Winwood knows why he's singing. When it works, it suggests a nice paradox — relaxed and exciting at the same time. Original grade: B plus. **B**

Traffic: *Shoot Out at the Fantasy Factory* (Island '73). You'd think Muscle Shoals boys Roger Hawkins and David Hood would add a little spark, but they settle for a little swamp. Giveaway: "(Sometimes I Feel So) Uninspired." **C**

Trammps: *Trammps* (Golden Fleece '75). You know what they mean by calling this a disco group? They mean that all the fast songs sound pretty good and all the slow ones don't. Which means that Jimmy Ellis's gritty tenor isn't anything to dwell on but gets the job done. Thank Ron Baker, Norman Harris, and (drummer and occasional bass singer) Earl Young for giving Jimmy and the band eight quickies. And recommend their methods to other Philadelphians. **B+**

The Trammps: *The Legendary Zing Album Featuring the Fabulous Trammps* (Buddah '75). Among the attractions of this compilation of disco hits going back to 1972 are three snappy originals, Mr. Bass Man, a rock and roll version of "Zing Went the Strings of My Heart," and a disco version of "Sixty Minute Man" that divides him in two. Among the drawbacks are three soggy originals, all of them orchestral intros disguised as songs. **B+**

The Trammps: *Where the Happy People Go* (Atlantic '76). The five-minute version of Wilson Pickett's "Ninety-Nine and a Half" is the key to this album. Jimmy Ellis can't match the depth of the original, and neither can the rhythm arrangement, which is light, festooned with horn licks, fanciful if you like it and just fancy if you don't. But if you like it it's not only fanciful but functional — that is, danceable. As are the other six cuts on this album, the two forgettable ones as well as the four catchy ones. I'm not especially happy in the disco sense of the term, but I like it OK myself. **B+**

The Trammps: *Disco Inferno* (Atlantic '77). I hum the title track and admire three of the remaining five, but at a distance. One sharp figure of speech per song — next to "burn baby burn" my favorite occurs in "Body Contact Contract," where the "party of the first part" parties — doesn't make up for how forced they sound when they're bad — or admirable. **B**

Trammps: *Disco Champs* (Philadelphia International '77). In theory I'm glad their ex-corporation has repackaged *Trammps* as a pure disco album. In practice I get distracted during the breaks and don't find the new dance cuts any more appealing than the old ballads. **B**

The Trammps: *The Best of the Trammps* (Atlantic '78). In a time when real soul groups, especially of the uptempo persuasion, have become as rare as snail darters, the Trammps fill a gap. On album their tricks have worn thin, and "Seasons for Girls" is one more proof that they should never slowitdownalittle, but this compilation is the best of both their worlds — two extended dance tracks, including the undeniable "Disco Inferno," and radio-length versions of seven other songs. No meaningful lyrics here unless you count "Soul Searchin' Time" (I might), and Jimmy Ellis is a narrow singer enslaved by great precedents. But for rough-and-easy black pop, catchy top and bottom, this is it. **A−**

Happy and Artie Traum: *Happy and Artie Traum* (Capitol '70). This sounds like a great big warm thank you from folk music to the Band, as well it might — how else do you think these ringleaders of the Woodstock fraternity got to cut their own album with the big company? **B −**

Happy & Artie Traum: *Hard Times in the Country* (Rounder '75). If you're a sucker for folkie nonsense — ramblin' mythopeia, articulated sentiment, purty tunes — you might as well buy it from real folkies on a real, struggling folkie label. Bonus: "Gambler's Song," Artie's uncharacteristically ironic tale of anomie, which ought to be recorded by somebody who'll get it heard. **B −**

T. Rex: *Electric Warrior* (Warner Bros. '72). As an acoustic warrior, back when he spelled out his group's first name and did concept albums about unicorns, Marc Bolan was considered "progressive," which meant he was as foolish as Donovan but not as famous. A freak hit turned him into a singer of rhythmic fairy tales for British pre-pubes, exactly what he was always suited for, and the great "Bang a Gong" extends his subject matter into the rock myth itself, which has its limits but sure beats unicorns. Now if he'd only recycle a few more pop readymades I could stop complaining about fey. **B**

The Troggs: *The Troggs* (Pye '75). Yeah, I own their greatest hits from the '60s, and I'm proud of it, but this is strictly for the dimwits liberation front. In general, I like rock and roll because it takes brains. **C**

Robin Trower: *For Earth Below* (Chrysalis '75). Is he experienced? He's a retread, and the best thing I can say for him is that he makes me remember the verve, humor, and fluidity of the original. **C −**

Robin Trower: *Caravan to Midnight* (Chrysalis '78). Over the years somewhat disappointing sales have convinced Trower that maybe all the people who found themselves stultified by his Hendrix clonings were onto something. On this album, therefore, he's made a point of mixing the vocals way up, so that the Paul Rodgers clonings of lead vocalist/second banana James Dewar can actually be discerned by the casual listener. Yug. **C**

Doris Troy: *Doris Troy* (Apple '71). Like most of the backup soul sisters making solo moves these days — I count at least six on my review shelf right now — she could be any of the others, but she's got some extra savvy. The production picks and chooses, melding straight blues and gospel with its soul tricks. Troy shares songwriting with names like Harrison, Starkey, and Stills — whose "Special Care" is the only song here that sounds as fresh as the ASCAP oldie "Exactly Like You." Original grade: B plus. **B −**

William Truckaway: *William Truckaway* (Reprise '72). Another affable pop-jug production from Eric Jacobson (Lovin' Spoonful, Critters, Sopwith Camel, Blue Velvet Band, Norman Greenbaum). As always, the auteur with his name in big letters has a mild voice and a mild sense of humor; in this case, he used to be in the Sopwith Camel and cuts his pastoral whimsy with a synthesizer. The backup is Jacobson's usual charming studio corn. I could listen to one of these a year forever. **B +**

The Andrea True Connection: *More, More, More* (Buddah '76). Forget Donna Summer — this is the real disco porn. She's covered on the cover right up to the clavicle, her rhythms sound more binary than her producer's, and she can't sing a lick. But even if you haven't seen her movies, she projects an exhibitionistic suck-and-fuck tractability that links the two pervasive fantasy media of our time, and from such conjunctions Great Art arises. **B**

The Tubes: *The Tubes* (A&M '75). If Blue Oyster Cult is hard-rock comedy, as I once claimed, then this is heavy-metal hysteria — without Buck Dharma, which is one of the jokes. So ugly it may be an earmark. So ugly it may be the American version of Genesis. **B−**

The Tubes: *Young and Rich* (A&M '76). Since it's my instinct to detest this group, I was dismayed to catch myself chuckling at "Tubes World Tour," "Slipped My Disco," and even "Proud to Be an American." I was even more astonished to conclude that "Pimp" might be serious. Further investigation turned up no additional satisfactions, but revealed a movement away from Al Kooper's general parody of the hard and the heavy toward a more eclectic satirical style reminiscent of (they should be so funny) Stan Freberg. **B−**

The Tubes: *Remote Control* (A&M '79). Their knack for songwriting always surprises me, because they deserve worse, and on this album they provide it, drenching their material in the grandiose harmonies and pomp-rock keyboard textures that thrive in the Midwest, where many poor souls still regard these transparent cynics as avatars of the new wave. You think maybe Patti Smith would do "No Mercy"? **C+**

Tanya Tucker: *Would You Lay with Me (In a Field of Stone)* (Columbia '74). If you think the inflatable dolls they sell with the Orgy-Gell in the back of cheap skin mags are sexy, then you will doubtless find this fifteen-year-old wonder of nature the hottest thing since that waitress who brought you the screwdrivers the time you blew $220 playing blackjack in downtown Winnemucca. A cute little ass, better-than-average pipes, and Billy Sherrill's usual "who gives a shit if the title cut is commercial" country album. Up a notch for no strings. **B−**

Tanya Tucker: *Tanya Tucker's Greatest Hits* (Columbia '75). As if recalling Appalachian roots, the youngest superstar and sex symbol in country music history adds rape, murder, and bastardy to familiar themes like drunkenness, poverty, abandonment, and love-is-the-answer. Kid stuff it ain't. Her burred contralto is an

American dream, some weird hybrid of Buffy Sainte-Marie, Marilyn Monroe, and Will Rogers — dirty plainsong. But though I enjoy almost everything she does as soap opera — the bloodier the better — I don't believe a word. **B+**

Tanya Tucker: *Livin' and Learnin'* (MCA '76). The gain in assurance and excitement should put to rest all narrow-spirited suspicions that only Billy Sherrill's cracker acumen can shape Tanya's voice. But the voice remains a dirty one, which means that those songs that broaden her appeal by forcing her to play the ingenue tend to unfocus the persona behind subtler lyrics like Sterling Whipple's "Makin' Love Don't Always Make Love Grow." Highlights: two rockers, one from Fats Domino, the other from the Eagles. **B**

Tanya Tucker: *TNT* (MCA '78). The problem with Tanya's crossover is her functional but rather tiny brain — if only she had some real idea of exactly what she wanted to become, her pipes would put it across. Despite the heavy hoopla, the rock move here comprises three of the '50s classics that have always been her meat, and all that distinguishes this from earlier MCA Tanya is that Jerry Goldstein, her new intellectual adviser, has contributed three unusually bad songs. **C+**

Tuff Darts: *Tuff Darts* (Sire '78). Maybe Robert Gordon left this band to escape resident sickie John DeSalvo, one of those guys who sounds like he deserves to get fixed by the knife-wielding lesbians he has nightmares about. The only way to make their record more depressing would be to add a hologram of Gordon's replacement, Tommy Frenzy, whose slick blond hair and metal teeth now set the band's android-delinquent "image." Then again, you could take away Jeff Salen's guitar. **C**

Ike Turner: *Blues Roots* (United Artists '72). Amazingly, the title is pretty accurate — some of it's even twelve-bar. He's always played a mean, flashy guitar, and his deadpan is good for one moderately interesting LP. On the other hand, you should hear James Brown — or the Five Royales — sing "Think." Original grade: B. **B—**

Ike Turner: *Bad Dreams* (United Artists '73). After twenty years of raking it in from the shadows, he's finally figured out a way of applying his basically comic bass/baritone to rock and roll. Studio-psychedelic New Orleans, echoes of the Band and Dr. John, some brilliant minor r&b mixed in with the dumb stuff. My God — at the moment he's more interesting than Tina. Original grade: B plus. **B**

Ike & Tina Turner and the Ikettes: *Come Together* (Liberty '70). Tina is more convincing when she's growling out Ike's songs about her sexual appetites (I sure couldn't handle her) than when she's belting out Ike's songs about the social fabric ("Why can't we be happy like we used to be"). She's also more convincing when she's growling out a Stones song about her sexual appetites than when she's belting out a Sly Stone song about the social fabric. Still, their vogue has been good for their music — the level of effort here is so high that the sole throwaway works as a coda that brings the record back down. And the rock covers take some strain off Ike — especially when Tina sings a Beatles song that's about both her sexual appetites and the social fabric. Original grade: A. **A—**

Ike & Tina Turner: *Her Man . . . His Woman* (Capitol '70). Elevated by the Rolling Stones into mythic status among white people, the Turners are now haunted by their profligate recording habits — Capitol is the tenth label to release an I&TT LP in the past two years. Granted, most and maybe all of them are better than this, a humdrum blues runthrough (with big-band horns and fake-symph strings) on which Ike claims authorship of such works as "Dust My Broom" (here yclept "I Believe") and "Ten Long Years"

(here yclept "Five Long Years"). Apparently it was cut some years ago for Cenco (?) Records. The Turners are currently contracted to Liberty, have authorized product out on A&M and Blue Thumb, and caveat emptor. **C**

Ike & Tina Turner: *Workin' Together* (Liberty '70). There's a pretty fair remake of "Ooh Poo Pah Doo" in between the two great cuts on this album — the easy-to-rough "Proud Mary" (with Ike rolling in back) and their first successful "peace and love" "generation" song, appropriately entitled "Funkier Than a Mosquita's Tweeter." Someone named Eki Renrut contributes a pretty fair do-rightman song. And Tina tries valiantly to sing her way out of some gunny sacks. **B**

Ike & Tina: *What You Hear Is What You Get* (United Artists '71). Those who regard Tina as Aretha with good legs should listen to her rasp through "I've Been Loving You Too Long" and "Respect" for the finale of this live-at-Carnegie double — her true grit isn't good for much power or warmth. But she and Ike really put their increasingly unfashionable rough-and-greasy notion of soul out there, and despite the speeches, backup singers, and guitar demonstrations a lot of their show is captured on disc. The band crackles, Tina is more intense than in the studio versions, and Ike provides basso humoroso commentary. And not only that but they eat each other! Right on the stage! Time: 59:42. **B+**

Ike & Tina: *Nuff Said* (United Artists '71). The title tune is performed by the Family Vibs, formerly Ike & Tina's Kings of Rhythm, formerly Ike Turner's Kings of Rhythm. They deserve the honor. Here Tina's screeching becomes painful, not because it's rough but because it's out of tune. As for Ike, he's out of tunes. **C+**

Ike & Tina: *Feel Good* (United Artists '72). In which Tina finds her more-than-match in all-night bikers, gentle pimps, and other wonders of nature — what, no strong-but-silent bandleaders? And then demonstrates that equality is more than Writing Your Own Songs. **B−**

Ike & Tina Turner: *Nutbush City Limits* (United Artists '73). Tina hasn't regained her voice, which makes this recovery a certain rather than a likely fluke, but I find happy accidents in every cut except maybe "Drift Away." Highlights include the nutball title hit, a stripped-down "River Deep, Mountain High," a tribute to East St. Louis's "Club Manhattan," and "That's My Purpose," keyed to a line I happen to be a sucker for: "Let your face be the last I see." **B+**

Ike & Tina Turner: *Greatest Hits* (United Artists '76). I prefer *Come Together,* which this duplicates only on the title cut, but I like the way the sides are split between rock and soul/r&b here. Best moments: the Ikettes harmonizing on "A Fool in Love" and Ike and Tina slurping on "I've Been Loving You Too Long." **A−**

Ron Turner: *Ron Turner* (Folkways '74). This folkie throwback supports the argument that it's easier to play the outlaw if you don't need roadies with pack mules to lug your amplifiers across the wide open spaces. Armed with a twelve-string and a sense of humor, Turner obviously yokes his imagination to felt experience rather than production schedules, and his flat monotone is often pretty droll. He makes rock and roll sound even bleaker. **B**

Tina Turner: *Acid Queen* (United Artists '75). Her rock myth reconfirmed cinematically, Tina quickly turns out two from the Who (only fair), two from the Stones (who else?), and one from Led Zep ("Whole Lotta Love," brilliant, I trust R. Plant has his big twelve-inch in a sling at this very moment). With bass lines lifted whole from the originals the singing almost doesn't matter. And what rocks

most mythically? I. Turner's cleverly entitled "Baby — Get It On." **B**

Stanley Turrentine: *In the Pocket* (Fantasy '75). This is the sound track for a romantic comedy featuring Henry "Hank" Aaron as a bank vice-president whose hobby is private investigation. While "digging" into billiard-licensing payoffs, he falls for a lady eight-ball hustler (Leslie Uggams) who happens to be the daughter of Mr. Big, played by Barry White. Aaron decides to go crooked, but you know he'll never achieve the power or vulgarity of his father-in-law. Neither will Gene Page, who arranged this claptrap for Turrentine, a saxophonist whose fat, self-indulgent tone is apparently demanding the worst these days. **D+**

20/20: *20/20* (Portrait '79). Just about all of these dense, cleverly constructed tunes would sound great on the radio. If they have some other reason for being, though, neither lyrics nor vocals — which seem to avoid both banality and its opposite as a simple matter of power pop taste — let on what it is. When CBS breaks a few hits off this we'll remember it as a classic. But CBS won't. **B+**

Dwight Twilley Band: *Sincerely* (Shelter '76). These days I suppose anybody who can construct hook-laden pop-rock songs — half good, half better — without schlocking them up qualifies as a walking treasury of people's art, like Taj Mahal. But because his natural habitat seems to be the studio (a forty-track when he has his druthers), this does smell a little like a museum. **B+**

Dwight Twilley Band: *Twilley Don't Mind* (Arista '78). If the twelve-cut debut was notable for its songs, this nine-cut follow-up puts the emphasis on sound — a deep, rather eerie, yet undeniably pop sound that reminds me more than anything of the Flamin' Groovies' *Supersnazz.* And as with the Flamin' Groovies, the sound creates a distance between Twilley and his hooks. But even though I can make up neat theories about how Twilley evokes a comparable distance in the lyrics, I certainly prefer *Supersnazz*. Original grade: B plus. **B**

Dwight Twilley: *Twilley* (Arista '79). Twilley's first two albums were marginally fascinating because of how obsessively he synthesized the Southern and British pop-rock traditions — like a cool Alex Chilton, or (only we didn't know this yet) a Nick Lowe who worked too hard — and because so few bands were bothering with the kind of catchy '60s-AM songs that Twilley turned out by the half dozen. Well, scratch the catchy part — both the Records and the Knack, to stick to the lightweights, have songs on the radio that cut anything on *Sincerely*, which is a lot catchier than this. And while you're at it, scratch Phil Seymour, Twilley's former rhythm section and harmony group. And add Jimmy Haskell doing Paul Buckmaster imitations. And think dark thoughts about the Raspberries and Eric Carmen. **C+**

Conway Twitty: *Conway Twitty's Greatest Hits Vol. I* (Decca '72). "My reasons for cheating, they're as good as lies can be," laments Conway in a properly ironic tag line for this concept-album-cum-compilation. Reversal follows upon reversal, but in the standard pattern the husband does wrong and then suffers hideously as the wife follows suit. Very convincing — right down to "Fifteen Years Ago," cunningly designed for everyone who ever thought he or she wouldn't get over it after a month of hideous suffering. **A−**

Conway Twitty: *Conway Twitty's Greatest Hits Volume II* (MCA '76). Twitty has grown artistically, which I guess is admirable in a forty-three-year-old country singer. I can only guess because although I'm glad he's traded big-ballad stolidity for honky-tonk stretch and catch, I'm not so glad he's writing his own songs. Too often he muddles country's adult themes with the teen romanticism of his early rockabilly success, and sometimes he's just inept — in "The Games That Daddies Play" a seven-year-old makes a speech that could have been written by the seven-year-old's therapist, while in "Don't Cry Joni" there are plot details that could have been devised by a seven-year-old. **B**

Conway Twitty: *The Very Best of Conway Twitty* (MCA '78). For me it's simple. I like Conway on classic — which means guilt- or pain-ridden — cheating songs. I don't like him so much when he starts comparing his wife invidiously to some idealized Linda, Georgia, or honky-tonk angel. And on ordinary country songs he's a slightly better than ordinary country singer. **B**

Conway Twitty: See also Loretta Lynn and Conway Twitty

Tyla Gang: *Yachtless* (Beserkley '78). Punk has not been good for former Duck Deluxe Sean T. because it's meant urbanization. I have nothing against the slick, hooky power chords his pub-rock has evolved into, not in theory. But when his charming if overly mythic tales of fireballs and West Texas running boards evolve into "The Young Lords" (give me a break, Bruce Springsteen) and "On the Street" (give me a break, Bob Geldof), I begin to crave recognizable human detail. **B−**

Bonnie Tyler: *It's a Heartache* (RCA Victor '78). Maybe the title smash doesn't deserve to end up a one-shot — Tyler's songwriters, Ronnie Scott and Steve Wolfe, show a gift for the Nashvillian pain-of-love lyric. But if there's another hit hidden away on this album, it's gonna bore us all stiff inside of two weeks. **C**

UFO: *Force It* (Chrysalis '75). Heavy metal that's not hard to take? What? Well, the whole first side moves so smartly you could almost mistake it for rock and roll. Original grade: B. **B−**

UFO: *Obsession* (Chrysalis '78). I've admired their forward motion and facile riffs, so it's my duty to report that they've degenerated into the usual exhibitionism. Theme song: "Lookin' Out for No. 1," a turn of phrase that's becoming as much of a watchword in late '70s rock as "get together" was in the late '60s. **C−**

U.K.: *U.K.* (Polydor '78). John Piccarella: "What the guys in U.K. apparently don't understand is that it's not impressive or difficult to rock out in 9/4 — it's impossible." **C+**

Ultravox: *Ultravox!* (Island '77). "I want to be a machine" is their slogan, and with Eno producing one would hope for the best. But only on "My Sex" do they go all the way; more often these tough-surfaced post-Velvets songs identify with "the wild, the beautiful, and the damned." Eno helps them sound like a machine regardless, but unlike Eno they don't seem to enjoy it much. Which calls their humanity into question. **B**

Ultravox: *Systems of Romance* (Antilles '78). This time these guys have mastered their concept. John Foxx's detached, creamy baritone works against the instrumentation's electronic cast for a streamlined rocksy music that suits titles like "Dislocation" and "Someone Else's Clothes." But unlike Bryan Ferry Foxx talks as if he's detached clean through, unlike Brian Eno he's encumbered by delusions of existential significance, and unlike both he's never funny. **B+**

The Undertones: *The Undertones* (Sire '79). Nice lads, nice lads — suddenly the world is teeming with nice lads. I like their punky speed and adolescent authenticity, but I'd prefer the reverse — among adolescents these days the speed takes care of itself, while finding something besides teendom to write about is a problem. **B+**

Utopia: *RA* (Bearsville '77). Todd Rundgren solo is a conundrum — a jaded, youthful pop technocrat whose inconsistency can be passed off as creative exuberance. Todd Rundgren bandleader is a disaster — a humorless rock progressive whose scientific know-how adds no saving details to his arid futurism. Roger Powell's circa-2001 improvements on the Hammond B-3 organ dominate as usual — it's not for nothing that Todd refers to the sun as "Ra, holy synthesizer." The first side is bad, the second unspeakable, yoking an appallingly unimaginative eighteen-minute "fairy tale" about stolen harmony to an infuriatingly impotent seven-minute preachment about Hiroshima. Why must those few rockers who espouse moral ideals do it so ineffectively? Oh, I know, mustn't criticize — just go out and achieve "Eternal Love." **D+**

Van Halen: *Van Halen* (Warner Bros. '78). For some reason Warners wants us to know that this is the biggest bar band in the San Fernando Valley. This doesn't mean much — all new bands are bar bands, unless they're Boston. The term becomes honorific when the music belongs in a bar. This music belongs on an aircraft carrier. **C**

Van Halen: *Van Halen II* (Warner Bros. '79). Never let it be said that popular styles don't evolve — in the wake of Kiss and Boston, this is heavy metal that's pure, fast, and clean. No mythopeia, no bombast, and even the guitar features are defined as just that. So how come formalists don't love the shit out of these guys? Not because they're into dominating women, I'm sure. **C+**

Dave Van Ronk: *Van Ronk* (Polydor '71). Although I've always thought Van Ronk was hard to listen to —after all, his range is about half an octave — what he does with songs by fellow "nonsingers" like Peter Stampfel, Leonard Cohen, and Randy Newman makes me think some more. He shoots his shot at big-label production here, and now and then the orchestration (not to mention the material) turns surprisingly schmaltzy, but for the most part this shouted melee of song collection is a riot. **B+**

The Velvet Underground: *Loaded* (Cotillion '70). The Velvets are to Manhattan what the Rascals are to New York — that is, they really make "Rock & Roll" (a title), but they're also really intellectual and ironic. Lou Reed's singing embodies the paradox even on beat-goes-on throwaways about cowboys and trains. Other subjects include drag, poverty, not loving nature, and the new age, mysteriously connected to an over-the-hill actress who would like her old age back. **A**

The Velvet Underground: *Live at Max's Kansas City* (Cotillion '72). If this is all that remains of the legendary 1970 engagement, I'll take my memories. The (mono) sound isn't bad for a record mastered from a Brigid Polk cassette, but that's not to say it isn't bad, and though I'm not one to cavil about out-of-tune guitars, this time I notice. Notable performance: Lou Reed's cover of the Maureen Tucker classic "Afterhours." **B−**

Velvet Underground: *1969 Velvet Underground Live* (Mercury '74). It's nice to have a decent-sounding live record of the legend, especially one that adds a few new songs — notably "We're Gonna Have a Real Good Time Together" — and choruses to the canon. This is a more impressive testimonial to Lou Reed than any of his solo LPs. And if it's not as essential as any of the four studio albums, it does provide an overview of the band's music: deadpan, demotic, jaded, oddly sensationalistic, primitive both harmonically and rhythmically and all but devoid of flourishes, always hard-edged and usually quick, never slow and heavy at the same time. Original grade: B plus. **A −**

Tom Verlaine: *Tom Verlaine* (Elektra '79). In which he deploys backup choruses and alien instruments, the kind of stuff that bogs down all solo debuts, with modest grace and wit. And continues to play guitar like Captain Marvel. Neater than Television, as you might expect, but almost as visionary anyway, and a lot more confident and droll. Inspirational Verse: "My head was spinning/My oh my." **A −**

The Vibrators: *Pure Mania* (Columbia '78). This has been raving without letup ever since it arrived at my house as an import in September of '77. Mixing raw vocals and relentless tempos with hooks that should strike familiar chords among over-twenties, it's a way into the punk style for seekers after pure musical rush. Those who listen to lyrics may regret, as I do, that they care so much about sex, since despite the distancing and pacing their s&m interests are clearly more than a flirtation with the absolute — they're narsty. Then again, so were the Velvets'. And this remains good new-fashioned rock and roll at its wildest. Original grade: A minus. **A**

Village People: *Macho Man* (Casablanca '78). Watch out, Ted Nugent, or these you-know-whats (I'm sure I don't) are gonna knock you off the cover of *Creem*. You're not the only one who can make up stories about eating it raw. **C**

Village People: *Cruisin'* (Casablanca '78). I give up — I've never been capable of resisting music this silly. At least this time they're not singing the praises of "macho," a term whose backlash resurgence is no laughing matter, and the gay stereotyping — right down to "The Women," every one a camp heroine of screen or disc — is so cartoonish that I can't imagine anyone taking it seriously. As for all the straights who think "Y.M.C.A." is about playing basket-ball, well, that's pretty funny too. But what happens when Victor Willis follows Teddy Pendergrass into sololand and reveals the wife and 2.4 kids in his closet? Original grade: B **B +**

Village People: *Go West* (Casablanca '79). At first I dismissed this as market fatigue — it's hard to act like you're still discovering your formula on your fourth album in twenty-one months. With no help from a peaked-sounding Victor Willis — shouters should avoid even the appearance of laryngitis — it came off as a tuneless disco tribute to John Philip Sousa that omitted the "Stars and Stripes Forever" cover only because Jacques Morali doesn't control Sousa's publishing. But now I kind of enjoy it. *Cruisin'* was dumb, and this is an advance — a quantum leap in dumbness, without even risque puns to distract from Victor's metronomic cries. Although I have my doubts about this "skin-diving" stuff myself. **B −**

Gene Vincent: *Gene Vincent* (Kama Sutra '70). Vincent was never a titan — his few moments of rockabilly greatness were hyped-up distillations of slavering lust from a sensitive little guy who was just as comfortable with "Over the Rainbow" in his normal frame of mind. And despite what the '50s revivalists believe, this comeback is a return to form only in the formal sense — simple songs, Tex-Mex backing. Some of it's very sweet — Doug Sahm meets "Over the Rainbow." But even when he slavers he does so quietly. **B −**

Eddie "Cleanhead" Vinson: *The Original Cleanhead* (BluesTime '70). A worthy introduction to one of the cleanest — and nastiest — blues voices you'll ever hear. He also plays alto sax with the solid adaptability of a territory man who's been on the road since the '40s, although not as cannily as Plas Johnson, who together with Joe Pass heads a committed supporting cast. How's that again, Cleanhead?

You've been balled a long long time? Original grade: B plus. **A −**

Eddie "Cleanhead" Vinson: *Kidney Stew Is Fine* (Delmark '79). Cut in the early '70s with an all-star band featuring T-Bone Walker and Jay McShann, this was winning various grand prix in Europe as *Wee Baby Blues* long before it was released here. More tentative and human-scale, more felt perhaps, than *The Original Cleanhead*, it sacrifices power and presence as a result, but the material is tough and funny, Vinson sounds loud enough, and at times Walker threatens to steal the record. **A −**

The Voices of East Harlem: *Right On Be Free* (Elektra '71). Producer-manager Jerry Brandt has done a pretty good job of recording this untransportable troupe of twenty or so black adolescents. Except for an unnecessary "Proud Mary" and an embarrassing "Let It Be Me" (a/k/a "Let It Be Us"), it shouts and almost jumps, just

like church, or a basketball tournament. Michael Jackson Award: Kevin Griffin on the 6:45-minute "Shaker Life." Original grade: B. **B −**

Mark Volman and Howard Kaylan: *The Phlorescent Leech & Eddie* (Reprise '72). They've learned their lessons well, ripping off riffs from everybody — what can you say when two slapsticking ex-Mothers steal a melody from a Graham Nash protest song? — and filtering it down into the finest pasteurized mush. For some reason, it sounds a lot like the Turtles. A charming exercise in the deliberate throwback category, a true artyfact. Recommended: the Hawaiian novelty, "Nikki Hoi." **B +**

Voyage: *Voyage* (Marlin '77). The ultimate kitsch — travelogue disco. For instance, what udderlike instrument do you think might be featured on "Scotch Machine"? **B**

Porter Wagoner & Dolly Parton: *The Best of Porter Wagoner & Dolly Parton* (RCA Victor '71). There are real pleasures here, but they're chiefly vocal. The surprises are few, the jokes weak and infrequent, the sentimentality overripe ("Jeanie's Afraid of the Dark," yeucch), and the best song's by Paxton, not Parton. In short, a lousy ad for couple-bonding, though whether Porter is repressing Dolly or Dolly holding out on Porter I wouldn't know. **B**

Bunny Wailer: *Blackheart Man* (Island '76). This isn't what they mean when they say protest music is boring, it's what they mean when they say protest music is subtle — only they don't, which is what's wrong with protest music. The content of the lyrics is as straightforward as Rastafarian thought can be (not very), but the spirit reveals itself slowly — "Fig Tree" is Jamaican Blake, "Oppressed Song" Jamaican Brecht, and "Fighting Against Convictions" simply Jamaican English, the autodidactic patois of a "common" criminal. And the music — well. We've come a long way from reggae's "primitive" days, haven't we? The interweave of mixed-back horns and multiple percussion is as gratifying and elusive rhythmically as it is harmonically, Bunny's singing is endlessly sinuous, and if you think you never want to hear another version of "This Train," you're just wrong. Original grade: B minus. **A−**

Bunny Wailer: *Protest* (Island '77). Neither Bunny's voice, strong by Jamaican standards but no soul shout, nor reggae's persuasive but rarely irrefutable rhythms, are suited to the more forceful (or is it just louder?) procedures of this follow-up. The decrease in compassion, consolation, and — most directly to the political point — inspiration is less a matter of the words themselves than of how they're sung, but never on the last record did he resort to such radio-preacher pretensions as "the rock of discretion/Will calm the floods of conflict." Not to mention an antiabortion line. **B**

The Wailers: *Catch a Fire* (Island '72). In the mid-60s, when these Jamaicans were also known as the Rude Boys, they covered "What's New Pussycat"; now their anguished rhythms and harmonies suggest a rough spiritual analogue to the Rolling Stones, with social realism their welcome replacement for arty cynicism. At first I distrusted this nine-cut U.S. debut — it seemed laid back and stretched out in the worst album-as-art tradition. Now I notice not only that half these songs are worthy of St. John the Divine, but that the Barrett brothers' bass and drums save those that aren't from limbo. Original grade: B. **A**

The Wailers: *Burnin'* (Island '74). This is as perplexing as it is jubilant — sometimes gripping, sometimes slippery. It's reggae, obviously, but it's not mainstream reggae, certainly not rock or soul, maybe some kind of futuristic slow funk, War without the psuedo-jazz. What's inescapable is Bob Marley's ferocious gift for melodic propaganda. It's one thing to come up with four consecutive title hooks, another to make the titles "Get Up Stand Up," "Hallelujah Time," "I Shot the Sheriff," "Burnin' and Lootin'." Original grade: B plus. **A**

The Wailers: See also Bob Marley & the Wailers

Loudon Wainwright III: *Loudon Wainwright III* (Atlantic '70). Wainwright writes with more precision and imagination than any other singer-songwriter of the current boom, and his melodies stick with you. He sings and plays with such authority that even though this record features only voice and acoustic guitar it's powerful musically. But. The failures of the talented are always painful, and this is very strained. He's smart enough to integrate syntactical contortions into his style, and to match them vocally, but they still make you wince sometimes. And there's no emotional maturity to go with the verbal control, no sense of kindness or ease. I enjoy this record quite a bit, but I admire it more, and sometimes I don't like it at all. **B−**

Loudon Wainwright III: *Album II* (Atlantic '71). In which Wainwright untwists the dense associations — usually too literal and/or analytic to qualify as metaphor — that made his first album so hard to take, though for those who'd like to sample the mode "Be Careful, There's a Baby in the House" is as good as it gets. He may make you laugh, but he's not trying to be funny — this is bitter stuff whether he's trying to persuade a groupie to save his life or to explain that an old friendship has gone from backslap to handshake. **B+**

Loudon Wainwright III: *Album III* (Columbia '72). In which the whiz kid relaxes with a pleasant folk-rock band and admits that the chief use of epigrammatic wit is humor, thereby consenting to be funny right out. He also allows himself a few moments of genuine lyricism, sees fit to steal a song from Leiber & Stoller, and also appropriates a melody from "Sweet Little Sixteen." His reward? "Dead Skunk," a song redolent of the pop success he seeks. The misanthrope grows older. Very encouraging. **A−**

Loudon Wainwright III: *Attempted Mustache* (Columbia '73). First he was a failed poet. Now he's a successful comedian. Maybe someday soon he'll put it all together and become a successful poet, but this will do — the fact that "Dilated to Meet You" and "Lullaby" and for that matter "The Swimming Song" are funny doesn't mean they don't add to the great store of human wisdom. And as I recall, Chuck Berry made do with something similar for quite a while. **A−**

Loudon Wainwright III: *Unrequited* (Columbia '75). Since most people can't absorb the head-on impact of Wainwright's conjugal details — how do you confront an accusation like "You told me that I came too soon but it was you who came too late"? — the second side of this album, recorded live, tends to sound a little yockier than it should. On side one, however, the mockery has just the right edge of self-flagellation and is balanced off by a gentleness without which he might seem a little spoiled. In other words, the balance of pleasure and pain he's been seeking for five years. **A−**

Loudon Wainwright III: *T Shirt* (Arista '76). Loudon seems to be approaching sanity as he approaches thirty, and while that bodes well for his career it won't help his (you'll pardon the expression) his art much. He needs one song as astonishing as "Rufus Is a Tit Man" every time out. **B+**

Loudon Wainwright III: *Final Exam* (Arista '78). The renewed bite here seems more a sign that producer John Lissauer has a knack for the exquisite programmatic effect — check out the Roches' demure buffoonery on "Golfin' Blues" or the way the band calls Loudon "Mr. Guilty" — than that Wainwright is once again willing to apply his scalpel to himself. It was always brave, painful jokes like "Motel Blues" and "Kick in the Head" that gave the rest of his funny stuff its strength, and their absence from his two most recent albums may be why even his best new songs sound like one-liners rather than comic classics. Lotsa great one-liners, though. **B+**

Tom Waits: *Closing Time* (Asylum '73). Waits has been around — one of the two songs that make this album is about driving home at dawn in a '55 Chevy, the other about contacting a girlfriend of forty years before. With his jazz-schooled piano and drawling delivery, he resembles Randy Newman more than such fellow inmates as Jackson Browne and David Blue — Newman feigns feelings for the purpose of mocking them, while Waits exploits an honest sentimentality which he undercuts just enough to be credible. He doesn't carry a tune as well as Newman, though, which gets to be an annoyance on side two. **B+**

Tom Waits: *The Heart of Saturday Night* (Asylum '74). Last time he was an urban romantic with a good eye who you would have figured for a Ferlinghetti fan if you'd thought about it. This time he begins to sound like a Ferlinghetti imitator, and while nostalgia for past bohemias sure beats nostalgia for past wars, it's still a drain and a drag. I mean, there might be more coverable songs here if maudlin melodies didn't merge with neon imagery in the spindrift dirge of the honky-tonk nicotine night. Dig? Original grade: B minus. **C+**

Tom Waits: *Nighthawks at the Diner* (Asylum '75). When he really works at evoking the swizzle-stick blues, Waits is so full of shit Port-O-San ought to name a model after him. Fortunately, this one's long on patter — first live double in history where you skip the song to get to the next intro. (And some of the songs are worth

going back to.) Original grade: C plus. **B**

Tom Waits: *Small Change* (Asylum '76). Waits has developed into such a horrible singer that sometimes I think his stentorian emotionalism is deliberate, like the clinkers he hits in "The Piano Has Been Drinking." This doesn't affect his monologue songs one way or the other, but it tends to detract from those with melodies. **B−**

Tom Waits: *Foreign Affairs* (Asylum '77). I like the poetry-with-jazz for "Jack & Neal," the mumbled monologue "Barber Shop," the Anglophile "Foreign Affair," and a duet with Bette on "I Never Talk to Strangers." But I get off the trolley at "Potter's Field," a production number for a high-rolling nightstick who crossed "from the Bronx to the River Styx." With his genre sleaze and metaphorical melodrama, Waits is a downwardly mobile escapist who believes that Everyman is a wino and Everywoman an all-night waitress who turns tricks when things get rough. The problem isn't the subjects themselves, but that for all his self-conscious unpretentiousness he inflates them. Which I guess is all we can expect of a schoolteacher's son who's been searching for his own world since he was old enough to think. **B**

Tom Waits: *Blue Valentine* (Asylum '78). Waits keeps getting weirder and good for him. As sheer sendup, his "Somewhere" beats Sid Vicious's "My Way" his way. But I'm not always sure he understands his gift — these lyrics should be *funnier*. And "Romeo Is Bleeding," easily my favorite among his Chandleroid sagas of tragedy outside the law, is more effective on the jacket than when he underlines its emotional resonance in song. That's not weird at all. **B**

Wendy Waldman: *Love Has Got Me* (Warner Bros. '73). Female chauvinism and a young lifetime's worth of melodies drew me to Waldman's reflections on trains, pirates, horses, show business, and of course love.

Then Carola pointed out that this was the kind of woman who not only pronounces Mexico Mehico — as in "Gringo en Mexico" — but who flings back her right arm and says "Ole!" as she does so. One reason I married Carola is that she's not much interested in trains, pirates, or horses. Show business and love are universals. Original grade: B plus. **B −**

Howard Wales and Jerry Garcia: Hooteroll (Douglas '71). Organist Wales gets top billing because this all-instrumental project is his — he wrote and no doubt conceived it. Now guess why Garcia gets any billing at all. Admittedly, the astral diversion is no worse than the Dead's. But the laid-back funk sure is. **C +**

Jerry Jeff Walker: A Man Must Carry On (MCA '77). Walker's Austin-based cult reputation has so much to do with looseness and charisma that it took a live double-LP featuring poetry readings and chicken imitations to convince me the man deserved it. Definitive. **B +**

Sammy Walker: Song for Patty (Folkways '75). Walker's amazing early Dylan soundalike isn't an imitation, it's a charming tribute, and the highly recommended title cut exemplifies his (by now) all but unique fusion of novelistic eye and political heart. (Fusion, hell — I'll settle for either.) But he is a windbag, and no matter how hard he tries he's never funny. Original grade: B. **B −**

T-Bone Walker: Very Rare (Reprise '73). Jerry Leiber and Mike Stoller put so much loving labor into this double-LP that it came out too tricky — the big band and the small band and the famous sidepeople and the new songs are all quite tasty, but they distract from what ought to be the business at hand. Of course, since T-Bone is singing more with his brain than his larynx these days, that may have been the idea. But I'd trade all the solos here

except maybe Dizzy Gillespie's on "Evening" — and there are lots of good ones — to hear T-Bone play guitar on every cut. **B −**

Joe Walsh: So What (ABC '74). No artist this inconsequential should risk such a title. **C +**

Joe Walsh: But Seriously, Folks (Asylum '78). Well, "Second Hand Store" is fairly likable, but keep it to yourself — a follow-up would ruin everything. "Life's Been Good" is not only Summer Song '78, it was born to be a novelty one-shot, and that it happens to say more about the tribulations of stardom than all the concept albums ever devised on the subject just goes to show how deeply significant AM radio can be. **C +**

Joe Walsh: The Best of Joe Walsh (ABC '78). 'Twixt James Gang and Eagles Walsh justified his existence by developing his own brand of spacey, tuneful guitar schlock. I admit that it sounds like nothing else. But I can't imagine why anyone would want this much of it. **B −**

War: All Day Music (United Artists '71). I'm beginning to find that their slow groove has a winning depth of character — B. B. Dickerson and Papa Dee Allen get as personal on bass and congas as most rock and rollers do on guitar and piano, and their chants often say more than rock's so-called poetry. Nice to have a couple of hits for purposes of identification, too. But their very slow groove, the one that takes over side one with "That's What Love Will Do," makes me think they take the whole idea of Vanilla Fudge too seriously. **B +**

War: The World Is a Ghetto (United Artists '72). According to all my own theories, I should love this big Afro-roots band with the number one album, but it's hard. Jazz pretensions are one problem — "City, Country, City" has a firm bottom, but it's thirteen minutes long, and up top is mush. And if "That's What Love Will Do" was Vanilla Fudge, "Four Cornered

Room'' makes me think they're trying to start their own genre — blackstrap-rock, they could call it. Original grade: C plus. **B**

War: *Deliver the Word* (United Artists '73). One-two-three green light. Resume normal speed. A literal change of pace. Neither snow nor rain nor heat nor gloom of night stays these couriers from the swift accomplishment of their appointed rounds. Get it? **B+**

War: *War Live* (United Artists '74). I thought they might conceivably cut it live, but even in the studio they stretch their tunes like Sherman tanks at a taffy pull. Only ''Ballero,'' which is not a bolero, and ''Lonely Feelin','' which is not a slow one, are worth their weight in plastic. **C+**

War: *Why Can't We Be Friends?* (United Artists '75). I like the way ''Low Rider'' does its bit for fuel economy, but the rest of the good stuff disappoints: the title hit is greater on the radio, ''Heartbeat'' is greater by the Wild Magnolias, and the salsa section of ''Leroy's Lament'' gets lost on a record that's a laid-back revision of their basic shtick. They're better off heavy. Original grade: C plus. **B−**

War: *Greatest Hits* (United Artists '76). This band lives up to its name. The powerful, deceptively torpid groove evokes the pace of inner-city pleasures like ''All Day Music'' and ''Summer.'' But however jokey and off-the-cuff they sound, they're usually singing about conflict, often racial conflict — the real subject of ''The Cisco Kid'' and ''Why Can't We Be Friends?,'' which many take for novelty songs. **A−**

War: *Platinum Jazz* (Blue Note '77). War's albums work — when they do — by alternating grooves with tunes. This compilation leaves the tunes on *Greatest Hits*, where they belong, and though most of the grooves that remain kick ass, four sides of them add up to the black Muzak this band has always lapsed into in its laziest moments. **C+**

War: *Galaxy* (MCA '77). The first side of the most unambitious album they've ever made works beautifully as what it is — P-Funk on thorazine, with the phrasemaking acuity of previous War records reduced to one title, ''Sweet Fighting Lady.'' Side two winds down from a pretty good hit single into fourteen minutes of carrying unambitiousness way too far. **B**

War: *Youngblood* (United Artists '78). I actually found myself paying attention to the dialogue on this soundtrack, a first, though I didn't ask for seconds. It's pretty coherent musically, too. But the level of the writing is suggested by the title of the best track, ''This Funky Music Makes You Feel Good.'' And the dialogue hardly makes up for that. **C+**

War: *The Music Band* (MCA '79). Fond as I might become of ''Corns and Callouses'' (in which ''Dr. Shoals'' is asked to fix souls) I think fading groove bands are ill-advised to spend most of an album singing about the joys of career. Better to brighten the groove, so the career can continue. **C**

Anita Ward: *Songs of Love* (Juana '79). You didn't really think she wanted to be the Supremes (much less the Toys or the Chiffons), did you? Nah — she wants to be Diana Ross, albeit without show tunes. Buy the single. **C+**

Dionne Warwicke: *Dionne* (Warner Bros. '72). ''Hasbrook Heights'' is no ''Walk On By,'' but it is an ambitious, honest song about the pleasures of the suburbs, where her chosen audience resides. Unfortunately, it's outnumbered by ambitious, dishonest songs directed at the same audience. Whether Hal David takes care of the liberal pieties himself (''Be Aware'') or passes them along from Jacques Brel (''If We Only Have Love'') and Lesley Duncan (''Love Song''), he's selling lies so blatant and boring that even his chosen audience must know it. And while Burt Bacharach's four arrangements (unlike those of Bob James and Don Sebesky, who get three each) are more tart and surprising than ever, too often he underlines ''meaning" with the little dramatic touches of someone who'd like to get into something classier than the record business, like the Broadway stage. Original grade: C minus. **C+**

Dionne Warwicke: *Just Being Myself* (Warner Bros. '73). Even in the heyday of Bacharach-David Dionne didn't make such terrific albums — the best-ofs were the prizes. So Holland-Dozier-Holland are doing all right: solid pop, with the rhythm up front and the strings often used percussively — though they do wash out on "I Always Get Caught in the Rain" (inclement weather is as bad for arrangers as it is for lyricists). Hook-of-the-month: the guitar riff on "You're Gonna Need Me." Original grade: B. **B−**

Dionne Warwick: *Dionne* (Arista '79). The voice is still magic — I even get off on her overdubbed backups — but who wants to listen to it through all this mush? Wait till the collaboration with Barry Manilow dries up, after two or three albums. Betcha Clive tries reuniting her with Bacharach-David around then. And around then they just might be in the mood to do it right. Maybe. **C+**

Grover Washington, Jr.: *Mister Magic* (Kudu '75). For the best-selling jazz album in the country, this is funktional enough. Washington plays a warm tenor in the pop jazz tradition of Gene Ammons, the rhythm section percolates danceably, and the result is sexy background music marred superficially by Bob James's strings. **B−**

Muddy Waters: *The London Muddy Waters Sessions* (Chess '72). Howlin' Wolf had the Rolling Stones for his London session, so how come Muddy only got Rory Gallagher, Steve Winwood, Rick Grech, and Mitch Mitchell for his? Maybe because this one was a money gig from the git-go. Anyway, only Gallagher — the sole committed blues player of the four — is exceptional, and Muddy sounds like the aging pro he is. One exception is "Blind Man Blues," with nice backup from Rosetta Hightower. The other is

"Walkin' Blues," featuring nobody but Muddy and Sam Lawhorn, who is from Chicago. Original grade: B plus. **B**

Muddy Waters: *Can't Get No Grindin'* (Chess '73). Muddy isn't the commanding presence he used to be, but despite the three instrumentals his writing puts this album across. "Love Weapon" and "Whiskey Ain't No Good" are slow ones he thought about, Willie Hammond's "Garbage Man" and the high-gear "Can't Get No Grindin' " classic shuffles. Come to think of it, one of the instrumentals is a classic shuffle too — you almost forgive him for putting "Dust My Broom" through an electric piano and calling it "Funky Butt." Original grade: B. **B+**

Muddy Waters: *Hard Again* (Blue Sky '77). Since the heyday of Chicago blues was midcentury, most of the classic blues LPs are collections of cuts; except maybe for B. B. King's *Live at the Regal* and Otis Spann's *Walking the Blues* (oh, there must be others, but let me go on) I can't recall a better blues *album* than this. The songs run the length of live performances — four of the nine over five minutes — without any loss of intensity, because their intensity depends not on the compression of the three-minute format but on the natural enthusiasm of an inspired collaboration. Waters sings as though his life depended on it, Johnny Winter proves with every note how right he was to want to do this, and James Cotton — well, James Cotton doesn't open his mouth except to make room for the harmonica, which sounds just great. Original grade: A. **A−**

Muddy Waters: *I'm Ready* (Blue Sky '78). Not as ready as you were last time, Mud, but don't let it worry you — it's always harder to get hard again again. **B**

Muddy Waters: *Muddy "Mississippi" Waters Live* (Blue Sky '79). Age cannot wither nor Johnny Winter whelm the elan of this boyish man. It may not last forever, though — he really seems to mean "Deep Down in Florida."

Sun shines every day, you can play in the sand with your wife, and maybe work on a slow one called "Condominium Blues" in your spare time.　　　　　　　　　　　**B+**

Johnny Guitar Watson: *A Real Mother for Ya* (DJM '77). Watson has been perfecting his own brand of easy-listening funk for years, and this time he's finally gone into the studio with his guitar Freddie and his drummer Emry and a bunch of electric keyboards and come up with a whole album of good stuff. The riff-based tracks go on too long but go down easy and the lyrics have an edge. Granted, Watson can't match George Benson's chops, but this is dance music, chops would just get in the way. And I prefer his Lou-Rawls-without-pipes to Benson's Stevie-Wonder-ditto.　　　**B+**

Weather Report: *Weather Report* (Columbia '71). *In a Silent Way* played mostly for atmosphere. The Milesian demi-jazz of side two sounds pretty finky (no misprint intended), but the tone-poem impressionism of side one does its mysterious work. Highlight: the opening mood piece, "Milky Way," in which two *Silent Way* vets, soprano saxophonist Wayne Shorter and pianist Joe Zawinul, make sounds that suggest a carillon approaching a time warp.　　　　　　　　　**B**

Weather Report: *I Sing the Body Electric* (Columbia '72). Significantly less Milesian than their debut, which is impressive but not necessarily good — the difference is that this is neater, more antiseptic, its bottom less dirty and its top less sexy. I find myself interested but never engaged, and I'm sure one piece is a flop — "Crystals," described by the annotator as *"about"* time. Sing the body electric and I'm with you. Sing the body short-circuited and you'd better turn me on. **B**

Weather Report: *Sweetnighter* (Columbia '73). Ask yourself: What kind of a jazz (or rock) (or jazz-rock) group would conceive its sonar identity

around electric keyboards and soprano sax? A pretty dinky (not dunky) one, right? So while I'm pleased that they're going for a drum groove a little solider than anything Dom Um Romao can move and shake, I'm not surprised that they get it only — just barely, in fact — on "125th Street Congress." And that "Boogie Woogie Waltz" is fatally cute, ace improvisations and all.　　　　　　　　　　　　　**B**

Weather Report: *Mysterious Traveller* (Columbia '74). Not bad, not bad — but is that all there is? Maybe what makes the traveller so mysterious is that he doesn't go anywhere in particular. Not even with Alphonso Johnson pushing like hell from underneath. Original grade: B plus.　　　**B**

Weather Report: *Tale Spinnin'* (Columbia '75). I used to be cowed by these guys, but all they are is Jeff Beck with liner notes. I mean, wouldn't you know that the finest fusion band in the land would be altogether too damn fine? Yoked to these tunes and concepts, their solidest rhythm section to date — Alphonso Johnson on bass and Ndugu on (trap) drums — only underscores their subservience to technique.　　　　　　　　　　　**B−**

Weather Report: *Mr. Gone* (Columbia/ARC '78). I don't think it was the advent of Jaco Pastorius that triggered the band's ever more fusoid tendencies. Professional evolution, that's all. Like *Black Market* and *Heavy Weather*, this is short on rhythmic inspiration (four different drummers, no percussionists) and long on electric ivory. When I'm in the mood I can still get off on its rich colors and compositional flow. When I'm not I think dark thoughts about Muzak and Yurrup.　　　　　　　　　　　　　**B**

Weather Report: *8:30* (Columbia/ARC '79). The live double their more bemused admirers have awaited for years is indeed Weather Report's most (if not first) useful album. But it also defines their limits. This is a band that runs the gamut from the catchy to the mysterioso. Joe Zawinul is the best sound effects man since Shadow Morton.

And when he gives himself room, Wayne Shorter can blow. **B+**

Bob Weir: *Ace* (Warner Bros. '72). Weir can be preachy and screechy, but Robert Hunter's homiletics ("Playing in the Band") make up for John Barlow's post-hippie know-nothingisms ("Walk in the Sunshine"), and "One More Saturday Night" isn't any less a rockabilly epiphany because it strains Bobby's vocal cords — that just adds a note of authenticity. With Barlow redeeming himself on the elegiac pre-hippie fable "Cassidy" and Keith Godchaux sounding like a cross between Chick Corea and Little Richard, this is the third in a series that began with *Workingman's Dead* and *American Beauty*. Original grade: A. **A−**

Bob Weir: *Heaven Help the Fool* (Arista '78). It should surprise no one who's kept an eye on Weir over the years that he manifests himself here as an El Lay country-rock crooner with studio-duperstar backup. But I bet thousands of Dead heads are lying to themselves about it right now, while at the same time Dead haters equate him with Richie Furay and Michael Murphey. Predictably, Weir is better — funnier, more feeling, harder to predict. But how much better can an E. L. c.-r. c. be? **C+**

Bob Welch: *French Kiss* (Capitol '78). When "rock" gets this creamy, it functions as disco for racists, people who'd rather play soft-core dominance games than dance anyway, and the classy lady flicking her tongue in the general direction of our classy artiste's ear lobe has the right idea: aural chic. 'Tis tuneful, though, and probably helps one get through the ironing as pleasantly as the Doobie Brothers do. **C+**

Leslie West: *The Great Fatsby* (Phantom '75). Whaddaya mean, is Leslie West a singer? Is the Pope Jewish? Do bears hum in the shower? And why has that hairy guy in the wet vestments forgotten the tune to "Ave Maria"? **C+**

Wet Willie: *Wet Willie's Greatest Hits* (Capricorn '77). Alone among Southern boogiemen, the Willies have avoided country as in c&w for country as in funk, and their rhythm section gets away with it — drummer Lewis Ross and bass player Jack Hall are all juke-joint bump-and-grind. In a better world they'd be rednecks in a soul band, but as it is they're stuck in a group with two problems — singer and songs. (Oops, forgot the guitarist, which isn't hard.) Jimmy Hall supposedly combines Ronnie Van Zant's discretion with Gregg Allman's power, but to me he sounds like a cross between Chris Youlden and Lonesome Dave Peverett — with an authentic accent, of course. And although their one lucky strike has been the reggaeish "Keep On Smilin'," most of the time they strive fruitlessly for r&b tunes as inescapably elementary as the here-included "Shout Bamalama" and "Grits Ain't Groceries." I guarantee you that Little Milton isn't going to return the favor and cover "Leona" or even "Baby Fat." But maybe Stoney Edwards would do "Airport." **B−**

The Whispers: *The Whispers* (Solar '79). They've been around forever because they're real pros, but that's all they are. Vocal-group fans will probably enjoy — check out these titles — "Lady" and "I Love You" and "Welcome into My Dream," though I hope they stop at the sanctimonious "Song for Donny" and the pallid "My Girl." But what makes this a breakthrough is the three dance tracks. The great one, "Out the Box," was written and coproduced by Leon Sylvers. In the great Sylvers tradition, you could almost mistake it for something you missed on *Destiny* or *Off the Wall*. **B**

Bobby Whitlock: *Bobby Whitlock* (Dunhill '72). Whitlock's mindless, indefatigable soul-straining was essential to Derek and the Dominoes, yet even though the usual pack of musical demigods accompanies him here, all that comes through is the strain. Proving that even in rock and roll unmitigated mindlessness is never really indefatigable. **C−**

Barry White: *I've Got So Much To Give* (20th Century '73). White's hustle is to combine Isaac Hayes's power with Al Green's niceness, and he succeeds, in his way, but the synthesis has its drawbacks — tends to compound his humorlessness and mendacity as well. But as a fait accompli he has quite a bit of silly charm, and does he lay down some powerful tracks. Nor is his style as far removed from soul music as white soul conservatives (myself included) first assumed — the bass pulse has a Latin oomph undiminished by its fat-man's pace. And is that a barrelhouse harpsichord on "Bring Back My Yesterdays"? Very, er, eclectic. Original grade: C. **B**

Barry White: *Can't Get Enough* (20th Century '74). Inspirational Cliches: "doin' our own thing," "different strokes for different folks," "rather fight than switch." Inspirational Emphases: "very important," "very very very very true," "truly truly." Inspirational Epithet: "hope-to-die woman." Inspirational Drum Sound: *"thwop."* **B−**

Barry White: *Just Another Way to Say You Love Me* (20th Century '75). With product as uniform as White's, subtle differentiations take on unlikely incremental significance — I'd swear he's a shade more turgid verbally and sluggish musically. And so would several hundred thousand others, apparently — his last album went number one, while this failed to crack top ten. Statistics never lie. **C+**

Barry White: *Barry White's Greatest Hits* (20th Century '75). The man's commonness is as monumental as his girth, and that's no insult — Barry White may not be Good Art, but neither is Mount Rushmore. It took real creative will to shape *Reader's Digest* virtues and that face and body into a sex symbol. On record, the symbol has weight because White manipulates studio technology with as much originality as — no insult once again — Mitch Miller: the strings-versus-rhythm dynamics, as well as his much-maligned baritone, resonate with physical authority. It's a little early for a best-of — he proceeds at a rate of two hits per album. But as someone who considers his raps entertaining one-shots and prefers his songs at top forty length, I'm delighted anyway. And though the token rap isn't his best, it does feature his greatest line: "I don't want to see *no panties.*" **A−**

Barry White: *Barry White Sings for Someone You Love* (20th Century '77). His two previous albums having slipped precipitously (last one didn't even make top *hundred*), White here recoups by hiring out the songwriting and acceding to such fads (in a style he damn near created) as the ticking cymbal and the tocking horn chart. Not to mention addressing his title to a male audience. Where's your integrity, man? **C+**

Barry White: *Barry White the Man* (20th Century-Fox '78). For those with a high giggle threshold, White's best music in years should prove a more than acceptable fuckalong. That's the A side. On the B side he essays "Just the Way You Are." **B**

James White and the Blacks: *Off White* (ZE '79). This is pretty good to dance to, but like so much disco music it gets tedious over a whole side. And the chick singer — probably somebody's girlfriend — certainly doesn't help. **B−**

Tony Joe White: *Tony Joe* (Monument '70). Because he sticks to his roots, White has those who don't trust rock-as-art all hot and bothered. Well, I don't trust rock-as-art myself, but I don't trust these bayou set pieces either. White's tales of spiders, widders, conjure wimmin, and wayward rich girls all sound like I've seen them on television, only there they had endings. Nor do the Otis Redding and Junior Walker covers teach me anything new. The John Lee Hooker is better. As are "Save Your Sugar for Me," about teenage sex, and "Stockholm Blues," about a songwriter from the bayous who goes somewhere in an airplane.   **C+**

The Who: *Live at Leeds* (Decca '70). This band has never even tried to simulate stage power in the studio except on its raw debut, which makes side one, with its first-ever recordings of two key live covers and the first version of the classic "Substitute" available here on LP, doubly valuable. But side two extrapolates the uncool-at-any-length "Magic Bus" and the bish-bash climax of "My Generation," which has to be seen to be believed. I much prefer the raw debut.   **B**

The Who: *Who's Next* (Decca '71). With its acoustic guitars and drumless bits, this triumph of hard rock is no more a pure hard rock album than *Tommy*. It's got more juice than *Live at Leeds*. And — are you listening, John Fogerty? — it uses the synthesizer to vary the power trio format, not to art things up. Given Peter Townshend's sharpness and compassion, even his out-front political disengagement — "I don't need to fight" — seems positive. The real theme, I think, is "getting in tune to the straight and narrow," and comes naturally to someone who's devoted a whole LP to the strictures of hit radio. Another sign of growth: the love songs. Original grade: A plus.   **A**

The Who: *Meaty Beaty Big and Bouncy* (Decca '71). In England, this is a greatest hits album. In the U.S., where some of these songs have never been released and most have never made the charts, it's a mishmash revelation. The programming defies comprehension — why not try to get the mod anthems on one side and the loonies on the other, or go for chronology? But I'd love it if only for "Anyway, Anyhow, Anywhere," which in 1965 redefined the punk machismo of "Blue Suede Shoes" and "The Wanderer" against pioneering break-'em-up feedback that has rarely been surpassed. Also welcome are the original "Substitute," the self-explanatory "I Can't Explain," and songs about masturbation, dressing up like a girl, and other spiritual quests.   **A−**

The Who: *Quadrophenia* (MCA '73). Unlike *Tommy*, this one really is a kind of opera — first you get to know the music, then you sit down with the libretto and concentrate for eighty minutes. Even with the synopsis (as brilliant a piece of writing as Townshend's ever done) and lyrics, its account of a young Mod's "double schizophrenia" can be pretty confusing, partly because confusion is his subject. The music is cluttered with horns and unnecessarily shrill, so that — despite its considerable melodic (and motivic, as they say) pizzazz — you don't play it for fun. But if Townshend's great virtue is compassion, this is his triumph — Everykid as heroic fuckup, smart enough to have a good idea of what's being done to him and so sensitive he gets pushed right out to the edge anyway. Original grade: A.   **A−**

The Who: *Odds and Sods* (MCA '74). Although Peter Townshend's genius (well, for once that's what it is) glimmers through on every one of these leftovers, all that glimmers is not gold, which is why most of them have been in the can for between three and seven years. The great exception is "Little Billy," a cheerful, cruel smoking-is-dangerous-to-your-health song that the American Cancer Society chickened out on; it'd make a great public service ad on *The Who Sell Out*. There are also two pretty fair rock life songs — and "Long Live Rock," a strained variation on that overworked theme. And to balance off the two pretty good devotional songs there's "Faith in Something Bigger,'' which could serve as Nashville filler. Original grade: C plus. **B**

The Who: *The Who by Numbers* (MCA '75). This record is more depressing than my dispassionate grade would indicate, not just because from the Who we expect better — do we, really? — but because its runaway fatalism invites dispassion. Peter Townshend has more to say about star-doubt than David Crosby or even John Lennon — he's not only honest but exceptionally inquisitive, and he's got a knack for condensing complex ideas. But despite their apercus songs like "However Much I Booze" and "Dreaming from the Waist" circle around so obsessively that they end up going nowhere; I don't expect answers from the seeker, but I do expect him to enjoy the questions. No surprise that the two songs that break out of the bind are "Blue Red and Gray" (which means satori) and "Slip Kid" (about one more imagined teenager). **B+**

The Who: *Who Are You* (MCA '78). Every time I concentrate I get off on some new detail in Daltrey's singing or Townshend's lyrics or Entwistle's bass parts — though not in Moon's drumming, and I still don't relate to the synthesizer. But I never learn anything new, and this is not my idea of fun rock and roll. It ought to be one or the other, if not both. **B+**

The Who: *The Kids Are Alright* (MCA '79). I prefer the originals, but this isn't a bad sampler. All of the songs are good, many are classics, and the relative roughness of performance has its attractions even if the relative roughness of sound doesn't (most of them are from live dates never intended for vinyl). One thing I'd like to know, though — if he's so "vital," how come twelve of the fifteen Townshend compositions are from the '60s? **B**

Wild Cherry: *Wild Cherry* (Epic/Sweet City '75). This is regarded by the pure of heart as a racist vulgarization, but although I'll go along with the argument that the hook on "Play That Funky Music" isn't the rhythm track but the words "white boy," I insist that it's real hard to vulgarize Graham Central Station. Sure the performance is a bit on the crude side, but the relationship is more that of Grand Funk to Cream than of, say, Jim Dandy Mangrum to Sly Stone. **C**

The Wild Magnolias: *The Wild Magnolias* (Polydor '74). Produced by Willie Tee, with Snooks Eaglin letting you know he's on guitar and semi-amateurs "Bo" Dollis and "Monk" Boudreaux shouting the vocals, here's some Mardi Gras music a little louder and jammier than we expect from Tee's Crescent City rival Allen Toussaint. In fact, it's the most boisterous recorded party I know, two sides of dancing fun that wears down only slightly as it slips into "Saints." This is not only what I always wanted the polyrhythm kids on the bandstand and benches of Tompkins Square Park to sound like, it's also what I always wanted Osibisa and the Ohio Players and maybe even the Meters to sound like. **A−**

The Wild Tchoupitoulas: *The Wild Tchoupitoulas* (Island '76). Here we have eight songs about dressing up in Indian costume on Mardi Gras; many of them are also about fighting with other Indians. You've probably heard the New Orleans nonsense patois before, and maybe the irresistible melodic elements, too, although I can't tell any more, because I've played this "repetitive" record so many times it sounds like where they all started (which it may be). For a while, I believed side two inferior, but eventually a longing for "Big Chief Got a Golden Crown" set in and now I prefer it for listening. Side one is the best non- (or anti-) disco dance music in years — it had folks who'd never heard it before shouting "Indians here they come" at a thirtieth birthday party. Allen Toussaint produced, the Meters played, and mighty kootie fiyo. **A**

Don Williams: *Greatest Hits* (ABC/Dot '75). In which this new country honcho — who as a founder of the Pozo-Seco Singers competed in the '60s downhome sweepstakes with the likes of Jim McGuinn — casts about for a style of gentleness that suits him. At its worst his torpid singing has all of Johnny Cash's monotonousness and none of his majesty. But he does reject the ranker strains of corn.   **B**

Don Williams: *The Best of Don Williams Volume II* (MCA '79). Because I can't get behind him as a role model for Eric Clapton, and because he's at least as shrewd as Tammy Wynette, I've resisted Williams's mild vogue, but this collection can't be denied. He may not be the modest homebody he pretends to be, but he sure does project a convincing image of romantic-domestic contentment, complete with separation, sex, and second thoughts. Both the care of the songwriting and the assured, conversational lilt of the vocals divide the sentimentality from the sentiment. Unsinging heroes: composers Bob McDill and Wayland Holyfield.   **A −**

Hank Williams, Jr. and Friends: *Hank Williams, Jr. and Friends* (MGM '75). Williams moved his country heritage towards rock and roll shortly after a confrontation with death on a mountain, and here the transformation conveys that kind of conviction. In fact, the authority of Williams' voice and persona, plus the good sense of his songwriting and selection, focuses an Allman and a Marshall Tucker and the Charlie Daniels into what I'm sure will stand as the best Southern-style rock of the year. No kidding — if you don't find Grinderswitch a suitable replacement for the Brothers, here's yours.   **A −**

Hank Williams, Jr.: *The New South* (Warner Bros. '78). Dear Up-and-Comer: OK, pretty good for a country-rock album — more spirited than your second, less inspired than your first. But let me mention a few things. The Atlanta Braves are not, repeat not, or-dinarily identified with the Old South. Rain gets to be a pretty tedious symbol of life's tribulations. The road gets to be a pretty tedious symbol of life's changes. And if you want to get away from Dad, well, I know it'd be a lot of trouble to change your name, but maybe you could do a whole album that doesn't refer to him at all. And you could stop doing his songs, too — it's bad luck that the best cut here is the one he wrote, now isn't it? I mean, you really could use a new exemplar. Good luck finding him or her. (Signed) Roll on, Dean. P.S. Not Waylon Jennings, either.   **B**

Hank Williams, Jr.: *Family Tradition* (Elektra '79). Since "To Love Somebody" isn't exactly Hank's kind of song, I guess he wasn't kidding when he disavowed the Ray Ruff-produced side of this. On the other hand, "Family Tradition" (guess who that's about) leads off the other side, and it *is* exactly Hank's kind of song. Exactly. That's not so great either.   **C**

Hank Williams, Jr.: *Whiskey Bent and Hell Bound* (Elektra '79). At times his son-of-an-outlaw obsession is worse than shtick, but here he does justice to the formula. Two candid songs about women tell you more about his sexism than he knows himself, two others explain why he's in that mood, the covers from Gregg Allman and George Jones define his parameters, and "The Conversation" — with Waylon Guess Who, about Guess Who, Sr. — doesn't make you gag once.   **B +**

Lenny Williams: *Love Current* (MCA '79). His first single, "Shoo Doo Fu Fu Ooh," was a young singer's whoop of triumph from the top of the world. It seemed to promise many more. But after three mediocre LPs — the first still the best — I've given up. Williams's subsequent tries at simple, ecstatic black pop have sounded like expert imitations, and most of the time he's just a love man, doing his best to shore up songs that were made to be broken. Never thought I'd believe he was better off in Tower of Power, but I do. **C+**

Otis Williams and the Midnight Cowboys: *Otis Williams and the Midnight Cowboys* (Stop '71). In which an old r&b pro (the Charms, remember?) who used to sing harmony on King's country releases heads an all-black country band in a passionately subversive union of two disparate but parallel modes. Granted, his slightly melismatic tenor doesn't equal Charley Pride's penetrating baritone on "Is Anybody Goin' to San Antone" or "Wonder Could I Live There Anymore." But Charley would never deliver the "come here boy" in "Muleskinner Blues" with such sarcastic relish. Original grade: B plus. **B**

The Tony Williams Lifetime: *Turn It Over* (Polydor '70). I'm being complimentary when I say that though *Led Zeppelin II* is infinitely more cumbrous and stupid it packs the same sheer clamoring rock presence. Of course, drummer John Bonham insists on breaking the mood with a solo, while drummer Williams improvises continually on a steadier beat than is ordinarily acceptable among jazz devotees — when he, Larry Young, John McLaughlin, and Jack Bruce all play together it's impossible to distinguish front and back or melody and rhythm. "Right On," two orgasmic minutes of raveup energy and master chops, almost makes me believe in his quavering, enigmatic vocal lines. Unfortunately, though, it doesn't make me want to listen to them, perhaps because he uses his voice to pronounce words. **B+**

Tony Williams: *The Joy of Flying* (Columbia '79). For months I've had the nagging suspicion that this special-guests showcase might be that oddity of oddities, a good fusion album. But it's only an interesting one, featuring a duet with Cecil Taylor that has nothing to do with fusion and including among its snappy complexities a snappy tune that is actually fun — the lead cut, Jan Hammer's "Going Far." Rest assured that Hammer redeems himself tout de suite on George Benson's "Hip Skip," which like most of what remains is snappy and complex and cloyingly high-tech in the great fusion tradition. But Ronnie Montrose's arena fusillades — unlike Benson's articulate tripe — are also fun. And not only is Williams equally comfortable with Cecil and snappy and heavy metal, he's worth listening to no matter what's in the foreground. **B−**

Bob Wills and the Texas Playboys: *For the Last Time* (United Artists '74). Recorded under Wills's supervision until he suffered a stroke before the last day's sessions, this double-LP doesn't represent the band at its peak. But though earlier recordings of most of these classic tunes are at least marginally sharper, it certainly captures the relaxed, playful, eclectic Western swing groove that Wills invented in the '30s. And Merle Haggard does sing lead on three cuts. **B+**

The Deirdre Wilson Tabac: *The Deirdre Wilson Tabac* (RCA Victor '70). For all of side one this trio (two women, one man; two whites, one black) makes Stax-Volt sound easy — with the help of svengali Sonny Casella, and despite traces of cocktail jazz, or maybe it's soul. Side two topples into the martinis, or maybe it's soup. Original grade: B. **C+**

Larry Jon Wilson: *New Beginnings* (Monument '75). A sleeper from a previously unrecorded Georgian who looks to be around forty. Capsule portrait: he named his crippled son after his father, a dirt farmer who moved to the city with misgivings, and Bertrand Russell, both of whom he "knew and loved." The record is as original as you might hope, catchy and fresh-sounding despite overlays of schlock intended to hook the country audience. I wish I could say it was promising as well, but I suspect not. The drawback to rediscovering home truths, which is definitely Wilson's calling, is that when the excitement fades — and even a modest career takes its toll — the reaffirmations turn back into platitudes. That has already begun to happen on the weak cuts here.   **B+**

Jesse Winchester: *Jesse Winchester* (Ampex '70). A Memphis boy who now resides in Canada for the usual reasons draftables reside in Canada, Winchester shares with his Southern-identified Canadian producer Robbie Robertson a knack for renewing the traditional in songs that rock and yet are (a title) "quiet about it." The clincher is "Yankee Lady," the most dangerous gotta-hit-the-road-now-babe song ever because it makes male chauvinism seem emotionally responsible — you really feel that fate has betrayed the bread-baking and winning paragon of the title, not her gentle love slave Jesse.   **A−**

Jesse Winchester: *Third Down, 110 to Go* (Bearsville '72). Winchester's first LP was apolitical on the surface and not without its conservative tendencies, but its brooding lyricism and barely contained ferment reflected the force of will it took for him to flee this country. Here the frustrations of exile seem to have gotten to him — he sounds involuted, willfully slight. The title is a football fan's version of "(Stuck Inside of Montreal with the) Memphis Blues Again," and even more telling is the way he feels about fatherhood: "I can't get out of that." Original grade: C plus.   **B−**

Jesse Winchester: *Learn to Love It* (Bearsville '74). Jesse sounds well. His singing has taken on character and humor and the new songs are pretty good. Yet there's something depressing about his resigned good cheer. Can domesticity be this disappointing — even domesticity confined within a draft resister's Canada? Only if you believe to your Mississippi soul that you were born a rambling man.   **B−**

Jesse Winchester: *Let the Rough Side Drag* (Bearsville '76). *Third Down* and *Learn to Love It* were thin but never less than pleasant, mostly because Winchester is such a warm, astute singer. This is a shade thinner, and when Ol' Jess goes MOR with "As Soon as I Get on My Feet" or transforms "Brand New Tennessee Waltz" into a straight country tune, it's less than pleasant.   **C+**

Jesse Winchester: *Nothing But a Breeze* (Bearsville '77). One reason Winchester disappointed after his first album is that he was conceived as a singer-songwriter, expected to deliver a couple of gems and five or six semi-precious stones a year. Finally seeing him live with his cheerful, comptent band was a revelation — suddenly he became a country singer who could also rock out. He proves it on this LP, which is, however, short on semiprecious stones and entirely gemless — although "Gilding the Lily" turns a cliche the way only a popular song can and the foolishness of "Rhumba Man" borders on brilliance.   **B**

Jesse Winchester: *A Touch on the Rainy Side* (Bearsville '78). Winchester has made a couple of pretty good albums (the first and the fifth), three uneven ones (two, three, and four), and a real stinkeroo (say hello to number six). The only thing that might make the lyrics more annoying would be for the music to induce you to notice them, and the best song on the record was done a lot better eight years ago by Tony Orlando.   **C−**

Wings: *Wild Life* (Apple '71). McCartney is coming to terms with his own fluff — the overproduction sounds less cluttered this time — but it's still fluff, and not even goosedown. Maybe the thrill of leading his very own band has him distracted. (Yes, Linda is in it — that's the good part.)   **C−**

Wings: *Venus and Mars* (Capitol '75). Superficially, which counts for a lot with McCartney, his New Orleans venture is his most appealing post-Beatles album — straight rock and roll with a few pop detours and one excursion into "When I'm 64" nostalgia.

So clear in its melodies, mix, and basic pulse that his whimsical juxtapositions — robots on Main Street, Rudy Vallee cheek by jowl with Allen Toussaint — sound like they might make some sense. Don't get me wrong — they probably don't, because McCartney's a convinced fool. But when the music is coherent it doesn't matter so much. Original grade: B. **B+**

Wings: *Wings at the Speed of Sound* (Capitol '76). The only substantial talent in this group is bassist-producer Paul McCartney, and he's at full strength only on the impassioned "Beware My Love," although "Let 'Em In" and "Silly Love Songs" are charming if lightweight singles, and "She's My Baby" sounds like an outtake from the "white" double-LP by McCartney's former group, the Beatles. In any case, the supporting cast is disgracefully third-rate. The vocals of guitarist Denny Laine are even lamer than those of McCartney's wife and keyboard player, Linda. Original grade: C plus. **B−**

Wings: *London Town* (Capitol '78). McCartney's lyricism is so capricious, so given to inanity and icky-poo, that only at its very best —"With a Little Luck" and the affectionate goof on "Famous Groupies"— does it come on strong. But from its slices of life to its romantic reassurances this is nowhere near as feckless as the Old *Band on the Run* claque claims — even on the one about the fairy who'll invite us to tea Linda adds a few harmonies that are as charming as they're meant to be. And at the very least you have to be impressed by how steadfastly Paul has resisted supersessions — he's been loyal to his group, which has now recorded longer than the Beatles. Original grade: B plus. **B**

Wings: *Wings Greatest* (Capitol '78). Twelve songs, five of them hits not on any previous Wings album, running 54:11 in all, replete with rhythm shifts and subthemes and counterplots and flights of fancy and forays into abject nonsense. In short, pop for potheads. All I could ask is a stylus-width scratch across "My Love." **B+**

Wings: *Back to the Egg* (Columbia '79). Whew. Sixteen titles on an untimed LP that must run forty minutes if not fifty — or seventy-five. When he's on, Paulie's abundant tunefulness passes for generosity. Here he's just hoping something will stick. **C**

Edgar Winter: *Entrance* (Epic '70). Better you should graft bebop harmonies and solos onto a rock (or even art-rock) trunk for your jazz fusion than arrange rock and not-so-rock songs for a Stan-Kenton-goes-to-Nevada bouquet. If only Edgar didn't try and conceal his mild-mannered vocal tendencies behind that shriek. And if only he scatted and soloed like a brother. Original grade: D. **C**

Edgar Winter: *Edgar Winter's White Trash* (Epic '71). So this is that hard-ass roadhouse rockaroll, eh? Sounds like overkill to me, which I guess is very Texas, but I figured in Texas they'd be too real to mistake hysteria for a good time. And since when do they rhyme "subjective" and "objective" down there? Or wonder whether the world will be saved by Mr. White or Mr. Black? **C**

The Edgar Winter Group: *They Only Come Out at Night* (Epic '72). This may be heavy, but it's fast, which means real rock and roll after the attempted progress and hyperboogie. And instead of hyperthyroid Jerry LaCroix we get Dan Hartman, who knows enough about songs to come up with "Free Ride," and Ronnie Montrose, who knows enough about guitar to get by. Not only that, but Edgar's found a midrange. And not only that but he wears lipstick, eye makeup, and a cheek stud on the cover. **B**

The Edgar Winter Group: *Shock Treatment* (Epic '74). A lot of heavy pop talent concentrated in this group —Rick Derringer, Dan Hartman, wow. Too bad about Edgar. At least when he brought out his saxophone you could say he was different.

Which is no doubt why he spends so much time with his synthesizer.   **C+**

Johnny Winter And: *Johnny Winter And* (Columbia '70). Ex-popstar Rick Derringer represents the North — real-McCoy rock guitar, contentless AM songs, dumb vocals (watch out Steve Miller here comes Dino Valenti). Ex-bluesman Winter represents the South — spacey ex-blues guitar, formless FM songs, exalted vocals. (and you thought spacey ex-blues was an insult). Result: best metal since *Layla*.   **B+**

Johnny Winter And: *Live* (Columbia '71). Except for the eight-minute "Mean Town Blues," which damn near transforms John Lee Hooker's shuffle into a stumble, this is what every live album ought to be and all too few are: loud, fast, raucous, and to the point. But except for an intense "Good Morning Little School Girl" it doesn't get any encores.   **B−**

Johnny Winter: *Still Alive and Well* (Columbia '73). Winter will never be an especially personable singer, but I like what's he's putting out on this monkey-off-my-comeback: two late-Stones covers, plenty of slide, and a good helping of nasty. Nastiest: the Delta-styled "Too Much Seconal" and "Ain't Nothing to Me," dedicated to the subversive notion that sometimes the impassivity of country music is a little sadistic. White blues lives: the best and heaviest track is a Hoodoo Rhythm Devils song.   **B+**

Johnny Winter: *Saints and Sinners* (Columbia '74). I think what puts me off this otherwise searing assertion of rock and roll prowess is the engineering. Rick Derringer has done the standard live-sound job, in which echo is amplified into unnatural "depth," and theoretically that's fine. The average live-sound band is too busy doing promotional tours for its current album to worry about material for the next, but here the songs are lovingly chosen — there's even a good one from the pitiful Richard Supa. Rock and roll the way

Johnny likes it, however, was meant to have a human dimension, and since he has trouble projecting irony or intimacy anyhow, a lot of these die a little when Derringer mixes them into heavy cuts.   **B**

Johnny Winter: *John Dawson Winter III* (Blue Sky '74). Those who considered *Saints and Sinners* a masterpiece of hard rock and roll should find this satisfactory. I prefer to figure out why Helen Reddy's version of "Raised on Rock" scores two out of a possible three on a credibility scale of ten while Johnny's gets one. (Hint: showbiz kids relate to rock-schlock more authentically than albino bluesmen.)   **C+**

Johnny Winter: *White, Hot and Blue* (Blue Sky '78). He was lionized as an authentic bluesman when *Rolling Stone* discovered him in 1968, and that's how he ended up — only a racist would deny his feeling for this music. Feel is something else. When he's entertaining, he's derivative; when he's original, he sounds shrill.   **B−**

Steve Winwood: *Steve Winwood* (Island '77). Combined with Stomu Yamashta's ersatz electronic classicism on *Go,* Winwood's chronic meandering seemed vaguely interesting. On its own again, it just seems vague.   **C−**

Wipers: *Is This Real?* (Park Ave. '79). Three guys from Portland (Oregon, but it might just as well be Maine) who caught on to punk unfashionably late and for that reason sound like they're still discovering something. Which hardly makes them unique — there are similar bands in dozens if not hundreds of American cities, many of whom send me records. What distinguishes this one is Greg Sage's hard-edged vocals — detached but never silly, passionate but never overwrought — and economical one-hook construction.   **B+**

Wire: *Pink Flag* (Harvest '78). The simultaneous rawness and detachment of this debut LP returns rock and roll irony to the (native) land of Mick Jagger, where it belongs. From a formal strategy almost identical to the Ramones' this band deducts most melody to arrive at music much grimmer and more frightening; Wire would sooner revamp "The Fat Lady of Limbourg" or "Some Kinda Love" than "Let's Dance" or "Surfin' Bird." Not that any of the twenty-one titles here have been heard before — that would ruin the overall effect of a punk suite comprising parts so singular that you can hardly imagine them in some other order. Inspirational Prose: "This is your correspondent, running out of tape, gunfire's increasing, looting, burning, rape." Original grade: A minus **A**

Wire: *154* (Warner Bros. '79). Predictions that these art schoolers would turn into art-rockers no longer seem so cynical. Their gift for the horrifying vignette remains. But their tempos are slowing, sometimes to a crawl, as their textures venture toward the orchestral, and neither effect enhances the power of their vignettes, which become ever more personalistic and/or abstract. **B**

Wishbone Ash: *There's the Rub* (MCA '74). The journeyman English blues-cum-heavy group of whom it has been said: "When they come out on stage, they seem to be holding their guitars like machine guns, but pretty soon you realize it's more like shovels." **D+**

Witch Queen: *Witch Queen* (Roadshow '79). Here Gino Soccio's disco goes pop, with the help of the Muscle Shoals boys and three jumpy, skillfully extended blasts from the riff-song past — Redbone's "Witch Queen," Free's "All Right Now," and T. Rex's "Bang a Gong." It's nowhere near Muzaky enough to desecrate material so unpretentious, but except for Barry Beckett's chunky piano break on "Bang a Gong" it doesn't add much, either. **B**

Bill Withers: *Just As I Am* (Sussex '71). With faultless production from Booker T. — even the strings are taut — this is an unusually likable and listenable middlebrow soul LP. As befits a strummer of acoustic guitars, Withers is more folk than pop, and when he adds folk seriousness to a gospel fervor surprising in such an apparently even-tempered man, he makes titles like "I'm Her Daddy" and "Better Off Dead" take on overtones of radical protest where other singers would descend into bathos. I don't find that even standout cuts like "Ain't No Sunshine" and "Grandma's Hands" reach out and grab me, but except for a letdown toward the end of side two the flow sustains. Original grade: B. **A−**

Bill Withers: *Still Bill* (Sussex '72). Wither has created the most credible persona of any of the upwardly mobile soul singers, avoiding Marvin Gaye's occasional vapidity, Donny Hathaway's overstatement, and Curtis Mayfield's racial salesmanship. He sounds straight, strong, compassionate. And don't be fooled by "Lean on Me" — he's also plenty raunchy and he can rock dead out. The self-production here is adamantly spare, with Ray Jackson furnishing the hook of the year on "Use Me," one of the few knowledgeable songs about sex our supposedly sexy music has ever produced. Original grade: B plus. **A**

Bill Withers: *Bill Withers Live at Carnegie Hall* (Sussex '73). Hearing Withers urge the audience on, as drummer James Gadson and pianist-arranger Ray Jackson drive their crack combo, really wipes out the man's MOR aura — nobody else in the music combines hard rhythms and warm sensuality so knowingly. A natural shouter who raises his voice judiciously and a deliberate, wryly moralistic rapper, his authority comes through even when you can't see him frowning mildly in his unshowy Saturday-night sports clothes. Two of the five new songs lean on friendship themes, and that's one too many, but the old ones are live indeed. Knockout: the encore, "Harlem/Cold Baloney," all 13:07 of it. **A−**

Bill Withers: +*'Justments* (Sussex '74). Most of side two sounds like Roberta Flack, which disappoints me even though it probably doesn't surprise anyone else, Withers included. Well, I had my hopes for this man, but then, so did all the Roberta Flack fans, every one of whom must love "Lean on Me." Side one, I'm happy to report, begins with a nasty song to a trendy fox who wants Bill to see a shrink! Keep it up, Bill! And he does! Pretty much. For one side. Recommended, but barely. **B+**

Bill Withers: *The Best of Bill Withers* (Sussex '75). Unfortunately, Withers the Balladeer has had more hits than Withers the Rocker. But the compilation demonstrates forcefully that both share the same convictions. And the two cuts from +*'Justments* gain power as a result. **A−**

Bill Withers: *Making Music* (Columbia '75). The slippage is suddenly a landslide. As songs, all of these tracks except "I Love You Dawn" and "The Family Table" are potentially enjoyable. But most of them are so fragile that one surge of the orchestrations Withers used to resist so steadfastly sweeps them into the mawk. Even "Make Love to Your Mind," a seductive lyric about not getting down (right away), goes on for so long you're afraid the man may overplay his hand. **C+**

Bill Withers: *Naked and Warm* (Columbia '76). Here Withers returns to the simple ways of his past, working five or six musicians for the kind of hard groove that doesn't have many parallels in black music these days. And almost succeeds in obscuring the continuing dearth of songs — there are only eight here, and the one that runs 10:46, a paean to L.A., includes a couplet about Disneyland that even I, a convert to Withers's plainspeech, find embarrassing every time out. Recommended single: "Close to Me." **B**

Bill Withers: *Menagerie* (Columbia '77). "It's a Lovely Day" is his biggest hit since changing labels, and this compromise between the mush of *Making Music* and the muscle of *Naked and Warm* his biggest album. The compromise is an honest one, the success earned. I wish I could say they made me happier. **C+**

Bill Withers: *'Bout Love* (Columbia '78). In which Bill acquires a melodist (Paul Smith) and a theme (see title). He should dump 'em both. And if he's in some sort of group therapy, he should dump that too. **C**

Howlin' Wolf: *The London Howlin' Wolf Sessions* (Chess '71). A supersession with a conscience, or maybe just a reason for being, in which a whole raft of rich English rock and rollers — the cream: the core band is Clapton, Winwood, Wyman, and Watts — get behind the man who taught them their shit if anyone did. The material is classic, the playing early Stones with chops — committed to a slightly speedy shuffle, a little lighter and more ornate (horns on two cuts) than the old Chess stuff. Wolf's voice sounds a little light as well — doesn't threaten to shatter the bones. Maybe he didn't want to scare the white boys. **A−**

Howlin' Wolf: *The Back Door Wolf* (Chess '73). There's more art, as it is called, in this sixty-three-year-old man's large intestine than is likely to pass through Sunset Sound in a month. Can you imagine Steve Stills or one of those guys coming up with a *title* as bold as "Coon on the Moon," much less turning it into a fierce, ominous cry of ironic pride. The Wolf hasn't been in such good bellow for years. Suggestion: get rid of the electric piano player. Original grade: B plus. **A−**

Stevie Wonder: *Signed, Sealed and Delivered* (Tamla '70). Sometime in the past (can it be?) eight years, Little Stevie became Big, and so did his frantic one-smash-a-year style — wheezes, shrieks, and all. Consistent Motown albums are rare, and Wonder is still an immature ballad singer, though at least now he's covering "We Can Work It Out" (some ballad) rather than (I'm not making this up) "The Shadow of Your Smile." All the good stuff here is stuffed onto one great side — the most exciting music by a male soul singer in quite some time, and it fits no mold, Motown's included. Original grade: A minus. **B+**

Stevie Wonder: *Stevie Wonder's Greatest Hits Vol. 2* (Tamla '71). Most of these songs hit the charts in a big way before Stevie turned twenty-one last May. Because he's grown up fast, the love lyrics are less teen-specific than a lot of early Smokey, say, but the music is pure puberty. Stevie's rockers are always one step ahead of themselves — their gawky groove is so disorienting it makes you pay attention, like a voice that's perpetually changing. The ballads conceive coming of age more conventionally, and less felicitously. But he sure covered Tony Bennett better than the Supremes or the Tempts could have, now didn't he? Original grade: A minus. **A**

Stevie Wonder: *Where I'm Coming From* (Tamla '71). Wonder produced and (with his wife, Syreeta Wright) scripted this escape from Berry Gordy's plantation, and as you might expect it's not entirely successful. Unlike his corporate masters, though, Wonder prefers sins of commission — he's always out on a limb, and if that means "classical" flutes and images like "ride the thorny mule" it also means the zany, stuttering autoback-talk of "I Wanna Talk to You" and the possible Sammy Davis cover "Take Up a Course in Happiness," not to mention the most expressive synthesizers yet recorded. And unlike the manumitted Marvin Gaye, Wonder never sounds like a simp — the sentiments may be stale, but their textures are fresh. **B+**

Stevie Wonder: *Music of My Mind* (Tamla '72). Making the most of the inevitable, Motown boasts on the back cover that "this album is virtually the work of one man" — he plays everything but one solo each on guitar and trombone. Sure could teach John Fogerty a thing or two about multitracked

spontaneity — this music is mercurial above all else. Just like the blind genius he's always compared to, Wonder transcends taste. But because the specifics are less inspired than the gestault — which is not to say I don't love "Love Having You Around" and catch myself enjoying the regrettable "Superwoman" — it doesn't quite hold together. **B+**

Stevie Wonder: *Talking Book* (Tamla '72). The artist breaks through and takes control, though not in that order. Suddenly he's writing better ballads than he used to choose, and not at any sacrifice of his endearing natural bathos (if you have doubts about "Sunshine of My Life," try "Blame It on the Sun"). "Maybe Your Baby" and "Big Brother" continue his wild multi-voice experiments but come in out of left field. And "Superstition" translates his way of knowledge into hard-headed, hard-rocking political analysis. Original grade: A minus. **A**

Stevie Wonder: *Innervisions* (Tamla '73). It's neither Wonder's attraction to cliches nor his proud belief that he's the peer of anyone who can read this that leads him to render his mental life in a visual metaphor. It's because he's got no use for abstraction — he's technical/physical rather than logical/ conceptual. Here once again he treads the fine line between glossolalia and running on at the mouth. Any suggestion that the bitter defeats of "Living in the City" are as unfactual as the "dream come true" of "Golden Lady" is simply irrelevant, because both are the truth — and unless he's snuck one past me and "Golden Lady" is about the sun, which would be interesting, that song is the worst one here. This is music that makes you believe in faith, almost like Stevie, who only knows that leaves turn from green to brown because he's got no choice. Original grade: B plus. **A**

Stevie Wonder: *Fulfillingness' First Finale* (Tamla '74). What made Wonder's last two albums so gorgeous was the carefree indecorum of the ballads, which broke the rules with supremely indulgent self-confidence and only became more beautiful as a result. But this time the slow ones are less carefree than aimless: Only "They Won't Go When I Go" gets lost altogether, and most reveal substantial charms in the end, but we really shouldn't have to look so hard for them. The two great cuts, meanwhile, get across mostly on momentum — "You Haven't Done Nothin'," about "the nightmare/ That's becomin' real life," and "Boogie On Reggae Woman," about boogieing on. Original grade: B plus. **A −**

Stevie Wonder: *Songs in the Key of Life* (Tamla '76). It's no accident that the rich, hortatory one-man music of "Love's in Need of Love Today" is counterposed against the more intimately devotional one-man music of "Have a Talk with God," or that when the theme turns sociopolitical in "Village Ghetto Land" Stevie's synthesizer turns from African sounds to an ironic (though elegant) string-quartet minuet — the calm detachment of which is rudely interrupted by a jazz-funk tribute from Stevie's Wonderlove band, which then moves into the danceable black-music tribute "Sir Duke." And in themselves the words are much funnier and trickier than the sociospiritual bullshit of Maurice White or Kenny Gamble; as validated by the wit, pace, and variety of the music, they come close to redeeming the whole genre. **A**

Stevie Wonder: *Stevie Wonder's Journey Through the Secret Life of Plants* (Tamla '79). Like most great popular composers, Wonder is an appalling "serious" one. With their one-world instrumental flourishes and other sound effects, the presumably synthesized "orchestral" passages that dominate the first two sides are like bad (!) David Amram at their best (!) and some justifiably anonymous Hollywood hack at their worst. (Major exception: "Race Babbling," especially when it glances a presumably synthesized horn riff off presumably synthesized voices and ostinatos.) And only

two of the four songs on side three, which defenders of this album admire, are worthy of *Key of Life*. But on side four Wonder's indomitable open-heartedness finally breaks through the mawk. "A Seed's a Star and Tree Medley" is even more foolish philosophically than most of the rest of the album, but its elan makes Stevie's vitalism palpable, so that even the presumably synthesized orchestral passages that wrap things up sound ardently schmaltzy instead of depressingly schlocky. Still, next time I hope he aims lower. **B −**

Ron Wood: *I've Got My Own Album to Do* (Warner Bros. '74). For a few minutes I thought Ron's version of "Far East Man" was co-composer George Harrison's. What can this mean? It means the next Rolling Stone ain't no Keith Richard in the vocal department. It also means that in the future he would be well-advised to stay away from Krishna. **C +**

Ronnie Wood: *Now Look* (Warner Bros. '75). Just like former Face and co-Ronnie R. Lane, Wood has something English-folk about him. But with Lane it's deliberate — Wood sounds modal because that's the groove his lost pitch instinctively reverts to. This collaboration with producer-composer Bobby Womack is good for one major love song ("I Got Lost When I Found You"), several minor ones, and a lot of melodies that sound familiar when heard again. Just wish they didn't sound so accidental as well — might help me hum 'em. **B**

Ron Wood & Ronnie Lane: *Mahoney's Last Stand* (Atco '76). Better moaning bottlenecks than singing strings, but soundtrack music is soundtrack music even when the movie remains invisible, and we all have access to more meaningful background noise. **B −**

Ron Wood: *Gimme Some Neck* (Columbia '79). Ron sounds more Dylany on his new Dylan ditty than Dylan has in a while, and he sounds even better on a song about getting saved (which

Dylan didn't write, praise the Lord). He's also induced Roy Thomas Baker to let him and the boys off with a mix as dirty as their rock and roll. But this is a man who should never sing two songs in a row. And he should stay away from lyrics about the perfidy of woman, too. **B−**

Roy Wood: *Boulders* (United Artists '73). Wood puts his heart into his multitracking — even plays a robot and makes you feel for him (by which I mean the robot). Then, on the very next track, he impersonates a grandma picking dexterously if erratically on her banjo. These are conceits, but they're successful conceits — as substantial as Loudon Wainwright's, say, and more tuneful. And when they're Move-style conceits you can gallumph to them. **A−**

Roy Wood's Wizzard: *Introducing Eddy and the Falcons* (United Artists '74). Catchy though it is — and why shouldn't it be, with Wood appropriating hooks if not entire melodies from the likes of Del Shannon, Elvis Presley, and "Little Darlin' "? — this collection of iron pyrite oldies may be the most pointless English import since the bowler. On *Boulders*, Wood exploded the forms he exploited. Here he falls victim to the *Grease* syndrome — in paying tribute to the teen emotions that fueled rock and roll he comes dangerously close to condescension. Original grade: C. **B−**

Roy Wood: *On the Road Again* (Warner Bros. '79). I once thought it spoke well of Annie Haslam and all her renascent octaves that they'd kept this gifted recluse interested for so many years. But on the evidence of these would-be Move outtakes — and the would-be *Boulders* outtakes of 1976's *Mustard* — I gather that it doesn't take much to divert the fellow. **C**

Woodstock (Cotillion '70). "I left one thing out of my Woodstock article," says Tom Smucker, author of a good one. "I left out how boring it was." And though you can be sure it's not like being there, this three-record set does capture that. As is inevitable in a live album featuring stage announcements, crowd noises, and sixteen different artists, not one side is enjoyable straight through: CSNY are stiff and atrociously flat in their second gig, Paul Butterfield sounds wasted, Sha Na Na should never record, Joan Baez should never record, and so forth. But a substantial proportion of this music sounds pretty good, and three performances belong to history: Ten Years After's "I'm Going Home" (speed kills), Joe Cocker's "With a Little Help from My Friends" (mad Englishman), and Jimi Hendrix's "Star Spangled Banner" (wotta ham). Also, the stage announcements and crowd noises are better than most. **B**

Woodstock II (Cotillion '71). I don't understand why, but Butterfield, Baez, and especially CSNY all sound more together on these selections than they did last time. I do understand why there's a whole side of Hendrix, and it's not the amazing ritual repetitions of "Jam Back at the House," but I'll settle — he makes what would be an engaging but dispensable piece of history into something more. **B**

Working (Columbia '78). Broadway is as obsessed with leisure as any other pop bastion, and I have no doubt that one reason this show failed was its subject, which it does justice to at least half the time. The best lyrics describe a character's own peculiar job, rather than generalizing about his or her line of work; whether it's the luck of the draw, the state of the art, or the moral superiority of women, the actresses have more touching stories to tell than the actors. All the songs flirt with sentimentality, which means the good ones can make you cry. Worth preserving. **B+**

Link Way: *Link Wray* (Polydor '71). The creator of a feedback experiment called "Rumble" that beat the Yardbirds to it by six or seven years must have turned hippie on his own as well, though his headband reflects birth loyalties to the Shawnee nation. These days he runs a three-track recording shack in rural Maryland where he and some fellow spirits put together this blues- and country-rooted document. The playing (not much feedback) is better than the vocals is better than the songs, and on the whole it's pretty dumb. But I have to grant that the man sings about getting crucified by the Establishment as unselfconsciously as a back-porch bluesman sings about trains, which must be worth something. Right? **C+**

Link Wray: See also Robert Gordon

Wreckless Eric: *The Whole Wide World* (Stiff '79). Like the Only Ones' *Special View*, Eric's U.S. debut sifts the duds out of two years' worth of U.K. singles and LPs to arrive at a stylistically unified compilation album — though the thirteen tracks list seven different producers, they cohere, because Eric hasn't had time to outgrow his own impulses. The voice mewls and scratches like a cat in a broom closet, but the melodies get out, and the lyrics are a lot less hapless than they pretend to be: beneath the girl-shy fool lurks an ironic paranoid of devastating subtlety. **A-**

Betty Wright: *I Love the Way You Love* (Alston '72). You'd never guess it from "Clean Up Woman," but this album is the perfect union of the Betty who has worked in the Alston studio since 1964 and the Betty who won't be nineteen until September 21 — teen love in all its moral passion and sweet concupiscence. Does her voice shoot upwards on "I'll Love You Forever Heart and Soul" because her spirit is soaring or because he just touched between her legs? Both, I hope. **B+**

Betty Wright: *Danger High Voltage* (Alston '74). In which the entire T.K. Productions gang — Willie Clarke, Casey & Finch, Little Beaver, Tommy Thomas, Clarence Reid, Bo Horne — pitch in on six prime Miami originals and native-sounding imports from Detroit, New Orleans, and New York. Like all but the greatest girl-group voices of the '60s, Wright's not an original stylist, but she's never sounded brighter or sassier, and she's always sounded bright and sassy. On her own "Tonight Is the Night" she also sounds sad, happy, confused, determined, virginal, and horny. Original grade: B plus. **A-**

Betty Wright: *Explosion* (Alston '76). Inevitably, she's turning into a warm, perky soul pro, and given how unfashionable simple soul has become we ought to be grateful. But the only times I'm on my knees are on "I Think I'd Better Think About It," in which she resists temptation — to infidelity rather than mere fucking by now — and "If I Ever Do Wrong," in which she thinks some more. **B**

Gary Wright: *Extraction* (A&M '71). The title means Spooky Tooth has lost Jersey — New Jersey, I guess I should say. Get it? Does that mean he's lost his roots or is returning to them? Anyway, he bites the bullet like a real American. Not too incisive, though. Get it? **C+**

Gary Wright: *Footprint* (A&M '71). Like his mentor, George O'Hara, Gary makes his spiritual home right next to his musical one, close by that great echo chamber in the sky. But unlike George he writes anthems that are forthright and tuneful — why, even "Give Me the Good Earth" is down-to-earth. The ecology-minded will also approve of "Love to Survive" and "Stand for Our Rights," both of which are vague enough to appeal to every constituency. Cosmic-commercial lives. **B**

Gary Wright: *The Dream Weaver* (Warner Bros. '75). Supposedly, the artistic breakthrough here is that Gary has transcended the electric guitar. Some breakthrough — good thing Lee Michaels never took up with a synthesizer. Although if he had he wouldn't have pimped it off to (and I quote) "the astral plane." **C**

O. V. Wright: *The Bottom Line* (Hi '78). With its unabashedly country (i.e. rural) singer and its back-to-basics Willie Mitchell production, this one has soul nostalgiacs hot and bothered, but I find the material thin and like it mostly for its oddities: the tribute to Guy Lombardo; the sexy mama who refuses to go, as opposed to get, down by declaring, "I don't do windows"; and the old man who defines love as "a misunderstanding between two damn fools." **B**

Robert Wyatt: *Rock Bottom* (Virgin '75). I'm at a loss to describe this album of "drones and songs" conceived and recorded after Wyatt's crippling accident except to say that the keyboards that dominate instrumentally are of a piece with his lovely tortured-to-vulnerable quaver and that the mood is that of a paraplegic with the spirit to conceive and record an album of drones and songs. **B+**

Tammy Wynette: *Tammy's Greatest Hits Volume II* (Epic '71). While no one was looking, that stand-by-your-man gal was writing a female identity song: "The Only Time I'm Really Me" (is when I'm asleep — and presumably dreaming). Which is almost cancelled out by one of the most appalling divine justice songs in that godforsaken subgenre: "The Wonders You Perform" (at least it's not about her husband). Beyond those two it's the best of the usual — her sultry resignation has archetypal power when the ideology isn't too repellent. It's more archetypal on her first best-of, though. Time: 27:05. **B**

Tammy Wynette: *Tammy Wynette's Greatest Hits Volume Three* (Epic '75). Songs like "(You Make Me Want to Be) A Mother" are why so many women more honest than Tammy don't want to be mothers — makes having a child seem like losing a self, and defines having a self as manipulating others. Though it was written by two men, I credit Tammy with enough autonomy to blame her for it. And would add (somewhat paradoxically) that the only time this compilation comes to life is during the song about her children and the song to them. Time: 28:02. **C+**

Tammy Wynette: *Womanhood* (Epic '78). In which Billy Sherrill performs (or permits) a miracle: five good songs on one side. (Nobody ever accused Billy of thinking big.) On side one, we learn about virtue sorely tempted, the limits of sisterhood, music as emotional communion, virtue abandoned, and the limits of professionalism. On side two, Tammy confuses Wolfman Jack with John the Baptist and then retreats into the commonplace. With country albums, you take what you can get. **B**

Tammy Wynette: *Greatest Hits Volume 4* (Epic '78). Nothing like d-i-v-o-r-c-e to bring out the independent woman in you — the only marital-commitment song here is about having an alcoholic husband. And where in her domestic-paragon phase she was beginning to sound prim, here she ranges from forthright to positively hot, torching up her tales of star-crossed sex as if she's just learned how to masturbate. Point of interest: Billy Sherrill's latest collaborator on Tammy's material is George Richey, Tammy's latest husband. Time: 27:49. **B+**

XTC: White Music (Virgin International '79). Although it took a year and a half for this debut album by the premier English art-pop band to get released in the States, two Andy Partridge songs on side one aim directly at the American market — "Radios in Motion," which mentions Milwaukee, surely isn't about the BBC, and the avowed purpose of "Statute of Liberty" is to get a look up her skirts. The third, "This Is Pop," is why he missed — radio programmers resent anyone telling them their business, especially subversives who favor herky-jerk rhythms, jerky-herk harmonies, Lene Lovich radar noises, and depressing subject matter. Colin Moulding's songs, on the other hand, are aimed at bored Yes fans, which is why he missed — the lad doesn't know that Yes fans *like* being bored.   **B+**

XTC: Go 2 (Virgin International '79). Last time they were calling it white music, this time they've released a dub version, and what can you call that except au courant? Or here's another one. It's Andy Partridge who puts the pop in their art-pop, right? If you can tell me whether his "Meccanik Dancing" is pro or con, I'll prove to you that his "Life Is Good in the Greenhouse" means it.   **B−**

XTC: Drums and Wires (Virgin '79). My reservations about this tuneful but willfully eccentric pop are ideological. With its playful clash of cross-currents (crossed wires, really, to go with the jingle drums) it's just a "Complicated Game"— like everything else under the sun, Andy Partridge believes. This idea is an attitude rather than an analysis, and it assures that the music's underlying passion will be strictly formal. But I like games, especially those — like Clue or categories or three-handed hearts or this record — which require concentration but not lifetime dedication, and Partridge and Colin Moulding are moving toward a great art-pop mean that will set standards for the genre. Catchy, funny, interesting — and it rocks.   **A−**

Yachts: *Yachts* (Polydor '79). You have to hand it to a group that can give itself such a ridiculous name and then come up with credible songs called "Yachting Type" and "Semaphore Love." Actually, most of these songs are pretty credible, even (or especially) the one structured around the word "tantamount." Funny boys, no doubt about it. But their biggest joke is a mock-snooty, mock-operatic rock-crooning style that I'm not eager to hear again. **B–**

The Yankees: *High 'n' Inside* (Big Sound '78). These New Yorkers play it fast and loose enough to dismay pop technicians and even offend people a little. Indeed, I was already hooked on their boisterous Strangeloves/Standells tribute when it struck me that maybe Jon Tiven's wandering pitch, which I find cute, meant the record was warped. It's more likely, though, that his voice has begun to change in his mid-twenties, inspiring him to cover "Bad Boy" (well) and write (a good) one called "Take It Like a Man." A hit that proves once again that rock and roll is about having the spirit, knowing the tricks, and taking the risks. Ivan Julian is DH. **A–**

Yellow Magic Orchestra: *Yellow Magic Orchestra* (Horizon '79). Yeah yeah, I know, synthesizers are the electric guitars of the future — they're "progressive," just like all the Europop here. But what about the corny swing melodies? I mean, in between sound effects these guys sound the way Walter Carlos might if he worked a lot of interfaith weddings. **C+**

Yes: *Time and a Word* (Atlantic '70). I delayed judgment on the weedy harmonies and genteel virtuosity of their debut, mostly because they covered the Byrds and the Beatles, who flirted with weeds and gentility themselves. This time they cover Richie Havens, synopsize Kahlil Gibran, and insert orchestrations that cry out for the fine hand of Dmitri Tiomkin. Answer to title quiz: "now" and "love." **C**

Yes: *The Yes Album* (Atlantic '71). Jon Anderson, who delivers the inane Con III lyrics with prissy expertise, and Tony Kaye, whose keyboards run the gamut from vague to overweening, are the bad guys. Bill Bruford, who rocks the rather fancy tempos and signatures, and Chris Squire, best when he gets a good interlock going with Bruford, are the neutrals. And new guitarist Steve Howe makes the record worth hearing if not owning. His commentary throughout "Yours Is No Disgrace," his live acoustic solo "The Clap," and his duet with himself on "Würm" (that's German for "worm," in case you're interested) make the first side almost interesting, and he's at the heart of the album's one great cut, "I've Seen All Good People," where all their arty eclecticism comes together for 6:47. **B–**

Yes: *Fragile* (Atlantic '72). I certainly prefer Yes's rock-classical synthesis — in which tricky intros, swooping dynamics, and intense textures are integrated into a self-sustaining (and -propelling) electric framework — to ELP's flashy chopsmanship. "Round-About" is a triumph right down to its nature-mystic lyric, the rhythm players each contribute a viable composition, Steve Howe remains a marvel, and even the rearranged Brahms from new keyboard player Rick Wakeman is tolerable. But isn't there supposed to be more to art than great contrivance? Original grade: B plus.   **B**

Yes: *Close to the Edge* (Atlantic '72). What a waste. They come up with a refrain that sums up everything they do — "I get up I get down" — and apply it only to their ostensible theme, which is the "seasons of man" or something like that. They segue effortlessly from Bach to harpsichord to bluesy rock and roll and don't mean to be funny. Conclusion: At the level of attention they deserve they're a one-idea group. Especially with Jon and Rick up front. Original grade: C. **C+**

Yes: *Tales from Topographic Oceans* (Atlantic '74). Nice "passages" here, as they say, but what flatulent quasi-symphonies — the whole is definitely less than the sum of its parts, and some of the parts are pretty negligible. I mean, howcum they didn't choose to echo Graeco-Roman, Hebrew, and African culture as well as the lost Indian, Chinese, Central American, and Atlantean ones? Typical hyperromantic exoticism is one answer, and everybody would know they're full of shit is the other. Original grade: D plus.   **C**

Yes: *Going for the One* (Atlantic '77). The title track may be their best ever, challenging a formula that even apologists are apologizing for by now with cutting hard rock guitar and lyrics in which Jon Anderson casts aspersions upon his own "cosmic mind." But even there you wish you could erase Rick Wakeman, who sticks strictly to organ pomp and ident noodles throughout, and elsewhere Steve Howe has almost as little to say.   **C**

Yipes!: *Yipes!* (Millennium '79). This Wisconsin band is nowhere near as yucky as name and packaging suggest — how can you hate someone who complains that Californians "got no ceilings on their cars"? Subjects of other cartoons — some simpleminded, some not — include class rivalry, being white, and the cold war. The problem is leader Pat McCurdy, who has one of those "good rock voices" that enable the artiste to shout in tune but don't permit much nuance. You can almost see him curling his lip and raising his eyebrows whenever a joke comes up. Oh well.   **B−**

Mighty Joe Young: *Mighty Joe Young* (Ovation '76). If Young's voice weren't as gruffly workaday as his guitar, he might be a threat — he's got a knack for the blues subject, from mama-in-law to barbecue to what money can buy. Even with the stupid string synthesizer butting in, this is a solid, coverable groove album. And the Johnnie Taylor medley kicks it off naturally.   **B**

Neil Young: *After the Gold Rush* (Reprise '70). While David Crosby yowls about assassinations, Young divulges darker agonies without even bothering to make them explicit. Here the gaunt pain of *Everybody Knows This Is Nowhere* fills out a little — the voice softer, the jangling guitar muted behind a piano. Young's melodies — every one of them — are impossible to dismiss. He can write "poetic" lyrics without falling flat on his metaphor even when the subject is ecology or crumbling empire. And despite his acoustic tenor, he rocks plenty. A real rarity: pleasant and hard at the same time.   **A+**

Neil Young: *Harvest* (Warner Bros. '72). Anticipation and mindless instant acceptance made for critical overreaction when this came out, but it stands as proof that the genteel Young has his charms, just like the sloppy one. Rhythmically it's a little wooden, and Young is guilty of self-imitation on "Alabama" and pomposity on the unbearable London Symphony Orchestra opus "There's a World." But those two excepted, even the slightest songs here are gratifying musically, and two of them are major indeed — "The Needle and the Damage Done" and the much-maligned (by feminists as well as those critics of the London Symphony Orchestra) "A Man Needs a Maid." Original grade: B. **B+**

Neil Young: *Journey Through the Past* (Reprise '73). The film is as yet unreleased, which judging from the still on the cover — hooded horsemen carrying cruciform staves — is just as well. Its "soundtrack" has one virtue: eccentricity. Except for the apparently unfinished "Soldier," the standards, the Buffalo Springfield numbers, and the Young songs are familiar, but not in these versions, many of which are also apparently unfinished. Scholars will be grateful for the source material; the rest of us will settle for the 15:51 of "Words," which occupies all of side three. **C+**

Neil Young: *Time Fades Away* (Reprise '73). This is no desperate throwaway or quickie live album. Loud and dense but never heavy, singing with riffs concocted from the simplest harmonic components, it's squarely country, yet it never hints at nouveau-rockabilly good times. The opener, "Don't Be Denied," is an anthem of encouragement to young hopefuls everywhere that doesn't shrink from laying open fame and its discontents. And the finale, "Last Dance," evokes the dayjob hassles that pay for Neil Young tickets, suggests alternatively that "you can live your own life," and then climaxes in a coda comprising dozens of "no"'s wailed over a repetitive back-riff. It must have been strange to watch fans boogieing slowly to this mournful epiphany. But with the Stray Gators (driven by ex-Turtle Johnny Barbata instead of ex-Dylanite Kenny Buttrey) doing as much for Young's

brooding, wacked-out originality as Crazy Horse ever did, it sure is exciting to hear. **A**

Neil Young: *On the Beach* (Reprise '74). Something in his obsessive self-examination is easy to dislike and something in his whiny thinness hard to enjoy. But even "Ambulance Blues," an eight-minute throwaway, is studded with great lines, one of which is "It's hard to know the meaning of this song." And I can hum it for you if you'd like. **A−**

Neil Young: *Tonight's the Night* (Reprise '75). This should end any lingering doubts as to whether the real Neil Young is the desperate recluse who released two albums in the late '60s or the sweet eccentric who became a superstar shortly thereafter. Better carpentered than *Time Fades Away* and less cranky than *On the Beach,* it extends their basic weirdness into a howling facedown with heroin and death itself. It's far from metal machine music — just simple, powerful rock and roll. But there's lots of pain with the pleasure, as after all is only "natural." In Boulder, it reportedly gets angry phone calls whenever it's played on the radio. What better recommendation could you ask? **A**

Neil Young: *Zuma* (Reprise '75). Young has violated form so convincingly over the past three years that this return may take a little getting used to. In fact, its relative neatness and control — relative to Y, not C, S, N, etc. — compromises the sprawling blockbuster cuts, "Danger Bird" and "Cortez the Killer." But the less ambitious tunes — "Pardon My Heart," say — are as pretty as the best of *After the Gold Rush,* yet very rough. Which is a neat trick. **A−**

Neil Young: *American Stars 'n Bars* (Reprise '77). The first side, recently recorded, is Young's rough-and-tough version of L.A. country rock, featuring a female backup duo called the Bullets and climaxing with "Bite the Bullet," his sharpest cut since "Tonight's the Night." The second is a journey through the past that perhaps should have stayed in the outtake can. On one tune, Neil turns into a salmon while masturbating in front of the fireplace; on another, he and Crazy Horse somehow take the wind out of "Like a Hurricane," which blew everybody away at the Palladium last fall.   **B+**

Neil Young: *Comes a Time* (Reprise '78). In which the old folkie seeks out his real roots, in folkiedom. Not only is this almost always quiet, usually acoustic and drumless, and sweetened by Nicolette Larson, but it finishes off with a chestnut from the songbook of Ian and Sylvia — not just folkies, but Canadian folkies. Conceptually and musically, it's a tour de force. Occasionally you do wonder why this thirty-two-year-old hasn't learned more about Long-Term Relationships, but the spare, good-natured assurance of the singing and playing deepens the more egregious homilies and transforms good sense into wisdom. The melodies don't hurt, either — Young hasn't put together so many winners since *After the Gold Rush*. Now that it's been done right, maybe all those other guys will hang up their Martins and enroll in bartending school.   **A**

Neil Young: *Decade* (Reprise '78). As usual with compilations by album artists, I prefer the original LPs in both theory and practice. But this triple is done with care right down to the packaging and commentary. The five previously unreleased songs range from pretty good to pretty great, the sides cohere stylistically, and I'd rather hear "Ohio," "Soldier," "Helpless," and "Long May You Run" in this context than in any other.   **A**

Neil Young: *Rust Never Sleeps* (Reprise '79). For the decade's greatest rock and roller to come out with his greatest album in 1979 is no miracle in itself — the Stones made *Exile* as grizzled veterans. The miracle is that Young doesn't sound much more grizzled now than he already did in 1969; he's wiser but not wearier, victor so far over the slow burnout his title warns of. The album's music, like its aura of space-age primitivism, seems familiar, but while the melodies work because they're as simple and fresh as his melodies have always been, the offhand complexity of the lyrics is unprecedented in Young's work: "Pocahantas" makes "Cortez the Killer" seem like a tract, "Sedan Delivery" turns "Tonight's the Night" on its head, and the Johnny Rotten tribute apotheosizes rock-and-roll-is-here-to-stay. Inspirational Bumper Sticker: "Welfare mothers make better lovers."   **A+**

Neil Young: *Live Rust* (Reprise '79). John Piccarella thinks this is the great Neil Young album, Greil Marcus thinks it's a waste, and they're both right. The two discs are probably more impressive cut for cut than *Decade*, but without offering one song Young fans don't already own. I prefer the studio versions of the acoustic stuff on side one for their intimacy and touch. But I'm sure I'll play the knockdown finale — "Like a Hurricane," "Hey Hey, My My," and "Tonight's the Night," all in their wildest (and best) recorded interpretations — whenever I want to hear Neil rock out.   **A−**

The Youngbloods: *Ride the Wind* (Raccoon '71). What hath folk-rock wrought? Or is it Marin County, or "owning" your own label? A lot of third-hand Barney Kessel and/or Dave Brubeck that couldn't have second-billed at the Half Note in 1957 plus some very occasional vocals from ol' Jess, who sounds like Mel Torme after 2000 micrograms and three months of Diet No. 7. Country vibes don't mean spilling your seed on the ground.   **D**

Zabriskie Point (MGM '70). Includes selections, most of them instrumental, by Pink Floyd, the Grateful Dead, Kaleidoscope, the Youngbloods, Jerry Garcia, John Fahey, Roscoe & Holcomb, and Patti Page. Is considerably deeper and more coherent than the Antonioni film of the same name.   **B −**

The Mothers of Invention: *Weasels Ripped My Flesh* (Bizarre/Reprise '70). Talk about "montage" — the construction here is all juxtaposition, the composition all interruption. Together with some relatively straightforward instrumentals and "My Guitar Wants to Kill Your Mama," the album's two finest strokes — a metal remake of Little Richard's "Directly from My Heart to You" and "Oh No," a devastating reply to "All You Need Is Love" — would make for a highly enjoyable album. But if Brecht considered pure enjoyment counterrevolutionary, Zappa considers it dumb — that's why he breaks in constantly with dialogue and vocal or electronic sounds whose musical interest/value is essentially theoretical. I find most of these engaging enough to think I might want to listen again some day. But all that means is that I enjoy it, quite moderately, in spite of itself.   **B +**

Frank Zappa: *Chunga's Revenge* (Bizarre '70). Like Bobby Sherman, Zappa is a selfish exploiter of popular taste. That Bobby Sherman wants to make money while Zappa wants to make money and emulate Varese is beside the point — if anything, Zappa's aestheticism intensifies his contempt for rock and its audience. Even *Hot Rats,* his compositional peak, played as much with the moods and usages of Muzak as with those of rock and roll. This is definitely not his peak. Zappa plays a lot of guitar, just as his admirers always hope he will, but the overall effect is more Martin Denny than Varese. Also featured are a number of "dirty" jokes.   **C +**

The Mothers: *Fillmore East, June 1971* (Bizarre '71). The sexist adolescent drivel that hooks these moderne mannerisms should dispel any doubts as to where Big Mother finds his market — among adolescents and sexists of every age and gender (bet he gets more adults than females). It must tickle Frank that a couple of ex-Turtles are now doing his dirty work. Probably tickled him too to split the only decent piece of rock and roll (or music) here between two sides. Original grade: D plus.   **C −**

Frank Zappa: *Waka/Jawaka — Hot Rats* (Bizarre/Reprise '72). With Sal Marquez playing "many trumpets" all over "Big Swifty," there are times you could drop the needle and think you were listening to recent Miles Davis. That's certainly what Zappa's been doing. But where Davis is occasionally too loose, Zappa's always too tight — he seems to perceive only what is weird and alienating in his influences, never what is humane. Also, Sal Marquez doesn't play trumpet(s) as good as Miles.   **B**

The Mothers: *Over-Nite Sensation* (DiscReet '73). Oh, I get it — the soft-core porn is there to contextualize the serious stuff. Oh, I get it — the automatic solos are there to undercut the serious stuff. Oh, I get it — the marimbas are there to mock-trivialize the serious stuff. But where's the serious stuff?   **C**

Frank Zappa: *Apostrophe (')* (DiscReet '74). Disillusioned acolytes are complaining that he's retreated, which means he's finally made top ten, but that's just his reward for professional persistence. If anything, the satire's improved a little, and the title piece — an improvisation with Jack Bruce, Jim Gordon, and rhythm guitarist Tony Duran — forays into quartet-style jazz-rock. Given Frank's distaste for "Cosmik Debris" you'd think maybe he's come up with something earthier than Mahavishnu, but given his distaste for sex you can be sure it's more cerebral instead.   **B−**

Frank Zappa/Mothers: *Roxy and Elsewhere* (DiscReet '74). You can actually hear Zappa thinking on "More Trouble Every Day," and "Son of Orange County" is an uncommonly understated Nixon tribute. The rest is the usual eccentric cliches, replete with meters and voicings and key changes that are as hard to play as they are easy to forget.   **C+**

Frank Zappa and the Mothers of Invention: *One Size Fits All* (DiscReet '75). Zappa's music has gotten a little slicker rhythmically — which is what happens when you consort with jazz guys — but basically it's unchanged. And his satire has neither improved nor deteriorated — if his contempt would be beneath an overbright high school junior, there's also a brief lieder parody that I'd love to jam onto WQXR. What's changed is the tastes of his erstwhile lionizers — they've gotten bored with his repertoire of stylistic barbarities. Us smart people just got bored faster.   **C+**

Frank Zappa/Captain Beefheart/The Mothers: *Bongo Fury* (DiscReet '75). This sentimental reunion album, recorded (where else?) in Austin with (what else?) additional L.A. studio work, is dismissed by Zappaphiles and 'Fhearthearts alike, but what were they expecting? Perhaps because there's a blues avatar up top, the jazzy music has a soulful integrity, and though it's embarrassing to hear the Captain deliver Frankie's latest pervo exploitations, the rest of the songs are funnier because he's singing them.   **B**

Frank Zappa: *Sleep Dirt* (DiscReet '79). For what it's worth, I thought I'd mention that this collection of outtakes showcases more good music than any Zappa album in years — including its companion piece, *Studio Tan,* which features a twenty-minute narrative called "Greggery Peccary" that could make me defend El Lay. Maybe the secret of *Sleep Dirt* is that Frank doesn't talk on it. But that didn't help *Orchestral Favorites*.   **B−**

Frank Zappa: *Sheik Yerbouti* (Zappa '79). If this be social "satire," how come its sole targets are ordinary citizens whose weirdnesses happen to diverge from those of the retentive gent at the control board? Or are we to read his new fixation on buggery as an indication of approval? Makes you wonder whether his primo guitar solo on "Yo' Mama" and those as-unique-as-they-used-to-be rhythms and textures are as arid spiritually as he is. As if there were any question after all these years.   **C**

Warren Zevon: *Warren Zevon* (Asylum '76). I am suspicious of singer-songwriters who draw attention to phrases like "hasten down the wind," and I would suggest a moratorium on songs about the James Brothers that don't also rhyme "pollution" and "solution." But I like the way Zevon resists pigeonholes like "country-rock" while avoiding both the banal and the mystagogical, and I like quatrains like: "And if California slides into the ocean/Like the mystics and statistics say it will/I predict this motel will be standing/Until I pay my bill."   **B+**

Warren Zevon: *Excitable Boy* (Asylum '78). The further these songs get from Ronstadtland, the more I like them. The four that exorcise male psychoses by mock celebration are positively addictive, the two uncomplicated rockers do the job, and two of the purely "serious" songs get by. But no one has yet been able to explain to me what "accidentally like a martyr" might mean — answers dependent on the term "Dylanesque" are not acceptable — and I have no doubt that that's the image Linda will home in on. After all, is she going to cover the one about the headless gunner? **A −**

Joel Zoss: *Joel Zoss* (Arista '76). As an unmistakably genuine artist who is unmistakably limited and unmistakably easy to dislike — his manipulative moan reminds Carola that "there are worse things in men than machismo" — Zoss raises the question of whether nice, bright product isn't sometimes preferable to realized art. Personally, I'll take good Anne Murray any day. **C +**

Tapper Zukie: *Man Ah Warrior* (Mer '78). Dub has certain affinities with heavy metal, which may be why the only album of the stuff I've ever played much is Big Youth's first, *Screaming Target,* now five years old and never released in the States. Ace discophile Lenny Kaye has compiled this set from the same period, which means that the mix is less volcanic than in recent dub, the vocals more buoyant. Zukie is fresh enough to really enjoy putting a rap down, too, so he doesn't sound doombound, verbally or musically. Sample segue: from "Simpleton Badness" to "Archie the Rednose Reindeer." **A −**

ZZ Top: *Rio Grande Mud* (London '72). Significant that the only memorable song by (or from, rather) this no-organ Allmanesque trio — "Francene," a small but deserving hit — was not written by the principals. Let's just hope it isn't very significant. [Later on Warner Bros.] **C**

ZZ Top: *Tejas* (London '76). Touring the way this band does tears you up by the roots, until the digs at *Rolling Stone* assume an authenticity lacking in the tales of the Pan-Am Highway. But this is the first trio to hark back to country music as well as blues, and they're brawnier than anything that comes out of Austin. You think Kinky Friedman will cover "Arrested for Driving While Blind"? [Later on Warner Bros.] **C +**

ZZ Top: *The Best of ZZ Top* (London '77). "10 Legendary Texas Tales," the cover claims, but that's another tall one. "Jesus Just Left Chicago" is more like it — these boys obviously believe that even sonsofgod get the blues. And by concentrating all their favorite steals in one place come up with a not-bad boogie album that can stand in for five lousy ones. High point: "Tush" (hey, I thought that was Jewish). [Later on Warner Bros.] **B**

ZZ Top: *Deguello* (Warner Bros. '79). These guys got off the road for real — sounds as if they spent all three years playing the blues on their front porch. The strident arena technique is gone, every song gives back a verbal phrase or two to make up for the musical ones it appropriates, and to vary the trio format they not only learned how to play horns but figured out where to put them. I've heard a shitload of white blues albums in the wake of Belushi & Aykroyd. This is the best by miles. **A −**

Subjects for Further Research

Kevin Ayers With his bananas and borrowed pataphysics, Ayers has always been an oddball's oddball, and his best-regarded work has never been released here. At the proper time, whateverhesingsillreview.

David Bromberg He's certainly overrated by his cult — what cult artist isn't? — but I think rock and rollers are too hard on him. You have to give some credit to a Jewish boy with glasses who makes his living doing Blind Willie McTell imitations and then begins a song: "When I got up this morning I had Someone Else's Blues."

Can Next to Henry Cow, this durable (and variable) German contingent is art-rock's most genuinely avant-garde band, adapting Stockhausen and Coleman to rock rhythms and sonorities in a way that is usually interesting if rarely (in my experience) compelling. All this and their own studio in Cologne without touching the American market or gaining any reliable American distribution. The almighty Deutschmark.

Bruce Cockburn This born-again Episcopalian (he's the type who appreciates oxymorons) is genuinely literate as well as genuinely musical. But I've been boycotting poetic types who admire the Church of England ever since escaping John Crowe Ransom as an undergraduate.

Nick Drake I'm not inclined to revere suicides. But Drake's jazzy folk-pop is admired by a lot of people who have no use for Kenny Rankin, and I prefer to leave open the possibility that he's yet another English mystic (romantic?) I'm too set in my ways to hear.

John Fahey Fahey is immersed in country blues, from which he derives his own unique guitar music — eerie, funny, stately, and incredibly calm. The best tranquilizing music I know, because instead of palming off a fantasy of sodden deliverance it seems to speak of real reserves of self-control inside the American psyche. That said, I'll add that tranquilizing music has never been a priority of mine. The only one of the albums on his own Takoma label I listen to is the first, *The Legend of Blind Joe Death*. My real favorites are *Of Rivers and Religion* and *After the Ball* — both orchestrated, both long out of print on Reprise. Avoid the Vanguard stuff, which tends to wander — and boy, can he wander.

Fatback Band I once blindfold-tested Fatback along with a dozen other members of the State Department's Committee on Jazz, Folk and Popular Music. Every one of us got the funk. When I returned home, however, I could never find that groove again.

Rory Gallagher After a decade-plus on the road he's earned his blue dues card. A real rock and roller, too — he's avoided the lassitude of John Mayall, the boogie boredom of Savoy Brown, the power madness of Foghat. I often notice a good song or two when I play his records, too. Just never remember what they are.

John Hammond It's not true that Hammond never developed his own style — his distinctive slur is very much a function of his unique vocal embouchure (he has a slight speech impediment). It offended rock critics — including me — not just because it seemed like a condescending mouldy-fig romanticization of the broken-down bluesman but because it wasn't forceful enough for rock and roll, as if he'd turned Junior Wells into John Hurt. I've never kept many of his records and suspect they still suffer from interpreter's disease — it's almost impossible to make every song new. But I wouldn't be altogether astonished if in twenty years he sounded almost as good as Junior Wells.

Donny Hathaway "Bourgeoisification at its genteel worst," I once called the Atlantic best-of, and while I'm no longer comfortable with that judgment it suggests why most white rock critics find him so impenetrable. Hathaway was a synthesizer of limitless cultural aspiration — he could never have contented himself with the classbound pop fantasies of Ashford & Simpson, whom I much prefer, and unlike, say, Nancy Wilson, whom I really can't stand, he conveyed a sense of roots. Perhaps the idealistic credulousness of a project that incorporated pop, jazz, a little blues, lots of gospel, and the conservatory into an all-over black style is linked to the floridity that mars much of his work.

John Lee Hooker Greil Marcus's comment on the Hook's *Detroit Special* says it all: "Hooker has put out scores of albums in his thirty-year career; all I've heard are good, because all I've heard feature his crawling kingsnake guitar, his pounding foot, his stoic, doomy rage." My own favorites are on ABC/Bluesway, especially 1969's *Simply the Truth,* which leads with "I Don't Want to Go to Vietnam," and 1972's *Never Get Out of These Blues Alive,* which has Van Morrison, Luther Tucker, Mel Brown, Elvin Bishop, and "T. B. Sheets." I can also say I've never gotten into *The Cream,* his 1978 live double on Tomato. But I wouldn't think of arguing my case on the merits.

Keith Jarrett Not a rock musician. Sometimes I'm not so sure he's a jazz musician either.

Waylon Jennings "Waylon lets you know he has balls by singing as though someone is twisting them," I wrote about the self-serving "Ladies Love Outlaws" in 1972, and although I've softened some — actually enjoy him when Willie's there to cut the grease — his macho melodrama will always rub me the wrong way. Allow me this prejudice. His admirers speak fondly of 1975's introspective, Jack Clement-produced *Dreaming My Dreams,* cut before his stance became a marketing procedure.

Albert King I've always found myself unmoved by Albert's broad-beamed variation on B.B.'s blues, but I've never been convinced that this was Albert's fault. It's generally believed, though, that the man's best stuff was cut for Stax in the '60s; he spent most of the '70s trying to go pop, with predictable results. For an eloquent defense, see Robert Palmer's notes on *Albert King Live* (Utopia '77).

Kool & the Gang Amelodic hitmakers, jazzbos who couldn't improvise, these primal funkers were too funking primal for me in the early '70s, their artistic heyday. Listening to their various best-ofs now, I can hear that it was arcane rhythms and silly novelty hooks that got them onto (black) radio. But the dance floor is obviously where to figure such music out, and though I like individual cuts — "Jungle Boogie" and "Hollywood Swinging" especially — I doubt I'll make sense of it until some DJ takes me by surprise.

Leo Kottke Much as I admire John Fahey, I'm no aficionado of the school of solo guitar he inspired, and though I once complained that Kottke lacked Fahey's "courage and clarity" I think what I really meant was genius — and I have no idea what that means. If a guest were to request Kottke I'd play Capitol's *The Best* twofer, which I enjoy under duress — the sides he doesn't sing on, that is.

The Last Poets The original rappers' first commitment was political, not rhythmic — an old story in protest music that fails to move its theoretical constituency. But they sure had a better beat than Pete Seeger.

John Martyn John Piccarella: "The shameless romance of his singing is balanced by his own tough-minded guitar style, which explores the wide range of tonal possibilities inherent in an acoustic instrument amplified and modified by various electronic devices." But Piccarella also mentions Martyn looking "as if he were seeing more of God than Jerry Garcia ever had," and that's the rub.

Magma An art-rock band with its own mythology — big deal. But these guys have also made up their own language. One night when I was painting my auxiliary record shelves I put on *Attahk* and started laughing out loud. I'm told *Attahk* is one of the fast ones, though.

Joe McDonald The proud author of "Bring Back the Sixties Man" has dated worse than John Sebastian because he has no pop sense. I liked *Paris Sessions* a lot in 1973 and it still sounds OK, but it's hard to, er, relate to the self-righteous feminist songs of a man who's subsequently proved much more dedicated to self-righteousness than to feminism. Still, he has a knack for the topical, and with Phil Ochs dead we may learn to appreciate him once again.

Yoko Ono She tried to go pop eventually, but only after a long layoff, on 1980's *Double Fantasy,* did she get it right. Before that came scads of avant-garde fiddle-faddle. Much of this — try "Fly" — is still unlistenable, some "interesting" in the wake of Eno-style ersatz ethnicity. But on parts of her *Plastic Ono Band* — "Why," featuring John and Ringo, more than "AOS," featuring Ornette — she anticipated punk jazz by a decade.

Shakti They sure sounded better than late Mahavishnu. And some believe "India" — about a woman rather than a country, I'm pleased to report — suggests a new sensuousness in John McLaughlin, which I hope is true; he's always been something of a cold fish. But I feel about L. Shankar the way I do about Ravi, which is to say: ?.

Rosalie Sorrels Though she recalls too many I-gotta-move-babe male precedents, Sorrels projects an idiosyncratic, independent female persona — sexual and ultimately even maternal, but no more a folkie earth mother than Joanne Dru in *Red River*. On record, however — for Sire, Paramount, Philo — she's been too quirky for her own good. And that country quaver does wear after a while.

Southside Johnny and the Asbury Jukes I've never found that Johnny Lyons's flat, nasal voice was up to his ambitions — his albums are good for two or three cuts apiece, if that. But because I've always admired his dedication to r&b new and old — he's fun on stage, and remarkably open for a traditionalist — I don't have the heart to dismiss his records with a quip. At least that's what I tell myself. Maybe I don't have the stomach to dissect them one by one.

Candi Staton Maybe she really is a victim of the very songs she sings — though not that one, or "Young Hearts Run Free." But her reputation for stiffing onstage makes me think there's something radically self-effacing about her — something the richest and sexiest voice can't quite make up for.

Steeleye Span Anglophiles (and real English people, which is not tue same thing at all) admire their respectful electric interpretations of traditional British music with an untoward passion. Maybe I will too someday. But at the moment the only cut of theirs I've ever noticed is the much-despised "To Know Him Is to Love Him."

Leon Thomas In the early '70s, the only time the former Pharoah Sanders vocalist has had a solo recording career, I thought his yodeling vocal expansions turned scatting "into an atavistic call from the unconscious." But without rejecting his yodel I came to prefer his shout — his collaboration with Oliver Nelson on "Disillusion Blues" over the one with Sanders on "The Creator Has a Master Plan." Meanwhile, my reservations about his muddleheadedness became firmer. Only *Legend* and *The Leon Thomas Album* remain on my first-run shelves, though I wouldn't advise against any of the others.

Townes Van Zandt   Texas's resident singer-songwriter (I use the term generically) has always struck me as unreasonably doleful, but when I played his live album to ascertain just how unreasonable I noticed him cracking jokes and talking blues, including a side-splitter about fraternities (not fraternity). Made me take his melancholy more seriously. Unfortunately, I also caught him singing "Pancho and Lefty" as if it had no melody (a big mistake, just ask Emmylou) and uttering the phrase "harlequin mandolins harmonize helplessly."

Cris Williamson   The most gifted of the lesbian folk-rockers (let's call a spade a spade) who gravitated toward Olivia Records in the mid-'70s, she sang and arranged *The Changer and the Changed* with unmistakable grace. But the organically self-righteous aura of community she and her sisters gathered around themselves was meant to protect them from me and everyone else with a penis, and it worked.

Bobby Womack   Sam Cooke gave him a heritage and God gave him a voice. He had songwriting credentials ("It's All Over Now") and big ideas (*Communication, Understanding, Facts of Life*). He played guitar all over *There's a Riot Goin' On*. And from the sweet reason of "I Can Understand It" to the reggae remake of Chris Kenner's "Something You Got" he had plenty of moments. But I've never found an album of his I wanted to listen to — including the often disappointing *Greatest Hits*, which features his "Sweet Caroline" but not (there's still some justice) his "Close to You."

Charles Wright   Expressing himself solo or with his Watts 103rd Street Rhythm Band, Wright had a talky vocal style that made him sound even more oddball than the other funk pioneers. I took him for a singles artist around his 1970 heyday, but recently I found an LP in a discount bin, and now I suspect I was wrong.

Distinctions Not Cost-Effective
(Or: Who Cares?)

AC/DC No sexual preference implied.

Ambrosia Nominated for several engineering awards.

The Babys Their demo was a videotape — in 1976.

Brownsville Station They weren't smokin' in that boys' room—just taking a quick dump.

Terry Callier The black Jim Webb, only warmer — and less talented.

Climax Blues Band Did you quit yet? Did you quit yet?

David Allen Coe Has never killed me.

David Crosby/Graham Nash See Graham Nash/David Crosby.

Tim Curry Hotter than Meat Loaf.

Rick Derringer The first cut on his solo debut was called "Let Me In," and it should have. Later he started trying to knock down the door.

Earth Quake Their "Friday on My Mind" (on *Beserkley Chartbusters*) cut Bowie and the Easybeats. The rest was Saturday-night swindle.

Focus Out of it.

Frijid Pink Not to be confused with the Frost — at least not if you come from Detroit.

Gentle Giant The first "progressive" band ever produced by a "progressive" radio programmer — AOR theoretician Lee Abrams, who was to the '70s what Mitch Miller was to the '50s.

Graham Central Station I ask you, is Sly's bassist going to name his spin-off Graham Cracker?

The Grass Roots I found only one of their many hits tolerable — 1967's tragically inaccurate "Let's Live for Today."*

Sammy Hagar He covered Patti Smith's "Free Money." He also covered Donovan's "Catch the Wind." And this is a heavy metal guy.

Peter Hammill/Van Der Graaf Generator Jon Pareles argues that if we honor high school punks we should also honor high school poets. I say we stick to high school punk poets.

Michael Henderson   A very great bass player.

Peter Ivers   When he failed to cross Sparks and Randy Newman, he mutated into Rodney Bingenheimer.

Paul Kelly   One great song — "Stealin' in the Name of the Lord" — was good for a decade's worth of rep. And the song wasn't all that great.

Jackie Lomax   He was soulful, he had blue eyes, and it wasn't enough.

Harvey Mandel   Ron Wood made better solo albums. And Bill Wyman came close.

The Manhattans   I recommend their 1980 best-of, but for albums I'll take the Chi-Lites. Or the Detroit Emeralds. Maybe even Boston.

Phil Manzanera   Randy California made better solo albums. And Jay Ferguson came close.

The Moody Blues   In 1970, while under the influence of marijuana and my new Toyota, I bought "Question," which sure beats Mantovani, reportedly their greatest influence.

Giorgio Moroder   As a solo artist he was the Ross Bagdasarian of his time, but without Alvin Chipmunk who could care?

Michael Murphey   No longer needs borrow his Cadillacs.

Graham Nash/David Crosby   See David Crosby/Graham Nash.

Nazareth   If they were a carpenter you'd really get them confused with Lazarus.

Oregon   Deciduous.

The Partridge Family   At least the Osmonds were a cultural presence. All David Cassidy had going was nice nipples and prime time.

Pearls Before Swine/Tom Rapp   I never understood who they/he thought they/he were/was throwing their/his accretions at/before.

Player   Why didn't they just call themselves Pimp and get it over with?

Kenny Rankin   Invented folk-jazz.

Terry Reid   Persistence beyond the call of talent.

Renaissance   Truly pseudo-genteel art rock — they get into the country club, where the Moody Blues would be blackballed by some opera-lover.

REO Speedwagon   When the banality achieves a certain density, I thought, velocity no longer matters. Then they began to score hit ballads.

Cliff Richard   Everyone knows the only great rock 'n' roll record ever to come out of England was by Lonnie Donegan.

Biff Rose   Still stoned.

Sadistic Mika Band   Don't let the name worry you — it's a transliteration of the Japanese "No Pope, daddy-o."

Ben Sidran   Beware of Ph.D.s playing rock and roll. Or jazz. Or blues. Or whatever it is.

Sons of Champlin   Their claim to fame was as Haight-Ashbury's first rock band. They regrouped so stubbornly they may yet be the last.

John David Souther   Souther sounds insipid until you listen close. Then you realize he isn't that nice.

Michael Stanley Band   Cleveland's answer to Pere Ubu.

Ray Stevens Like Jerry Reed, a novelty artist with lover-boy delusions, except that even when he was hot he was lukewarm.

Stuff Stuffing. Or anyway, backing.

Sutherland Brothers and Quiver Not as in "Shakin' All Over" — as in "I shot an arrow in the air."

Third World Great name, but too often Fifth Wheel would be more accurate.

Jim Webb Spent the decade sitting in his paper cup.

West, Bruce & Laing Move me no mountains.

Paul Williams The best thing he ever did in his life was say he looked like a gym teacher from Bryn Mawr.

Meltdown

Angel
Barclay James Harvest
Blackmore's Rainbow
Bloodrock
Cactus
Camel
Stanley Clarke
Cold Blood
Al DiMeola
England Dan and John Ford Coley
Lewis Furey
Hamilton, Joe Frank & Reynolds
Jan Hammer
Judas Priest
Kayak
Eric Justin Kaz
Klaatu
Lighthouse
Jon Lucien

Lucifer's Friend
Chuck Mangione
Van McCoy
Montrose
Nektar
Shawn Phillips
Pamela Polland
Jean-Luc Ponty
Pure Prairie League
The Scorpions
Sha Na Na
Bobby Sherman
Spyro Gyra
Starz
Toto
Triumvirat
Uriah Heep
Rick Wakeman
Lenny White

ROCK AND ROLL.

A BASIC RECORD

LIBRARY

The Fifties and Sixties

The lists that follow, dominated by standbys that have given me pleasure for years, are for context — where my judgments are coming from — as well as guidance. They've taken some relistening, but not the kind of scrutiny that went into the body of the book, and they're less than comprehensive, based largely on albums in my non-collector's collection. Nevertheless, similar criteria apply. I've named records, not artists — great, listenable records as opposed to important ones, records rarely marred by humdrum cuts. I've included urban blues because it differs from rock and roll only in stylistic rigor and target audience, and ignored country music because the styles only began to merge fully in the '70s (honky-tonkers like George Jones and Hank Williams — not to mention Country Jerry Lee — are/were more rock and roll than Willie Nelson, but singer-songwriter Nelson is definitively "rock"). Certain faves (*More Chuck Berry*, Aretha's *I Never Loved a Man*) have been passed over to avoid duplication with best-ofs. There are twenty-five LPs from the '50s and seventy-five from the '60s because those round numbers are about where the quality begins to tail off.

As suits what was basically a singles music, all but three of the '50s selections are greatest-hits albums, most of them put together in the '70s. I've omitted such classic multiple-artist compilations as *18 King Size Rhythm & Blues Hits* (Columbia), *You Must Remember These* (Bell), *History of Rhythm & Blues Vol. 3* (Atlantic), *Echoes of a Rock Era* and *Golden Goodies* (Roulette), and *American Graffiti* (MCA) in favor of twenty-five forty-fives by artists whose LPs — if they exist at all — didn't make the grade. A lot of best-ofs show up in the '60s as well because outside of the fab five — Beatles-Dylan-Stones-Who-Redding — great albums-as-albums were rare before 1967. The good old days? We'll never know.

THE '50S: SINGLES

The Big Bopper: "Chantilly Lace" (Mercury)
The Bobbettes: "Mr. Lee" (Atlantic)

The Cadillacs: "Speedo" (Josie)
The Channels: "The Closer You Are" (Whirling Disc)
The Chantels: "Maybe" (End)
Danny and the Juniors: "At the Hop" (ABC)
The Del Vikings: "Come Go with Me" (Dot)
Bill Doggett: "Honky Tonk" (King)
The Five Satins: "In the Still of the Night" (Ember)
Bobby Freeman: "Do You Wanna Dance" (Josie)
The Gladiolas: "Little Darlin'" (Excello)
Dale Hawkins: "Suzie Q" (Checker)
Screamin' Jay Hawkins: "I Put a Spell on You" (Okeh)
The Heartbeats: "A Thousand Miles Away" (Rama)
Ivory Joe Hunter: "Since I Met You Baby" (Atlantic)
Little Willie John: "Fever" (King)
Johnnie & Joe: "Over the Mountain, Across the Sea" (Chess)
Mickey & Sylvia: "Love Is Strange" (Groove)
The Monotones: "Book of Love" (Argo)
The Penguins: "Earth Angel" (Dootone)
The Rays: "Silhouettes" (Cameo)
Shirley & Lee: "Let the Good Times Roll" (Aladdin)
The Silhouettes: "Get a Job" (Ember)
The Teenagers: "Why Do Fools Fall in Love" (Gee)
Ritchie Valens: "La Bamba" (Del-Fi)

THE '50S: ALBUMS

Chuck Berry: *Chuck Berry's Golden Decade* (Chess)
Chuck Berry: *Chuck Berry's Golden Decade Volume II* (Chess)
Ray Charles: *What'd I Say* (Atlantic)
The Clovers: *Their Greatest Recordings: The Early Years* (Atco)
The Coasters: *Their Greatest Recordings: The Early Years* (Atco)
Bo Diddley: *Got My Own Bag of Tricks* (Chess)
Fats Domino: *Fats Domino* (United Artists)
The Drifters: *Their Greatest Recordings: The Early Years* (Atco)
The Everly Brothers: *History of the Everly Brothers* (Barnaby)
The Five Royales: *The Five Royales* (King)
Buddy Holly/Crickets: *20 Golden Greats* (MCA)
Jerry Lee Lewis: *Original Golden Hits — Volume One* (Sun)
Little Richard: *17 Original Golden Hits* (Specialty)
Ricky Nelson: *Ricky Nelson* (United Artists)
Carl Perkins: *Original Golden Hits* (Sun)
The Platters: *Encore of Golden Hits* (Mercury)
Elvis Presley: *The Sun Sessions* (RCA Victor)
Elvis Presley: *Elvis' Gold Records* (RCA Victor)
Jimmy Reed: *The Ultimate Jimmy Reed* (BluesWay)
Huey Smith et al.: *Huey "Piano" Smith's Rock & Roll Revival* (Ace)
Joe Turner: *His Greatest Recordings* (Atco)
Gene Vincent: *The Bop That Just Won't Stop (1956)* (Capitol)
Muddy Waters: *Sail On* (Chess)

Sonny Boy Williamson: *This Is My Story* (Chess)
Howlin' Wolf: *Chester Burnett A.K.A. Howlin' Wolf* (Chess)

THE '60S

The Band: *The Band* (Capitol)
The Beach Boys: *Endless Summer* (Capitol)
The Beach Boys: *Wild Honey* (Capitol)
The Beatles: *Meet the Beatles!* (Capitol)
The Beatles: *The Beatles' Second Album* (Capitol)
The Beatles: *The Early Beatles* (Capitol)
The Beatles: *Something New* (Capitol)
The Beatles: *Rubber Soul* (Capitol)
The Beatles: *Sgt. Pepper's Lonely Hearts Club Band* (Capitol)
Bobby Bland: *The Best of Bobby Bland* (Duke)
James Brown: *"Live" at the Apollo* (King)
James Brown: *"Live" at the Apollo Volume II* (King)
Buffalo Springfield: *Buffalo Springfield Again* (Atco)
The Byrds: *The Byrds' Greatest Hits* (Columbia)
The Byrds: *The Notorious Byrd Brothers* (Columbia)
The Byrds: *Sweetheart of the Rodeo* (Columbia)
Ray Charles: *Ray Charles' Greatest Hits* (ABC)
Ray Charles: *Modern Sounds in Country & Western Music* (ABC)
Sam Cooke: *The Legendary Sam Cooke* (RCA Special Products)
Creedence Clearwater Revival: *Willy and the Poor Boys* (Fantasy)
Donovan: *Donovan's Greatest Hits* (Epic)
The Drifters: *The Drifters' Golden Hits* (Atlantic)
Bob Dylan: *The Freewheelin' Bob Dylan* (Columbia)
Bob Dylan: *Bringing It All Back Home* (Columbia)
Bob Dylan: *Highway 61 Revisited* (Columbia)
Bob Dylan: *Blonde on Blonde* (Columbia)
Bob Dylan: *John Wesley Harding* (Columbia)
Bob Dylan: *Nashville Skyline* (Columbia)
The Flying Burrito Bros.: *The Gilded Palace of Sin* (A&M)
Aretha Franklin: *Aretha's Gold* (Atlantic)
Marvin Gaye: *Super Hits* (Tamla)
Jimi Hendrix: *Are You Experienced?* (Reprise)
Jimi Hendrix Experience: *Electric Ladyland* (Reprise)
Jimi Hendrix Experience: *Smash Hits!* Reprise)
The Impressions: *Vintage Years: The Impressions Featuring Jerry Butler and Curtis Mayfield* (Sire)
B. B. King: *Live at the Regal* (ABC)
The Kinks: *The Kinks' Greatest Hits* (Reprise)
The Kinks: *Face to Face* (Reprise)
Love: *Forever Changes* (Elektra)
The Lovin' Spoonful: *The Best . . .* (Kama Sutra)
The Mamas and the Papas: *Farewell to the First Golden Era* (Dunhill)
Martha and the Vandellas: *Greatest Hits* (Gordy)
The Marvellettes: *Greatest Hits* (Tamla)

The Miracles: *The Miracles' Greatest Hits from the Beginning* (Tamla)
Moby Grape: *Moby Grape* (Columbia)
Wilson Pickett: *The Best of Wilson Pickett* (Atlantic)
The Rascals: *Time Peace: The Rascals' Greatest Hits* (Atlantic)
Otis Redding: *Dictionary of Soul* (Stax)
Otis Redding: *The Best of Otis Redding* (Atco)
Otis Redding: *The Immortal Otis Redding* (Atco)
Smokey Robinson & the Miracles: *Greatest Hits Vol. 2* (Tamla)
The Rolling Stones: *12 x 5* (London)
The Rolling Stones: *The Rolling Stones, Now!* (London)
The Rolling Stones: *Out of Our Heads* (London)
The Rolling Stones: *Aftermath* (London)
The Rolling Stones: *Between the Buttons* (London)
The Rolling Stones: *Beggars Banquet* (London)
The Rolling Stones: *Let It Bleed* (London)
Diana Ross & the Supremes: *Anthology* (Motown)
Sam and Dave: *The Best of Sam and Dave* (Atlantic)
The Shirelles: *The Shirelles' Greatest Hits* (Scepter)
Otis Spann: *Walking the Blues* (Barnaby)
Phil Spector's Greatest Hits (Warner/Spector)
Dusty Springfield: *Dusty in Memphis* (Atlantic)
Howard Tate: *Howard Tate* (Verve)
The Temptations: *The Temptations' Greatest Hits* (Gordy)
Joe Tex: *The Best of Joe Tex* (Atlantic)
The Velvet Underground: *The Velvet Underground & Nico* (Verve)
The Velvet Underground: *The Velvet Underground* (Verve)
Dionne Warwick: *Golden Hits/Part I* (Scepter)
The Who: *The Who Sing My Generation* (Decca)
The Who: *Happy Jack* (Decca)
The Who: *The Who Sell Out* (Decca)
Jackie Wilson: *Jackie Wilson's Greatest Hits* (Brunswick)
Stevie Wonder: *Looking Back* (Motown)

The Seventies and 1980

Below is a year-by-year listing of every '70s LP I've graded A minus or better — that is, every one I recommend (more or less) unequivocally. They appear in roughly descending order of quality, though I make no guarantee as to the permanence of the mood that pertained while I was preparing the lists. I've added a list for 1980, and omitted the grades themselves. The total number of albums to qualify each year is indicated in parentheses.

1970 (56)

Derek and the Dominoes: *Layla* (Atco)
Sly & the Family Stone: *Greatest Hits* (Epic)
Randy Newman: *12 Songs* (Reprise)
Van Morrison: *Moondance* (Warner Bros.)
Neil Young: *After the Gold Rush* (Reprise)
James Brown: *Sex Machine* (King)
John Lennon: *Plastic Ono Band* (Apple)
Aretha Franklin: *Spirit in the Dark* (Atlantic)
John McLaughlin: *Devotion* (Douglas)
The Velvet Underground: *Loaded* (Cotillion)
Dolly Parton: *The Best of Dolly Parton* (RCA Victor)
Al Green: *Al Green Gets Next to You* (Hi)
Creedence Clearwater Revival: *Cosmo's Factory* (Fantasy)
The Grateful Dead: *Workingman's Dead* (Warner Bros.)
The Insect Trust: *Hoboken Saturday Night* (Atco)
The Beatles: *Hey Jude* (Apple)
Van Morrison: *His Band and the Street Choir* (Warner Bros.)
Tracy Nelson: *Mother Earth Presents Tracy Nelson Country* (Mercury)
The Stooges: *Fun House* (Elektra)
Miles Davis: *Bitches Brew* (Columbia)
Fleetwood Mac: *Kiln House* (Reprise)
Janis Joplin: *Pearl* (Columbia)
Fairport Convention: *Unhalfbricking* (A&M)
Delaney & Bonnie & Friends with Eric Clapton: *On Tour* (Atco)

Gladys Knight & the Pips: *Greatest Hits* (Soul)
Captain Beefheart and the Magic Band: *Lick My Decals Off, Baby* (Straight/Reprise)
Love: *False Start* (Blue Thumb)
Lee Dorsey: *Yes We Can* (Polydor)
Ann Peebles: *Part Time Love* (Hi)
The Doors: *13* (Elektra)
Joni Mitchell: *Ladies of the Canyon* (Reprise)
Johnnie Taylor: *Johnnie Taylor's Greatest Hits* (Stax)
Bob Dylan: *New Morning* (Columbia)
Jerry Butler: *The Best of Jerry Butler* (Mercury)
Creedence Clearwater Revival: *Pendulum* (Fantasy)
Eddie "Cleanhead" Vinson: *The Original Cleanhead* (BluesTime)
The Temptations: *Greatest Hits, Volume 2* (Gordy)
Jerry Lee Lewis: *The Best of Jerry Lee Lewis* (Smash)
Rod Stewart: *Gasoline Alley* (Mercury)
Booker T. & the M.G.'s: *Greatest Hits* (Stax)
MC5: *Back in the USA* (Atlantic)
Otis Redding/The Jimi Hendrix Experience: *Historic Performances Recorded at the Monterey International Pop Festival* (Reprise)
The Grateful Dead: *American Beauty* (Warner Bros.)
Jesse Winchester: *Jesse Winchester* (Ampex)
The Beach Boys: *Sunflower* (Brother/Reprise)
Ike & Tina Turner: *Come Together* (Liberty)
The Beatles: *Let It Be* (Apple)
Loretta Lynn: *Loretta Lynn Writes 'Em and Sings 'Em* (Decca)
Canned Heat: *Future Blues* (Liberty)
Mother Earth: *Satisfied* (Mercury)
Delaney & Bonnie: *To Bonnie from Delaney* (Atco)
James Brown: *Super Bad* (King)
Nolan: *No Apologies* (Lizard)
Charlie Rich: *The Fabulous Charlie Rich* (Epic)
Allen Ginsberg: *William Blake, Songs of Innocence and Experience* (Verve/Forecast)
Big Brother & the Holding Co.: *Be a Brother* (Columbia)

1971 (45)

Miles Davis: *Jack Johnson* (Columbia)
Ray Charles: *A 25th Anniversary in Show Business Salute to Ray Charles* (ABC)
Rod Stewart: *Every Picture Tells a Story* (Mercury)
Sly & the Family Stone: *There's a Riot Goin' On* (Epic)
John Lennon: *Imagine* (Apple)
The Rolling Stones: *Sticky Fingers* (Rolling Stones)
The Who: *Who's Next* (Decca)
Led Zeppelin: *Led Zeppelin IV* (Atlantic)
Joni Mitchell: *Blue* (Reprise)
Jimi Hendrix: *The Cry of Love* (Reprise)
Wilson Pickett: *The Best of Wilson Pickett — Vol. II* (Atlantic)
Joy of Cooking: *Joy of Cooking* (Capitol)
John Prine: *John Prine* (Atlantic)

The Mahavishnu Orchestra with John McLaughlin: *The Inner Mounting Flame* (Columbia)

Nils Lofgren/Grin: *1 + 1* (Spindizzy)

Tom T. Hall: *In Search of a Song* (Mercury)

Stevie Wonder: *Greatest Hits Vol. 2* (Tamla)

Delaney & Bonnie: *Motel Shot* (Atco)

Nilsson: *Nilsson Schmilsson* (RCA Victor)

Crazy Horse: *Crazy Horse* (Reprise)

Hound Dog Taylor and the HouseRockers: *Hound Dog Taylor and the HouseRockers* (Alligator)

Jackson 5: *Greatest Hits* (Motown)

Clarence Carter: *The Best of Clarence Carter* (Atlantic)

Bonnie Raitt: *Bonnie Raitt* (Warner Bros.)

Helen Reddy: *Helen Reddy* (Capitol)

Van Morrison: *Tupelo Honey* (Warner Bros.)

The Who: *Meaty, Beaty, Big and Bouncy* (Decca)

Howlin' Wolf: *The London Howlin' Wolf Sessions* (Chess)

Faces: *A Nod Is as Good as a Wink . . . to a Blind Horse* (Warner Bros.)

The Stylistics: *The Stylistics* (Avco)

Carole King: *Tapestry* (Ode)

The Doors: *L.A. Woman* (Elektra)

The Move: *Message from the Country* (Capitol)

Jimi Hendrix: *Rainbow Bridge* (Reprise)

B. B. King: *Live in Cook County Jail* (ABC)

Michael Hurley & Pals: *Armchair Boogie* (Raccoon)

Miles Davis: *Live Evil* (Columbia)

The Chi-Lites: *(For God's Sake) Give More Power to the People* (Brunswick)

Ray Charles: *Volcanic Action of My Soul* (ABC)

David Bowie: *Hunky Dory* (RCA Victor)

Sir Douglas Quintet: *The Return of Doug Saldana* (Philips)

Dolly Parton: *Coat of Many Colors* (RCA Victor)

Leonard Cohen: *Live Songs* (Columbia)

Bill Withers: *Just as I Am* (Sussex)

1972 (49)

Rolling Stones: *Exile on Main St.* (Rolling Stones)

Paul Simon: *Paul Simon* (Columbia)

Manfred Mann's Earth Band: *Manfred Mann's Earth Band* (Polydor)

Bonnie Raitt: *Give It Up* (Warner Bros.)

Joni Mitchell: *For the Roses* (Asylum)

The Kinks: *The Kink Kronikles* (Reprise)

Aretha Franklin: *Young, Gifted and Black* (Atlantic)

The Wailers: *Catch a Fire* (Island)

Steely Dan: *Can't Buy a Thrill* (ABC)

Stevie Wonder: *Talking Book* (Tamla)

Mississippi John Hurt: *Last Sessions* (Vanguard)

Bob Dylan: *Bob Dylan's Greatest Hits Vol. II* (Columbia)

Bill Withers: *Still Bill* (Sussex)

The Chi-Lites: *Greatest Hits* (Brunswick)
Delaney & Bonnie: *The Best of Delaney & Bonnie* (Atco)
Mott the Hoople: *All the Young Dudes* (Columbia)
Al Green: *I'm Still in Love with You* (Hi)
Curtis Mayfield: *Super Fly* (Curtom)
Rod Stewart: *Never a Dull Moment* (Mercury)
Bette Midler: *The Divine Miss M* (Atlantic)
Howard Tate: *Howard Tate* (Atlantic)
Van Morrison: *Saint Dominic's Preview* (Warner Bros.)
James Brown: *There It Is* (Polydor)
Richard Thompson: *Henry the Human Fly* (Reprise)
Ann Peebles: *Straight from the Heart* (Hi)
Johnny Shines: *Johnny Shines* (Blue Horizon)
Jimi Hendrix: *Hendrix in the West* (Reprise)
Buddy Guy & Junior Wells: *Buddy Guy & Junior Wells Play the Blues* (Atco)
Chris Smither: *Don't It Drag On* (Poppy)
Elton John: *Honky Chateau* (Uni)
Randy Newman: *Sail Away* (Reprise)
John Prine: *Diamond in the Rough* (Atlantic)
Joy of Cooking: *Castles* (Capitol)
Al Green: *Let's Stay Together* (Hi)
Peter Townshend: *Who Came First* (Track)
Dr. John: *Gumbo* (Atco)
George Jones: *The Best of George Jones Vol. I* (Epic)
Grin: *All Out* (Spindizzy)
Loudon Wainwright III: *Album III* (Columbia)
Brinsley Schwarz: *Nervous on the Road* (United Artists)
Manu Dibango: *Soul Makossa* (Atlantic)
Conway Twitty: *Conway Twitty's Greatest Hits Vol. I* (MCA)
Janis Joplin: *Janis Joplin in Concert* (Columbia)
Nitty Gritty Dirt Band: *Will the Circle Be Unbroken* (United Artists)
Paul Pena: *Paul Pena* (Capitol)
Charlie Rich: *The Best of Charlie Rich* (Epic)
The Paul Butterfield Blues Band: *Golden Butter: The Best of the Paul Butterfield Blues
   Band* (Elektra)
Todd Rundgren: *Something/Anything* (Bearsville)

1973 (47)

Al Green: *Call Me* (Hi)
New York Dolls: *New York Dolls* (Mercury)
Jimmy Cliff et al.: *The Harder They Come* (Mango)
Wilson Pickett: *Wilson Pickett's Greatest Hits* (Atlantic)
Lynyrd Skynyrd: *Pronounced Leh-nerd Skeh-nerd* (Sounds of the South/MCA)
John Prine: *Sweet Revenge* (Atlantic)
Sly & the Family Stone: *Fresh* (Epic)
Africa Dances (Authentic)
Janis Joplin: *Janis Joplin's Greatest Hits* (Columbia)
Al Green: *Livin' for You* (Hi)
Steely Dan: *Countdown to Ecstasy* (ABC)

Stevie Wonder: *Innervisions* (Tamla)
Neil Young: *Time Fades Away* (Reprise)
Asleep at the Wheel: *Comin' Right at Ya* (United Artists)
Bruce Springsteen: *The Wild, the Innocent and the E Street Shuffle* (Columbia)
Bill Withers: *Bill Withers Live at Carnegie Hall* (Sussex)
Slade: *Slayed?* (Polydor)
Mahavishnu Orchestra: *Birds of Fire* (Columbia)
The Move: *Split Ends* (United Artists)
Coulson, Dean, McGuinness, Flint: *Lo and Behold* (Sire)
Bonnie Raitt: *Takin My Time* (Warner Bros.)
Led Zepplin: *Houses of the Holy* (Atlantic)
Tom T. Hall: *The Rhymer and Other Five and Dimers* (Mercury)
Spinners: *Spinners* (Atlantic)
Roy Brown: *Hard Times* (BluesWay)
The Who: *Quadrophenia* (Track)
The Kinks: *The Great Lost Kinks Album* (Reprise)
Mott the Hoople: *Mott* (Columbia)
Laura Lee: *The Best of Laura Lee* (Hot Wax)
James Brown: *Soul Classics Volume II* (Polydor)
Marvin Gaye: *Let's Get It On* (Tamla)
The Hollies: *The Hollies' Greatest Hits* (Epic)
The Allman Brothers Band: *Brothers and Sisters* (Capricorn)
Manfred Mann's Earth Band: *Get Your Rocks Off* (Polydor)
Elliott Murphy: *Aquashow* (Polydor)
Frederic Rzewski: *Coming Together; Attica; Moutons de Panurge* (Opus One)
Roy Wood: *Boulders* (United Artists)
Howlin' Wolf: *The Back Door Wolf* (Chess)
Charles Bevel: *Meet "Mississippi Charles" Bevel* (A&M)
Marlo Thomas: *Free to Be . . . You and Me* (Bell)
Derek & the Dominoes: *In Concert* (Atco)
Miles Davis: *Miles Davis in Concert* (Columbia)
Loudon Wainwright III: *Attempted Mustache* (Columbia)
Mike Seeger: *The Second Annual Farewell Reunion* (Mercury)
Esther Phillips: *Black Eyed Blues* (Kudu)
Swamp Dogg: *Gag a Maggott* (Stone Dogg)
Taj Mahal: *Ooh So Good 'n Blues* (Columbia)

1974 (47)

New York Dolls: *In Too Much Too Soon* (Mercury)
Steely Dan: *Pretzel Logic* (ABC)
Big Star: *Radio City* (Ardent)
The Wailers: *Burnin'* (Island)
Randy Newman: *Good Old Boys* (Reprise)
Andy Fairweather Low: *Spider Jiving* (A&M)
Gram Parsons: *Grievous Angel* (Reprise)
Van Morrison: *It's Too Late to Stop Now* (Warner Bros.)
Joni Mitchell: *Court and Spark* (Asylum)
Eric Clapton: *461 Ocean Boulevard* (RSO)
Eno: *Here Come the Warm Jets* (Island)

Thomas Jefferson Kaye: *First Grade* (ABC/Dunhill)
Richard & Linda Thompson: *Hokey Pokey* (Island)
Bob Dylan/The Band: *Before the Flood* (Asylum)
The Wild Magnolias: *The Wild Magnolias* (Polydor)
Velvet Underground: *1969 Velvet Underground Live* (Mercury)
Miles Davis: *Get Up with It* (Columbia)
Lynyrd Skynyrd: *Second Helping* (MCA)
Labelle: *Nightbirds* (Epic)
Stevie Wonder: *Fulfillingness' First Finale* (Tamla)
Millie Jackson: *Caught Up* (Spring)
Miles Davis: *Big Fun* (Columbia)
Hound Dog Taylor and the HouseRockers: *Natural Boogie* (Alligator)
Lou Reed: *Rock n Roll Animal* (RCA Victor)
Bob Dylan: *Planet Waves* (Asylum)
King Crimson: *Red* (Atlantic)
Raspberries: *Starting Over* (Capitol)
Bryan Ferry: *These Foolish Things* (Atlantic)
Willie Nelson: *Phases and Stages* (Atlantic)
Parliament: *Up for the Down Stroke* (Casablanca)
Linda Rondstadt: *Heart Like a Wheel* (Capitol)
Loretta Lynn: *Loretta Lynn's Greatest Hits Vol. II* (MCA)
John Cale: *Fear* (Island)
Alice Cooper: *Alice Cooper's Greatest Hits* (Warner Bros.)
Leonard Cohen: *New Skin for the Old Ceremony* (Columbia)
Average White Band: *Average White Band* (Atlantic)
Betty Wright: *Danger High Voltage* (Alston)
The Mighty Clouds of Joy: *It's Time* (ABC)
Neil Young: *On the Beach* (Reprise)
Mary McCaslin: *Way Out West* (Philo)
Gladys Knight & the Pips: *Claudine* (Buddah)
Moe Bandy: *I Just Started Hating Cheating Songs Today* (GRT)
Earth, Wind & Fire: *Open Our Eyes* (Columbia)
Shirley Brown: *Woman to Woman* (Truth)
Ry Cooder: *Paradise and Lunch* (Reprise)

1975 (40)

Bob Dylan/The Band: *The Basement Tapes* (Columbia)
Dolly Parton: *Best of Dolly Parton* (RCA Victor)
Al Green: *Al Green's Greatest Hits* (Hi)
James Talley: *Got No Bread, No Milk, No Money, but We Sure Got a Lot of Love*
   (Capitol)
Neil Young: *Tonight's the Night* (Reprise)
Patti Smith: *Horses* (Arista)
Bonnie Raitt: *Home Plate* (Warner Bros.)
Bob Marley & the Wailers: *Natty Dread* (Island)
Bob Dylan: *Blood on the Tracks* (Columbia)
Bruce Springsteen: *Born to Run* (Columbia)
Steely Dan: *Katy Lied* (ABC)

Eno: *Taking Tiger Mountain (by Strategy)* (Island)
Fleetwood Mac: *Fleetwood Mac* (Warner Bros.)
Funkadelic: *Funkadelic's Greatest Hits* (Westbound)
The Staple Singers: *The Best of the Staple Singers* (Stax)
Elton John: *Rock of the Westies* (MCA)
The Stylistics: *The Best of the Stylistics* (H&L)
Toots and the Maytals: *Funky Kingston* (Island)
Roxy Music: *Siren* (Atlantic)
Andy Fairweather Low: *La Booga Rooga* (A&M)
Lynyrd Skynyrd: *Nuthin' Fancy* (MCA)
The Meters: *Cissy Strut* (Island)
Gary Stewart: *Out of Hand* (RCA Victor)
Funkadelic: *Let's Take It to the Stage* (Westbound)
Sonny Rollins: *Nucleus* (Milestone)
Beserkley Chartbusters Volume 1 (Beserkley)
Leonard Cohen: *The Best of* (Columbia)
Parliament: *Mothership Connection* (Casablanca)
Loudon Wainwright III: *Unrequited* (Columbia)
Barry White: *Barry White's Greatest Hits* (20th Century)
The Allman Brothers Band: *The Road Goes On Forever* (Capricorn)
Bill Withers: *The Best of Bill Withers* (Sussex)
Neil Young: *Zuma* (Reprise)
John Cale: *Slow Dazzle* (Island)
John Prine: *Common Sense* (Atlantic)
Amazing Rhythm Aces: *Stacked Deck* (ABC)
Pink Floyd: *Wish You Were Here* (Columbia)
Terry Garthwaite: *Terry* (Arista)
Stoney Edwards: *Mississippi You're on My Mind* (Capitol)
Spinners: *Pick of the Litter* (Atlantic)
Bobby Bare: *Cowboys and Daddys* (RCA Victor)

1976 (47)

Michael Hurley/The Unholy Modal Rounders/Jeffrey Fredericks & the Clamtones:
    Have Moicy! (Rounder)
Eno: *Another Green World* (Island)
The Wild Tchoupitoulas: *The Wild Tchoupitoulas* (Island)
Ramones: *Ramones* (Sire)
Creedence Clearwater Revival: *Chronicle* (Fantasy)
Dr. Buzzard's Original Savannah Band: *Dr. Buzzard's Original Savannah Band* (RCA
    Victor)
David Bowie: *Station to Station* (RCA Victor)
Kate & Anna McGarrigle: *Kate & Anna McGarrigle* (Warner Bros.)
Graham Parker: *Howlin Wind* (Mercury)
David Bowie: *Changesonebowie* (RCA Victor)
Graham Parker: *Heat Treatment* (Mercury)
Miles Davis: *Agharta* (Columbia)
Stevie Wonder: *Songs in the Key of Life* (Tamla)
The Modern Lovers: *The Modern Lovers* (Home of the Hits)
Burning Spear: *Marcus Garvey* (Island)

Arlo Guthrie: *Amigo* (Warner Bros.)
Mighty Diamonds: *Right Time* (Virgin)
Ohio Players: *Gold* (Mercury)
War: *Greatest Hits* (United Artists)
Mott the Hoople: *Greatest Hits* (Columbia)
New York Shakespeare Festival: *Threepenny Opera* (Columbia)
Patti Smith Group: *Radio Ethiopia* (Arista)
Bob Seger & the Silver Bullet Band: *Night Moves* (Capitol)
K.C. & the Sunshine Band: *K.C. & the Sunshine Band* (T.K.)
Funkadelic: *Hardcore Jollies* (Warner Bros.)
Aerosmith: *Rocks* (Columbia)
Hound Dog Taylor & the HouseRockers: *Beware of the Dog* (Alligator)
Al Green: *Full of Fire* (Hi)
Billy Swan: *Billy Swan* (Monument)
Gil Scott-Heron and Brian Jackson: *It's Your World* (Arista)
Ike & Tina Turner: *Greatest Hits* (United Artists)
Fairport Convention: *Fairport Chronicles* (A&M)
Son Seals: *Midnight Son* (Alligator)
Grin: *The Best of Grin Featuring Nils Lofgren* (Epic)
The Rolling Stones: *Black and Blue* (Rolling Stones)
Hot Chocolate: *Man to Man* (Big Tree)
Lynyrd Skynyrd: *One More for the Road* (MCA)
Raspberries: *Raspberries' Best Featuring Eric Carmen* (Capitol)
Bob Marley & the Wailers: *Live!* (Island)
George Jones: *Alone Again* (Epic)
Hi Rhythm: *On the Loose* (Hi)
Esther Phillips: *Confessin' the Blues* (Atlantic)
Boz Scaggs: *Silk Degrees* (Columbia)
Harold Melvin & the Blue Notes: *Collectors' Item* (Philadelphia International)
Gasolin': *Gasolin'* (Epic)
Bunny Wailer: *Blackheart Man* (Island)
James Talley: *Tryin' Like the Devil* (Capitol)

1977 (56)

Television: *Marquee Moon* (Elektra)
Kate & Anna McGarrigle: *Dancer with Bruised Knees* (Warner Bros.)
Fleetwood Mac: *Rumours* (Warner Bros.)
Sex Pistols: *Never Mind the Bollocks, Here's the Sex Pistols* (Warner Bros.)
Ramones: *Rocket to Russia* (Sire)
Andy Fairweather Low: *Be Bop 'n' Holla* (A&M)
Parliament: *Funkentelechy vs. the Placebo Syndrome* (Casablanca)
Ornette Coleman: *Dancing in Your Head* (Horizon)
Al Green: *The Belle Album* (Hi)
Hot Chocolate: *10 Greatest Hits* (Big Tree)
Funkadelic: *The Best of the Early Years Volume One* (Westbound)
The Beach Boys: *Love You* (Brother/Reprise)
The Beatles: *The Beatles at the Hollywood Bowl* (Capitol)
Ramones: *Ramones Leave Home* (Sire)

Roxy Music: *Greatest Hits* (Atlantic)
John Cale: *Guts* (Island)
Lynyrd Skynyrd: *Street Survivors* (MCA)
Paul Simon: *Greatest Hits, Etc.* (Columbia)
Muddy Waters: *Hard Again* (Blue Sky)
Richard Hell and the Voidoids: *Blank Generation* (Sire)
Ray Charles: *True to Life* (Atlantic)
George Jones & Tammy Wynette: *Greatest Hits* (Epic)
Talking Heads: *Talking Heads 77* (Sire)
Johnny Shines: *Too Wet to Plow* (Blue Labor)
Freddy Fender: *The Best of Freddy Fender* (ABC/Dot)
Moe Bandy: *The Best of Moe Bandy* (Columbia)
George Jones: *All-Time Greatest Hits — Volume I* (Epic)
Iggy Pop: *Lust for Life* (RCA Victor)
Richard & Linda Thompson: *Live (More or Less)* (Island)
Johnnie Taylor: *Chronicle — The Twenty Greatest Hits* (Stax)
Joe Cocker: *Joe Cocker's Greatest Hits* (A&M)
Lou Reed: *Walk on the Wild Side — The Best of Lou Reed* (RCA Victor)
Bizarros/Rubber City Rebels: *From Akron* (Clone)
The Jam: *In the City* (Polydor)
Fela and Afrika 70: *Zombie* (Mercury)
Taj Mahal: *The Taj Mahal Anthology Volume One* (Columbia)
Merle Haggard and the Strangers: *Songs I'll Always Sing* (Capitol)
Elvin Bishop: *Raisin' Hell* (Capricorn)
Al Green: *Greatest Hits Volume II* (Hi)
Joe Ely: *Joe Ely* (MCA)
Asleep at the Wheel: *The Wheel* (Capitol)
Brian Eno: *Discreet Music* (Antilles)
Bette Midler: *Live at Last* (Atlantic)
Garland Jeffreys: *Ghost Writer* (A&M)
Gary Stewart: *Your Place or Mine* (RCA Victor)
Tavares: *The Best of Tavares* (Capitol)
The Scruffs: *Wanna' Meet the Scruffs?* (Power Play)
Merle Haggard and the Strangers: *A Working Man Can't Get Nowhere Today* (Capitol)
The Guess Who: *The Greatest of the Guess Who* (RCA Victor)
Graham Parker and the Rumour: *Stick to Me* (Mercury)
Peter Townshend-Ronnie Lane: *Rough Mix* (MCA)
Philip Glass: *North Star* (Virgin)
Kraftwerk: *Trans-Europe Express* (Capitol)
Bonnie Raitt: *Sweet Forgiveness* (Warner Bros.)
Ashford & Simpson: *So So Satisfied* (Warner Bros.)
Iggy Pop: *The Idiot* (RCA Victor)

1978 (62)

Blondie: *Parallel Lines* (Chrysalis)
Wire: *Pink Flag* (Harvest)
Talking Heads: *More Songs About Buildings and Food* (Sire)
The Rolling Stones: *Some Girls* (Rolling Stones)

Nick Lowe: *Pure Pop for Now People* (Columbia)
Elvis Costello and the Attractions: *This Year's Model* (Columbia)
The Clash: *Give 'Em Enough Rope* (Epic)
Neil Young: *Comes a Time* (Reprise)
The Vibrators: *Pure Mania* (Columbia)
Neil Young: *Decade* (Reprise)
Captain Beefheart and the Magic Band: *Shiny Beast (Bat Chain Puller)* (Warner Bros.)
Funkadelic: *One Nation Under a Groove* (Warner Bros.)
Ramones: *Road to Ruin* (Sire)
Joe Ely: *Honky Tonk Masquerade* (MCA)
Lee Dorsey: *Night People* (ABC)
Television: *Adventure* (Elektra)
Ashford & Simpson: *Is It Still Good to Ya* (Warner Bros.)
Pere Ubu: *The Modern Dance* (Blank)
Willie Nelson: *Stardust* (Columbia)
Bob Marley & the Wailers: *Kaya* (Island)
Steve Reich: *Music for 18 Musicians* (ECM)
Willie Nelson: *Face of a Fighter* (Lone Star)
Parliament: *Motor-Booty Affair* (Casablanca)
Dave Edmunds: *Tracks on Wax 4* (Swan Song)
David Johansen: *David Johansen* (Blue Sky)
The Steve Miller Band: *Greatest Hits 1974–78* (Capitol)
Billy Swan: *At His Best* (Monument)
David Behrman: *On the Other Ocean/Figure in a Clearing* (Lovely)
The Trammps: *The Best of the Trammps* (Atlantic)
Ducks Deluxe: *Don't Mind Rockin' Tonite* (RCA Victor)
Professor Longhair: *Live on the Queen Mary* (Harvest)
Ian Dury: *New Boots and Panties!!* (Stiff)
Merle Haggard and the Strangers: *The Way It Was in '51* (Capitol)
The Marshall Tucker Band: *Greatest Hits* (Capricorn)
Spinners: *The Best of Spinners* (Atlantic)
Max Romeo: *Open the Iron Gate* (United Artists)
Al Green: *Truth n' Time* (Hi)
Earth, Wind & Fire: *The Best of Earth, Wind & Fire, Vol. 1* (Columbia)
Raydio: *Raydio* (Arista)
Big Star: *Third* (PVC)
Albert Collins: *Ice Pickin'.* (Alligator)
Shoes: *Black Vinyl Shoes* (PVC)
Johnny Paycheck: *Greatest Hits Volume II* (Epic)
Pablo Moses: *I Love I Bring* (United Artists)
Tom Robinson Band: *Power in the Darkness* (Harvest)
Warren Zevon: *Excitable Boy* (Asylum)
Michael Mantler: *Movies* (Watt)
Brian Eno: *Before and After Science* (Island)
Patti Smith Group: *Easter* (Arista)
Loleatta Holloway: *Queen of the Night* (Gold Mind)
The Yankees: *High 'n' Inside* (Big Sound)
Steppin' Out: Disco's Greatest Hits (Polydor)

Son Seals: *Live and Burning* (Alligator)
Robert Ashley: *Private Parts* (Lovely)
The Carla Bley Band: *European Tour 1977* (Watt)
Ornette Coleman: *Body Meta* (Artists House)
Mary McCaslin & Jim Ringer: *The Bramble and the Rose* (Philo)
McKinley Mitchell: *McKinley Mitchell* (Chimneyville)
The Residents: *Duck Stab/Buster & Glen* (Ralph)
Steve Gibbons Band: *Down in the Bunker* (Polydor)
Tapper Zukie: *Man Ah Warrior* (Mer)
Rodney Crowell: *Ain't Living Long Like This* (Warner Bros.)

1979 (59)

The Clash: *The Clash* (Epic)
Pere Ubu: *Dub Housing* (Chrysalis)
Neil Young & Crazy Horse: *Rust Never Sleeps* (Reprise)
Lynyrd Skynyrd: *Gold and Platinum* (MCA)
Van Morrison: *Into the Music* (Warner Bros.)
Nick Lowe: *Labour of Lust* (Columbia)
Arthur Blythe: *Lenox Avenue Breakdown* (Columbia)
Air: *Lore* (Arista Novus)
Michael Jackson: *Off the Wall* (Epic)
Donna Summer: *On the Radio: Greatest Hits Volumes I & II* (Casablanca)
The B-52's: *The B-52's* (Warner Bros.)
Burning Spear: *Harder Than the Best* (Mango)
The Roches: *The Roches* (Warner Bros.)
Graham Parker and the Rumour: *Squeezing Out Sparks* (Arista)
Donna Summer: *Bad Girls* (Casablanca)
Tom Verlaine: *Tom Verlaine* (Elektra)
Dr. Buzzard's Original Savannah Band: *James Monroe High School Presents Dr.
   Buzzard's Original Savannah Band Goes to Washington* (Elektra)
Talking Heads: *Fear of Music* (Sire)
Marianne Faithfull: *Broken English* (Island)
Buzzcocks: *Singles Going Steady* (I.R.S.)
Chic: *Risque* (Atlantic)
XTC: *Drums and Wires* (Virgin)
Pretenders: *Pretenders* (Warner Bros.)
Wreckless Eric: *The Whole Wide World* (Stiff)
The Only Ones: *Special View* (Epic)
Shoes: *Present Tense* (Elektra)
Neil Young & Crazy Horse: *Live Rust* (Reprise)
Cory Daye: *Cory and Me* (New York International)
Steel Pulse: *Tribute to the Martyrs* (Mango)
Linton Kwesi Johnson: *Forces of Victory* (Mango)
Si Kahn: *Home* (Flying Fish)
Chic: *Les Plus Grands Succes de Chic/Chic's Greatest Hits* (Atlantic)
Dave Edmunds: *Repeat When Necessary* (Swan Song)
Fashion: *Product Perfect* (I.R.S.)

Don Williams: *The Best of Don Williams Volume II* (MCA)
Living Chicago Blues Volume I (Alligator)
Millie Jackson: *Live and Uncensored* (Spring)
Culture: *International Herb* (Virgin International)
Roxy Music: *Manifesto* (Atco)
Ian Hunter: *Shades of Ian Hunter: The Ballad of Ian Hunter & Mott the Hoople*
  (Columbia)
Mutiny: *Mutiny on the Mamaship* (Columbia)
Lene Lovich: *Stateless* (Stiff/Epic)
Terry Allen: *Lubbock (on Everything)* (Fate)
Henry Cow: *Unrest* (Red)
James Brown: *The Original Disco Man* (Polydor)
The Brides of Funkenstein: *Never Buy Texas from a Cowboy* (Atlantic)
Smokey Robinson: *Where There's Smoke . . .* (Tamla)
David Bowie: *Lodger* (RCA Victor)
Blondie: *Eat to the Beat* (Chrysalis)
Elvis Costello and the Attractions: *Armed Forces* (Columbia)
Heartbreakers: *Live at Max's Kansas City* (Max's Kansas City)
Taana Gardner: *Taana Gardner* (West End)
Tom Robinson Band: *TRB 2* (Harvest)
ZZ Top: *Deguello* (Warner Bros.)
Irakere: *Irakere* (Columbia)
James Blood: *Tales of Captain Black* (Artists House)
Midnight Rhythm: *Midnight Rhythm* (Atlantic)
Eddie "Cleanhead" Vinson: *Kidney Stew Is Fine* (Delmark)
George Jones: *My Very Special Guests* (Epic)

1980 (49)

The Clash: *London Calling* (Epic)
Talking Heads: *Remain in Light* (Sire)
Prince: *Dirty Mind* (Warner Bros.)
Tom Robinson: *Sector 27* (I.R.S.)
Wanna Buy a Bridge? (Rough Trade)
John Lennon/Yoko Ono: *Double Fantasy* (Geffen)
Jon Hassell/Brian Eno: *Fourth World Vol. I: Possible Musics* (Editions E.G.)
Chic: *Real People* (Atlantic)
Bruce Springsteen: *The River* (Columbia)
Professor Longhair: *Crawfish Fiesta* (Alligator)
Gang of Four: *Entertainment!* (Warner Bros.)
Alberta Hunter: *Amtrak Blues* (Columbia)
Robert Ashley: *Perfect Lives (Private Parts): The Bar* (Lovely)
Public Image Ltd.: *Second Edition* (Island)
The Jacksons: *Triumph* (Epic)
Captain Beefheart and the Magic Band: *Doc at the Radar Station* (Virgin)
The Feelies: *Crazy Rhythms* (Stiff)
John Prine: *Storm Windows* (Asylum)
Michael Hurley: *Snockgrass* (Rounder)
Stevie Wonder: *Hotter Than July* (Tamla)

Robert Jr. Lockwood & Johnny Shines: *Hangin' On* (Rounder)
The English Beat: *I Just Can't Stop It* (Sire)
The Psychedelic Furs: *The Psychedelic Furs* (Columbia)
Dollar Brand: *African Marketplace* (Elektra)
Pere Ubu: *The Art of Walking* (Rough Trade)
Henry Cow: *Western Culture* (Interzone)
The Undertones: *Hypnotised* (Sire)
Joy Division: *Unknown Pleasures* (Factory)
Aerosmith: *Aerosmith's Greatest Hits* (Columbia)
Rap's Greatest Hits (Sugarhill)
Joe "King" Carrasco and the Crowns: *Joe "King" Carrasco and the Crowns* (Hannibal)
Neil Young: *Hawks and Doves* (Reprise)
Rockers (Mango)
Smokey Robinson: *Warm Thoughts* (Tamla)
X: *Los Angeles* (Slash)
Gil Scott-Heron and Brian Jackson: *1980* (Arista)
Steel Pulse: *Reggae Fever* (Mango)
The Clash: *Black Market Clash* (Epic Nu-Disk)
Bootsy: *Ultra Wave* (Warner Bros.)
Popeye (Boardwalk)
T-Bone Burnett: *Truth Decay* (Takoma)
Donna Summer: *The Wanderer* (Geffen)
The Brains: *The Brains* (Mercury)
B. T. Express: *Greatest Hits* (Columbia)
Rockpile: *Seconds of Pleasure* (Columbia)
The Suburbs: *In Combo* (Twin/Tone)
Lydia Lunch: *Queen of Siam* (ZE)
Bunny Wailer: *Bunny Wailer Sings the Wailers* (Mango)
Teddy Pendergrass: *TP* (Philadelphia International)

Acknowledgments

The number of friends, acquaintances, publicists, and editors who have made a tangible contribution to the Consumer Guide must total over five hundred. For eleven years I've asked people what they're listening to, played records for strangers in the hope of garnering new shreds of insight, and stolen ideas, facts, and wisecracks shamelessly. Even to name only those who've helped get the material into book form would be impossible, and I apologize to anyone I've left out.

One of my biggest hassles was obtaining out-of-print albums. Essential to this task was my upstairs neighbor Vince Aletti, whose vast black-music collection saved me many hours of searching; I should add that I've been picking his brain since 1970. John Morthland, Tom Hull, Joe McEwen, Stephen Holden, and my sister Georgia Christgau perused my outline and suggested additions from their own shelves. Boston's incomparable Jeep Holland, whom I've never laid eyes on, generously opened his hoard of rarities to me. Tom Smucker, also an upstairs neighbor, offered jokes, advice, and emotional support as well as pieces of plastic. Others who lent me records — sometimes dozens, sometimes just one — include Billy Altman, Michael Beinhorn, Karin Berg, Alan Betrock, Barry Cooper, Karen Durbin, Ken Emerson, Gary Giddins, Eliot Hubbard, Greil Marcus, Dave Marsh, Steve McAvoy, John Milward, Richard Mortifoglio, Paul Nelson, Jon Pareles, John Piccarella, Kit Rachlis, John Rockwell, Don Shewey, Davitt Sigerson, Danny Stanger, Chip Stern, and Roger Trilling.

As diligent consumers soon discover, records that are still in the Schwann catalogue can be even harder to find than out-of-print items, and here company publicists prove invaluable. Special thanks must go to Eliot Hubbard of Epic, whose heroic interactions with CBS's New Jersey warehouse kept me working in the worst days of August. Barbara Pepe at RCA, Liz Rosenberg and Stacy Greene Mizrahi at Warners, Paula Batson at Columbia, Suzanne Scivoletti and Sherrie Levy at Phonogram, Bill Schubart at Philo, Caroline Prutzman at ABC and EMI/UA, Andy McKaie at Arista, and Joanne Toker and Pat Cox at Atlantic did discographical research as well as obtaining records for me. Kathy Schenker at A&M, Maureen O'Connor and Doreen

D'Agostino at Capitol, and Lynn Kellerman at MCA tolerated many more phone calls than were necessary. My appreciation also to Irene Simmons at Island, Terry Hinte at Fantasy, and Bruce Iglauer at Alligator.

Needless to say, I employed many secondary sources in my search for dates and other facts, of which the most useful were the monthly *Schwann Record & Tape Guide* and Joel Whitburn's annual Record Research breakdowns of the *Billboard* charts. Special thanks are due Brock Helander, who allowed me to refer to his unpublished *Rock 'n' Roll to Rock: A Discography,* and to Paul Crapo of Schwann for lending me a copy. Also of value were Ed Naha's revision of Lillian Roxon's *Rock Encyclopedia, The Rolling Stone Record Guide,* Norm N. Nite's *Rock On, NME's Illustrated Encyclopedia of Rock,* and Phil Hardy and Dave Laing's *Encyclopedia of Rock.*

I've also benefited from extensive editorial assistance. At *The Village Voice,* M. Mark taught me that my most gnomic conceits could be sharpened and clarified, while David Schneiderman was generous with the time off it took me to complete what I'd started and regain my sanity. Bob Cornfield talked me through numerous crises of confidence as well as taking care of business with the kind of honesty and taste I've always dreamed of in an agent. M. Mark, David Schneiderman, Kit Rachlis, and Laura Tillem offered comments on a sample chapter. Greil Marcus did the same, and then — incredibly — proceeded to offer comments on all the other chapters as well, reading through the entire manuscript and catching too many howlers in the process. Georgia Christgau organized the original Consumer Guides from *The Voice* and *Creem* into a workable draft, and proofread galleys along with John Morthland. Roger Trilling handled permissions with a savvy I could only expect to find in a manager I wish did more journalism. Parke Puterbaugh was a sharp-eyed and sensitive copy editor. And James Raimes brought the project to Ticknor & Fields, watched with alarm as it ballooned past its estimated proportions, and then cut with a tact and forebearance I ordinarily encounter only in other writers. I don't think he got what he bargained for, but I do think he likes what he got, and I'm flattered.

Finally we come to the spot customarily reserved for spouses — the without-whom-I-could-not-have paragraph. Well, this one's for real. Carola Dibbell has heard thousands of records she doesn't much like since 1972, and if that sounds easy, try it for a week. Thousands of times I've asked her, "How does this sound to you?," and thousands of times she's told me something I needed to know — often that the record is a nonentity, always one of the hardest things to get a bead on. Her ideas — especially her amazing ability to find words that evoke voices — can be found in hundreds of entries; phrases and more from her own published criticism can be found (unattributed) in a few. In addition, she's edited the rough draft of virtually every review in this book, applying her jargon detector and her slapstick wit to writing that would be several quantums drearier without her. It's her encouragement and her literary conscience that have made the Consumer Guide something I've gotten prouder to look back on over the years.

How does this look to you, Carola?

Credits